MAGICAL KNOWLEDGE

BOOKS ONE, TWO, AND THREE

FOUNDATIONS: THE LONE PRACTITIONER

THE INITIATE

CONTACTS OF THE ADEPTS

BY JOSEPHINE MCCARTHY

TaDehent Books
Exeter
2021

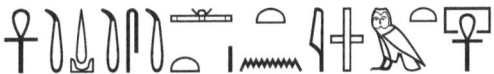

Copyright 2021 © Josephine McCarthy

All rights reserved

Without limiting the rights under copyright reserved above, no part of this publication may be reproduced, stored in, or introduced into a retrieval system, or transmitted, in any form or by any means (electronic, mechanical, photocopying, recording or otherwise) without prior permission of the copyright owner and the publisher of this book.

Originally published in three volumes by Mandrake of Oxford:
Magical Knowledge Book II: The Initiate (2011)
Magical Knowledge Book I: Foundations/ The Lone Practitioner (2012)
Magical Knowledge Book III: Contacts of the Adepts (2012)

Second editions originally published in three volumes by TaDehent Books:
Magical Knowledge Book One: Foundations: The Lone Practitioner (2020)
Magical Knowledge Book Two: The Initiate (2020)
Magical Knowledge Book Three: Contacts of the Adepts (2020)

Published as a single volume by TaDehent Books (2020)

Reprinted as a paperback by TaDehent Books 2021, Exeter UK

ISBN 978-1-911134-60-2

Cover image by Stuart Littlejohn
Typeset by Michael Sheppard

Dedicated to Frater Acher
and to my husband Stuart Littlejohn

Acknowledgements

I would like to thank the following people for their friendship, love, support and critiques, for without these people, this work would not be possible: Toni, Tony, Catherine, Jon, Andrea, Nusye, Jane, Anne H, Frater Acher, Michael for all his hard work, Cec, Cassandra and Leander.

I would also like to thank the helpers, workers, trustees, and student council of Quareia for keeping me on my toes: you guys are awesome.

Contents

I Foundations   1

Introduction   3

1 The world of magic and magical training   5
- 1.1   Things to consider   5
- 1.2   Magical systems old and new   8
- 1.3   Duality and ethics in magic   11
- 1.4   Approach to training: selfish versus non selfish   13
- 1.5   So why do we do magic?   15
- 1.6   Personal development   15

2 The pitfalls and traps of magic   19
- 2.1   Oath taking   19
- 2.2   The tying-in of energy   22
- 2.3   Blockage of knowledge   23
- 2.4   Past lives and genetic threads   25
- 2.5   Candy shop magic   28
- 2.6   Glamour, control, and ego   30

3 Power and magic   33
- 3.1   Boundaries   33
- 3.2   Working with power   35
- 3.3   Loss of ego   36
- 3.4   Power drunkenness   39
- 3.5   The power dynamics of ritual and vision   40
- 3.6   Using inner power   42
- 3.7   Outer power: ritual   45
- 3.8   High ritual   46
- 3.9   Visionary action   47
- 3.10   Inner worlds and actions: cause and effect   48
- 3.11   Justice, balance, and karma   51

4 Inner contacts and inner beings — 57
- 4.1 Human inner contact: dead or alive? — 59
- 4.2 Living contacts — 60
- 4.3 The roles of destroying deities and demonic powers — 62
- 4.4 What we can do — 63
- 4.5 Thought forms and passive enlivening — 65
- 4.6 Golems — 67
- 4.7 Passive enlivening — 68

5 Visionary magic — 75
- 5.1 The first step of visionary work — 76
- 5.2 Tips and things to think about — 77
- 5.3 The Void — 79
- 5.4 Vision of the Void — 79
- 5.5 The next step: discovery of the world — 81
- 5.6 What are boundaries? — 83
- 5.7 Practical methods for foundation training — 83
- 5.8 Practical visions and background information — 84
- 5.9 The Vision of the Inner Land — 85
- 5.10 The Goddess in the Underworld — 89

6 Ritual Magic — 95
- 6.1 Group rituals — 96
- 6.2 The lone ritual — 97
- 6.3 Altars — 99
- 6.4 Implements — 101
- 6.5 Ways of working with the implements — 103
- 6.6 The sword — 105
- 6.7 The wand — 105
- 6.8 The cup — 106
- 6.9 The shield — 106
- 6.10 The basic tuning of ritual tools — 107
- 6.11 Basic consecration method — 108
- 6.12 Developing your relationships with your ritual tools — 110
- 6.13 Basic ritual patterns and exercises — 111
- 6.14 Opening and closing directions and working spaces — 112
- 6.15 Creating a directional space — 114
- 6.16 Establishing the gates and tools — 115
- 6.17 The Pentagram as the magical human pattern — 119
- 6.18 The ritual of building the Hexagram — 123
- 6.19 Hexagram ritual — 124
- 6.20 Bringing in inner contacts to the directions — 132
- 6.21 Triggering the gates and the contact of the east — 133

6.22	Contacts in the south	135
6.23	Contacts in the west	137
6.24	Contacts in the north	138
6.25	Inner contacts and their issues	140
6.26	Establishing power flows across the directions	141
6.27	Moving energy from one inner direction to another	142
6.28	Moving energy from an inner direction to an outer object	143
6.29	The web of power	146
6.30	Designing a ritual	149
6.31	Designing a lone ritual	153
6.32	Constructing a lone ritual using inner contacts	154

7 Developing Tarot skills — 157

7.1	A reading	158
7.2	Shuffling	158
7.3	Layouts	159
7.4	The Tree of Life layout	160
7.5	The Landscape Layout	164
7.6	Tarot Taboos	170
7.7	Keeping yourself and the deck clean	172
7.8	A method for cleaning a Tarot deck	173
7.9	Cleaning yourself	173
7.10	Tasks for getting good at Tarot	174
7.11	Magical dynamics of Tarot, both good and bad	175
7.12	Cards as doorways	175
7.13	Narrowing fate	176
7.14	Responsibility	177

8 Summary — 179

8.1	Prejudice	179
8.2	Discernment	179
8.3	Glamour	180
8.4	Self-responsibility	180

II The Initiate — 183

Introduction — 185

9 Accessing the Inner Worlds — 187

9.1	Accessing beings: making a contact	190
9.2	Human inner contacts	192

10 Practical methods for working with angelic beings — 195
10.1 So how and why do we work with them? 198

11 Working with deities: pitfalls and approaches — 203
11.1 Forms of deity 204
11.2 Working with the deity 205

12 Working with ancestors — 211
12.1 Time jumping 213
12.2 Family ancestors 214
12.3 The ancestral vision 215
12.4 The family 218
12.5 Guarding the children 219
12.6 Tribal ancestors 220
12.7 Cultural ancestors 223
12.8 The vision of Tin Hinan 224
12.9 Practical use of ancestral work 225
12.10 Time and intention 226
12.11 Interactions with ancestors 227
12.12 Vision of meeting the ancestors 229
12.13 Dynamics 230

13 Accessing and working within the Faery Realm — 233
13.1 Short vision for accessing the Faery Realm 234
13.2 Longer vision of the Faery Realm 235
13.3 Work 238
13.4 My own discovery of faeries 240
13.5 Magic, faeries and sex 244

14 Polarization: magical dynamics and partnerships — 249
14.1 Polarity within magical partnerships 252

15 The physical implications of practising magic — 259
15.1 Treating impacts 260
15.2 Working with balance 262
15.3 Food 264
15.4 Practicalities while working 265
15.5 The effects of inner contact on the endocrine system . . . 267
15.6 The future 272

16 Inner landscapes of the people and the land — 275
16.1 Energetic load-sharing: a short look 280

17 Magical protection: working methods — 285

| | 17.1 | So when do you use banishing and talismans? . . . . 286 |
| | 17.2 | House protection . . . . 289 |

18 Sigils and seals 293
- 18.1 Angelic and demonic sigils 293
- 18.2 Deity sigils 296
- 18.3 Magical seals 297
- 18.4 Platonic solids and geometric shapes 300
- 18.5 Mandalas 302

19 Inner world parasites 305
- 19.1 Dealing with and removing parasites 307
- 19.2 Emotional parasites 309
- 19.3 Sexual parasites 309
- 19.4 Magical parasites 310
- 19.5 Parasites of the dying 312
- 19.6 Minor parasites 313
- 19.7 Removing parasites: practical application 313
- 19.8 Summary 315

20 Removing ghosts and other unwelcome guests 317
- 20.1 Types of hauntings 318
- 20.2 Land-based entities 320
- 20.3 Possession of a house by demonic forces 323
- 20.4 Possession from an object 325

21 How to deal with simple magical/psychic attacks 327

22 Dismantling Hermetic or Kabbalistic curses 331
- 22.1 What is a Hermetic/Kabbalistic curse? 332
- 22.2 How do curses affect the victim? 333
- 22.3 So what about protection? 335
- 22.4 Dismantling the curse: working methods 338
- 22.5 What do they look like on the inner? 340
- 22.6 How are curses taken off? 341
- 22.7 What is the cleanup procedure? 343

23 Short tour of the Tree of Life without Kabbalah 345
- 23.1 So what actually is the Tree of Life? 346

24 The Structure of the Abyss without Kabbalah 351

25 The eighteenth-century pattern of initiation in Britain 359
- 25.1 The Walk of Initiation at Stourhead, Wiltshire 360

| | 25.2 | The Stourhead initiation . . . . 361 |

26 Working with Sleepers 367
	26.1	So what are sleepers? 367
	26.2	Are the sleepers still active? 369
	26.3	Communing with sleepers 372
	26.4	Vision for contacting a sleeper 376
	26.5	The future 377
	26.6	Bridging 378

27 Death and Birth 383
	27.1	Death 384
	27.2	So what happens when a person dies? 385
	27.3	The death vision in detail 386
	27.4	The Bridge 389
	27.5	The Plains 390
	27.6	The Mountain 391
	27.7	The awakening into rebirth 393
	27.8	Practical working methods 394
	27.9	Physical practicalities 395
	27.10	Birth 396

28 Using tarot as a working tool 399
	28.1	Layouts 401
	28.2	The use of tarot in healing 406
	28.3	The health layout 409
	28.4	Making a contacted deck for magical seership 416
	28.5	Minor layouts 419
	28.6	Creating your major cards 419

29 Working methods for leading group visions/workings 423
	29.1	Contacts 424
	29.2	Energy dynamics 425
	29.3	Reality or imagination? 426
	29.4	Snatched energy 427
	29.5	Different strains for different places 428
	29.6	Picking up maps from written visions 429
	29.7	Clearing up 430
	29.8	Creating a vision from a personal experience 430
	29.9	The vision of the goddess Tefnut in Ethiopia 431
	29.10	The vision of Metatron and the Abyss 434
	29.11	Vision of the elders 436

30	The inner aspects of consecration	443
30.1	Born or touched	443
30.2	Pros and cons	444
30.3	Physical and magical effects	447
30.4	Training versus nature	448
30.5	Lines	450
30.6	What is the future for such consecrations?	450

31	Afterword	453

III The Adept — 455

Introduction — 457

32	Methods of working with temples and deities	461
32.1	Deities: working practice and power dynamics	462
32.2	Working with Deities in the Temple Environment	464
32.3	Finding the Doorway	465
32.4	Creating a window for the deity	466
32.5	Work on site or move the site? How to move a Temple	470
32.6	Deity versus Divinity in a magical temple space	475
32.7	Visionary ritual action	476
32.8	Visionary movement	479
32.9	Summary	481

33	The magic of the fire/volcanic temple	483
33.1	The use of volcanic magic	484
33.2	The path to working with volcanic/fire power	485
33.3	Visions of the volcanic temples	486
33.4	Going into the city beneath the waves	487
33.5	The cave in the centre of the world that links all volcanoes	492
33.6	The vision of the cave	496
33.7	The contact of the sword maker	499
33.8	The work with swords	500
33.9	The vision of the sword maker	501

34	The power and magic of utterance, sound and sigil	507
34.1	Vision: the mediation of sound at the edge of the Abyss	511
34.2	Utterance in the temple	514
34.3	The vision of utterance in the temple	516
34.4	The vision for the creation of magical sigils	519
34.5	Working with the sacred sigils and alphabet	523

| | 34.6 | Sacred alphabet . . . . 524 |

35 The magical dynamics of fate — 527
	35.1	Vision of the conception of a soul out in the stars 530
	35.2	Chess and the Inner Temple 532
	35.3	The board game 533
	35.4	Summary 543

36 How to work with angels — 545
	36.1	Bound angels 546
	36.2	Religious angels 549
	36.3	The consecration of the cathedral 551
	36.4	Religious angels of recitation 553
	36.5	The vision of recitation 553
	36.6	Human angels 556
	36.7	Sandalphon/Synadalphos ("colleague") 557
	36.8	Vision of the Companion 557
	36.9	Metatron 559
	36.10	The vision of Metatron and the Abyss 560
	36.11	Natural angels 562
	36.12	The vision of the Metatron Cube 563
	36.13	The Archon and the Aeon 569
	36.14	Working advice 570
	36.15	Vision of the pattern of death 570

37 Practical methods for creating ritual tools — 573
	37.1	Consecration of tools in the deepest part of the temple . . 573
	37.2	Consecration ritual/vision for a consecrated Sword of Justice 574
	37.3	Ritually enlivening the scabbard 579
	37.4	Placing a being within the sword 583
	37.5	Bridging a being into a tool 584
	37.6	Awakening Divinity in substance 585
	37.7	Summary 588

38 The magic of the Underworld — 589
	38.1	Vision of the Goddess in the Cave and in the Abyss 592
	38.2	The Sisters at the back of the North Wind 597
	38.3	Vision of the Sisters at the back of the North Wind 598
	38.4	Origins of humanity in the Abyss 604
	38.5	Methods of descent 608

39 Functioning as an adept — 613
| | 39.1 | Service . . . . 614 |

39.2	Practicalities of living as an adept	618
39.3	Working within a tradition	620
39.4	The future: passing on the teaching	621

IV Appendices 625

A The consecration of salt and water — 627

B A recitation for a basic exorcism — 629

C Making a Specific Talisman — 631

D What does magic do? — 635
- D.1 The complex web of fate and time — 636
- D.2 Magic and fate in action — 637
- D.3 Magical consequences: an example of magic in action — 638
- D.4 A checklist of advice for beginners — 642
- D.5 Some things to think about — 643

E The magical understanding of good and evil — 645

F The directions in Western magic — 651
- F.1 Background — 651
- F.2 The magical directions — 653
- F.3 The current magical use of the directions — 654
- F.4 Nineteenth-century Europe — 656
- F.5 The sixteenth century — 669
- F.6 The modern structural approach — 676
- F.7 Dynastic Egypt — 677
- F.8 Right hand path, left hand path — 696

G The Book of Death — 705

H Advanced Decoys — 731
- H.1 Personal decoys — 732
- H.2 False doors — 734
- H.3 Time decoys — 736
- H.4 Oppositions — 739
- H.5 Copper as deflection — 741

I The prehistory of magical development — 743
- I.1 Magic and its forms — 745
- I.2 The series of unfortunate events — 747

I.3	People and responses	751
I.4	Early ritual solar circles	757
I.5	Chambered tombs in Northern Europe	763

Part I
Foundations

Introduction

The work of the lone practitioner is very hard but extremely rewarding, and it really and truly puts you on the path of powerful magic. Nothing is done for you, you are not babysat through your training, and your path of work is something that comes from your choice alone, not the dictates of a group. It also allows a magician to forge his or her own path in a direction that is perfect for them.

In truth, the life of a magician tends to be a mixture of group and lone practice. Sometimes groups are put in our path for a length of time for us to learn something, and other times groups and teachers evade us so we are thrown back on our own resources and initiative. Magic, like life, does not start and end in a group: we are born alone, and we die alone. We walk the path through life and magic with people around us, sometimes very close to us, but ultimately our development and practice is within ourselves.

The first and last rule of magical development, for both beginner and experienced practitioner, is discernment. That word should be tattooed on everyone's forehead so that it is the first thing you read each morning when you look in the mirror. As we grow into adulthood and maturity, we learn how to spot the con artist, the possible dangers in life, the good things, the bad things, and the just plain stupid things. We learn as children not to talk to strangers, not to stick our fingers in electrical sockets or touch live wires; we learn to be careful near cliffs, near bears, and not to poke rattlesnakes. So why the hell don't we carry that lesson of maturity into magic?

Some people approach magic with all the wisdom and foresight of a curious three year old. And as a result of that quaint naivety, they end up drained, depressed, and parasited. On the other hand, if you approach magic with extreme cynicism and over caution, you will never get anywhere. There needs to be a balance between caution, curiosity, an open and exploratory mind, and a good inner alarm system. A good bullshit meter will also shave years off your search for learning. There is a tremendous amount of bullshit out there, and keeping an awareness of that fact will be very helpful. There are also wonderful things out there, excellent books, great teachers, and amazing experiences waiting to be had.

At the end of the day, your magical path is what you make it. What path you forge through magic is based upon your decisions and actions, not what system it is that you follow. I hope that in some small way you find this book helpful. I am sure you will find things in it that you do not agree with, which I think is healthy. I just hope that you also find things in this book that are helpful to you, or which at least will challenge your thinking or make you look at your own practice through different eyes.

Magic is the most beautiful path to tread. It can be rewarding, terrifying, challenging, and fascinating. Magic has been a part of my life since I was very young, and I can say that it has enriched my life to a level that is almost indescribable. I cannot imagine a life without magic. The path was, and still is, tough. It has mainly been walked alone, with the odd eccentric teacher thrown in my path when I needed them, and it has challenged my courage, strength, and values to levels that almost broke me at times. I think it has made me a better person, and it most certainly made me feel whole: it has been like coming home. Magic is my life.

Chapter One

The world of magic and magical training

1.1 Things to consider

The first exposure of a person to magic these days is usually through a book or a film sparking our desire for something which we all know instinctively, deep inside us, is powerful, natural, and true. Gone are the days when lords of the manor secretly held all the mysteries of ritual magic and villagers held the magical secrets of the land powers. In the last hundred years, magic has gone public. It has appeared in college courses, night classes, how-to books, films...the list is as endless as a compulsive shopper's wish list. And therein lies the secret: magic is power, true magic, real magic. It is powerful, intense, and dangerous. It is beautiful and inspiring, and it brings us closer to ourselves.

Although the average person in the street is exposed only to the cotton candy variety of magic, their instincts, deep instincts, tell them to fear it or desire it. Such fear is of course partly grounded in the fears fed to us as children, and the propaganda fed to us by the church. Yes, magic is dangerous in its full potential; yes, it can do damage to the soul if misused; and yes, there are unethical people out there who use it. But the same could be said of a car. And if a child gets into a car, the worst thing that could happen is they take the handbrake off and roll. A car needs keys, and it needs skills to drive it. Once those skills are honed to a fine art, they can be used for great good or great bad. They can also be used simply to do a necessary job.

The majority of people who are first drawn to magic fall into either the witchcraft collection of paths (Wicca, Trad Craft, etc.) or the ritualist collection (Golden Dawn, OTO, etc.). Online courses

1. THE WORLD OF MAGIC AND MAGICAL TRAINING

and book series proliferate and eventually people find their way to a local group or a more solid course of study. From that point, they usually join a coven or a lodge.

The commercialization of magic has brought about a massive change in how magic is approached and why. It has been watered down to make it more palatable, it has been discussed in psychological terms to make it more believable, and it has been presented to make it the panacea for all ills. Dogmas have been reinforced, snake oil pocketed, and profits made. Magic is so much more than that. Magic is the power that flows from unbeing into being. Magic is the space between objects, planets, and cells. Magic is the logic of the universe.

Many of the systems of magic that have developed over the millennia were originally designed in relation to the land on which the magician lived and what culture he or she was immersed in. The cultural relationship with Divinity was the vessel that held the magical system, and religion/magic were one and the same thing. The separation between Deity and magic is a relatively recent thing in human history, and it has been a slow but sustained split in the various schools of magic.

This movement away from the central culture and religious expression of the people slowly developed magic as a hidden power that was potentially evil, and something that only 'bad' people do. This attitude developed steadily in the monotheistic religions: we can see the progression from Moses, Aaron and Miriam, the mythical three magicians who mediated magical power in a battle for their people, through to Jesus who used magic, along with other religious revolutionaries of that time (Simon Magus is one good example), to the purging of all magical and mystical texts and people during the expulsion of the heretics in both Judaism and early Christianity. It was at this point that magic and religion in the Western world parted ways.

Because of this expulsion of heresies, magic became furtive and mobile. It was passed on quietly from generation to generation by people who moved around from one land to another. So for example, Jewish people travelling around Europe took their own brand of magic with them and began practising and teaching it upon the new land where they lived. This had a great effect upon the people whom they interacted with, and magical wisdoms were passed back and forth and sometimes melded together. One very good example of this is Italy in the 15th century when Sephardi Jews were cast out of Spain and ended up in Italy via Libya. The interaction between Libyan Berbers, Spanish Catholics, and Jewish Kabbalists is very apparent in the magic of that time, which eventually gave birth to the Keys of Solomon.

The magic of those Kabbalists from the fifteenth and sixteenth centuries still has a great deal of influence on the magic of today: some magicians consider the Keys of Solomon and related texts the cornerstone of certain types of magic. Egyptian writings relating to magic and religion that were unearthed in the 1800s by archaeologists and esoteric 'romantics' also play a heavy part in modern magic. Today, people follow those paths of magic because they are known and they work. But how valid is that?

Magic is an expression of power and an expression of how that power relates to you, your environment, and your ancestors. Magic is the interface of the land and Divinity; it is the power of the elements around you, the power of the sun and moon, the air that you breathe, and the language of the unseen beings, both benign and malicious, that are living alongside you. With all that in mind, how valid is it to then try and interface with this power by using a foreign language, foreign deities, and directional powers that have no relevance to the actual land upon which you live? The systems will work, and sometimes very powerfully, but to what effect on the land and upon ourselves? I am not saying that to use these systems is wrong; I use them in various ways myself. But I think it is important to also be very mindful of where you are and what you are, and to build upon that foundation.

If you were beginning to practice magic in steps, instead of copying something from another land, stop and look at what is around you. Where is the water in relation to you, where are the plains or grasslands, where is the sun, where are the burials, where are the mountains? Look at what ancient things are around you: what ancestral contacts are there? Do you have cemeteries, cairns, ancient remains, burials, castles, etc.? Look at maps to see what natural springs are around you. Are there any caves? If you are in a city

1. THE WORLD OF MAGIC AND MAGICAL TRAINING

that is modern and vast, like an American city, look into its history to see what is there. It is often not easy to find the ancient stories of a land, but if you dig with intent to work with it, then powers will begin to awaken to help you.

When I lived in Tennessee I had a hell of a job trying to find local information, but after digging relentlessly I did come across some very interesting details that really slotted together very well and gave me a template for my work upon that land. Another very important point to consider is manners. If you work to find what is actually on the land, and who was there before you, how they did things, what their legends were, etc., then you will find that quite powerful forces begin to swirl around you in response. You will be led to places to experience things, and the natural powers of magic within the land will open up to you. It is important that if these land powers awaken to you, that you are acutely aware of the manner of your communication towards them, and that you are always respectful (so that they do not eat you).

1.2 Magical systems old and new

One of the major problems that has repeated over and over within magical circles is the quick disintegration of a true magical system into either a commercial New Age venture, or the older story which is an infighting, agenda-driven lodge. The first happens when the power input is imbalanced, and the second usually happens either for the same reason or because the person who was holding it all together died. Both pictures (and these are just two examples of what can go wrong, there are many more) display an inherent imbalance in the foundation of the system. Why the inherent imbalance? Because the foundations are built on shaky ground.

A great many magical systems work from the ground up. Kabbalah, for example, trains the neophyte to slowly climb the Tree of Life[1] through study, ritual, and meditation. This works from the stance of the human body, which is a finite physical container for the soul, reaching up towards Divinity. This creates a drag upon the

---

[1] The Tree of Life is a map that outlines how Divine power manifests from unbeing to being.

body and is also like swimming up a stream against the tide. When you work from the ground up, you are working within the burden of manifestation, and you have to carry that manifestation as an inner burden as you attempt to journey back to the threshold of Divinity (the edge of the Abyss or Daarth).

The spirit naturally travels *down* the Tree on its journey into and through life. If you repeat this journey in a conscious way, you are more able to interact magically with the process, the beings involved, and the powers as you pass from unbeing into being. Dion Fortune was a great advocate of this method, and from my own personal magical experience, I would say it is a far more powerful method which for me unlocked a great many of the magical secrets hidden within its structure.

And yet, going from Malkuth upwards is the 'official' way to work the Tree. I am not saying that it does not work to study going up the Tree, but what I am saying is that it flies against the Tree's natural flow (which is not actually a tree or anything even remotely to do with trees). The other problem I see in Kabbalah training is that it encourages intense mental study which creates a trap whereby the mind is constantly swirling around concepts that only the deeper inner spirit of a person can truly open.

The second aspect of a shaky foundation is the magical container, i.e. the philosophies, myths, and rituals that the system sits upon. Most Western magic comes from a line of systems that developed out of mystical Christianity and Judaism, with some Greek, Roman, and Egyptian threads thrown in for good measure. If you look into the deeper historic and magical aspects of these threads, then the first thing that becomes apparent is the lack of proper polarity i.e. exclusion of women in their full power and the heavy reliance upon sovereignty power, which is essentially a power grab[1]. We have magical systems developing through a male line that is connected to religious and mythical patterns of power grabbing. Both patriarchy and matriarchy are imbalanced expressions of power and can both express power imbalances through their actions, something that we have witnessed repeatedly throughout history.

---

[1] Egypt, of all the ancient cultures still present in modern magic, is one that is more balanced in terms of gender power.

1. THE WORLD OF MAGIC AND MAGICAL TRAINING

The other problem with basing magic upon these mythical and religious foundations is that by the time the classical era came along (i.e. Greek and Roman times), these ancient patterns were already falling apart. The same pattern repeats over and over in the Mediterranean and Near East cultures from about 500 B.C. onward (much earlier in some cases). These cultures and their degenerated myths are what our current magical systems are based upon.

So how does a neophyte or new initiate navigate such a vessel, and do they actually need to? A system by which a person can learn about power structure is vitally important: if they are forewarned about the vessel's pros and cons, i.e. that it is cracked, then much learning can be brought out of working within such a container. The important step is to realize when it has given all that it can give: then it is time for the initiate to step away and move on.

There are also a great many lessons that can be learned from working with an unbalanced system and learning firsthand why it is imbalanced. Most people have a complex bag of learning needs when they first approach magic, and the imbalanced paths can place those learning needs right in the face of the initiate if they choose to look. It's all about evolution.

That is not to say that we should stick with imbalanced paths because we can learn from them, any more than we should take heavy drugs to learn why not to take them. Some people need that 'in your face learning'; others have different burdens of learning that they need to shoulder. The adepts have a chance, if they take it, to strike out and wipe the slate clean by working on structural methods of learning magic that do not rely on these imbalanced paths. It is very hard work, but it does provide a healthier ladder for the initiate to climb, and it is a form of magical service to the next generation.

For the neophyte or new initiate, the onus is to look beyond glamour and comfort zones, to find a system that is clean and as balanced as possible. Many of the magical systems present a wonderful glamour that attracts seekers like a golden grail. It is up to the seeker to look beyond, and to question what it is they are actually looking for. If it is pure glamour, then such magical systems will suffice. If it is true magical learning a beginner seeks, then the search will become much harder and will have less outer gratification.

But with the quickly changing world in which we live, and with its more flexible way of being, there are many magical adepts from a variety of systems who are throwing the old order to the winds and trying to experiment, research, and build more relevant and efficient working and learning practices. The previous generations who attempted such vessel building often reverted to drawing upon history, myths, philosophies, and more recently, psychology, in their attempts to forge new paths. I feel the problem with such approaches is that by reaching through texts and histories we are already back to the issue of shaky foundations. This is going up the Tree from ground level, trying to swim against the tide. The answer, I feel, is to reach into the inner worlds, into the land, and to access the deeper inner soul of ourselves to get an inner perspective of how magical power flows into our world. That way, the adept can see at what point in the process the power begins to distort, and begin to work on a vessel that plugs that distortion or dispenses with it entirely. By working on the construction of a magical system before the powers manifest physically, the outer expression of that power finds its own natural form, one more in harmony with who we are and where we live.

1.3 Duality and ethics in magic

The major issue that people hit when they begin serious magical study is duality: light and dark, good and bad, the right and left hand paths (a dyslexic's nightmare). Such separation of the two streams of power is inherently unhealthy and immediately creates an antagonism of power (although that antagonism can be seen as a power source by some magical paths). Either path studied to any depth will create an imbalance within which the natural flow of power will try to reharmonize itself. When this 'rebalancing' manifests itself without the conscious actions or intentions of the magician, it can have a destabilizing effect upon the magician and will play out in a number of ways either through the life path of the practitioner or through their bodies as mental or physical imbalances. If a practitioner consciously engages the opposing flow of power through action and intent, it can have a more productive and educational effect without quite as much devastation.

1. THE WORLD OF MAGIC AND MAGICAL TRAINING

Another way of avoiding such imbalances is to completely sidestep the polarization and approach the light and dark equally, or to walk a path that works with beings unconditionally. The same method is also employed in the interaction of beings in the inner worlds and outer worlds. Instead of viewing a being as inherently 'good' or 'bad,' the practitioner works with each being without judgement and understands that every being has its role in the picture of existence. Just because a being or a being's expression of power is bad for humanity or a human, that does not make it 'bad'; it is all relative.

In practice this means working in all worlds with all beings in an appropriate way and simply understanding how they affect us and how we affect them. Through that understanding you may choose to not work with certain beings because of how they affect us. That is not the same as the practice of subduing, pinning, or binding a being just for being itself because it is considered 'dark.'

If a being of great power is causing chaos, the first question to ask is *why*. If it is simply doing its own thing in the greater pattern, then it should not be interfered with just because we do not like it. If it is out of place because some human ritual action drew it in, then it should be quietly put back where it belongs. If it has been bound ritually into service by a human action and is causing chaos, then it must be unbound and put back where it came from. If is has been released from a natural process of binding by ritual magic, then it needs to be put back into its binding. It's like returning things to factory settings.

Some beings, particularly strong ancient powers, are bound naturally by the evolution of the species and the planet. To release them for conditional reasons is highly dangerous as they do not operate on our 'frequency' and can cause untold damage. This can manifest, for example, as a practitioner summoning and releasing ancient powers from the depths of the Abyss. It is all very 'glam' but it creates a hell of a mess. And this is one of the approaches that has created such imbalance in the world of humans: we cannot stop fiddling to suit ourselves.

Practitioners follow a path of light or dark, then from there, summon, banish, or bind beings that fit with their agenda. This is reflected in the Tibetan Buddhist practice of teaching respect for all beings, but then binding powerful beings into conditional service. Not healthy at all. It is much healthier, but harder, to meet and work with such beings on an equal footing, unconditionally, powerfully, and with respect.

In practical modern terms, the magical practitioner would learn about all the various orders of beings, meet them on their own turf and learn the dangers of certain types of beings. From there, a wider understanding of how power and consciousness can develop, which in turn leads to healthier and more balanced practices.

1.4 Approach to training: selfish versus non selfish

Magic is simply the manipulation of power to elicit a change. The change can be conscious or unconscious, conditional or unconditional. Magic moves power from A to B, it awakens powers and forces, or it sends them into hibernation. It evokes emotional responses, affects the human body, changes the flow of fate, brings things into being, and sends them into unbeing. It can build structures in other worlds, and it can be used to interface with beings from other realms.

So immediately you can see how easily misused magic can be if someone with no ethics, loads of patience, and natural talent decides to walk down that path. Such a path does have its downsides, however.

There are two ways to approach magic: the intelligent way, and the not so intelligent way. To approach it the not so intelligent way, the neophyte uses magic to obtain that which his personality is too weak to achieve alone without effort. As the neophyte progresses, the temptation, then justification, to use magic to achieve whatever is needed becomes greater and more normalized. If the magician is slighted, hurt, or otherwise upset, then they will revert to aggressive magic to attack and punish. Magic is used to draw in a lover, money, fame, and to settle disputes: the list is as endless as man's stupidity.

If this path is taken, there is no fatherly god sitting on a cloud wagging a parental finger. Life is not quite so easy. What

1. THE WORLD OF MAGIC AND MAGICAL TRAINING

happens with such an approach to magical work is that the personality gradually gets weaker and the spirit gets flabbier. We learn, strengthen, and mature from the everyday normal physical knocks, hardships, and disappointments that life puts in our path. Using magic to shortcut those lessons leaves a person emotionally, spiritually, and magically illiterate. The personality that uses magic to handle everyday issues and problems is the same as the personality of a long-term drug user: their emotional age becomes stuck at the age they started 'using.' They do not develop the 'inner skin' that life knocks can give us, therefore they become vulnerable to inner parasites that feed off emotive, magical, and sexual exchanges. Those parasites then use that energy to 'cross-dress' in an effort to convince the practitioner that they are magical contacts or deities.

The combination of a retarded emotional age and inner parasites results in a very unhealthy and unhappy individual who 'bottoms out' in their magical power: it levels off at a dead end and they get stuck there. It is nature's way of saving humanity from its own idiots.

A more intelligent way is to approach magic like learning a craft that has an ancient heritage, and a lot of responsibility attached to it. If it is approached with a sense of respect and a sense of service, of wanting to be useful, then although such a path is not as materially rewarding in some senses, it is a very powerful path indeed. A respect for the Divinity within all things, a respect for the beings of all the different realms without judgement or prejudice, and a respect and willingness to protect/serve the world of nature around us are all foundations of approach which put the neophyte on a path of true magical adeptship. It then links him or her to those who have walked the same path of service for millennia, and ensures that the magician has what they need in order to do their work.

It is not a fluffy bunny path by any means: the practitioner often serves deep and high in the Abyss, facing great danger. Such a path brings with it difficulties and challenges but it also brings with it great learning, power, and maturity. The magician must be able to cross all realms, commune with all types of beings, and fight their corner in deep magical combat when needed. All of this needs to be done without any emotion.

1.5 So why do we do magic?

Humanity has an ability that many other beings, both physical and not physical, do not have: we can move power and consciousness from A to B. We can initiate action, pressing the red button so to speak, which many other beings cannot do. Every being has its inner action, and when all the beings and actions are put together you have an orchestra. Our part is to start the ball rolling and move power around. Magic forms a threshold and filter for power, it shapes it, patterns it, gives it form, and brings it out into our world. It alters the flow of inner power and with ritual and vision we can effect change in that power to give it boundaries and use it to a specific end.

With that in mind, the magician can use that ability to serve himself, or to serve the land, culture, community, or Divinity. It will work regardless of the intention, but the long-term outcomes both for the individual and the land upon which they reside will be different. Often the magician will change their intent over the years as their personality matures. Sometimes, of course, that doesn't happen and the magician stays on their original path of intent, be it good, bad, or indifferent.

1.6 Personal development

There is a stream of people who are drawn to magic because religion has failed them in some way or other, and yet they are deeply aware that there is more to the world than Kentucky Fried Chicken. Often people have mystical, magical, or power/sight experiences that show them, at a deep personal level, that there are streams of power that are not obviously apparent, and they begin to explore those streams.

In general, the Western culture in which we live is underpinned by a sense of powerlessness: the government runs our lives, the churches, mosques, etc. control our access to Divinity, and social constraints discourage use and expression of power. When a person chooses not to play a part in that circus, they look elsewhere for a path to power. Some people begin that path in search of their own power, some begin in search of knowledge, and some approach that path from a sense of deep instinct.

1. The World of Magic and Magical Training

The beginning of the path in magic is very much about personal development, be it spiritual, intellectual, or self determination. This is the first rung of the ladder and it has many dead ends woven into it at a deep magical level regardless of the type of magic it is. These dead ends are designed to trap someone and teach them a lesson that is needful for their development. Some stay in those traps indefinitely (the inner weeding process) and some eventually get the message at a deep level and haul themselves up on to the next rung of the ladder.

The 'dead ends' on the first rung of magic are often related to our relationship to power, glamour, and ego. We all go through it in one form or another and most climb out of it with a very red face, ready to move on, lesson well learned. There is nothing wrong in making mistakes and doing silly things, it is all part of the learning process. The first rung teaches us about ourselves, our weaknesses and strengths, our true desires and fears, and the real extent of our ability to be honest with ourselves. Remember the words over the door to the temple: Γνῶθι σαυτὸν "know thyself."[1] The threshold of the temple must be crossed with the intention to be willing to look in the mirror with an open mind and see what is really there.

If we approach the 'outer mysteries,' which is the first rung of the ladder, with that openness, then we begin the focused evolution of the soul, which takes up the rest of our lives. Because the outer court of magic, or the outer/lesser mysteries contain methods of divination, methods of lone and group ritual, using magical tools and methods, and the study of magical history, there are many who approach the first ladder and get stuck in these outer court skills. They can pull a few tricks, impress people with their titles, dress in cool clothes, and have strange symbols around their necks: it is a dead end for the ego. Some get stuck there for a time and climb out, and some stay there indefinitely.

When the initiate climbs out of that dead end, they look back and see the power traps and the allurement of the ego: they then have to face their weaknesses. That is a major step forward and is of great value to the developing magician: when you know your own weaknesses, face them and address them, you are far less vulnerable to the dangers lurking in magic.

---

[1] **pausanias-gnothi-seauton** 10.24.1

Higher octaves of the same experience revisit the neophyte in a variety of ways until all the layers are peeled away. There is nothing wrong with ego, indeed it is something that is needful in our society and for ourselves: it is a natural and healthy part of our psychological make up. It only becomes a problem when it becomes the 'truth' to us and we are unaware of it. The first layers of training expose the weaknesses, then the strengths, of our egos. It takes fragmented egos and solidifies them, making a person confident with awareness from within, as opposed to trying to obtain confidence and power through outside actions.

When that rung of the ladder is finished with, the new initiate climbs onto the next rung which is a higher octave of the first. The magical work becomes more about the group, or the community, or the lodge. The same traps are present, just in a more subtle dressing. The magical work becomes more focused through ritual and vision, through the use of the elements/tools, and the introduction to beings. This brings with it, particularly for the naturally inclined magician, the ability to begin to move power around, contact inner beings and affect the world around them in small ways. They learn how to manipulate power and the very shiny dead end appears. Some magicians, at this phase, become very enamoured of their own power ability and sense of importance. It is the all-singing, all-dancing messiah trap. Their ability to impress people is strong and they begin to be held in awe by people who are not of their level of knowledge. Some climb out of this dead end, again red faced and a little wiser. Some do not and become new age pop star/goth/guru/Merlin flavoured magicians who effectively feed off the surrounding neophyte's energy.

The initiates who do not get stuck in this trap, or who climb out of it, learn how to use their ability and technique for the good of their community, land, nation, lodge, or group. At this phase, initiates are also sometimes given the responsibility to teach early neophytes, which in itself is a major learning opportunity. It is only when we have to teach something to another person that we really begin to see the mechanics of power, technique, and method.

If the initiate is not part of a magical order or group, i.e. a lone practitioner, the same power dynamics occur as it is an integral part of the way inner power flows. Things are put in your path, and you either learn from them or you don't. If you learn, more powerful things are put in your path and you step forward to the next training session. This rung is the usual one where initiates decide to leave the group or stream and go it alone. It is a harder path, but can for some be a much more powerful one.

The next and more powerful rung is the one of service to the long-term planetary powers and to Divinity. This is the level where magic and spirituality truly come together, and the adept becomes a bridge of Divinity/universal power (not deity). The service is rarely conducted within a lodge or group, but becomes either a very lonely path or a path whereby others of similar level are brought together from different streams to do a 'job,' which can often span a whole lifetime. It fully dispenses with the dead end of egos because the simple nature of the work often demands a silence in the outside world. This is not an oath form of secrecy; rather it is a knowing that there is nothing to be gained and all to be lost by advertising one's actions. This is where the old saying 'cast ye not pearls before swine' comes into play. If you tread this path carefully, then others of similar service are put in your path to work with. If you become stuck in the dead end, it forms into a stronger messiah trap and the whole 'Illuminati of the modern age' bullshit rears its head.

Each rung has its own steps within it that expose our weaknesses and strengths, and the rungs flow in a natural power manifestation rather than being imposed by human structures. The groups and lodges often have their own self designed lessons, but in truth, life itself places the more powerful traps at your feet to see how you handle them. Power has a way of working, and it will flow regardless of how we try to shape it, funnel it, or use it. By taking a lone path, the initiate essentially hands over the lessons to be learned to a higher teacher (fate) and it can take a very strong sense of focus and self examination to walk the lone path. Hence it is harder, but infinitely more productive.

Chapter Two

The pitfalls and traps of magic

2.1 Oath taking

Once the neophyte is crossing the road to become an initiate, one of the first major issues to raise its head regardless of whether the person is a member of magical group/lodge, or a sole practitioner, is the issue of oath taking. At some point, once a person has begun to show any ability to work in the inner worlds, the need for oaths will raise its head. There are many reasons why oaths are asked of a magician, and to be honest with you, most of the reasons are a load of bull. There are a small number of reasons to take oaths and a very limited list of whom that oath should be bound to. There tend to be three basic types of oaths, the oath to a group, the oath to a deity or power, and the oath to a landmass. Within those categories there are many variants and subcategories with enough red tape to keep you going for months.

The first basic type of oath I mentioned is the oath to a group/lodge/fellowship. This type tends to cover secrecy, honour and obedience towards the group, the work, the leader or all three. I am personally very uncomfortable with such oaths as they are easily misused, often connected or attached to curses, and are not necessary. If there is work being done in the group that is of a nature that is best not discussed, one would hope that magicians working at that level would have enough intelligence and magical maturity to know to hold their tongues without being sworn on pain of death. If such an oath is needed, it reflects upon the weakness of the group and therefore states that they should not be doing such work anyhow. If the oath is sworn to the leader, then it is possible that a power grab situation is happening where the leader is manipulating the members. Oaths are often asked for when there is something to hide: remember that.

2. THE PITFALLS AND TRAPS OF MAGIC

Another unhealthy reason for oaths is an age-old adherence to drama and intrigue. It puts the members in a 'special status' of a secret society, or a brotherhood: it is very appealing to a teenager, but again, it serves no real magical purpose. When we come to the issue of magical knowledge that some feel should be withheld or kept secret and preserved, even then the path of oath taking, I feel, is still not justified. Those who are unprepared at an inner level cannot understand magical knowledge; it reveals itself to a seeker only when the seeker is ready to receive it fully. Some naturally talented people can unravel magical text and usually promptly blow themselves up. But the taking of oaths under these circumstances can be very unhealthy both for the practitioner and the magic itself.

The other very important issue regarding oath taking is that it disengages the individual's important learning curve regarding knowing when to keep silent and when not. The institutionalization of magical learning over the centuries has created a framework whereby the individual is not allowed to develop their own self discipline, their own inner strength; nor are they given space to develop individually at their own pace. When someone who is immature begins a path of practice that will potentially take them to strength, knowledge, and power, they will show off and brag about it to their peers who are not involved in such a path. Life will teach such a person a lesson of maturity, which will be painful and embarrassing if they are perceptive. If they are not perceptive, but are self absorbed, they will continue to expose themselves to ridicule as they parade their path like a new coat. That will trap them magically at that stage and they will not develop much beyond the basics.

As the initiate matures, they usually become very aware that it is pointless to try and discuss magic outside of the community of magicians: their silence becomes self-imposed. As the initiate progresses onto being an adept, they begin to see how magic is just another name for what is, basically, the power of the universe. That power is addressed in terms of religion, magic, physics, and biology, etc. When the adept talks about magic to a priest, or a theoretical physicist for example, it is very possible to have in-depth magical conversations where you realize you are both talking about the same power, but you are both just using a different vocabulary. Hence the need for secrecy falls away. It's all about discernment, which is one of the major necessities in magic.

And this is why, for me personally, I have no qualms about writing certain texts and making them available: the lack of secrecy ensures that the information goes where it needs to. Of course, there are certain parts of magic that I do not write about not because I have some archaic need for secrecy, rather it is because it serves no necessary purpose to put such work in a public domain.

The rules and regulations that abound in magical groups/lodges are outdated and follow a mentality of control and hierarchy. We need to move a little beyond that and mature a bit spiritually.

The other pitfall with oaths is the inner impact or binding that can affect the spirit and life path. Some magical oaths are constructed to be more than just a promise—they can become ritual binds that will trigger curses if that oath is broken. Sometimes, many times in fact, neophytes or new initiates are bound by ritual oaths to obedience and secrecy. Then they discover that the group or lodge is corrupt and is involved in magical practice that goes against the ethics of the individual. The ritual oath means the person who is oath bound cannot warn others, challenge the behaviour, or seek support, however confidential. It puts the individual in an ethically difficult situation in that they can potentially become silent witnesses to all manner of magical abuses. The side-effect of such a curse-bound oath is that they also become complicit in the unbalanced act and take on some of the energetic interplay that is tied to the ritual actions. Leaving the group is sometimes not enough to sever from the oath, so it pays to be very choosy about what oaths one takes, and to whom.

Deities rarely, if ever, ask for heavy oaths: they may ask you to do something or commit to something for a length of time, but that is not an oath, it is an agreement. You can simply agree or disagree to such a request: some people interpret such requests as a need for an oath when really, it is not. Often the interpretation of such a request as a need for an oath is based upon the individual's cultural behaviour which ultimately has no bearing on the magical relationship between a deity and a magician: we think it is the right thing to do when in fact it is counter productive. Be very mindful that if you swear an oath, you cannot back out without repercussions.

2. The pitfalls and traps of magic

2.2 The tying-in of energy

This is something that most people do not realize when they attach themselves to a magical path, group, or deity, and that is by partaking of that path, you are in effect tying yourself energetically to that path for a length of time. That can happen naturally or can be imposed upon you. It happens naturally when you begin to work with a specific God or Goddess, your energies become interwoven with the magical interface that allows that power to interact with humanity.

The more energetically sensitive you are, the deeper the impact upon your spirit. The same happens naturally when you work on a piece of land for a very long time, particularly if you also live on that land—you become entwined with its energy structure. This was the mechanism that was used in times past to accommodate sleepers within the land. It strengthens the interconnection with the land, and the power of the land flows through the practitioner as they mature in magical knowledge and skills.

The tying in of energy is also done intentionally when people join some magical lodges or groups. Their energies become connected, usually by way of a group ritual initiation or oath of allegiance, to the egregore and the magical structure that upholds the group. This can become extremely unhealthy as the balance of the whole structure is only as balanced as the person or persons upholding the group. Any action initiated by the leader is energetically tied to all its members so that the action is in effect fuelled by the members. If this is done with consent, then all well and good, and people sometimes learn some hard lessons. If this is done without consent, as is often the case, then irreparable damage can potentially be inflicted upon the energetic systems of the people. Most often this action without consent is done without bad intent, and sometimes without understanding, but nevertheless the results can take many years to untangle.

Because of these types of pitfalls and problems, it is wise to not get into oaths until you are absolutely sure what it is that you are getting involved in. It pays to look from an inner point of view as well as an outer point of view, and if a person is not able to do that, then that in itself is an indication that oaths should not be taken. As for the tying-in of energies, it is prudent to develop one's energy sensitivity as a priority when working/learning magical skills.

With a heightened level of sensitivity, it is harder for a 'tying-in' of energy to be imposed upon you, and the more ground foundation work one does the more solid the practitioner becomes. With that solidity comes boundaries, which are of paramount importance in magic. Without boundaries, one is quickly drained of energies in a variety of ways and can be potentially exposed to powers that can seriously unbalance a sensitive mind. Anyone who walks a magical path must understand from the very beginning that you are ultimately responsible for yourself and you are not going to be protected from the results of your own bad decisions.

If you are walking a solitary path, the rules are the same. Inner contacts can initiate all the same problems that outer groups can, and one should proceed with caution and common sense at all times. The solitary path is something that does have less in the way of pitfalls but is much harder to walk. The development however of a solitary magician is often fused with far more power than a group path if the solitary magician has good inner and outer boundaries, and lashings of self discipline.

2.3 Blockage of knowledge

This is a favourite form of power manipulation in groups and lodges. The leader or the 'inner court' members effectively block the neophytes and initiates from accessing certain lines of power 'for their own good.' I find this arrogant and elitist. There is nothing wrong in unfolding the training in steps and ensuring that each person develops a strong foundation and good working practice. That is different. When someone who is being grounded in the foundations of magic, and they have natural talent, or have done this at some 'other time,' the foundation training will awaken certain things within their consciousness which will allow them to access deeper inner realms and contacts. This is the hallmark of a true initiate: they find the inner keys for themselves. Many lodges hold very tight control over inner contacts and inner temples, locking out all but a few adepts, the chosen ones, which in effect mummifies the line of magic. This disengages the natural development of progress within the initiate ranks and keeps them disempowered. The result is a group of initiates who cannot access new realms and new contacts

2. THE PITFALLS AND TRAPS OF MAGIC

for themselves, and who often cannot step beyond the 'allowed' contacts. Such controlling behaviour is degenerate and unforgivable.

The other form of blocking power that can happen in groups is where all the members are deliberately blocked from accessing the inner worlds in any way other than what is given to them. This can be done by giving the initiates certain meditations or visions to do that effectively block them from inner worlds and contacts. It is often done furtively, and in a way that would not arouse suspicion. I have personally witnessed an eastern 'Lama' giving out a group meditation that was designed to stop the practitioner accessing power from the land. People trusted his robes and gentle smile and did not stop to think for a moment what it was they were doing. I was appalled by the arrogance of the man, that he did not even try to hide what he was doing, but instead sugar coated it with new age sweetness.

Thankfully such behaviour is not widespread and most blocking happens when the teacher feels superior and justified in such actions. I don't feel that there is such a justification; such 'nannying' of an initiate stops them from learning important lessons. Many initiates who are not strong enough to handle deeper inner contacts often cannot get them anyhow. If they are able to make the contacts but are not grounded enough to work with them, they will either shut down naturally, or they will fragment physically or mentally just enough for them to drop out of that path.

Such power blocking is there to stop that from happening. But I do feel that, in the long-term pattern of spiritual development, it is an important phase to go through if it is necessary. By protecting a person from their actions, their natural inner evolution is suppressed, and they do not really learn why not to do something. If they have been warned, then that is enough, they have to make the choice, not the lodge. Usually I have found that when the work begins to really pick up pace and the power levels rise, people who would be unsuitable for the work suddenly cannot get to the meetings. The inner contacts that are being worked with usually filter out unsuitable candidates, and they tend to be better judges than I, so I trust that filtering.

The blocking of power for a solitary practitioner is not really an issue, as there is no one there to block him. If the lone practitioner is not capable of handling a contact, they will not get that contact. If one is being blocked from getting into somewhere or making contact with an inner being, it is usually because the inner 'do not disturb' sign is up for a reason. To this day, I sometimes find that I cannot access something, or sometimes I am booted out of the inner worlds. Usually within twenty-four hours I find out why—I would have an infection, or have energy building up for something else to be done, or there was something unhealthy going on and I was being filtered out of it.

2.4 Past lives and genetic threads

Something that rears its head very quickly in magical training is the issue of past lives, ancient souls, and blood lines. In our modern world of disconnected communities and disempowered people, it is wonderfully alluring to hearken back to another life/personality/time when things were different. For a weaker personality, this can provide a refuge from the real world, where a person can be 'something' of importance.

It is important right from the outset to be able to distinguish reality from fantasy and the lines can get blurred very easily. Yes, magic will exhume past living experiences, yes it will wake up other times when you have lived and yes it will also kick start genetic knowledge held in your blood (along with feuds, quests, and unfinished business). But such awakening has to be approached very carefully and with a level head. 'Past' is not 'better,' it is just a memory that can be useful or not.

The mechanism of remembering 'past living' experiences in magic is intended to enable you to access magical learning and wisdom that you acquired in other lives so that you can integrate that learning in a present day setting and use it consciously—that way you not constantly reinventing the wheel. However, that process is not like having 'facts' unearthed in your mind; it is more of a 'deep knowing' where you *know* how to do something, you just don't know *how* you know. Before I go on to talk about how such memories can be used in magic, let's look at what can go wrong, and often does.

2. THE PITFALLS AND TRAPS OF MAGIC

When people begin to reach back through time, or the magic awakens old dormant memories and skills, how that person reacts to the awakening will decide whether or not that person moves any further along the path of true magic. It is one of the 'swirls' that catch people on the climb up the ladder of magical training and like so many other swirls, they can be spectacular in their presentation. The amount of people who get trapped at this phase and think they are Akhenaten, John Dee, Aleister Crowley, Dion Fortune etc. is just mind-boggling. They spend the rest of their lives trying to recreate a past that never existed, or to live in a past culture that has no real relevance in today's world. Who cares if you were John Dee in another life? You are not now, so get over it.

Memories can do many things when they emerge, and the first thing to be wary of is getting into the glamour and drama of another life. It does not matter who you were, all that matters is the skill set that you have access to, awareness of any outstanding patterns that need to be addressed (and I mean magically, not psychologically) and any ongoing jobs. The ongoing jobs are not usually something that emerges early on in a magical training. The deep timeless consciousness of the soul only usually brings that to the fore when it is finally time to get back to work, and that can often be many years into the magical life of someone. It never presents as a formed 'job'; rather the magician is compelled by some deep instinct to follow a certain action or path. Emerging skills, work and memories never come fully formed or with detail—when the past emerges, it emerges in shadows, fleeting senses and a deep *knowing* that cannot be verbalized. If someone presents a past emergence of skills with full details, names, etc. then it is more likely that subconscious fantasy and escapism is driving such experiences.

Access to the magical skill set is often the first thing to emerge from other lives. The skills initially emerge unconsciously and will have been triggered by the practitioner's involvement in a situation that demands such a skill. You are put in a situation that is new to you in this life, but you will feel like you are slipping into a comfy old favourite pair of slippers. You will be on home turf and will be able to access things you didn't know that you knew. When that happens, is it best to expand that opening by going into silence through meditation, so that it can emerge naturally. Sometimes, the door can be opened

2.4. Past lives and genetic threads

by a specific event, but what comes after that needs to be approached with care and intelligence. Powers and skills need to emerge in their own time without being forced and if the ground is prepared by stillness and meditation, and an 'openness' to allow nature to do her job, then the skills will emerge as needed.

An example. When I was a youngster, a man called Dr Gupta, a doctor in Bradford who was running a small research project, hypnotized me. I regressed quickly which was not expected or intended, and the major thing to come out of it for me was the emergence of the void. I was talked into a space 'between lives' where I was still, silent, and in a place of profound power. I did not have the vocabulary to properly verbalize what I was experiencing, but the experience itself stayed with me and changed me forever. It opened the doors within me, and skills started to spill out. They came out slowly, though, emerging over a twenty-year period that allowed me to properly integrate them and build upon them. I never consciously at any point tried to actively engage the skill memory, which to be honest with you is something that never occurred to me anyway during those years—I was far too young to understand what was happening. I tended to bumble my way through things, blissfully unaware most of the time of what the hell was going on around or even within me.

If you do try to actively engage the memories, they filter through your present day mental vocabulary and you can quickly get trapped in the 'story' as opposed to engaging the skills you actually need. Anything that you try to force under such circumstances will shut down on you as power just does not flow like that. Magical development in general has a basic rule—focus on what is directly in your path and the rest of it falls into place as you go.

Outstanding patterns are things that begin to emerge as the magical development of the individual progresses. By outstanding patterns I mean events that play out, often mirroring mythical patterns that are much bigger than ourselves. I am not talking particularly about personal behaviour patterns, but rather patterns of power that play out through families, lodges, races and cultures. When we recognize what is happening, we can choose to get back on the hamster wheel of the pattern or we can opt to look for more

2. THE PITFALLS AND TRAPS OF MAGIC

imaginative solutions to our small part in the play—what can we do to change the cycle for the better?

Often recognizing a pattern and consciously deciding not to partake of it is enough to break the cycle. The most common patterns are ones of war, conflict, magical infighting, and rival temple powers. To dive back in to 'do your bit,' or 'defend the ancestors' adds to the pattern, which feeds power to all the beings that have a vested interest in keeping the pattern going. One of the maturing factors of magical development is the conscious decision to find better, more balanced ways to resolve your part in the pattern. By focusing on your own actions, you allow the deeper powers to run through the pattern as a whole. Often the best action is not actually part of the pattern, but a small, regular act of service to uphold or help the beings that are working within the fate pattern. This in turn is mirrored in the magical development of the adept who finally gets to a stage of realizing that most of the time, magic is not the appropriate action to take.

The longer and deeper you do magic, the less of it you do—it becomes very clear that most of the time is it just interfering with a bigger pattern. This is why certain lines of adepts choose unconditional magic in service: you turn up, lend a helping hand, then leave without ever knowing what the hell you just did. That way, it is very hard to interfere or impose your own opinionated action upon a situation.

2.5 Candy shop magic

This is a term I use for the practice of buying into any and all magical paths, books, courses, workshops, outfits, jewellery, haircuts, T-shirts... The person hops from one book to another, from one path to another, constantly looking for the next power fix and glamour image. One week it's Chumley, the next it's Fortune, Enochian magic, Egyptian magic, and so on. I am not saying that someone should stick only with one path because that is equally unhealthy. But there needs to be a sensible, solid consistency in the initial learning so that something can take root and begin to grow. We have to learn the rules and gain a foundation with roots before we can break them.

2.5. Candy shop magic

This is obvious to anyone who has studied any classical discipline to a professional level. Once you know one system of work well from the inside out, then you can throw that structure away if needs be and access virtually anything even remotely on the same frequency. So lodge secrecy regarding contacts becomes obsolete: once you have worked in depth with inner contacts, you can access just about anyone or anything. You don't need to have the contacts handed to you: just go get them for yourself.

If you are a lone practitioner, it is even better—though it is harder. The lone practitioner needs to find an initial, foundational training mechanism that will teach them inner and outer pattern making and skill sets, provide boundaries, and help develop self discipline. It takes a lot more work because it all has to come from within you; but it is far more rewarding if you achieve it, and certainly more powerful. You also do not end up with the sometimes-ridiculous rules, poor quality work, and low-level dross that often accompanies group beginner training.

Once that foundation is there and inner contacts have been made and worked with, and solid skills have been developed, then it becomes interesting to go and look at these various systems. The truths and flaws quickly become apparent in a way that would not have been so obvious in the early stages of the initiate. That way, you can read interesting ideas and be challenged and informed, and view everything with a critical eye.

There is too much written about magic by people who have no real inner experience. They rely on other books, history, philosophy, and myths to come to their conclusions, rather than direct experience. A beginner would not realize that is what is happening, but an initiate who has experience of deeper inner work will immediately spot the flaws in such a text and move swiftly on.

The other problem with the candy shop approach to magic is that the various paths that are dived into and out of often don't mix well, and from a power point of view can be antagonistic. Mixing deities that are not connected, with a form of magic that is not connected to them, can result in anything from total failure to a power kickback that unbalances the practitioner.

2. THE PITFALLS AND TRAPS OF MAGIC

Yes, power does have the potential to work in such a way, but only when done with a deep and full knowledge of the ingredients that are being put together. A trained classical musician, for example, can write a crazy piece of orchestrated music using unusual instruments and make it work. Why? Because they know how the rules of sound work. Someone who is just messing about with instruments and can sort of play one enough to busk is not quite the same. The outcome will most probably be noise. The same goes for power and magic. Learn the deep rules first, then push the boundaries.

2.6 Glamour, control, and ego

The three 'magic' words. These are the biggest of all of the pitfalls. Magical paths and individual teachers can present themselves in a very glamorous way. They draw power around themselves, people look up to them, and they begin to behave like rock stars. They then start to try and control their adoring 'fans' with unnecessary rules and demands of submission, which in turn feeds their ego. Groups similarly shroud themselves in secrecy, club rules, and ranks. They appear as mysterious and have goals that you are told you may be able to aspire to, but will possibly never reach...guaranteed to draw an audience.

A wide-eyed young aspirant sees what they perceive as power and they begin to emulate it so that the next generation of egomaniacs is ready and waiting. It's the same pattern as cult behaviour, and people fall for it all the time. Such leaders get away with really bad behaviour because people will turn a blind eye. More often than not, they will actually try to excuse or even copy such behaviour.

This sort of approach to magic weeds out people from powerful magic and keeps them in magical primary school. If you are starting out on a magical path either with a group or alone and you find yourself adoring some teacher, leader, or adept, then remember one thing: their shit stinks just the same as yours does. And if they are playing on the glamour, they are probably not quite as powerful as they would have you think. Power does not need glamour. Power is hard work, like chopping wood. It burdens you with responsibility, it

2.6. Glamour, control, and ego

challenges you and your actions on a daily basis, and then it puts you to work.

When you approach a magical path, do not disengage your common sense. Use the same early warning systems you do in everyday life. Do not believe everything you see and are told: personal experience is everything in magic. And never ever hand over your power or will to someone else.

Chapter Three

Power and magic

Magic is about working with power. It is the calling of power, the manipulation of power, and the moving of power from A to B. The forms that we work with in vision and ritual—the names, beings, and objects—are all just vessels for the power; they are just matrices that interface between conscious power and humanity. It is very important to understand this when walking a magical path: it is all power, and nothing more.

When we first tread a magical path, we are often swept up in a tide of rituals, beings, magical objects, visionary inner worlds, and inner contacts. Our conscious mind is kept busy with the 'inner' reality show and that allows our minds to interface with Universal Power. But the clutter of human magic, all its accoutrements, is just a dressing that presents itself until our consciousness becomes malleable enough to work without it.

Eventually, as an ageing adept, the work becomes a wordless, formless, but highly focused movement of, or interaction with, power that flows through a pure inner and very powerful instinct: we become a conscious part of the Universal Power. But a practitioner of magic has to go through the various long and often difficult stages of training and development to get to such instinctive work: through the structure, the magician finds the nature of power. Why? Because that is how our consciousness works.

3.1 Boundaries

The first skill that is paramount when working with power is boundaries. If you have no boundaries for the magic, then it will overtake you and destroy you. Another word for these boundaries is *frequencies*. When you work in a particular magical stream, you connect to a certain *frequency* of magic so that, when you are correctly tuned to that frequency, you only pick up what is part of that path. This is very important, because such a defined tuning blocks out many unhealthy inner beings, realms etc. that could be parasitical or damaging. It allows the magician to learn and grow in a relatively safe environment. The longer that path has been walked, the more tuned and focused it is, and the safer it becomes. Such boundaries can also be self-imposed for a new magician learning alone, providing this is approached with careful thought.

The boundaries themselves present as self-imposed restrictions on what action is taken, what element of power is worked with, and what inner visions or outer rituals are done. Add to this a regular daily practice of meditation, and the potential magician will be on the right path. The restricted path should be a longer-term endeavour, not a two-week burst of enthusiasm that quickly vanishes.

For example, let's say a person wishes to train themselves in magic. After learning the very basics of the ritual patterns that work with the directions (boundaries) and observing what is around them, they would slowly start to build upon those ritual patterns in defined stages. From a visionary point of view there would be one place, usually a place of learning like the Inner Library, where they would go in vision on a weekly basis. There would be one simple ritual that is done regularly until its power begins to flow, and a daily meditation to train and discipline the mind. Boundaries—i.e. a ritual pattern such as a directional one, or a pentagram or hexagram pattern—contain the power so that it begins to build, allowing the new practitioner to slowly adjust physically to being in the presence of power.

The simple vision or ritual often gets cast to one side in search of something more powerful and interesting, and such action is a dead end that pulls the prospective magician off the tracks. Some of the simplest rituals are the most powerful, once the magician has learned the deeper frequency of the ritual and can interact with it. For me, the most powerful ritual of all is the lighting of the candle. It opens all worlds, all times and gives me access to focused power that is unfiltered.

The inner vision of the Library has a bit more freedom for a budding magician because all the books in the library are in fact the consciousness of many magicians, mystics, and priests/esses throughout time. It is possible to interact with these wise minds and learn a great deal. Working within the visionary confines of the Library allows the spirit to interact with inner contacts in a variety of ways while still maintaining boundaries.

The combination of a daily simple stillness meditation, a twice-weekly ritual working with a specific pattern, and twice-weekly visits to the Inner Library is a good foundation training that will seriously build inner muscle over a year. Working within such a restriction over a year will build an inner battery for power and will give the practitioner a solid, basic foundation to work from. During that first year, it would be wise to not read tons of magical books, but to work with a small selection within one field. It is important that the ritual and visionary experiences of the practitioner, in the early stages of their training, are not influenced by the writing of others: it is vitally important that the reading is done *after* the experiences, not before.

The other very important and often overlooked boundary that is needed to work with power is a physical discipline. This can take the form of anything from physical training in martial arts, dance, athletics, etc. to dietary restrictions, yoga, etc. It is also good to do a regular physical service, whether that entails tending a patch of land, looking after a few graves of local ancestors, or gardening for an elderly neighbour. Doing something that sometimes you do not want to do, but have to, is very good for self-imposed boundaries. Service is very important in magic, as it teaches us not to be selfish—a quality that is not good to mix with power. Physical discipline builds up strength, and enables the body to process large amounts of power, and the service builds stamina. With strength and stamina, power can flow unfettered through a human and be mediated to whatever situation needs it.

3.2 Working with power

If someone just wants to dress up in outfits, wave around wands, and utter incantations they really don't understand, then power will never be an issue for them. If, however, a prospective magician truly wants to know how to engage power, work through the worlds, and interact with the many beings of the inner realms, then they really need to learn how to interact intelligently with power.

Once a magician has learned how to connect with power, they need to know what to do with it and how to do it. A common mistake that people make when dealing with power is that they identify themselves with it and take it on as a mantle. This quickly leads to a messiah or magus syndrome where they put themselves on a pedestal and quickly self-destruct: they become parodies of what they aspire to. Some also try to power grab, i.e. hold on to the power themselves and not let others engage freely with it. This also brings about degeneration, and the inner worlds eventually disengage from such individuals.

Those are the most common mistakes. The subtler ones to watch for are where the power begins to fragment parts of the mind and/or body that are not able to hold it. This can happen through wilful stupidity or blissful ignorance. If someone is ill and does not realize, and they work with a high level of power, then the power will find the weak point in the body and smash it wide open. It will do the same to any emotional or mental weakness or frailty; hence the need to be physically and mentally solid before working with higher levels of power.

3.3 Loss of ego

This is a very important step in the path to working with magical power, and that is the ability to loosen the grasp on the ego. This is talked about frequently, often in very philosophical terms, in a variety of spiritual and magical traditions. Such traditions often take it too far so that people are expected to lose the very essence that defines them in magic.

To 'lose the ego' in a healthy way means to have conscious awareness of what a small player you truly are in a very big show, and when you get a taste of power, to understand that to connect with such power is actually normal—it does not mean you are chosen or special. By understanding this, the next step, which is to drop the need to control, is far easier to swallow. Surrendering control of a situation is a major step in working with large amounts of power, because without such surrender, the power cannot truly flow.

We limit ourselves by our need to contain power and make it do what we want it to. Our imaginations and ability to look at the longer-range prospect of an action is so limited that we cannot possibly mediate the full flow of power and contain it. We end up in a losing battle with nature and the forces that flow all around us. And when those forces do things we do not like and we cannot control, we label them as evil. Such behaviour is a pattern within humanity that rears its head from the smallest issue to the biggest project.

But by relinquishing control, we then have to approach power either unconditionally, or in harmony with everything else. When we step beyond the toddler phase of 'its all about us,' we then begin to see how these vast powers, which can be horrifically destructive, are also regenerative and are just doing their jobs. The same goes for smaller powers that flow through magic: when they flow in balance, regardless of their outcome, we must learn to live with and around that power, rather than contain or manipulate it.

A good example of this is the tale of Lilith. This power, which is a hive consciousness, is the force of storms/the wind in the desert, which often brings death to the weak. This power, identified in some desert cultures as female, and in others as male, also began to be connected in near eastern myths with parasitical powers that induced sexual dreams in god fearing Jewish men (it was her, they cry, I didn't do anything...yeah right). Often such 'evil winds' or destructive storms do have beings that flow with them, that are parasitical in nature, but they are the 'hangers on' not the power of the storm itself (like the ticks on the back of a ferocious dog).

Back to Lilith. So the power of the destructive storms, or the winds that blow in disease and death, became feared, reviled, and 'amulets a many' were created to keep her/them/it at bay. But no-one ever stops to ask what true function this destructive power has in our world.

The power of the storms is about keeping the land healthy, and the tides of death are nature's way of taking out the very old and very young. It is a tough, but natural way the land keeps populations of various species in check. So instead of battling the storms with magic,

3. POWER AND MAGIC

how about learning to live with them in a healthy way? How about learning about their power and working with them in service–or at least how to get out of their way without trying to attack them head on? By doing so, the magician learns to tune into the power, and will even feel it coming: he will feel its intention, its path, and its force, and will be able to act accordingly. Should he work with it? Hunker down? Become invisible to it?

Such a magical connection with the land and power was adeptly displayed by the Adaman Island's aboriginal Indians, who live on a string of islands in the Indian Ocean. When a tsunami hit, they were already safely tucked away at the top of the hills. They moved hours before the giant wave hit. They were in tune with the land and talked to the sea. They knew the earthquake was coming and they knew the sea was coming, so they got out of the way.

So, back to the Near East. Lilith was presented as a female demon; she was reviled and hated, and vast numbers of people prayed against her. This in itself builds up a huge, collective antagonism which only makes the visitations by such powers more aggressive. How much simpler it would have been to acknowledge the power of the storms, and live and work around them, and to take responsibility for population control so that land powers would not need to do so instead.

It's all about keeping the balance. When you begin to work magically with deeper powers, such issues will come to the fore; and we have to be very careful indeed to ensure that we are working with the power in a balanced way, not in a selfish or egotistical way that will strengthen and encourage imbalance. It's about changing how we think about power. If we take the time to watch, listen, and learn, then the powers of nature have incredible lessons to teach us about how power works and what our parts are in such power displays. Most of the jobs of a magician are about restoring balance—they are very simple, very unglamorous, and not very useful for getting laid or acquiring a new car.

3.4 Power drunkenness

One of the major dangers of doing high magic without foundations, scruples, or commonsense, is blowing one's fuse in a spectacular, all-singing, all-dancing fashion. If someone has natural ability and they play with powerful magical rituals or visions, then they may get hit. If they have no boundaries or foundation, or they lust for power, then they will be blown apart.

When people get their first taste of real magic, it can be like a drug if there is no internal discipline within the practitioner. Such a taste then becomes an addiction, and magic is done just because they can do it, to prove something to themselves, to impress others, or to draw things to them. When they succeed, their ego becomes inflated and common sense goes out of the window. Just as amphetamine can give people a false sense of importance and greatness, so can magical power. It will hike you up on a great high and you will plateau before you crash unceremoniously to the ground. The crash can come in the way of degeneracy, idiocy, or mental instability. It can be fast and spectacular or slow and insidious, but it will come one way or the other. History is littered with tales of magicians degenerating slowly into rotting heaps, literally blowing themselves up, or becoming parodies of themselves.

But what causes the power drunkenness in the first place? Weakness in the personality. Everyone has a weakness of some sort or another, which is not really the problem. What does cause the problem is when there is a weakness in the body, mind, or personality and the person does not address it in any way. It is ignored, denied, dodged, and compensated for—which points to someone who is not ready to know himself. And that takes us back to the words initiates read as they enter the sanctum: *know thyself.*

If you have a weakness and you are aware of it, then you take that weakness into account when you begin to work on something magically. If you know that weakness will interfere with a magical job, then you withdraw and wait until you have strengthened. Just being aware of a weakness goes a long way towards dealing with it. We all have them, without exception; the trick is to know what they are and what you have to do to strengthen that weakness. This takes us back to the self-discipline issue, which is one of the earliest lessons in the magical path, and one of the most important qualities in a magician. If you know your weakness, and you focus on addressing that weakness while also walking a magical path, then power drunkenness will not be a major issue.

In the end, how we approach power dictates how we will approach magic, and in turn how that magic will affect us and everything around us. This is why the initial path of magical training or self-learning should be slow and precise. Get those feet firmly planted in the earth, and remember how much it hurts if you stick a wet metal fork into a plug socket.

3.5 The power dynamics of ritual and vision

A major question, for beginning and experienced magicians alike, is when to use inner powers (visions and beings), when to use outer patterns (rituals and tools), and when to cause an effect simply by observation or participation. There is no easy answer to such decisions; no hard and fast rule to make them clearer. I feel it all depends on the person, situation, and intent. The more you immerse yourself in a magical life, the more fluid and chameleon-like your path becomes. Humanity is the one that makes hard and fast rules...and humanity is the one that hits such barriers like a truck travelling at high speed. In real terms, the universe is an ever-changing, diverse, and confounding power that is infinitely harmonious.

Major keys to working with inner powers are being able to adapt and change, to know when to question the rules and when to follow them, and following one's instincts. It is important to understand that most outer ritual will not really work well without the inner plug stuck in the socket: without inner fuel, they become psychologized rituals and feel-good imaginary actions. Inner fuel comes either from a person's natural mediating abilities or their trained skills in visionary magic.

There are cases, however, where prefabricated rituals, ones that have been used before with inner power, will work properly when performed without any inner connection. When a ritual is *contacted* it becomes a single beacon of power. After that, if the ritual is repeated exactly, it is connected back to the original ritual: they become one

3.5. The power dynamics of ritual and vision

and the same action. The ritual passes through time and every time the ritual is performed, it manifests the original ritual with all its contacted power. This is why ancient rituals, when conducted exactly to the prescribed pattern, will work. What is happening is not a reenactment or repeat but a *reconnection* to the original ritual so that its power continues down through time. This was understood and demonstrated very well in ancient Egypt: they knew that a certain ritual had to be exact, with the original tools, words, timing, etc. That is because they knew that performing the ritual in this way brought the original ritual, with all its contacted beings and power, through time and up to their present day. They also knew, for the most part, what you could change and still ensure the ritual behaviour worked.

Maintaining ritual this way ensured that the power and structure stayed in place, and that the ritual would work even if there were a generation of priests who had no contact ability. If they did everything in the ritual as they should, the contact would work, because the ritual would be passing through time and connecting to the original. This was also very important because the preparation involved in opening a power contact, and the energy needed to maintain that contact, would have been massive. The rituals were not minor issues: they maintained the rivers, the weather, the birth of new generations, and the health of the crops. If any of those failed, then the population would die. So the rituals had to draw in deities and associated beings that had the power to work in harmony with such flows of nature, as opposed to antagonistically fighting them. To manifest that level of contact, with multiple deities over a year cycle, was an incredible amount of work. There is no way that such rituals could be done from scratch year-in, year-out: the pressure would have wiped out the priesthood.

The way to get around the risk of priestly burn-out was to ensure that the contacted ritual could travel through time, so it would only need to be *triggered* again year after year. To take the ritual through time with its contacts, it had to be repeated exactly, with the same tools, the same words, the same everything. Then it became joined with the original: the power and contact would flow through time and through the repeated action. The patterns of those rituals are still imprinted in the inner worlds, and can still be awakened with the right skills and tools. In today's world, the same technique can be used: once a contacted ritual is created, it can be revisited if recreated exactly.

3.6 Using inner power

The foundation training in visionary ('astral') work opens the consciousness up to the deeper powers that run through magic, enabling them to flow through the inner landscape of the practitioner. The deeper into the inner realms a magician goes, the less intricate the rituals need to be. The human consciousness becomes more fluid through visionary work, allowing the mind to stretch out and interconnect with all the patterns of power that flow around the outer world. Once the mind becomes comfortable and able to handle the stretches of worlds and power, it slowly becomes entwined in the inner patterns of power: this is the 'plugging in' phase of visionary magic. This can take anything from a couple of years to many years to achieve this, depending on how flexible and stable the practitioner is. The mind needs to be disciplined and yet unfettered at the same time. Once that stage is reached, wherever the mind goes, power truly follows.

Let's break this down a little. The steps towards accessing inner power are simple and very hard work. First the mind must be disciplined, and then the imagination must be loosened. From there, once the basic ability is in place, the practitioner needs to learn about how they individually perceive the overall structure of the inner worlds. Many books have been written over the years about how many astral planes there are, what colour they are, etc., but in reality the living, breathing universe is not quite that accommodating. Things are not so neat and tidy; hence the need to be flexible, and to not be indoctrinated before you get your feet off the ground. The best texts to read, to get an idea of the weirdness of the inner worlds and its attendant beings, are the *Revelations* of John of Patmos, the book of *Ezekiel*, the Egyptian *Book of Gates*,[1] and the Egyptian *Coffin Texts*.[2] What you are reading in those vision and ritual texts are true glimpses as to the reality of the strangeness of inner power. They are

---
[1] For a recent translation and commentary aimed at a magical audience, see **mccarthy2017**.

[2] For an English translation, see **faulknercoffintexts**.

3.6. Using inner power

not allegories, or hints; they are direct descriptions that are literal, though they are filtered through the religion and culture of the writer: the mysteries are hidden within text indeed!

The first stage of visionary or astral work, once the basic skills are in place, is acquiring the connection with humanity's stored knowledge and an interface with Divinity. Humanity's stored knowledge is what the Theosophists called the Akashic records and what others call the Great Library. It is the consciousness of all learning that has been done by humanity, and it is the wisdom and knowledge of those who have gone before us. It is also a filter for new understanding flowing out of the Void: it passes through the Library before flowing into the minds of those ready to receive it. Where does that new knowledge come from? I haven't a bloody clue, to be honest with you.

In the Great Library, what we perceive as books, scrolls, etc. are in fact fragments of magicians, priests/priestesses, scholars, inventors, healers, etc. The part of them that held the knowledge in life was jettisoned at their death and that part of them passed into the Great Library. If you wish to learn something of depth, that is where you go. It is also a place where one can access many different temples throughout time, various inner adepts and a variety of streams of magic and religion. All those threads come together in this powerful place of learning and wisdom.

This is why it is a good thing for a new practitioner to spend at least the first year of their training simply going into the Library and making contact with the teachers and their various skills. Often an inner adept will put a book 'into' you, which means they have connected you to the knowledge and teacher that is that book. Its lessons will slowly unfold over the years and that is one of the major keys to the library: you don't go pick up a book, read it and go, oh! The books flow into you and unravel in their own time. It can take anything from a few weeks to many years. I am still unravelling things I was plugged into back in the early 90s.

The progression from the Great/Inner Library is usually a natural one. The practitioner is guided from the Library to other places, usually inner patterns of outer temples. From there, they are slowly introduced to the various realms and beings. This is the greatest

3. POWER AND MAGIC

form of education, as it is solely the responsibility of the magician to direct their own learning—and it is coming from inner sources, not outer classes or programs. The practitioner occasionally gets outer confirmation of their inner training when they come across a book in the outer world that talks about what they have experienced on the inner. It is always far better to get it yourself through inner discovery and then have outer confirmation, than to learn from a book or outer teacher and have to take their word for it. Go find out for yourself!

The period of active visionary work can take quite a few years and there is no real way of speeding that process up. It will take however long it needs to take. From that solid visionary aspect, it will slowly become apparent that you can slip into inner realms quickly and without vision, just by thinking about them. This is where the inner and outer minds are coming together, and the consciousness is becoming fluid. During this phase, the practitioner flows between solid inner visions, interacting with beings in vision, and simply thinking about them and being there. Again this phase will take as long as it needs to take and will run parallel to similar developments in the ritual work, which we will discuss below.

Gaining the ability to interact with an inner contact just by thinking about them is a very important achievement, as it demonstrates the ability of the magician to be able to truly hold themselves in more than one world at once. Having the body in one world and the mind in another is one thing, but having the mind in two places, interacting in both places at the same time, shows that the inner powers are preparing to truly flow from outer to inner in a constant conversation of power.

In practical terms, a practitioner would be walking around a sacred site (or the supermarket) and could be holding a conversation with someone while also interacting with the power site and talking with the inner contacts there—and *also* be interacting with the inner pattern of the sacred site. Balancing the mind as it goes in so many directions at once is a key skill which takes many years of practice, and it quickly becomes very clear why anyone with mental instability should not do magic: they would fragment very quickly under such strain.

It is also at this phase where the inner vision and outer ritual come together. As the magician is walking around the temple conducting a ritual, so they are also walking in the inner worlds weaving the power and interacting with the inner beings that are connected with the ritual. The two actions work simultaneously and allow power to flow back and forth, manifest to unmanifest, in a dance of power.

3.7 Outer power: ritual

In magical practice, outer power mainly expresses itself through the use of ritual action. When a new practitioner begins to explore magic, the first thing they usually encounter is ritual. At first the ritual seems to be a dramatic action that bonds the group, focuses intention and attention, and specifies, through action, a magical intent. This layer of ritual was quickly taken up by psychologists and is used to unravel certain issues through action and intent.

The next layer of ritual that surfaces in magic is the layer by which the practitioner repeatedly assigns a certain direction, altar, object, or statue a specific power and identity. This is the first step on the bridge to connecting with true outer power through ritual. The mental intent married to a ritual action kick-starts the wheels of power into action. The power this produces heavily depends on either the mental focus of the practitioner or the embedded pattern of ritual in the object or direction.

An embedded pattern of ritual is an inner pattern that has built up over time. Engaging this pattern through magical action and intent will trigger the pattern, regardless of the ability of the practitioner. It is a bit like a neuro-engram: a pattern of action repeated many times, in exactly the same way, will create specific memory pathways in the brain. Once that engram pattern is in place, the need for conscious action goes and the action becomes an automatic response. So it is with magical patterns repeated over generations in the same place and in the same way. The magical reaction of the ritual power moves from conscious to automatic. This was probably one of the reasons why, in many ancient temples that worked with high levels of magical power, only the highest initiates

3. POWER AND MAGIC

were allowed to access the inner court or sanctum. This restriction stopped the idiots from waltzing in and pressing the red button.

It is interesting to note that in some ruins of ancient temples, these patterns are still operating. It is as if the temple was abandoned so quickly that the priests never had time to shut them down. Those who have the knowledge or keys to the ritual will still be able to operate the temple's magical power. Many other temples, though, are tightly shut, and their ritual patterns have either been dismantled or have been ritually sealed.

The next step on from working an engrammed ritual is a ritual of conscious engagement. This type of ritual relies heavily upon the visionary or inner response skills of the practitioner. A ritual of conscious engagement is where the practitioner works *through* the object or direction, through ritual action and speech, to connect with inner powers drawn in to assist with the ritual intent. As a practitioner approaches a direction/altar, from an inner point of view as well as an outer point of view they call for the power or consciousness that they wish to work with. This is the first stage of vision and ritual coming together as a working method. So the outer ritual prepares the space and tunes the frequency needed, it puts the practitioner and/or objects in a certain pattern, then uses vision to bridge inner power/contacts into the pattern so that the ritual is conducted on both inner and outer planes through direct intent and action. This is a very effective way to work that shares the burden of power out between soul, mind, and body. The patterned outer structure of the ritual takes up some of the impact and spreads the power out into a more manageable job.

3.8 High ritual

What I term high ritual does not involve impressive scripts, velour robes, and gold fabric headdresses (god forbid); rather it is a form of ritual that is one of the highest frequency methods of working without blowing yourself up. In high ritual there are many things going on at once, and the practitioner has to carry burdens on many levels as they work. The outer ritual carries on as normal, but at the same time the practitioner is also doing the same outer ritual action in an inner temple in vision, while also mediating and/or interacting with power, contact, and pattern in their own realm.

Any use of speech must be conducted while also talking to the inner contact, deity, and/or power with the mind. At the same time the practitioner will be expected to conduct ritual action both in vision and in body. It can take many years to achieve this skill, but maintaining an equal distribution between outer action and inner action is one of the least impacting ways of doing powerful work. It is working to the scales of balance. If large amounts of power are worked with, then both the mind and the body will take the impact.

3.9 Visionary action

This type of action is a step on from high ritual and is where the lines between vision and ritual completely merge and the spearhead of the action is intent. Visionary action needs a very pliable mind, a focused body, and a deep familiarity with power. One of the hallmarks of powerful magic is that the more powerful the magic, the less formed the action, vision, and ritual. So when your mind and body becomes truly comfortable with power, it has no need of elaborate rituals and visions to navigate through magic; instead it develops a sense of 'touch' for want of a better word, where everything moves in a natural way with a little stewarding. It is a bit like homeopathy or cranial osteopathy; a little conscious movement goes a long way.

For example, calling in a power or deity is done in the ritual space by first standing very still and tuning into the rhythm of the space. The magician then reaches with the mind through the space for the rhythm of the power she wishes to draw in, and by using a movement, reaches out both inwardly and outwardly to connect and flow with that power. It becomes a Tai chi-type motion where the body and mind flow like a river to commune and connect with power and consciousness. The intent governs everything, so it becomes an awareness of power with intent and nothing more. A physical motion interrupts the stillness of the tuned space, gathers the power, and moves it by way of focused body movement. This is probably where the use of mudras came in when Bharat Natyam was still a form of ritual action and not New Age entertainment.

3. Power and magic

When the mind becomes tuned to this level of action, it can effect change or connection just through the action of observation. Simply 'being' or observing with intent in a ritual space will effect change. It is a controlled use of power to effect change rather than a random result from a passive action. The only prerequisite is the level of focus and magical experience in the person doing the observing. Without that level of experience, the observation or presence simply elicits a random change by nature of the human presence: the change cannot be directed or focused for a specific action or outcome.

This dynamic can be seen when a magician who has experience of inner and outer ritual visits a sacred site, temple, church, or a dramatic ritual reenactment. The mere presence and observation by the magician brings change to the power pattern. If the magician has no specified intent other that to acknowledge the power of the place, then the change will be unconditional—whatever is needed for the site—but it will not be random. If the magician observes with intent, then the intent will trigger specific powers into action. Hence the more experienced the magician is, the less they seem to do (and without velour robes and golden headdresses).

3.10 Inner worlds and actions: cause and effect

Usually when people embark upon a mission to learn and practice magic, they give little or no thought to what the long-term consequence of their actions will be. We have all been there in one form or another, and most of us develop beyond that, but some do not. Some people do magic to get what they want and to control their universe; some people do magic to affect the world according to their agenda; some do magic because that is how they breathe; and some people have no clue why they do it, just that they are driven down a particular path and they go with the flow. All of these, plus many more reasons for doing magic, have positive and negative effects on the individual and the worlds around them. I say worlds because magic not only affects the outer world, its ripples pass through all the worlds in one way or another.

3.10. Inner worlds and actions: cause and effect

Any act of magic will have an effect through the worlds to a greater or lesser degree, because magic is the tuning fork of the universe: it is the vibration that effects change far beyond our understanding of the original action and allows us to perceive and interact with power. Our very limited understanding of the universe prevents us from seeing the vast multilayered highways of consciousness, power, and substance; how they interact, and how their interactions trigger more highways, patterns, and expressions. Just as we are all apparently moving faster and away from the ground zero of the Big Bang, so magic expands and accelerates from its initial action.

When you do a simple magical act the first time, it is weak. But over the years, as your consciousness strengthens and your ability to perceive subtler 'vibrations' from the tuning fork of the universe strengthens, so the revisited act gets more and more complex in its expression. A simple magical act can become a profound, complex, and many-layered catalyst.

My personal deepest experience of that is with the lighting and tuning of the candle flame. The intent to light a candle to prepare the space for a ritual act developed from a simple action to an act of bringing into physical manifestation an elemental expression that lights through all worlds and all times: it becomes the Light of Divinity within everything. And that is the biggest clue to all magical acts: in its true expansion, all magic is an expression of the power of Divinity. By Divinity I do not mean deity, but the inexplicable ultimate conscious power of the Universe. When you start to meddle with such power, it bodes well to use a bit of foresight and common sense.

Let's bring it a bit closer to home and look at it in more practical terms. The inner and outer worlds are not separate realms; they are intricately interwoven, like a bolt of fine linen. Anything you do energetically in one realm affects many others. It's that simple. The action/reaction seesaw between the worlds is a strange and interesting one, and the way it all balances is very curious. Small, highly focused actions create massive energetic responses. Large, diffuse actions create little response. The more condensed the power, the heavier the result has to be to balance the seesaw.

3. POWER AND MAGIC

A beautiful pattern example of that is the Tree of Life. The first three spheres on the Tree of Life balance out the rest of the seven spheres. That is because the first 3 spheres are Divine power undivided (sphere one), and Divine power divided (spheres two and three) The other seven spheres are the processes and presences by which that Divine power polarizes and forms itself from unbeing into being (substance, the world).

The Tree is a good expression of the acceleration of magical/Divine power as it expands, changes frequency, and becomes more diffuse and complex. The tenth sphere is the fully externalized expression of power, i.e. our world, and beyond the tenth sphere are the actions of time (past, present, future).

So 'inner power' is denser energetically but has no physical expression of itself in our understanding of the laws of physicality, whereas 'outer' power is more diffuse, has less density energetically, but has a stronger physical expression that we can perceive. Thus a small amount of inner power is balanced by a much bigger expression of outer power.

The other thing that becomes obvious from a magical point of view is that there is not just inner and outer; there are many other layers of power expression in between that all interact. In magical terms, pure Divine power is on one end of the seesaw and all expressions that come from that power are on the other. On the Tree of Life, this translates to three expressions of Divinity that have issued from the pure inner power on one end of the seesaw and life/death/all of creation is on the other. Did you get that?

That translates in magical practical terms thus: a conscious interaction with a small amount of inner power creates a much bigger expression or reaction in the outer world. The closer to the source of the inner power you get, the more profound and powerful that interaction becomes, with long-term consequences for the physical world. But it also depends upon the frequency that the magician is 'vibrating' at (remember the tuning fork of the universe?). So if you go back to the lighting of the candle it would go something like this:

The magician lights a candle with intent to tune a sacred space. The magician is in the early days of magical work, so he has not consciously interacted much with that 'tuning fork' magic, therefore his 'vibration' is currently tuned to physicality more than anything. Therefore, he does not perceive the real power behind the magical action: he cannot perceive the density of inner power in its pure form.

As the magician continues to interact with the magic away from the physicality, i.e. in vision (no physical act), so his vibration begins to change, as he moves his consciousness into nonphysical realms. This allows him to perceive nonphysical power and with that perception comes more understanding, which leads to more interaction in the inner worlds.

The more he practices lighting the candle, the more he begins to perceive the power as it moves away from the initial point of action, and the diffuse complexity of that power expression is seen and interacted with. This in turn builds momentum in the vibrational change of the magician, so it becomes a conscious interaction between the ever-expanding magical inner power and the magician. Through that interaction, the consciousness of the magician begins to flow with that highway of power expression, and there comes a point whereby the magician can revisit or observe the initial expression of inner power triggered by the very first lighting of the candle with intent. The magician is now vibrating at a frequency where he can fully perceive its power to the best of human ability. Hence the act becomes more and more profound, greater power is perceived, and the direct long-term energetic consequence of the action is now observable. This is why magicians who work deeply in the inner realms do less and less magic as they mature—but when they do initiate a magical action, its long-term effects can be considerable.

3.11 Justice, balance, and karma

The minute one begins to walk a magical path and starts to interact and influence the 'tuning fork of the universe,' one takes on the responsibility of justice/karma. Why? Because a magical action has consequence, and you bear responsibility for that. It is also important to understand that when you step properly onto a magical path, fate and cause and effect come into a very sharp, fast focus. I don't know why or how, only that I have observed it repeatedly in myself and other magicians for decades.

3. POWER AND MAGIC

Justice, karma, and balance are words that do not often pop into the heads of people first walking a magical path, as the focus of intent is more often directed towards the acquisition of power, skill, and peers. I have had interesting conversations with elderly occultists regarding the subject of justice and karma, and I think the misunderstandings that often arise in such conversations come from the lack of understanding of those two words: karma and justice.

Justice is about power in and power out: a better word for justice would be *balance:* to balance the Scales. The Scales, like the Tree of Life, have to be kept as balanced as humanly possible so that the practitioner can handle power safely without getting blown up. The deeper into magic or spirituality you go, the stronger the need for justice/balance in your life. If you live completely within the physical realm, then the Sword of Justice[1] is slow and diffuse. The more you reach into the inner worlds through magic or spirituality, the more focused, pronounced, and densely powerful the Sword of Justice becomes. When you take on specific magical responsibilities as an adept, then the Scales become very finely balanced indeed, and knowingly taking a false step will result in swift results. The lesson of the unfolding energy will be sharp and to the point. And it will not come in the form of punishment, but in the form of bitter understanding through experience.

Justice is not about morals: it is about how power works, and being responsible with that power. If you do something that you know damages, hurts, or deprives someone, then your 'power-scales' are at a deficit. As a magician, when you interact with the inner worlds, you automatically engage the rule of magical justice, known as the rule of Ma'at in ancient Egypt. Universal consciousness and fate will trigger to place things in your path to teach you why your actions were unbalanced, so that you learn from bitter experience. That is a lesson that is hard to forget. Then, once the learning is in place, the energetic scales must be rebalanced. This is achieved by putting you in a situation whereby you observe an energetic 'debit,' and you are given an opportunity to put your own action or energy into a debit to turn it into a credit. Again, this is not about a moral or ethical

---

[1] The Sword of Justice is a magical term for cause and effect at a deep magical level.

3.11. Justice, balance, and karma

code which is more about culture and beliefs, and there is no 'daddy god' stood over you to teach you a harsh lesson.

Rather, it is about the complex weave of fate, power, and how magic flows. We are all heavily interwoven far more than we realize, and what we do to something outside of ourselves becomes mirrored in our own pattern of fate and existence. Similarly, what we do to and of ourselves becomes mirrored around us. This is a deep and profound fragment of magical knowledge: we are all of each other, and we are an integral part of everything that is around us. This is the deeper esoteric wisdom behind the saying *if you want to change the world, change yourself.* The truth of that statement goes far beyond the realms of feel-good psychology and New Age mantras where that statement is usually touted (and heavily misunderstood). It eventually becomes a raw personal experience where the adept finally starts to see beyond the veil of illusion in our physical world.

The deeper you go into inner magic, the more profound the effects of justice become. If you reach through the inner worlds in an unbalanced pursuit of power and you are not ready from an inner point of view to handle such power, you will blow yourself up. Cause and effect. Put hand in fire, hand get burned. Such magical cause and effect can manifest either as literally going mad from the power, becoming ill, losing everything, or being shut down magically. If you are totally incapable of handling large amounts of power, or powerful contacts, then the inner safety switch is thrown, and you are left in the dark. This is done by the deeper part of you and is for your own good: you literally blow a fuse and end up in the dark.

If you have the natural or trained potential to handle vast amounts of power/contact and you go after that power in an unbalanced way, then you will be treated to a reaction that we perceive as a very hard lesson: the two most common possibilities are going mad or dying. Because you potentially have the ability to hold power, the inner fuse does not flip and the power flows into an unbalanced vessel and tips it over. Its all about personal responsibility, cause and effect; it's not about punishment.

This has been one of the biggest misunderstandings regarding the role of karma. Some people perceive the laws of karma to be based around an idea that your life is preordained, nothing can be changed

3. POWER AND MAGIC

and any shit in life you get is because you were bad in another life. That is not true and is a total misunderstanding of the law of karma. The law of karma is the same as the law of Ma'at or justice: everything works in a complex balancing act, or chaos ensues. The law of karma is the law of cause and effect, which translates practically into responsibility and understanding the natural consequences of actions.

In magical practice, if you curse or attack someone, then you are put into a dance of rebalancing the scales with that person: your respective fates become entangled until the energy and fate deficits are equalized, one way or another. A skilled magician has to make the informed decision as to whether it is worth the long and often complex entanglement, which can last for years.

If you magically interfere with nature for conditional human ends, then the results of that action will be set in motion and there is nothing that you can do to stop it. One you realize that your simple thoughtless action is spreading out and causing untold damage, you cannot say sorry and stop it. You will have to observe the long unfolding of that action. And because your energy went into the initial action, your energy will be drawn upon throughout the unfolding of the action until it has run its course. This connection of energy to an action is the part that most people do not understand. The connection of energy will manifest in many ways, and the more profound the magical action, the more energy it will draw from you until it has fully run its course. With so much of your energy going in a justice/balance direction, it will leave you energetically in deficit. This will manifest as inner weakness that will make you vulnerable to an endless list of imbalances, both energetic and magical.

If you try to compensate for such imbalance by using magic to draw more energy to you, or to enlist the help of beings, or to counteract the imbalance, then the imbalance will get longer and more pronounced as you draw more and more beings and power to your unbalanced orbit.

The best advice is either hunker down, accept the results of the energetic deficit, and learn a hard lesson, or consciously engage the unfolding alone, and work unconditionally in magical service to help rebalance the scales. This can be done when working in ritual or vision by being willing to allow whatever is necessary for a person, situation, land, or nation to flow through you and out into the world: working as a bridge without necessarily knowing what it will do. This is not work for a beginner, but as a practising magician, if you find yourself in deficit from magical work that went feral, it can be a good way to rebalance the system.

Working unconditionally, without specific intent or agenda, allows the energy to flow where it needs to and puts you in situations that will truly give you an opportunity to rebalance things. Often we can make things much worse by intentional actions that we think will bring about rebalance but actually do not. This is because our understanding of the wider reach of a magical act is often shortsighted, and working blind with justice/balance will sidestep such lack of understanding. This is one of the deeper reasons why the statue of Justice is blindfolded: humanity cannot often perceive the whole picture, and we need to work blind, unconditionally, trusting the flow of universal power to guide our hand. We surrender to the tide of universal power and yet keep our awareness focused so that we can learn from the events that manifest. That way, you will rebalance your scales and learn some good lessons.

Chapter Four

Inner contacts and inner beings

Studying and practising magic will at some point or other, depending on which system of magic you are working with, bring you into direct contact with inner beings, i.e. beings/consciousnesses that are not part of you or your own psychology (or your granny or the cat). These beings are part of the holism that is creation, and just because you cannot see them with your eyes does not mean they are not there. The magical interaction with these beings usually takes the form of visionary work, ritual invocation, or both.

Practising magic will bring you into contact with all sorts of inner beings over the years, and some of them will work with you in long-term working partnerships. The most common working contact tends to be a contact that was once human, i.e. either they are dead and have chosen to stay in the inner worlds as a contact for humanity, or they are living contacts in their own time and place, working in the inner worlds as a contact. Sometimes there are human inner contacts that were part of a lodge, temple, or order while in life, and after death they carry on their work with their order, acting as a go-between or bridge between the inner and outer worlds. In the early stages of working with inner contacts, these are usually the type of inner contact or priest/ess that is brought through. They are worked with the most in earlier stages of magical work because their agendas, magical lines, etc. are well known and usually fairly transparent.

Then there are contacts that are ancestors, contacts that are land beings, or deities, elemental beings, animals, or hybrids of all of them. Some of the ancestral contacts are very ancient beings from before our form of humanity or from a different form of humanity. There are ancient beings that seem to be part human and part something else. Whatever the contact is, it is important not to get sidetracked by

4. INNER CONTACTS AND INNER BEINGS

wanting to know who/what/where they are. You are brought together to do a job, not satisfy your curiosity or aid in agendas and theories.

There are inner contacts that are deep ancient combinations of human, deity, and land power. These contacts are usually tied to a specific area and mediate the power of a particular force, such as a volcano, a fault line, a lake, a temple, a mountain, etc. They probably started out as a human who worked intensively with land and the faery/land beings connected to the site. Upon their death, this local magical shaman/witch would have continued to work with the local faery or land being: often the land or faery being will have merged with the human as they work from the realm of death. Slowly, over the years, the working union creates a merged form, which then presents as a local deity. These contacts are powerful to work with, but they still contain the frailty of the human spirit along with all its inherent issues and hang-ups. That is why it is wise to tread carefully with a contact that presents as an ancient local deity, as most often they are composite beings.

Because of the spiritual propaganda of monotheistic religions, almost all inner beings are considered evil and dangerous. Then you have the modern psychological 'slant,' which states that these beings are all parts of our psychology. These two primitive stances not only serve to separate us from interacting with these powerful beings, but they also create a deep imbalance that affects all of humanity. All beings have a purpose and are intimately interconnected: when we actively participate in this orchestra, harmony rules.

Some beings create life and sustain power, others kill, damage, or cull life forms. The need for light and dark, life and death, health and disease is paramount to the harmonic balance of the universe. When we step away from our role within that orchestra, like all other parts of nature it quickly flies out of balance and nature triggers a counterbalance in an attempt to rebalance the scales of existence. We see this nature response all around us everyday. The more we cling to life at any cost and insist on overpopulating, overconsuming and overbuilding, the more nature and the balance of power responds with destruction: the natural scales of balance in action.

There is also a whole level of inner contact that is human, or human in origin, and this level of contact sort of survived the monotheistic 'slash and burn' conditioning by being referred to as saints. People in church ask them to intercede on their behalf, and yet do not think of them as inner contacts or feel that they can just chat to them, ask them questions, etc. Only in deepest darkest Catholicism will you still find people chatting and even offering part of their meal to a 'saint.' This is a form of working with an inner contact, just in the most difficult and unproductive way. In reality, human inner contacts span a whole complex weave of contact that is as fascinating as it is useful.

4.1 Human inner contact: dead or alive?

There are a variety of forms of inner contact that are or once were human. The first we will look at is the contact that once was human. Often these people were priests or priestesses in their lifetime. They were probably teachers, but what they all have in common is that they were and are all adepts in the Greater Mysteries. When an adept (and I mean a real adept, not a weekend course and paid a lot of money, or read a lot of books 'adept') dies, their knowledge of the death passage, and experience of working in death while alive, allows them to make informed choices regarding whether to reincarnate or stay in the inner worlds to work as an inner contact. If they choose to stay out of the life circle and act in service as an inner contact, they will pass into a level of consciousness that is on the same 'frequency' for want of a better word, as the inner temples and Inner Library. Living magicians who have a connection to them, or people working on that same frequency, will be able to find them and work with them both in vision and ritual.

If a beginner wishes to reach an inner adept as an inner contact, then they would need to be walking a similar magical path, or one that has enough cross-connections so that the same magical vocabulary is used, and which has similar intent. For example if you wanted to reach W. E. Butler, or Dion Fortune, then working in the Western Mysteries in some form would give you the right frequency and vocabulary for productive communication. That is, if they want to work with you: sometimes they may just tell you to piss off. But if you were studying Vodun, or Siberian Magic, or Indonesian Magic, then trying to reach such Western contacts through non-Western systems would most likely not work.

But if you are working in a particular path of magic in your learning process, then it is better to go into the Inner Library in search of a contact if you are working in vision, or work in your temple space if you are working through ritual, and call for an inner contact who can guide you in what you need to know during this phase of your learning. This is far better than reaching for a specific named magical 'star' adept. If you ask unconditionally for help, then the teacher who is best equipped to help you will come to your aide. Some of the famous adepts were indeed brilliant magicians, but like all of us, many had their baggage also. Then there are the ones who were great writers and communicators, but magically left a lot to be desired. Some adepts became famous just by virtue of their ability to sound like they knew what they were talking about, even when they did not; and some just because they had money and were able to get their work in print. So do not try and reach for a 'name': just ask for help.

4.2 Living contacts

Contacts that are alive and in their own time are the most fascinating to work with. How this works is as follows: an adept works through vision and ritual, offering themselves in service as a contact to assist in particular magical tasks that are relevant to them, or working unconditionally when they 'hear' a call for help. They work through the inner worlds in vision, usually while also working in ritual, appearing in the inner or outer magical space/temple as an inner contact. They can be from the same time as you, or from your past or future. It is a fascinating and little understood area of contact magic.

When you work with living inner contacts, there are certain things that you need to bear in mind when approaching such a contact. Firstly, do not assume that because he or she is a magical adept that they will be all-knowing, all-wise and all-ethical. Nothing could be further from the truth. Some of the most screwed-up people I know are also gifted magical adepts. When you are working with a living adept, you have to be aware that because their consciousness is rooted in a living body somewhere, their spirit will be subject to all the emotional baggage that the chemical soup of neurotransmitters inflicts. So if that adept has mental/emotional problems, then you will be on the receiving end of whatever instability they express in daily life.

You will also be exposed to any inner parasites—or worse—that are hitching a ride on the adept. If that adept has a magical tie or oath binding upon them and their communication with you breaks that oath, then you will be subject to any whiplash from that oath breaking. So you can see that working with living inner contacts can be fascinating, but also riddled with dangers and potholes. If you are going to do this sort of work, a very good eye for bullshit, lies, and unhealthy spirits is paramount.

If you do not wish to have your call answered by a living adept, then you can plainly say so in your call through the worlds. As an aside, it would be wise to use similar common sense when you are looking for a teacher in your own time, in the flesh. Again, just because a magician is brilliant doesn't mean that they are also mentally balanced. And just because an adept says that they are a good person doesn't really mean that they are; it just means that they could be a good liar. Again, it is all down to the bullshit meter, also known as discernment. That meter works well when you are not desperate for something. If you have a desperate longing for magical learning, then call out that desperation while in the Inner Library, which has many filters attached to its inner form to filter out unhealthy people. Life doesn't have those filters: you have to provide them for yourself.

I have worked as an inner contact in rituals both in real time and in the past and the future. Physically it can be very draining, but it does expand our understanding of inner contacts when this form of work is done.

4.3 The roles of destroying deities and demonic powers

In times past, cultures worked closely with destroying deities and demonic powers along with creative deities and other beings. A very good example of such harmonic balance was the Egyptian concept of Ma'at, which was both a deity and a concept of balance. Destroying deities were respected and worked with to keep the balance, and the actions of such destroying deities in a proper context were respected and accepted. Humanity attempted to live with, and adjust to, such destroying principles, until humanity realized it could manipulate, bind, and clash with such powers to their own advantage. The transition from respecting power to attempting to harness and control it was a degenerate step for humanity, and has led to the mess that we are now in. These destructive beings bring disease, war, death, and natural disasters that keep living beings in check. So how, as magicians, can we work with such powers?

The first step is to understand these powers, their functions in our world, and our own responsibility. The outer manifestation of a destroying deity is a human-constructed interface (a form, statue, attributes, etc.) that we used first to communicate with, then control the deity/being. Over the generations, as human power agendas changed, so did our explanations of the mythology, image, and function of the deity. So, for example, a Near Eastern female destroying power of the desert and bringer of disease[1] was transformed, by religious spin, into a sexual predatory vamp that ate babies and turned men mad. The more that people formed that image in their minds, the stronger that construct became, until a parasitical being was more than happy to step into that role, thus making it a 'reality.' The original power still raged in the form of desert storms and disease, but the focus of the people was not on that natural power, but on the image of the 'sex vamp' baby killer that was reviled. By deflecting our attention to a parasite deity form and away from the natural power, we didn't really learn to respect that power, nor learn how to get out of its way. We also didn't learn to look carefully at what that conscious power was doing and why. If a

---

[1] Lilith.

human population does not keep itself in check and balance with its surroundings, then from a magical perspective, the conscious powers of that land will do it for us.

Instead of respecting the destroying power of a landmass, we build cities in its path so a storm, earthquake, or flood can wreak havoc with our population. It is much better to build with foresight and care in such an area, to limit our expansion in a sustainable way, to commune with the inner power behind the natural manifestation, and to learn to respect it. That tuning into the natural power helps us to build a relationship with it so that we get advanced warning of oncoming potential disasters so that we can get out of the way.

Similarly with respecting the need to keep a population in balance, the need for nature to inflict death and disease lessens. With fewer babies there are more resources, and there is often better communal parenting. There are still examples of this happening in Stone Age cultures scattered around the world, (the Adaman Islands, the Amazon, etc.) although they are almost extinct now from civilization encroaching upon their resources. Nature does still intervene where she can, though. When a population is getting out of control, female babies abort more often and the population generally gets more aggressive. When there is a threat to the population, i.e. natural disasters or major stresses, all but the strongest male babies abort, whereas more female babies survive. This ensures a better chance of species survival.[1]

4.4 What we can do

The first and probably most important step would be to develop a working practice whereby the magician works with beings in their own place and time rather than dragging them into our world if they do not naturally live in our realm. The second would be to work consciously in cooperation with the beings and powers that do express themselves through our world. This can be done by working in cooperation with weather powers (as opposed to controlling and manipulating them) and building respectful relationships with

---

[1] The Culled Cohort theory of Dr. Ralph Catalano, professor of public health at the University of California, Berkeley. See for example **bruckner2007**.

4. INNER CONTACTS AND INNER BEINGS

them. By working this way, you slowly begin to understand the inner dynamics of these powers and the effects that they have on human consciousness—effects that stretch far beyond simple weather patterns. The same can be said of land powers, beings of this world, and deities. By stepping back and looking at what these powers actually bring to the world, and looking beyond our own needs and wants, we begin to see an intricate dance of consciousness and power that constantly keeps the land, and all living beings, in balance. That does not mean that these beings will favour our survival; rather we will begin to understand that death and destruction is all part of the health of the land and all species.

Accepting that a storm, weather pattern, or disease outbreak is doing a needed job, and learning how to operate with and around that power rather than clash with it, changes how we view our roles as humans. By changing how we perceive those roles, we change the impact it can have upon us, and we end up rolling with the punches and learning. Taking an active role in assisting the power can change the way we view such disasters. It doesn't stop them, but they become a bigger part of us. And the nearer towards a healthy balance we move, the less likely are such expressions of power to devastate us.

One way of taking an active role in balance with the land is to first come to know the land upon which you live in intimate detail. Walking the land, visiting the water, the hills, learning where the weather patterns come from and go to, tuning into fault lines and the seasons...all of these actions benefit the land upon which you live, and help you enter a working relationship with the land and its inherent beings. If you live on land that has ancient burials, it will teach you about where the places of death and life are. Visiting the burials and talking with them, honouring the places of death, and giving gifts of food to the places of life are all simple acts that help build a relationship with the land. Once that communion is established, then communing with the storms, the sun, the moon, the caves, the rivers, and the trees will connect you to the larger tides of consciousness that flow through the land.

The next step beyond passive communion is active listening through instinct, inner contacts, and body reactions. Through listening we begin to build an active conversation with the powers around us, which enable us to have deeper magical relationships with the immensely powerful beings that manifest through the landscape. Our imagination builds an interface of characters that enables us to understand these powers in a more human way; and as long as we do not try to control them, a working relationship can build where the storms, seas, rivers, etc. communicate their tides of power and alert us to any imbalance. Through this relationship we can begin to learn what the role is that we need to take up in our dance with these forces.

What becomes a human/animal type interface is usually an intermediary being that becomes the voice of the power and acts an interpreter between humanity and the nature force. That intermediary will step into the interface we have created (i.e. an image, statue, form), and if there is specific, focused magical intent to create such an interface for a mediator, then any opportunist and potentially rogue beings will be filtered out. The more established the intermediary becomes, the more it fuses with the nature power so that it become intertwined with the nature force. So when we commune with the goddess of the river, the interface translates needs and actions between humanity and nature. Some of the more ancient nature deities are still active and do respond to human interaction. They will, if a relationship is built with them, warn of coming fluctuations of their power, (i.e. storms, floods), communicate their needs for honouring/care, and will be keen to express outrage at human actions that cause imbalances.

By working closely with these beings, we can build up a better understanding of the tides and flows of the powers within the land around us, which in turn can educate us as to how to live alongside these powers properly, rather than harnessing, controlling, and manipulating them. They will show us how to act to trigger rebalance as unconditional catalysts , and warn us as to the difficulties that will be experienced for us in that rebalancing process.

4.5 Thought forms and passive enlivening

There are areas of magic where it is considered an integral part of the art to create and develop thought forms. These are used for a number of tasks, including guarding, attacking, watching, etc. Thought forms

4. INNER CONTACTS AND INNER BEINGS

are beings created straight from the imagination of the magician and powered by the magician's own energy to fulfil his or her agenda. Such practice takes a lot of mental discipline to ensure that the thought form stays under control. Thought forms can go feral very easily, and their antics are fed by the magician's own energy, which can result in a major energy deficit on the part of the magician. The stability of the thought form is only as good as the mental focus and stability of its creator, as it is basically an extension and projection of their imagination.

For any magician capable of creating and fully controlling such a thought form, it makes much more sense, and is far better energetically, not to create a form outside of oneself, but to project directly from the central imagination without a separation of identity. It is far more effective and easier to control. However, such practice by a magician who has any sort of mental or emotional instability or immaturity is very probably going to result in a major fragmentation of the personality at some point.

The other problem that can arise from the use of thought forms, when created in a lodge setting, is the question of energy source. Unscrupulous lodge or group leaders can engage the group in the creation of a thought form or inner structure, then use the energy of the group to power such creations. It's a form of scapegoating. The group's energy creates and feeds the thought forms, and also takes the consequences of what the thought form does. If it goes feral and does damage, kills etc., then it is the group which carries the energetic burden, not the leader. This is sadly a common practice of some larger, more public lodges that have a huge membership that involves initiation. The small inner group creates the form and the rest of the membership take the fall for what goes wrong.

Personally I think thought forms are more trouble than they are worth, and it is much better and safer to work with real inner beings (as opposed to created ones) on magical projects and jobs. Creating thought forms can very easily lead to digging very deep holes for oneself that take a lot of energy and effort to deal with. The other issue with thought forms, particularly if they are used to attack someone, is that their combat power is only as strong as the mental focus and life force of the person who created and is powering them. If the victim happens to be stronger, then the attacker is liable not only to have wasted a lot of energy for nothing,[1] but the person or group can potentially put their egregore at risk. If the thought form is connected to the egregore as an energy source, then a skilled victim can not only dismantle the thought form, but track the umbilical back to the egregore, then dismantle the egregore itself. So all in all, I really think they are a total waste of time.

4.6 Golems

A step up the skill ladder is the making of a golem. Contrary to popular belief, golems are not manifest beings that we can see with the eye; they are inner beings created out of the element of earth and enlivened with the sacred breath and the word of power, usually written on the forehead but sometimes in a hidden place on the clay body. The power of consciousness is in the clay body, but it is the 'inner' body of the golem that then goes out to do its masters bidding. So it is a soulless being which is a slave to its creator.

Destroying a golem is fairly straightforward, but it must be done correctly. Finding that actual clay body and erasing the word of power from it will not destroy the golem, it will only destroy the being's link to the physical realm—and will also free it from its bind to its maker. To be rid of the golem, the word of power must be located on its inner body and wiped out at that level. To wipe off the Aleph from the word Emet leaves Met, which is death, and as such destroys the golem. It is ritually sent back into the earth whence it came, and if possible the clay figure is similarly destroyed.

The making of a golem takes a great deal of energy, as it uses your essence to operate: you breathe life into it and it works from your 'sacred breath.' Golems are usually not put to good use, are dangerous, and are akin to putting an AK-47 into the hands of an immature, short-tempered idiot with an axe to grind.

It is good to remember that in truth, you never get away with a silly or vicious act: there is no punishment or judgement, true, but there is usually a massive energetic payback at some point, and I have watched such situations with people over and over again. If you

---

[1] Ever spent a bored afternoon swatting feeble thought forms sent from a disgruntled lodge? Great fun!

really have to have a go at someone, just bloody well punch them and have done with it!

4.7 Passive enlivening

Passive enlivening is a very interesting phenomenon that I have had some interesting results with. I have also seen some epic disasters as a result of this technique. There are two main forms of passive enlivening, intentional and unintentional. Let's take the unintentional first, as that one can create the most spectacular boo-boos.

Unintentional passive enlivening is the accidental creation of a door in an object or image that a being steps into and begins to interact with the humans around it. What causes this unintentional door/threshold to appear is either the natural ability of a human or thoughtless action by a trained magician.

If, for example, you are a highly trained magician who is used to working in the inner worlds and conversing with many different types of beings, then the ability within you to mediate, call, and access different worlds and beings is probably very strong. So if, for example, you mindlessly begin to chat with, say, an ornamental statue of a deity, being, or person, then there will come a point when said statue or image will begin to chat back. The process from behind the scenes goes a little like this: magician gets bored and talks to statue, the fact that the magician is programmed from an inner sense to reach through worlds means that whenever there is conversation, ears prick up, thresholds are created, and doors are opened. Whatever you do with your imagination as a magician has magical potential. But because it is unfocused, there is a good chance that a passing parasite, dead person, or faery/land being with a warped sense of humour picks up on the communion potential and steps into the statue to use it as an interface.

The other possibility is that the magician unconsciously creates a thought form that resides in the image or statue, which again has the potential to go feral or become the vessel for passing beings looking for an interaction meal. The deeper the magician works in the inner worlds and communes with inner world beings, the more potential

4.7. Passive enlivening

there is for such things to happen. It has happened to me a few times...I talk to things all the time.

Sometimes when you get someone who has natural ability or was magically adept in another life and is not aware of it in this life, beings will walk into statues and images in attempts to connect with them or build a relationship which often ends up being parasitical in nature. I have observed this in children who have natural ability: their teddy is a wee bit more than the shop advert claimed...

The long and short of it is, if you are going to talk to inanimate objects, make sure it is intentional and that you are ready for a being coming through and talking back.

Intentional passive enlivening is an interesting magical technique that involves picking or making a statue or image and beginning to treat it as though it is a real being as opposed to an object. With focused intent, time, and the right form of communion and repetitive interactions, the being you are reaching for will at some point begin to commune with you through the object; or a being will mediate between you and the target being, using the object as a window. This is a different method from ritual enlivenment or magical entrapment, but it can be just as effective.

The mechanism of how it works is simple. The statue or image is obviously an image of a known being, god, goddess, or person, and you talk to the image as if you were talking directly to that being on a daily basis. Because of the focused intent, the repetitive action, and the relative conversation, all done by a person with inner connections, pathways of inner communication on specific magical frequencies begin to form and open. These strengthen with each day of communion, and usually first attract a type of mediator being who acts as a preparer and go-between for the communion. As the contact becomes established, then the deity/being that the image represents begins to commune and interact through the image. Then the enlivening is complete.

So what can go wrong? Oh hell, loads of things. The mishaps can range from feral thought forms, to hungry parasites, to aggressive and territorial beings, to demanding deities that refuse to go and demand your attention and homage day-in, day-out. Sometimes these deities have a limited shelf life, in that they will commune with you for a while and will then pack up and go once they have achieved what they wanted or have become convinced that you are an idiot (or both). Because it is all done passively, i.e. as part of everyday life, the whole situation can be especially hard to deal with, as they embed themselves into your living environment.

On the other hand, you can passively enliven objects and images to bring through guardian beings that will watch your home and warn you of inner intrusion, power build-ups, and other odd happenings. They may wish for something in return: I had a wonderful hardworking guardian being who loved shiny things, for example.

This is also a technique used within the Catholic Church, as opposed to ritual enlivenment. The statue of the saint is prayed to constantly and over a period of time a being connected to that consciousness steps into the image and begins to interact or intercede. The blessing of the object and the 'dedication' ensure that a specific line of communication opens slowly, as opposed to random beings stepping in. It is not as effective or powerful as the earlier Egyptian ritual methods of bringing through deities into statues. That technique was far more powerful and enduring. The essential difference between the two methods is that passive enlivening needs near constant communication for the bridge to stay open. Once the communion stops on the part of the human, then the doorway for the inner contact starts to fade away.

With specific ritual enlivenment, it is totally different. Ritually, a fragment of the consciousness of the deity is brought into substance and stays there while ever that substance exists. It is the root of the concept of transubstantiation in Catholicism.[1] An ancient statue of say, Sekhmet, is very likely to still have echoes of her power within that statue. If the magician, who is adept at inner communication, visits a museum, then it is very likely that they will pick up on the calls and demands of such deities as they try to communicate through statues. It is important to note that the power is within the original statue that was ritually enlivened, not the generic image. So a copy of the image will be just an image and nothing more.

---

[1] Christian rituals, particularly from the Roman Empire—i.e. Catholic ones—are fragments of earlier Pagan rituals.

4.7. Passive enlivening

It is good to remember this when you buy or obtain an ancient relic that is ritually enlivened. It is not an ornament or magical plaything; it is real, potentially powerful, demanding, and possibly dangerous. When you get bored of playing with that deity and want to partake of the New Age shopping frenzy for gods and goddesses, be aware that the being that is bridging through the image or statue may not have finished with you and will not be prepared to let go until it is ready. There is a whole major can of worms that can be opened with such behaviour.

The single most important thing to remember when you create a thought form, a window for a being etc., is that the action is caused solely by you. Any chaos, destruction, major change in fate, anything that upsets the balance of order is your responsibility alone. That doesn't mean you can say sorry, or that you can stick a finger up at the universe...well, if you do it will be ignored, it means that energetically you are responsible to set the balance right.

People assume, mainly because of the religions of today, that 'God' is a conscious being who is like a parent, that God will smile indulgently at his naughty creations and let them off with a smack. That is not correct, and it never ceases to amaze me that people think that way. Divinity is power, universal power that flows through everything and enlivens or destroys. It has no emotion. It operates through a rule of balance within an imbalanced world, and beings operate within that world to constantly keep the plates spinning. Fate is tied up with this path of constant striving for balance, and what we call karma is the dynamic that operates through life to balance the scales. In real terms, the very powerful beings i.e. archangelic beings, are aware of balance and imbalance and they are driven to action from that standpoint. It has nothing to do with emotion.

Beings that have physical form do have emotions and inner beings that once had physical form or an inner projection of form, also have emotions. This makes it easier for us to interact with this type of being than the major angelic powers and beyond, where emotion is not their greatest quality. So beings that are close to us, who help or hinder us, can come across as nurturing or destroying. We respond to this output of emotive interchange by building relationships or interactions with these beings, and one of the lessons to be recovered from such interaction is the understanding that we basically haven't

4. INNER CONTACTS AND INNER BEINGS

a clue what we are doing and every time we act, we usually mess it up.

If you create a thought form or enliven an object that causes destruction where destruction was not needed, that creates an energy deficit that you have to fill. You would carry the burden of that deficit and the energy would leak from your life, or your belongings, or anything else that can fill that void. Or it may be filled by someone else who then draws upon your energy. The twists and weaves of these energy dances are awesome in their complexity. If, however, that deficit was needed, then your actions will have fulfilled a need through your magical work. Because of this complex dynamic, one can become paranoid about every action one takes, which is not a productive way forward. A better approach is either to work unconditionally with inner contacts, or to double check you work first using divination.

Working unconditionally with inner contacts is a method of work that you can come to once you have built up a good working relationship with inner contacts that you trust. You agree to work unconditionally for what is needful, and they put things in your path that need to be dealt with magically. For example, with enlivening an object, you will have a perceived magical need that has to be attended to, or they will have a job for you. An object or image will be placed into your path for you to work with, and you would mediate whatever is necessary from the inner worlds into the object. So you can see how trust is a major thing with this method: you really have to know that your inner contact is solid and legitimate.

Double checking work before you commence is another method of dodging scales chaos. If you need to bring something through or create something, obviously it has to be for a purpose—doing this type of magic just because you can is the path of the immature idiot. However, once you have decided that it really needs doing, then it is time to check the short- and long-term outcomes of such actions. The way to do this is through Tarot or through using your own designed deck, which is usually more specific and accurate. That way, you cannot kid yourself that such work needs doing. You must always look at the long-term consequences as well as the short-term immediate outcome of the problem, as magic can ripple for generations and cause chaos in the future.

4.7. Passive enlivening

I use both methods, unconditional and double checking. There have been many times that I was convinced a certain action was needed, but then when I checked it, the long term outcome was very bad for all concerned, so I didn't do it. The eventual solution often plopped down in front of me when I wasn't expecting it. This is the other interesting thing about working deeply in magic and the inner worlds: the beings that keep the balance of power in and out begin to work closely with you. They often block you from work when it is imbalanced, and can on rare occasions nanny you through certain situations. This is not because they care about you; they are ensuring that the flow of energy is going where it needs to.

Similarly, if you go too deeply into the inner realms and get too close to the threshold of Divinity, then the major beings that keep the world in balance, the Archon and the Aeon[1], will knock you back and probably blow your body fuse so that you cannot do that again. Their job is to keep humanity and the core power of Divinity apart.

---

[1] Archon and Aeon are Greek words. Archon is the masculine present participle of the verb stem αρχ, meaning "to be first, to rule." Aeon is from the Ancient Greek αἰών, "age, eternity." Magically these are two opposing forces that create a boundary of tension allowing existence in time. To push beyond that boundary would take the magician out of existence.

Chapter Five

Visionary magic

Visionary magic is the use of the imagination to structure a door whereby the magician can pass into the inner realms or what is sometimes called the astral realm. It is an ancient form of magical practice, though I was surprised to read an academic article the other day which claimed it was a new form of magical practice. Nothing could be further from the truth: the article was unfortunately written out of ignorance. The use of structured vision combined with ritual, as opposed to spontaneous vision, is one of the most powerful and ancient ways to conduct magic.

The methods were usually passed from teacher to student, as the easiest way to gain this skill is through resonance; and the keys to the visionary paths were written into many ancient texts. And this is one of the greatest joys when treading a magical path as a student: coming upon an ancient text or painting and seeing or reading the keys of the vision before you. You recognize them instantly, not because you studied them, but because you had direct experience of them.

Without visionary techniques to access the inner realms, magic gets stuck on the ground like a plane without an engine. The power that fuels ritual comes from inner flexibility, which in turn comes from visionary work conducted regularly over a period of time. Meditation prepares the mind for visionary work by teaching the student how to still their minds and learn focus. From that focused point the student learns first how to access thresholds within themselves and later, thresholds to the inner worlds.

Meditation can take a very simple form, and the simpler the better. Learning to breathe calmly and freely without force is the first step. Sitting still, be aware of the breath as it regulates its own rhythm. Once that is achieved, then counting the out-breath up to ten then going back to one and starting again is the next step. If the mind wanders even slightly during the counting, then the student should start back at one and count the breaths up to ten again. From there, seeing the in-breath as white smoke and breathing out black smoke while counting focuses the mind further into a specific action. Again, if the mind becomes distracted, go back to one and start over again. This simple breathing exercise should be done morning and night until it can be performed without distraction, without wandering of the mind or constantly shifting the body. One does not have to assume difficult or odd poses, but the back must be supported to ensure clear breathing.

When the student has become accustomed to the breathing exercise then it is time to turn the mind inwards to the inner centre or threshold of the Void within. This can be focused upon as an inner flame, which burns quietly within your centre[1]. After starting the meditation with the breathing exercise, see a flame burning quietly and calmly within. Just hold the focus of the flame with no other thought and sit silently in the presence of that flame. Once that image has been established, then see water beneath the flame, held naturally as if by a membrane that has no description other than it holds water. Once the combination of inner flame and water can be held in meditation without distraction then it is time to make the step from meditation to vision.

5.1 The first step of visionary work.

Visionary work can quickly be taken up by the mind as a browsing pastime, which must be avoided at all costs. This discipline has become much harder for young people who have been exposed to years of video games: the mind expects to be playing, changing focus, etc. The focus of meditation trains the mind away from such distractions and allows the natural visionary skills of the human to surface.

---

[1] The centre of your torso.

5.2 Tips and things to think about

When first starting with visionary work and working with written-out visions, it can be difficult to remember the sequence and the important steps. One way to work with such texts is to record the vision, then to follow the recording in your mind, but allow for spontaneous images or events that may emerge unexpectedly: these visions are maps, but what you encounter on your journey can be unique to you.

When you record a vision to listen to, give yourself gaps of silence, where you can experience things, and where you can take your own time to move into the vision. Where there maybe two minutes of spoken text, often the actual vision can be ten or fifteen minutes long. Give yourself plenty of silence at key points in the journey.

I would strongly suggest, however, that you do not allow yourself to 'play out' in your imagination by deviating from the path of the vision, or intentionally creating scenes or people that you wish to psychologically project. This work is magical: it is not psychological pathworking. These visions are not about your psychology, but are interfaces with real inner powers, so treat them with caution and respect, as a great deal of power can flow through them.

The general rule of thumb is: always treat what you see in vision as real, unless you start to get the 'Disney channel.' Treating all imaginative interactions as real breaks down the barriers that our culture erects in us where we end up questioning everything. That shuts down the bridge of communion with the inner worlds very quickly. Once you have become used to working in vision, certain aspects of the vision will begin to solidify, and you will start to recognize what is real and what is just your imagination. Eventually you will learn to filter your own imagination out naturally so that interactions are clear and powerful.

Another important rule to remember is not to use the vision as entertainment; and do not veer from the intended vision and vanish into flights of fancy. Too many people follow their curiosity or flights of fancy, and end up losing their contact as they play in a pool of imagination.

5. Visionary Magic

It takes great discipline to develop the inner muscle for true visionary magic. This is one of the places where a need for self-imposed boundaries comes in. Once that discipline is in place, then it is far easier to go on exploratory missions, as you will very easily be able to ascertain what is a real contact and what is not, and you will be able to access many inner realms without danger of letting your imagination take over.

Keeping a diary of your visions and experiences is very important so that you can go back and look in years to come. Any small details that crop up unexpectedly, or seem meaningless, write them down also. It helps you to remember the vision, and what happened, what contacts where made, and what your responses were. Then, later on, when you are reading about the subject matter and you come across something that you saw in vision, it will help to confirm your experiences. And this is another exciting part of visionary magic: you will see, hear, and meet many different types of beings, and they will teach you or tell you things. Later, such information will manifest in the outside world, or something they predicted will happen. It is a wonderful feeling when you are first venturing into the inner worlds and you get absolute solid evidence for yourself that it is real and it works. Many years later, I still smile when that happens—which is often.

The other way to work with such visions, if you do not wish to record them, is to work out the details of basic key points in the vision, which are like critical points of the map. It is important to know where you are going, how you get there, and how you get back.

And here are some basic tips:

1. Do not lie down to do these visions. Sit up so that you do not fall asleep.

2. Turn off phones, music, the television, etc., and close doors so that you will not be disturbed.

3. Light a candle and meditate briefly before a vision to still your mind.

4. When you have finished the vision, blow out the candle, get up, and walk around to ground yourself.

5. Don't come to rely on recordings. Once you have been in vision to a certain place a couple of times with the aid of a recording, then it is time to start working without that recording. Learn to develop your own inner navigation skills.

5.3 The Void

To begin with the student needs to learn how to access the deepest and yet simplest mystery within visionary magic and that is the Void[1] from which All flows into the worlds and to which All flows back. It is the beginning and end of all magic, and this cannot be reiterated enough. It is within us and within everything around us: it is the threshold of existence. It is represented within the Tarot as the Fool card, which begins the Major Arcana and should also end the Major Arcana.

It is a keystone visionary exercise that deepens in its intensity over time and can become a central foundation stone for all visionary and magical work. It is also a very useful vision: if you need to vanish quickly from inner visibility in an emergency, knowing from experience and practice how to suddenly put your mind and inner consciousness into the Void without preparation is a major skill. The moment your mind immerses itself in the Void, you effectively 'vanish' from the inner radar.

The vision of the Void also has immense mystical depths to it once it has been worked with over a long period of time. The Void is a bottomless space where eventually you begin to truly understand your eternal nature.

5.4 Vision of the Void

See a flame within you and be with it quietly until your mind is still. It is a flame that does not burn, a flame of existence, a flame that nourishes you. The flame rests in the centre of your body, and it can appear big or small,

---

[1] In Egyptian mythos this is known as ⟨hieroglyphs⟩ "the Nu": the inactive, still water that all things rise out of. (**pinch2002; allen1988.**)

5. Visionary magic

bright or gentle. It is a flame that feels familiar to you, a flame that gives you strength.

Once you are still, see the flame grow bigger until it is all around you and spreads out beyond your body. Stand up in the flame and feel the power of the flame of life flow through you. The flame does not burn you, but refreshes you, and your spirit recognizes the feeling deep within you. From that still place, see yourself stepping through the flame, stepping into nothing. You step through the fire's threshold to find yourself in a place that has no time, no sound, no light, no movement, no image: it is truly nothing, and yet you can feel so much in that space. It is a feeling you cannot describe, a feeling of potential that is waiting.

In this place, you realize you have no boundaries, no body, and no earthly life. In this place your spirit is not locked into the form of your body: you have freedom to flow, to expand, and to awaken. This is the threshold of the eternal soul. Feel yourself spreading out in the nothing, drifting and expanding in stillness and silence. You are everywhere in this place, and yet you are nothing. You are all things and none, drifting in the silence and stillness.

In this place, you feel the power of all being flow within and all around you. Do not let your mind wander into thought patterns, just bathe in the stillness until you are ready to come out. When you are ready, be aware of your earthly life and your human form. Feel yourself slowly come back into the shape of your earthly body, and when that is complete, see the flame as a wall of fire before you. Step into the flame, bathing in its energy. Slowly bring your consciousness back to the flame that sits deep within you, in the centre of your body. Be aware of yourself sitting quietly, with the flame within you and a candle flame close by you. Be aware of your breathing, be aware of your surroundings, and when you are ready, open your eyes.

This vision of the Void should be worked with every day until it becomes second nature. It is the most powerful vision and yet the simplest that you will ever use. Over time you will learn how to access this place in an instant, just by tuning your mind to the feeling and space of the Void, which will instantly put you in a deep and still place. If you are ever in a dangerous inner situation (like having a demonic Titan being rushing towards you with teeth bared) it can instantly put you in a place and state where very little can touch you or get a hold of you. If you are in the total stillness of the Void, and are spread out beyond the confines of your body, then there is nothing for an inner being to grab: you have no boundaries, no form, and your consciousness is suddenly out of their frequency. This vision must be practised regularly throughout your magical life and never forgotten or cast to one side. It has saved my life on more than one occasion.

Once you can go in and out of the Void with no distraction and with ease, then it is time to practice the same meditation/vision while walking and with your eyes open. After a few years of practice, you can walk down a busy high street full of noise and distraction and yet be still within the Void as you walk. You will affect the energy of everything around you by mediating the stillness and silence, calming down chaotic energies as you pass by.

The Void vision, along with the breath meditation, prepares the mind and soul for the hard work of visionary magic. And it truly is very hard work, both physically and spiritually. Moving power around at great depths and heights needs a body and spirit that is strong, focused, disciplined, and able to work under any circumstances. The simple Void vision is the first step in that preparation.

5.5 The next step: discovery of the world

Before the student begins to delve into magical structures it is important to be aware of one's own inner surroundings, i.e. the inner manifestations of the land upon which we live. The inner landscape of the land and the immediate realms surrounding that landscape are important foundations for any magical work to stand upon. It is pointless reaching for the moon if you do not know what is in your own backyard. This can be accessed first through a series of simple

5. VISIONARY MAGIC

but potentially profound visions, then worked with in basic ritual to ground, root, and develop the magical mind.

It is also important for the student who begins the path of learning visionary magic to be aware of the necessity for inner and outer boundaries. These boundaries do not have to be in place forever, and indeed as each generation develops, the need for boundaries will change depending upon the consciousness of the student and the culture in which they live. These early boundaries are to safeguard the mind and spirit of the student: natural visionary students can be drawn into vision haphazardly to satisfy their curiosity or to push boundaries early on. This opens the student up to the dangers of parasites, feral beings, and the latent imbalances within their own personality. Visionary work carries great power with it, and when dealing with any great power, "Caution!" should be an ever-repeating mantra.

Once the boundaries are in place, the student can begin to learn the inner highway code of conduct, the basics of 'stranger danger,' and safely find the pathways to various realms without too many mishaps. In times past, magical lodges had very strict boundaries in place, and in many lodges those same boundaries are still in place, but the original purpose for them seems to have been forgotten. Those boundaries reflected the consciousness of the time, and although we have moved on in the way we think and feel, such boundaries have not kept pace with the evolution of the spirit and mind.

Some lodges still use a very slow and cumbersome ladder of inner contacts, along with strict grades, top-heavy rituals, and an abundance of rules, regulations, and secrecy oaths. New contacts are rarely sought, and the health and balance of the current contacts is rarely challenged. Instead, only the information given by the contacts is challenged, and this is usually conducted through trance mediumship or scryers with the occasional foray into vision. Such a working pattern traps the flow of power into a small pot. The rigid reliance upon a small group of recent human inner contacts, communed with through a tight hierarchy, strangles the potential for deeper, older, and more profound nonhuman contacts. It also potentially blocks more ancient human contacts that can be worked with directly, rather than through a 'chain of command.'

If we truly want to move forward, then the initial boundaries need to keep pace with our minds and spirits, without losing the quality of the protection that boundaries can give. Magic is moving closer and closer in small steps towards recognition of the power of nature in a mature, respectful manner as opposed to an older attitude of dominion and control. Nature can be utilized magically to create boundaries, which gives us a purer and more malleable form to work with.

5.6 What are boundaries?

In visionary magic, the 'boundaries' are the paradigm that you work in. The landscape, the contacts, the method for opening the contact, and the method for closing the contact all create a format to work within. If the path is newly forged, i.e. you constructed it, then it is more important to take one's time over the vision, and to be mindful of building up the paths, structures, and images carefully so that they strengthen. The danger is, if it is a new path and the person walking the path has little or no experience in visionary magic, that the ability to differentiate between real and imaginary, and healthy and unhealthy contacts will be weak. Forging new paths is not a good idea for someone who does not have a lot of experience in visionary work, and who doesn't understand the inner structures and dynamics of inner places and beings.

My personal belief is that if you work initially within frameworks that have been previously used, then you can hone your skills properly before striking out alone in discovery. In established visionary structures, boundaries, contacts, ground rules, and power are already solid which will allow you to progress.

5.7 Practical methods for foundation training

Once the ability to be still and meditate have been accomplished, and the Void is accessible without the imagination drifting, then it is time to learn some foundation visions and rituals to train the mind and body in preparation for magical work. The following method/path for a basic foundation is just one of many, but it is one I have personally worked with and taught for a very long time, so I am fully aware of its strengths and weaknesses. It is a series of methods and visions that have been worked with for many generations, and many Western Mystery magicians will recognize fragments of this path.

The structure of the foundation training in this path is geared towards training the practitioner to be able to access certain inner temples and inner contacts that have long-term connections to both our own land and the mixed culture that we live in. Once work has been established with the contacts gained from these visions, then the practitioner will begin to get a deeper understanding of some of the other magical paths that are around us today—the deeper into the inner worlds you go, the less difference you will find between cultures, religions, and magical paths. Starting with a base foundation also gives you the techniques and methods to be able to expand your own magical work with strength, knowledge, and foresight.

5.8 Practical visions and background information

Once the technique of inner visionary work has been established, then it is time to go through various realms to learn about them, make inner contacts, find inner teachers, and so forth. The first place to venture to is the place closest to home, i.e. the inner landscape that is all around you. Getting to know the land upon which you live is a very important step towards grounding, service, and also to learning your own place in the grand scheme of things.

The vision of the Inner Land is an ancient mythical vision that takes us to the depths of the inner landscape in the Northern Hemisphere. It does not look at the ancient presentation of the particular land you live on; it presents an ancient 'template' for want of a better word, an inherent inner pattern that flows through most landmass in various ways. It is the visionary version of looking at the ancient inner DNA of the living land. I have worked with this vision in many different countries, and did it in a way that would allow for different presentations to emerge should the pattern be wrong for that land. However, besides some slight differences in the trees, the pattern always worked in the same way.

Wherever you are, this vision will link you deep into the ancient memory of the land. It works with the inner pattern and spirit of the primal forest before humans encroached upon it—you are essentially meeting the ancient collective ancestor of the forests. Bear in mind that many places today in the northern hemisphere that are desert, were once covered in trees, so do not worry too much if you currently live in desert.

If you live in the southern hemisphere then you will have to experiment with this vision and see where it takes you, as I have never worked magically in the southern hemisphere. If the forest slowly fades off and another landscape emerges, and you recognize it as an ancient representation of the land you live on, then work with what appears. Afterwards, write down everything you saw so that you can build up a record of the presentation of the ancient land pattern.

Record the following visions so that they guide you through the vision until you know your way there and back without help.

5.9 The Vision of the Inner Land

Light a candle, close your eyes, and be still.

With your inner vision, see a flame burning quietly within you, the flame that burns at the edge of the Void. In vision, reach with your hand into your inner flame and cup a fragment of it in your hand. Reach out with your hand in vision, and carefully join your inner flame with the inner flame of the candle.

As you look at the candle flame with your inner vision, the flame grows bigger until it is big enough for you to step into. Step into the flame and let the flames lick around you. They do not burn you; they cleanse and refresh you as you bathe in the sacred element. You stay in the flame for a moment, enjoying its power and bathing in the flame of life. When you are ready, step forward through the flame and you will find yourself within the Void. This is a place out of time, a place with no movement, no sound, no time. As you drift in this place, you allow your daily life to fall away until it is the eternal you that drifts in this

5. VISIONARY MAGIC

special place. You feel the potential of all things in this quiet space, and you feel the stillness within yourself.

You form intent in your mind to venture into the inner world of the land where you live. With that focused intent, step forward out of the Void and find yourself standing on ground, with a slight wind in your face. You find yourself on the edge of a tall, ancient forest where the trees seem to stretch up to the clouds. The forest is silent except for the sound of running water, and as you look around you find a small stream that weaves its way through the forest. You follow the water as it weaves in and out of the ancient trees, and you feel as if you are being watched as you walk. The deeper into the forest you go, the more your body starts to react to the surroundings. You begin to recognize certain scents, and long-buried memories flit in and out of your mind, but they do not stay with you long enough for you to fully grasp what it is you are remembering. The more you walk, the deeper your memory of this place becomes, and the more your everyday life falls away.

Eventually the stream tumbles into a clearing, and you step into the light after the darkness of the forest. Before you is an image of intense beauty. An ancient gnarled and twisted giant tree grows out of an outcrop island of rock and earth, which is in the centre of a small lake. On the other side of the tree and island is a horizon with a stunning sunrise, and the waters of the lake seem to cascade over the horizon and tumble down into nothing. The tree emits its own light, which shines out among the trees, and in the shadows, tiny bright beings seem to dart and hide.

Walk to the edge of the water and put your hand in the lake. The water feels bright, full of life and power. The tree senses your presence and you can feel it reaching out its thoughts to you. The tree asks you to sing. You begin to sing songs that you know but as the power of the water and trees surround you, a deeper sound emerges from

5.9. The Vision of the Inner Land

within you and you begin to sing the sound that is your soul. The sound flows out of you and across the lake.

Everything around you begins to emit sound, and the sounds of each tree, each rock, the water, each being, all joins with your sound to create a wonderful harmony. Out of the forest come beings that are a part of this land, a part of this world, and they each have a sound too.

They sing their sound, and the vibrations of their sound resonate deeply with yours, and you realize that these beings are connected to you somehow. They are ancestors of your genetic line maybe going back millions of years but in this place, there is no time: it is the eternal forest that walks slowly across the face of the earth.

One of the beings comes forward and touches you on the forehead and allows you to touch them. You commune together, telling each other about the way that you live. Spend some time in silent communion with this being.

After the communion has ended, it is time to leave. You will be able to come back here whenever you need to, but always treat this place with respect: it is the sacred inner landscape of the planet and must be protected.

You have an urge deep within you to dive into the water, which you do. You swim towards the horizon and you find fishes swimming alongside you, who also communicate with you. They are the guardians of the Great Tree. You swim until you come to where the water falls into nothing and you fall with the water, falling through space, through time, and through the Void.

You fall and fall, and your mind is peaceful and relaxed as you fall, and the water cascades all around you. The longer you fall, the more you become aware of the water all around you, travelling with you. The water seems to fall through you, joining with the water within your body, filling you with life and vitality. You begin to lose the sense of falling, instead becoming filled with a sense of being water. Its soft silence fills you with a deep peace, and you float within the dark, still water. You *are* the water, you are flowing in all directions, you are the stillness and silence. You drift in the water of the Void, being at one with the water.

Slowly you become aware of a golden light like the sun shining on your face, and you remember your humanity. You remember that you are alive and in the Void. You remember your own flame within, and you remember the candle flame that burns close by. You remember your body and your inner flame begins to burn brighter. You remember the chair in which you were seated and you feel the boundaries of your own body. Slowly you sink into your body awareness, and your awareness of the water fades away. Remember the trees, remember the lake, remember drifting in the water, and when you are ready, you open your eyes.

The vision of the Inner Land takes you into the heart of the inner landscape of our world as it is in our era, which means the last five million years. The inner interface of the land has many differing presentations, just like the outer landscape, and the tree, lake, and forest is just one of them. Working with that interface of the forest gives us a deeper connection to the trees, water, and beings that are all around us. It takes us to the threshold of existence of the forest, where it flows in and out of the Void, and allows us to interact with the consciousness of the land at a much deeper level.

Humanity historically has created animal/human images as deities in an attempt to communicate with nature. Going into the inner land itself and communing with the inner forest/water in a more natural, non-verbal, non-ritualized communication allows us to truly connect energetically to the land and to interact with that power at a very deep level. The inner landscape is also a natural form of egregore, an inner storage of energy for the land and all beings upon and within it. It can act as a 'reset' button for balance when worked with magically; and the longer the magician works with this vision, the more layers of depth and application they will find.

Once you are familiar with the vision, it is very rewarding to go and do this vision in a forest where there is water. Where I live there is old woodland with springs that emerge out of the roots of some of the trees, so that some of the trees are surrounded by water. Sitting in the silence of the woodland and doing this vision is extremely powerful and beautiful, and it has brought me much closer to the land around me. This vision connects us to the land upon which we live and helps to tune us into the earth that we serve.

5.10 The Goddess in the Underworld

The next vision that would make sense to follow on from the inner land is one that connects us to that part of human consciousness where the power of ancestors and deities come together. First you start from zero (the Void), then you learn about the land upon which you stand, after which you learn *what is the power held within that land.*

The Goddess in the Cave is an ancient visionary doorway to the Underworld Goddess who absorbs and expresses, among other things, the female ancestral consciousness that sleeps within the land. This presentation of an old goddess has many layers to it, the ancestral layer being the most superficial and immediate. Beyond that layer, the magician can build a relationship with this power to reach through the ancestral layer to commune with the female deity power that is inherent upon and within that land. She is also a guardian and gatekeeper of the deeper underworld, an advisor and teacher; and when angered she is the rage that destroys everything in her path. Always approach this power in vision with respect and caution.

Her power is expressed in cultures around the world in very similar forms as a powerful and often older woman, goddess, or queen who resides in an underground cave that houses a pool of water or a river. The following version is based upon the form that resides in the British Isles, but this template can be used to access the same type of consciousness in other lands. The vision, if you have true contact, will adjust and display the signature characteristics of the land upon which you live. It may need working with a few times for the unique signatures and imagery of your own land to emerge in the vision, but patience works wonders. You will notice that this vision does not use the Void as an access point, but goes directly into the Underworld. If you wish to follow a path of visionary magic,

5. Visionary Magic

then eventually you will learn many different ways to access the inner realms. Each way has its own advantages and reasons for use.

> Light a candle, close your eyes, and be still.
>
> With your inner vision, see a flame burning quietly within you, the flame that burns at the edge of the Void. In vision, reach your hand into your inner flame and cup a fragment of it in your hand. Carefully join your inner flame with the candle flame. As the two flames merge, the flame grows bigger and the floor beneath the flame fades away. The flame plunges into the Underworld and you lean over to look down and watch the flame. As you look, you see very old and worn steep stone steps carved out of the side of the tunnel and you climb into the darkness, staying close to the wall as you begin to climb down. The steps pass by old roots, rocks, and sweet-smelling earth as you climb deeper and deeper into the darkness. The flame has landed below you and you carefully step your way down towards it.
>
> The steps go around and around as you climb down, and the light of the surface world fades into the darkness as you aim for the flame below. You eventually come to a stop at the bottom of the tunnel and look around. The flame casts a glow that allows you to see into the darkness. To one side you see a large crack in the rock face, and you squeeze yourself through into a very narrow passage between two rock faces. The flame follows you and together you make your way down the narrow, twisting, descending path that is taking you deep into the land. The flame goes ahead of you, and a few yards ahead it seems to vanish around a corner, leaving you in total darkness. This is a darkness so deep you have never experienced anything like it before. There is nothing to see, nothing to hear, just a total still darkness. Stretch out your arms to touch each side of the rock face around you, and walk carefully, feeling the floor before you with your feet.

5.10. The Goddess in the Underworld

The path goes around a corner, and a faint green light glows from a crack in front of you. Squeezing once more through a rock crack, you emerge in a cavern where the rock walls emit a very faint green glow. To one side of the cavern is a pool of water, and on the far side of the cave is an old woman who seems to be asleep in a large rock throne that is covered in shells. Her long white hair appears to be growing into the rocks around her, and her robes are full of sleeping creatures. Between her and you, the floor is littered with sleeping animals, birds, bees, and insects. Very quietly and carefully, you pick your way through the sleeping family to the water and wash your hands, face, and mouth in the water. If you are urged to, get into the water and completely wash yourself: you must be clean before you stand in front of the Mother.

As you stand back up and turn to face the old woman you see that she has one eye open and is watching you. She beckons you to her and holds out her hand, expecting a gift from you. Reach into your pocket and give her whatever appears in your hand. Once she is happy with her gift, talk with her and tell her about yourself, and about the land where you live.[1] Listen carefully to what she might have to say and try to remember it. When you have both finished, thank her and then carefully pick your way back through the sleeping animals to the entrance of the tunnel.

By the door is a lit candle, and the old woman tells you to take it with you to light you way back. As you go back through the narrow tunnel that leads to the stairs back to the surface, you notice for the first time that ancient carvings are etched out on the rough rock walls. The carvings continue all along the walls and up along side the stone steps: look at them as you climb back to the surface world. One etching may possibly stand out to

---

[1] If you are recording this, give yourself plenty of silence time at this point of the recording.

5. VISIONARY MAGIC

> you. Try to remember it, so that you can work with it and learn about it.
>
> As you emerge back into your own world, go and sit back in your chair before the candle flame. Look at the candle flame with your inner vision and allow its stillness to wash over you. In that stillness you remember your experience, the things that were said to you, and the signs, sigils, or beings that you saw. Once you have recovered your memory, open your eyes and look again at the candle flame. When you are ready, blow out the flame.

The visions above are from a very specific line of magic that has been operating in the Western world for a very long time. Many of the visions from this line have been in operation for thousands of years, but they are not a dogmatic magical line that must be followed. They are the accumulation of many lifetimes of visionary exploration that was often expressed through a religious, mystical line. It is important to remember that for millennia magic was a major part of the inner mysteries of priesthoods and priestesshoods, and was tightly interwoven with the spirituality of ancient cultures. It is only since the advent of Christianity after the second century A.D. that it became separated from spirituality and became a path of its own.

The reason I mention this is to ensure the understanding that ritual and vision, and the methods of operating them, are bound by the dynamics of the inner and outer worlds, not the rules and regulations of magical lines, lodges, and religious paths. They are a part of our existence and as such were respected in the ancient temples for those capable of operating them. The peoples of ancient times stated that their method of ritual and vision was tied to their specific deities not because of dogma, but because it was literally true. Their deities, rituals, and magic emerged through their consciousness from the powers of the elements and land all around them. To work with a foreign method often brought magical chaos, as it was designed and emerged from a very different land power, and that in turn birthed new lines of work for both good and not-so-stable purposes. We see examples of that mismatch in today's magical

5.10. The Goddess in the Underworld

practices, but I think that mismatch is slowly fading away as it catches up with our modern mobility and melting pots.

The Egyptians gave us our first record of one culture using the magic of another in the pyramid texts of King Unis (2450—2300 B.C.) where Proto-Canaanite spells were used alongside Egyptian ones.[1] Much later in dynastic Egypt, influences from Persia, Greece, and Rome inserted themselves into the Egyptian magical structure. It changed both the magic and the approach, and as the old died off in the Late Period, the new emerged. However as a magician who has worked these various systems, I see that the Egyptian system lost a great deal of its stability and strength with this process. The new hybrid that emerged was a totally different and much lesser magic.

It's an interesting question to see how our mobility of both mind and body affects our relationships with the land and its powers, and how mobile those powers will become in light of our constant interactions with foreign lands, cultures, and peoples. I know that certain powers from other cultures operate with me very well on this British landmass, whereas other foreign powers that I have tried over the years to work with out of the context of their land have failed miserably or been unstable. It is all about experimenting, making mistakes, learning though experiences, and, most of all, using your common sense.

---

[1] steiner2011

Chapter Six

Ritual Magic

There is one very interesting dynamic that comes into play with a lone ritual: there is no audience to play to. Because magic demands a certain amount of imagination and creativity, it can open the door for drama queens who perceive their ritual roles as a performance and play out their little power fantasies. By doing that, the power raised by the ritual stays in the realm of psychology and doesn't move any further than that.

So what is happening in a ritual? Well it all depends on what you want to achieve, how you are doing it, and with whom you are doing it. From an inner point of view there are a variety of kinds of ritual that all work magic in different ways and at different power levels. There are types of rituals that sustain inner patterns, rituals that create inner patterns, and rituals that tear apart certain patterns. There are rituals for the whole community, rituals for a working group, and rituals done by a sole worker or a very small group. Each magical tradition has its signature form of ritual that is used to interface with power and work patterns, but the underlying principle is generally the same.

In this ritual section you will find that some of the rituals have strong visionary elements to them as well as ritual action. When working and learning as a lone magician, you have to establish your own inner contacts as opposed to getting them from a lodge or magical line/group. This can be triggered by combining vision and ritual together, which is usually a more advanced way of working, but it can benefit a lone magician in the earlier stages of their magical development.

In this chapter, visionary ritual is present where it is needed, mainly to develop inner contacts, bridge inner power into

6. Ritual Magic

implements, and to develop the directional gates. The rest of the ritual exercises/patterns use less visionary content.

6.1 Group rituals

This is the most common form of ritual and is usually the type of ritual that involves a group of people and onlookers. Although it is not directly relevant to a lone practitioner, it is important to understand they dynamics of the different forms of magical ritual.

The group ritual is often a mythical reenactment which is keeping an inner path trodden, and therefore keeping it open in the consciousness of the people. The large community ritual ensures that an energetic link is kept between the land/temple/deity/beings and the people. That way, the path of communication, energy, and cooperation is kept open by following the ritual footsteps of those who came before us.

The main source of power in this type of ritual is in the reenactment. By walking a path already trodden, contacts and powers woven into that original pattern are energized and interacted with. The trodden path becomes a window over the generations until it is like a program whereby you throw the switch and all the lights come on. From an inner point of view this is one of the weakest forms of ritual magic, because although there are more people and it is a well established pattern, it is usually a dispersed form of magical pattern that works through the characters of the myths and is kept in a tightly humanized form. So there are stories, deities, beings, and actions all represented by human players through which the power is quickly dispersed.

A more powerful form of this kind of ritual is one whereby a small group of magical mediators undertake the ritual and the community passively watches. What makes it more powerful is two things, the first being that the ritualists are not doing a drama reenactment, they are actually partaking of the original action from an inner point of view. This means the action that they ritually take only happens once from an inner point of view: they are magically returning to the original event. The second thing that makes this more powerful is that the community audience is drawn upon as a power source. Their passive observance allows the ritualists to draw upon the energies of all those present to create a large battery to power the ritual. This technique was often used in the ancient world, and it survived in the form of the early Catholic high mass, in which the congregation had no part in the sacred part of the mass and were merely bystanders there to provide energy. The mass developed over time to include the congregation more, thus dispersing the power expression that the ritual awoke.

A new form of this ritual can be established by using a mythical pattern or a newly written script and reenacting the ritual in exactly the same way each year—such consistent action builds an inner path so that power can flow through it.

In more modern times, the communal ritual has also become a vessel for self help and psychological therapy, and while that is valid in itself, it is not a form of ritual magic: it does not create an interface with an inner being or landmass and the ritualists. Instead it creates a link between the outer and inner self of the individual.

6.2 The lone ritual

A lone practitioner must establish, from the very beginning, a sense of focused intent and stillness so that the method of ritual is established from the start with no showmanship, and also with a sense of integrity. Although such an undertaking is very difficult for someone working on their own while trying to learn, it reaps huge benefits in the future years when the practitioner has developed a strong, unique, and focused skill of ritual pattern making.

The first thing that is important in a ritual is to know the physical directions of the space in which you are working, and to be clear about which direction or directions you are using and why. The reason for this is that each direction has a certain quality of power that flows through it, and that flow of power will affect your work. The definitions of directional powers vary according to which tradition or magical method is being used, but in the northern hemisphere they are generally expressed as:

6. Ritual Magic

East air, utterance, sword, birth, seed, the creation of something;

South fire, wand, creativity, solar, the way ahead, the path to the future;

West water, emotions, cups or vessels, the threshold of death, the harvest;

North earth, land, the ancestral dead, the underworld.

Of course, there are variants upon these themes: some more modern magical systems place the sword in the south, probably due to the aggressive nature of most solar religions and deities. I suppose that the sword would be at home in either east or south. In the east it brings through the power of guardianship, necessary limitation, justice, and focus, and in the south the powers of battle and war. On top of such variants is the fact that the powers in the directions can be very fluid at times and have elements of each of the four powers within themselves.

It can get very confusing for beginners, so I feel the best approach, if you are serious about magical study and development, is to work with one system of directional pattern until you are completely at home with it. Then once that foundation is laid down, you can begin to experiment and explore.

For example, in one place where I worked magically for a while there were springs to my west, but the power that flowed out of those springs was not healing or emotive power but was the power of female spirit warriors (they show up a lot in northern Europe). No matter what work I was doing, if I worked in the west, a very powerful female warrior presence made herself known in no uncertain terms. So that was the power I worked with in the west. You have to be flexible and able to adjust your work to enable natural patterns of power to flow.

A very important point to remember is that the powers that flow through the directions are not the consequence to your attributions; rather they are expressions of the powers that flow through the land, and beyond that, the inner worlds. If you persist in trying to impose a pattern of power upon a direction that does not mediate that power in a balanced way then you will have a build up of disharmony that will ultimately sabotage your work.

It is also pertinent to be clear to yourself in your ritual and magical work as to what depth of magical connection you wish to work with. If your focus is strictly limited to nature work, the elements, ancestors, etc. such as in witchcraft, folk, or tribal magic, then your directional pattern needs to be rooted in the land and ancestors around you. If your focus in magical work stretches beyond that, to the inner worlds, the underworld, stellar powers, and angelic, demonic, or Divine powers, then the magic becomes very different. The land pattern is the foundation stone upon which you stand, and the directional powers and access points worked with are far deeper than any land connection. Thus, the directional pattern worked in ritual becomes more about those deeper powers and less about the landscape around you. For example, the east would be worked with as a gateway for creation, new birth, a new pattern of magic, and the Inner Library, and deities whose power is about utterance and learning. You can see how the land, the solar and lunar cycle, and the seasons and elements are not really the focus of that directional work.

The ability to adapt and be fluid with how you work ritually does not come easily for most people; but once you have established patterns by working repeatedly with them, and you are able to feel powers flowing back and forth, then you will be able to learn what works and what doesn't—if you pay attention. If you are working with the wrong power in the wrong direction, then you will be made aware of that fact in no uncertain terms.

6.3 Altars

Altars are for working on. They are not a New Age store display, so it is best not to fill them with tons of magical crap. It would seem to be in vogue these days to use an altar as an expression of yourself and your beliefs, so they are filled with statues, trinkets, crystals, and all sorts of product. That is fine if your altar is about your beliefs or is about your own personal psychology. If your altar is there for magical work, then such displays are extremely counterproductive: anything on the altar has to have a specific magical function and reason for being there. If a magical altar is clogged up with stuff,

6. Ritual Magic

then it becomes a poorly focused lens at best, and a disaster waiting to happen at worst.

Altars are thresholds for power and communication, so if you fill them with loads of tat, then the streams of contacts and powers will be confusing, fragmented, or may even block the work you are trying to achieve. If you want to do a magical display, fine, do it on your dresser, but leave your altar as a clear working space with only the essential items upon it.

Those essential items would be:

- the element which you use as a focus and doorway (e.g. a candle flame, a bowl of water, a rock);
- whatever magical implement you are using (e.g. a sword, a wand), and any object directly relevant to what you are currently doing (e.g. paper inscribed with sigils, an ancestral bone).

If you have things that are 'charging' or 'pending' then they go to one side of the altar.

If you wish to work only in relation to a particular deity then an image or statue of that deity with be on the altar too. One word of advice, though: if the altar has a deity upon it, then the altar is the domain only of that deity and nothing else. Any work that is not directly related to that deity can possibly be blocked by the narrow field of contact such work can invoke. This is where the separation of devotion and pure magic comes in. One suggestion that has worked well for me is if you are working with a particular deity, have an altar just for them then have a magical working altar that is separate.

If you work with a few different deities, do not stick them all together on one altar; rather they should each have their own 'territory.' The reason for this that each deity is a doorway and the altar is a threshold. Keeping things clear and simple ensures there is far less likelihood of the deity statue itself becoming parasited (where a parasitical being moves in and pretends to be the deity), and it also keeps the magic clear, precise, and on point.

If you can keep the same table or surface for an altar, then that will help to build up the patterns and focus the power. However if you cannot, then an altar cloth that is used only for magical work can suffice. I have used that method many times over the years when it was not possible to have a dedicated altar: I had a specific cloth that I would lay out on a table, or even on a stack of books, to do my magical work. And it all worked perfectly well.

There are also methods for working magic using floor patterns and no altar, which again is about the establishment of patterns in a space. It can be a bit difficult, though, if you need to use implements. Once the techniques for opening, closing, mediating, and raising power are well established, and the magician has good focus, then an inner flexibility emerges whereby you can work anywhere, at any time, and eventually without any implements or tools. But first the rules need to be learned so that they can be thrown away.

6.4 Implements

The traditional way to acquire one's magical implements is a way that very rarely occurs these days in the rush to consume and have everything you want when you want it. It would often take many years to acquire the implements, and they would come one at a time when the path of power that the implement mediates crosses yours. Sometimes the implements would come into a magician's life before they had decided to study magic and it would stay with them, quietly ticking in the background until the magician finally realized what it was.

The sword would be given or come to a person after they had learned the lesson of justice and had acted with honour in the best way that they could in a dangerous situation. Once the person had done all that they could for themselves, the sword would arrive as backup, protection, and teacher. The wand arrives always in unusual circumstances and heralds the path of learning about fire/solar/serpent magic. The cup is given to the magician as a token of love, and not necessarily couple love: it can be any form of love. It can also appear as a cauldron of regeneration, appearing when the magician is in a place of needing regeneration after battle or is about to undertake service to heal others. The shield, which can also be a rock, bone, or sigil, teaches about protection, the land, and your

6. Ritual Magic

place upon the land, and again turns up when you have exhausted your ability to defend yourself in an honourable way. From this you can see why such a method was not fashionable and was cast aside.

Methods changed when the need arose to fit the acquisition of the implements to the rigid structures of magical grades that became very fashionable through the influence of Freemasonry. Texts began to spring up with formalized ways of making and finding your magical implements so that the magician, not magic, had control over the pace of an individual's magical development. In today's world there are many variants upon the theme with courses, books, and workshops that show you how to make/find and consecrate your implements, down to the all-out commercial 'get it all here' occult shops where you can simply buy implements.

To find a sense of balance with magical implements, I feel a good way forward in today's world is to give fate a chance to put these implements in your path, but also to be proactive. One way to do this is to flow with the momentum of magic rather than against it by slowly building up your four implements over time by starting with one and working around the directions/elements over a long period of time with the one implement working in each direction and the centre. For example, a budding magician would first perhaps find a sword and begin to work with it until they have got a very good understanding as to how it works. Not only does that stop the gluttony of wanting it all at once, it allows a person to work in depth with one line of power so that they have an excellent grounding before they move on to the next implement.

Don't feel that you have to work to a rigid rule of developing your implements in step with the rule book of which comes first and why; and don't feel that you need to have all the implements in order to do the work. It is you and the magical thresholds that create the magic: the implements are tools and work associates that come when the time is right. They work with you and draw you in when you are ready to open up to their power. In truth, you cannot force an implement to work for and with you, as the power of the implement comes partly from within yourself and your own fate pattern. It will open within you when you are ready, not when you want it to be. This ensures that people cannot tap the true depths of magical power that these tools hold until the practitioner is in a space where they can truly access and understand its power. Until that point is reached, the implement lies dormant no matter what you do with it.

My first implement arrived on my doorstep as a teenager and I had no idea what it was. It was this implement more than anything else that led me on to a true path of magic and it took a while before I finally realized what it was and how it worked—I can be a bit slow on the uptake sometimes. The sword turned out to be the sword of the original Golden Dawn Temple (Horus no. 5) from Bradford, Yorkshire. Next came the cup, ten years after the sword arrived; and the wand appeared under very strange circumstances twenty-two years after the sword first made its appearance. My shield only turned up a year ago, some thirty years after the sword popped up.

What I did discover over the years is that the actual implement itself is not that important; it is the power within that implement that is the true tool that you work with. That power, once it has appeared properly in your life can be transferred out of one physical implement and into another. So you may have more than one sword, for example, over your lifetime; but the power that resides in those various swords is one and the same original power. This only happens, and is only workable, if the original implement came to you through fate/magical pathways.

The transfer of power from the original implement to a new one is a technique to protect the power should something happen to the implement itself. Another quirk that happens is that the implements change as you do, and as your knowledge and understanding of implements deepens, so the instruments and tools of your craft change and transform with you. For example, when your work with a wand gets to a deeper level, often the wand will break and another one, with a deeper and more profound expression of the same power, will cross your path. The transfer of power is sometimes automatic, and sometimes initiated by the practitioner.

6.5 Ways of working with the implements

Different traditions have variants upon the theme of magical implements, of how they work and what you do with them. It is pointless for me to go into any depth on the different traditional methods, as I do not have working experience of every tradition out there, and I do not write about things in theory, only in practice from direct experience. It is also important to note that just because you have the implement does not mean that you will learn its secrets straightaway. In truth, learning the true power and purpose of a tool can take many years, and can even evade understanding throughout a lifetime. The best way to move forward is to begin working in a disciplined form with the tool. The more experience you gain, the more flexible you become with your working methods. It is at that point that the tool can truly begin to commune with you and teach you about its power.

But it is vitally important to establish a pattern of work with boundaries first, so that you can learn within a contained field. Those that try to dive into complex ritual magic straightaway either fail to penetrate the power, or if they are naturally very talented, will learn a great deal but in a very harsh way that could permanently damage them.

Magical implements are used in roughly two forms, one ceremonial and one magical. The ceremonial use of implements in magical ritual is where the sword, cup, wand, and shield are used in a *representative* way. The sword etc. takes up a ritual function that represents an action or power connected to the powers/deities that the ritual centres around. This is true for about fifty percent of magical ritual paths, and also includes various forms of witchcraft, religions, etc.

The magical use of an implement is where the implement (e.g. the sword) is 'awakened' by a specific consecration that merges it with the 'original Magical Sword,' or the power has already moved into the sword and is naturally fully 'awakened.' Between those two extremes, there are ritual methods of working with a virgin sword that by nature of the repeated ritual work, the sword begins first to tune to the 'original Magical Sword' then slowly through that tuning actually *becomes* the original Magical Sword.

The awakened implements do not *represent* anything. Rather, they are working members of the team and contribute power, knowledge, and contact to the ritual. They are conscious beings in their own right.

The following descriptions of the implements list their magical awakened attributes that are found in the wide spectrum of the Western Mysteries. Remember, just like ritual and visionary patterns, everything in magic has many different layers, and just when you think you have learned all you can about a magical pattern, a deeper layer will present itself. It is truly a lifelong learning process.

6.6 The sword

The power of the sword is something that has a deep resonance with the lands of the United Kingdom, along with the stone and cup or grail. Legends of magical or sacred swords reach back in Irish and British history just about as far back as you can go. Similar sword, blade, and spear myths and magical themes flow through many different cultures, and these mythic patterns give you an idea of the most superficial layer of a magical sword.

One of the recurring themes of some of these sword legends is that the sword is not to be wielded in battle, but held in justice or sovereignty. In magical terms, the sword is present in the ritual as a fellow worker and is used as a focus of power, or as a guardian, or used to confer sovereignty, power, or consecration. It is not wielded in the sense of a weapon, but used in accordance to its line of consecration. There are also times where the sword has been consecrated and enlivened to become a window for a particular being. In such a case, just the unsheathed presence of the sword is enough to affect a power flow and influence a ritual. When a magical sword has become a consecrated window, it is very important not to wield that sword as a tool. It is not a tool but a being, usually very powerful, and able to create disaster if misused.

6.7 The wand

The wand is usually a branch of a tree, and holds the power of that tree for the use in magical ritual. It can also be one of the tools of kingship, with its connection to the Royal Oak of Britain being just one example. The consecrated wand, or wand from a sacred tree, is, like the sword, a being in its own right, and is most often used as a focus tool. The intent of the magician in the ritual is focused to a fine point, which is then jettisoned into action in some cases by the directional use of the wand.

6.8 The cup

Using the cup in ritual when it has been consecrated affects the fluid that is placed within the cup. It is used for blood, wine, water, and as a consecrated vessel, brings about transformation to the fluids within the cup. Traditionally in magic the cup is associated with womanhood, the womb, and love. In actual magical practice I have not found this to be the case. What I have found, working with a variety of consecrated vessels, is that the cup is connected to powers that regenerate warriors, like the cauldron of regeneration. I live in an area of many cold springs, and I have found that the power of these springs is more akin to the powers of Valkyries than it is to love and motherhood. Whereas the sword and wand can work as actual beings, I have not personally found that with the cup; but I have found that used properly, it is a very powerful tool of transformation.

6.9 The shield

Just as it sounds, the shield is there to protect, to hide, and to deflect. A consecrated shield will protect you from things that you cannot cope with, but it will not blindly protect you in the way an unconsecrated shield would. That is good. Too much protection is a dangerous thing in magical work, and an intelligent shield can add to the power of a ritual without putting you in long-term danger from overconfidence. Five years ago I would have maintained that magical shields are not beings but tools. I changed that stance after a shield came to me that is very much a sacred being, fierce, powerful and very much its own boss. In ritual it is there as a worker, doing its job without interference from me or anyone else. It blocks certain streams of damaging power and also acts as a power storage unit, holding power until it is needed.

As always with such powerful things as consecrated objects, you can only learn so much from another person or book; you will truly learn the qualities, consciousness, and powers of implements by long-term use and observation. I used to be very sure of myself and make pronouncements about certain tools and powers, but over the years practical long-term experience has shown me that our understanding of magic in all aspects is extremely limited and we will never be able to properly quantify it, control it, or pronounce certainties about it. So anything that is read in this or any other book is a fraction of the true understanding of magical power and should be used only as a guide until one gets to the stage in magic where you have learned the rules, learned the powers, and are beginning to walk out on your own path.

6.10 The basic tuning of ritual tools

A basic tuning of ritual tools is a simple contacted tying-in of the ritual tool to the inner powers that work through ritual implements. It is the run-of-the-mill magical sword, cup, wand, and shield setup, and the tuning methods tie in the magical power needed for the implements to work properly. It is not a consecration of magical implements, but it is a step in that direction. In the early days of magical training, it is much better to work with attuned magical tools first so that you can gain a good understanding of how tools work and why, before you then progress on to working with consecrated tools. The various methods of consecration of magical tools are discussed in the third book of the Magical Knowledge series, *The Contacts of the Adepts*.[1]

The first thing to note is that when you get an implement ready to attune, you cannot pre-judge what direction it is going to work in. To try, even at an advanced level of work, to impose a pattern or action on a magical implement is just sheer folly. It is important to understand right from the beginning that although there are particular attributes in Western magic given to specific directions, in truth all the directions and their powers are fluid and the inner contacts connected to the implement will more or less choose which

---

[1] mccarthy2020c

6. Ritual Magic

direction you will work in. Sometimes the implement will be worked with in a traditional direction, but sometimes an instrument will gravitate towards a direction that such an implement would not normally be connected with.

The following method can be used for any of the four implements and will connect the implement up to an inner contact, which will mediate power from the inner direction to the implement. Whichever directional power you work with, that is what will flavor the magical tool's power. To gain the basic skills needed to undertake such a working, if you are not used to working ritual while also using vision, it would be a good idea to practice some of the basic ritual exercises that are listed later in this chapter first. They will give you a deeper understanding of how vision and ritual come together in the simplest terms and will give you a chance to develop the necessary focus needed to attune objects.

6.11 Basic consecration method

First cover the ritual object in dry salt and leave overnight. In the morning, recite the exorcism and blessing of substance over the tool (provided in Appendix B).

Have four altars set up, and a fifth altar or freestanding candle in the centre of the room. Each altar should have a candle upon it and nothing else. Starting in the east, go to the altar and stand quietly before the candle. Feel yourself stilling and connecting to a silent flame burning at the edge of the Void. When you are ready, using your inner vision, reach inside of yourself to your own deep inner flame, and cup a fragment of the flame upon your hand. Use this inner flame to light the inner candle and once the inner candle is lit, then light the outer candle.

Stand before the flame and close your eyes. Using your imagination, see beyond the flame and see a gateway on the other side of the altar. Using your inner voice, ask for an inner contact to come to the threshold of the east to assist with work, and see the gates slowly swing open. You see a priest, priestess, or inner contact slowly

6.11. Basic consecration method

walking towards you. They stop at the threshold of the gates, which is also the threshold of the altar. Thank them for being here, then walk to the south.

Repeat the action in the south, the west, and the north until all four directions are lit and there is an inner contact in each direction waiting to work with you.

Light the central candle, which is the flame at the centre of all being, then pick up the ritual tool you are wishing to consecrate. Instead of going to the traditional directions for that tool (e.g. west for a cup), starting in the east, go to the altar and place the tool on the altar, then place your hands upon the tool. See how the tool feels. Then pick up the tool and hold it over the flame to the inner contact who is waiting for you, and ask them if this tool is the tool for that direction: are they willing to work with it? They will either say yes or no. You may not get a defined answer straightaway, in which case you move on to the next direction. If all four directions are undefined in their answer, then you go around again. Another method of choosing the directions is to simply walk up to each direction holding the tool. You will either attracted or repelled in the various directions. Either way, one direction will really stand out for that tool.

When you have chosen the right direction, take it to the altar and hold it over the flame. The inner contact will place a hand over the object or they will take it from you and do something to it. If they place a hand upon it, place your hand over their hand and feel a power passing from them, through you, into the object. This process will take a long time or a short time: there is no way to tell beforehand. Once they have finished, place the object on the altar and go out of the room. The inner contacts need clarity to complete the power transfer, and it is easier and better if there are no humans in the room. The power is all passed by touch and resonance.

You will get a very clear indication of when the object has been completed. At that point go back into the room, and, starting in the east, say thank you to the inner contact for their work. Let them withdraw, close the gates by seeing them close in your mind, and blow the candle out. Repeat this in the other directions, and lastly in the centre.

Now you must learn how to work with the implement. It will be a combination of its traditional use plus the quality of the direction that it was worked in. It is also possible that a being was put in the object by the priesthood, but if that has happened it will be very obvious right from the start. A good way of learning about the tool is to open the direction that it has been tuned to, then go through the gates in vision with the object in your hand with the intention of communing with the priesthood of that direction. They will teach you all that is possible for you to learn about working with your tool.

6.12 Developing your relationships with your ritual tools

Learning how to work with the tools in ritual is not straightforward, particularly if you are working with enlivened tools that are essentially vessels for beings that will work with you. My advice is to learn the ritual basics first, i.e. how to open and close gates, how to bring a contact to the threshold, how to create patterns and trigger them (e.g. the Hexagram ritual, pp. 124–132) and how to work with energy/power by moving it around. The exercises in this chapter will give you all the basics in these foundation skills, and as you work with them and practice them, have your tools around you as passive presences. So, for example, have the sword by the east altar (always point down or laid down when a passive presence), the wand or staff by the south altar, the vessel on the west altar, and the shield or stone on the north altar.

This will enable the tools to slowly tune into the magical pattern and build up their connections with you. Once they are fully integrated into your pattern and you have the basic ritual and visionary skills, you will find that you slowly become aware of how, when, where, and why the tools should be used. Allowing the skill of tools to unfold naturally this way, instead of through prescribed rituals, will allow your magic to develop at its own pace. Remember, ritual tools are not theatre props to wave around; rather they are companions to be activated for specific jobs, not integral parts of every ritual you do.

For example, the sword may come into use when you need it to guard something, or when in ritual you need to limit the presence of a power or contact. Held point down in the left hand, the sword will limit (not block) power and contact around you so that you do not become overwhelmed. The vessel can be used to contain substance or energy during a ritual. The staff can be held (left hand) as a companion worker in visionary ritual or as an extension of your left arm. The shield/stone protects you. If you are working with a shield stone, then it would be placed at your feet; if you are working with a wooden shield, then it can be placed behind you (to have your back) or used as a central altar. If you are working with a cloth shield, then it can be draped over your shoulders to protect you during potentially dangerous work, or you can stand upon it as an enclosed ritual protective space.

6.13 Basic ritual patterns and exercises

The following is a series of exercises, starting with the simplest, that will train a person in the basics of pattern making and the methods of combining vision and ritual, and will prepare them for acquiring deeper ritual skills. The following methods are the ones that I often used to train apprentice and initiate magicians, and are the ones I know work well for a student.

Instead of laying out actual 'work' rituals for people to try, I have pulled together a series of exercises that train the magician in the inner power dynamics of how energy moves around, how contacts actually work, and what is happening from an inner point of view when the magician recites during ritual. If the outer ritual has no inner power base, then it is just a dramatic display with wishful thinking. However, if the inner energy and contact dynamics are learned first, then when the magician actually comes to perform a ritual, and uses the inner techniques learned in these exercises, then the ritual will become a major power action.

6. RITUAL MAGIC

The following working methods and suggestions are not hard and fast rules, but they all come from a system that works well. Once you have understood what is actually happening in these exercises and tasks, then their underlying principles can be grafted onto whatever other system you feel draws you the most. The reason for this is that the methods are magical techniques, not magical dogmas from a particular path.

6.14 Opening and closing directions and working spaces

This is the first skill that is needed to begin to develop magical sensitivity of the veils between the worlds, and to be able to wake up and put to sleep the magical space. In a deeper truth, a space cannot really be closed down from the inner worlds: it doesn't really work that way. However, barriers can be put up and lines drawn. On a surface level these act as closings and openings. But if a powerful being, human included, wanted to get into the inner space of a magical temple, if they were skilled enough it would be almost impossible to keep them out by closing the space. More powerful and ingenious methods would be needed. I tell you this only to ensure that a) you get a reality check about magical abilities versus powerful beings, and b) that you also get a deeper understanding about how space actually works.

The opening and closing of a magical space creates a 'tuning' frequency so that the room, the land, and any attendant beings will prepare for what is about to happen. It is like focusing a lens. By changing the frequency of a space, any inner 'static' from the building or passers-by, human and otherwise, gets tuned out. The room and the person working in the room moves from an everyday frequency to a different 'working' frequency. The outer effect is that the space becomes quiet and the people working become 'invisible' to casual passers by. The more this is built upon, by regularly opening and closing in a specific space, the more the room becomes tuned. I stopped closing my dedicated working spaces many years ago, for a variety of reasons, which allowed a certain tuning to develop within that space that became deep and profound. Such depth provides its

6.14. Opening and closing directions and working spaces

own deep protection and makes the work invisible to all but those on the same frequency. Other people who work in the same tradition, or who are naturally psychic, will pick up on the space as they walk past: they will 'feel' the silence.

The opening of the space method is simple and yet becomes very profound the deeper the magician goes into the inner realms. Remember this profundity when you execute this method: have respect for its simplicity, which will allow it to open out the true depths of power hidden in this simple action.

The following action needs a candle and a box of matches. Preferably you would work with an altar, but this is not necessary.

> Before you light the candle, stand in total silence and stillness. Close your eyes and begin to see with your inner vision. From that stillness pass into the Void and deepen that stillness within yourself. Feel yourself losing the boundary of your body and have a sense of your spirit spreading out through space. Once you are deep within the Void, see a flame in the distance come slowly from the depths of the Void towards you. When it gets closer, see your own inner flame resonate within you. Reach within yourself of a fragment of the flame and cup it in your hands. Light the inner candle flame, then open your eyes, staying in the Void, and light the outer flame. Stand before the flame for a moment with eyes open, but seeing yourself still in the Void. See the power of the Void spill out of the flame into the room until you and the room are in the void.

This action, when built up over time, can become an extremely powerful action that can be used in many ways for many reasons. It should become obvious why the use of visionary training is very important right from the very beginning. The two, vision and ritual, are inextricably linked in higher magic, and they balance out power to make it more manageable when used together.

So, the next step is to tune the directions. Magical work can be done though an almost limitless list of directional patterns. Most traditions have their own directional pattern of one sort of another,

6. Ritual Magic

and some are more obvious that others. For example, the directional use of the pentacle shape would be a five-directional pattern, and many witchcraft groups use a four-directional pattern to denote the elements and seasons. I use either one, two, four, or five directions, depending on what I am doing.

6.15 Creating a directional space

Just for the sake of training I will do this exercise in a five-directional pattern. This pattern gives acknowledgement to the inner powers of the land around us. Once this pattern is learned and worked with ease, then specific directional patterns that do specific jobs can be attempted. By using a foundation learning like this, good skills are learned from the very beginning that will help the magician learn how to move power around from A to B, and how to open doors deep into the inner worlds while retaining a physical conscious presence in our own realm.

> Set up the space with a candle in each of the four directions and one in the centre. They can be on altars, boxes, or just on the floor. Make sure the paths to each candle are clear and that you have a long taper. Ensure your phone is turned off and the door locked, pets out, etc. so that you will not be disturbed.
>
> Light the candle in the centre of the room, using the method that takes you into the Void. Once the flame is established within the candle, then, taking a flame for the taper from the centre flame, go to the east and stand before the candle. Again be aware of the Void and be still. When you are still, light the candle with the taper, and also 'see' with your inner vision the inner flame settling on the candle. Once that is done, do the same in the south, west, and north, ensuring each time that you take the flame from the centre. The world flows in and out of the Void, and the directional patterning reflects that through the centre candle.
>
> Once all candles are lit, sit in the east facing the east candle. Be still and allow the power of that direction to

flow to you. It will be very faint at first, and it usually takes a great deal of practice for it to become discernible. Repeat the exercise in each of the four directions, then the centre. The more you do this, the more you will become aware of how different the powers are in each direction.

When you are ready to close it down, start again in the east. Be still, and using inner vision, see yourself take the inner flame back into yourself; then blow the candle out. Repeat this action in the south, west, and north. Finally stand before the central flame, and take the inner flame back into yourself. Be aware of the Void within you, and of the flame burning within the Void. The two flames become one. Then, gently blow out the central flame.

If possible this exercise should be done daily, or at least a couple of times a week, so that you can really build up the inner connection with the directions and their powers.

6.16 Establishing the gates and tools

This ritual is the next step on from developing the directional space. This ritual builds upon the last one and starts the magical construction process of bringing the gates/thresholds of the inner worlds to your working space. It also starts to ritually establish the directional pattern for the magical implements: the relationship between the tools, the directions, and you as the magician.

If you do not have a dedicated workspace (who does, these days?), use either small fold-down tables as altars, or whatever furniture is nearby. I do not have a dedicated space to work in, and when I need altars I use specific altar cloths which I place on piles of books, a chair, and a fold-down table. The key is to have a working candle in each direction, and to get used to working directionally in a space.

Altar cloths do not need to be a special fabric, I used a white bed sheet that I cut up into squares, and I mark each cloth with its direction by putting a tiny E, S, N, or W in a corner.

6. RITUAL MAGIC

Start in the east. Whenever you work directional magic, always start in the east. This is where the power opens, and it also helps you to tap into a ritual pattern that has been used for millennia. The pattern you create will resonate with the ancient pattern and will be fuelled, stabilized, and brought to life through this resonance.

When you walk into the room, walk a full circle around the central altar, walking clockwise, then approach the altar in the east. Always walk clockwise to build up that flow of power, and never approach the east altar directly: always walk a full circle before you start any initial ritual action.

> Approach the east altar and stand before it. Take a few moments to close your eyes and still yourself before you begin to work. When you are ready, open your eyes and light the candle. Stand for a moment before the candle and try to empty your mind. After a few minutes, take a step or two back, turn and walk to the south altar, and repeat the action: stillness, light the flame, be silent for a few moments. Repeat this in the west and the north.
>
> When you have finished in the north, step back, turn, and go to the central altar. Repeat the action. Once all the candles are lit, walk a full circle around the central altar, then approach the east altar.
>
> Stand before the altar and close your eyes. Imagine that you see two large gates beyond the altar. Take your time. Build up the image, note if they are made of metal or are wooden doors: allow an image to build. When you feel you have a nice strong image of an east gate, take a step back from the altar, turn, and go to the south. Repeat the action in each direction. You may find that each gate in each direction is different: each direction will have a unique type of gateway.
>
> Once you have finished in the north, turn to the central altar, stand before it (facing south), and close your eyes. Imagine a large column of fire that reaches up beyond the ceiling and stretches into the stars, and it also plunges

6.16. Establishing the gates and tools

down into the Underworld: a column of fire that is like an axis that goes through all the worlds.

Open your eyes, walk a full circle around the central altar, and approach the east. Place your hands upon the altar at either side of the candle flame, and look beyond the flame.

With your eyes open, use your mind's eye to imagine the east gates. Using your voice, utter the following words:

"I acknowledge the gates of the east, I acknowledge the angelic threshold of the east, and I acknowledge the wind of the east."

Step back from the altar, turn and walk to the south. Repeat the same exercise, using the words:

"I acknowledge the gates of the south, I acknowledge the angelic threshold of the south and I acknowledge the fire of the south."

In the west, do the same and repeat the words:

"I acknowledge the gates of the west, I acknowledge the angelic threshold of the west and I acknowledge the water of the west."

And in the north:

"I acknowledge the gates of the north, I acknowledge the angelic threshold of the north and I acknowledge the stone of the north."

When you have finished in the north, take a step back, turn and stand before the central altar. Remember the visual of the column of fire and utter the words:

"I acknowledge the central fire that flows through all worlds, all times, and all substance; I acknowledge the angelic threshold of the Void, the threshold of Divinity as it flows through all things, and the light of all living beings as it flows from the stars to the Underworld."

Close your eyes and imagine the stars in the sky above you. Imagine the earth below you, the east wind to your

6. RITUAL MAGIC

left, and the western water to your right. Be aware of the power of fire in the south before you, and of the power of the earth in the north behind you. Imagine a spark or flame deep within your centre, a light that stretches up to the stars and down to the earth. It meets in your centre in the form of a small flame within you. This is the spark of Divinity within all things, and it embeds the pattern of the central axis not only in the centre of the ritual room, but also in the centre of your own body. The use of the word Divinity does not denote a deity; rather it recognizes the Divine creative and destructive power of the universe.

Build up that sense of the elemental powers in the directions around you. Open your eyes and look at the central flame. Hold out your arms and declare:

"The sword will be my left hand, the cup will be my right hand, the fire of inspiration before me, and the rock of my ancestors behind me."

Drop your arms and walk a full circle around the flame/central altar. Once you have done a full circle, go to the east, and turn to face the central flame. Hold out your arms and declare:

"The wand of creative fire and the future in my left hand, the shield of the ancestors and the past in my right hand, the cup of humanity before me and the breath of God behind me."[1]

When you have finished, walk a full circle around the central altar and go to the east. See in your mind's eye the gates of the east. Blow out the candle, and see the gates vanish. Step back, bow to acknowledge the powers, and repeat this action in the south, west, and north. Step back from the north, bow, and turn to face the central flame.

---

[1] Eventually you will learn to do this magical positioning with the powers and tools for all the directions, but two directions is enough to get you started. Eventually you will be able to use this directional and elemental tuning within seconds by simply thinking about it, but that skill is built through repeated use of this ritual in the early stages of training.

Stand before the central flame and see in your mind's eye the column of fire that reaches through all of the worlds.

Notice that in the centre of the column, where the candle flame is, there seems to be a small void: a nothing in the centre of the light. Utter:

"I acknowledge the Void in the centre of the light, the nothing from which all comes."

Blow out the candle flame and bow.

Sit down and close your eyes. Meditate for a few moments to still yourself, and be aware of the directions around you: the east to your left, the west to your right. Remember the elements in each direction: air, fire, water, earth, and the light in the centre. Remember the magical tools in each direction: the sword, wand, cup, and shield. Remember the Void in the centre of the flame. Allow those images to rise, then fall away from your mind, until you are simply seated in the room. Remember what the room looks like. See the room's door in your mind's eye, its walls and its contents; and see yourself seated before the central altar. When you are ready, open your eyes.

Starting in the east, collect up the cloths, fold them up, and wrap them around the candles or put them carefully in a box. They must not be used for anything else. Put the room back into its normal state.

6.17 The Pentagram as the magical human pattern

The Pentagram is a shape that has been used ritually in many different ways, and was a beginner ritual used for training by the nineteenth-century Order of the Golden Dawn. The pentagram is the pattern of a human, and the hexagram is a pattern of the Divine.

This version of a basic pentagram ritual pattern establishes the magician as a human working in a magical pattern, working in time, and working with the inner and magical powers that flow around them. It is like a 'return to magical factory settings' ritual that tunes

6. RITUAL MAGIC

you and the space around you. When you feel threatened or out of balance, it is a simple and old ritual pattern that can bring you back into focus.

You will note that unlike the Golden Dawn pentagram ritual, it does not project outwards. You do not draw the pentagram in the air; rather you awaken the pattern within you. It is more subtle than tracing the pentagram outwards as a shield: it strengthens the magical power within and around you. It doesn't shield you; you *become* the shield.

This ritual can be used as a beginning to more complex rituals in order to bring yourself into focus. It can also be used with other pentagram rituals to provide a more solid foundation for the magical act.

> Set up your work space with the four directional altars and one in the centre. Go around the directions, starting in the east, and, using the methods you have already learned, light the lights and see the gates opening. With each direction, after you acknowledge it and as you see its gates open, become aware of a figure coming through those gates and standing on the other side of the altar. Do not try to put an identity upon them or communicate with them; just be aware they are there as passive presences. Once all four directional gates are open, go and stand before the central flame/altar facing south (so the east altar is to your left).
>
> Hold out your arms to the sides. Throughout this section, keep your arms outstretched, even as you turn. They will start to hurt. Get over it. Keep your shoulders down and your elbows held and that will help. When you stand, stand with your legs apart so that you make the pentagram shape with your body.
>
> See in your mind's eye the magical sword in your left hand, handle up, blade down. See in your right hand the cup. See in your mind's eye above you the Hexagram, and below you the earth sign. See before you in the south a

6.17. The Pentagram as the magical human pattern

road going off into the distance with a full sun. See people behind you: the ancestors.

Recite:

"In my left hand, the sword of Justice and balance. With my left hand I give to bring balance. With my left hand I release to bring balance. My left foot stands upon the stone of restriction, the grindstone which forges my future. Saturn is my grindstone."

Recite:

"In my right hand, the vessel of regeneration. With my right hand I receive to bring balance. With my right hand I accept in order to bring balance. My right foot stands upon the threshing floor which receives the gifts and blessings of my harvest. Pluto is my threshing floor."

Recite:

"Behind me is time past, the ancestors who walked before me. I release whatever is necessary to them. Before me is the future, the path I will forge. I accept whatever is necessary for that path."

Turn around to face the north altar while still keeping your arms outstretched.

Recite:

"In my left hand is the sword of balance that is given to the vessel in the west. In my right hand is the vessel which receives the sword from the east. With me is my past, the blood of my past, and those who birthed me. Before you and in honour of you, I hold the power of the sword and the vessel in your name. Beyond me is the future. My path is forged by the grindstone of the future, and my past is measured by my harvest upon the threshing floor."

Now turn and face the central altar in the pentagram stance with your arms still outstretched (stop whining!).

Recite:

"Above me is Divine Power, the father that gives breath. To the east is the power of the sword. Below me is Divine

6. Ritual Magic

> Substance, the mother that receives the breath. To the west is the power of the vessel. Before me is the future, lined with the noble ones. Behind me is the past, and the angel who guards me. Within me is stillness. I Am (your first name). I Will Be."
>
> Stand in the pentagram position in silence and think about all the powers and dynamics that are around you. When you are ready, drop your arms and bow to the central altar. Starting in the east, go to the east altar, bow to the inner presence there in thanks for holding that space for you, then blow out the candle. Repeat in the south, west, and north, then finally with the centre candle.

When you worked with the Pentagram ritual, you placed a Hexagram over your head, which is the mark of the Divine breath as it flows from unbeing into being, from no substance to enlivening all substance (creation). Now we will work the Hexagram itself, and learn how that symbol/filter tells us about that first step of the breath of Universal Power as it breathes out of the Void, out of unbeing.

As the breath of Universal Power is uttered out of the Void ("In the beginning was the Word") it hits its first filter which enables it to pass into form, into creation. That first filter is something we understand via the magical symbol of the Hexagram.

The reason we approach this filter through a magical symbol is that our tiny minds are really incapable of truly understanding the sheer complexity of this creation process. Working with the symbol of the Hexagram, breaking it down into its power dynamics, then reassembling it helps our brains to process what is actually happening.

This first filter, the Hexagram, is about Divine Power that has done its first division. Just like a fertilized human egg starts life by making a first division, so also Divine or Universal Power first divides into two: positive and negative, male (releasing/giving) and female (accepting/containing). This creates an opposition of power, a tension which allows form to exist. Everything in creation is polarized; everything in creation has a tension which creates energy and movement.

The Hexagram teaches us about this basic foundational dynamic. Without that understanding, we fall back upon giving Divinity a human face, emotions, and 'humanlike' reactions. This is a great folly, and it has no place in real magic (or mystical religion). Deities have such qualities, but Divinity does not. Divinity has consciousness, but it is of a nature far beyond what we can understand. Through working with the Hexagram, the magician slowly learns how this polarized dynamic works, and learns how power can have consciousness without being humanlike.

Before we can work with deities as magicians, we must first learn about the powers of Divinity itself. This power flows through everything in creation, and therefore flows through all of magic. It flows through every magical action, every thought, every movement, and once you come to understand these flows of power, how this intricate balancing act works, you can then engage that understanding in advanced magic so that your work flows in harmony with creation and not against it. You work with creation; you do not try to control it.

Once the magician has worked with this ritual pattern for a while, they will slowly begin to understand how the Hexagram works, what powers flow through it, and how it is then applied in various magical streams. Its actions are often sadly misunderstood in modern magic, but if you reach back to much earlier forms of magic and magical religions, you will begin to see its use subtly hidden within certain religions and magical texts.

This is a long ritual that works with utterance and moving around the space. If you wish to work with it, study the steps and words, and practice it without the candles, altars, etc. until you feel ready and able to do the ritual with the space tuned and active, and all the gates open.

6.18 The ritual of building the Hexagram

The ritual is in two parts. The first part is about understanding power in and power out, about Divinity in its polarization and its echo within ourselves. In the first part we learn how these polarized powers work with and flow through the directions, and how those polarized forms can be put together and overlaid to create a filter of creation/destruction, power in/power out, a filter of power balance and harmony.

This in turn creates a simple but effective flow of power that the magician can then engage with in their work. It is a flow of power that is balanced, and that can be approached from a variety of angles depending on what work the magician is going to do. The second part of the ritual is about how that pattern is then triggered and brought to life, and how the magician can become immersed within the magical Hexagram pattern.

6.19 Hexagram ritual

Open the directions by lighting the candles in each direction and visualize the gates in each direction. When you have been around all of the directions, return to the east altar and stand before the candle flame. Place your hands upon the altar (or hold them up) on either side of the candle flame and look beyond the flame. With your eyes open, use your mind's eye to see the east gates open. Using your voice, utter the following words:

"I acknowledge the gates of the east, I acknowledge the angelic threshold of the east, and I acknowledge the wind of the east."

Step back from the altar, turn, and walk to the south. Repeat the same exercise, using the words:

"I acknowledge the gates of the south, I acknowledge the angelic threshold of the south, and I acknowledge the fire of the south."

In the west, do the same and repeat the words:

"I acknowledge the gates of the west, I acknowledge the angelic threshold of the west, and I acknowledge the water of the west."

And in the north:

"I acknowledge the gates of the north, I acknowledge the angelic threshold of the north, and I acknowledge the stone of the north."

When you have finished in the north, take a step back, turn, and stand before the central altar. Remember the visual of the column of fire and utter the words:

"I acknowledge the central fire that flows through all worlds, all times and all substance, I acknowledge the angelic threshold of the void, the breath of Divinity as it flows through all things, and I acknowledge the light within all living beings as it flows from the stars to the underworld."

Close your eyes and imagine the stars in the sky above you. Imagine the earth below you, the east wind to your left, the western water to your right. Be aware of the power of fire in the south before you, and of the power of the earth in the north behind you. Imagine a spark or flame deep within your centre, a light that stretches up to the stars and down to the earth, which meets in your centre in the form of a small flame within you.

Turn and go to the east altar. With your eyes open, in your mind's eye, see the gates of the east wide open. Turn and face the central flame. You are going to trace a triangle in the air.

With your right hand, pointing with your first two fingers, starting with your arm outstretched high above you, recite:

"In the name of the Great Father..."

Now bring your point down to the right hand corner:

"...and in the name of the Great Mother..."

Now trace your point to the left hand corner:

"...and in the name of the great Spirits,"

Trace your point back to the top to complete the triangle:

"...I give."

Walk a full circle around the central flame, then go stand before the altar of the west. With your eyes open, in your mind's eye, see the gates of the west wide open. Turn and face the central flame.

Now you are going to trace an inverted triangle. With your arm outstretched, pointing to the left corner recite:

"In the name of the Great Mother..."

Trace your point across to the high right corner:

"...and in the name of the Great Father..."

Trace your finger down to the low bottom of the triangle:

"...and in the name of the Great Spirits..."

Trace your point back to the high left corner to complete the triangle:

"...I receive."

Walk a full circle clockwise around the flame, then stand before the north altar. See in your mind's eye the gates of the north wide open. Turn your back to the altar and face the central flame.

You are going to repeat the inverted triangle. Starting with the high left corner, recite:

"In the name of the Great Mother..."

Trace your point across to the high right corner:

"...and in the name of the Great Father..."

Trace your finger down to the low bottom of the triangle:

"...and in the name of the Great Spirits..."

Trace your point back to the high left corner to complete the triangle:

"...I Come From."

Walk a full circle clockwise around the flame and stand before the south altar. See in your mind's eye the gates of the south wide open. Turn your back to the altar and face the central flame.

6.19. Hexagram ritual

You are going to trace an upright triangle. With your right hand, pointing with your first two fingers, starting with your arm outstretched high above you, recite:

"In the name of the Great Father..."

Bring your point down to the bottom right hand corner:

"...and in the name of the Great Mother..."

Trace your point to the left hand corner:

"...and in the name of the great Spirits..."

Trace your point back to complete the triangle:

"...I Am Going To."

Walk a full circle around the flame and stand upon the first cross-quarter, the space between the north and east altars.

You are going to trace both triangles, one at a time. With your right hand, pointing with the first two fingers, starting with your arm outstretched high above you, recite:

"In the name of the Great Father..."

Bring your point down to the right hand corner:

"...and in the name of the Great Mother..."

Trace your point to the left hand corner:

"...and in the name of the great Spirits..."

Trace your point back to complete the triangle. Immediately use your point to draw a circle from the apex of the triangle and finish the circle at the upper left hand corner, in order to begin the second triangle, the inverted triangle. Recite:

"In the name of the Great Mother..."

Trace your point across to the high right corner:

"...and in the name of the Great Father..."

Trace your finger down to the low centre of the triangle:

"...and in the name of the Great Spirits..."

6. Ritual Magic

Trace your point back to the high left corner to complete the triangle. Recite:

"...We are."

To conduct the second part of the Hexagram ritual, take out the central altar and candle, or move them to one side and put out the central flame.

Go back and stand at the northeast cross-quarter. To start with, you are going to repeat the declaration of the two triangles, but with one difference at the end.

With your right hand, pointing with the first two fingers, starting with your arm outstretched high above you, recite:

"In the name of the Great Father..."

Bring your point down to the right hand corner:

"...and in the name of the Great Mother..."

Trace your point to the left hand corner:

"...and in the name of the great Spirits..."

Trace your point back to complete the triangle. Immediately use your point to draw a circle from the apex of the triangle and finish the circle at the upper left hand corner, in order to begin the second triangle, the inverted triangle. Recite:

"...In the name of the Great Mother..."

Trace your point across to the high right corner:

"...and in the name of the Great Father..."

Trace your finger down to the low centre of the triangle:

"...and in the name of the Great Spirits..."

Trace your point back to the high left corner to complete the triangle. Recite:

"...We are, and from 'We,' I shall become."

Walk around the directions, going from the northeast cross-quarter, past east, and all around until you come back to the east. Stand before the east altar, hold out your arms to the sides, and recite:

"I call upon the powers of the east to witness the giving of Divine Breath into life."

Step back and bow. Turn and go to the south altar. Stand before the south altar, hold your arms out before you, and recite:

"I call upon the powers of the south to give safe passage to the Divine Breath onto the path of life as it vanishes into the mists of the future."

Step back and bow. Turn and go to the west altar and hold your hands out before you in a cupped position. Recite:

"I call upon the powers of the west to witness the receiving of Divine Breath into substance."

Step back, and hold your cupped hands to your chest as if they hold something, and bow. Turn and go to the north altar. Stand before the north altar, hold down your arms, open your hands as if to release something to the ground, then with both hands pointing to the floor recite:

"I call upon the powers of the north to witness the release of the Divine Breath back to its source."

Step back and bow. Turn and walk around the directions then stand in the west with your back to the west altar and recite:

"Powers of the directions, you are my witness. I have announced the passage of the Divine Breath from its first aspiration, to its containment in the vessel, then its passage back to the Source. I declare that I understand. I am a vessel. I am life. I contain the Divine Breath within me and I honour that Divine Breath that gives me life."

Take a deep breath in. Focus your mind on the direction east that is opposite you, and that the air you breathe in flows from this magical direction, then exhale. Take a step forward and take in another breath, breathing in the

6. Ritual Magic

air from the magical direction of east, and then slowly exhale. Repeat this action until you are standing in the centre of the directions, where the central candle flame would be.

Turn and face the south, feet apart. Raise your arms straight up above you, arms straight and locked. Bring your arms down, outstretched to the sides, keeping your arms straight, and follow your left hand with your eyes, so that your eyes and head face east while your body stays facing south. As your left hand reaches east, it lands palm facing up, while your right arm, without bending, lands west with the first two fingers of the right hand pointed. Ensure that your hands, eyes, and head all move at the same time, in harmony, so that your left hand and your eyes land east at the same time.

Bring your right hand above you (centre, top of the triangle), then bring it down to the east, across to the west, and back to above to make the 'up' triangle.

Recite as you do this action:

"The Divine Breath that brings life to form flows from the east; the father gives."

Imagine the up triangle hanging in the air before you. Bring your hands to your chest (containment: you are the vessel). Now walk around to the other side of the triangle (passing on the east side of the triangle). Stand facing north.

Extend your arms up above you, inhaling as you do so, with arms straight, bring your right arm down to the east, right hand landing east, palm up, with your head following your right hand so you are looking east. The left hand moves straight down in front of you to point at the floor with the first two fingers pointed. This is all done as one harmonic movement.

With the left hand, trace the down triangle starting 'down/point' to west, as the hand moves to the west, the head turns to the west, and you exhale and begin to recite.

Ensure the head and hand arrive west at exactly the same time: head stays west. As you recite trace west to east, east to down. As the hand arrives at 'down' the head is set straight looking north.

As you do the action, recite:

"The Divine Vessel in the west that contains the Breath: the Mother receives. The wind that blows from the east finds the vessel of the west."

Drop your arms by your side (release). Close your eyes. See in your mind's eye the hexagram hanging before you. With your mind's eye, see a flow of power/energy come down from above and from the east at the same time, joining with and filling the east half of the hexagram (along with the east & up section of the space) with a golden light. As the power settles in the east half of the hexagram it flows out of the east side of the hexagram, flows towards and through you, and vanishes behind you. As it flows towards you it turns red, passes through you, and vanishes through the south gate.

In your mind's eye see the red flow back out of the south gate behind you, and pass into you on your west side. As it passes through you and leaves you, it turns into a bright white light that dazzles you. It flows into the west side of the hexagram, filling it with a very bright pure light. It also fills up the west direction and down section of the space. The bright light flows out into the north before you until the hexagram and the space around you is totally empty. The dark hexagram outline hangs before you, filled with emptiness.

Close your eyes (if they are not already closed for visualizing) and take a step forward so that you are standing in the space of the empty hexagram. With your eyes closed, clear your mind. Feel the nothing all around you. Feel the blackness, the space without time, motion, light, sound: a total black stillness. Stay in that silence for as long as you feel you need to.

6. RITUAL MAGIC

> When you are ready, take in a deeper breath and hold it, eyes still closed. Take a step forward, open your eyes, and breathe out, all at the same time. Then recite:
>
> "I am born of the Void, the breath that breathes life out of the nothing, the breath that contains everything. I step into life with the Divine breath flowing through me."
>
> Turn and face east. Step to the altar, blow out the candle, and bow. Repeat in the other directions going clockwise until the room is dark and silent. Stand for a moment in the darkness and silence. Be aware that this ritual is about the birth of life, of Divinity breathing life into substance. Be aware that the Divine Breath flows through you. Your breath and your words have the power of Divine Consciousness flowing through them. Use that breath wisely and with balance.

Once the magician has worked with the directions, the gates, the Pentagram, and the Hexagram, then it is time to start working in visionary ritual to learn how to connect properly with inner contacts, and how to work with moving energy around. These are all basic magical principles that draw upon the physical (ritual) and the inner (vision) together in order to achieve something.

Once the magician can work comfortably with these methods, then the techniques themselves can be adapted for a variety of different magical applications. They are core principles of magical work, like building blocks that can be worked with in all sorts of different ways.

6.20 Bringing in inner contacts to the directions

Once you have established the directions, the next phase of development, both of the room and your training, is to learn how to open the thresholds for an inner contact. This will not work straightaway unless you are a natural medium: it is something that has to be built up in the room and within yourself. If you are working with someone who has worked with contacts for a long time, then the resonance of working with a contacted magician opens out the connection within yourself. This is one of the sad facts for lone magicians: most skills in magic are passed on through resonance. But you can develop the skill within yourself with hard work. That work includes practising opening the thresholds and reaching over them for a contact.

If you work regularly with the lighting of the flame and opening the directions, then reaching using inner vision for the contacts, it will build up a pattern within the space that will slowly open out for contacts. The contacts reached for in this exercise are specific contacts that are safe and educational to work with. Do not be tempted to reach for your own idea of a contact, or some being you have read about: to do such work requires a great deal of inner skill that usually only comes after years of work. Yes, you may be able to reach those contacts, but you will not be able to control how they operate in your space or get rid of them easily. You also leave yourself open to parasitical beings that will latch on immediately and will be hard to get rid of. Learn with patience, which will give you a strong and clean foundation. This method uses visionary techniques to establish contact, but then the contact is worked with ritually.

6.21 Triggering the gates and the contact of the east

> Light the candle flame in the centre of the room and tune it to the Void and your flame within. Using inner vision while walking around, take the inner flame from the centre and light the inner candle on the altar of the east while physically lighting the outer candle using a taper which you light from the flame in the centre of the room. Do the same in the other directions working clockwise: east, south, west, north.
>
> Once all the directions are lit, go back to the east. Stand with both hands upon the altar, or hands out if there is no altar. The candle is the threshold between the worlds. With eyes closed, using your inner vision, look through

6. Ritual Magic

the candle flame and see beyond it the faint details of the inside of an ancient building with columns.

Most of the room is obscured by mist. Call with both your inner and outer voice for a teacher or contact of the sacred utterance. Focus your vision on the mist. Slowly a person emerges out of the mist and stands on their side of the candle, looking at you. Tell them in your mind who you are, and that you want to learn the skills of the Mysteries. Then physically put your hand beyond the flame and into their realm. They will possibly touch your hand in vision or make some sort of contact. Once you have made contact and told them why you are there, ask them if they would be willing to work with you over a period of time. If they agree, fix their image in your mind: their visual description will be what enables you to reestablish contact in the future. The contact may ask you to cross the threshold, and if they do, you will step over into what looks like the courtyard of a great temple with large doors, beyond which is the Great Library. Do not go any further for now, but concentrate upon building up the visuals of the contact so far. Once the contact is steady, then you can pass through the great doors and encounter the learning and the contacts who reside in that great temple.

When you are ready, thank the contact for being there and step back from the candle. Circle the room clockwise so that you walk and acknowledge the south flame, west flame, and north flame. When you come back to east, bow to the threshold, close your eyes, and take the flame back into yourself, then blow it out. Repeat the same in the south, west, and north. Finally stand before the centre, take the flame into yourself, and then blow it out. The flames all merge with your inner flame, which in turn merges with the Void within.

It may take a few goes until you 'see' a contact with your inner vision, as it is a difficult thing to do. Some people never see but sense and 'feel' a contact. That is fine; just remember the 'feeling' of that particular contact and use that feeling as a way back to them when you next work in the direction. It is something that needs to be built up, and the more you work with it, the stronger the contact will become. You are using your imagination to build a window that a contact can step through. The basic image is taken from your imagination, but it is not random. It is a quite complex inner procedure that in itself is quite fascinating. The inner and outer lighting of the flame with intent is the first step. That lights up the flame in the inner worlds. The intent behind the lighting creates a particular frequency that begins to narrow the field of contact. The use of a specific image, for example the ancient building with columns, tells the inner worlds that you are looking for a contact from the ancient Temple Mysteries. This way, any inner being picking up on your flame knows your intentions. Using your imagination to form a human figure out of the ancient buildings narrows the field of contact even more to a human of the Mysteries operating within an ancient building (temple).

That focusing of the lens through thought and intent creates a tunnel for a contact of the Mysteries that is willing to work with humans. The contact will use your inner image to dress itself, so that you can interact. Once you have a solid working connection with the power in the east, then it will be time to approach a contact in the south.

6.22 Contacts in the south

The visionary steps used in each directional working begin in the same way, and overall are very similar; the aim of such similarity is to develop a specific working method that builds over time.

> Light the candle flame in the centre of the room and tune it to the Void and your flame within. Using inner vision while walking around, take the inner flame from the centre and light the inner candle on the altar of the east while physically lighting the outer candle using a taper which you light from the flame in the centre of the room. Do the same in the other directions, working clockwise: east, south, west, north.

6. Ritual Magic

Once all the directions are lit, go back to the south. Stand with both hands upon the altar, or hands out if there is no altar. The candle is the threshold between the worlds. With eyes closed, using your inner vision, look through the candle flame and see beyond it the faint details of the inside of a circular space with a fire in the centre. Most of the area around the fire is obscured by mist. Call with both your inner and outer voice for a teacher or contact of the sacred flames.

Focus your vision on the mist. Slowly a person emerges out of the mist and stands on their side of the candle, looking at you. Tell them in your mind who you are and that you want to learn the skills of the Mysteries. Then physically put your hand beyond the flame and into their realm. They will maybe touch your hand or make some sort of physical contact. Once that contact is made, step over the threshold and you will find yourself walking to a circular space within a clearing or a building where there is a fire or flame in the centre, and priests, magicians, or inner contacts standing around the flame. Go to the central flame and reach within yourself. Cup a fragment of your inner flame and add it to the central flame. Once you have done this, step back. The contact that you made will reach into the fire and give you a fragment back of the central flame. The exchange of fire connects you deeply to the fire at the centre of all flames in the south, and will give you a thread of connection with the priesthood in this direction.

Follow the priest who will lead you back to the threshold of your altar: the contact will work with you both at that threshold and in that direction.

When you are ready, thank the contact for being there, and step back from the candle. Circle the room clockwise so that you walk and acknowledge the west flame, north flame, and east flame. When you come back to south, bow to the threshold, close your eyes, and take the flame back into yourself, then blow it out. Repeat the same in the west, north, and east. Finally stand before the centre, take the flame into yourself, and then blow it out. The flames all merge with your inner flame, which in turn merges with the Void within.

The contacts in the circular space are a template of inner contact for the many different priesthoods who are connected with fire power. Working with them in a non-cultural, not heavily formed way will allow you to learn basic skills without agendas.

6.23 Contacts in the west

Light the candle flame in the centre of the room and tune it to the Void and your flame within. Using inner vision while walking around, take the inner flame from the centre and light the inner candle on the altar of the east while physically lighting the outer candle using a taper which you light from the flame in the centre of the room. Do the same in the other directions working clockwise: east, south, west, north. Once all the directions are lit, go back to the west. Stand with both hands upon the altar, or hands out if there is no altar. The candle is the threshold between the worlds.

With eyes closed, using your inner vision, look through the candle flame and see beyond it the faint details of a lake with a small island in the centre. Most of the lake and surrounding forest is obscured by mist. Call with both your inner and outer voice for a teacher or contact of the sacred waters. Focus your vision on the mist. Slowly a person emerges out of the mist and stands on their side of the candle looking at you. Tell them in your mind who you are and that you want to learn the skills of the Mysteries. Then physically put your hand beyond the flame and into their realm. They will maybe touch your hand or make some sort of physical contact. Once you have made contact and established why you are there, ask them if they would be willing to work with you over a period of time. If they agree, fix their image in your mind: their visual description will be what enables you to reestablish contact in the future. You may cross the threshold and stand upon the edge of the waters briefly to gain a feeling of the power that resides there.

When you are ready, thank the contact for being there and step back from the candle. Circle the room clockwise so that you walk and acknowledge the north flame, east flame, and south flame. When you come back to west, bow to the threshold, close your eyes, and take the flame back into yourself, then blow it out. Repeat the same in the north, east, and south. Finally stand before the centre, take the flame into yourself, and then blow it out. The flames all merge with your inner flame, which in turn merges with the Void within.

6.24 Contacts in the north

Light the candle flame in the centre of the room and tune it to the Void and your flame within. Using inner vision while walking around, take the inner flame from the centre and light the inner candle on the altar of the east while physically lighting the outer candle using a taper which you light from the flame in the centre of the room. Do the same in the other directions working clockwise: east, south, west, north. Once all the directions are lit, go back to the north. Stand with both hands upon the altar, or hands out if there is no altar. The candle is the threshold between the worlds.

With eyes closed, using your inner vision, look through the candle flame, and see beyond it standing stones surrounded by mist. Call with both your inner and outer voice for a teacher or contact of the sacred standing stones. Focus your vision on the mist. Slowly a person emerges out of the mist and stands on their side of the candle, looking at you. Tell them in your mind who you are and that you want to learn the skills of the Mysteries. Then physically put your hand beyond the flame and into their realm. They will maybe touch your hand or make some sort of physical contact. Once you have made contact and established why you are there, ask them if they would be willing to work with you over a period of time. If they agree, fix their image in your mind: their visual description will be what enables you to reestablish contact in the future. Once the contact has been made, step over the threshold to find yourself in a dark cave with a priestess standing in the half-shadows. Tell the priestess that you are there to learn about the powers of the North and commune with her.

When you are ready, thank the contact for being there, and step back from the candle. Circle the room clockwise, so that you walk and acknowledge the east, south, and west flames. When you come back to north, bow to the threshold, close your eyes, and take the flame back into yourself, then blow it out. Repeat the same in the other directions, working clockwise. Finally stand before the centre, take the flame into yourself, then blow it out. The flames all merge with your inner flame, which in turn merges with the Void within.

Establishing the contacts and the pattern of ritual behaviour in the room builds the ability to work in a contacted ritual, as opposed to a non-contacted ritual. The difference between a contacted ritual and a non-contacted ritual method is as follows:

In a non-contacted ritual, you work ritual patterns, read invocations, and enact ritual movement in order to achieve a specific aim. Sometimes the ritual intent is to bring a being or deity into the space for communication. In a contacted ritual, you open the ritual, then invite the contacts from one or all of the directions to assist in the ritual at the threshold between the worlds. The ritual then commences as normal while communicating with the contacts as if they were officers in the ritual. A third form of ritual in this particular stream of work is a combination of the inner and outer ritual: this is where a contacted ritual is conducted both in the outer world and inner world simultaneously. I will talk about that later.

6. Ritual Magic

Before I go any further with the ritual techniques, I want to cover certain issues regarding contacts.

6.25 Inner contacts and their issues

When you work with the pattern of contact that is listed above, you will hopefully be tapped into a series of contact lines that are very much about learning and guidance. The contacts from these directional patterns tend to be fairly straightforward in their dealings with our world. However if you do branch off in search of other contacts, ensure that what you are reaching for is a known quantity i.e. if you are interested in Setian priests, then reach for that contact (south or east probably) through the directional work. But don't just call for anyone: use your everyday common sense, and do not invite a passerby into your work.

If a contact becomes demanding, wants blood, worship, your energy, etc., then back off: you have probably picked up on a very intelligent cross-dressing parasite that wants dinner. They are very clever and will show and tell you what you want to know in return for a dinner, but like all unhealthy beings, they tend to be greedy and once you give willingly, they will begin to take more than you can afford to give. If the contact presents as a very grand, showy, all-powerful deity, teacher, or wise being, then chances are that it, too, is a being dressing up. Inner contacts tend to be down-to-earth, have a strange sense of humour, do not dress up in grandeur, and don't tend to demand your firstborn.

Deities are a different matter: you may want to think very carefully before bringing in such power in the early stages of your work. When you do begin to work with them, it is much better to work with them in terms of working partners where they are the stronger, respected partner. If you get into inner contact with a deity and offer them worship, then you may be in for a lot more trouble than you bargained for. They will try and take over you life and will be extremely demanding, and when you wish to move on, often they do not and will try to force you to stay with them.

The other thing to remember about working with inner contacts is to ask questions: lots of questions. Use your everyday sense to interpret the answers. Engage the same rules you use in everyday life, and do not take everything at face value. In short, when dealing with inner contacts, use your common sense and treat them the way you would treat an outer teacher. They are not gods, all-knowing, or even all-good or all-bad: they are beings trying to convey information to continue an agenda which may or may not match your own.

6.26 Establishing power flows across the directions

This is the beginning of learning how to move power around, which is a principal skill within magic. Once you are used to lighting and closing the flame in the directions, then it is time to begin learning how to move a power from one direction to another, and how to establish paths of power from one direction to another.

This is basic magical technique that is not particularly linked to any specific tradition; it is just a method for working with power that can then be adjusted to work within most ritual traditions. The basic concept of moving inner power from A to B is learned, along with learning how to put power into an object and also how to take it out. The skills can then be transplanted into different magical traditions to enliven and strengthen workings. These inner skills were not written down but taught person-to-person, passing down the line between people who had inner ability. These days human consciousness has become far more malleable, which enables a person to be able to use exercises and patterns to build inner skills and to train themselves.

So why would you want to move power from A to B? Ritual magic is about the changing of the inner and or outer structure, energy, or pattern of the world around us. One useful tool is the ability to move power around so that you can bring power through from the inner worlds, work with it, focus it, then put it into something that you are doing or making. One of the many other reasons for moving power around is the rebalancing of a flow of magical power, or putting the energy into someone who is sick, or to raise extra power to fuel your work. The one thing to remember is that if you are handling large amounts of power, it will really hurt you physically afterwards. You

6. RITUAL MAGIC

will not feel it during the work, but it will hit usually the day after. Your muscles will feel as if you have worked out in the fields for twelve hours without a break, depending on how much power you were throwing around. So do bear that in mind, when you decide to do such work: once you get to the stage of manipulating and working with inner power, it is hard labour.

6.27 Moving energy from one inner direction to another

This exercise is something that must be built up over a series of weeks or even months until you develop the sensitivity to truly feel and be aware of what is happening. The release and movement of the energy itself is not that hard; the perception of it *is*. Again, this is one of those things that can be triggered in someone by resonance, but if you are working alone then you have to build it up yourself. At the beginning of any of these exercises it is very difficult to discern what is real and what you have imagined. Don't worry about that; just work at it and let the imagination create its window. You will know for certain when it has worked, as your arms will hurt like hell and you will be exhausted the day after. Moving energy from one place to another is hard work. It is the same as moving boxes: the heavier the energy, the harder the work, and the more the muscles hurt. What is very interesting is that when you carry a heavy box you can see how the muscles are working and why they are tired. When you move energy, although it has no physical expression that we can discern, it still seems to engage the use of the body's muscular system, and thus causes muscle exhaustion.

> To begin the exercise, light the central candle using the usual method, then go around and light the four directional candles: east, south, west, north. Once all four are lit, go back to the centre and be still for a moment, feeling out as to which two directions would be best to work with. Once you have decided which direction you will receive the energy from, circle the directions clockwise until you get to that direction. Be aware of the contact that you work with in that direction, and using

your inner vision, reach through the flame to that contact and call them in. When they appear, ask them if they would be willing to help you in this work. If they agree, put out your hand to them and ask for the energy to be placed in your hand. Once you have got it, ask the contact which direction it should go to. It might be the same one that you chose, or it might be a different one.

Carry the energy in your hands working clockwise around the directions until you come to the receiving direction. Once you are at the receiving direction, call for the contact of that direction. When they emerge on the other side of the flame, pass the energy over to them. They may give you something back to carry to another direction. When you have finished, go around the directions acknowledging the flames and contacts, and one by one put the flames out, starting in the east and working clockwise.

When you have mastered this technique, then it is time to work without the visionary aspect:

Do the working as before, but do not reach for any contact in any direction. Simply go to the direction, reach over the flame, and verbally ask for the power of that direction to be in your hands. When you take it to the receiving direction, simply release the energy. Once the work is finished, then go around the directions again and close them down one by one.

6.28 Moving energy from an inner direction to an outer object

This is an interesting exercise where you gather power from a direction using the above methods, but instead of releasing it to a direction, you release it into an outer object, which is then worked with. This exercise is training for the inner aspect of consecrating ritual objects and enlivening deity statues. Because of the impact on

6. RITUAL MAGIC

the human body such work can have, it is important to practise it slowly, building up the power levels little by little so that the body adjusts gradually to the inflow of power. This is a really important step and must not be skipped: allowing the body to adjust to inputs of power is vitally important so that the body is able to adapt. If the body is slammed by power that it has no ability to disperse, then the impact on the organs can cause permanent damage.

Most of the time when a person first begins to draw energy out of the inner realms, the amount of energy handled is minuscule unless they are a natural mediator. If you are a natural mediator, as I am, then you can inadvertently pull through large amounts of energy straightaway. This does wonders for the ego, but it causes a good deal of damage to the body, which can be, and often is, permanent. I know: I was that idiot experimenting, and I sustained damage, and it was not the only time. I bumbled my way through numerous experiments in the early days, a completely unaware loose cannon, and I damaged myself many times. Heed my warning and don't be the egotistical idiot that I was. Youth is no excuse!

Anyhow, back to the training exercise.

> Go to a nearby river, field, or forest and get a stone. If you live in a city, get yourself out into the country, choose a rock, and bring it home. Take note of where you got it from, because you are going to have to take it back. Once you have your stone, go to your altars and put the stone in the centre by the central flame. Light the central flame, light the directions, and go around the directions tuning yourself and the altars in by visiting each altar and acknowledging the direction's flame and contact. Once each direction is tuned in and the room feels still and balanced, go back to the central flame and pick up the stone.
>
> Hold the stone and 'feel it' with your imagination. What does it feel that it needs? The stone is like a record-holder for the land where you took it from. If there is a power deficit in that area, then it will reflect through the stone. Once you have established a link with the stone by feeling what it needs, go around each direction, starting in the

6.28. Moving energy from an inner direction to an outer object

east. Pause at the altar and feel if the stone is drawn to that direction. Go around each direction. You may have to go around a few times until you are sure which direction it is drawn to. It will be drawn to the direction that holds the power it needs.

Once you are in that direction, place the stone by the flame and reach over the flame for the contact. Once the contact appears in your mind, tell them your intention with the stone and ask for the energy. They will hand it to you over the flame: collect it in your hands. The contact withdraws, and you pick up the stone and allow the energy to flow into it.

Once all the power is in the stone, place it back in the centre by the central flame and leave the room with all the candles still going. This allows the inner contacts to do whatever is needed for the stone with no human interference. You will feel when it is time to go back into the room. Go around the directions, thanking the contacts in each direction, and blowing out the candles. Leave the stone there if it will not be disturbed, and as soon as you can, take the stone back to where you found it.

Out of curiosity, go back and visit the area every couple of months or so, and keep a record of happenings in the area. The power will unfold there over a year or so. The energy, because you worked unconditionally, will do whatever is needed, good or bad. By working unconditionally, I mean that you did not specify anything to the contact, just whatever is needed for that area. By doing that, what was truly needed was put in the stone, be that regeneration or destruction. If you try to conditionally set the energy i.e. healing, regeneration, etc., then you are bypassing what the land actually needs and placing your limited human expectations upon a landscape that is beyond human comprehension.

A lot of high magic is about moving power from A to B, and often not really knowing what it is doing. Past generations of magicians used to insist that beings and powers did what they wanted; but our human understanding of how power actually works and what will happen is so limited that it is often more productive to allow the inner contacts to do their job properly, to allow nature to do her job properly, and to take our place in the machinery instead of being egomaniacs and trying to drive something we cannot truly comprehend.

The exercise of the stone will truly prepare you for creating power tools, waking up sacred spaces and temples, and consecrating objects and people. The stone will require a small amount of energy, and if you do it a few times with different areas and stones, or containers of sea or river water that is returned, then you will find that the amount of power you are given increases each time. This slowly builds inner muscle and enables your work to develop.

6.29 The web of power

The inner web of power is the next phase on from moving power around, and is the inner basis for many rituals. A well-established outer ritual that follows certain patterns will automatically instigate what I call the 'web of power,' and often outer ritualists will not be aware of it unless they are sensitive; but the practical learning of how it operates, and how to consciously work with it, greatly enhances the overall strength and success of ritual. It basically plugs in the outer ritual to an inner power source to ensure all the lights go on. When conducting an outer ritual, if the ritualist is aware of, and consciously enacting, the web of power, then it will ensure that the ritual operates at full capacity.

A word of caution: once the skills of the transfer of power have been mastered and used in ritual, then you will set off a large cascade of inner action and reaction by using them, so be very careful what you use this power for. If you use this method to power a ritual that attacks, destroys, heals, etc. purely for your own agenda, then be ready for the backwash to possibly flow over you. If you start to mess with higher levels of power for silly reasons (such as fuelling vendettas, exacting revenge, and gaining power, wealth, or a larger sex organ) then you will learn a hard lesson fast in a way where there is no going back. It's not about punishment for doing bad, which does not happen in the inner worlds; it is about the results

6.29. The web of power

of causing a power imbalance which will flow through you and often destroy you. Because of this, most adepts do not teach these methods of working with power. I disagree: those who need this work will develop it properly, and those that get destroyed...well...it's a self culling mechanism of humanity: all the idiots get wiped out.

Once you have read the structure of this inner work, then the outer ritual can be written to slip over the top of it, like clothing. Just ensure that when you do write the ritual, that it works in harmony with what the inner web of power is doing and that the power sources you are calling upon in the outer ritual do actually work in harmony together. You do not want to be in the middle of a ritual and have two deities break out into a marital dispute or turf war!

In this instance, we are going to work the web of power around a ritual function that benefits something or someone unconditionally. It can be a stone, a bowl of water, or yourself. If you use a stone or water, then the unconditional need will be for the land that you then place the stone upon or pour the water on. If it is for yourself, then be aware that if you get it to work, it will bring whatever is necessary for you, be that good or bad. So if you are stuck in a rut that you have not made an effort to get out of, or if you are living in a situation where you are not letting go of something, then it will instigate things for you, often with very painful results. However, in the long run it will benefit you, as it is what was needed to move you along your path.

> To begin, light the flames in the centre and the four directions, and open the contacts in the four directions so that all the inner contacts are present. Starting with the east, go to each direction, and ask the contact for whatever power is needed for the land or you. Hold your hand out over the flame until you feel a power begin to build in your hand. Once it is there, take that power, seeing it as a line of power, light, or flame in your hand, and walk to the central flame, joining the line and flame using outer hand movements as well as inner hand movements. Return to the east and draw a line of power off the flame in the east and carry it with you to the south

and connect it into the south flame. So there should be a line of power going from east to centre, *and* east to south.

Repeat the same action in the south, linking a line of power to the centre, and also taking a line of power with you to the west. Keep working until each of the four directions are connected together and each direction is also connected to the centre.

Then work in the centre. Standing before the flame with your back to the northeast cross-quarter, raise your arms up to the skies and call the power of the stars above to flow down your arms and into the centre. See, with your inner vision, power streaming down from above you, flowing down your arms. Place your hands over the flame in the centre and see the line of power from above connect to the central flame. Once that is connected, point your hands to the floor and call upon the power of the Underworld to flow up through you, lifting your arms up slowly and seeing lines of power draw up from below you. Once you see the lines of power in your imagination, connect them to the central flame. Place your hands on either side of the flame and see with your inner vision lines of power running from each direction, above and below, into the flame in the centre. It will look like a web of power.

See the web, and build its brightness and strength with your imagination. Once it is strong and you can feel its power (and don't rush, this stage may take time), either hold the stone into the flame (if you are working with stone) or your hands on either side of the flame, and see the stone or yourself connect to the centre flame. See the web of power flowing into and finishing in the stone or your own centre; and stay in that vision until you strongly feel the connection.

If you are doing this work upon yourself, stand for a good length of time, feeling the directions flow into you, the power reaching every part of you and affecting your spirit.

See the central flame passing into you and joining with your inner flame until you are the centre of the web.

If you are using a stone, then see the power collect within the centre of the stone and see it at the centre of the web. To finish with the stone, leave it in the centre by the flame, and leave all the flames working. Go out of the room to let the stone 'cook' in the power. You will know when it is finished: you will feel it all switch off. When that happens, go in, put out the directions, and say thank you to the contacts, collect the stone, and go put it out on the land.

If it is yourself you are working on, sit down with your back to the central flame, with your back touching the central altar, or close to the flame if it is on the floor. Close your eyes and meditate with the power all around you. Feel into the depth of the power, be still with it, and feel it fill every corner of your body and mind. Spend as long as you like there: you will feel when it is all finished. When you get to that point, stand and put out the lights, starting in the east and finishing in the centre. See each flame seek refuge within you as the outer flame is extinguished. It would be advisable at this point to go and have a sleep so that the power can really embed itself within you without distraction.

If you are using this as an inner skeleton for a ritual, first link all the flames and directions up as described, then begin your ritual. Don't forget to close all the lines down afterwards.

6.30 Designing a ritual

Note: it is important, as a lone practitioner, to know how a group ritual is actually built and written. Once that method is understood, it is easier then to convert the method for lone use, which will be discussed later.

Once you have worked with the directions and powers/contacts within those directions, then it is time to look at the structuring of a ritual.

6. RITUAL MAGIC

The first thing to decide is what the ritual is for. Is it a ritual to gain something? Is it a ritual to honour or worship something? Is it a ritual to do a job? Is it a ritual to mark passage? We talked earlier about the different kinds of ritual, and it is important to have a very clear idea within yourself what it is you are trying to achieve. It is also important to ensure that if you are designing a ritual that has a certain number of key players within it, that you can actually get that number of people to work with you. If you are a group that is established in a particular format of magic, then it is very important that the ritual is compatible with the power flow and frequency of any deities or inner contacts you work with.

The first step of putting a ritual together is not the writing of the words that will be used, but the decision regarding what directional powers you will be working with and whether you will use an altar or altars. From the minute you decide the ritual pattern that will be used, the inner contacts, if you have been working with them regularly in exercise, will begin lining up. The formation of pattern and intention is the strongest trigger in ritual, and everything else hangs upon those two driving forces. Once the directional layout and pattern of power flow has been set—i.e. what directions are going to be used, and in what order/flow—the next step is to think about what, if any, implements will be used and why. Ensure that everything you decide is for a magical reason, not a 'showing off' reason. Drama and theatre do have a place in outer ritual (seasonal passage, for example) but for deeper, more powerful rituals they become major distractions and drains on power. The choice of implements should be directly related to the job in hand and the powers that will be used.

Once all of that has been chosen, then it is time to write the ritual speeches if there are any to be used, and to allocate people to their jobs and positions. Dates can be important, but I have found, purely by accident, that if you do not concentrate upon a particular date/moon passage etc., then the ritual will line itself up with all manner of star alignments. Of course, if you are designing an outer ritual, say a solstice ritual, then it must be done on the solstice. But if it is not a seasonal outer ritual, do not limit the powers of the work by trying to force some timing: trying to time a ritual for a full moon to use its power is a limited way of thinking. Set the date according

6.30. Designing a ritual

to when you can get the room and the people together; the inner contacts will do their job in nudging you to the right date.

A good example of this was a time when I was training magicians in the USA. It was time to do a consecration on a group of experienced workers, and there was only one weekend in that season when we could get together. Closer to the date, our room booking fell through and we had to take another date. During that weekend, someone who was an astrologer pointed out that we were working during a massive star alignment and we all really felt its power working with us. I would never have known about it, and therefore would not have lined up the ritual to use its energy. The inner flow of power ensured that we did indeed match up with the alignment so that full power was available. That has happened many, many times to me over the years, so I have learned not to try and control the situation too much.

If things like dates, people dropping out, and room disasters happen in the run-up to a major working, don't panic: there is usually a good reason for it. People will drop out or be stopped from arriving if they are not meant to be there for one reason or another: its all about being flexible and going with the flow. If they are not absolutely critical for the ritual, then go on without them and improvise. Eventually you will get an inner sense about times, people, etc. in regards to success or otherwise in ritual situations. Instinct plays a major part.

Any ritual speech should be to the point and without dramatic flourishes that sap energy. There can be a tendency in magical work for people to copy the overly dramatic and flowery speeches of rituals from past times. There is a danger of people losing concentration and energy by giving them extensive speeches and dramatic roleplay that have no actual real power purpose. Think very carefully about your words and tone, and the implications of any words you use. If you are talking in ritual to a being, power, or deity, are you using words of worship when you are actually looking for a coworker? If so you will confuse the situation, yourself, and the being you are talking to. And that is also a very important point: when you write a ritual speech, who is it you are actually talking to, and why? Its all very nice being clever with your prose, using puns and clever poetic metres, etc., but that is not the point of speech in a ritual. The point of speech in

6. Ritual Magic

ritual is to communicate directly with a power, or to state intent. If the speech does not do one of those two things, then it is a waste of time and energy. (The exceptions to that rule are social ritual and ritual dramas.)

Write your ritual speech with care and thought, use no unnecessary words or declarations, and never ever say something in a contacted ritual that you do not mean or do not really intend to carry out. Contacted ritual means that there are inner powers there with you, and what you say will be taken as gospel. It is not a game, and if you have real contacts there then you will be held to your word—*to the letter.*

Ensure within the writing of the ritual that there are spans of silences so that the officers/workers can commune with the inner contacts in the directions to ensure that the ritual is fully contacted and is working at all levels. In reality, the more powerful a ritual becomes, the more silences it has. The most powerful rituals are conducted in total silence. Any communion is done silently with the inner contacts and the energy is channelled through action and thought rather than word.

When you have done the ritual, it is important during the decompression time that each of the members voice their experiences and also write them down. In a contacted ritual there is much that goes on behind the scenes, and each member will often see or experience a fragment of the whole. If everyone expresses their experiences, the fragments can be pulled together to show a bigger, more complete picture. It is also important to write down those experiences so that when the ritual begins to actually do its job, any mistakes can be gone over, and any flashes of inspiration can be checked against the notes. It is also very common in contacted rituals for people to forget what happened within a day or two. This dynamic becomes more pronounced the more inner contacts work within the ritual. Because of this, it can become crucial that at least one person documents what happened, and what people saw and felt; then later, what the results of the ritual actually were.

6.31 Designing a lone ritual

The only difference in the structure of the lone ritual is that you work with inner contacts and yourself. It is very possible to have inner contacts working in the directions for and with you; and once you have built up experience in connecting with inner contacts, then it becomes a natural progression to have them working in the room with you. The major difference in rituals with inner contacts as opposed to humans is that with a human-based ritual the humans interact with the inner contacts at the threshold (i.e. at the candle flame, which acts as a threshold signifier). In a lone ritual the inner contacts are actually brought into the room to work with you in your world.

Before I explain how that is done, it is important to understand whom you are actually working with. We have looked at inner contacts earlier, but when you are building up a series of rituals for a larger purpose, the frequency of the buildup can alert other types of inner contacts who will time in and work with your rituals. The more experienced you are at working, the more frequently this will happen. When the ritual is being put together—and when it has a major reason for being put together, as I said earlier—certain frequencies begin to flow through the inner worlds and calls for workers can go out naturally, or that call can be made consciously by the magician. That frequency is not only picked up by inner adepts, teachers, workers, and beings; it can also be picked up by other human magicians and adepts living in their own time and place. The result is that when the ritual commences, workers from inner worlds, outer worlds, and other times come together to complete a task.

It has happened to me many times where I have been called to work, and I am drawn in vision to ritual happening somewhere, and I appear out of a direction to work. I have also worked many rituals within a lodge or group and had living inner contacts come into the ritual who are adepts working in vision from a distance.

A digression: A good example of this is a magical consecration of adepts that was taking place in Baltimore. I had a sick child at home in the UK and could not fly out with my then magical partner to conduct the consecration. We usually worked as a team, with me in the north and him in the south, and inner contact priests in the east and west. When the ritual commenced, I sat down in my quiet

6. RITUAL MAGIC

room in the UK and the adepts began the ritual. I consciously went in vision (called 'astral travel' by some) and took my place in the north. I consecrated thirteen people: the thirteenth person seemed very bright, and to my shock immediately vanished from my vision as soon as they were consecrated. A fourteenth person tried to stand before me, but something was wrong: they did not have the inner markings of an initiate upon them. I challenged them and the person changed appearance and showed themselves as the land being they really were: they had tried to gatecrash! A couple of hours later, my partner called to say that all had gone well, everyone had been aware of me, and all twelve had been consecrated. I told him I had actually consecrated thirteen people, not twelve. It all became very confusing. He went back to the group who were taking a lunch break and told them. One person put their hand up and related a story of a local initiate who had died during the summer, a person who was deeply magical and who would have made a great adept. Later that night my partner called again, related the tale, and asked me to describe the thirteenth person, which I did. The descriptions matched: I had consecrated the recently dead initiate. She probably went on to become an inner worker, and the consecration she received connected her into the long line of adepts that she could draw upon. It has never happened to me since, but it was the most curious happening!

6.32 Constructing a lone ritual using inner contacts

The basic construction of the ritual is the same: there is very little difference until you come to the officer part. If you need input from another being, decide what direction you would need them to come from and what sort of power they would need to wield.

So if the ritual is to lay the foundation or the building of a temple space, then a temple ritualist or esoteric mason would be a good inner contact to work with. When you begin writing the ritual, keep that need in mind so that you can construct an outer call into the direction (east, for an esoteric mason) for the inner contact to help you. The inner work that is needed to draw in such a contact is as follows:

6.32. Constructing a lone ritual using inner contacts

Light the central candle in the working space and go into silence. Using your inner vision, walk from the central flame to the east, and light the inner candle using the flame that burns within you as a fire source. Once the inner candle is lit, call through that flame into the inner direction of east for a contact to work with you in the construction of a temple. Once that is done, open your eyes and physically light the candle in the east, and utter the same request outwardly. Leave the candle going for as long as you can, and if it is safe to do so, keep a candle lit in that direction while you are designing and writing the ritual. When you do put the candle out, see the inner candle as still being lit, functioning as a beacon for a worker.

When the ritual is actually performed, call out for that contact to come into the space and work with you. What will happen, if you are successful, is that during the ritual you will start to find that you know things and are prompted to say or do things: this is the inner contact nudging you and guiding you. You will feel the power levels of the working space go right up as the contact adds to the power of the space. Don't forget to thank them. Offer your hand in their work in return should they need it, and be aware of them as a contact when you next go to the direction they came out of. It is very difficult with inner contacts to tell if they are living somewhere in their own time or if they are truly dead inner contacts. Being able to tell the difference takes a while, but you will eventually be able to differentiate.

It is also possible, once you are well versed in ritual methods, to pass in vision through the directions and into someone's working space to assist them in ritual, should they request it. It is all done through visionary methods, and you will get to see how the inner patterns of ritual work: it is like a wonderful weaving of power with living beings as the frame and energy as the thread.

Chapter Seven

Developing Tarot skills

Tarot is an important tool in the skills bag of a budding initiate, and it is a versatile tool that has many applications. It is of course used for divination, but it can also be a great teacher in the steps of inner development and the patterns of the magical world. The one thing to remember, above all things in card divination, is that the success depends upon the relationship between you and the beings that use the cards as windows.

Some card decks are mere vocabularies, some decks are icons of deities and powers, and some decks are extensions of your own magical ability. The trick is knowing which deck is which. Every form of deck has its limitations; then you add your limitations as reader. There is the limitation on sight: most sighted people see through the keyhole: they see a segment of the truth or the future, not the whole picture. That is why prophecies can seem so terrible and Armageddon-like. If you look at say, the current situation in Iraq, and you look at it through a keyhole, then the small section of totality that you see *is* your whole picture: hence it looks like the end of the world. When you 'see' potential future events in the cards, you have to keep in mind that you are seeing only a small fragment of totality.

The best way, I feel, to approach Tarot, is to just get on and start working with the deck. If you are new to Tarot it can be daunting, but playing with the cards, looking them up, and trying layouts and readings, are all things that will slowly teach you your own unique way path to divination.

This chapter is about learning how to just get on and do, to get you walking down a path where Tarot will reveal itself to you as you go. You never stop learning with card divination: every time you think you have cracked it, another layer appears, and off you go again. That is because you are learning about the universe. I have been using cards since I was twelve years old, so I have been doing it a wee while, and I am still learning.

7.1 A reading

The best way to learn about Tarot is to do readings: to practice the skill from the very beginning. It is a tool for extending your mind, and like any new tool, practice is the way to perfect your skill in using it. To get a good foundation in Tarot it is best to choose a simple, straightforward version of the Rider-Waite deck. This is the most commonly used deck and it will give you a good understanding of the basic structure of Tarot. With a basic version of the deck and a straightforward book on the meanings of the Minor and Major Arcana, you are ready to begin the long and fascinating path of Tarot. Don't fall into the trap of trying to make it a deep meaningful and mystical part of your training; if you do you will miss most of the truly magical aspects to this line of the work.

Divination is a natural part of humanity and the more you try to mystify it, the more you will become mystified and confused. The more you treat Tarot as an everyday part of your existence, the more comfortable you will become with it. The keys of the Mysteries are hidden among the images of the Rider-Waite deck, but not in a way that you can crack them like a code; the Mysteries do not work like that. Just let them surface naturally over the years. Their meanings will change as you change.

7.2 Shuffling

How you approach shuffling the cards can be just as important as any other aspect of working with Tarot. Everyone develops their own shuffling technique, but there are some points to consider in order to help the shuffling be successful.

One key factor is to ensure that you are fully focused on the question in hand as you shuffle. Do not be distracted by talking or allow your mind to wander: keep the question foremost in your mind as you work the cards. Also keep in mind as you shuffle what layout you will use: you need to focus on the question and the layout.

One good method for doing this is to work with your eyes closed. As you shuffle, think about the question, the layout you are going to use, and imagine you are searching for something through a mist. Use your inner vision and imagination to create the sensation of trying to pierce a veil.

As you develop your own technique, you will find that after the initial shuffle, your hand action begins to slow down so that the cards are placed more precisely in their order. Once everything is in the right position you will feel them 'lock' in place. The accuracy of a reading relies on the focus of intention you hold as you work the cards.

Once your deck is ready, then work from the top of the pile and place each card out. Once you have become accustomed to working with the cards, you may find that the answer you were looking for seeps into your mind even before you lay the cards out. It is as if you get a preview of what is coming. Not all readers have this experience, but for those with a strong natural ability, the flavour of the reading often emerges in the reader's mind before the cards are laid out.

Once you have laid out the cards, take a moment to look at them in their positions. Remember, the meaning of the card and the meaning of its position should be read together. Go through the cards one by one until you get to the end, then go back to the beginning. Often a card and position will not make any sense until you have looked at the whole reading; then the meaning starts to unfold. If there is still something you are not getting, sometimes it works to sit quietly and say to yourself, "okay, tell me about this." Write down the reading so that you can go back to it after a few hours, and look again. What I have always found is that when in doubt, the simplest interpretation is often the right one.

7.3 Layouts

The next most important thing after the deck is the layout. Little thought is given to layouts, yet they are the most important part of the act. The layout is part of the deck: it puts the cards in context, and without a proper layout the deck becomes inaccessible. Two things that set a reader up to fail are a badly-designed deck and a badly-designed layout. Some decks and layouts are created as works of art, or philosophical musings, or experiments in magical dogmas. None of those decks will work to the degree that a properly focused, functioning deck would. So choose with clear thought. The more generalized the layout, the more generalized the answers and insights will be. I work with a variety of layouts and choose which one to use according to what I actually need to know. I use specific layouts for questions regarding health, exorcism, and ritual, and more general layouts for other questions.

Let's look at a selection of general layouts that can be used for a wide variety of questions while also helping to imprint certain patterns of the Mysteries. Both of the following layouts have their roots in patterns of the Greater Mysteries.

7.4 The Tree of Life layout

The Tree of Life layout (fig. 7.1) is one that is used in a teaching capacity in many of the better occult schools and lodges in the West. Not only is it fairly straightforward as a layout for gaining information, it also slowly instils the inner pattern of the Kabbalistic map of the inner pattern of our world as humans, which is what the Tree of Life is. By using it in a regular divinatory way, the subconscious begins to absorb the little clues and snippets of information that always surface regarding the mystery of the Tree as you use it.

There are many deep and meaningful insights into the Tree of Life layout, but if you get yourself tangled in them too soon and in the wrong way, you will not be able to get straightforward, decent readings, so the following interpretations for the layout are simple and straightforward. Their deeper meanings will surface to you when you need them to.

So let's look at a reading to see how it works. Let's say that a person is trying to choose between two houses to buy. One looks better than the other, but the buyer gets a weird feeling from the better-looking house. The buyer is a magician who will be working magically in the home, so it is important to take that factor into

7.4. The Tree of Life layout

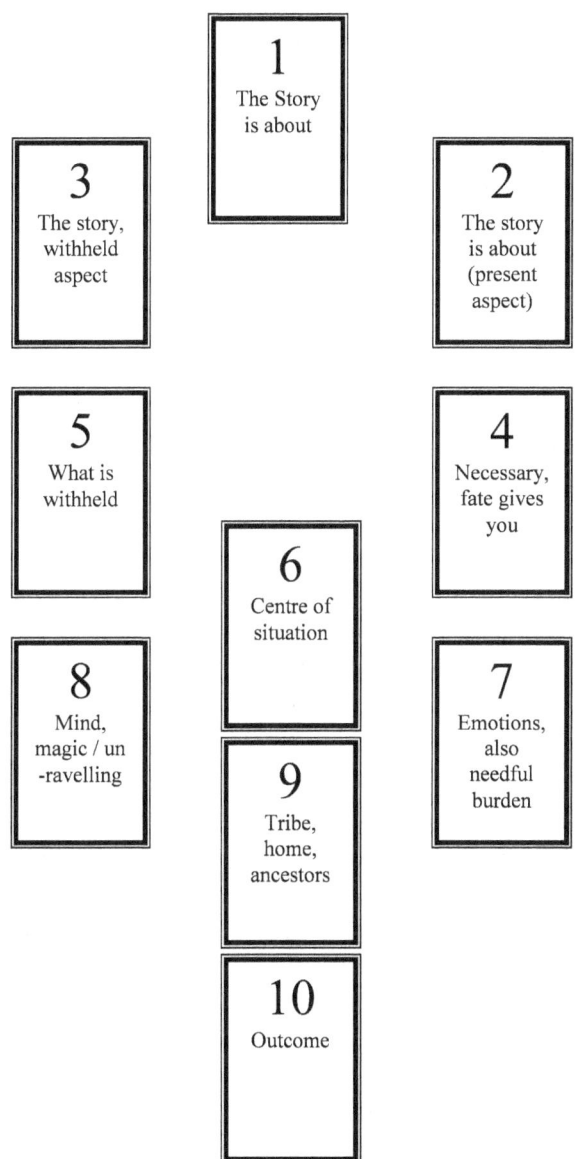

Figure 7.1: The Tree of Life layout

7. Developing Tarot skills

considerations. The question is: "show me what it would be like living in the better-looking house."

Overall the reading (fig. 7.2) states that the house would be a working place, not a resting place, and would be very hard work to live in, but would teach the person a lot. So let's break it down. The first three cards tell us that the story is about something that costs a lot of money and provides a sense of security (ten of coins), that has to do with stability (four of coins), but that also has an unknown quantity or has hidden things (Moon).

The central three cards tell us that it is a place that needs work and will be a place of service, not socializing (three of cups withheld). The service (Hanged Man) alongside the tower tells me that the property expects a lot of magical work and service for the land, building, and community.

The ten of wands tells me there is a lot of magical power there, and that one would need focus and discipline to enjoy living there (queen of swords in emotions), but that it is the perfect place for a magician to live (Magician in the position of the home/tribe). The Star as the outcome tells us it is the start of a whole new path of learning. So as a reading I would interpret it as saying that it would be a good and powerful working space, but that it would need a lot of tuning work first, and that it would not be a relaxing place to live in.

How the question is asked is very important. Asking "what would it be like living in the better-looking house?" gives you many answers in one. It showed what it would be like to do magic in that house, and it showed what sort of house it would be like as far as relaxation and regeneration is concerned. If the question had been, "is that the best house for me to buy?" then the answer could have been in relation to financial investment, the quality of the building, or one's family life, or one's general happiness, etc.: the options are endless and so do not give a straightforward answer.

If the reader is really stupid they would have asked, "which is the best house to buy?" Firstly, the deck cannot tell you which house is better, as there are no cards that can possibly identify either house in this situation. It also leaves open an extremely wide door in respect

7.4. The Tree of Life layout

Figure 7.2: Tree of Life example reading: "Show me what it would be like living in the better-looking house."

of whose opinion matters as to which is the best house: the cards? you? the postman? And best house in what respect?

So you can begin to see how the question is really important and has to be precise and to the point. Remember, you are asking your questions to a set of cards that has a limited vocabulary, not to a human.

7.5 The Landscape Layout

Another layout, which is also based upon magical patterns and gives general information, though somewhat more detailed information than the Tree of Life, is one I call the Landscape or Desert layout (fig. 7.3). It is based around the inner landscape of humanity, and looks at the inner powers that operate through our lives as well as life and fate dynamics that play out in any given situation.

This layout gives you more specific information regarding the location, timing, and influences upon a situation, and what dynamics are at play, both at the present and in the future. Its positions are as follows:

1: Foundation The body or land.

2: Union The second position, crossing the first, tells us what power or people dynamics we are currently dealing with.

3: Star Father What is coming in the long-term future, a pattern that is still being formed in the stars. If resolution is on its way, but will take some time, then that will show here; however if the problem is going to be prolonged, then that will also be indicated here.

4: Underworld What has already passed away down into the depths and will not be coming back any time soon.

5: Gate of the Past This is the threshold of what is now in the immediate past. In this position of the threshold, whatever is in this position has the potential to return at some point in the future, but for the moment is considered past.

7.5. The Landscape Layout

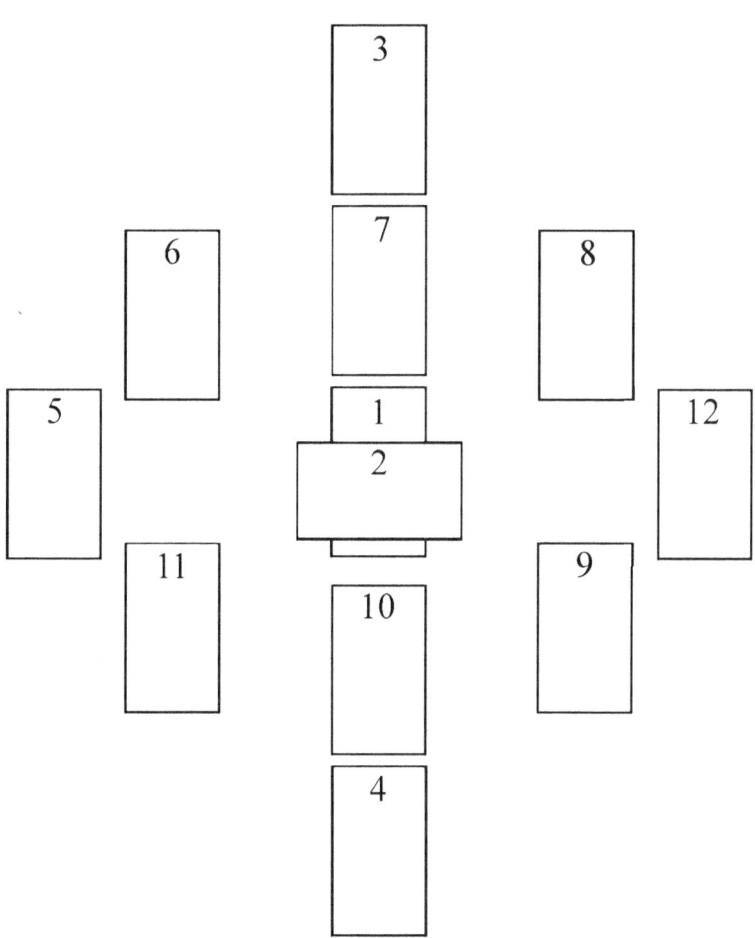

Figure 7.3: The Landscape or Desert layout

6: Wheel of Fate The current pattern of fate or action that is playing out. This could be a struggle, a cycle of magical work, a period of renewal, etc. This is the path you are currently on unless you do something to change your path's direction.

7: Grindstone The hardships and difficulties that must be overcome. On the current path that is indicated in the sixth position, there are bound to be hardships, difficulties, and barriers that must be overcome. These are shown in the seventh position and must be endured if you are to continue in the fate direction you are currently travelling.

8: The Inner Temple What is coming directly into your landscape from the inner worlds. All magical attacks, inner contacts, work programs, inner support, deities, etc. will show here.

9: Home and Hearth What influence in your inner landscape is potentially affecting your home and/or family surroundings, or *vice versa*. If there is a haunting, bad energy, or difficulty in the home environment, then it will show here.

10: Unraveller What is falling away or starting to decline. If you have defeated something or it is starting to leave your body or fate path, then it will show here. It is travelling towards the Gate of the Past and will finally vanish into the depths. If, however you do not meet the challenges that appear in the seventh position, then any difficulties that show in the tenth position will come right back to challenge you until you get the message.

11: Sleeper Dreams and/or sleep. What your deeper unconscious mind is dealing with, and what is happening to you in your sleep.

12: The Path Ahead The way ahead. The immediate outcome to your question. (For a longer-term outcome, look to position three.)

So let's have a look at this layout at work, using the same question as we asked in the previous reading. The results of the reading are illustrated in fig. 7.4.

7.5. The Landscape Layout

Figure 7.4: Inner Landscape or Desert example reading: "Show me what it would be like living in the better-looking house."

7. Developing Tarot skills

1: Ace of coins on Foundation. This tells us that the body of the subject matter is earth (bricks and mortar).

2: Devil on Union. Is a relationship with a powerful consciousness, an entity, or a major temptation.

3: Ten of wands on Star Father. What is being formed in the future of this place is power.

4: Fool on Underworld. What has fallen into the Underworld and therefore the past is the Fool: foolish emptiness.

5: Knight of cups on Gate of the Past. This card, and the previous one, combine together to suggest that the previous owner was a man who was too emotional and unstable to be able to operate the powers in that land/house properly. This gives you insight into how power lines up for the magician: because there is a possible future with the magician in that house, power is already starting to line up in the inner worlds ready for the decision.

6: Wheel of Fortune on Wheel of Fate. The current trend is that a partnership of house and magician would change old patterns in both the person and the property.

7: Nine of wands on Grindstone. What would have to be overcome is the level of power, nine of wands, and its potential danger. The lesson of this position is to tread wisely and learn a major lesson about handling power. This position, which I call the Mountain or Grindstone, never gives you more than you can cope with, but it will push you to your outer limits.

8: High Priestess on the Inner Temple. This property has active inner lines and there is a contact which is female.

9: Five of swords on Home and Hearth. The home will not be a peaceful place to rest in. The five of swords indicates arguments and irritations, not major disruptions, but enough to know that you will not get much peaceful downtime in that house.

10: **Nine of swords on Unraveller.** Difficulties with negative or difficult power are slowly fading into the past. This means that working within such a difficult house will most likely strengthen you to the point whereby such negative power will not affect you too greatly in the future. I have personally found that the nine of swords and nine of wands often appear in a reading together, and when they do, they can signify that the negative powers flowing to you are not a natural flow of power: they are being sent by human force, be it magic, ill wishing, or deception. In this reading, I would say that the person asking the question is on the receiving end of some unhealthy or negative magic, and this house will help the person learn how to handle power and how to get strong enough to deal with such nasty actions.

11: **Eight of swords on Sleeper.** The person who sleeps in this house will have almost continuous nightmares. It will be a dynamic of the magical activity in the house. In such circumstances the worst thing anyone could do would be to take sleeping pills. When such activity shows in the dreams, it is saying that the person sleeping will actually be working hard fighting unhealthy energies, which will be part of the service work for that property. If the person takes sleeping pills then it will render them helpless in the face of such power, and will damage them. That will probably be why the previous tenant was emotionally unstable. In such situations, although there will be bad nights, the tenant will probably have enough sleep to keep functioning. I once lived like that for five years: I used to go to a motel every so often for a couple of days, just to sleep peacefully.

12: **Hanged Man on the Path Ahead**. The Hanged Man is service and self-sacrifice. It is showing that basically going to live in that house will be training for powerful service that is in the future.

To sum the reading up, I would tell the person that if they chose that house, it would be bloody hard work. They would learn a lot, get no peace, but would come out the other end fighting fit and able to take on anything the world could throw at them.

Readings are a mixture of the cards, the positions, and common sense. They will not do all the work for you: as a reader you have to also allow your own sight to kick in and let *it* fill the gaps, rather than platitudes and wishful thinking.

7.6 Tarot Taboos

There are a variety of Tarot taboos, some of which are useful and some of which are just plain silly. Often the taboos are stated in Tarot books without any explanation of how they developed. This makes it difficult to differentiate between what should be noted and what should be ignored: in the end, personal experience and common sense can be the only way forward without sensible explanation. Let's have a look at the most common taboos.

A reader cannot read for themselves

This is just not true. It is difficult to step back and be impartial when reading for yourself. Most of the time when readers read Tarot for themselves, they are looking at common, low-level questions such as whether they will get a lover, money, or a job. Such questions are not only a waste of time for an initiate but also take the attention away from necessary work and down the blind alley of trying to control one's universe. If a reader does not like, or does not believe, what the cards foretell, then they will read them again and again until the results become more palatable. That is an easy road to get stuck down, but if you use your common sense, you can read pretty well for yourself: the key is to be detached. And that is a larger aspect of magical training in general: to be able to put wants and needs to one side, and to be able to look at a situation from an unemotional standpoint. We have to be able to look outside of ourselves and beyond ourselves: that way we can use the information we are given in a calm, dispassionate way that will ensure its balanced and productive use.

7.6. Tarot Taboos

The cards need to be wrapped in a certain coloured silk

To which my reply is "oh, whatever." No, they do not. For years I kept my cards wrapped in a plastic bag and had them shoved at the bottom of my bottomless purse that also had a spanner, a screwdriver, wooden nickels, pepper spray, raisins, and various other bits and bats that were totally unconnected but often came in useful. It is helpful but not essential to have a piece of cloth that you can lay the cards on when you do a reading. On an outer level this protects the cards from whatever is on the table surface (or floor: I often read on the floor). It also stops the energetic gloop that can accompany some readings from seeping onto the working surface.

You cannot read after dark

Really? Cough...

The cards must only be shuffled by the person asking the question

Who shuffles the cards is completely up to the style and wishes of the reader. Personally I shuffle the cards for whoever wants a reading. I don't like other people handling the cards and leaving their residue upon them: it interferes with my ability to have a clear working communion with the cards. But that's just me. You have to work out for yourself which one works best for you. When I first started reading as a young girl, I noticed that when people shuffled the cards, the cards would get a buildup of sticky inner goo that made me feel uncomfortable. So by about the age of eighteen, I stopped letting people touch my cards at all. But then I know very successful readers who never shuffle the cards themselves.

The person you are reading about, or for, needs to be there with you

Wrong. You are the only thing that puts limits on what and who you can read for. The key to reading about anyone and anything is to focus your mind very clearly on what you want to know or who you are reading about, then do your reading. Some readers can only

7. Developing Tarot skills

read for someone if they are there in front of them, as they need to be able to 'read' their energies, etc. But that is a personal and individual thing, not a regular restriction. There are no limits on for whom, about what, or when you can read: the only limit is the imagination of the reader.

However, do bear in mind any issues of privacy and ethics, and also of energetic entanglements in other people's stories. I do readings for friends when it is necessary, and they are rarely in the room with me. Often they are in a different country entirely. It works no differently from having them there with me.

7.7 Keeping yourself and the deck clean

One thing that does happen in readings, no matter whom or what the readings are about, is that the cards will accumulate a kind of inner dirt or residue. This manifests itself as the cards feeling grimy and sticky. It is important to gain sensitivity towards inner residue and dirt, as it could prevent a whole lot of magical health problems in the future. The best way to get the feeling of inner dirt is to wash your hands with soap and a handful of salt, then go to a thrift store or junk store and handle old things like rings, statues, etc. Your hands will feel sticky or grimy. Another way to do it is to salt clean your hands, then handle your own Tarot deck if you have used it a lot. Notice how it feels and how it makes your hands feel. Clean the deck and then feel them again: they will feel completely different. Smudging can help maintain a deck after each reading, but it does not clean a deck as thoroughly as salt. Using smoke to maintain the deck after each reading will ensure that they do not need salting quite as much. A lot of people use sage because it is what Native Americans use, but that is not a part of my culture nor my practice. It is always better to try and use something that is relevant to your own magical path. I use Frankincense mixed with a tree resin that comes from an evergreen tree in the Romanian mountains (exotic, huh?).

7.8 A method for cleaning a Tarot deck

Keeping a deck clean is simple but necessary and should be done regularly if you use your deck a lot. You will need a plastic Tupperware-type long container and a large bag of salt. To clean the deck, just put all the cards in the container and pour the salt over them until they are covered. Then move them around so that the salt gets in between the cards, and when you are sure that they are well covered, put the container with the cards in a safe place overnight. The following morning, take them out of the salt and give them a good shake to get the salt residue off. Spread them out on a cloth to air for an hour. After that, they should be ready for use again.

To smudge your cards, have some frankincense or a similar resin burning on charcoal and hold the cards over them, moving the cards around to ensure that all of the cards are touched by the smoke. Then 'wash' your hands in the smoke. If you use a cloth to wrap the cards in, then ensure that you wash the cloth regularly and that some salt is in the washing water. I also dab frankincense essential oil on the cloth that I wrap my deck in, and that keeps them nicely clean. There is no ceremony to cleaning cards: it is just regular maintenance. Some books will tell you that there are many complex ritual ways to clear cards with invocations, etc. Just remember that drama sells books more than reality and common sense.

7.9 Cleaning yourself

The first rule for keeping yourself clean after a reading is to wash your hands with salt and soap as soon as you have finished. Do not do, or touch, anything else until you have cleaned your hands. If the reading session was particularly hard or the subject matter was very unhealthy, then also rub some salt over your 'third eye' area, then wash your face. If you were doing a series of readings on powerful magical subject like demonic issues, or difficult readings like around a suicide, then not only must you clean your hands and forehead, but you must also clean your whole body. You will need to take a consecrated salt bath to clear off any residue and any connections to

7. Developing Tarot skills

beings that may have latched onto you. The instructions for doing a salt bath are listed in Appendix A.

7.10 Tasks for getting good at Tarot

Developing skills in Tarot is like developing skills in any other form of art: it's all about practice. The first step to developing a good practice routine is to keep a log of readings. Every time you do a reading, copy down the layout and cards that came out, then write down your interpretation. Date it, and don't forget to also write down the question asked. Do this as a major discipline for at least five years, and keep the log books tucked away safely so that you do not lose them. Whatever it was that you read for, when the actual event happened, write down the actual physical outcome underneath the reading so that you can look to see how accurate or not you were. If you were off-base, then look at the reading again, look at the positions of the cards, and look at what actually happened. The cards with show you how they were interpreting the event, then you will be able to see where you went wrong in your interpretation. One great lesson you will learn from this, above all other lessons, is that the cards are always right: it is your skill as an interpreter that may be at loss. You will learn far more from your mistakes than you will from studying any book, and keeping a reading diary is a major way of ensuring that learning.

Once you have your diary in place then you need to do readings that you can later look back on. Doing many readings on a wide variety of subjects that you can follow up on is a great way to learn. So for example, if there is an election coming up, do readings on each candidate, look at their next twelve months, at their health, their family life, and ask if they will be elected or not. Record all of the readings in your diary, then a year later look back at the answers the cards gave and how you interpreted them. Do year readings for celebrities, for public figures, etc. so that you can track outcomes through the media. What you may find is that although you ask to see the next twelve months, you may be shown the next major happening in their life, which may be further away than twelve months. Just bear that in mind, and if it has not happened after twelve months, keep watching.

I was working with a Tarot group in Cambridge Massachusetts in the nineties and we were looking at political figures of the time. We looked at Clinton, as it was coming up to election time, to see if he was going to get in. We also did a twelve month reading. The reading showed a hidden daughter figure who would cause a scandal. Obviously now we know it was not a hidden daughter, but the public knowledge of the affair took longer to come to light, so at the end of the twelve months we saw nothing that related to the reading. It came out a wee bit later. Sometimes it can come out *years* later; hence it is important to keep all your diaries so that you can look back. It is also a good idea to use readings to track your magical development and do readings on a yearly basis to monitor your magical training.

Read about anything to stretch your ability and the deck's ability to push beyond boundaries. Look into death, and ask questions that would not occur to you normally to read about. Think carefully about how you phrase your question so that you get a clear answer. Ask about the health of a body organ in someone, about the future history of a car...anything that you can verify in the future. The more readings you do on a wide variety of subjects, the better a reader you will become. There are no limits. Just understand that your ability to interpret the readings will probably be off for a few years, and that the skill of interpretation will possibly take years to perfect. So don't freak out or freak someone else out over a reading's conclusions, because there will be a big chance, particularly in the first couple of years, that you may be incorrect in your assumptions.

7.11 Magical dynamics of Tarot, both good and bad

When you read Tarot beyond just the silly everyday "am I going to get rich?" readings, there are a variety of energetic and power dynamics that come into play that you need, as a reader, to be aware of.

7.12 Cards as doorways

The first and most important point that you always have to keep at the back of your head is that when you do a reading for a being or

7. Developing Tarot skills

a realm, doing a reading and laying out the cards opens a porthole to that being or place. This only happens if you have been working and training in visionary magic: once you open the door to the inner worlds, it never really shuts. So when you 'read' about a place or being, the door that was propped slightly open becomes opened wide and any beings involved in that realm can come through if they are allowed to.

In magic, intent and focus of thought is everything (which should be a mantra and also written in large letters upon your forehead). That focus and intent can be used to create boundaries that will enclose a reading and make it safe. If you are reading about an issue that involves other worlds or beings, ensure that you light a candle and focus it on the Void or upon the magical pattern of the magical working space. Even if you are nowhere near your magical working/patterned room, lighting the candle with the focus of that room will superimpose it over the place where you are doing the reading. You tune the two places together so that you are working in a magical space with boundaries.

If you are communing with a being through the reading, or looking for answers relating to the being, then working within the boundaries will make it safer. You can ask the being direct questions using the Tarot, but when you have finished, ensure that you mix the deck up well to break up the reading, and that the deck is immediately put in salt to break any hold the being may have upon the deck. They can use decks as windows into our world, which is often not a good thing. Also ensure that you wash yourself properly with salt after such a reading.

7.13 Narrowing fate

The other dynamic that can become a problem for a magician using Tarot, is the narrowing of fate. When you read for a situation the first time, a variety of options of future outcomes may present themselves. The more a reading is focused on a specific event and read for over and over, the more the fate options are closed down and the final future outcome is set. This can be very dangerous, as it can take away the chance for inner powers to flow through a fate situation to assist in a magical path. The advice is: only repeat a reading or try a reading on the same question from a different angle if you did not understand the original outcome the first time around. Do not keep asking the same question: you run the possibility of damaging future options.

Another, more important dynamic with the narrowing of fate with readings is the dynamic of interrupted fate. If you happened to have pissed off a very skilled magician (which is something I did a lot in my younger days), they may launch a magical attack upon you that changes your fate. If you are under such an attack then it is important to keep an eye on your fate path by way of readings. If it is interfered with, then you can work out through readings how to restore the fate to what it looked like before the attack, or as close in as you can get to restoring it.

7.14 Responsibility

This is something that is very important in the field of divination in general: whenever you peer into the future (or past, Tarot works both ways) you carry a great deal of responsibility, not only due to the magical dynamics previously discussed, but also in the way of privacy and compassion. If you are doing a basic reading for someone, do it with him or her alone and with no one else in the room. What transpires in that room is private and should always remain so. Never read couples together: that was a mistake I made when I was young. Often people are dishonest to each other, and it will show in a reading. So diplomacy can be very important, as can tact and compassion.

Someone who was learning the skill of Tarot once offered me a reading, and he wanted to practice on me. He was what I would call an archetypal Asperger's-type with no social skills, but very good sight. He told me that in my late forties I would be terribly ill and could possibly die in my fifties, but that there was a chance I would survive. I was already aware of this situation that was coming, but the way he put it so bluntly, with such cold lack of emotion, caused me to give him a very harsh telling off. If he had come out with something like that to a person off the street he could have driven them to suicide, or at least deep depression.

7. Developing Tarot skills

I was cursed very seriously a few years back (by a disgruntled ex-husband) and it altered my life path considerably. My body was badly impacted by the strength of the attack (the energy of many students was used), and along with more usual life stresses and an inherited autoimmune disease, it has shorted the lifespan that I would have had. There is a possibility that I could die in my mid-fifties, but then I could get knocked over tomorrow. I have no problem with that prediction, and I trust the inner contacts that I work with to guide me through this period of my life—and as long as I complete the work I promised to do, then it really is not such an issue. If I am meant to survive, then I will. If not, it has been a wild life! The problem that I had with the reader is that he was not aware that I was okay with this situation, and it had not occurred to him that I might find it disturbing. That lack of awareness makes him a loose cannon in magical terms, and he should not be reading for other people (which I told him in no uncertain terms). All in all, Tarot, both as a deep magical tool, and as a 'fortune-telling' tool, has a lot of responsibility attached to it. The basic overall advice is to use your common sense and think very carefully about the impact that your words may have!

Chapter Eight

Summary

Walking the path of magic is something that will change you profoundly forever if you walk the very narrow and powerful path that it lays before you. There is knowledge to be found in the most curious places, and many teachers have fragments to pass on in one way or another. But to really condense advice down to a few paragraphs for those starting out in magic, or struggling alone in their training, well, that is a challenge! So here goes...

8.1 Prejudice

Don't assume that because someone dresses in fancy robes and has grand titles and loads of books out with New Age publishers that they are going to be useful or good teachers. Similarly, don't think that because someone looks normal and does not have a fancy-sounding name that they do not have something to teach you. Remember, the Goddess often appears as a bag lady on the street, and the grumpy old man in front of you on the train is really an angelic being! Magical learning can often come from the strangest of places.

8.2 Discernment

The greatest skill of all. Learn to read with discernment. Choose your books wisely, read their words with your bullshit meter on full blast, and if what is written seems to be using complex, confusing, and archaic language, then chances are the writer has not got a clue.

8.3 Glamour

One of the biggest magical traps of all. When you learn how to work with contacts and power for the first time, the realization of what is possible becomes overwhelming, and you can end up walking straight into the glamour trap. There are two sides to the glamour trap: being glamorized by someone, and glamorizing yourself. Being glamorized by someone is where you are easily taken in or impressed by their abilities to the point that you begin to hero-worship or guru-worship them. This is very unhealthy and unnecessary. It is one thing to be impressed by someone; it is another to worship them. Do not go down that route: it can lead to a very unhappy ending. Humans are humans. Respect is great; pedestals are not.

8.4 Self-responsibility

One other very important thing to remember that will really help you move forward on your magical path is self-responsibility. If you mess up, you are to blame, no one else. When things go badly in our lives, or we do stupid things, it is easy to turn around and blame everyone and everything around us for our failings and misfortunes. But by doing that, the process of learning through experience is short-circuited, and we end up going nowhere. It can sometimes take a lot of soul-searching to see how we often bring things down upon ourselves, or to see how we dodge responsibility where we can. But that is something that cannot be done for very long on a powerful magical path: at some point, you will be put in a situation where you must face yourself. So to make life easier, it is much better to be true to yourself: accept the harsh reality of your part in the wrongdoing or disaster that has befallen you, and move on.

I hope this book has been useful in some way or another, and that you discover some of the wondrous and truly amazing things that lie in wait for those who step out onto the path of Magical Knowledge. For those who are reading this and wish to truly follow a serious magical training, I and my fellow magicians have produced a free training course that takes you from apprentice to adept. It is a self-study course: you put in the hard work, you reap the benefits. It can be found at www.quareia.com.

8.4. Self-responsibility

Hence man is now a microcosm, or a little world, because he is an extract from all the stars and planets of the whole firmament, from the earth and the elements; and so he is their quintessence.

— Paracelsus [1]

---

[1] waite1894

Part II

The Initiate

Introduction

Once you have been initiated into or have been working at any depth in a magical or spiritual line, there are certain things that will start to happen to you: the inner contacts will begin to include you in their job listings and things will be put in your path for you to sort out. If you decide to be totally self-serving, then this peculiarity will fade off and they will eventually leave you alone. Just bear in mind if you do that, they will also leave you alone when you don't want them to.

But if you rise to the challenge, then more things will be put in your path and the tasks that will be thrown your way might have no connection to the stream of magic/spirituality that you are initiated into or working on. You become a worker in their eyes and they will give you jobs: they don't care what robes you wear or who's books you read.

This book is about methods, approaches and techniques that can be used regardless of what tradition you are from, as it is a book that shows you the world from the back door: a view into the boiler room of the universe. This is where adepts work from, whether they are Western Mystery adepts, Mystical Christian adepts, or Pagan adepts. It doesn't really matter because once you get past the surface details, the skills and techniques are more or less the same, and the beings that you will encounter are most definitely the same.

Instead of taking you by the hand and spoon-feeding you details, visions and a step-by-step guide, which is a stage you should be past now, these chapters look at potential pitfalls and suggest good working methods, approaches and how to tackle common problems. There are practical parts where you are shown how to develop certain tools, but in general the idea is to move beyond the beginner shuffle and progress to more advanced working methods.

Introduction

Once you have got your head around using working methods without specific structures (i.e. traditions) then you start to look at the tradition that you are an initiate of in more depth. You start to see the inner pattern that holds that tradition together and the blueprint of the structure that was used to build it. Once you look at a tradition this way, you start to see its strengths and weaknesses, and it begins to expose the reasons why certain things within that tradition are the way that they are. It helps you to understand the best way to work within your tradition, and the most positive way to move forward with the work as a part of the new generation.

A tradition that grows as a result of the magical development of its initiates and adepts is a tradition that will survive the many ups and downs that all magical and spiritual groups go through. The more balanced a tradition, the less infighting, power games and glamour it expresses and that balance comes from the maturing of the skills of the adepts over time and sometimes generations. It also encourages offshoot development which keeps the original group healthy by pruning and by satellite development instead of mummifying and degenerating the line of magic as a result of no innovation.

> What is a magician?
> 'One who does magic' is the Magician's reply.
>
> What is a magician?
> 'One who stands at the centre of everything' is the Developing One's reply.
>
> What is a magician?
> 'One who reflects the golden rays' is the Foremost One's reply.
>
> What is a magician?
> 'One who is I,' replies the Divine.

Chapter Nine

Accessing the Inner Worlds

Making contacts without the use of temples, rituals and patterns

Magical and spiritual traditions have developed working structures over hundreds of years to enable the practitioner to gain access to the inner realms in one form or another.

Without inner access, most magical work is pointless as it is not 'plugged in' or connected. The outer ritual must have an inner mirror, an inner connection through which power, contact and action can flow. Some traditions and working methods dispense completely with the outer ritual/action and focus purely on the inner structure/action. Some use a mixture depending on the desired outcome. There are traditions that work with only outer ritual and evocation methods, using complex patterns, rituals, incantations and sigils.

The less inner work that is done in a temple/lodge, the less power manifests and therefore the more fragmented the practitioners and work become. This usually manifests in ego squabbles, tantrums, power games, sexual manipulations etc., which are all symptoms that something is badly wrong with the inner power structure.

Over the years various methods of accessing the Inner Worlds (also known as astral travel) have developed and have matured according to the consciousness of the people involved and the consciousness of the culture of that time. As our minds have become more pliable, so our inner abilities have become more flexible and able to 'imagine.' TV, computers, phones, and internet have all changed how we perceive communication and how we use our imagination. This in turn has changed how we use our inner abilities and how our imaginations work in a visionary sense. Magical working methods have to catch up with this change and flex accordingly.

9. ACCESSING THE INNER WORLDS

There is also a movement that has been developing in the magical community over the last hundred years or so to move away from ritual structures, deities, temples, etc. and move back towards nature, the land, the Faery Realm and the ancestors: returning to the garden. Unfortunately a lot of those movements have fallen back upon the need for structure and have mirrored the ritualist groups in one way or another using directions/attributes/priests/magical sigils/patterns etc. We have been civilized for so long it is as if we have forgot how nature actually works, and how we can attempt to work naturally within the inner structure of nature.

So, if you want to access the Inner Worlds but do not wish to continue using the age-old patterns, then what do you do? You cannot just sort of float around in the Inner Worlds hoping to bump into someone: that is just silly and dangerous.

In Western culture, using drugs to catapult yourself into the Inner Worlds is also not that bright, unless you know exactly what you are doing and where you are going. Really the only safe way to work in the Inner Worlds using drugs is if you are working within a cultural/religious structure that is designed for such use i.e. shamanic/native cultures.

Hallucinogenic drugs strip a layer of protective skin from the consciousness and allow you to see and access places that you would normally be blocked from seeing (for your own good usually). When you go magically into vision, you develop inner 'muscles' (for want of a better description) that uphold and protect you as you work. If you bypass this natural but lengthy process of strengthening by using drugs, you are often thrown straight to the threshold of your existence. This means you come face-to-face with the angelic being that straddles life and death, which often presents as a large many-headed snake being with many eyes (sound familiar to all you acid/ayahuasca /DMT heads?).

An inner adventure without complex rituals, sigil patterns, drugs or annoying drum-banging sessions: what do you do? You go back to the source of humanity itself.

For those who have done magical/spiritual inner work, you will have your own version of the Void. This is a deeply profound place from which all flows and to which all returns. And if this is a place from which all comes, then everywhere in the Inner Worlds is connected to this place: therefore everywhere can be accessed from this place. All elements also flow from this place, and the Void is within all elements: hence the use of an element (fire, water, earth, air) as an access point to the inner worlds.

To work in this simple form, the practitioner must have good mental focus: there is no pattern/temple or easy visual aid to fall back on. As you start the vision to access the Inner Worlds, you must be clearly intent on where you are going. That intent is the key to everything: the mind is the car that takes you there and it has a route finder if you know how to use it.

The key to this method is the ability to go into the Void and be there in total stillness and focus. That ability frees up the mind and strengthens the inner focus that enables the imagination to open the door to anywhere. Going into the Void creates stillness and allows the mind to disconnect from the outer world. From that point of stillness, the intent of place can be focused without interference. As soon as the mind connects to that place, the practitioner steps out of the Void and begins to walk towards their intended destination.

Even if you are trying to gain inner access to an outer place that you know well, it is good working practice to still go through the Void. This creates an inner discipline and also creates the inner stretching that is necessary for such inner work. This practice also replaces the need for lengthy patterned visions or preparations.

For example, say I wish to access an ancestral sacred site near my house from an inner point of view. I can choose to access it as it is now, i.e. the inner expression of the site complete with the inner contacts there, be they faery/land/elemental beings, or I can access it back in time when it was used by my ancestors. What matters is the clear intent when stepping into the Void. At first, spend time in there stretching, dropping the daily life and returning to an eternal stillness. That frees the spirit and allows it to flow naturally between the worlds.

Another good stretching method is also taking your time getting there once you step out of the Void. Don't step out of the Void straight into the middle of where you want to be. Step out onto a road or walkway and take a little time walking there. This inner

9. Accessing the Inner Worlds

dynamic in important for the success of the vision/contact, but also has a protective effect on the body: it doesn't get so impacted if you take your time.

When you have finished with the contact you don't have to spend as long going back as you did getting there. What is important is that you make sure that you are clean and balanced before stepping back into the void to get home. If you have worked at healing someone, clearing someone, bridging death, or connecting with beings in the Abyss, then the chances are you are pretty gunked up and need a clean up. Use something that is within the realms of that vision: a stream, river, hot springs, etc. and take a bath/wash.

Once you step back into the Void, let the vision fall away from you and feel your earthly self reemerge before you step out of the Void back to where you first started.

9.1 Accessing beings: making a contact

Making an inner contact from scratch, without the interface of a temple/ritual/structure or pattern, can be quite daunting to someone who does not have a natural ability to connect with inner contacts. Usually inner interaction with a power site will also connect the practitioner to a contact. However, there is an interesting way of working that reaches out for an unknown contact in a place: it is almost like 'feeling' for a connection. The method relies once again on a sense of stillness and connectedness: this developing awareness helps to filter out parasites and other undesirables, enabling the inner senses to be selective and discerning.

You can either go into the Void with the specific intent of connecting with a particular being/person at a set place/time, or you can go into the Void with the intent of connecting with a particular type of being. If you do not know the contact but wish to reach out for one then you have to use the method of 'homing in on a beacon' in the Void. This entails going into the Void/stillness with some intent, e.g. to meet an ancestor, then reaching out in the Void for a time in that ancestor's life when they cried out to the universe for help, or when they mediated a great deal of power. The cry for help creates a beacon that lights through the worlds and attracts the attention of

9.1. Accessing beings: making a contact

beings that flow in and out of the Void in service. You can pick up on that beacon and appear before that ancestor, but you must be prepared to help them.

If you are looking for an inner teacher who is connected to magic/ritual/spirituality then you must use those patterns, which is a totally different story. But if you are wishing to reach back before such patterning, then you can use the beacon method.

All in all, it is always about intent, not allowing self-limitation, and developing total focus. With these skills you can more or less go anywhere and connect with anyone. This is the reason why mystical sects and powerful magical groups insisted upon physical discipline, self-sacrifice, aestheticism and meditation: these skills develop the ability to focus with intent, to not be fragmented by desires (which is a great protection from parasites) and to not be easily frightened.

We do not have to join a monastery for twenty years hard labour, but we can use our everyday life with intent to develop and hone such skills for inner use: it just takes more self-discipline and awareness of everything that is around us. This in turn heightens our abilities to connect with inner contacts. The more you stretch out your everyday awareness of who is around you, the more you become aware of beings in the Inner Worlds. We spend so much of our time cut off from each other and closing our personal space that we slowly end up closing off our inner ability to commune with consciousness: thus when we reach out to inner contacts, it is a terrible struggle.

Learning how to be open, to have thinner barriers around us without being eaten alive by every draining person and parasite, teaches us to be able to flow through the worlds and be receptive to the slightest whisper from inner contacts while retaining our energetic health and integrity.

A different method of passing into the inner realms and making contacts is to pass through the Void with the intent of going to an Inner Temple, the Abyss, the Desert of the Tree of Life, or the great Inner Library. All of these places are human constructs of consciousness from millennia ago and have been used by magical workers of many different traditions for hundreds if not thousand of years. Because they are well-trodden paths, as soon as you focus that intent within the Void and step out, you will find yourself before that inner structure.

Gaining access is a different matter and depends largely upon your intent. If you are allowed into these places, you will make contact with the beings and adepts that work there. Again, the whole story is about discipline of the mind, focus and intent. Discernment is also a necessary quality to have when working in vision. You wouldn't trust a stranger in the street, but people seem to think that because a being manifests itself in the Inner Worlds, it must be powerful, wise and willing to communicate with you. That is a fantasy and it would be far better and much more productive to simply use your common sense. Parasites abound in the Inner Worlds just as they do in the outer world.

9.2 Human inner contacts

There are a variety of different human inner contacts, but the most common ones are people who became true adepts in their own lifetime and upon their death chose to stay in the Inner Worlds as teachers rather than come back into the cycle of life and death once more.

Being a true adept means that a person has let go of their mortal existence and has allowed true spiritual maturity to flow through them: they are spiritually as well as magically adept. It does not mean that they are all knowing/all powerful, but they carry less shit than the rest of us. The further and longer they spend in this inner state, the less connection they have to everyday earthly existence. Most inner adepts quickly let go of their life pattern and do not hold the personality with all its inherent failings any longer. However, this is not always the case.

There are some magical adepts who have learned to navigate death properly, and have chosen to stay in the Inner Worlds as a contact or teacher. They are often still heavily connected to their magical group/lodge/order and can often try hard to continue to wield power in the outer world through their priests and priestesses. They retain their personality, with all its problems and issues, but it slowly begins to distort.

9.2. Human inner contacts

As they move further into death this can become a problem, as they lose full understanding of the earthly life without losing the wish to have power in that realm. If the person was unbalanced in their earthly life, then that imbalance can sometimes get a little worse as the person becomes more desperate to cling to power.

In between those two extremes are a wide variety of people working as inner contacts and teachers, some with good intent, some with bad, and some unconditionally. With this in mind, if you make or pursue contact with an inner teacher, use your common sense and discernment. Choose an inner teacher in the same way you would choose an outer teacher, although often inner teachers, as with good outer teachers, find you when the time is right.

They stay with you only as long as they can teach you something, and when you have learned what they had to give you, they tend to boot you out. This is good and healthy. Any teacher, inner or outer, who holds onto you or allows you to cling to them, is not the sort of teacher that you need.

Some lodges work with specific inner adepts who were once outer adepts in the order. This is a classic mistake as the adept is approached in vision as the personality they were before they died. To work in this way limits both the adept and the group as the adept is constantly trapped in the dressing and knowledge that they had in life. The adept needs time after death to drop the outer pattern of their life, which then allows the deeper part of their consciousness, which has many lifetimes of knowledge, to surface and get to work. Once they return to the lodge, they are often not recognized for who they used to be, but who they are now.

Finding these inner contacts often happens by accident after you have screamed at the universe begging for help. The universe usually let you hang a while, just to cook, before you are connected with help. The more you do inner work in the flavour of service, the more help seems to reach out to connect with you, but you do have to ask. And then there are the junction points in life: times when people and power seem to all come together at the right place and you connect deeply with them.

There are also inner human contacts that are alive in their own space, working in service. Just because you make a connection with

9. Accessing the Inner Worlds

someone in the inner realms does not mean they are dead: it might mean they are in the inner realms too, and your paths have crossed.

These people are in their own place, doing their own tradition, and offering help/contact to those who need it. There are also the ones who reach out from curiosity, and the usual rules apply: be wise about those with whom you choose to connect. But useful stuff can flow back and forth between cultures and traditions.

There are also human contacts who are in their own place and their own time, reaching through the Void, out of time, for contacts, or offering help as an inner contact. At first when you make an inner contact it can be difficult to discern who is what from where and when. But as the contact deepens and you get to know each other, it then slowly becomes clear who is what.

The more you work and the more experience you gain, the more you will be put into the path of others that you can help. When someone cries out for spiritual help, that cry echoes throughout the Void, and as you pass through the Void during your meditations, you hear them or are drawn to them. If that happens, then follow the call and step out of the Void in the direction of the call.

Be aware that when you do that, the person or group that sent out the call may not be aware that you are also human in your own time and place. They might expect you to be all knowing/all powerful and ask impossible things of you. Don't go into lengthy explanations that you are actually from Michigan and work in an office: that would freak them out. Just quietly do what you can and ignore the rest before gracefully pulling away from the contact. Always disconnect from such contacts by going back into the Void to rebalance yourself.

Chapter Ten

Practical methods for working with angelic beings

In magical work, you will come to a point where the need to work with angelic beings cannot be avoided as they are the threshold keepers, the bridges, as it were, to certain forms of power. There are many different approaches to working with angelic beings and most of these tend to be a part of a religious/magical system.

The most common approaches to angelic beings in the western world are Kabbalistic, Christian and Islamic. The pagan systems tend to reflect these three monotheistic systems usually with a bit of Greek or Egyptian mythology thrown in for good measure. In ritual magic the Kabbalistic and Greco-Roman are the most commonly used approaches, using the names, attributes etc as a precursor to invocation.

Some magical systems simply invoke these beings, and when they are successful the beings emerge into this realm and look at the magician. The magician looks back and the angelic being waits for the working request. Nothing happens except that the magician, in terror and awe of the immensity and power of this being, freaks out and begins frantically waving their arms about in a futile attempt to create a banishing sigil. Usually though, if a person doesn't know what they are doing, nothing tends to happen other than a puffed-up ego and some rather impressive recitation.

Certain magical systems have tight structures for working with angelic beings which filter the power, and shape it to the needs and wants of that group. This is probably a safe if ineffective way to work with angelic beings and while not an awful lot can be done, not a lot of damage can be done either.

10. PRACTICAL METHODS FOR WORKING WITH ANGELIC BEINGS

The exception to that rule is pure Kabbalah: the system is tight and heavily filtered, but can, when used properly, bring immense amounts of angelic power into our world. Luckily such a system takes a lot of time to learn and practice, which filters out most idiots. There are however, the occasional 'high-level' Kabbalists who still use these beings to carry out their own personal agendas.

So can you work with these beings without all the names, rituals, patterns, etc.? Well, the answer is yes. It's not easy, but it does allow the worker to interact with an angelic being without the human-made filters or bindings: you have to rely totally on the angelic being to create its own filter so that its power will not destroy you.

Before we go any further, let's go over some basic facts: Angels are not fluffy light beings: They are immensely powerful, large and strange-looking beings often presenting with many heads, many eyes, loads of wings, sometimes in a serpent shape, sometimes half-beast, and sometimes as cubes or spinning Wheels of fire. Their voices are powerful enough to destroy buildings or kill people.

Angels are hive beings: they are often made up of many fragments which are all the same being. All of the parts together make an archangel. When we humans work with angelic beings, often what we are working with is a fragment or tiny part of that being. That is all our feeble bodies can handle without self-destructing.

Angelic beings have no emotion: they do not discern 'good' or 'bad,' they simply do their job. If their job is to destroy, and you point them at a city, they will destroy it, if you ask in the right way. (That's the knack, knowing how to ask: it's like trying to get spending money out of a parent...)

They do not have a wide range of perception: they basically see only what they are programmed to see. What this means is that they have a needlepoint type of consciousness that tends to do one thing or one stream of actions, and do it extremely well. They do not understand or perceive much out of their field.

There are many orders and types of angelic beings. Some work closely with humanity, some work occasionally with humanity, some stay well away, and some are not even aware of our existence. An angelic being is the threshold for the consciousness of a planet, it is the threshold for the consciousness of a grain of sand, a puff of air, a tornado, an animal, a tree, a rock...hopefully you get my point.

There are certain angels, usually named angels, who have been magically bound into service over the centuries or even millennia. Regardless of what their bound action is, they are dangerous as they are operating from a standpoint of human manipulation and not their true purpose.

The binding of angels (it happens with demons too) stretches right back to Mesopotamian and Egyptian magic, and it is also used in Tibetan Bon magic: it is powerful, dangerous and corrupt. A lot of the named angels that appear in Kabbalistic magic have been bound into human service as temple guardians, providers of power and as assassins. To sidestep this problem, it is better to work with angelic consciousness without using a name/presentation: go deeper to the source of angelic consciousness without human form and you will begin to touch upon clear, true angelic power.

As an adept gains more magical knowledge, they will come across bound angels more and more. This is an attempt to put the adept in the path of work, and they will be expected to recognize the bindings and take them off. It's a hell of a job, but well worth it if you or a group succeeds (although the physical fallout afterwards really sucks and can last weeks). Then you get to see and interact with true angelic power.

Without an angelic threshold, nothing can pass from formlessness to form, nothing can manifest in our physical world. We pass through angelic consciousness when we are born and we pass through them again when we die. We perceive this as seeing them helping us and they work in every aspect of life and death. They are the thresholds of power in the temples, and the threshold of power within our bodies.

They do not do your gardening for you, nor do they do marriage counselling. If someone is advertising that they counsel marital problems with the help or channelling of angels the person is either a con artist or a naïve person who is being played with, probably by parasites. Do remember that many other beings cross-dress either to get what they want or just for the hell of it. Faery beings in particular have a twisted sense of humour, and will pluck an image from your head and dress like that. Parasites will dress like angels if that gets you

10. Practical Methods for Working with Angelic Beings

to open up your energies for 'healing': there is always some hapless New Age victim who has more money than sense.

10.1 So how and why do we work with them?

Working with angelic beings can be useful in many instances: the most obvious is within death or birth. They can also be worked with when tackling demonic powers, heavier intelligent parasites, when bringing through deities, lifting death curses, building or dismantling sacred buildings, communing with Divinity, searching for the balance of the scales, and for the passing on of consecrated lines. Basically if the work is heavy dude stuff (that is, of course, a technical description!) you pull in the angelic beings to help you.

There are magicians who use/invoke bound angelic beings to gain personal power. This creates an inherent weakness in the magician, both emotionally and magically. If you draw something from outside yourself to make you more powerful then you have failed: you are drawing on a power that is not yours, so you are in fact, not more powerful, just more dependant. That creates a major weak spot in the person and the magic.

The best and most profound way to work with angelic beings is to keep it simple and powerful. First off, you need to be focused because there is no ritual to tune you and hold you. You also need to be clear about whom you are trying to reach and why: make sure you get the right angelic being for the job. For example it will do you no good whatsoever to work with the angelic being of water to lift a curse placed by a fire priest. You need to use appropriate angels to do the job, which means you need to know your angels, and you need to know the structure of what it is you are working on.

So you need to know your elements (each element and direction has an angelic being), know your thresholds, and be simple and clear about your intention. Most of the angelic beings that are taught about in Kabbalah and Christian mythology will not be of much use to you in that their functions are not really the sort of skills that can be used by us: they are often bound into skill areas that are dangerous and nasty. But there are a few that can be useful, and these are the ones we work with: hence it is important to know your angels.

10.1. So how and why do we work with them?

The way to reach an angelic being is the way that it is possible to reach most things: going through the Void. Most people brush the Void off as some benign concept, not fully understanding what it is or what it does. They prefer instead to reach out for complex, glamorous and overstuffed visions.

The Void is within everything and is the basic root of everything: therefore it can be an access point to virtually anything. All that is necessary is absolute concentration and focus. You go into the Void with specific intent, shedding your surface life and allowing the eternal you to expand to the surface. Once you are in that totally still place and the focused intent is held, the contact emerges through the Void.

Before we go any further, another point I would like to make about the use of the Void is that because you shed your earthy existence when you go into the Void (which should be a daily maintenance exercise) you are far more able to work face-to-face with an angelic being: you are not bound by the limits of your earthly life if you drop it when you go in. This is why, when you first approach the Abyss, you are asked by the angelic being if you are willing to give up your life. You have to have that clarity: you must cling to nothing and be able to let go of everything.

Going into that timeless space puts you back closer to your natural state, which is a formless, powerful soul. You can take much higher levels of power impact in such a state without doing too much damage to yourself.

You reach out in the Void for that angelic contact and when it emerges before you, you step into it. There are two ways of working with these beings: one is to work within the being, which appears as the being working within you, with its arms through your arms, etc. The other way is to step through this being, and to emerge out the other side with a fragment of that being coming with you as an ally or coworker.

When you step into these angelic beings, it is a good idea to stop for a little while and stay in their energy. It allows you to acclimatize to their power and allows them to get a good grasp of you and what you are about. Show them in your mind what you wish to achieve, and the tools that you need to do the job will emerge out of the being

10. Practical Methods for Working with Angelic Beings

for you. Just make sure you leave those 'tools' behind when you have finished: they are a fragment of a fragment of the being itself, and you do not want those hanging around your consciousness afterwards.

Once you have established contact and you are ready for work, step with the being out of the Void and off to where you are going to work. When you have finished, you reverse your action and go back into the angel, remembering to release all the fragments and tools that came with you. Then you step out into the Void for rebalancing before stepping out from the Void back into your earthly life.

When you have worked with such powers, your body will of course have some impact. If you have worked through the Void and trusted their filters, you will not be seriously damaged, but you will have some physical impact that will need rest and maybe even treatment. Sometimes if you work inside archangelic beings it can knock the deeper part of you off-balance and the best way to be 'put back' is to be treated by a cranial osteopath.

If you have a homeopath who understands inner work, then that will be good also. The reason for the homeopath needing to understand inner work is that when you do such deep inner work it changes you at profound depths and changes how your body responds to things. Homeopathic remedy pictures become meaningless and the choice of remedy has to be made using different tools and a different way of thinking.

After a powerful working with these beings, rest is the best thing. And do not eat meat for a few days if you are a carnivore: the life that the animal led will impact you for a few days. Passing through an angel can heighten your inner senses for a while and everything can become loud or bright, and your 'sight' can become a great deal stronger. Sometimes the opposite happens and it feels like you have a bag on your head for a few days: everyone's body reacts differently, but it sure does react!

One thing to be careful of when you begin working with these beings: do not become carried away by the power that you have access to. Most silly egomaniacs tend to be blocked from working with these beings by nature of their inability to be disciplined. But any worker can get sucked in if they are not careful, particularly when you realize just what potential level of power you are accessing. I

10.1. So how and why do we work with them?

have seen some great priests destroyed or turned into parodies of themselves by grabbing power from, or abusing the power of these beings.

Just remember when you work with these beings it is always best to work in service for others or for the land: unravelling, unbinding, opening gates, etc. If you instigate a new action using these beings, then you are starting a new pattern of fate and because you have used these threshold beings, the pattern is powerful: the backlash could be immense.

Chapter Eleven

Working with deities: pitfalls and approaches

If you are working in the realm of magic, no matter what form you use, at some point you are going to work with a deity or deities. Different traditions have different approaches and all have their strengths and weaknesses. The one approach we will not go into is the psychological approach (that the deity is only a creation of man and we work with the idea of a god to explain things). The reason for not looking at this form of deity work is that it falls more in the realm of therapy that it does magic.

One method of approaching this type of work is the devotional form, where a priest or priestess aligns themselves with, or is initiated into, a steam of magic associated with one deity or a close family of deities. This is where the act of magic moves closer to a religious movement, so that spirituality and magic becomes a combined path.

The relationship between deity and priest/ess is often structured and intense: the priest/ess is required to maintain certain devotions, tasks, and emotional/sexual restrictions. The deity patterns will often dictate how the priest/ess conducts their daily lives, and whom they socialize with.

In today's pagan community, it also affects how the priest/ess dresses, acts, does magic, etc. It can become an all-consuming identity. The deeper octave of this is when the priest/ess opens themselves up for the deity to step into and co-habit their body. This is done for a few moments at a time, although some particularly strong and stupid ones do tend to carry around destroying deities for a few months or years. This can have a little bit of a toll on the human body, to say the least!

11. Working with deities: pitfalls and approaches

But that form of devotional service, to me, is more religious than magical (which is a system that magic grew out of). When you work magically with a deity or deities, another approach is more one of working colleagues who are better qualified than you, like working with elders, only stronger. Deities are by nature polarized consciousness and the nearer to humanity they are, the more polarized they become.

11.1 Forms of deity

There are many different forms of deity. Some are divine expressions of the land that flow through a semihuman form (taken from their environment and our consciousness). Then there are the polarized parts of Divinity that appear in more or less the same expression all over the world: they do not appear similar because they are all from one place or people, it is more likely that they are similar because that is what people see when they go into the inner world.

Some are the Divine expression of the people, and some are ancient ancestors/kings/queens/elders who have become deified over thousands of years.

If for example a major priest or adept opts out of the circuit of death to become an inner contact, then sometimes that contact becomes more than the original person: their human form becomes a conduit for a greater power which in turns becomes a deity expression either by virtue of its actions, or by the reflection of the people they serve.

So before you go to work, know who and what it is you are working with. The reasons for this are many: if you are working with a polarized form of Divinity, it/he/she will have a set repertoire of skills, powers and needs in return for help. These forms of deity are the most powerful and have to be worked with most carefully. They will often want devotion and allegiance: there you have to decide if you want to be a worker or devotee.

If you want to be a worker, then you have to justify your wants and needs to the agenda of the deity. They will not just do what you want, rather they will do what you need to accomplish your work provided the work fits with their ethics and actions. In return, they will often put things in your path that they want you to work on.

When you are working with a deity that is an expression of the land/people, it/he/she will have a narrow view of the world and they will only be able to operate within that view and that environment. If you want something that is within their field, then they will work with you if the time/place/action is right. They will often not work with you for things that do not serve/help/feed them. They are there to keep a balance of sorts in that land: if your actions fit that, then all is good, if not, you will be told to piss off.

The gods/esses that have developed out of ancestral consciousness or an ancient king/queenship are interesting to work with as they are closer to humanity and have a deeper understanding of what our tiny minds are about. The only problem with that is if you get one that is not a 'goodie.' Now, you cannot go by their historical myths: I have repeatedly found with these types of deities that they often got bad press by later generations, or that their identities were often false. Many times the fluffy bunny deities turn out to be just downright evil (in the nicest possible way of course).

You have to work with them to find out who they are and what they are really like. The relationship will often be one of: if you do this for me, then I will do this for you. Just be careful what you get sucked into and don't get glamorized, and ignore the promise: if you do this I will give you endless power...uhuh...

One interesting aside when working with this type of deity is hearing their version of history. They will often want to tell you about their time, what happened, who they were and what they did. It can make a lot of nonsensical myths suddenly make perfect sense, and the sense often resonates with what is happening magically today. Power works in octaves: what was happening to them is probably happening now in some way, and the lessons they learned can help us too.

11.2 Working with the deity

Overall, working with deities is powerful and interesting, but can be dangerous both physically and spiritually. You have to use your common sense and remember that you are a worker: by doing so,

11. WORKING WITH DEITIES: PITFALLS AND APPROACHES

you opt out of the often unhealthy role of devotee which can become a relationship that ultimately weakens you.

If you work with deities for your own personal power/gain, you will do pretty well up to a point, but the limits are put in place by you and the deity. If it is solely for your needs, then the power that will be raised by the deity will be only enough for one person at the end of the day. If you are working in a wider service, then you will be given the power you need to do your job and the harder/more dangerous the job, the more power flows into you.

By being a worker as opposed to a devotee, there are fewer limits on whom you can work with and when you work with them. You work with them when there is need and the rest of the time you get on with you magical life and they get on with theirs. There is none of this getting up at four a.m. to feed raw pigs' liver to the sacred cat after banging a gong six times while standing on your head: life is a little too short for that.

Just be aware that if you work with a variety of deities, that you do get some that don't like each other (their powers clash) and it can turn into a workplace filled with bratty hormonal temperamental gods who refuse to work with you if you work with 'that one': a little discernment goes a long way.

When you work with deities, there are many different ways that you can practically work with them to achieve things. You can work with them in vision, you can work with them through images or places, you can raise them to work in the room with you, or you can be a complete idiot and bring the deity into yourself to achieve something.

When I was young and stupid, as opposed to now where I am old and stupid, I had the bright idea of bringing Kali through. At first I had the intent to bring her through into a painting. I set about preparing, pulling the power in, setting it all up, and then I began the weave that brings the Goddess through. I painted her, but she wanted a sculpture of herself to move into. So I began the sculpture. By this time I had already been working for twelve hours, but I could not stop. I worked through the night and the Goddess flowed into me as I worked. I held her in my body for about twenty-four hours while I worked and then finally bridged her into the sculpture and painting.

11.2. Working with the deity

The day after the working I got sick. Then I got sicker. Then it turned into scarlet fever and I became dangerously ill. I went bright red (the colour of Kali) before then developing rheumatic fever. It took six weeks to recover and stop peeling, but the illness left permanent damage.

I got the message: yes you can bring a deity through, yes it hurts and does damage when done properly but without a structure for it to flow through.

As usual I learned the way I have always learned: when they say don't press the red button, I invariably do. It was an important lesson though, and it taught me a lot about Kali. By having her flow through me, I felt her at her depth and felt all the parts of her that are not written about or expressed in images. I learned to work with her properly from that experience and I think it was invaluable. I would go through it again, but this time I would have antibiotics on standby!

Over the years, many things have dawned on me since that silly weekend, and I slowly learned how to work sensibly and powerfully with deities without trashing myself too much.

The painting that had Kali in it ended up to being too much for the house and anyone who went anywhere near it. It had to eventually go into the fire to release the power within it. Interestingly from an astrology point of view, that was the beginning of my Pluto transit. Dude, I know how to blow up in style!

Discernment is a really good skill to have around deities: the closer they are to humanity the less likely they are to tell the truth if they do not get their own way, and they will try and manipulate you to get what they want. Boundaries have to be drawn from the earliest days.

The other really important thing to be aware of is that if you feed and water the deities, they will get stronger. Again the closer they are to humanity, the more they mirror the needs of a human: they want food, water, trinkets, power and sex. Be careful what you give them because certain power/energy can dictate how they react to certain situations. Look into their history and you may find clues regarding how they eat/act.

The most fascinating way to work with a deity is to reach for the old gods which means going down into the part of the Abyss where

11. Working with Deities: Pitfalls and Approaches

the older deities sleep. As newer gods and goddesses emerge and work with humanity, so the older gods sink down into the land to sleep. You can reach them either by going deep into the Underworld, or by going down the Abyss to where their power is asleep.

The ancient gods that worked with other forms of humanity also sleep there and the beings that you can meet and work with become fascinating. Sometimes they want you to go down to them to work with them and learn from them. Sometimes they want you to bridge them so that they can rise out of the Abyss and walk once more upon the surface of the earth. That takes a lot of hard work but is also a form on service.

Some of the ancient gods are still in our realm simply because their images are still here and their temples till exist, even if they are in ruins. Just that image and Inner Temple bridge allows their power to stay with humanity, so it is much easier to reach and work with them. That is why it is so easy to work with the Egyptian or Tibetan gods: they are still in our minds and landscape.

The much older gods who no longer have images or temples in our world are harder to reach and nearly always have to be accessed through the Underworld or the Abyss. When you work with these ancient gods, be aware that their relationship with humanity was probably different to what we expect today, in fact they might have even worked with a different form of humanity and not understand us at all.

They might ask you to do things that are way off our radar or repertoire of actions and if that happens, you have to just say no. You will have to teach them about your form of humanity and what our culture finds acceptable and not acceptable. So when the deity offers you limitless power in return for the decapitated heads of the men of the tribe of whatever, you have to politely point out to them that we don't really do such things anymore (unless you are a far right wing Republican, in which case it might be plausible).

The skills and knowledge that they can bring to us are interesting and useful, and the view of modern humanity can be useful to them. I think they mostly look around at our world and decide that the pit of the Abyss, with all its demons, is probably a safer place to be.

11.2. Working with the deity

At the end of the day, you shouldn't really need to use deities that much: it's like taking an anti-aircraft missile to crack a nut. Depends really on what you are doing and what you want to achieve.

Chapter Twelve

Working with ancestors

As soon as we pass into the inner realms, the little things with which we surround ourselves fade away. Our excuses to ourselves, our fantasies and our deliberate blindness all fall away, leaving us no option but to see ourselves as we truly are. This is not a spiritual revelation that happens overnight. It is a slow but steady awakening from which we cannot retreat.

We gradually begin to see the true consequences of our actions, be they good or bad, and we are unable to turn from them. 'Sorry' is a word that does not exist in the Inner Worlds. If you cause something to happen, you and you alone are fully responsible for the full unraveling of the consequences of your action. No matter how long, how many lifetimes, how many regrets you have. It is not a punishment, merely a cause and reaction. It is the natural law of power and balance.

Ancestral work is one of the hardest things to do, mainly because of the emotional baggage usually passed down through families, but also because of the energetic dynamics of the work. When you do ancestral work, you are not truly working with an individual but a whole genetic line that flows through both the past and the future.

Modern concepts of ancestral work are taken from tribal and shamanic practices without the accompanied wisdom of land, beings and power. Tribal ancestral work consists of working or communing with a being that is not particularly your ancestor, but is a composite being made up of human, faery and land consciousness. Most ethnic shamans or tribal magicians understand this without rationalizing it, because the consciousness of the people is such that it operates from within a holism.

A land spirit connects with a human at birth, and the tribal consciousness is woven into the child from the moment it draws

12. WORKING WITH ANCESTORS

breath. So when the person dies, the consciousness of that land being is still there and operating within the structure of the human identity. It is this being that is worked with as an ancestor within a tribal cultural setting. It is not masquerading as an ancestor: rather, it upholds part of who that human was in one life, echoing the soul that has since moved on.

Sometimes, the person themselves waits at the threshold of death: not moving all the way through death to rebirth allows the ancestor to continue communion with his family and tribe. This quickly becomes unhealthy, though, if the spirit refuses to move on and is holding onto lifetime grudges, wants or ambitions. Sometimes they wait for a while, until they have achieved something in service for the tribe, and then they move on.

A second form of ancestral contact is working with ancestors within the world's many ritual burial mounds. In this case, the ancestor is still present in a spirit form for us to work with. They are there to do a job within a certain span of time, usually connected to the welfare of the land. The greatest tragedy occurs when archaeologists, in their pursuit of the past, hack into and remove the bodies of these sleepers. When a body is removed from its ritual sleeping place, the interaction between the sleeper and the land is ended.

So what are sleepers and how do they get there? A sleeper is a person who has opted to step out of the cycle of birth and death to act as a threshold or inner contact between the tribe, the land and the Inner Worlds. The death would have been a ritual slaying with the permission of the victim. Please note that later sacrifices, like those found in Central America were a degenerate form of this tradition, and forced sacrifices are relatively modern in history. What we see in the Inca culture for example are the twisted remnants of what was once a sacred Mystery.

The ceremony of ritual slaying would make sure that the spirit of the person did not pass on, but stayed within the body that was usually, but not always, buried in the earth. A mound was built around the sleeper: it was revered as a sacred place. The seers of the tribe would establish contact with the sleeper and the sleeper would guide the tribe by acting as an intermediary between the inner contacts, the deities, and the people.

Some sleepers were there as guardians of the land. Their spirit would guard the land or sacred enclosures, keeping the land healthy and strong. It is ironic that in today's world, which has the most need of these sleepers, we dig them up and stick them on public show. Not only is this a terrible indignity, but it strips the land of the interaction between humanity and the sacred earth. All inner protection that the land and tribe jointly enjoyed is destroyed out of greed and curiosity.

12.1 Time jumping

The most common form of ancestral work is working with the ancestor in their own time. You are not working with a dead person who is hanging around just for you to contact them. You are reaching out of time, passing through timelessness to connect with a person in their own life. Such work affects all the generations that come after that person.

This dissolving of the barriers of time is the key to ancestral work. So what is time? It is a condition that is bound by substance, movement, gravity. Our everyday life on the surface of the planet is bound by a series of rhythms and cycles. These cycles denote time, a linear time that starts at A and finishes at B. We accept this as a whole reality: the 'be all and end of life.' And with that acceptance comes the concept that life has no inner pattern or existence outside the physical body. And if we look at the world simply from that physical plane, then it is not that far from the truth.

But the world is not just a physical plane. There are many levels of consciousness, many forms of existence and energies that exist without physical expression that we can perceive. The physical substance is merely the outermost expression of being: the end of the line, so to speak. Once you stretch beyond the physical substance, to the inner consciousness, then gravity and time have no meaning. They are simply laws that govern substance, but they do not govern reality.

Stepping out or beyond the base physical reality frees a person from the bonds of time. It allows them to experience the true expression of consciousness without its strictures of substance.

To step out of time, you must take your consciousness beyond the world of substance. Doing that is simpler than it sounds. Tuning into the inner flame and passing through the flame into the Void obviates time immediately: allowing you by the power of disciplined thought to move freely through time. This is not a theory. It is an active working technique.

12.2 Family ancestors

Next comes the question: why would you do ancestral work and what you would use such a working for? Working through and with your ancestors is probably one of the most profound and powerful ways to work on tribal/family issues. It is also an effective way of working on one's own internal issues beyond the usual mundane gripes that we carry.

When you trace back and work with an ancestor, you are given the opportunity to interact and transform the negative and difficult patterns that become so entrenched. These patterns trickle down through the generations and affect everyone in their path.

As the generations flower, the original situation that manifested the pattern is forgotten, but the effect still lives on from generation to generation. Simply finding the original cause of a family pattern of behavior can go a long way towards healing that pattern.

The other great joy of this particular work is that it often uncovers surprises. It is work that is often undertaken by people who have no real idea of who their family is. It enables them to track back through their line and reconnect with their ancestral and tribal line. No matter how fast we live and how independent we consider ourselves, there comes a time when the rootedness of blood becomes important.

The following vision takes you back through your line to a place within the history of your family: to a point in time where you can interact with and learn from your ancestors.

It is a vision that should be done more than once, so that it builds in power and connection.

12.3 The ancestral vision

Light the candle flame and watch the flame for a few seconds before you close your eyes. See the candle flame before you with your inner vision and be aware of the breath of life that flows through the candle flame: the divine flame that manifests on the edge of the Void.

With your inner vision, see the room in which you sit fall away and you find yourself out in a field of grasses and flowers. Beside you are a knife, a fire, and a bowl of water. You will see the sun rising before you in the east. Be aware of that direction and of the west behind you. Be aware of the north and south, of the earth below and the stars above. Be aware of yourself sitting in the center and within your center is the sacred flame of all being.

In your inner vision, pick up the knife and slice across your hand causing blood to flow. Hold the blood over the bowl of water and allow your blood to mingle with the water. When your hand stops bleeding, hold it near the fire to cleanse the wound.

A crow circles above you and then dives down, hitting the bowl of water causing it to spill onto the ground. The liquid flows out of the bowl and creates a stream of blood and water that flows off into the distance. The stream grows and grows until it becomes a river that you fall into and the current pulls you along. You allow the current to carry you as the water flows over your face. The taste of blood reaches your lips and the water gets deeper and deeper as you are pulled along.

When you feel that you are about to drown, your hand touches a branch and you hang onto it. Hauling yourself up out of the water, you see that you are hanging onto an old gnarled tree that is bent over and many of its branches are trailing in the river. Pulling yourself out of the river, you roll on the grassy bank and rest.

As you lie steaming in the sun, you hear voices in the distance. Something within you recognizes the voices, even through the language may be strange. You get up and walk towards the voices, pushing through taller and taller grasses as you go. The surrounding trees seem to bend down to join the grass, creating a wall of green that you must push through. As you emerge on the other side, you

12. WORKING WITH ANCESTORS

will see a person standing in a clearing, looking around as if they have just heard something.

Approach this ancestor carefully, taking in the situation around them and acting accordingly. Commune with your ancestor, and tell them about yourself and your world. Ask the questions that need to be asked. Offer help and advice where you can, and be of assistance to your ancestor should they need it.

At the end of the interaction, step back and tell them that they will be remembered in the future. Allow the ancestor to walk away from you and wait until they have vanished. Then it is time to push deeper into the forest as you reach further back through time.

The further back you go, the denser the forest will be. The journey starts to take its toll on your body and your muscles begin to feel as if you have carried heavy weights. Push yourself forward until you reach a clearing in the trees.

As you emerge from the forest, you will see people sitting around a fire. Go and sit with them quietly and watch the flames. One of those in this gathering looks at you intently, and recognizes you as someone from the future.

The seer looks around the group for someone who is connected to you. When the seer recognizes which member of their community is your ancestor, the seer stands and walks towards you. With one arm outstretched, he or she asks you to follow as they turn and leave the fire. You are led a short way to a tent or structure and told to wait.

The seer leaves, and then returns shortly with someone at their side. This person is told that you are here and that you wish to commune with them. The seer places a hand on your head, and a hand on your ancestor's head. He or she acts as an interpreter between you and your ancestor.

When the communion is over, the ancestor leaves and the seer turns to talk to you. The seer tells you of the tribe and its problems, and asks you—as a person of the future—if you have any advice that you can give. Do your best to answer honestly and clearly. If you do not have an answer, then you must say so.

In return, the seer offers you advice for your life or family. Take the advice into your heart where you can unravel it and make it

12.3. The ancestral vision

appropriate for your own time. The seer then places a hand over your eyes. Through the hands of the seer, you are empowered with the seer's sight. The landscape and way of life is revealed to you as you look around. The seer also looks into you and sees your world.

When the time comes to leave, you begin to feel tired. Your body feels so tired that you can hardly stand up. Finally, your legs give in and you lie down on the soft fresh earth. Sleep comes heavily upon you and you drift in a state of total relaxation. The seer stays beside you and sings a lullaby to you in a language that your body understands, even if you do not.

The earth seems to cover you over and the grass grows all around you. A feeling of deep peace descends upon you as you lie in communion with the earth. You become aware of a presence beside you, as though it flows from the earth that is all around you.

The presence touches you deeply and you begin to weep tears of love and compassion. The presence is your first ancestor, the source of all patterns that run through you. You merge and mingle together as one, feeling the planet turn through time as you lie in union.

Your tears reach the surface of the earth and become flowers, turning their faces to the sun and blossoming. All awareness of your time-bound life falls away and all you are left with is the timeless union of blood within the earth.

As you lie together with your first ancestor, you hear a voice calling out your name. The sound echoes through the earth, vibrating within the rocks and causing you to stir. You want to reach out for the sound, but you need help.

An instinct deep within you causes you to push your hand and arm up through the earth to the air. Your arm emerges out of the rich earth and grasps onto someone's hand. That someone pulls on your arm, pulling you out of the earth.

As you emerge, you find yourself standing before a future ancestor, someone from your own future who has reached through time to commune with you. Be with this person: pass on all that you can. The future ancestor looks deeply into you and sees a pattern within you that you were not aware of. It is something that you acquired in your present life and it can affect generations to come.

They reach out to help you with this pattern and you must choose to allow them to assist you with the letting go and recognition of what that pattern might be.

Visions of scenes within your life, issues that you cling to and emotions that are becoming difficult parade before your vision and the future ancestor helps you to look at these objectively. Your body feels the transition as you let things alter and change.

Before you can commune further, the future ancestor falls back into a mist and vanishes from your sight. You hear the flow of the river which rages like a torrent all around you. You look down to find yourself standing on an isthmus, almost surrounded by the water that flows on all sides.

The water laps around your feet and pulls at you to leave. Reluctantly you dive back into the river and swim towards the setting sun. As you swim, you become aware of fires that burn on both sides of the river. Some are bonfires lit for the ancestors, and some are natural fires.

The flames build up around you until it seems that you are swimming through fire: the fires burn around and within you: cleansing and purifying you as you reach back to your own time.

You emerge out through the central flame and find yourself back in the room where you first started. You take you seat and look at the central flame. Around you, you see the rivers of water and blood flowing into and out of you, vanishing off into the far distance. When you are ready, open your eyes and look at the central flame.

12.4 The family

A major part of ancestral work is bound up with our present day families. When you care for an elder or child within the family, you are caring for the family ancestors. All those who have gone before live on in one way or another through our lives. A thread of their experiences and patterns are carried down the line of blood and will be passed onto the future generations. It is our responsibility to make sure the right patterns carry on and that unhealthy ones are brought to conclusion in our lifetime.

One of the many ways to do this is through the children: protecting them magically as they develop and ensuring that old patterns are not repeated. Often just the sense for a child that they are totally safe from all things is enough for them to have space to blossom and grow to their full potential.

The following vision is one for working with the children within your family. It is something that I have used for many years with my own children and my family's children. I do it periodically as a form of service to my family.

12.5 Guarding the children

This is a vision of ancestral responsibility, the sharing of the burden of protection for the future generations. It is usually conducted within your own family or tribe and must not be done with any other family group without permission.

Light a candle and close your eyes. See the flame before you and see a flame deep within you. The more you focus on the inner flame the more it draws you inward until you find yourself in the Void that is at your centre.

As you stand in the stillness and silence that is within, you hear a baby cry. The cry gets louder and louder and pulls upon you, urging you to step forward. You recognize something within the cry and something within you tells you that a child of your blood cries out in the dark for protection.

Stepping forward you pass over the threshold of the west and find yourself stood before the bed or crib of a child. The child is crying and is distressed. You sense danger around the child: either inner or physical danger, maybe even serious sickness.

As you look at the child, you see a pattern of energy that you recognize: the child feels a little like you. You realize that this child is of your family or tribe, and that you have responsibility as an ancestor to protect them.

Reach out your hand and place it lightly on the child's head or shoulders. When you have established the contact with them, feel for the child's inner flame, seated deep within them. Cup the child's inner flame in your hand carefully and respectfully.

Now feel the deep inner peace that always visits you when you reach into your inner flame. Allow that peace and stillness to flow over the child as you mediate silence from the eternal inner flame: the flame of Divinity.

The child begins to settle down and fall asleep. You, as ancestor, stand guard over the child as they sleep. As you watch the child slumber, a song rises up from deep within you and you begin to quietly sing. The child relaxes more and more as you sing, and the sound carries around the room creating a pattern of protection that swirls around the child.

Faery beings from outside creep closer to listen to the song and you also become aware that all the creatures around the building are listening to your voice. The song tells of the child's heritage, the blood of the tribe and the gifts that the child can carry forward for the future.

You begin to get tired and just as your eyes begin to close, you feel a hand on your shoulder. Another ancestor of your blood stands beside you and offers to take over to watch as the child sleeps. You may or may not recognize them.

The ancestor takes position beside the child and begins to sing as you quietly back out of the room. Turning, you find yourself on the threshold of a wall of fire that is the threshold of the Void. Stepping over the threshold, you suddenly remember a time when you were a small child and you were frightened. You remember a sensation of someone coming to watch over you or protect you and you remember your fear being taken away. When you are ready, pass through the Void back into the room where you first started and blow out the candle.

12.6 Tribal ancestors

When I talked earlier about the blending of a land spirit and an ancestor, I suddenly realized that this was probably the basis for a lot of localized legends of strange-looking humans that would help the community.

When I lived on a reservation, I did come across all sorts of stories and legends that are based in the land there. Although the

12.6. Tribal ancestors

local tribes did not come from this particular patch of land, (they were previously living about sixty miles south) they would go to the area once a year in gathering to hold ceremonies and reunions.

While in sweat one evening, I had a vision of a great spider that was busy weaving the lodge. I talked to her and asked her who she was. She told me she was the Tou'piah, or great grandmother. I thought this strange, as this particular tribe does not look well upon spiders: they are seen here as bad. I told her this and she just laughed and then became serious.

She showed me another version of herself, as an old woman and went onto tell me about how the local Jesuits did horrific damage, as everywhere else, but that they had also managed to change the beliefs of the local tribe. She was sad that her descendants had inherited such mistruths as traditional facts. I told her there was nothing I could do about it: I was a guest in the lodge and it was not my place to interfere.

After the sweat, I told the medicine man who had led the sweat what I had seen and heard and he nodded sadly. I described the old woman and he told me that was the original matriarch of the family who owned the lodge. She had died in her early fifties and had been a strong protector of the traditions and songs of the family. I asked him about the local fear of spiders and he shrugged saying that he was not from here, and his tribe saw spiders as powerful medicine. So I have to assume that the great grandmother was raised before that particular propaganda was pushed about by the Jesuits.

After that encounter, she would appear whenever I sweated in that lodge and she would show me things that were about to happen. The only problem was the images she was showing me were presented in a way that I could not do much with the information unless a person connected to that happening was in the lodge.

Once I was sweating and I suddenly saw a head-on collision between a car and a truck. I was so shocked and it was so real that I started to panic. After that sweat round, I went to the spring to try and calm down. I told the sweat leader what I had just seen. He asked me if I recognized anyone or even knew the car. I told him that the car was familiar but that was all.

12. WORKING WITH ANCESTORS

I knew the Tou'piah was frustrated with me because I didn't recognize the people in the car. Later I found out that the doorman's (the man who guards the entrance of the sweat lodge) family had been in a head-on collision with a truck just at the time we were sweating. The spirits of the lodge were trying to help but there was too much of a disconnection for it to work.

And this is the problem today: too much disconnection. The tribal disconnection was done deliberately. I hadn't realized this until that point in time. I had always thought that the Catholic Church pushed aside the tribal culture just out of ignorance and saw it as mindless stupidity. But after what I had experienced in the lodge, I wasn't so sure about that any more. It seemed to me after living and working with tribal people that their power had been specifically and deliberately dismantled.

By simply turning spiders into bad things, they singlehandedly disconnected the local tribe from their ancestral contacts. None of the tribal people in the lodge, other than the medicine man, had any contact with the Tou'piah. If anyone had natural sight, they would shun such a connection away immediately out of fear. Clever.

Usually what has been told to us to avoid (spiders, the Underworld, the dark, etc.) are all powerful things that should be explored. Working with and for tribal ancestors becomes a task of not only protecting the family and unravelling past patterns, it is also a task of reeducating us away from religious propaganda and allowing the spirits and ancestors to speak once more.

If you are from a tribal community, one of the ways forward for this path is to visit the graves of the community that went before you. Be with them, talk with them, take them gifts of food/herbs/stones and establish a connection with the continued line from past to future.

This is also something that can be done if you wish to respect and acknowledge the ancestors of an area where you live. I visit the local graveyard regularly here and commune with the ancestors here. They guide me in many things and I am grateful for their contact. In return I keep their memories alive and tend their resting places.

12.7 Cultural ancestors

In Algeria is the ancient city Abalessa, former capital of the Hoggar region. In Abalessa there is the tomb of the famous Tuareg queen Tin Hinan (she who came from far away).

There are legends in Libya that Tin Hinan was an Amazon queen, and that the Amazon warriors were heavily established in North Africa a long time before the Amazons of Northern Turkey. The Berbers, of which the Tuareg (aka Imuhar) are a tribe, call themselves Amazigh in their language. There is definitely a strong similarity between the words Amazon and Amazigh.

Women in Tuareg society are the holders of property and power. It is a matriarchal society in which only the women are literate and they are the keepers of history through stories and poems. They were also fierce warriors and the first Arab invasion in A.D. 700 was fought off by a band of warriors, male and female, led by a woman.

To the Berbers, Tin Hinan is their mother, their founder: indeed even today she is still called 'mother of all.' She became the Mother Protector, first ancestor, to the Berber people and her tomb is still a place of pilgrimage and worship.

So great was the respect of the tribes for this woman that her tomb was never desecrated: she was buried with multiple gold and silver bangles, and her body was covered in precious jewels. When the tomb was finally excavated by westerners, not only did they find this fabulous wealth, but they also found evidence that the tomb was used for healing sleep and visions by the local tribes.

People would travel great distance to lie by her tomb and sleep with her. Their dreams would be recounted in poems that would be passed down the generations of women.

This is a wonderful example of true ancestral work. And because there is such a long tradition of work with Tin Hinan, it is a line of consciousness that we can tap into, respectfully, to learn about how to honor our own ancestors and the land.

12. WORKING WITH ANCESTORS

12.8 The vision of Tin Hinan

Light a candle and close your eyes. With your inner vision see the candle flame and as you watch the flame, it grows into a fire. The room in which you are seated falls away and you find yourself seated around a camp fire at night with a group of women. They are wrapped heavily with many layers of dark cloth to protect them against the fierce sun during the day and the harsh cold of the desert night. Their faces bear the marks of tattooing and as you look at their tattoos you realize that one of them can see you.

The rest for the women is over and someone calls for the night march to resume. Some of the women grab torches from the fire and hold up the fire to light the way for others. As the women walk through the dark they sing a song which tells you the history of their first queen: their mother.

You walk with the women, listening to their songs until the dawn begins to awaken. Your feet are heavy from walking, and the dawn pulls at you to sleep. One of the women puts a hand to your back to keep you walking and you struggle to continue against an overwhelming urge to sleep.

As the sun rises, you see a large mound ahead of you and upon the mound sits an ancient brick structure. The women snake up the mound and enter a low doorway one by one, extinguishing their flames before they enter. When it is your time to enter, you stop and take off your sandals before entering the gathering place.

All of the women sit, laugh and unwrap leaves which they hand around to each other. Someone hands you a small bunch of leaves and motions for you to chew them. They taste bitter on your tongue and yet the bitterness is refreshing after the desert.

A strange but pleasant feeling flows over you and your tired feet and your muscles relax as the magic of the leaves unfolds within you. Without thinking, you lie down and close your eyes. You become aware that the other women are also lying down and preparing to sleep.

Immediately sleep pulls you deeply and you begin to dream. You are pulled through the floor into a tomb with a woman lying as if asleep on a beautifully carved wooden bed. Flowers and jewels lie all around her and a bone knife has been laid beside her. Her robe reaches down to the floor and you instinctively kneel and touch the hem of her robe.

Her power flows through her robe and into you, filling you with a sense of awe. She is a queen, an embodiment of the Goddess, and as such you know that you must give her a gift: something worthy of a great queen. You hold out your hand and whatever appears in your hand you must be willing to give her. You lay the gift at her feet and a guardian steps forward out of the dark shadows to place a hand upon your shoulder.

The guardian tells you that this place is sacred to all women: this is the tomb of one of the great sleeping queens. The guardian instructs you to lie down and he places a hand over your eyes.

You immediately fall into a deep and refreshing sleep. As you sleep, you can feel hands massage you and heal you. Old wounds and old illnesses surface and then vanish under the powerful touch. A deep peace descends upon you as you join in sleep with all the great sleepers hidden around the world.

The sleep reaches through time, and every time that you have ever closed your eyes and gone to sleep, you realize that a part of you has unwittingly come here. In future, you will be able to reach this place in your sleep if you wish, so that you can lie with the great queen and bathe in her healing power. In return you must always remember her and keep her name alive.

Now it is time to return. Someone calls your name and you find yourself waking from a deep healing sleep. You remember the candle flame that is before you and you remember the room in which you are seated. When you are ready, open your eyes.

12.9 Practical use of ancestral work

Connecting with the old ancestors can be useful from a learning point of view. Learning to work without temples, priests/esses and deities can be difficult when we come from a culture that is based around hierarchy, temples and worship.

But the old ancestors did just that: the ordinary people of the land thousands of years ago worked from a premise that anyone can leave an offering for the Earth Mother, that everything around them was sacred and therefore there was no use for a temple, and that Divine Being was everywhere and in everything: every rock, spring, tree and mountain was sacred and treated as such.

This is no revelation, but we have, as a magical community in the west, taken that knowledge and then fashioned robed rituals, hierarchies, priesthoods, temple spaces, etc., in an effort to give a familiar form to an ancient magic.

But to connect back through thousands of years to a pre-temple people who lived without such structures is really useful. Some of the most powerful magical teaching acts through resonance: that is to say, being in the same space, working alongside someone allows magical knowledge and power to pass from one spirit to the other.

So to go back through time and work alongside someone who is partaking of such magic is powerful. Being in the middle of a working teaches us much more than reading about something. It also puts many things in context and a new understanding begins to dawn. Going back through time in vision takes discipline and focus. You have to be sure you are not going to be disturbed (turn your phones off) and not be tired. Don't drink coffee too close to the working (coffee blocks some inner powers) and obviously don't drink alcohol for a few hours before working.

12.10 Time and intention

Do you have to specify a time to reach back to ancient workers? Basically, no. The intention to go back to before temple structures will open out a certain pathway for you to walk. Then what will happen is that your spirit is drawn to the most powerful happening around that time period. This is the easiest way to stretch back. When there is a powerful magical happening, it sends out ripples throughout time, and your spirit can home in on it like a beacon. You do not need to know what time you are in, you are not there to prove a point.

Picking up on the power beacon along with the intention is usually enough to take you to where you need to be. The other signal that flows out through time is the magical request. I am sure you have also done this at some point in your life: called out to the universe for help. When this happens and if it is powerful enough, the call flows through time and as you pass through the Void with your intention of going back through time, the call echoes through the Void and you pick up on it. Just be aware that when this happens, you are not a tourist: you will be expected to help in what may be a difficult and dangerous situation.

The method of passing through the Void with the intent of time jumping is a good, clean, clear way of working that protects you from all sorts of nasties and will also help your spirit to become more pliable while staying intact. We will look at this in more depth in a moment.

12.11 Interactions with ancestors

So how do you behave with these ancestors? What or who do they think you are? If you are stretching back beyond temple structures, be aware that you are going pretty far back and that the concepts, magical ways, culture and even physical make-up will be different. Be careful about how you present yourself: by this I mean be focused, clear and simple in how you envision yourself, for this is how they will see you. If you are festooned with magical baubles, talismans and protective spirits, they will think you are a lunatic at best, and a danger at worst.

Present yourself in a simple way, i.e. in a simple physical form, with a clear heart. Also be aware that past ancestors are not New Age fluffy pink nice old grannies. Life has always been tough and full of people with greedy agendas, so be on your guard and use your common sense. If they have sent out a calling beacon for help then you are less likely to trip up and bump into shamans looking for an easy target. They will be glad of the help and in return will forge a good contact with you for knowledge exchange: remember that this is always a two-way street.

If you are going back by focusing on a burst of power (i.e. a powerful event that you can be drawn to) be a little careful until you know, by the feel of it, what that powerful event was. Make sure for example that it was not some massive slaughter for sacrifice or war. You could end up becoming someone's dinner! You do not have to

12. WORKING WITH ANCESTORS

take all that is offered, you do not have to give all that is demanded and you do not have to do what is requested if you do not think it is right. If you have landed somewhere in time where you feel you are way out of your league, break the contact, leave the room and go take a bath.

An ancient working space is useful as a focal point to access back through time so. So before trying to do this work in vision, it is helpful if you are able to physically go to one of these spaces (an Iron Age fort, a stone circle, a sacred hill, an ancient burial, etc.). If you are unable to go to one of these sites then choose one that you feel a deep connection with: learn about it, fix its qualities in your head and put up a picture of it so that you see it regularly.

For example, there are a few ancient sites close to where I live, so when I am working with ancestors I reach out through the Void for contacts or power surges that are connected to one of those sites. They may end up coming from somewhere else, but they have a connection to that site, or were visiting it at some point. It is a good way of working in the early days of time jumping as it gives focus and roots to the work connection.

As the work deepens, you become used to trotting back and forth and then experimenting wider, so that your range opens out. It often happens through inner necessity rather than idle curiosity.

Once you have made an inner connection with your outer site it is time to go to work. Choose your working element (stone, bowl of water, flame) and keep that candle/stone/water bowl only for this work. Place your element before you and prepare yourself for work. If you are using fire then light your candle. The easiest way to build up this work is as follows:

Prepare for work with an element (flame or bowl of water, etc).

Still yourself and move through the element into the Void, the place of nothingness from which all things flow forth and to which they return. Spend time in the Void connecting to the sense of nothing, stillness and silence. Be aware of flowing through all things in this place. Focus on looking for a power burst or call connected to a site you have been working with and when you sense it, turn towards it and step out of the Void.

See yourself stepping into mist and walking towards the power source or call. When you meet the ancestors, commune with them and do what they need. When you have finished use the fire (ancestors often reach for contact in front of a fire) as a focused doorway back into the Void: from the Void step back through your element into your working space to conclude your visit.

The following vision can be used to approach ancestors at a sacred place if you haven't been able to establish a call.

12.12 Vision of meeting the ancestors

Still yourself by going into the Void: spend some time in the stillness, being aware of yourself as a timeless being, as a being of service. Be aware that you can pass through all structures, all time, all places: your consciousness has no boundaries.

Stepping out of the Void you find yourself walking through a mist which obscures everything around you. Hold to a clear intent to reach the sacred place you have chosen to visit. The sacred space you have chosen emerges out of the mist and you walk to the centre of it. You can see nothing beyond the sacred enclosure, as the land is surrounded in thick mist.

Using your inner vision, you stand up with your arms outstretched, and begin to turn. You turn and turn, with the mists swirling around you, allowing the power of the Void to flow through you and out into this most sacred place. As you turn you begin to feel an immense build-up of power swirling around you, and you feel the power of the Underworld beneath your feet flowing up through your body to the stars, and the power of the stars flowing down into the Underworld. You turn in the centre of this flow of power, acting as a fulcrum of power as it flows through the worlds.

You hear a voice calling out and you begin to slow your turning until you come to a stop. The power slows down and as you look around you see many people stood in a circle. One who is sighted sees you and comes forward to you. At first they think you are a land spirit, but you must tell them that you are a person from another time who wishes to learn from them and also help them.

The sighted one asks you what you need to learn and you commune with this elder to learn what you need for your service. In return, you tell them things of the future that will assist them in their spiritual lives. You can also act as an inner contact or worker for them, assisting them to heal or work on someone, or to act as a death worker for someone who is dying or recently dead. They will show you what they need from you.

When you have finished you withdraw from the group, walking into the centre of the space and stilling yourself. Be aware of the Void and of stillness. See yourself passing from the sacred space into the Void, letting all the work you have done fall away from you, and allow yourself to rest for a while in the stillness.

The knowledge that you were given lies within you and will surface when needed, but for now it passes from your mind as you drift in the stillness and silence. When you are ready, step out of the Void and back into the room where you first started. Focus on the element before you as you slowly come back to consciousness and when you are ready, open your eyes.

12.13 Dynamics

The dynamics of ancestral connection is always a two-way affair. At this stage of the work it is about service as well as learning, and time jumping is a major part of this service. We are bound by time only by virtue of our physical existence. As soon as we pass into the inner states of consciousness, then the mind has no time boundaries and we can flow back and forth. In practical terms, working through time can be hard on the physical body and you must be ready for the impact exhaustion afterwards.

The further back you go in time, the harder it can be to understand what the contact is trying to communicate. This is mostly because our consciousness is so different from the consciousness of the ancients. Just the speed at which we think and process is far in excess of the processing abilities of our ancestors. But then again they have a deeper and more anchored sense of connection from which we can truly benefit.

Our inner abilities have a great deal more elasticity than the people who went before us. This has accelerated over the years so that, within just two generations, the work has become far more pliable: magical work that we now find fairly easy was a terrible struggle for those working only a hundred years ago.

To go back in time we have to be aware of the subtle as well as obvious differences and adjust our communications accordingly. Because of our flexibility in working with power, which is probably a side product of our modern existence, we can often do tasks that the ancients would find incredibly difficult. When we appear in a certain time in a sacred space, that time is often determined by a call from the ancestors who reach out to the Inner Worlds for help. That call for help flows through the worlds, and as we reach back for that ancestral contact, it puts us both on the same frequency. Our spirits respond to the call (hence the hearing of a voice as we turn in the centre of the sacred space).

The need for working with ancestors seems to take on a natural flow of its own. There are tides within the land, tides within the races of people and tides within families that sometimes all come together to create a porthole for working. You will be pulled in dreams, thoughts and ideas, and that is when you know it is time to do this work.

It can also be important to tune into this work at certain times of the year, like the solstices or equinoxes. Learn to trust your inner instincts with the work: if it is right you will be almost obsessively drawn to the work. If it is not the right time, you will not be able to get it together to get the work done, regardless of what the New Age reconstructionalist calendars tell us. This is all about learning to tune into to the tides, to the inner natural patterns and to the voices of all those who work around the world in and out of time. Every person who makes that step to inner service becomes connected at a deep level. The more you work the more you become aware of them in their own time and place, doing similar work to yours. It is a bit like being a part of a large insane family!

As you work more and more through time you will find that some of the other workers begin to appear in your own work as inner contacts, appearing at a time when you need help or guidance during

12. Working with ancestors

a healing or working. The call for help, when it is truly needed, never goes unanswered.

Chapter Thirteen

Accessing and working within the Faery Realm

The Faery Realm is a part of our world, overlaid and hidden within the landscapes that are all around us. Some magical streams of work ignore this facet of inner work which is a shame and a great loss: we are surrounded by many orders of beings and all of them and us have a part to play in the great scheme of things.

A simple way to access the Faery Realm is to look at the landscape around in which you live. You can access the Faery Realm via a hill, a forest, a rock or a spring. Once you are in the Faery Realm, the central point of focus is usually the crossroads at which is a standing stone, which is actually the Goddess in one of her most powerful forms.

This way of accessing the Faery Realm is not the only way by any means, but it is simple, effective and has no baggage attached to it. It is important however that the first doorway to the Faery Realm is connected to the land upon which you live. The reason for this is that the contact needs to be real, connected and able to flow in a two-way relationship. Connection with the Faery Realm means working with the land, birds, animals and plants that are all around you regardless of whether you live in the country or a city.

Connecting with faeries brings about a relationship that is interdependent and active. They will want you to do things for them and the land. In return they will work with you, help you and teach you many things. They often want feeding, entertaining and companionship. You cannot do this if you are working in a way that is not connected to your everyday existence.

Look for an access point around you that you can build upon. Use the following two visions to build up the inner connection point

13. Accessing and working within the Faery Realm

for faery contact. From that connection point flow many paths within the faery realm, which take you to many different forms of contact, beings and landscapes. I use the Void as a threshold to many different places, including the Faery Realm, because it is a clear, clean place of peace, which puts us in a better frame of mind to meet other beings. The second vision takes you through a more traditional access route through the upside-down tree: an ancient and powerful image that is found throughout the British Isles (e.g. Woodhendge).

13.1 Short vision for accessing the Faery Realm

Use a flame, bowl of water or a rock as an elemental focus. Be aware of yourself passing through the element into the Void where you allow your daily life to fall away and a sense of stillness to wash over you. Take your time to feel yourself expand in all directions, feeling yourself reach out while breathing through the Void.

When you are still and calm, step out of the Void, seeing yourself walking upon a path that leads to a hill, a large rock or a tree. As you get closer to the access point you see a small crack in it that you hadn't noticed before and you squeeze yourself through, passing into a dark damp tunnel with a faint light at the end. As you walk in the darkness you become aware of many eyes watching you, and many whispers surrounding you, but you cannot hear what they are saying.

You emerge into the light of a grassy plain with a low hill in the distance and a standing stone at a crossroads up ahead. Walk up to the standing stone and place you hands upon it. You will feel it breathing under your touch and you become aware that the stone is a living being. You prick your finger and place a drop of your blood upon the stone and a drop of your spit in offering: in response the stone begins to change shape. The stone becomes a woman who sings in many tones at once, as if calling.

Many beings approach from the four pathways in response to the call and you see faery beings of all shapes and sizes approaching you warily. They stop at a short distance and wait for what you have to say. Commune with them, offer them a gift of your service and listen well to their reply. If they ask you to do something, then make sure that you are willing to do it in your own world, as they will hold you to your promise.

They offer you a gift in return and you also commune with the woman. When you have finished, return the way you came, and when you emerge out of the rock/tree/hill, see a misty area in the path and walk into the mist. It will take you back into the Void. Be still in the Void for a little while, remembering what you have just done and when you are ready, open your eyes.

13.2 Longer vision of the Faery Realm

This vision is a vision that you can use regularly to connect with the Faery Realm and build a relationship with the beings of that world. It goes down through the Underworld (its back door being in the Abyss) and gives you access to a much older ancestral faery consciousness. Once you have been to this place by the 'front door,' it is then interesting to access it by going down the Abyss to the place where this consciousness now rests. It is important to note at this point that faeries are not cute little half-dressed prepubescent Victorian constructs, they are strange, often wild-looking beings of various sizes from little to extremely large.

Sitting quietly, be aware of the inner flame that burns deep within you. As your awareness of the flame builds, reach within you and bring out a fragment of the flame, holding it before you. The fragment of flame lights up the space in such a way that you can see things that were previously hidden.

As you look around with your inner vision, you see an opening in the floor that falls down into the Underworld. The fragment of flame plunges down the hole and you follow. As you fall, you become aware of many different scents that you recognize. They all evoke emotions, and yet the precise memory of these familiar scents evades you.

Deeper and deeper down you fall, twisting around the directions as you pass roots, earth and stone. The flame falls below you and lights your way and in the dim light you become aware of beings falling with you, keeping you company as you pass through the earth and into the ancient Faery Realm. The beings that are falling with you start to shout loudly that they are nearly home. You begin to

13. ACCESSING AND WORKING WITHIN THE FAERY REALM

pass tree roots as you fall and finally you pass tree trunks. You fall through a forest of upside-down trees and emerge in a strange land of great beauty. The friends that fell with you land beside you gently. Before you can speak to them, they vanish leaving you alone.

All around you is grass and flowers. Many trees hang down from the sky, reaching for the grass. The light comes not from the sky, but from the ground below your feet. In the distance there are many hills and standing stones. One particular stone stands out for you and you set off walking towards it. Faint singing whispers all around you and as you listen, you hear that the song is advising you where to go.

On your chosen path, there is a stone blocking the pathway. Something tells you, deep within you, not to walk around the stone, but to touch it. Reaching your hands out, gently caress the stone, which moves under your touch. A wild power emanates from the stone and you realize that this stone is special. Before you can draw breath, the stone transforms into a tall muscular woman who blocks the path.

Her eyes bore into you, seeing everything that is hidden within. She looks at your intentions for seeking the Faery Realm. She looks for a deed that was done without selfishness. If she is happy with what she has seen, she opens her arms to you. Her body scent evokes memories, long since forgotten, of your babyhood. The nurturing of the mother's breast flows from her as she invites you to embrace her.

Stepping forward towards her, you pass through her and she vanishes. The mother of all being has awoken you to life and you now see the landscape through different eyes. All the plants, trees, flowers and bushes show themselves to you as tall beautiful beings that uphold the earth. Many creatures dart in and out of the forest that has appeared all around you.

The stones move and breathe as many strange and wondrous faery beings tend them. All around you is vibrant life in balanced communion. Reach down to the earth and scoop a handful up. The scent of earth is that of the Mother who stood in your path. The scent of nurturing fills you and you lie down on the earth to embrace your Mother.

All of the faery beings lie down with you and each one places an arm around another until one of them places an arm around you. The

13.2. Longer vision of the Faery Realm

spirits of the plants, trees, flowers and stones all participate in until every living thing is joined, united in honoring of the Mother. A sense of communion and family flows strongly through you as you realize that all the beings assembled are truly your brothers and sisters.

A gentle rain starts to fall. The community of beings starts to separate and enjoy the soft falling water. The faery beings dance with the raindrops, and all the plants and trees open themselves out to receive the life giving water. The rain falls all around you and also falls through you. Much that is incoherent, unbalanced, suppressed or inappropriate is washed from you by this rain. What falls from you is taken up by the earth and transformed.

When the rainfall stops, a hand reaches out from the earth, holding something out for you. The hand of your first ancestor holds out your imbalances: they have been transformed by the rich earth. Opportunities for learning from what you have relinquished are offered to you. Take the offering and place it within you, where it will unfold slowly throughout your life.

The assembled faeries are beginning to dance through the forest and they call upon you to join them. Holding out your arms, you follow, dancing and singing as you pass ever deeper into the forest. Someone grabs your hand and dances with you. A faery being has chosen you as a companion and should you choose to upkeep this friendship, it will be your companion throughout life.

As you dance, your faery companion asks about your life in the surface world. It asks you what you eat, how you play, where your favorite tree is. In turn, you can ask about life in the Faery Realm.

A call sounds out and the dancing stops. Your companion tells you that it is time for you to leave the Faery Realm and return to the surface world. The assembled faeries accompany you back to the tree, and ask you to return to them again. They tell you that when you return, all you need to do is call out your name when you have jumped from the tree. Your companion will hear your call and will come to greet you. They will escort you to the many places within the Faery Realm and teach you about their world.

Your companion offers you a gift as you prepare to leave. It is something from the Faery Realm that will help you learn more about nature in the surface world. In return, you must make the gift of a promise to the assembled faeries. Whisper your promise, and the faeries will whisper it back to you.

Now it is time to leave. You jump up into the tree, catching onto a tree branch as you start to climb. Carefully climb through the branches until you reach the hollow trunk. Many of the faeries climb with you as you enter the tree hollow and ascend to the surface world. The fragment of your flame is hovering at the roots of the tree, guiding you back. The closer you get to the surface world the more you begin to be aware of the pollution, both physical and psychic of the world in which you live.

The faeries who climb with you begin to sing sad songs as they climb, telling of all the terrible things that have happening on the surface of the earth. It is only then that you realize the faeries are carrying work tools. They tell you that they are going out into the surface world to tend what is left of the flowers, the trees and the creatures. They advise you on how you can help on your own land—small things that you can do to help these beings in their never ending work.

Finally, you emerge back in the surface world, back where you first started. The fragment of inner flame returns back to its source deep within you, and you feel its refreshing power flow through you. Remember the promise that you made, and remember the ways that you can help maintain the land where you live. Also remember the gift that was given to you, and the friends that you made. You can return to the faery realm, back to your friends, whenever you feel it is appropriate.

To complete this vision, if you are indoors, go outside. Take off your shoes and feel the earth beneath your feet. If you are in a city, find a park or a patch of wasteland that has grass. Remember the scent of the Mother and those powerful beings that are the plants and flowers. Honor them quietly.

13.3 Work

Once you have established contact, you will find that things start being put in your path, sometimes literally! If you need something for your work, it will start to appear around you if you truly need it.

13.3. Work

The more you work with the local tree, rock, spring, hill etc., the more of a conversation will seep into your dreams, visions and waking life.

You will start picking up instincts regarding 'good' areas and 'bad' areas, places that need cleaning up either literally or from an inner point of view. Follow your instincts, listen to the voices within you and go with those feelings. You will often be asked to pick up litter, move rocks, clear springs, walk hills, sing, dance, put out honey, fruits and nuts for the faeries and birds. You also may be asked to change how you feed yourself and what you drink.

The processes that happen from faery work can totally transform a person's life for the good, and often bring us much closer to the land and creatures that live on and in that land. You will learn to heal creatures, how to feed and guard them, how to birth faeries and live among them whilst living in the human world.

Faery work is entwined with the environment: they are one and the same thing. So once you have gotten over the 'tourist' agenda and are ready to go into the Faery Realm to work rather than gawp, you will be offered many jobs that really need attending to.

These 'jobs' take many forms including the unwinding and dismantling of religious patterns: pre-1800 Catholic and Anglican churches in Europe tend to have ritual bindings and pinnings in the foundations that trap beings within the land and block access for faeries to the surface world: they hold the ancient powers down so that they cannot be tapped into. This is often displayed in churches by images such as St. George and the Dragon, St. Patrick and the serpent, St. Michael and the dragon, etc.

When the Romans came, they used Apollo to suppress, pin and block the dragon power of the Bright Goddess in the British Isles, just as they had done at Delphi. Ancient Britain was a place of oracles, warriors and druid priests who worked with the weather, and the Romans wanted to pin and control that power just as they pinned and controlled the oracle at Delphi and other places of power. Later this pinning method was absorbed into the Early Roman Christian church: the pin became the cross of Christianity and the sword of the saints that pinned the ancient dragon power down through rituals designed to destroy or imprison that power forever.

Churches were built upon sacred enclosures, groves were cut and mounds were dug up. This ritual entrapment also blocked a lot of faery access to the surface world. It did not stop it by any means, but it did interfere with the natural balance of power and order, leaving the land unbalanced and disconnected. Dealing with this disconnection is one of the most common requests voiced by the faery beings of the land of Britain. The other is sweet food, which of course is an energy source!

Song is another faery request that is often put to humans. Music and song have great power: we are creatures of spiritual harmonics, as are faeries, angelic beings, and the land itself. The harmonics flow back and forth, energizing, strengthening and balancing the land. The best way that we can contribute on an external level is to play natural instruments (rather than recordings of psychedelic trance stuff) and to sing with a clear heart. Words are irrelevant—it is the sound that draws all consciousness to the fire to listen.

It is a bonding mechanism and also a healing tool in a non New Age sense: sometimes beautiful tones cross all war lines, all mountains of adversity and all manner of hatreds.

13.4 My own discovery of faeries

When I was a kid, I was very much the loner. I was way too weird for other kids to want to play with me and I wasn't interested in the things they were interested in. My idea of heaven was to spend all day outside in the woods alone, hanging out with the trees and the creatures.

I had a rough mountain pony called Topper (because no matter how bad other ponies were, he could top that). He had one wall eye (blue eye) and a mean temper. He bolted when he got bored and loved to suddenly break out into a flat out gallop and then just as suddenly slam on his brakes and put his head the to the floor. I would, of course being bareback, slip down his neck every time and land flat on my back in the mud. He loved it: what power!

So everyday I would spend a couple of hours trying to catch him until one day I decided not to chase him, which was what he wanted, but to sit quietly in the forest where he had dumped me and wait for

13.4. My own discovery of faeries

him to come to me. Day after day I would sit among the fallen trees and thick broom bushes, laying back in the weak European sunshine, and wait for the brat to get bored.

During that time I began to watch the squirrels and the birds. I loved talking to them in my mind and I would hold long imaginary conversations with them. Once such day I was deep in conversation when I saw a wild rabbit. I had never seen a wild rabbit before and I was fascinated.

During my childhood the government had seen fit to release a disease that would wipe out the rabbit population which had grown out of control. The rabbits often died a terrible agonizing death and I can remember when I was young, about 5 yrs old, seeing the last death throws of a rabbit in the road. My father covered my eyes and told me not to look.

To see a wild healthy rabbit in the late sixties/early seventies was rare. I watched him, thinking he was the most beautiful thing I had seen. Something happened at that point in my life, that instant. Something opened deep inside me and I looked around and saw just how beautiful everything was in this forest. Everything had life, a bright dazzling life that just was bursting with something that I didn't even have the words for.

That day I felt like I had seen God for the first time. I was nine years old and everything I touched, the trees, the plants, even Topper spoke to me in a silent voice that made me feel like I was hearing for the first time. It was that moment that I became aware that there was something else in that forest with me: something that was not bird animal or human. I could feel it, I could hear it, but I didn't know what it was.

Later that day, I went home and was busy watching my mother. She would often be gone for long periods of time so when she was around, I would sit and watch her: sort of filling myself up with her. I started to try and tell her what had happened that day, but it blurted out in a clumsy way.

I didn't have the words in my brain to describe what had happened. But what I did get was that I thought there was something else there in the forest with me that day. Could it be a ghost? No she replied, it sounds like they were faeries. She told me next time I went

13. Accessing and working within the Faery Realm

out to the forest with topper and took a pack lunch, I should share some of it with them by leaving them the best and sweetest foods on a tree stump.

I did just that. Then I hid to watch and see if I could catch a glimpse of them coming to get their food. I had put out some grandma buns (my grandmother's special recipe) and some plot toffee (a bittersweet toffee made with dark treacle and made only in the months of October and November), my favorite. But alas, no one turned up except an excited crow. I kept waving him off the food and he would just caw at me.

I was so disappointed. I so wanted to meet with the faeries. I told my mother of my abysmal failure and she smiled a wide smile. "No Josie, they don't eat like we do, they take the strength out of the food and leave what's left for the creatures. And you can't see the faeries with these eyes: you have to look at them in a different way. They don't have bodies like we do, they are like Adam and Eve were before God gave them skin and threw them out of the garden. The faeries were never bad so they didn't get skin and they are still in the garden."

But I wanted to see them! I did learn to feel them however. One of my favorite games as a child was the Mayday precession. It was something we did every year where I lived and we would all have a large picnic afterwards. And I loved to recreate it. I would get our family statue of the Virgin Mary and dress her up in flowers with a flower crown. I would place her on a book and parade around the garden with a sheet tied around me like a robe and in my arms was the flowered Virgin resting ceremoniously on my father's history book. I sang the old may song to her as I paraded with my two bemused cats following me with suitable dignity. "Oh Mary we crown thee with blossoms today, Queen of the Angels and Queen of the May."

And something else followed me, I could feel them. Something that liked what I was doing and sang with me. And that feeling of companionship grew. And it also saved my life many years later when as a teen I was walking through a dark alley and was told by them urgently to run. I ran like the wind. I found out the day after that the Yorkshire Ripper grabbed a student from that alley around the time

13.4. My own discovery of faeries

I was walking through there, and he tortured and killed her. It could have been me.

They began to talk to me, to tell me about the trees and the wind and the horses. None of it was like conversation talk, it was not like talking at all. It was something else. At the time I wrote a poem about them which didn't survive the ravages of time, but one line I can remember from it is "hear the whispers, mumbles and cautions, silent eyes that watch and wait." That was probably the best description that I could give. Wherever I went I could hear them and feel them, and they gave me a knowing.

And they taught me how to talk to birds. My mother knew how to talk to birds and it was not unusual to have a wild blackbird furiously banging on our window in the morning as it looked for my mother.

Since that time I too have tended to birds, both wild and exotic. Some have come to me with terrible injuries and the faeries have always helped me to find the way to treat them and get them better.

When I was in my early twenties, I went through a phase of thinking that my childhood interactions with the faeries was just the imagination of a lonely child. I even went back to my forest as a young adult, just to look and convince myself that it was all in my head. The place, which I called the Blue Lagoon, had seemed to me in my childhood to be a deep wild forest with a beautiful lagoon and some mysterious ruins.

When I returned I found a small patch of woodland with a dirty pond full of trash and the remains of an old house: nothing romantic at all. At that point I stopped putting out food for the faeries (something I had done ever since that wonderful day) and began an inner fight with myself. It didn't last long. And they won.

Faeries are a part of everyday life, particularly if you live out in the country. I lived for a few years on the edge of preserved wilderness in West Montana and faeries really make their presence known there. They come in a variety of shapes and sizes there, some look human whereas others have no human features or shapes at all. I lived near a place where two mountains come together and form a strange-looking canyon. A powerful underground river rushes out from the side of the mountain and falls many feet before it carves a path through the forest and valley.

Working in that area, by the falls, is powerful: the spirits of the land and the Goddess are apparent there. It is on tribally protected land which ensures that there will never be buildings there, and that the spirits of the land will be undisturbed. I went to the falls often and it was my favorite place to do a Faery Realm meditation.

But look around you, even in the city. They are there and would really benefit from contact. Feed them, tend them and tend the birds and animals around you. None of them are pests, they are all creatures in balance.

13.5 Magic, faeries and sex

There is a whole area of work that is about bringing through special beings, be they human, faery or otherwise. It is not written about much as it can be misused and it is a difficult subject to broach. Whenever sex and magic are put together, doors open that can quickly lead a person down silly, dangerous, or just plain stupid roads.

To work with sex and magic, you need to be in a place of maturity, with a sense of responsibility and balance. Believing that sex magic will bring you power, a great sex life, or power over others is a sign that you really should not be doing it. The results of this type of magical work are not about the participants, but for the spirit or door that is being opened by the process. When a couple makes love in a magical way, it can open up major doorways to many worlds to allow a spirit to pass into our world. Pregnancy is not just about human babies: it can be about birthing many things. But like any pregnancy, it carries with it a great deal of responsibility.

In the ancient world, sacred sex with a priestess would make sure the bringing through of a future sacred king: that is, reaching through the worlds to find the soul that is most suitable for the job. Ancient history is littered with tales of special births: babies born that are of a deity and a human, or half faery and half human. And seeing as we already have more humans than we could possibly need on this trashed planet, I will go more into the creating and birthing of faeries rather than anything with human form.

13.5. Magic, faeries and sex

Traditionally, faeries are conceived by two people who make love in a sacred way while the woman is menstruating, and the male is mediating a faery being. It is not that a 'faery ovum' is placed in her womb: it is that the nature of the woman's body as a vessel, coupled with the power of the moonblood and the focused intention/mediation opens a door through which a faery being can step into the outer world from the inner world. It is most certainly not the only way a faery manifests itself, in fact it is probably the rarest way, but it is an interesting way. The faery being takes on some of the human 'personality' and has more of an alignment with the human world than other faery beings.

The being does not have a gestation period, as there is no physical body. But the being will clamour for contact and will ask for a physical window to be made for it to have a more open connection with the human world. This can be achieved by making a model, painting a picture, anything which gives the being eyes and ears to look out of. It uses the statue or painting as a window through which it can better commune with humanity.

This is similar in process to deities and statues/images. The image is made and the consciousness of the being steps into it to use the image as a means of connection. This is not the same as a being that has been trapped or bound into an image or statue or even a person: that is a totally different process that I think is unethical and dangerous. It is used by Tibetans, was used by the ancient Egyptians, and sometimes still happens in various religions around the world.

So the window gives a connection with the world. To break that connection the window must be destroyed. That will not destroy the being, only its tool of connection. So it bodes well to think carefully before you bring something through in this way: like sulky teenagers, they are not so easy to get rid of once birthed.

The urge to do this creation is spurred by an ancient stirring within us to reach back to a time when we were properly connected with faeries, animals, and the land. It is within our nature to be a part of the whole, to be 'in the Garden' and as such we strive both consciously and unconsciously to reconnect somehow, someway.

Particularly earth-based paths have become interested in the idea of sex with faeries, which is a whole minefield in itself. I won't go

13. ACCESSING AND WORKING WITHIN THE FAERY REALM

into it in any detail as I personally feel it can easily become seriously imbalanced and parasitical. If you get the urge to experiment in such a way, I would suggest that you think long and hard about opening your energy levels with a being that you don't know. Would you sleep with a stranger off the street?

Sex is a major opening of power portholes and can enable the person to move quickly and effectively through the worlds, and can open deep powers within ourselves: hence the use of sex with Tantra. But such opening of power can quickly go wrong if there is not a sense of focus, balance and harmony. The person that declares that they sleep with a faery lover because their husband is impotent/ignores them/screws only sheep, is saying that they are happy to sleep with random strangers. Just because the faery being has no body it does not mean that there is not an energy exchange: and under such imbalanced conditions, the chances are that such a union is heavily parasitical.

The rules of health, disease, energy parasites, power surges, and bringing through souls that apply to sex between two humans also apply to human interaction with faeries. So common sense and self-respect are important things to think about.

There are many stories of people who are half faery from mixed unions but how does that work if the faery has no body? Well...When you make love, it opens up the worlds. The purer (and I don't mean moral, I mean spiritually clean...as in no rape/parasite sex, goats or chickens...) the love making, the higher up the Abyss the porthole opens. When you make love as a woman and the man who is making love to you is mediating a faery being, there is a chance that as the porthole opens, it opens on the 'faery' frequency as opposed to the 'human' frequency. This, again, is a method within Tantra (it's not really about bizarre-looking sex positions...). So the child that fruits from such a union has spirit elements of faery as well as human.

Mixed being marriages are talked about in the Old Testament: for example, humans and Titans (ouch...) and there are many lines that flow through humanity today.

Obviously the rule about the porthole also works in reverse: the more degenerate the sex, the more likely a bottom feeder will come through. And that moves onto an important point if you do magic and you have inner ability: having a condom on or being on the pill only stops human babies coming through. The sex act can also bring through many beings that have no physical manifestation: it depends on what is going on in your head (scary thought) when making love in a magical way. The imagination is an extremely powerful tool and if your imagination is used regularly for visionary magic, then it will click into work mode under such power conditions as sex. Hence the biblical saying that if it is in your thoughts, then the deed is already done. That is how magic works.

So back to faeries...if you are used to mediating powers and beings, then that is how you could birth a faery. Just be aware that if you make it, you are responsible for it and you have to learn to live with it/them.

Chapter Fourteen

Polarization: magical dynamics and partnerships

When working with magical beings of any description, eventually the issue of polarity will come into play: we are by nature polarized beings and as such are vulnerable to any imbalance in any direction. Our physical universe is made up of positive and negative, so you would think that as a species we would have got such power dynamics down to a fine art. Wrong! With the advent of monotheism everything else went out of the window as far as western spirituality goes (and also a large chunk of eastern spirituality). That movement, which started in the late Bronze Age, gave us the concepts of good and evil, day and night, and one true god ruling over all (a megalomaniac storm god who gets pissed off easily: yeah, good choice).

Now, such thinking is in itself polarized, right? Well, yes, apart from the all-knowing god, but because the polarization revolves around issues that we are told threaten our souls (bad, evil, Satan) we stay on the side of good, light, god, etc. So we become one end of the pole both spiritually and culturally, which is extremely unhealthy and unbalanced. Polarized 'light/good' power also, by nature of the stresses and tensions in the universe which keeps everything spinning and manifesting, attracts the opposite of the 'good,' 'light' in an attempt to balance itself.

We cannot be one end of a polarized scale as it is unhealthy, and we cannot be unpolarized and be in life: you have to be the fulcrum in the middle, a balance of both ends of the pole, and also a fulcrum between polarity and non-polarity. Is that possible? Well, magically yes it is possible, and it is one of the magical ideals that many strain towards.

14. POLARIZATION: MAGICAL DYNAMICS AND PARTNERSHIPS

For example: if you are looking to work with major power beings, like say, the Barakiel (and make sure you have a bloody good reason to work with these dudes...they are no lightweights), then you have to have a strong and balanced expression within your magical being of polarization, negative and positive: this will strengthen and compliment your physical polarity and in turn will protect your body from the massive impact that can happen when you work in vision with this order of being. They are totally unpolarized: they are unconditional beings of pinpoint consciousness and power i.e. angelic beings. To work safely with them for any length of time or to partake of their power, you must reach and work with their polar opposite i.e. the polarized version of the same power.

This is where the knowledge of working in the Abyss comes in handy, and the knowledge of the beings that inhabit the particular levels of the Abyss is even handier. The Barakiel are a high order of angelic beings that operate within the consciousness of the stars and the lightning: they are bright pinpoint power and must be balanced by something of similar status and quality. The Barakiel are one of the orders of beings traditionally 'one step away from God and held above all others.' So, who do we know who is of angelic consciousness, is bright, close to Divinity and a high level of power while also being of the earth and polarized? Lucifer.

Lucifer, the bright one, Venus, the brightness upon the earth, the light that goes and comes back (dark, light, dark...polarized, not constant) is traditionally about the earth, the land, solidity, sexuality, an angel close to god that is deep within the earth/Underworld.

Note: The casting down story of Lucifer comes from the story of the king of Tire and also the Babylonian king (*Isaiah* 14:12) which in turn comes from an older Canaanite story about the falling of the morning star into the Underworld. The linking of Lucifer to this older myth explained to people why there is a bright angel in the depths of the earth. This brightness is a major power that flows out from the earth, and the angelic consciousness known as Lucifer is the threshold being for it to manifest at the depths. The power itself (which is not Lucifer) is a polarized manifest Divine power that flows out of the land, the opposite of the unmanifest God. In the Near East this power was known as Shekhinah and in Britain was known as Brigh or the Bright one. Both were expressed as feminine.

So, if you work with the being Lucifer, you learn to work with that brightness in a stable polarized way, drawing it right through your body and processing it at a cellular level. This way, when you stand before the Barakiel and ask them to work with you on a task, your body, particularly your endocrine system stays in one piece and you don't end up frying all your nerve endings. (The lightning power that hits the earth is also the lightning power that carries messages around your nervous system)

The other thing to think about is the actions of the beings themselves: the Barakiel are defenders of the innocent, they help victims who are attacked with demonic or other magical power: they are the defenders just as the Irin are the judges. So the Barakiel are probably not good beings to use if you are seeking their power to do dodgy stuff.

The same rules of polarity work in reverse: if you are working a lot with powerful conditional polarized beings, then you need to balance yourself by working with unconditional unpolarized beings like angelic beings. By not doing this, you can fall into the usual trap of becoming unbalanced and you could eventually turn into either a nutter or a not nice sorcerer or both.

This is where the whole thing of demons comes from: they are not bad beings: they are powerful conditional polarized beings who like to push buttons (not unlike we humans). If you are balanced and you stretch in each direction as you work, then their conditionality and perchance for button pushing will not affect you.

But our society is a one sided society that views the world as good and evil and has a religious/cultural pattern that encourages fear whenever power is expressed: if it is from the depths of the Abyss, or a demon, then it must be evil/bad and must be destroyed, or if the person wants to rebel, then the demon is a bad being that the practitioner can use to be 'bad.'

All conditional beings have the capability to be good or bad or indifferent. What we call from them, how we react to them and what we do in conjunction with them will decide whether bad or good comes from them. And then you get into the mire of what is good anyway? Good and bad is relative to what culture you come from and what time you live in. So you have to start to tread carefully as things

14. POLARIZATION: MAGICAL DYNAMICS AND PARTNERSHIPS

are not so black and white: there are many different shades and how we behave influences how other beings will react to us.

Most beings that we would consider demons are an ancient consciousness that we can barely begin to understand. They are dangerous (not evil), seductive, powerful and some are out of place in our everyday physical world, and some have a defined role in our world. But the same can be said of angelic beings: our views are heavily coloured by our cultural programming.

So in practical terms, how to you keep the balance?

The basic simmered-down version is: if you are working with conditional polarized beings that are powerful, then do some opposite work to balance it out: connect with unconditional beings also. So if you are working with ancient gods, demonic beings, old ancestors, deeper faery beings etc., then do some angelic work or star power work to balance yourself.

If you have to work a lot with angelic beings or formless power, then balance it out with Underworld beings of the same level of power, or with elemental beings, faeries, etc. Your body will tell you what you are doing wrong: the thyroid often reacts to the surges of unbalanced power (along with the hypothalamus) and the practitioner ends up with either a dead metabolism or a sky high fast metabolism with added OCD.

It is like body building: too much bulky short muscle can look impressive but you cant really do much with it, just as someone who doesn't do anything at all has no muscle tone: the body and spirit need a little of everything to bring about balance, learning and strength.

14.1 Polarity within magical partnerships

Working magically in a partnership can be a wonderful and powerfully rewarding way to do magic. However, like all partnerships and relationships, it can be fraught with potholes, tripwires and the odd smack over the head with a 2 by 4.

When you have worked alone magically for any length of time, you begin to realize that there is a wide section of magic that really needs to be done with a member of the opposite sex. The need

14.1. Polarity within magical partnerships

for opposition is not about sexual preference, it's about the actual physicality of the human body. The way that a female body is put together ensures that it can handle certain types of power regardless of the sexual preference. The same goes for men: it is about the physical filter, the body, not the sexuality.

But one of the side issues that comes into play quickly when talking about magical partners is the use of power and how it affects the people around us. When you work with a power exchange, it creates a powerful bond between the priest and priestess: it is a conversation that becomes, by its nature, intense and intimate. That is not to say it becomes physically sexual, our bodies can interpret the energy as sexual, when in fact it is a conversation of energy.

For this reason, before any magical work is embarked upon, the actual relationship with the priest or priestess needs to be looked at carefully, and what the implications would be for people on the periphery. This is why some of the most powerful magical working relationships are between couples. If a priest and priestess are working at a deep energetic level, and they are not partnered in a relationship, a bit of a tangle can develop.

The spouse or long-term partner of the priest or priestess can sometimes pick up on the power exchange and respond subconsciously at a deep level by pulling away from the depth of intimacy as a self-preservation mechanism. And because it is not about sex, the dynamics become confusing for the non-working partner, and can create disharmony within the relationship that cannot easily be addressed. Nothing wrong is being done, but still the non-working partner feels uncomfortable at an instinctive level.

If the priest and priestess are also married, that takes away one bag of worms but opens another, much deeper bag of issues that would need to be harmonized for successful long-term work to occur. The first hurdle, particularly if both priest and priestess are strong magically and also have strong personalities, is the one of hierarchy. If they truly honor and respect the qualities of the other partner, and are prepared to make up any shortfall, then this level of problems will not occur.

Unfortunately this is the first stage of collapse that powerful magic usually initiates: when working with true magical power at any depth,

14. POLARIZATION: MAGICAL DYNAMICS AND PARTNERSHIPS

the first thing it will do is highlight weaknesses, prod issues and open cracks. Magic is like water: it will find the weakest part in the wall to come through. That is why, when working with high levels of power, you need to be clear, balanced and have your act together, otherwise it will slowly destroy or degenerate you.

What can happen is that as the power starts to build over months or years, one or both of the partners begins to become glamorized by the power (messiah syndrome) and starts to look down on the other partner. This was common in the last generation where historically, the men at the forefront of magic treated their partners like shit. They would become famous names and the wife/priestess would be pushed behind the screen.

This became more apparent with the advent of commercial workshops (the Company of Hawkwood, for example): suddenly the priest magician was exposed to many more people than the habitual little local group and they were worshipped like gods. The partners, although magical equals, were pushed into the shadows which immediately damages the harmony of the power exchange. It was not all male priests that behaved this way, it also happened publicly with female esotericists.

Such a problem can be sidestepped by equally sharing the work both privately and publicly, and if one partner is working silently in a group setting, upholding the power for example, or mediating the contacts, then such work is publicly acknowledged. In private, the problem can be sidestepped by power sharing: taking specific responsibility for certain parts of the magic, and taking the time to step back and allow the other partner to forge on with the work. At an everyday level, such dynamics can be mirrored, which truly enhances the magical dynamic.

This is something that equal rights action has actually damaged: if everyone is supposed perform the same function then everything becomes a mess and a power struggle. Some women in New Age and magical communities see attacking men and making them feel inadequate as part and parcel of the 'Goddess' movement. It isn't. It just creates resentment. The same goes for magical communities in which men treat women as subservient: it's wrong, it's unhealthy and it doesn't make for good magic.

14.1. Polarity within magical partnerships

Having specific areas in magic and life where one partner excels, and areas within magic and life where the other partner excels, creates a harmonic situation where both parties hold power, and both parties learn to also yield power to the other. The partnership, from a magical point of view, becomes an octave of the scales: both sides are equal in their inequality.

So, having survived the first hurdles, the priest and priestess then really get down to the intricacies of polarity and how it works. The early and interesting form of polarized energy exchange is the load share in the buildup to a piece of work.

When a powerful magical working is planned, from the moment the time and date is set, the inner side of the magic begins to work. The energies are beginning to stretch out and will start to affect the partners in various ways. This is where the necessity for male and female bodies comes in: the different bodies bring in and hold power in different ways.

Because of a woman's womb, she can hold and grow power within her to quite a high level. Men can bring through the catalyst that triggers the power within the woman to go from dormant to active: thus magic is born. In a practical sense this can create temporary issues (or sometimes a holocaust!) in the home while the magic is being 'cooked.'

Of course, there are always the exceptions to this scenario: men who hold and cook power and women who bring through strong sudden energy bursts.

Once the power is released within the working environment, it is woven between the partners as a power sharing activity. While ever the couple keep the understanding that they are working as a composite being, then the magic will work through them in a more or less balanced way depending on what you are doing. Should one or both parties begin to tiptoe down the road of ego, then a power struggle will ensue and the partnership will possibly begin the downhill slide toward destruction unless they realize what they are doing and pull back.

That downhill plunge is usually brought about by lack of respect for the other partner, or an inflated sense of self-importance brought about by imbalanced working practice. The other thing that a couple

14. POLARIZATION: MAGICAL DYNAMICS AND PARTNERSHIPS

should be aware of is that such disharmony can come about if they are being messed with by beings who don't want such a partnership in action. This usually happens when the couple is working in the field of parasite removal or exorcism: it's the grimiest, hardest and most dangerous side of esoteric service work, so usually couples who work in this field tend to be pretty well versed in such issues.

If a couple is striking out in that field for the first time, it is important for them to know that this is a major feature of the operational problems for that line of work. Major grounding, common sense and balancing work is needed on a regular basis to keep the energy and polarity balanced and healthy.

The interesting feature of polarity work is how the two bodies distribute the burden of power, often without conscious thought or decision. Upon the commencement of a line of work, each partner will begin to manifest some expression of the buildup of power. It is important to recognize this as soon as possible for what it is and take steps to work with the buildup rather than struggle against it. However the buildup manifests will give a clue about how to handle it. The skill is handling the buildup without dispersing it.

A version of this still lingers on in old esoteric circles where it is considered bad to have sex before a ritual: the energy is leeched off by the sex act leaving the priest drained of energy that was needed for the work.

Nature is often a good balancer and walking out in the forest, on the moors, or by the sea if it is possible is a good way to balance out when there is a power build up. Creative expression is another way, as is gardening, planting, making things with your hands: all are ways that any power buildup can be handled along with plenty of rest. It is all a matter of finding the action that will not take the power away from the magic, but will stop it blowing your head off (or killing each other) before the magic is completed.

Each partner will carry a certain load and it is not always a fair distribution: it is what is needful for the work. Sometimes one partner will be weighed down to the point of exhaustion with the burden of the power, while the other one is left relatively untouched. In this circumstance it is important that the energetic partner tends and cares for the burdened partner: the energy dynamic will switch

14.1. Polarity within magical partnerships

around and the longer the couple works together the more complex and interesting it will become.

For example if one partner has a chronic illness and there is some power building, the power will go to which ever partner needs to be processing that power for work. If it happens to be the ill partner, then the other partner will often take on the burden of illness symptoms, leaving the ill partner free of symptoms and able to do the power carrying that is needed.

Such energy swapping is fascinating and really calls into question the nature of boundaries and how energy actually works; and it opens out the possibility for chronic illness to be load-shared between people.

All of these dynamics are dependent on the basic respect, honour and care that each partner gives to the other. With such a partnership, the potential for great and powerful magic is limitless: polarity when used correctly can create a whole new level of consciousness that could potentially take us as a generation onto the next step of magical development.

Chapter Fifteen

The physical implications of practising magic

If you spend a lot of time doing inner work or working in the inner realms, then sooner or later you are going to feel the impact of such work. When you work in realms that are close to our realm, the impact can be minimal or even positive: what is close to ourselves (i.e. ritual and outer court magic) takes little energy and has little impact upon the body and mind. The further away from your own realm you stretch, the harsher the impact on the human body.

In past times in the magical community, much more ritual/outer court work was done than visionary/inner work, and this acted as ballast to ground and root the magician. It then began to devolve into an almost exclusive use of outer court action (ritual, talismanic magic, scrying, etc. In more modern times (i.e. in the last century), more vision was used but in a lot of cases it was psychological pathworking, or visualizations that were constructed from a psychological base and which did not stretch out of the self: hence they had no impact and a therapeutic outcome.

Some magical lodges used astral travel with a limited core of the group: the Golden Dawn Sphere group was a classic example. The only problem with this is that the inner connections are channeled through a small number of people who then wield the power and it creates an imbalance in general within the initiates. (It is only balanced when all do outer and inner work.) This dynamic alone can blast apart a magical lodge regardless of the other issues or problems that are so common in magical groups.

But some magicians realized the potential of using inner visions more often and at greater depth: they had major results and magic leapt forward another notch on the evolutionary scale. Instead of

15. THE PHYSICAL IMPLICATIONS OF PRACTISING MAGIC

a long preparation, complex seals/ritual and incantations to finally bring the consciousness of an angelic or demonic being to them in the physical realm, magicians realized they could go through a variety of stages in vision to come face-to-face with an angelic being and have a conversation with it. This development unknowingly brought with it an impact both on the magician and the environment around them.

One modernish magician who worked ceaselessly to develop this method and used it at length during the Second World War was Dion Fortune. She worked tirelessly in ritual and vision to keep back the magical inroads the Germans were trying to make into Britain, blocking their powers and invoking the ancient warriors of the sacred land of Britain to defend the realm. She paid for such work with her life.

Intense inner work is processed through the endocrine system and through the immune system. Too much deep work too often, without the right protections, rests, or supports, will eventually collapse the system, leaving the magician burned out and chronically exhausted. The other major problem that can affect magicians is the impact and infestation of unhealthy beings if the magician is working at any great depth in the Abyss: the infestation becomes physical and mental if precautions are not taken in the work.

15.1 Treating impacts

Sometimes working at depth either deep in the past, deep in the Abyss or far out with or within Archangelic beings is necessary, and if this is done frequently the impact will show by exhaustion, depression, brain fog, and muscle aches. Such work, particularly if it is frequent, will drain the body's vital energy leaving little left for the proper running of everyday functions.

Homeopathy is one effective way of coping with magical impact and if used correctly can usually divert most impact to the outer organs like the skin, and drive the body to refuel in a healthy way (food and sleep).

Now before you go rushing off to the shops to buy a homeopathy book, one thing to think about is that when you do a lot of magic, it changes how your body responds to deep and subtle

15.1. Treating impacts

powers. Homeopathy, cranial osteopathy and similar treatments are processed differently by a body that has become accustomed to power so the usual remedy pictures and indications have no meaning and cannot be used. The substance choice has to be more poetically and magically approached. (Which is why magicians of times past would study alchemy.)

Some research is often necessary to look into various substances from a magical point of view: the magician is led down the path of the alchemist. It becomes handy to learn about transformation through substance catalysts, the 'personality' of substance, and also about the magical history of substances.

For example, when inner impact or an inner porthole is staying open and affecting the body, homeopathic potencies of nitric acid can often close the contact down. Where violence or demonic power is coming through and cannot be closed off, homeopathic stramonium can sometimes help the body to calm down. When a serious blast of inner power hits, usually during attack, the homeopathic sarcodes of Pineal and Pituitary at 30c or 1M will buffer the impact.

But in a longer term scenario, it is important to know how to look after the body while it is under magical stress, and how to monitor the body so that you are alerted quickly if something is going wrong. Often magical impact will mirror illness to the point of serious physical symptoms, but when it has become so entrenched in the body, the chances are that long-term damage has already been done.

The endocrine system is the first threshold of impact, so there you would watch closely to monitor any changes that are going to escalate. In women, one of the first changes to occur is disturbance in the menstrual cycle: the cycle of bleeding starts to time in with the powerful workings rather than with the natural rhythms of the body. In both men and women, variation in sex drive is a common thing to appear. Then the appetite becomes disturbed along with the regularity of digestion and a change in sleep patterns.

The use of herbs can also be useful in supporting a hardworking magician, especially ones grown and harvested by yourself: you gain a working relationship with the plants and by communicating with them, you can begin to understand the deeper qualities of the plant, and what it can offer you. Shamanic magicians have used plants for centuries not only to protect and heal them, but to assist in visions if it is needed: not everyone has instant or easily accessible inner sight.

Magic can do many strange things to the body, it can also manifest certain powers that impact your body in the same way a toxic substance would. For instance, if you are working a lot with a power like Mithraism, or Apollo, or any major solar male deity, then eventually the body will begin to manifest the symptoms of gold toxicity. Such details can be easily passed by these days as most people are not aware of the pictures of metal toxicity: our everyday environment does not usually expose us to such things. And again, it becomes apparent that a form of alchemy is needed for a serious magician: you need to know the properties of gold, mercury, lead, silver, the various acids, and the numerous poisonous power plants.

In the case of gold toxicity from overworking with the solar powers, you would first look at homeopathic gold: Aurum Met is a interesting remedy from a magical point of view.

When looking at these substances for magical treatment, it is important to look at the mental and emotional pictures of the remedies as this is where the damage is usually most obvious when the imbalance comes from magic. Similarly with herbs and flower essences, the mental/emotive picture tells the largest tale of where the power is doing damage. It is common when a person begins to connect to certain streams of power, for the imbalanced form of that power to begin to express itself through their mental/emotional imbalance: this is where the gurus, messiahs, and 'senior most high magi' are born.

15.2 Working with balance

Avoiding such imbalances is usually the best way forward, and that can be achieved by pacing the work and spreading out the power across a variety of working methods. Ritual, vision, seeing, recitation, meditation and hands-on power transfer are all methods that can be used to achieve a certain goal. Using any one of these methods a lot can cause an imbalance and if one single method is used in excess it can cause illness, and sometimes severe illness.

15.2. Working with balance

Another dynamic that is interesting which can help to redress the balance of power is the use of completely exteriorized magic: a physical action with intent, when done by a magician who is heavily versed in visionary magic, can become powerful without much energetic impact. For years I could not figure out how this actually worked, I just knew that it did.

Eventually it became apparent that a magical worker who had connected in depth throughout the inner realms for a good length of time became 'connected' to an extensive collective of power and consciousness. When a magician did a simple physical action with magical intent, all the power of the collective flowed through the action.

If the connection to the inner collective is not there or established strongly enough, then the physical action does nothing. This then explained to me why all the writings from the sixteenth and seventeenth centuries on ritual, sigil and talismanic magic didn't work well in most instances: it didn't fail because the magic doesn't work, it would fail the magician didn't have the inner connections and power. By not publishing that fact it kept the practical application of power in the hands of those ready for it. Without inner power, it became a meaningless jumble of shapes and words.

If you have a lot of work that must be done, share it out with a partner (or group) if that is possible. Change your working methods frequently and balance out the methods you use so that intense inner work is balanced by externalized ritual. Take frequent salt baths and keep your working area and rest area clean, clear and balanced so that you do not have to deal with any little nasties anywhere.

If you work a lot on vision, vary the realms that you work in and the beings that you work with: don't become a stuck record or it will carve a groove in you that could damage you. It is also more fun to work with a variety of beings and it keeps the work fresh. It also makes it harder for other people to tap into your work or to interfere with it: being predictable is never good!

If you have to spend a lot of time swimming around in the depths of the Abyss, make sure you also do some lighter work like faery work to balance the load: it's all about spreading out in a harmonious way. If you do a lot of angelic work, then do some ancestral work to

15. The physical implications of practising magic

counter it. Failing that, a six pack of Guinness, the movie Hellboy, a large bar of chocolate and some good tobacco will do the trick.

Another thing to consider if you are doing tons of inner work is to get out on the land and recharge your batteries in nature. Working with animals, growing things, walking, swimming, anything outside and not man made will refill you and start you back on the path to balance. Lying on stones or on the earth is good for grounding and the sun can work wonders in cleaning you off (unless you live in Arizona, in which case it will just crisp you).

15.3 Food

What you eat is also important and can aid or prevent you from doing your job. If you eat a lot of toxic junk then of course your body will be in no state to do any sort of deep work for too long without it beginning to show. If you are young you can get away with it for a while, but as you get older, the ability to shrug off such poison begins to diminish and the toxic waste begins to pile up. The deeper the inner work, the more your body will react to the toxins and the sooner it will show the damage.

Working for lengths of time in deeper realms is like mountain climbing: you have to be fit, healthy and look after yourself to survive it. What you eat is the starting point to your health and what work you do defines what you can eat or not. If you want deep sensitivity in most realms and a high level of sight, then you will have more success if you are vegetarian or vegan. Meat is an anchor, it lowers your frequency and ties you closer to earth: it is perfect for you is you are a healer or you work out with the public a lot. It creates a barrier that stops certain powers from seeing you and it can help to give you ballast if you work pulling out parasites.

If however you spend a lot of your time chasing demons, conversing with angelic powers or Abyss diving, then meat can sometimes become a liability. In some cases it blocks your ability to work with these beings or even to see them, or for them to see you. It can also become a problem if it is not clean meat: if it has a lot of toxicity in the muscle fiber and also a lot of fear hormones released from suffering before its death, those hormones will play havoc with your adrenals and also affect how your energy is perceived on the inner. Wild hunted meat is the cleanest for magicians if you do eat meat. If you do not have access to that type of meat, try to find a local farm that sells its own meat.

The liability comes in when you are dealing with polarized beings and you are holding within you the flesh of a being that has gone through profound suffering before you ate it: you will appear to the beings around you as a form of monster. It's not about morals, ethics or anything like that: it's about working practice, tools and common sense.

I eat meat when I am doing certain types of work. Most of the time I do not eat meat because I work at depths where such a diet is not helpful, it blocks my sight and stops me getting into certain realms. I have no problem shooting, killing, skinning and eating an animal: it is good to know your food, know where it came from and what it truly is. And when I have to live in a city or work on a lot of people, then I need meat otherwise I would get eaten alive by every parasite going.

The other thing that can be interesting as part of your health regime is your water: recitation over water before you drink it is an old and powerful concept. The water absorbs the sacred power of the word and then you take it into yourself as nourishment. Again it is a strange form of alchemy: by using recitation you change the quality and power of the water, and as you take it into yourself, it changes you also.

15.4 Practicalities while working

When you are working, first make sure your working space is balanced, clear and ready for work. Whatever element you are working with, make sure it is also 'clean': water should be drawn from a river/spring or at least filtered, a flame should come from wood: matches where possible and not directly from a lighter, etc. and the candle should be simple, not perfumed or shaped like a being/person/hippo. Be aware of your directions and what is coming from those directions. Don't have power objects in the room if you do not work with them or you do not know what they are or what they

15. THE PHYSICAL IMPLICATIONS OF PRACTISING MAGIC

do. Also be aware that if you are doing deep magic and you have an object in your working space that is not compatible with your brand of magic, you can end up with an agitated energy in your room. For example if you are working in an esoteric Kabbalistic format, don't have a statue of Kali in your working space as the two don't magically mix well.

If you do bring magical objects into your working space, make sure that you fully understand what beings are in them, not just what they represent. Some tourist objects can represent one deity (like Ganesha, Kali, Shiva, etc. but can actually be holding a spirit from the local area where it was made, and the spirit will probably not have anything directly to do with the deity.

If you buy such an object, it is a good idea to magically strip it first. Or, if you want to work with that deity, strip the object and then put the deity in it yourself. The only time you do not need to do that is when the object has been properly tuned and used magically or spiritually. Some deity statues are blessed in temples and antique ones can often be enlivened with the deity form or personality. In this case just be aware that it brings that power through, and make sure that is compatible with whatever else you are working with, otherwise you might end up with a war in your workroom!

The other thing to watch out for, if you are working at any depth in the Abyss, is not to have objects that represent humans, spirits or animals in your workroom. A stray power can take up residence quietly if you are not observant with your sealing work, and you could end up with more than you bargained for in the cute fluffy teddy that is on your shelf. If the object has eyes, ears etc., the being can use that representation to move through and cause havoc. (Sometimes these powers get bored and think it's funny to move into a statue, doll or soft toy and annoy you.) I'm sure that anyone who has done any length of time as an exorcist will have come across a mask, statue or doll that has a little 'something' in it that is causing problems for someone.

Prepare your working space by the use of sound if you are going to be doing heavy work. Certain types of music and voice are superb at flattening spaces and preparing them for deep work. Chants, drums etc. are all sounds that affect the space and can create an energy that can make the work easier.

After you have finished working, close your work properly and then go have a bath and something to eat. Taking a bath with salt in it removes any stray energy that is around you, and food grounds you.

Above all, learn to listen to your body and respond to what it is trying to tell you. There is too much machismo in our society these days: people are expected to shrug everything off and are considered sissies if they look after themselves. That is a ignorant way of working: you last a lot longer and look good for a much longer time if you listen to and care of your body.

15.5 The effects of inner contact on the endocrine system

For a while I spent a great deal of time working in small experienced groups, pushing the boundaries of visionary magic from its then limited scope in the magical field. During the 80s and early 90s, visionary work was either approached from a psychological point of view, or was approached magically through long, drawn-out, prewritten scripts that were designed to guide the initiate through inner ritual paths and bore the shit out of them. Having said this, I have since learned that to take someone deeply into a place, or to approach a deep level of consciousness, a long, drawn-out path can sometimes stretch the consciousness of a practitioner and can facilitate a deeper contact.

I wanted to approach the work in a different way. I wanted the visionary work to reflect the reality and immediacy of stretching the consciousness from one world to another without allowing the imagination to 'play' in the psychological realm. This meant that I had to work only with practitioners that had enough internal discipline and experience to know the difference between real and imaginary contacts, and to work in uncharted territory.

One of the things that we all immediately noticed was that our bodies were preparing for the work a few days before. People began to get hungry and tired about 3 days before the work (the magical

15. THE PHYSICAL IMPLICATIONS OF PRACTISING MAGIC

tide going out). The day before the workings, women were beginning to bleed regardless of where they were on their cycle. This was of particular interest to me as it signaled that the female hormone cycle was directly involved in the distribution of power in a magical working.

This in turn raised questions about why the menstrual cycle was considered to be 'unclean' by the monotheistic religions (whereas the pre-Christian Celtic culture used the menstrual cycle as a power base for battle and magic). Did the 'unclean' status deflect attention from the power available to women at certain times of their cycle? In such cases, the power would be suppressed which in turn would force an unhealthy outlet for that power: pre-menstrual strain, tension, and rage. Anyhow, that is another topic altogether.

The morning of the first working day, everyone felt a massive inrush of energy ready for working. After the two-day working sessions, everyone would independently experience a serious slump to the point where most practitioners were unable to go to work at their day jobs the following day. The body was reacting as though it had worked physically hard for two days, even though the majority of the time people spent the day sat in a chair.

The first thing I noticed with myself and my fellow coworkers was that we had begun to react to certain substances and foods. Our bodies were becoming intolerant of minor depressants and stimulants. The deeper we worked, the more sensitive we became. Mediating a consciousness was also creating a 'burnout' situation throughout the endocrine system. The higher the level of being that was contacted or mediated, the harder the impact was upon the hypothalamus, thyroid and adrenals. The effect was a massive slowing of the metabolism, increase of appetite, increased need for sleep: the body acted as if it had severe prolonged fatigue. When the work was continued over months, muscle fatigue set in with a pattern that mimicked chronic fatigue. If the work undertaken was new, or was visions that had not been worked with for generations, then the physical impact was at a maximum. If the work was current or recent (last two thousand years) then the impact was minimal.

One of the interesting asides is that if the work included high-powered angelic/Tree of Life work, some people experienced burning

15.5. The effects of inner contact on the endocrine system

sensations and reddened skin. I did find, after about a year of this, that coffee, which is a power substance, would lessen the contact a lot and relieve the pressure on the body. The more coffee was drunk, the less the power impacted the body.

I started to track the effects of substances on the body using tarot. My reasoning was that if tarot (which I had been using since my early teens) showed the patterns of possible future paths, then it could show patterns of present paths within the body and where those present paths could lead. I devised a layout that was specific to the human body so that I could pinpoint the source of effects and the likely future pattern that the body would take from that substance.

To make sure that the system worked, I teamed up with a medical doctor[1] who was also familiar with magic. I tested the deck layout by looking at patients. She gave her patients a number and I had to read the body picture of that 'number.' The body picture was compared to the medical notes to see how accurate the deck reading was.

Over a period of time, what became clear from the readings and the actual bodily reactions of the magical workers is that the immune system via the thymus was being affected, as was the hypothalamus.

The immune system was kicking in and reacting to certain types of inner contacts as if they were bacteria or viruses. The primary immune system was not kicking in, therefore there was no sneezing or coughing. But the deeper immune reaction was surfacing in the form of fevers and inflammation. This was causing the weaker members of the groups to drop out.

It was noted that the body changed how it reacted to things. Most people became much more sensitive to allergens and medicines, and much more reactive to homeopathy. It was also noted by most members of the groups that the work seemed somehow to blur the boundaries of the body. This was a most bizarre situation in which a magical worker was inheriting or acquiring another person's physical symptoms: in their families, if someone was ill, the symptoms would move from the sick person to the magical worker if they were in close

---

[1] She was a DO, a doctor of osteopathy. In the USA, DOs do the usual medical training of a doctor plus extra osteopathic training. She had also completed an extra two years of cranial training.

15. THE PHYSICAL IMPLICATIONS OF PRACTISING MAGIC

proximity. The sick person would have a temporary reprieve. This was not done intentionally and in fact started to become a problem.

Using the deck, we worked out ways that this process could be blocked, but these didn't always work. We also found that you could work on one person to cause an effect in the other person, raising intriguing questions about the nature of illness and symptoms.

The initial impact upon the body seemed to be slowing of the metabolism. The body seemed to literally 'chunk up' in preparation for work, a cycle of work, or an impact.

Then an inrush of energy would accompany the work to the point where the thyroid seemed to go into overdrive. People working would experience a high level of energy, a lowered appetite, needed less sleep, would urinate more, and would be able to operate, think and process quickly. People would also have a sense of being 'hot' and/or burning, but this was not reflected in actual body temperature which stayed pretty stable.

Twenty-four hours after the working, the body's system would appear to crash. Temperature and blood pressure would drop, the person would need lots of sleep, and they would feel bruised and disorientated. They would feel cold, hungry and tired. Their hair would go dull and the person would seem to age. The reaction was as if the thyroid had slowed right down. It would take a week for the system to right itself.

Longer-term effects seemed to occur mainly in women and manifested as menstrual abnormalities, mood swings and thyroid dysfunction. The effects in people who were doing major work only two or three times a year seemed minimal, and in the longer term seemed to be beneficial. So there is also an issue of timing: space your workings out and basically do not do too much.

It was interesting to watch people over the span of fifteen years and see the long-term effects of the work and how it shifted their consciousness in a beneficial way.

Doing heavier work too many times did seem to have a chronic inflammatory effect upon the body. And people who had minor physical problems did experience a major flare-up of their conditions (asthma, IBS, etc.) if they did not approach the work correctly.

15.5. The effects of inner contact on the endocrine system

Longer-term patterns seemed to be more pronounced in women than in men. Men had a much lower reaction to the work than women did.

What I found interesting, though I have no idea how something like this could be looked at scientifically, was that people who had mental issues (depression, mental illness, OCD, etc.) did not last beyond a couple of hours into the work. They would feel physically (not mentally) sick and would often begin coughing terribly or would become nauseous.

What also became obvious, and this happened a lot, mainly to men, was that when the level of power went right up, a small number of people became emotional. Some became weepy or passive-aggressive (mainly women) and some became hostile or difficult (mainly men). Although interestingly in people with Celtic descent, the pattern seemed to reverse, which was weird and may have just been a hiccup...but that would make a fascinating study all on its own...the DNA determination about how a body reacts to power.

All of this was really interesting to observe because, after watching this a few times, I realized that they were reverting to childhood, mainly teenage patterns of behaviour, which took me back to the deck to look at the hypothalamus. Up to that point I have been looking at the thyroid, the adrenals and the thymus. When I realized that the endocrine system was freaking out in all directions I tracked it back to the hypothalamus.

The repeated picture was that as power flowed through the inner landscape and reached the body at a tissue level, it seemed to flow first through the hypothalamus which in turn affected every other gland in the body.

I treated people with a hypothalamus sarcode at 50M (when the symptoms were triggered by inner power, it needed a dose comparable with the inner power levels) level which gave a relief of symptoms temporarily but it didn't last more than a week. I also learned that the effects on the body were increased tremendously if they were thin. It would seem to put their system into freefall, with the blood pressure dropping dramatically and the thyroid then swinging from fast to slow.

If the person put on some weight, i.e. ballast, they seemed to stabilize better. The conclusion I came to was that high levels of

15. The physical implications of practising magic

work need only be approached sparingly, like a catalyst, and then subsequent work to follow up is done at a much lower level over a longer period of a time. That way, the body gets a healthy balance and in the longer term truly benefits from the work.

15.6 The future

Magical practice is speeding up along with our culture, consciousness and cars. If we wish to really push the boundaries of the Inner Worlds beyond what has been done in the last few hundred years, then we need to make sure that our bodies are suitably prepared and up to speed for such a burden.

Magical practice and knowing when not to do magic, diet, living conditions, body types, relationships and location all play their part and I feel that we are on a threshold of some extremely interesting times (unless all the dippy New Agers have their way in which case we all go poof in 2012). If we and the next few generations get it right, we could truly push the inner boundaries in a massive leap of magical evolution. It is up to us.

It is time to move away from the psychological structure of magic that was so beloved of those who working in the early twentieth century, and revisit some of the much older (Renaissance) approaches to magic, operating in a much more holistic way that includes practical alchemy, medicine, herbalism, astronomy, theology, anatomy, science, art and music.

Some new commercial magical books/systems do touch upon such things, but often under the veil of 'hidden wisdoms and secrets,' or misinterpreted or badly paraphrased text. Getting your range of knowledge on such subjects is best achieved by studying in-depth texts written by people who are well-versed or specialized in their particular subject matter.

A magical library should have, besides all the usual magical writings, a good selection of anatomy and physiology books, homeopathic *matera medica*, extensive herbal reference books, lots of ancient history, a good bible (Douay Rheims) and apocrypha, a concordance, elemental tables, basic geology, physics and geometry reference books, archaeology, historical and classical mythology, chemical tables, music theory and a good history of art book.

This way you are able to reference and source a lot of what is written about in magic. It brings a deeper understanding about what you are actually experiencing and where that experience is coming from. Some modern commercial magical books have 'facts' within them about history, mythology, medicine, etc. that are either misunderstood or taken out of context to fit an uneducated pet theory of the writer. As a classical education becomes less and less common, it is easier for such writers to get away with that type of behaviour.

The other sin that seems to happen a lot these days is plagiarism in the form of one generation of magical writers 'lifting' work from a couple of generations ago when such writing was a little more obscure. If you are well read, there is much less chance of you being taken in by such charlatans. With modern magical writers, always check their sources and do not be afraid to respectfully challenge them on their work and expect a coherent response. If they get hostile or defensive, that should be a really good sign that something is wrong. If they say they cannot discuss it because its secret, then they are highly likely to be full of shit.

Some magical writers feel that they have to give a history or source for their work when it actually comes from an inner source that they cannot identify. This is a difficult situation for them, as most people these days want to know about lineage, masters, etc. They are tempted to make up a source and end up getting themselves in a mess. My opinion in this matter is, if it works and it is balanced, then it doesn't matter if Mickey Mouse taught it to them. It always goes back to commercialism versus free work: if it is work that is done because it is right to do it and money is not part of the equation, then the work will be done and people who want a famous line of magicians can go look in the commercial glamour department. That leaves the serious workers to get on with magic that needs doing as opposed to magic that sells.

Chapter Sixteen

Inner landscapes of the people and the land

When you get into the depths of a person's spirit, you trip across what is known as the 'inner landscape.' This appears in the deep consciousness of the person as a landscape which reflects their physical and spiritual health. It is not imagined by the person and often people are not aware of them, but a person's mental, spiritual and physical health can be assessed and approached using this interface with the inner person.

Similarly, when you go into an inner landscape of the land, you can often see deeper issues that are affecting the land that are not obvious on the surface. Here you begin to see parallels between the human body and the land itself: they are octaves of each other and are constantly interacting.

Why is a human landscape a 'landscape' and not a body? I have absolutely no idea. All that I know is that when you go in, it is a landscape that you come across, not an inner body. I once got into cautious discussion with an osteopathic doctor about seeing this 'landscape' in a young person I had been working on.

In the USA, osteopaths are fully qualified doctors trained in hospitals/universities. I nearly fell over when she said that she had also seen such a thing and worked with it regularly in the course of her practice as a cranial osteopath.

When I first discovered the inner landscape, it was totally by accident, and happened while I was working on someone using vision. I saw a door in the brain and had to go in to see what was there. I found myself in a room full of boxes and filing cabinets, with piles of papers, bags and general mess. I started to clean it up and let some

16. INNER LANDSCAPES OF THE PEOPLE AND THE LAND

light in through the window. The chaos in this place reflected the character of the person I was working on.

A month later, I was working on them again and when I went back into this room that I had found, I saw grass trying to grow through the concrete floor and trees trying to get in the window. I figured that nature was probably better for a body, so I tore down the building and let nature in. A few weeks later when I went in, I found sparse, harsh moorland and a cold wind. The person I was working on was someone with heavy mental problems who was a sociopath. The work was having a curious effect, and the person began to get urges to spend more time out in nature, which I took to be a good thing.

So I became a landscape junkie and had to look at everyone's and anyone's. The next foray into a landscape was on a young girl with growth issues. When I got into her landscape I found a beautiful meadow, a river and lots of pretty flowers. But in the corner was a dark place where nothing grew, and there was a little girl huddled into the corner weeping. I was horrified by the pain this child carried.

I gently picked her up and laid her in the meadow with all the flowers, and then I went back to the dark place to try and lighten it. I could not trigger any change, so I bricked it up and planted roses around the wall so that the darkness could not come back. While I was doing this vision, the young girl whom I was treating, who was partially asleep, began to cry. I didn't wake her, but let her weep while I worked.

The effect was amazing: her growth issue suddenly wasn't an issue and she made major leaps both physically and mentally in the following months. I realized that what I was working with was powerful, it worked, and I needed to know more about it. I discovered that the weather in the landscape often reflected the short-term health of the immune system: if it was storming, then chances are they were about to come down with a virus.

If there were emotional problems, it would often show by overgrowth or lack of foliage, and if there were mental (i.e. chemical) problems, it would show by the appearance of man-made structures. Magical and psychic attacks showed by beings wandering around the landscape, or the appearance of shapes like Platonic solids. I was fascinated and worked hard taking things out, gardening, weather watching, etc. on anyone I worked on.

But after a couple of years of doing this work I began to notice something about the people I had worked on. When I got close to them, I got a feeling that I had intruded on something that was not supposed to be intruded upon.

I began to look deeper at these people from a magical sense and I began to realize that by dealing with major issues in their landscape, I had trodden their learning path for them: I had preempted the fate lessons they needed to tackle for themselves. Remember the sociopath with the filing cabinets? I now know, years later, that those files and boxes were blocking and containing unhealthy power so that the person could not access them. Reawakening the harsh landscape gave them access to a dark power, which they went onto wield mercilessly and aggressively. Their inner landscape had cluttered up and isolated that power until that person was ready to face it themselves. I had stupidly and arrogantly sidestepped a natural process.

There were only a few instances where I got a strong sense that I had stepped in and worked where someone was just too exhausted to deal with something: this was usually where they had been magically attacked by someone and were not able to cope with it.

In those instances I learned a great deal about magical attacks and what they looked like from an inner point of view. I was looking at them from an inner angle that I hadn't perceived before. It looked different from the 'inner' sight of the attack I was used to looking at. I then realized I was seeing the attack in its 'backroom' sense: I was seeing the actual construction behind the frontage, the nuts and bolts of the creation. This in turn gave me far more information that I needed to dismantle such attacks.

I learned eventually that if the landscape was not being affected by magic, but by illness, fate or a natural process, not to plough in and change it, but to stand, observe, and learn what I could from what I saw. It seemed okay to occasionally talk to the person in their landscape, to offer advice but not to take action. It gave me a much deeper insight to the person's issues, illnesses and mental states. It also told me a great deal about their spirituality: their soul was often reflected in the flowers.

Many things appeared in the landscape before they appeared in the body or mind, so it became a good indicator of what was coming and what needed to be addressed by the person. When the person tackled their issues themselves, the landscape changed and matured in a grounded, permanent way which was much healthier than having it changed by someone else. When an outside influence changed the landscape, it often obviated certain processes that were important for the person and therefore the change effected was temporary or incomplete.

Things that were wrapped over with vines were viruses, issues or parasites that the body had put into storage until it was ready to work on them and eject them. When I saw this I realized that the inner and outer immune system had to mature properly themselves so that they could strengthen. If I dragged off the viruses/parasites etc., the inner immune system was not dealing with them and therefore was not gaining experience and strength. It was like watching the effects of unnecessary vaccination.

One of the few occasions that can justify an intervention in the landscape is a full blown possession, which is almost impossible for the person themselves to deal with. Once the being has been removed, then the victim can keep an eye on their own landscape. What can make it so difficult for someone to get rid of a possession themselves is that the being will often begin integrating into the landscape itself and will no longer appear as a being at all. Everything you look at is probably a part of the being: that is a major job and as such is best left to an experienced exorcist.

The land also has an inner landscape, and the true health of the land, its power places, its illnesses and its issues can be identified by looking at its inner self. I really didn't think about this until I got back to the land of Britain after living abroad for eleven years. The land where I was born reacted the minute I landed and I felt its strengths, weaknesses and illnesses through my feet.

I felt really bad for having left the land for so long and made my mind up then and there to do what I could for the land as an apology. I began to look at the land in a deeper sense which showed the many areas of work that were needed. It also showed me the areas and realms where other people were already working or had been working for a long time. I looked closely at what was being done to see what I could learn and I watched how the land reacted to such work.

What I found truly fascinating was something I fell across just recently. I was walking across the Desert away from the Abyss in a magical vision when I saw cocoons on either side of me. Angelic beings and other strange creatures were bound up upon the land and looked strange indeed.

I asked the being I was walking with what these cocoons were and they replied that they were beings that had no place in the land at present because they were so destructive. When I came out of the vision, I later went to look at the land of Britain to see if those cocoons were simply in the inner realms, or if they were mirrored upon the land itself.

Sure enough there were beings trapped in rocks, in the roots of ancient trees, in bogs etc., and they were the same beings that I had seen near the Abyss. Then it occurred to me that the land worked upon the same mechanism as the human body: when invaded by a destructive consciousness, the immune system isolated and then bound that consciousness until it could be safely dealt with. It was fascinating!

I then started to look at the inner structure of the land in areas where there were buildings. To my amazement, some of the buildings appeared and some didn't. The ones that appeared had been there for hundreds and hundreds of years, but more recent buildings did not appear at all.

So then I looked at the land where my house is and some of the local houses appeared (some date back to the twelfth century) but mine didn't. Certain things began to make sense. I live on the side of a wild hill with ancient forest up above me and springs all around me. Living in the house sometimes is busy: many beings saunter through our house as if we didn't exist.

When I looked at the house from an inner point of view, it didn't appear: we were not in the inner landscape as the house was too modern so beings just didn't see us. They could probably feel us as

16. INNER LANDSCAPES OF THE PEOPLE AND THE LAND

they passed through the ancient forest, but they would not be able to figure out what they were feeling. So we were/are a main thoroughfare for all and sundry. The answer to this is to work in vision to build the house on the inner landscape so that we appear to all the beings tripping back and forth through the woods. First though, I have to figure out what effect that will have on the land in general before I make any more booboos.

But it does make for interesting thinking about what effect the houses have on the inner landscape when they do appear. Does it make it easier for the land to cope with such intrusion if it has incorporated it into its own pattern? Or does it ultimately lead to an imbalance that will express itself though the way the land lives and breathes?

What I think is important is to be at least aware of the overlays, imprints and changes that buildings, magical patterns and religious structures have on the living, breathing land and what we can do as a part of that intrusion to lessen the impact and restore what we can to a more natural state.

It also begins to raise questions regarding magical work that has been done over the years to affect the land in Britain in one way or another: the British Israelites are renowned for the amount of work they have done over the years to affect the land of Britain to suit their religious and political agenda. Similarly going back through time the Freemasons, the Golden Dawn, and way before that, the Normans and the Romans have all done their dirty work to affect the land in one way or another.

Similarly it also begins to raise questions about our own landscapes: how much does our magical and spiritual work affect the inner landscape, and is it really for the better?

16.1 Energetic load-sharing: a short look

The idea that we as beings are separate from each other is a misconception that feeds, among other things, a sense of helplessness and spiritual emptiness. Energetically, power is constantly flowing back and forth between people, the creatures around us and the land.

16.1. Energetic load-sharing: a short look

It is part of the communal soul and is the strength that drives the 'power in numbers.'

But our modern day culture has no place for such a 'truth': We have no words for it and we are discouraged from talking about it in general. And yet it is something that affects every sensitive person on a daily basis. If you are a magical worker, then the effect is massively amplified and can cause all sorts of problems.

Rather than talk about human energy boundaries in general, which is another subject all of its own, I want to focus in on the act of energetic 'load-sharing,' both conscious and unconscious.

Historically, this was one of the many uses of the storyteller or bard. The bard would go from place to place and recount tales of great acts of courage, battles with humans and non-humans, terrible tragedies, great joys and wondrous happenings. People would listen to these tales and be entranced, they would cry at the sad bits, be angry at the unfair or cruel bits, and be silent and still at the tragedies.

On an inner level, when people shed tears for the sorrow of others, the suffering of the original victim was shared by those who wept: the load became spread out. This way, the suffering of the individual was never more than they could bear. The more the story was told, the less was the burden on the victim's soul. And if the story was told repeatedly down the ages, then any terrible suffering became watered right down and the soul of the original victim could flow into and beyond death without the burden of pain.

This ensured that suffering was never allowed to impact an individual to the point that it would damage them permanently, and that the suffering would not become ingrained in the generations of their family: it kept the generations clear. Suffering was a group affair and was dealt with without the risk of lingering genetic damage. None of this was thought about consciously by the people, it was just the way things were done.

This method of load-sharing still survives today in various tribal cultures and in some of the Roma tribes around Europe. It is one of the reasons why people from these cultures will ask about the truth of a story or the root of a story. If a story makes a person cry, they want to know that their tears are going to the right place. If you cry

16. INNER LANDSCAPES OF THE PEOPLE AND THE LAND

at a story or film that is total fiction, where is the energy of those tears going?

Fragments of this instinctive behaviour survive in today's modern culture by the unconscious act of holding the hand of a dying person: it is not only about the reassurance of touch. Dying takes a great deal of energy and sometimes, in a slow and difficult death, the sufferer might not have enough energy to die. So the family sits around and takes turns to touch or hold the hand of the person dying: their energy is feeding the journey.

Babies, toddlers, old people, sick people, unbalanced people, all of these groups have a greater need for energy, and in the normal world they would be living in a multigenerational extended family/community where the load of energy that they need would be available to them, and the impact from providing that energy would not be too great for any one family member.

These days, such structures of family are almost gone and the burden of providing energy can fall upon one person.

Another and greater example of this load-sharing, at the other extreme, is the marriage between sovereign and the land: this is the basis for sacred kingship/queenship. Upon being consecrated as sovereign of the land, the energy of the land and the human become intertwined. The health of the land is echoed in the health of the king/queen and *vice versa*. If the sovereign becomes unbalanced, so will the land. The reverse also applies: if the land is imbalanced, so would be the sovereign. The job of the sovereign, in such a case, was to bring their body back into balance to rebalance the land. If they could not do that, then they would be sacrificed.

This was one of the reasons why the sovereign was held to such vows of marital honour, self-sacrifice, etc.: they had to be cleaner than clean. That way, they stayed in balance and so did the land. Whoever thought that one up obviously wasn't that in touch with humanity.

In today's world, sensitive people still engage in load-sharing, often without realizing. When a powerful event is about to happen that will have a lasting impact on society or the land, people often become tired and sleepy: they are giving up their energy for it to be used in the pattern that is being woven by fate.

16.1. Energetic load-sharing: a short look

Magically, this innate human ability to load-share is often taken advantage of by unscrupulous magicians, teachers, and leaders who literally feed off of their followers or students to fuel themselves or their magical agendas. This has become more common in the last few decades with the rise in 'guru' culture. It is also an energetic system used by churches and other religious organizations. Once you become a part of that organization, your energy becomes fair game to feed whatever being, egregore or structure is behind it all.

There is a positive side to such magical load-sharing, though. Some groups commit their energy through service to the land and the sacred places. Druid groups in particular who tend the sacred sites often become deeply connected to the land and their energies become entwined with the sacred places. To the sensitive person, it often means that they become deeply connected to a, and they can often feel if it is being abused or misused in any way: they become a communal part of the land itself.

I think that just having an awareness of such energy dynamics helps our bodies to field unhealthy or imbalanced situations, and that awareness also allows us to make informed commitments with our energy to the land, family, and community that we serve.

Chapter Seventeen

Magical protection: working methods

When people get seriously involved in a magical group, one of the first things they learn is how to protect themselves magically. After a while it becomes tempting for the magical student to cover themselves in protection at all times. They conduct the lesser banishing ritual of the pentagram and festoon themselves with protective talismans. This is of no help whatsoever if you truly want to progress into the depths of magic and experience what is truly out there. It is like sex with twenty thick condoms on.

The lesser banishing ritual of the pentagram is the most commonly used protection ritual in ritual magic. Its popularity dates back to the original Golden Dawn and is a good example of their clunky and overstructured approach to ritual magic. It was and is overused and ends up defeating the purpose of the work the magician is trying to embark upon. To do this ritual before a major working is essentially wiping out all the inner preparations that are going on in the Inner Worlds to meet and connect with your work.

So why and when do we need protection?

If your work is clear, your working space is properly maintained and you have good working practice methods, then there is no need for protection. Modern magicians in general are heavily overprotected and then they wonder why they cannot connect easily to beings in the Inner Worlds.

In the hospitals of days past, we used to wash our hands all the time, cover our mouths when we sneezed or coughed, burn infected waste and keep the area clean and tidy. Since the cutbacks in training and overuse of antibiotics, we don't bother with any of that so much. As a result, we have lots of resistant hospital infections. The same goes for magic: too much protection and too little practical experience ends up with vulnerable people who are likely at some

17. MAGICAL PROTECTION: WORKING METHODS

point in their work to come up against a real nasty and not be able to deal with it. It will brush your banishing ritual to one side like dust and then do as it will with you.

If you are constantly protected when you work, you are not learning to deal with minor nasties as they come along and you are not building skills, strengths and understanding of the more unsavoury side of the Inner Worlds. With these skills, strengths and understanding, you would be able to deal with most nasties that are put in your path. You will also begin to understand which banishings work easily and quickly, and which ones take time and too many tools.

Magical work should be approached in a clear way, with clear intent, good knowledge of what you are doing and in tandem with the right powers for the job. In such a setting you do not need protections: it is built automatically into the work you are doing.

Everyday magical rituals really do not need sealed spaces, banishments, etc. Far from it: the magician should be trained to work anywhere, at any time, with no tools or dressing. The natural protection comes from knowing what you are doing, where you are going and having good reasons for doing what you are doing. That way, all the natural structures, patterns and beings are there for you to work with and are not blocked by talismans or banishments. How could you possibly expect an inner contact to come and work in your space if you have sealed it, done a banishment and react immediately if some being does turn up?

I am not saying that you will never need these skills: you most likely will, quite a few times, but they should not be a daily part of your magical practice. And the regular wearing of a magical talisman for protection will create a weakness in you that will make it hard for you to function without one on.

17.1 So when do you use banishing and talismans?

Banishings are only to be used when something comes into your space and you have tried all other ways to get it to go. The first thing to do is not to react when a being moves into your space. Initially you need to find out what it is. Is it a parasite? Is it a dead person?

17.1. So when do you use banishing and talismans?

Is it an inner contact trying to work with you? Is it a nature being drawn to you by the magic it can see? Is it a lesser demonic type of being that you have inadvertently allowed into your space by playing around with portholes that you don't understand?

Once you have found out what it is, then you can ask it to leave, show it the way out, and give it a chance to go of its own accord. You can tell it (nicely) what will happen to it if it doesn't. If it chooses not to go, then you tell it to piss off. If it still doesn't go, then it is time to get rid of it. There are a few ways of doing this. The lesser banishing ritual of the pentagram does work, but it is clunky, time-consuming and needs tools. The other important thing to think about with a straightforward banishing is where are you banishing it to? It needs to simply go back where it belongs. It may have been called into this realm by other magicians and not know how to get back.

Some old Christianized versions of ritual space banishment and cleansings can be adjusted to work (Dion Fortune used a variant of this) using salt and water. Then there are visionary ways of taking the buggers out. I prefer this method, as it is more fun. I go in vision, give it one more chance and open a porthole for it. If it doesn't go I get a good hold of it by the scruff of the neck and take it to the Abyss where it is unceremoniously dumped back to where it came from. If it is a largish or powerful being, I call in angelic help, or dragon-based help.

Before I do any of this, I tune into a state that I meditate on regularly which is an expansion of the soul beyond the body: I regularly work on stretching out in all directions, becoming the boundary-less being that we are in our full glory: it makes it bloody hard to get a hold of someone if they have no ends.

If it is a really powerful nasty or a demonic being, then it is a good idea to work with angelic beings: they are really into putting these dudes back in the Abyss and they uphold your body to stop it getting impacted or intruded upon. But always make sure first that you fully understand why those beings are in your space and what drew them there. Just because a power is demonic does not mean it is 'bad': it might be doing a necessary job, in which case you ask it to go do it somewhere else because you are busy (and demons always make a mess on the carpet). These sorts of powers are incredibly

17. Magical protection: working methods

clever and intelligent, and are good at manipulating you around to their way of thinking: this is where you learn to be unemotional and unresponsive to bargaining.

Talismans are usually needed if you are not experienced at dealing with heavy beings and are going to a place that might be infested with them. By place I mean in the physical realm. If you are inexperienced in inner work, then you should not be going into dangerous inner places. Dangerous outer places are bad enough.

Talismans are good for kids, pregnant women, old people and sick people once they have been stripped of inner goo (talismans not only seal things from coming in, they also stop things getting out). Using talismans if you are a magician tends to weaken you and overprotect you. It is best to use them if you are doing nasty dangerous work and you are slightly ill.

Talismans are best homemade: ones that are sold in magic shops are a fancy waste of time. It doesn't need to look like anything: you can use virtually anything to make a talisman, but stone and metal hold the magic the best: it is what you put into it that is powerful. The ritualized sigil talismans are okay, but they are limited for today's world of magic: they were designed for a world that no longer exists and they are also created in a generic outer way with no inner content. The only way something like this will protect you from 'a heavy' is if it is interesting and the demon stops chewing on your head to have a closer look at the shiny pretty talisman.

To make a talisman is simple but takes focus and energy. There are many different ways to make them and many different powers that you can use to fuel them, but think carefully about what power you use. If you use a deity, then you might be in for more than you bargained for: if you wear the protection of a deity, it will expect you at some point to dedicate yourself to them, or at least do something major for them which might not be in keeping with your lifestyle.

If you use faery powers then you are truly nuts: they are conditional beings and they have a wicked sense of humor which is often at your expense. I wouldn't trust them to protect anything: its not that they will not do a good job, it's the other mischief they get up to in the meantime.

You can use angelic powers but be clear about what you are using: know your angels and don't overdo it as most are extremely powerful and are likely to blow you up. You need to work with one that specializes in protection and guardianship.

The other option is to work with inner contacts that you have and that are used to working with you. You can work around the directions, asking a contact in each direction to put something into the talisman to give you whatever protection you need. It is better for them to decide what protection you need, because if you specify things for them, then there is a chance that you will have missed something.

Before you work on your talisman, put it in salt to strip it. Work with the beings/contact to put the power in by letting them work through your hands: place your hand over the talisman as you work in vision or ritual with the contacts.

Afterwards put the talisman on and leave it on, don't take it off to shower, etc. They tend to run off of your body power so if you do not have it on, then it will power down. When it has done its job it will fall off, break or explode (which can be quite spectacular and impressive). In general though, it is better to build up your own inner immune system and get strong.

17.2 House protection

The issue of house protection can get interesting. The usual form for a magician is to have the house sealed so tight that a cat's fart cannot get through the protection. Living in such a protected environment is often not too healthy and can end up counterproductive.

My house is usually like grand central station: beings are coming and going all the time, dropping in to connect with me, coming for help, for sanctuary or to just rest a while. It is interesting to note that in Buddhist culture, the temples have wind chimes on their porches to attract ghosts at night: they draw the spirits to a friendly place of rest at night. So I scratch my head when I see people with wind chimes outside their homes...

When a magical home is kept clean and balanced, and you work as a priest/ess to all beings, then there really is no need to seal your

17. MAGICAL PROTECTION: WORKING METHODS

home. If they all get too much for me I just tell them all to piss off for a while and leave me alone. It is also interesting that if an inner intruder with bad intent comes near, the other beings will tell me so that I can watch the intruders, find out where they have come from and why, and then dispatch them promptly.

It doesn't hurt to have a spirit guardian outside the home, but just make sure that they allow in any being that is coming to you for help or sanctuary. We have some great ancient guardian beings that are native to Dartmoor so I just drop them a nod every so often and they keep an eye on the house.

This approach also gets you used to not reacting so much to intrusions, attacks, etc. If you are used to beings coming and going from your home and then one with a nasty intention comes along, instead of being repelled it is allowed to wander around a little so that you can study it and figure out what it is about and why. That way you get to know an awful lot more about people's intentions towards you and what their strengths and weaknesses are. If the baddie sent to you is not a construct (thought form) but a being, then you can often ask it (with bribery) who sent it and why.

If it is a thought form or golem, by observing it closely it will tell you a great deal about the person who constructed it, and what their weaknesses, strengths, etc. are: it is a part of their mind so you can use it to look closely at them. Golems as inner constructs only work on the victim when they do not understand how the sacred lettering of Hebrew works in magic.

The best way to avoid the regular use of protection is to have healthy, powerful and knowledgeable ways of working: even at a beginner phase, clarity works much better than protection. It is also important to have a healthy body. Like the outer immune system, the inner immune system needs to be strong and healthy: look after yourself inwardly and outwardly. Eat well, use herbs and resins burning around the house to keep it clean, use salt after doing readings to clean your hands, and put a bowl of salt in a room after a lot of magical work: it soaks up any magical residue.

Most of all, use your common sense. Don't invite weird beings into your home, don't wander into unhealthy inner or outer places, and don't indulge in parasite-infested pastimes: don't swim in cesspits and then wonder why you are a mess. A cesspit is any unbalanced magical system: books, teachings, biographies, etc. of unhealthy, parasitical or downright silly or nasty magical things.

The other main caution is: if you do magic at home, don't sit down and watch any exorcist movies that are based upon the real records, diaries, etc. of someone. There is a good chance that the original being, if portrayed well enough, can come through the movie and hook into you. The recreation of a real event can sometimes act like a doorway for the original being to pass through: it's like a passive form of invocation (as I found out...ouch!). No amount of protection would have stopped that. And it is bloody hard to pull a rabid demon out of yourself with no help. (Don't want to go through *that* again...)

The best protection of all is to use your common sense and some really awful perfume.

Chapter Eighteen

Sigils and seals

What they are, how they work and what to do with them

When you begin the study of magic, the first thing that smacks you between the eyes is the massive array of bizarre signs, weird shapes and alien texts.

When people first begin to work with signs and sigils, they often misunderstand what these signs are and how they work: they assume, in our fine modern world of psychology, that the signs/sigils stand for something or represent something. Wrong. That is not what they do and that is a bad way to start to try and work with them (can you see the wagging finger?): if you assume it stands for something because of its shape etc., then it will not work for you.

Sigils and seals once formed, become their own consciousness: they are beings within their own right. They are fragments of the power that they come from and they can work as a part of the hive being. So for example, if you work with an order of being that is powerful, and then later you want to work again with that same quality of power, but without the full-on nuclear power hit, then you would work with the sigil of that being in vision or in ritual: a fragment of it. The other way of working with these fragments is to string a few of them together so that they work in harmony and join their powers to create a specific form of magic, usually protective. Just make sure that the powers that you weave together get on: war raging will not a powerful pentacle make!

18.1 Angelic and demonic sigils

The sigil of an angel or a demon is like a fragment of their power, and also a key to their power when used correctly. When you want

18. SIGILS AND SEALS

to work with an angelic or demonic being, first you need its name or its sigil to bridge to this being. There are three basic ways to do this type of work: either you bring them to you, or you go to them, or you bridge them into something through the sigil or name.

The thing to remember, regardless of which way you go, is that these powers are not a joke: they will kill without thought and they will bring destruction down upon you if you prompt them to: you have to choose your words clearly. Doing a rite in a strange language like Hebrew or Latin might summon Metatron, but you might also order a pizza or a hit on your neighbour by mispronouncing what you are saying!

If you use the sigils to ritually bring the angel/demon to you, then be prepared to use a lot of energy, mess your room up and have fleeting contact. It's not an efficient way to work as you never get enough time to actually do anything, and the energy it takes to bridge that being into your world is not eco-conscious! And if you are successful and they decide they like it here and you did not attend your sigils correctly, they may decide not to go. Hmm, that could be a problem.

The second method is to go to them using the sigil. To do this you work in vision and use the sigil as a guide: you descend or ascend the Abyss or pass through the Void using the sigil as a key and a guide. When you are at the right area, the sigil will appear on the walls, or the one you are holding will glow. It is safer to commune with these beings and ask them to help you in their own realm and in their own form: they are not being squeezed into a human realm, which is not comfortable for them, so they are less likely to be pissy if you go to them.

This works well, the work does manifest out into the outer world and they operate at their own power level because they are on home turf. The problem is your ability to hold it together in the depths or heights of the Abyss. It takes a lot of energy (all angelic and demonic work will whack you one way or another: just find the least exhausting method) and it is more dangerous. You will have to know how to protect yourself without blocking your ability to work, usually by working with other beings, and will need to navigate yourself around without being distracted or glamoured. Once you find the area with the corresponding sigil, you make your connection with the being, sort out the task that drew you there in the first place, and then get out.

The third method, which doesn't work for everything, but does work well in some circumstances, is the pure use of the sigil. This is where you need to know the power levels of these beings, and be clear about what you need from them. If you are simply looking for their protection or their power to seal something, for example, then you would just use the sigil. The sigil itself holds the power of that being and allows you to draw a little upon it: it is like a mini-me. So if you are after sealing or protection, simply use the sigil on whatever needs protecting or sealing.

There is no fancy drama, ritual or anything else involved: just draw the sigil and it works. All the dressing is usually there either to look good, or because someone doesn't know that it is dressing. Most magic that we use today goes back to the sixteenth century and they were massive drama queens in those days: the more Mysterious it looked the more awe people held the magician in. I'm from Yorkshire, so I'm not into all that shit.

To work with demons or angels their sigils or names are important as part of the working tools, and they must be used correctly for it all to work. Just make sure you have a good reason to work with such beings and that you are fully aware of what they are and what they do. Luckily if you don't know what you are doing, it tends not to work, so stupidity can be a saving grace sometimes. If you are attracted as I am to red buttons, then I can tell you from burned experience: if you want to work directly with one of these beings, do your homework, do your inner workouts, and move thoughtfully and carefully.

Angels are just as dangerous as demons and demons can be just as helpful as angels: just make sure you know their job description! If you are still at the baby phase of wanting to use magic to get a big car or a big willy, or to smite the neighbours/ex-wife/boss, I would suggest you do not use these beings: you may be in for a major learning curve if you do.

Most common reasons to work with such beings is either in a war situation, i.e. world war: a good example of such work was Dion

18. Sigils and seals

Fortune and her Battle of Britain. It burned her body out and killed her, but she stopped the German magical elite from repeating the success of Claudius when he used Etruscan Apulu magic to conquer Britain (which he did successfully).

Other sensible reasons for working with such beings would be for major exorcism, working on a seriously magically bound or pinned land, to build or destroy a temple, etc. Big jobs, they are big job dudes: they will most certainly not tend your garden for you: that's a faery job.

18.2 Deity sigils

Divine sigils work in a similar way to angelic/demonic sigils: they are fragments of the original power: they are not representations of anything. They can be the source of endless hours of entertainment: watching someone trying to 'unlock' the key and discover what the sign really means can be good fun: maybe humans are just becoming too cerebral.

So you would use the sigil to mark things for example that need the protection of that deity, or belong to that deity. They can also be used as inner keys to get into places, a little like a VIP pass. They only work this way if you are given the sigil by the deity as opposed to looking it up in a book or off a statue. When you work with deities in vision they begin to interact strongly with you, and may offer you a sigil key that opens many inner doors for you so that you can go about your work. If the sigil is used in service for that deity, then it often develops into a priesthood mark that people who are priest/esses of that deity will have upon them. These marks appear upon the inner body of the person so that anyone with sight can see it. Other people who also bear that sigil will see it and recognize you.

Sometimes the sigil will have a shape correspondence to the deity, but most often it doesn't. The most famous magical sigil that corresponds to deity is the pentagram: the five pointed star. It has had many uses down the ages and is now an image used by a wide variety of pagans. It has an old and deep connection to the Underworld through its Sumerian usage: it was used as a pictogram to represent the Sumerian word Ub which meant cavity or hole. This is remarkably similar to the British Goddess Sul: Sul is an old Celtic word for hole, eye or gap and Sul is a goddess of the Underworld, of cursing and curse lifting.

So in that context, the pentagram could be used to access ancient Underworld deities along with all the other usage it has had over the years. It has been known to occasionally open the minds of sullen Nintendo teens who suddenly discover a world of rebellion, symbology and the hope of wild sex.

Deity sigils can be used in conjunction together to create a harmonic in physical manifestation. Using deity sigils from deities that are in harmony with each other is an age-old method, for example a pattern of the world by using deities from the directions and seasons. Once the pattern is created and the sigils in place, then the whole thing can be used to weave land magic by weaving the powers of the various deities together and keeping them in harmony.

Deity sigils can also be used to enliven a piece of land and infuse it with the power of that deity. A remnant of this is the use of corn dollies at planting. Drawing or etching out the sigil over a piece of land will bring the power of that deity right out into the land, which is maybe the source reasoning of the Cerne man and the white horses.

If you work with one deity and you use their sigil a lot, just make sure that you are doing it for the right reasons, i.e. because you have dedicated yourself to that deity for a span of time or for life. If you blindly mess about with deity symbols because it looks cool, then there will come a time when you become bored or the fashion changes. You will want to move on but deities are not that keen at being tossed aside so easily and can become pissed off or even vengeful. So if you decide to deck yourself with a certain deity sigil, make sure it is for a finite length of time and be aware of what you are wearing and why.

18.3 Magical seals

Magical seals, like the impressive ones used by eighteenth and nineteenth-century magical groups, are and were used for a wide variety of good and bad intentions. The use of magical seals stretches back far in to antiquity, to the world of ancient Sumer, Egypt and

18. SIGILS AND SEALS

Mesopotamia. Magically they were mainly used for protection, to seal something into a container, or to keep beings out of a building or area. They were used upon thresholds to affect the person who crossed them, and they were used around the neck to protect the body from invasion and impact.

Today's usage is more or less the same. The magical seals are made up of a 'sentence' of angelic/demonic sigils combined with sacred text and sometimes a deity sigil. The 'sentence' would sometimes be encased in an overall sign to contain it and pressurize it (i.e. make it more powerful and stop it being messed with). An ancient and impressive version of the use of magical seals is the Babylonian demon bowls which are vessels covered in script and glued together with pitch. Inside is often eggshell, human skull or bone with sigils and script upon it. This is a demon 'prison,' a trap in which a demonic entity has been trapped and sealed. The sigils and script around the bowl would encase the demon and stop it escaping.

The use of early sacred script or alphabet was deliberate: for example the letters of the Hebrew alphabet are considered by some to be expressions of G-D, they are sacred sigils which have the potential to bring through power themselves. That is to say that the letter itself has its own power. It is not dependent on anyone using it in a certain way to make it magical: it is magical itself. It is a part of an ancient movement of the magical power of air, of utterance, and remnants of that ancient Mystery still survive to this day in the form of the religions of the book and the word. So when you start to string these sacred letters together to form words combined with sigils, you are getting into some ancient and powerful working methods.

When you recite the letters as sounds, or write them as shapes, you are mediating a power of Divinity: a potent form of magic. If you use such magic without the deeper understanding, it will work if pronounced exactly right, but its true expression will evade you and the mediating of such power without understanding will eventually take its toll upon the body (ever noticed that non-Jewish Kabbalists who do heavy ritual nearly always end up fat?)

Such magical sealing is still in use today, although personally I find it easier to take demons back home and deposit them where they

18.3. Magical seals

belong rather than end up with a house full of containers that some idiot could open one day.

In modern magic, seals are most often used as protection. The wisdom of the constant use of protection is debatable but the seals do work when done properly using the right powers. It is best to use them when you have to do heavy magic and you are under the weather or under a major attack. The seals can be used as a wearable amulet: it can be drawn upon an object or marked out over an area.

Large magical seals are used in certain branches of magic to keep out spirits while the magician works. The seal would be marked out upon the floor or on the altar and it would keep out any beings other than the one being summoned.

One of the oldest magical seals seen around the British Isles is the swirls that cover some of the Neolithic tombs, stones and chambers. The swirl or series of interlocking swirls are extremely effective at sealing in power and trapping solar (sun temple) power. If the swirls are on the inside of the container, they will trap whatever is in there: the whole surface needs to be covered in interlocking swirls. If the swirls are on the outside and are shiny, then they will draw the being or power to them and the being gets trapped in the endless patterns as though mesmerized.

One of the dangers of magical seals is that life can become too comfortable and safe with them if they are used too many times for everything that you do. It is best to keep them for sealing in things that need to not see the light of day ever: it will guard something for you so that you can get on with your work.

An important factor in the decision to use seals that must be considered is the human energy cost. When you draw a seal or sigil for magical use with a specific intention, the seal draws upon your energy stores to 'power' itself. If you use lots of seals and sigils for trapping, drawing, whatever, then you are going to get drained after a while.

The other danger that can happen from the overuse of magical symbols is that you never get to learn to deal with all the various beings that are in the Inner Worlds. If you are so heavily protected that nothing can ever get near you, then you will end up never knowing any Inner World beings. This is a sad byproduct of the middle ages: people were and still are controlled by fear, and that paranoia of vulnerability seeped into magic as well as everything else in people's lives.

Our culture and the insidious effect of the church upon our consciousness breeds a fear of the unknown, of the Inner Worlds and all the beings therein. Most young magicians start from a standpoint of fear, and the magic develops out of that standpoint, hence the proliferation of amulets, protective pentacles and magical seals.

Like all magic, used sensibly in context magical protection is powerful, but it must be used from a place of knowledge and calm, not curiosity and fear. That way, you don't spend all your energy casting circles and summoning demons, only to freak out and banish them as soon as they appear: demons get confused if you do this and it gives the rest of us a bad name.

18.4 Platonic solids and geometric shapes

Magic is like a science: it is about learning how the universe works, what particles, powers and energies do, and it is about the realization that magic works like a mathematical poem. It is logical, it makes sense and it is a natural part of the universe. Physics and magic are basically the same thing with different names: they both work with and are aware of the powers that flow through space, and they are both littered with workers who are maladjusted. Some of the most interesting magical conversations I have ever had have been with particle physicists: but then, some of the most unintelligent dogmatic and down right stupid discussions I have ever had have also been with physicists: so I guess science and magic really are two sides of the same coin.

Platonic solids and geometric shapes often appear in magic simply because they are a natural part of our world. They are the purest form of a power expression in harmony with itself and when a being appears to you as a Platonic solid you know you have reached one of its deepest and most powerful forms. When the angel of death and destruction appears before you as a cube, you know you are in for a bit of a bumpy ride.

18.4. Platonic solids and geometric shapes

The forms that beings take to appear to us, i.e. wings, eyes, swords, teeth, fire, etc. is their way of talking slowly to us: they play down their size, cool their power and dress up from images in our cultural imagination so that we can interact with them and understand what they are about. If an angelic being appeared before you as a cube, you would blink and scratch your head before finding yourself fried to a crisp. If an angelic being appeared before you with a flaming sword, fancy armour, nice hairdo, big wings and a cheesy grin, then you know that the angel is really downplaying it for the ants (or it is a parasite dressing up for you).

The more you work the Abyss, the thresholds and the Void, the more you will begin to see that the Inner Worlds are like a conversation of pure form, of harmony, shapes, sounds and energy. The beings with faces, wings, horns, etc. are just our feeble way of trying to understand the enormity of that which is all around us.

So back to Platonic solids: if you see one in vision then chances are you are hitting an angel full on, or something connected with angels: Platonic solids or geometric shapes are often used as angelic sigils. If the angel appears to you in that form, then chances are it is safe for you if you can communicate at a level which uses no imagination or emotion: angels are really like Asperger's physicists. You will have to communicate in mathematics, physics and logic.

If you cannot communicate in that form, then it is best not to call them in that form: having a premenstrual emotional artist in the flows of power outputting, standing before a confused cube, is rather entertaining.

But those forms can be used to bring in that power to use at a impersonal level, so if you work that way it is usually in temple construction or a similar practical job. An ancient example of this is the Ka'ba: a perfect cube temple that stands at the centre of an ancient power site. Today it is the spiritual centre of the Islamic faith but before that time it was already an ancient structure that housed many deities.

Its legend is that it was built by Adam to the heavenly specifications of the Angels. It works in a specific way to do with utterance and the magical power of breath/sound, and the myth states that it was built to house paradise on earth. It is a balanced harmonic

18. SIGILS AND SEALS

form that mediates a pure power of air into the consciousness of humanity for us to work with: how much closer to paradise can we get?

When you think of geometric shapes in this context, and then you go back to the seals of Solomon and look closely, you can begin to see what people were reaching for. Just like all other sigils, they are powerful when used a certain way, but every shape must be exact and in the right combination, and used with the knowledge to unlock them.

18.5 Mandalas

Mandalas can become interesting tools simply from a learning point of view and although they don't really have much to do with western magic, I have come across a couple of things that are worth mentioning just because they can be converted for use. (I'm all into inner recycling: it saves time and mess to learn from others.)

A few years ago I was living in California and teaching in an art centre. In the rooms opposite me a small group of Tibetan monks were working away at building a mandala to cleanse the area over a series of days. I was fascinated and wanted to know what it was all about. I was fobbed off by the only English-speaking one who told me about creating pretty patterns to bring peace and then destroying them because nothing was permanent. I wasn't buying it: I could feel all sorts of powerful things going on in my backyard and I wanted to know what these people were doing.

So at the end of my class each day, I would go and sit in meditation where they were working and watch on the inner what they were doing. Only one of them, the eldest, picked up on me and would come and sit by me and probe to find out what I was about (the spy being spied upon...cool, huh?).

The land that the centre was built on was ground that had been devastated by gold mining and was hostile. I was interested to see what they could do, as the land there was quite badly out of balance and many nasties were wandering about on the inner planes there.

Over the days I watched as they created an amazing picture pattern. I was more amazed to see that the nasties were becoming

18.5. Mandalas

obsessed at seeing what was going on and were getting trapped in the picture. As they were trapped, the form of the picture seemed to change their ability to express themselves: they were being forced into an image form that they were unfamiliar with.

I had no illusions about the power of this culture and its ancient magic: I was fully aware of the depth of shamanic knowledge under the veneer of gentle monkishness and the 'harm no being' did not stretch to inner world beings at all (nor, it would seem, to dissenters, but that's a different matter).

I observed over the days many beings, good and bad, natural and demonic getting trapped in a beautiful, complex pattern that had them changing and shifting in an unfamiliar world of colour and form. I was expecting at the end, a ritual that would separate out the natural faery and land beings from the unhealthy beings, and free them back into the land, before putting the more demonic unhealthy beings, who had been raised by blasting, back to where they came from.

I was horrified when I watched the ritual breaking of the sand pattern and saw all of those beings, good and bad, have their inner patterns trashed and magically torn apart. They were cast into the river and I was furious: so much for Buddhist compassion. Their methods were grafted onto a foreign land that had already suffered much at the hands of men: they just added to it in their own way. In retrospect, I do not think for one minute that the monks were aware of what their actions were doing, nor do I think any of the destruction as a result of the ritual action was intentional: they were working on impermanence in a dogmatic ritualized way.

But, to get away from the personal story and emotion, it is interesting to see what a pattern can be used for and how it works. And once you have understood that, then you start to look at the ancient artwork in temples in a different light. If you study in more depth what sort of patterns where used where, what powers were used there, and what their opposing powers were, then you will start to understand what pattern does what to whom, and how you can use those patterns in your magical service.

The use of sigils in magic is a whole branch of magic on its own once you start to look closely at it, and it can take years for pennies

18. Sigils and seals

to drop about certain texts, images and patterns. But the more you learn about sigils, the more you approach them like the rest of magic: to be used sparingly and with intelligent understanding.

Chapter Nineteen

Inner world parasites

Just as the outer world is full of various parasites, so are the inner realms. Most are pretty harmless, some are needed for our survival and health, some are just annoying and some are just plain nasty and dangerous.

Our bodies are full of bacteria, viruses, fungi, and microbes that 'parasite' off of our energy but they also serve a purpose for us: a symbiotic relationship that helps the world go around. Problems arise when some of these beings get out of balance and overrun the body. The same rule more or less applies in the Inner Worlds and the two worlds are inextricably linked: don't make the mistake of trying to approach the Inner Worlds as something removed from our everyday outer existence: they are one and the same.

Bacteria have an inner consciousness, viruses can be seen and affected on the 'inner': whatever has an outer form also has an inner form. The rule doesn't always apply the other way around, which can make life a little complicated. Inner parasites sometimes have an outer manifestation, but a lot of the time they do not. They do however often leave a trail of outer effects that can be identified, and the trained eye can spot the telltale symptoms in a person, animal, or object pretty swiftly. (Unless you are like me and can stand looking straight at the salt while asking where the salt is: I was born as a woman with man vision).

Wherever there is energy, there is a parasite either feeding or trying to feed. That energy can take a variety of forms and some forms are yummier than others to a hungry parasite. Some parasites are intelligent, some are sort of intelligent, and some are morons. The sort of energy that attracts them can be anything from sex, violence, death, birth, hormone rises (young teens are particularly vulnerable) pleasure, pain, emotion (love, hate, anger, etc.) drugs, and so forth.

19. INNER WORLD PARASITES

Some people are more vulnerable than others, some are pretty much immune, and some people get terribly overwhelmed by these beings.

As far as inner work goes, parasites are usually pushed out by good working practices and a healthy magical operational method. They tend mostly to appear in the fluffy New Age parlours, attaching themselves to frail egos and masquerading as an 'ascended master' or an 'angel,' spurring their hapless victims to channel banal advice and feeding off the power rush the speaker gets when people give them attention or status.

The more dangerous parasites in the magical world tend to attach to egos in the magical world, feeding a loop of messiah ego, greed, and power lust. The fundamental magical and religious world is full of people who feel they are saviours, messiahs, adepts, and magi who deserve great things like power/money/status, and the parasite feeds off the feelings of power and ego. It also manipulates the victim to set up a feeding chain.

It is important to note at this point that if a person is on certain types of medications or drugs, it can allow the parasite to dig in deeper and feed freely. It talks to the host through the host's thoughts and feelings, spurring on their actions, paranoia, and greed. The more people join in the magical/spiritual group actions, the more food the parasite has. Hence cults, which have a high tendency to be parasited, tend to have secretive, paranoid, egotistical, and glamorous leaders.

Parasites can also inhabit a land area, feeding off of what happens there: hence the need to work in a clean, clear space. Some areas can be so badly infested that it is not worth trying to clean them up. Mental institutions that have been around for a long time are a really good example of a parasitic area, as are meditation/spiritual centres that allow anything and everything in.

Just building an awareness of these beings, what they 'feel' like and what an infested place feels like can be a useful tool in inner work, as at some point you will undoubtedly come head to head with one. It's like Kindergarten: the head lice are just ready and waiting! It is important to note that there is a major difference between a parasite, which is usually just annoying and draining, and a demon.

A demon is a totally different kettle of fish and most people, even in the magical worlds, will not encounter one in their lifetime.

19.1 Dealing with and removing parasites

Parasite removal has traditionally been the forte of Shamanism and similar tribal magic: magicians tend to ignore them at their peril and priests try to bless or banish them. But what are they?

Well, if you are a magical worker and you want to deal with and be familiar with all types of beings, then you need to become familiar with parasites along with all the other choice and yucky beings that live in our universe. A trip down the Abyss will teach you a lot about these beings, how they operate and why: If you are going to deal with a being, you need to know everything about it. Why? So that you do not shoot the innocent is the shortest answer. Knee jerk action is not a part of higher magic: intelligent communion is: beings are just beings, they only become 'bad' to us if they are in the wrong place in relation to our wants and needs.

Just because something looks nasty to us doesn't mean it's bad. If it's dark, it doesn't mean it's bad. If it is munching away on your energy, it doesn't mean it's bad: it just means they are probably in the wrong realm. Every being becomes parasitical in a way if it is out of balance or out of its proper environment. The job of a magical worker is to discern what it is, why it is doing something and what to do with it.

Most parasites find their way to our realm through a variety of portholes that we as humanity open up by our actions. Once they are in our realm, they can have all sorts of effects upon our lives, most of which are negative. But what they feed on tells us a great deal about what they are and where they belong.

In modern shamanism, the parasite is taken off, and is taken away by a helper being. There is no discernment about what that being is, why it is there, where it belongs, etc. Although these questions do not matter to the victim that really just wants the bloody thing off, it should matter a great deal to the magical worker.

Back to parasites. First what needs to be identified is its food source: what does it eat? Most parasites tend to feed off the energy

19. INNER WORLD PARASITES

generated by emotions, be they fear, anger, etc. Any strong emotion will provide a meal so the parasite quickly learns to manipulate the host into generating such yummy emotions. This can be achieved either through manipulating the host's imagination or through the manipulation of the host's endocrine system.

The endocrine system is the gateway of the body to the Inner Worlds: this is where magic is processed as it passes from inner impact to outer physical impact. Heavy magic tends to affect the thyroid, the pineal, hypothalamus and pituitary: the control centres of the body. This is why too much of a burden of heavy magic will 'burn out' the hypothalamus, thus rendering the magician vulnerable to all sorts of constitutional illnesses.

Parasites operating through the endocrine system will usually go for the adrenals (generating fight or flight mode) creating fear and stress, or through the reproductive organs, creating hormonal imbalances and feeding off the subsequent emotional rollercoasters. To dig into the endocrine system in such a way they need to be there for quite a long time and can be separated out from ordinary endocrine illness by a carefully approached list of questions regarding the emotional state of the host for a few years before the endocrine problems.

In general the body's immune system will evict the parasite before it manages to dig in so deep. But weakened hosts can have this sort of long term problem and it must be looked at carefully.

Most infestations present themselves through emotional, sexual, magical or violent outbursts, with lesser ones presenting through constant primary immune system triggering.

Let's have a closer look at the more obvious and dangerous parasite presentations. The reason I am looking at these more extreme ones is that the lesser ones tend to either be pushed out naturally, or some hapless modern shaman from Glastonbury will come along and pull it out. But the more extreme ones need not only taking out, but putting back where they belong and the pathway they used to get in must be closed up.

19.2 Emotional parasites

These parasites usually get in during an initial emotional situation like a divorce, death, failure etc., something that generated a lot of energy and made the victim visible and edible. They slip in and then begin to generate a feeding loop in which the parasite generates activity, usually through the imagination, that keeps the emotive flow going and the victim in the constant clutches of their despair. The victim feels severely depressed or angry, or in emotional pain, and the parasite settles in for nightly dinner.

Usually the first heads up that people get that something is wrong is that the victim is not getting over something: the pain continues, they spiral into the depths of dark emotions and nothing brings them out. Antidepressants at this stage will only disable the body's ability to shake this being off, so the infestation is actually made worse by the drug, often creating a suicide situation. So it is important, for both sides of the reasoning to make sure that the emotion is from a parasite as opposed to a chemical depression. The usual way to tell is if you take the parasite out, the victim gets better within hours. You can also use tarot to look if you do not have the inner sight abilities to look.

After an emotive parasite is removed, the victim will be emotionally frail for a few weeks, and will need a careful eye along with homeopathy or herbs to strengthen and rebalance their system. They will also need an input of energy as theirs will have been sucked dry, so energetically feeding them would be a good idea, along with closing up any holes that the parasite left behind. (For the actual removal method, see below.)

19.3 Sexual parasites

Sex is an act that generates a lot of visible energy and if that act is not protected, then every parasite within a hundred miles will come running for a piece of the action. Sexual parasites work primarily through the imagination though with time and practice they can begin to affect the sex organs directly. The emotive energy that is released with desire is a particularly potent energy and the parasite will do anything it can to keep that level of the first 'high' going. This drives the victim to find more and more ways to get that initial arousal 'hit,' with it fading as the parasite becomes normalized to the energy level.

A longer-term victim of such a parasite will have sexual problems in which little excites them and there is a constant searching for new ways to get a 'hit.' Again, one has to be cautious to ascertain if it truly is a parasite and not a hormone imbalance, although a long-term parasite will eventually begin to affect the hormone levels as it attempts to manipulate the body's chemical balance to suit its appetite. This is analogous to the recent discovery that viruses will affect the imagination, emotions and endocrine system to force the host into actions that will be favourable to the virus. Sound familiar?

19.4 Magical parasites

These little buggers are just downright nasty. They are initially attracted by the power of a magical or religious act that has been conducted without proper balance of power structures/patterns and inner contacts. These horrible things are the main reason for a magician to stop and think carefully if he/she should throw the known structure out of the window when doing high magic. If you forge into new territory magically, make sure you know what you are doing and that you are properly balanced in the way that you approach your work.

If not, the magical energy generated will attract a particular type of being that can wreak havoc around humans. They do not necessarily attach to the magician: they go for the nearest 'sensitive' and dig into their thoughts. So anyone who happens to be nearby who is a sensitive or seer is in real danger of these beings. They are a slightly higher order of being than the emotive or sexual parasite: their energy needs operate on a high frequency (hence you will find them deeper in the Abyss). Because of that, they tend to be far more dangerous: they feed off threshold energy, which for us translates eventually to death.

They will talk to their victims, isolating them from their families and friends, telling them they are in constant danger or that a particular person is evil. They will slowly manoeuvre the person into a state in which they think they have to kill someone for some real reason. Most people fight this and seek help. Unfortunately medical help will immediately drug them, which allows the being to dig in deeper. But if the person is not parasited, but is mentally ill, then they need the drug initially to calm them. So it is a difficult situation which must be handled carefully.

More often than not the victim will have been convinced by the parasite that anyone trying to help them is the enemy: these are intelligent beings who do not give up their hosts easily, and most be approached carefully. If they see you coming they will try to urge the victim to self-destruct so that they can have a gorge feed before bolting. My personal approach to someone who is infested with this type of being is to consecrate a scarf as a sacred stole, come up behind them and carefully, in a friendly manner, put it around their necks. This gives you a short time to talk to the human and explain what is going on and what you need to do.

With this sort of infestation, it is advisable to have a mental health professional assess the victim after the parasite has been lifted, just to be on the safe side. The victim will need a great deal of aftercare in the form of clean energy, good food, sacred baths and lots of sleep that is protected by a sacred flame. It is probable that the victim will have flashbacks, and will have echoes of the infestation at the same time each year for a few years. It is a good idea for the victim to preempt this by actively doing something like a spiritual cleanse at that time of the year.

Once you have cleaned the victim up, taken the parasite home and sealed up the porthole it used, try and find out what magical act or which magical person attracted the being in the first place. If it is an adult who should know better, try to resist the urge to beat the shit out of them: just let them know what their actions are doing.

The reason why those types of parasite should never be left in the host is that they are the order of being that will generate a lot of violence and emotion in people. They get into teens and mentally ill men: for some reason, it is rare for them to dig so deeply into mature women. When the being is lifted the difference is astounding and almost instant (within a couple of hours). One teen that I worked on who was suicidal, self-mutilating, hearing voices and planning death,

19. INNER WORLD PARASITES

looked terrible. I stripped the being out with a doctor present and the kid was totally different within two hours. They ate and slept for the first time in days, and awoke with little memory of what had been happening: the previous two weeks were a near total blank.

If you do not get such a dramatic reversal of symptoms, then the chances are it is not a parasite and the victim needs medical help.

19.5 Parasites of the dying

These parasites tend to move into old people and people in comas. They live off the life force of the dying, and off the sensations that they get to feel through the victim's senses. In return they block the natural mechanism that would allow the person to die: in effect they keep their host alive so that they can live through the body of the host. When a person is old or severely injured, the natural defence system against such parasites collapses and they can move in unchecked.

Sometimes they can get so ingrained in the person, that a natural psychic who is not used to such beings would assume that the original person had gone and another being had taken its place (which does sometimes happen). But more often than not, if you reach deep in, you find the original person squashed into a corner, unable to use their body and unable to die: it is a terrible situation for them and for everyone else concerned. If you take the parasite out, the victim will die. If you leave it in, the victim is stuck in no man's land.

In such situations, it is most compassionate to take them out. It is also the most ethical: you are restoring the human to their original fate pattern of death. Keeping someone alive at all costs is not a good thing to do. The family might want the person to stay alive regardless of the parasite, but it must be explained to them that their loved one is not really there much anymore, what they are holding the hand of is mainly a parasite. If there is enough of the human left, then they will survive the extraction. If not, they will die shortly after.

Under such circumstances, it is advisable wherever possible to include the family in the extraction process so that they have a sense of control and inclusion in such a difficult emotive situation. It would also be wise to protect the family from parasites at this highly emotional time.

19.6 Minor parasites

There are tons of minor orders of parasites that live off emotions, pain, sex, magic, drugs, drink, certain rhythms, and hormonal imbalances. The list is endless and the effects in general tend to be minor. Usually the body can eventually shrug them off naturally, or the host slowly realizes that their actions are creating a bad situation, and they change their lives accordingly. Some parasites come in useful and symbiotic relationships can develop, just as the bowel needs bacteria, so our emotive selves sometimes need help. In teen years kids become vulnerable to parasites, but unless they are particularly sensitive or open, it is best to help them deal with it naturally so that they build up a basic immunity to these beings. That translates to helping them identify what is them and what is the being: identify the 'food' source that is attracting it, and help the teen to decide how to change their environment and actions to make them less visible and less yummy.

19.7 Removing parasites: practical application

Obviously the first thing is that the person you are working on has to agree to be worked on: forcing an extraction is not such a good idea, unless it is a severe attack in which the victim is unable to ask for help: that is when you use a stole to give them time to think.

Never, under any circumstances, physically assault, handle or hit the victim in an attempt to drive out the being. Not only is this the Neanderthal method of extraction so beloved by Christian fundamentalists, it is also plain and simple assault.

The other thing when working in this way as a worker rather than a healer is that you will need to work in a partnership. There will be times within the session that two people will be needed.

Make sure that you are both clean, working in a clean space and that you both have a clear mind that cannot be messed with. It is a good idea to go into the Void or a similar thing within your own tradition to strip away your surface life and step into a deeper level of your consciousness before working: this ensures that there is nothing that the parasite can latch onto in you. Reach out within the Void for

19. Inner world parasites

the tools that you need for the job—just keep your intentions clear within your thoughts and the necessary tools will emerge.

The parasite worker will need to reach deeper into the Void and connect with angelic consciousness, usually an Angel of Air (see article working with angels) and have that being come out to work with you.

Within the partnership, one person should focus upon the human and the other upon the parasite. The worker who is tending the human never leaves the human's side, vision or otherwise, while the other worker takes the parasite and deals with the Void side of things. For example:

Human worker

Work in vision, starting at the top of the body and work your way down, looking deep into the body, around the adrenals, the heart, the thymus and the head. Once you have found the being, bind it: if it is one of the more intelligent magical beings, pass it to the parasite worker. Once you have cleared them of all parasites, pull out any umbilical cords or connections, seal them at all the access points and rebalance them by ensuring that the inner body is equal on both sides of the body's midline. (An imaginary line of balance that runs down the centre of the body)

Finally fill them with grounded earth energy and put them in a salt bath.

Parasite worker

When the being is handed to you, disable the being by using angelic binding with the Angel of Air. Immediately take the being to the Abyss by passing through the Void (or through your own version of such a place). You will need to descend into the Abyss to make sure that it goes where it is supposed to go. You can work with the angelic consciousness that resides within the Abyss to take you down and bring you back up again.

Once down at the level where the being belongs, release it and look around for a porthole or crack. You will recognize the light/scent/energy leaking into the Abyss from the human world that attracted the being in the first place. Seal up the crack, again using the angelic worker that is with you and take another look around just in case you can see something that caused the crack in the first place. If you identify the cause, and can deal with it simply, then deal with it at this point of the work. If it looks more complicated, or you cannot immediately identify the reason for the crack, then you must come back at another time and focus properly upon the problem. Just bear in mind, if you come back at a later date, you will need to reconnect with the being to get the sense of where the crack was.

Once all is finished, make sure that you both clean yourselves up properly and that the victim is closely watched and helped for a while by family and friends. Go back a few times to check up on them until you are sure they are strong and able to fend off another attack. At that point it might be wise to talk at length to them to find out how it got access in the first place and what could be done to avoid such a situation in the future.

19.8 Summary

I haven't gone into too much detail about working methods so that if you haven't a clue, then you will not be able to bumble your way through something and do damage. If you have knowledge or are a natural, then hopefully this section will help with ideas and working methods: either way, the idea is to stop people and make them think a little more about how these beings operate and why. They are not evil nasties: they are hungry out of place beings just looking for a home and a meal. I'm sure cows and pigs find human omnivores evil: it's all a matter of perspective.

I am also hoping that this section will encourage people to pause for thought before undergoing powerful magic, just to make sure that any hapless youngsters nearby don't get sucked in and end up with nasties inside them.

Chapter Twenty

Removing ghosts and other unwelcome guests

Sometimes unwelcome guests come into our homes and workplaces, creating anything from mild discomfort to outright chaos. Sometimes they were there all the time and we move into their 'patch' triggering a hostile response, and sometimes we move to an area or property that is sat on unhealthy, unbalanced or just plain dangerous land. To us that equals sleepless nights and many strange happenings.

Most of the time when people think they are being haunted, in actual reality, they are not. It is much rarer than people think unless you are unlucky enough to live in a place that is a magnet for such energy. In the British Isles for example, the relative number of powerful 'possessions' of houses is much less than the USA, even when you take into account the vast territory of the USA in relation to the small isle of Britain.

The reasons for this could be many: length of time of population and cities upon the land, amount of wild territory, reuse of sacred burial land as building land, etc. Whatever the reason, the USA is a far more haunted land than Britain, and its hauntings can be spectacular.

The different types of hauntings must be dealt with differently according to what type of being you are dealing with and why they are there. Do not automatically assume a presence is hostile just because it is there and rattling your windows: it might be trapped there, terrified of you and desperately trying to get out.

We react to hauntings in a hostile way because they can be frightening, and they are frightening only because of the lack of understanding of what is happening. Unless of course you happen to be sat upon one of the really nasty unbalanced sites that attract every parasite and lesser demon around for miles and they all end up in your kitchen: that's scary!

When dealing with beings in this situation, it is useful to have no emotion whatsoever when you are working. When dealing with unsavoury beings, no emotion is safe: there is nothing they can poke or play upon. Do not fall into the trap of feeling sorry for them, or being fearful of them, or even friendly with them: they do not belong in that space, so they have to go.

20.1 Types of hauntings

The first one to cover—and actually the least common of all hauntings—is the presence of a dead human. When someone dies, they tend to normally go through the death process and they might try to hang around the house of a little while before slowly fading off. Those that do hang around at home after a while should not be encouraged by loved ones left behind, no matter how tempting that may be. It prolongs an unhealthy situation for them and for the living. There are times however, particularly if it is part of the culture of that family, when dead people to stay connected to a family line as a guardian for a while. In these circumstances all is well and it isn't a problem.

Some humans die in a state of anger, greed, or with a need for revenge. These people in life tend to be types who find it hard to let go of anything and will hang on for grim death to anything that will allow them access to the living world. Their enormous output of emotional energy attracts parasites that begin to feed on the situation and may even try to impersonate the dead person to carry the haunting on even when the dead person has moved on.

The way to deal with a dead human is to go into death and deal with them face-to-face at that level (rather than an aggressive banishing ritual). It is much better to ask 'uncle Harry' to go and take him by the hand as you walk him into death to make sure he goes, than to ritually impact his soul by magical banishments. The method of working in death teaches them to stop and think about what is happening and what they are doing. If they go with you voluntarily, then they have learned and are moving on.

20.1. Types of hauntings

If you get an unhealthy dead person hanging around doing damage, then you get them by the scruff of the neck and frogmarch them through death. Again this is better than a ritual banishment, and it tends to work better anyhow. Sometimes a mass conducted by a Catholic priest will move a dead person on if the transubstantiation ceremony is used, but this depends on the skill of the priest and the dead person's reaction to the ceremony. If they are in tune with that faith, they can use the ceremony as an impetus to move on.

Many years ago I was contacted about a haunting in Manhattan USA. A woman could feel her dead husband standing over her in a rage night after night: she was sleep-deprived and stressed out. I went to have a look, as sometimes when people think they are under attack, they are not.

He was indeed there and angry. Before he died, he controlled a large businesses empire of which he was the cutthroat owner. They had begun the process of separating and had not approached it legally, but were about to. He was killed in an accident and was fuming that his wife was the sole beneficiary of all his estate: he had not got around to changing his will.

I went into the death vision to speak to him. When I found him, he presented himself as a man sitting inside a heavily armoured tank: this was his projection of himself as a dangerous man. I tried to talk to him while he sat in his tank but he would not come out and would not see sense. So I reached in and pulled him out by his collar. He refused to move, to stop attacking her or to listen to any sort of reason. I dragged him to the 'river,' made him drink lots, and then marched him over the 'bridge' into death. (To read about the death vision, see notes on death and birth.)

The haunting stopped immediately and never returned. I showed the woman how to cleanse her apartment from an inner point of view and how to tune it. She never had problems again.

Most hauntings by dead people stem from their frustration at not being able to finish something up, not being able to let go of family or belongings, or the need to pass information on. Once that has been achieved, most do move on, but some do stay as they want to stay connected to their old life. These ones really do have to be moved on.

20. REMOVING GHOSTS AND OTHER UNWELCOME GUESTS

Be aware though that sometimes the being that presents as a haunting is actually a parasite that is 'wearing' the persona of the dead person. The dead human was probably there for a while, but a parasite moved in and eventually took over the haunting so that it could feed off the emotions its presence generated in the living.

If you go into the death vision and you find that it is a parasite that is doing the haunting, you will need to separate it from the dead person's persona (a little like wrestling its coat off) and then take a firm hold of the parasite and take it into the Void to send it back to where it belongs. The persona that was stripped off like a coat will also need to go into the Void.

Once a home has been stripped of the presence, it will need cleaning from an outer and inner point of view, and then it will need tuning. This can be a simple affair using a simple flame, consecrated salt and water, and then bringing the power of the Void into the house. Music can be powerful in affecting a space, and calm sacred music can be used afterwards to just still the space and restore a sense of calm.

20.2 Land-based entities

These hauntings tend to be more dangerous and dramatic than actual dead people, and must be approached with caution and intelligence. If they appear suddenly after a span of normality in the house, the chances are it has either come in or been triggered by something brought into the house, or something happening at the house.

Sometimes these beings have been there for generations and are a part of the land. In that case there is nothing you can do about it and the best option is to leave. I lived in a house in north California for two years that sat upon a site that was terribly unbalanced and dark. All sorts of parasitical beings ran around the house messing with the family, and one bedroom was unusable because it was so badly haunted. No amount of cleansing, banishments, bribes and threats got rid of it. It came into people's dreams and fed them hatred, paranoia and general mental instability.

In the end we threw in the towel and moved. I later heard that on that street, people regularly went mad and one tenant had gone on a killing spree after spending time there. Yum! The being was part of that land, and was known to local Indians as the 'black snake.' It had been disturbed by the aggressive gold mining years before, which had brought it up to surface in a hostile manner. Later, a yellow fever camp sat upon that spot where people were forced to stay when they got ill. Many people died there in terrible circumstances which fed the whole unhealthy land pattern. There was nothing that could be done: that land needed to not have humans on it any longer: it needed to be left in peace to slowly compost and regenerate.

Most land beings that come into houses are attracted by a particular energy and the first step is to identify what attracted them in the first place. Sometimes rituals or magical work can attract them, which means you are not clearing your space or opening it without properly tuning it.

Sometimes the energy a teen puts out can attract them, or your house could be sat on an energy vortex (which sucks) or you could be unlucky enough to live upon a patch of land that is of death: that means it has a large area that is considered access to the Underworld. In those areas, the veils between the worlds are thin and it will be like living in Grand Central Station. In those types of cases you need to keep your house fully tuned at all times, have a sacred flame going at all times and do regular 'let's clear out the dead, confused and hungry beings' sessions.

In the USA, the native Indians knew about these areas and did not live upon them but instead they chose to bury their dead there. Nashville (in fact North TN in general) is a good example of this, as are Milwaukee and Chicago. These areas have lots of hauntings, lots of strange parasitical beings floating around, and consequentially have a much higher incidence of violent killers and mentally unstable people. The areas often stretch for hundreds of miles and affect anyone sensitive who lives in that area.

In Britain, stone circles, churches and Roman temples tend to adorn such places in an attempt to harness the power and use these Underworld entrances. These land areas are not 'bad' or 'evil,' they are just powerful: they mediate power that connects with death, the Underworld and the destroying element of Divinity within the land. So if you work with them in context, they are balanced and powerful.

20. REMOVING GHOSTS AND OTHER UNWELCOME GUESTS

If you try to live on top of them and raise kids, then you are in for a shock.

If it is not rooted totally in the land and you have something trying to eat your cat, giving lurid dreams to your teen and bothering you night after night by rattling things etc., the best thing you can do is send it back to the realm where it belongs. Praying at it will do nothing: it is probably not aware of human religions and it will wonder what on earth you are doing. Such beings often appear scarier than they actually are and some take great delight in dressing up in 'scary suits' taken from your imagination. These beings work through the mind and affect the mind the most, so you work with the mind to get rid of it.

First rule: no emotions. Second rule: total focus on what you are doing. Third rule: know where you are going to put it before you grab it. The best way is always to take them into the Void and release them there with the order for them to go back where they came from. Taking a being like that into the Void takes great focus as you are working with stillness, which is bloody hard if you have a wriggling screaming 'being' in your grasp.

Alternatively you can take it down into the depths of the Underworld and leave it there, hoping that it will not find its way back again. If it is particularly nasty, then if you have access to a fireplace or a fire pit, build a fire before you start. If you cannot get it into the Void, cast it into the fire to send it back to its own line.

Should you ever be silly enough to grasp hold of a being that turns out to be much more powerful and nastier than you thought (and this is something where I talk from personal stupid experience) go straight into the Void within you and expand your consciousness to the eternal soul that is you. It will not be able to keep a hold on you and will fizzle off you. If you know where in the Abyss it belongs, call upon the Sandalphon while in the Void and step out at the Abyss to put it back where it came from.

This underlines the importance of having the regular practice of meditating upon the Void or a similar concept. You need to do such a discipline every day if you are doing this type of work: only then will you be tuned enough to silence your emotions and mind, and expand your soul while in danger. It has to be a second nature act: it is not something that works if you have to think about it and struggle with it.

A good thing to do if you live on a power site is to go into the inner landscape and take a close look. You might have to 'build' your house into the inner landscape: sometimes these beings wander into the house because they do not know that the house is there. If it hasn't been there for long (and I am talking hundreds of years) then chances are the inner landscape is still forest or whatever is local. So beings wander around the inner landscape and find that a 'patch' has interesting and sometimes yummy energies to feed on. This is your house and your energy. Just as you cannot see them, they often cannot see you: you just feel each other. If the house is built in the inner landscape, then they can see you and will avoid you unless some bright energy attracts them.

20.3 Possession of a house by demonic forces

This is a rare occurrence, much rarer than people think: what most people think of as 'dark demons' usually turns out to be a land-based consciousnesses. If such an occurrence does happen, the approach needs to take on a series of defined steps. First you have to identify what drew them in. Beings of this power do not just wander blindly into a house: something summons them or they come in with something. Identifying the source will tell you a lot about what type of being it is and what to do with it. If it is aligned to a particular tradition or religion, then you must deal with it in that context.

Demons are not beings to mess with (no shit!) and must be dealt with angelically using the Abyss. If you don't know how to work with angels (or another culture's equivalent being) then don't try and do this level of clearing: you will get hurt. Only attempt this type of clearing if you know it is a weak form of demonic consciousness: anything bigger needs a fully experienced exorcist.

If you do know how to work with angels (and I don't mean the fluffy bunny New Age image of angels, more the bloody great big things with loads of eyes/heads/whatnot) but are not sure how to approach this sort of situation then follow these stages:

1. Identify the source.

20. REMOVING GHOSTS AND OTHER UNWELCOME GUESTS

2. Identify what element it is most aligned to.

3. If it has come in on a religious artefact, then work within the frame work (not the method, just the framework) of that religion if you can.

4. Use the archangelic beings most aligned to the being's elements, usually fire and air.

5. Be in the Void at all times and do not be teased out for anything.

6. Seal the room where you are working and open up the four directions.

7. Work through the archangelic fragments, so they are within you as you work, bind the being using recitation and take it to the Abyss.

8. Work with the archangel in the Abyss to take you and demon down to where it belongs. Do not harm it and do not have any emotion at any time. Do not listen to anything said to you, hold total focus on what you are doing at all times. Once you have found where it belongs, unbind it, seal up the crack into the human realm that allowed it out in the first place.

9. Clean yourself (sacred or ritual bath) and the space thoroughly afterwards and then consecrate the space.

10. Go into the Void and be still: allow anything to fall from you that doesn't belong with you.

11. Don't do anything for a good 10 days after. You need to be dense and to rest. This type of work takes an extreme amount of energy and can kill you if you do not approach it properly. The Inner Worlds must not exist for you for a while until your body has recovered. You will be tired, bruised, and will need lots of food and sleep for quite a few days after. Dealing with this type of being changes you forever and you have to be aware of that. You become battle scarred and more visible to that order of being in the future.

In real terms, it is best to leave this sort of work to an experienced exorcist. If this is an area of magical work that you truly want to learn, then you need to find an exorcist and apprentice yourself to them. I have written a handbook for exorcists, but it is a book to be used in tandem with actual training, or as a reference book for current practitioners.

20.4 Possession from an object

Occasionally people bring strange objects home that they found on holiday or in a junk store and do not realize that they have just brought home a statue or object that has a being living within or attached to it. It will wreak havoc in your home and the longer it is left to run around, the stronger it will get.

If you suddenly start to have strange things happening in your home, the first thing you ask is, "did anyone buy something or get something recently and bring it home?" If they cannot think, go into vision and look around the house on the inner. It will usually show up there. I have had a Hawaiian Ku marching around my house attacking my kids, along with various other strange and wonderful beings that caused chaos through curious acquisitions.

If you identify the source by looking at the 'inner' house, then that source has to go in the fire. Do not think for one minute that you can strip it out of the object because you want to keep the object: learning to let go is important! It probably cannot be fully stripped out and will need to be sent back to its own realm by going into the fire. So build a fire and burn it. Doesn't matter what it is worth: it is potentially dangerous.

It is a simple but effective way of handling these beings and it works instantly. The other way you can deal with it is to physically send it back where it came from. So if it is a religious/cultural piece, send it to a priest/ess of that religion with an explanation. They will give it a home and that will probably be where it belongs.

Having spiritual or cultural artefacts that are not tourist pieces and not of your own religion/tradition in your home is generally a bad idea. They can clash with what you do magically and that can have disastrous results. I have personally witnessed tragic events brought

20. REMOVING GHOSTS AND OTHER UNWELCOME GUESTS

on by someone conducting magic in a house full of religious magical statues from another culture where the two forms of magic clashed badly. The result was a freak house fire that had fatalities.

The golden rule with any of these situations is not to get emotional in any way, to stay focused and calm, and to know what you are doing. If you are out of your depth, then hand over the job to someone else. If you are ill, tired or hormonal, then don't do this work.

Chapter Twenty-one

How to deal with simple magical/psychic attacks

If you are a magical worker i.e. a teacher, priest/ess, healer, seer etc. in service to your community, then you are one of the unfortunate ones who lives life on the firing line. I use the term worker as opposed to practitioner, because if you are working in service, then it is a job and you are a 'worker.'

The magical worker, when acting as an interface with the Inner Worlds for the outer world, needs access at all times to inner contacts, the inner energies and to have extreme sensitivity to what is around them. You cannot do that and have protection on, as the protection will interfere to some degree with your ability to filter and mediate: it will lessen your sensitivity.

And yet if you spend your time taking off parasites, lifting curses, dragging groups of people around the Inner Worlds or peering into the future, then you will have regular natural splats and the odd directed attack from some unsavoury immature person. Usually the splats and attacks are fairly minor and do not take much to deal with, but if you are working a lot and are getting hit a lot, then the short term solution isn't really practical.

Natural splats (parasites, psychic sludge and grime) are dealt with by daily magical hygiene: use lots of salt when washing and take a blessed bath using salt after working. Don't put the same clothes back on, throw them in the washer and put clean clothes on.

Attacks are slightly different as they are so varied, usually emotively driven and can just be bloody annoying. Mostly they are badly done and have a short shelf life, but a few of them in succession can end up like a squeaky wheel or door: this doesn't really do any harm, but it drives you nuts.

21. How to deal with simple magical/psychic attacks

But attacks like that, simple and not dangerous ones, are a bit like the common cold: the body and soul can use them to process things, to strengthen your inner immune system and to give you an elephant hide. The common cold is often used by the body to process and dump all sorts of stored toxins and viruses, and an attack has a similar use for the inner you.

Not reacting or defending from an attack or attacks can put you into a very interesting space if it is done properly. When you first sign up to be a magical worker in service, there is a certain road you can take that has its own inherent protections, backups and knowledge bases. That road is the road of the inner servant/worker. It is not religious, not connected to any system and can be used within any magical or spiritual system that has similar ethics.

It is a simple case of opting out of day-to-day fate and putting your life in the hands of the Universe. There are a variety of ways to do this and the one I know best is the edge of the Abyss, communing with the angelic being within the Abyss, handing over your fate in service, and submitting to the power and knowledge of the Universe.

What this means is that past actions which have tipped the scales and need rebalancing are not processed by the usual means: this generally entails having to face, be confronted by or having a taste of your past misdeeds and acts of total stupidity. The submitting to the power of the Universe triggers the automatic basic protection, access to knowledge and ability to bridge massive amounts of power, but only when truly needed.

The protection is only from that which you cannot handle alone, or from anything which stops you from doing your job properly. The 'knowledge access' is the ability to tap into whatever information or knowledge you need to achieve your service, and it only comes to you when you need it: you often forget it afterwards (which is really, really annoying). The bridging of massive amounts of power is truly awesome and blows your socks off: but again, you have no control over it: it comes when needed and at no other time.

Instead, you work off your karma (for want of a better description) by being of service to anyone or anything that is put in your path. This also means not making money from it: it must be free from all energetic rules, ties, and balances, and also from any temptations.

In practice, this method allows the Universal power to get on with its job and you to get on with yours. I have found that not taking action against an attack becomes a powerful thing: the attacker gets to learn the hard way why not to attack by being allowed free rein to 'hang themselves.' This means that unstopped, they burn out and eventually have to face their own actions: you are allowing their true fate to continue by not interfering.

It also, with that thin veil of protection to stop too much accumulation, strengthens the worker by regular 'exercise.' If you are truly committed to a life of service, then you will be given lots of work to do and the tougher you get, the harder the tasks become. You strengthen by adversity, which enables you to deal with the real and serious nasty things that can happen in the many worlds around us.

It's strange: the deeper you go in magic, the more it becomes apparent that in ninety percent of cases, it should not be used.

One thing that is important to consider before you go tripping off heartily to the Abyss to declare your life of service is that the deeper the magic and power you have access to under service conditions, the faster and harder your 'karma' becomes. The act of stepping into the shoes of a worker is a profound one: you are held above all others in terms of the need for wisdom, maturity and integrity. If you knowingly do something that is harmful, vindictive or just plain selfishly wrong, then you will have the large hand in the sky swinging down to slap you bloody hard on the bum: your scale balancing is instant.

This has nothing to do with right and wrong, moral codes or anything like that: it is about cause and effect. With having such access to power, you move up the ladder of power evolution. With that move up the stakes get higher, the effects get stronger and the balancing gets faster. This is just about how power works. You need to have balanced scales, so to speak, to work deeply in service. That way, if you have to deal with serious demonic entities, there is nothing they can blackmail you with, threaten you with or jerk your chain with.

21. How to deal with simple magical/psychic attacks

And that is important for the safety of your life and the lives of those close to you.

Anything that you do towards another person or place creates an energetic pattern, so living a simple life free of complex illicit affairs, weird sex with goats, curse compulsions or Marks & Spencer's shoplifting sprees, tends to keep you fairly pattern free. And that in itself makes for a simpler life. So if you screw up, you will get the balancing action almost immediately and with bells on, just to make sure that you have got the message.

If you don't want to go down that route for the sake of protection, then the other option, which is simpler, but is less of a magical move up the ladder so to speak, is to go into the Void whenever you work and whenever you are attacked. This really should become a daily meditation in which you still yourself to such a point that any magic/being that is on or around you will immediately become apparent.

In that stillness, you learn to pause before reaction and take time to look at what it is that is on you. And I mean really look. Once you learn to look at magic in a clinical fashion without emotion, you will begin to see its construction, its signatures, its emotive content, etc. This tells you a lot about where it has come from and why. With that knowledge, you then slowly peel it off and let it vanish into the Void. Take no action towards the sender: don't even have emotion or thought regarding them: as a worker, the task of educating the sender will be taken care of by fate, not by you.

And that is also a point to remember: someone who has the immaturity to curse or attack will not truly learn anything from retaliation or punishment. They will only stop doing it when they learn why not to do it, and that wisdom is usually brought about by deep personal suffering. That suffering in turn brings compassion and maturity. You are not responsible for the development of someone's soul: you do not have access to their deepest self to see where the learning is truly needed. Therefore you turn that action over to the structure of fate and get on with your job.

The other option is to get a shotgun and every time someone magically attacks you, you blow their kneecaps out. But that can get messy.

Chapter Twenty-two

Dismantling Hermetic or Kabbalistic curses

If someone should ever curse you, just hope that they are an idiot and do not know what they are doing: that way you don't wake up dead...

Ritual curses that emanate out of the 'Western Mystery Tradition' have many forms that do many things, but what they all have in common is their source of structure. To dismantle a curse you have to work within the language that was used to build it, using the same tools and types of beings that the 'curser' used.

For this section I am focusing purely on curses launched from people who operate within the Hermetic, Western Kabbalistic magical forms. The methods discussed within this chapter will most probably not work if you were attacked by a true Jewish Kabbalist or Chassid, but then, what would such a religious person in Israel want with a hermetic magician in Bromley?

Also, if you are cursed by someone from one of the many old tribal traditions (not a New Age reconstruction)...dude...you're on your own...

One would think that someone who has reached the level of Major Adept in a magical tradition would have a little maturity about them and would not take to blindly attacking on the magical plane anyone who upsets their applecart. But unfortunately it does happen and we do have to learn to deal with it. Magical practitioners who have not reached such a stage of training can also probably pull together some sort of attack, but they are usually fairly minor and can be dealt with using common sense, an inner clearing and a lot of salt.

The types of curses that are outlined in this chapter are curses that are powerful and serious. A serious attack or curse needs careful

22. Dismantling Hermetic or Kabbalistic curses

thought and consideration. Make a wrong move and a carefully crafted curse could kill you. It's not a joke and it has nothing to do with belief: it is the construction and moulding of powers that uphold the universe and they will take you out if they are pointing at you.

22.1 What is a Hermetic/Kabbalistic curse?

A curse is a construction using patterns, beings, energies and shapes that are brought together to achieve a goal. That goal could be anything from stopping someone speaking, writing, walking or going to a certain area, to the extreme of killing someone or making them seriously ill. It can be used against a person, place or thing. The structure of the construct holds the intent, the being gives it life and action, and the energy runs it. Usually curses don't 'run out,' they will continue for as long as the energy source is going and until it completes its task. Sometimes they can run for generations.

Then there is the basic law of power mediation: to bring something from the inner to the outer it must pass through you first: the mediator or doorway for power is affected by what they bring through. It is a simple and basic law and everyone seems to forget it.

This universal law is not about morals, it's about the nuts and bolts of the universe and how the balance of power works. Every time you put something out, a pattern is created which has life of its own. It has to run to completion and cannot be stopped. If it has come through or from you, then you are inextricably linked to it (even if you attach a scapegoat to it to avoid the backlash) and it will affect your fate one way or another until it has run its course. This is the basis of karma, and this is why 'sorry' doesn't work: it's not about how you feel, what you think or what your morals are. If you jump on one side of the seesaw, the other side will pop up, it's called physics.

Another interesting side of this law is that once the pattern of the curse is released, that pattern is connected to the curser as a part of their being or 'fate.' If that curser should then go onto consecrate a person, that consecrated person also becomes a part of the pattern. Why? Because a true consecration flattens your own soul fate and you take on the mantle of the line into which you have been consecrated.[1] There is only ever one consecrated human in a particular line just as there is only ever one consecrated sword, cup, etc. So by the act of being consecrated, you become one with the consecrator which means everything that consecrator 'is' magically becomes a part of you—hence the need to be slightly picky when choosing which magical line to be consecrated into. A truly outstanding example of this is the consecrated line that runs through W. G. Grey.

Although that pattern cannot be stopped it can be redeemed: just because you inherit the line habit of cursing doesn't mean you too have to curse. You can choose to rebalance the seesaw by offering in service to dismantle the damage wrought by your fellow priests. This is somewhat of the redemptive basis for Christianity. You cannot be indifferent or opt out: if you are in the line where the consecrator cursed people, you will either curse or will lift curses.

The sensible choice is to lift them...But if you are in that inherited line, the stronger your inner abilities, the stronger the urge to attack will be. The rebalancing comes from having the strength to overcome the urges, and to not try and justify attacks to yourself. This resistance in turn pulls away energy from the parasitical beings that are often wrapped up in such unhealthy lines. The beings, like the line, are passed from generation to generation and they build their working knowledge of the human psyche as they go along: this enables them to find newer and juicer ways to lean on the urge to attack.

22.2 How do curses affect the victim?

So, you are unfortunate enough to have been cursed? That truly sucks! Curses affect their victims on many levels depending on what the curse was aimed at. If it was a simple curse to stop you communicating, or to isolate you or to stop you doing some activity, then no matter how hard you work or how good you are at something, unbelievable blocks will fill your path. The body will react to the curse, particularly if you are sensitive. Usually most curses are at this level as few people are truly nasty enough to curse to the death.

---

[1] N.B. Consecration is not the same as initiation or ordination.

22. Dismantling Hermetic or Kabbalistic curses

If you have been cursed to the death then your body will definitely react to it and you will also find yourself in the most bizarre accidents and close shaves. If the curser is good at what he/she does and you have no real protection, then you will probably die of a strange illness or you will be killed in an accident. (Don't you just love my positive outlook on life?)

If you have been cursed to the death and you have some real protection, then you will become ill and you will survive a series of close shave freak accidents. If you happen to be unfortunate enough to have a close family who are all magical or who are sensitive/physic/empaths, then it will spill over onto them too. They will suffer the same illnesses and accidents, most of the time not quite so strongly, but enough to cause concern.

By illnesses and accidents, I do not mean that if you stub your toe a lot and get lots of colds then you are cursed, I mean that if you suddenly begin to suffer from life-threatening illnesses for which there is no visible cause, and you are suddenly in near-fatal accidents, nearly get shot or do get shot, are attacked by muggers, rapists, wild animals and this is happening on a weekly basis, chances are there may be something wrong.

If you survive the initial attacks, then after a few months the body and the energies around you begin to shift and adjust around the curse: you begin to learn to live with it. It will mean that your life will be a string of bizarre accidents and strange illnesses, and people will react to you in negative ways. Your life will probably fall apart and nothing that you do in your outer life to improve your lot will work. So the curse goes from acute to chronic. If the curse is never lifted, then chances are you will die before the time you were fated to die and the life you live before that death will be full of suffering. Don't you just love positive thinking?

If it is eventually lifted, then chances are you will be left with physical and emotional scars or disabilities, and your lifespan will still probably be a bit shorter, just not as short as it would have been if the curse had not been lifted. The blocks in your life will fall away and any energy that has been blocked from you will now rush in like water escaping from a dam.

22.3 So what about protection?

Well, there are two major ways of protecting yourself: covering yourself with magical protections, or turning over your trust to the inner worlds. The festooning with magical protections works to an extent and only to the level of your own magical skills. If you are in for the long haul, then magical protections will take up a vast amount of your time and energy which in itself is dangerous. In the long term, it is not a good or wise option.

The best protection comes from beings that uphold the structure of the universe. If you call upon specific beings to protect you, then your level of protection will depend on what level of power you can use to interface with these beings: chances are the beings have far more power in their pockets if you just let them get on and do their job rather than giving them a set job description which is what a summoning basically is.

The way to do this is simple and yet complex: if you are doing inner/magical work, then make sure it is for the true service of the Universe: this in itself will bring a certain level of protection with it. Don't do the service just to save your own ass, though: do it because it is the right thing to do.

Call upon the power of Divine Being to guide you and to protect you from that which you cannot handle yourself: the curse will not be lifted from you, nor will your life get easier, but it will stop you being killed and it will put you within a loop of cause and effect. If you learn compassion, patience and generosity out of the suffering, then lifelines of compassion, patience and generosity will be thrown out to you to give you what you need and no more. It will not stop the learning or strengthening process that happens with chronic curses, but it will give you the chance not to be destroyed.

It all sounds spiritual, and that is because it is. Heavy death curses peel away all the pap from one's life and from one's magical experiences, and what you are left with is a view of the Universe. You learn that taking action in the inner and outer worlds, regardless of what that action is for, shortens and limits power. Witnessing and upholding the natural flow of action in the Universe however, exposes you to the true extent of power that flows through all the worlds: it is breathtaking.

22. Dismantling Hermetic or Kabbalistic curses

This is the magical basis for the religious saying, "let God deal with it." It does work, but only if approached the right way. You cannot turn over your responsibilities, nor can you dump your learning path. What will happen is anything that is truly beyond your ability to cope with will be dealt with, and the rest is up to you. It will teach you a lot, it will strengthen you and it will test you to the extreme of life, but it will not destroy you unless you let it.

Basic practicalities: don't do protection rituals, and don't summon beings to protect you. Go into the Void and learn to be still, call out for Divine Being to send you beings to help you in any way that you truly need help, and make these meditations and calls a daily practice. And in return, be truly of service/help to those around you who are placed in your path, and to the Inner Worlds. Learn to trust and communicate properly with the beings that work with you, let them do their job: don't try and direct them.

Don't do anything that triggers the various levels of the curse : i.e. going to places that you were bound from, seeing people you were blocked from, doing activities that were part of the curse (ie. writing, teaching, magical practice, etc. Go to ground for a while and be patient. Your body needs time to adjust so that you can survive in the long term.

Do not, under *any* circumstances get into the silly New Age Wiccan fantasy of 'sending it back.' A curse is not a poison pen letter: it is a heavily crafted piece of magical structure with a bloody great being attached to it. Not only will it blow your boat out of the water with tripwires, but you are also getting into a 'conversation' energetically with the sender. This will cause a deeper digging in of the relationship between curser and cursed, and the dance will continue for much, much longer. It will also obviate immediately any deep inner protection that you might be getting from the Inner Worlds.

To care for your body is important...and the following advice will sound like the exact opposite of what is healthy! You will need power substances that block certain energies and make you denser. So if you are a vegetarian, start eating meat. Coffee, tobacco and chocolate are all power substances that work in various ways to filter inner powers, which is why they were used by the priests and kings in the Central

22.3. So what about protection?

American cultures. Coffee is a wonderful blocking tool as it affects the serotonin levels, which is one of the things that inner attacks work through: the endocrine system is vulnerable during an attack and will probably burn out along with the immune system if it is a chronic curse.

Stay away from gambling, lotto cards, bingo, anything that involves you possibly gaining from chance: this obviates inner protection and inner providing. You can only be on one fate wheel at a time and by going onto the luck/chance fate wheel, you climb off the wheel where you have handed over your fate to a higher and more sensible power.

Stay away from alcohol, as it will open you wider to the effects of the attack, as will most drugs. Also anti-inflammatory drugs can be counterproductive as they seem to mess with the body's ability to cope with a full-on attack. When first attacked, the body can have an immune reaction as it will see the attack as an invading being, which it is, and will respond accordingly.

More usually, the victim quickly becomes sick with all the symptoms of a major acute infection (high fever, breathing difficulties, rashes, severe headache, etc.) but the blood tests will reveal nothing. Once the acute phase is over, the body will settle into a chronic illness mode and will slowly degenerate. The illness usually takes on the pattern of autoimmune disease without the usual blood markers. The illness can and often does become severe over a few years and even when the curse is lifted, the damage can take years to mend.

Don't do heavy inner work, don't frequent power sites, try to stay as invisible as possible until you can find someone to lift it. And that moves onto the next important point: do not try and deal with the curse yourself. No matter how powerful you think you are, most structured curses have booby traps that will trigger if the cursed person goes anywhere near them. Think of the curse as a nuclear bomb strapped to your abdomen: it is best to let someone else deal with it as they can look from a different angle to you and will see tripwires that you cannot see from your perspective.

This in itself is a bummer as people who have the true ability to lift such curses are not particularly thick on the ground, particularly in the higher echelons of the Western Magical World. Most of them these days have weakened themselves by selling out to the workshop and commercial publishing merry-go-round which by its greedy nature disempowers and disconnects people from deeper levels of power.

The other problem is that technical knowledge is not enough: the person needs to have access to true real power, needs to have an experience of working with many different types of beings and needs to have a strong sense of adventure so that they will not be easily scared off. In fact, technical knowledge is the least important thing in that someone with the correct qualities, connections and inner contacts can be given a technical crash course. But they have to be connected to a priesthood to draw upon: when a priest or priestess is consecrated into a tradition, they carry the power of the collective within them, which practically means collective contacts and collective power.

And if you eventually find someone with all those qualities, then they have to be willing to delve into danger: curse removal, like bomb disposal, is dangerous. It is also a lengthy, drawn-out process that can take weeks or months depending on its construction. Once the first layer is off, then the cursed person can work with the lifter if they are skilled enough, and then the dismantling will take less time and have less of an impact on the lifter. This is the other thing that tends to make it difficult to get someone to work on lifting a curse: it takes a lot of energy and has a massive impact on their body. It is hard graft work and like all hard work, it makes the body tired and sore.

22.4 Dismantling the curse: working methods

Note: there are parts of this section where I will deliberately avoid too much detail: for those who are too dumb to figure out why, putting out too much information about how curses are constructed would be a little silly, to say the least. Hopefully the middle ground will get the info to those who need it without giving it to those who want it.

"A curse is a construction using patterns, beings, energies and shapes that are brought together to achieve a goal." Hmm, so what does this mean in real terms? The use of Western Kabbalistic Magic usually moves into the realms of angelic beings and these beings are

22.4. Dismantling the curse: working methods

the most commonly used being for cursing. They are like point and click beings: you get their 'frequency,' use ritual to bind the being to the curse and off it will go. Demons on the other hand are a little trickier to use: they are closer down the pole to density (see section on the Abyss) so they have desires that can be used for bargaining. That makes them potentially unstable: they will seriously think about it if the cursed person offers them a better payoff. The same can be applied to faery beings: they like to haggle. So if the attacker is Hermetic and the curse is skilfully put together, chances are that the being involved is angelic.

The two most common elements of the angelic beings are fire and air. You can spend half a lifetime learning the names, attributes and family trees of various angelic beings, but to strip a curse off, what you really need to know is what element or attribute is it: is it an angel of fire? an angel of destruction? This knowledge is the key to the first stage of stripping off the curse.

And the more powerful the angelic being is, the less human its representation will be. The closer to humanity an angelic being is, the more sympathy it can have with humanity and the less likely it will be to allow the curser to bind it into service. The further up the Abyss the angel is and the further away from humanity it is, the less chance there is of it being even remotely interested in humanity. The point is, the further away and more powerful these beings are, the less of a humanoid shape they will have. Closer to humanity they tend to have eyes, wings, etc. The further away they are, the more they take on the appearance of Platonic solids, multifaceted complex shapes, or even mathematical structures. The truly devastating and powerful archangelic beings further up the Abyss tend to appear as their element or source construct: a tornado for air, a wall of flames for fire, etc.

It is prudent to note at this point that if someone has constructed a curse using this level of being, chances are they have a lot of ritual help (i.e. a group) and a lot of people to draw from energetically. The people might not be aware that their energies are being used in such a way, and that innocence has no effect on the curse: it will work anyway as they are just a battery to draw from.

22. Dismantling Hermetic or Kabbalistic curses

It is often a group gathering where the people are all focused on one thing for a period of time, like a workshop, teaching session or prayer session. It is irrelevant what they are doing, just that they are all together at one time, an element is present (a flame usually) and that there is a central point of focus (an action, ritual, meditation or prayer). Alternatively a large gathering of people who are on drugs can be used, but this is less focused and less reliable. This need for a large, focused group immediately cuts down the number of people who would attempt to construct such a curse as most people do not have access to such resources.

What that battery of energy does is launch the attack: working with such beings takes a great deal of energy and creates massive impact, therefore sharing the load is important.

The ritual itself can take many different forms, although there are some pretty old ones kicking about that are not too difficult to get a hold of, like the Pulsa D'Nora, but as I said before, the technical details are not that important: it's the contacts, inner ability and focus coupled with a power source that is needed.

The other ingredient for such an action is connection to an inner priesthood through a consecration. This is not a mandatory ingredient, but it will put a massive amount of power behind the attack.

With these ingredients, you can see that it is not simple and easy to curse someone, but such complexity makes it a lot easier to narrow down the search for the perpetrator. More often than not there are at least two people involved for a death curse, though singular attacks are not unknown.

22.5 What do they look like on the inner?

First you have to decide what is the safest way to look at them? Some heavy curses are tripwired to attack anyone who approaches them on the inner. You can use a tarot reading using the Tree of Life layout to look and find out what element of angelic being you are looking at. To get a clear answer you will first have to push aside any inner veils that hang around the situation and give false readings. A good way to do this is to ask the cards to tell you the truth, not what someone wants you to see: sometimes the simplest and most obvious method is the most powerful.

Once you know what type of angelic being upholds the curse, then you have to go into the angelic structure of that being and operate from within it: a fragment of that being will work through you and the being upholding the curse will see an angelic fragment, not a hyperventilating curse lifter! It is probably wise, when you do this, to have a partner working with you to hold the gates open and support you energetically. If you are terrified (which is a healthy state to be in when stepping through angels) the partner will carry the physical reaction to such fear so that you are not distracted by not being able to breathe.

When you look at someone one the inner who has been cursed, they look odd to say the least. Apart from the state that their inner energies are in, the curse itself can often look bizarre which can be off-putting and confusing to someone looking at them for the first time. The person is often surrounded by strange sigils or script: this is the binding that is spoken aloud, usually in Hebrew as it is a sacred language and holds power.

Then you will see either a being attached, around or even within them if a lesser being is used, or you will see a strange three-dimensional shape over their heads, which is the angelic being itself. Sometimes you will see the victim impaled by a magical implement and/or surrounded by wind/fire/rocks. Sometimes they are bound with concrete or tentacles if lesser elements/beings have been used, and sometimes, if they have really pissed someone off, they will have everything but the kitchen sink on and around them.

The area around them will often look like a war zone or a vacuum, as the curse will be affecting everything around them.

22.6 How are curses taken off?

The whole curse will not be taken off in one go: they are usually multifaceted, complex and may have been reiterated many times to strengthen them (some people are just so anal about their work: they keep going in and making improvements...sheesh!).

22. Dismantling Hermetic or Kabbalistic curses

The first thing you have to do is to strip off the angelic being. Once that is off, then the rest is just time and detail, as the angelic being hangs everything together. Next you have to cut off the power source without harming those people involved, and dispense with any parasitical beings that have come along for the ride. If the groups of people powering the curse are still ongoing, then you have to either keep cutting off the source of power, or you have to divert it to less dangerous uses. After that, it is a long road of stripping off layers of script using the angelic working contact you have, pulling out the magical implements and returning them carefully to the original inner implement, and then pulling off all the blocks, bindings, etc. that you find.

If you know who the attacker is, and they have something that belongs to the victim, chances are that object or bit of DNA (hair, etc.) is being used to direct the action. You will need to go in vision, find the object and take the inner form of the object into the Void where the inner imprint can no longer be used to launch a new attack.

Also, if the attacker is clever and devious, they will have constructed or trapped a scapegoat being to take any backlash, fate impact or energy kickback from the attack. This will appear to the lifter as a vastly inflated being that is not bright and is bound in slavery to the attacker. It will probably be attached to the site of the temple/working space that the attack is constructed in. It would be compassionate to unbind such a tormented creature and cut the cord that binds it to its master. It would also be wise to take it into the Void.

This whole process can take weeks or months. It is time consuming, exhausting and has to be done carefully and methodically. During this process you also have to be careful to make sure that if the attacker becomes aware that the curse is being lifted, that you take proper precautions to make sure that a new attack cannot be launched—and if it is launched, that it doesn't find its target. Usually the first time someone is attacked they are blissfully unaware of what is coming. The second time they tend to be a little wiser and are ready.

Another useful procedure that can be used if the angelic being attached is of a high frequency is to work in the realm of the Tree of Life. When the soul manifests in the position of Daath, it takes on a complex structure which is made up of angelic consciousness through which the soul manifests into life. Tracking up the tree of someone's soul will bring you to this structure and it is here where damage will show itself if high-level angelic beings have been used. The complex pattern looks a bit like a Metatron Cube and if an angel is still attached, it will show here. The trick is to take the shape of the angelic being off and repair the complex pattern back to its original form. The danger is not recognizing what is the threshold pattern for the soul and taking that off instead of the angel. If you are not used to working with angels and thresholds as geometric patterns, then this is a technique that would best not be used.

Seeing magical cursing at this depth is intriguing and educating. Most of the time, when someone has sent something of this depth, they are not fully aware of its power and complexity. They call up specific angelic beings that are bound and wind them into the curse. The rest happens automatically from much earlier constructions, which often the sender is not aware of. Magical names, patterns and invocations if used in the right way will do the job if there is inner energy behind them: it's a bit like ready-constructed software. The real danger is when you have a Kabbalist who really knows what they are doing, has a sense of justification and a bad simmering temper. The deeper their knowledge, the more dangerous they become.

22.7 What is the cleanup procedure?

The cursed person will be sludged, chronically sick and low on inner energy. They will need ritual salt baths, connection with nature, good food and time to rest and recover. The lifter must make sure that they clean themselves and the room well after each session. (Also make sure that before you start, the room and the house/apartment/temple that you are due to work in is clean, balanced and tidy: you must leave no corner for nasties to hide in or attach to.)

Just as curse removal takes time, so does the recovery and it can take months or even a couple of years, depending on how long the cursed victim was under attack, for them to recover and regain their full strength. What is important, however, is that they begin a regular meditation practice to bring their consciousness back into action. The lifter must also be aware that what they have undertaken was a massive physical strain and must rest/recoup adequately for a few weeks before taking on another such task. Thankfully, these situations do not happen often, not at this level anyhow.

Chapter Twenty-three

Short tour of the Tree of Life without Kabbalah

The Tree of Life structure was put together to map out the externalization of Divine Being into substance. It was also a working tool: by putting together a coherent structure that people could see, it allowed people to actively interact with and observe the power of that Divine Being. Because the structure reflects such power, it is complex and intricate: the more you look at a powerful pattern, the more you will see.

One of the problems with presenting such a pattern to humanity is that they will focus on the intricate patterns and take great delight in finding new and more complex patterns: they lose sight of the real power and what it is trying to express. Therefore you end up with lots of people who all know the spheres, the pathways, the names and interconnections etc., but they do not look at the passage of Divinity through the Tree or within themselves.

Today in modern magic, people are expected to learn the paths and patterns of the Tree of Life by learning words in a sacred language that they do not understand. That in itself disables a lot of the power that can be accessed. The sacred names do hold power within themselves but the spheres are not dependent upon that power: it is a filter that can be approached with a different sacred utterance or breath.

But the reason to move away from that Kabbalistic pattern is deeper and more important: any pattern, though it creates a safety net, also limits and shapes power, dictating how that power can be connected with. The patterns and networks create paths of thought that discipline the mind, giving focus and strength. But eventually, for the mystical mind, it limits the expansion of understanding and heavily filters the ability of humans to interact with Divinity and angelic beings.

Once that pattern has been fully learned, it becomes inherent within that human so that even if they walk away from that pattern, it still lives within them and still limits them to some extent. I do think that this was intentional as a protective measure, but I also feel that such a protective action is counterproductive for humanity. We always think we know better than the universe, rather than trusting such power.

The pattern can be loosely worked with, stripping it down to almost nothing and looking at the natural flow of power and how the natural inner pattern works. If such a thing is dangerous for someone, then the chances are that that they will not get it. This is the whole point of not limiting each other as humans: you can never really tell what a fellow human is truly capable of: it is not for us to judge, filter and exclude. Nature will do that naturally.

Using the structure as sparsely as possible enables the human consciousness to comprehend something so vast without cluttering it with dead ends, endless mazes and important sounding titles (which we all love so much...). If it is inappropriate for that person, they will not understand it, they will be blocked from it or they will lose interest. This is the most common trip-up for humanity. Real power is not glamorous: it doesn't twinkle and give us importance and it doesn't give status or titles. It is simple, hard work, and requires a lot of focus and perseverance.

23.1 So what actually is the Tree of Life?

It is a map that shows the power of formation from formless Divine Power to the world and everything in it. It is the progression from formlessness to substance: it maps the creation of the Universe. It shows the focused eternal soul descending into physical form and acquiring emotion, intellect and imagination. It shows where we came from and where we return to. The outer pattern of the Tree of Life in Kabbalistic terms is a reflection of a pattern that exists on the inner planes: humanity has just made it a little more complicated.

23.1. So what actually is the Tree of Life?

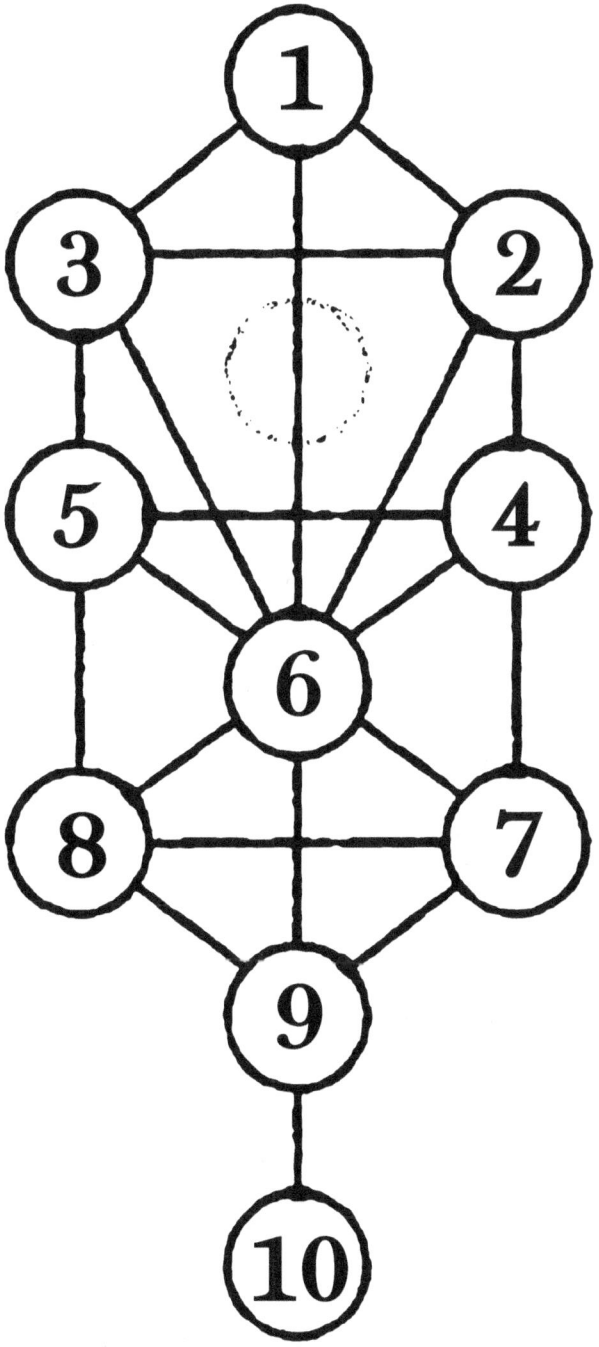

Figure 23.1: Diagram of the Tree of Life

23. Short Tour of the Tree of Life without Kabbalah

The first sphere is the first breath/act of consciousness out of the Void: it is Divinity unpolarized, poised on the brink of expression.

The second and third sphere are the separation of Divine consciousness into negative and positive. Without that split, life and the universe cannot happen as everything that takes on physical manifestation is polarized. This polarized Divinity stands (from our perspective) on the other side of the Abyss. The Abyss appears to us in vision as a vast crack in a Desert landscape, and essentially it is a dividing line between Divinity and the rest of creation/destruction (the Universe). It is also a place/state of storage and profound learning, hence its official Kabbalistic name is Daat.

Once Divinity crosses the Abyss, it begins the process of taking on form. The polarization that occurred before the Abyss is repeated and mirrored: Divinity becomes positive (forth sphere) and negative (fifth sphere) action and inaction, forward momentum and movement withheld. The fourth sphere is the 'forward into creation' power, and the fifth sphere is the 'brakes on the power of creation' or 'destruction.' Between those two spheres sits the sixth sphere which is the fulcrum that balances the two opposing powers. The three central sefirot provide the building blocks for the inner soul of the soon-to-be created living being/world: positive, negative and stasis between the two powers in tension. At this stage in the process of formation, for a vessel to begin forming to allow a soul to express itself in the physical realm, it must have inner dynamics that will link together the deeper powers of formation with time, substance and fate. Those dynamics are also part and parcel of the powers of the three central sefirot.

When you get to the seventh, eighth and ninth sefirot, you are now in to the 'production' area of mirror dynamics that are evident in all living things, and for us as humans, they are dynamics that flow through every aspect of our lives from how we act, how our bodies work, to how we operate within our fate paths. These three sefirot are very much about *how we live* and are dynamics that the magician can actively engage in their life and work. Sefirot seven and eight are our 'two feet' that carry us through fate and life, and they are powers of discipline/endurance and release/loosening. These dynamics in their deepest true sense is how our bodies work, and the same dynamics can be intentionally engaged in how we do our magic and how we live our lives.

23.1. So what actually is the Tree of Life?

The ninth sefirot is about fate patterns, genetic patterns, blood, ancestral lines, and also about our imagination, our emotions and our dreams: how we dream and imagine our lives to be. To exist, we are a thought first. The inner idea and pattern of the body is formed, then the ancestral/fate patterns begin to form.

The final sefirot is our living body, our world, our universe: it is everything around us. It is Divine Power manifest into human or physical form—the Divine Universal consciousness that, breathed out, takes on physical form and becomes a human body, a tree, a planet. This is the root of the teaching that 'God is in everyone' and we are all Divine Being. The tenth sphere is also the world, creation manifest, the vessel for life itself.

Now you have to keep in mind that the Tree of Life with its spheres and paths is simply a map of a creation process. It is not really a natural pattern, but it was created by a man as a way to formalize the pattern that is the expression of Divinity within humanity.

That map has now become complex to the point of ridiculousness and has almost come to a point of uselessness. The above description is an attempt to take it back to a simpler form. As humans we love to list things, organize things, pattern things and form groups, tribes and hierarchies. That immediately powers down our ability to truly experience the natural magical world around us, and to truly partake of that world without conditions. It is the stepping out of the Garden: by having to have knowledge and control, we obviate our ability to truly *know*.

Some of this harks back to former discussions regarding working with angels and the Kabbalistic filters. Kabbalah teaches certain patterns to open up a filtered threshold through which we can work with angels. But it limits how we 'see' that angelic being and how we work with it. That angel can only respond within the parameters that we set, which also limits the angelic being in its ability to interact and work with us. Now I am not saying that the Kabbalistic way of working with angels is not powerful: it most certainly is. What I am saying is that it limits us from the true scope of that being, both in our experience and how we work with it.

Working with angelic beings without the rigidity of that structure opens the door for that angel in all its true power. The angelic being itself determines how much of that power you will have access to through that door. It will give you access to what you need and no more. It will not stop your access based upon your intentions as there is no moral filter with these beings: if you can handle the power, then you will get access to it. If you cannot, then you will not.

And working with the progression of Divinity into humanity is much the same: if you can take the pressure of riding with Divinity as it falls out of the Void and into life, then you will go along with the ride and observe what truly happens. If you are not able to hold that level of power, nothing will happen.

Working through the Tree of Life pattern enables us to take apart what we see in a deeper experience and break it down into manageable parts for understanding. It also allows an observer or researcher to look closely at one aspect of the progression and zoom in on it. For example, from the Tree structure we can see that the pattern for mind and emotions are formed just before the body is formed. It has an inner as well as outer quality to it, but it is not part of the eternal soul, it is only an inner part of this life expression.

Chapter Twenty-four

The Structure of the Abyss without Kabbalah

The Abyss, like angelic beings, has been the territory of mystical Kabbalah almost to the point of exclusivity. The complexity of real Kabbalistic training has so many tangles, filters and dead ends that it can encourage the practitioner to become focused upon patterns to the extent of truly missing what they are attempting to work with.

Some of that structure was originally woven into the training methods as a safety valve, not only to discourage idiots and casual glances, but also to create a 'firewall' from an inner point of view. When you work with an Angelic being, you are potentially playing with a 'nuclear' type of power. The names, attributes, patterns, shapes and rituals filter and form the power that you work with, and dictate what method of interaction is used with such a being.

So you get a focused, filtered, power controlled contact that does specific things and does not move out of its structure. Although that is still powerful and dangerous, it is much safer to work with as a magical practitioner.

If you do not use these filters, shapes and patterns, then you are faced with the true power of the Angelic being in all its glory and you have to be extremely focused, unconditional and balanced. You also have to be willing to die if it is necessary.

This rule is also true for working in and with the Abyss. If it is approached with its magical filters then it can be worked with safely but in a limited and filtered way. The more patterns, attributes and rules we apply, the less of the Abyss we are able to access.

And yet accessing the Abyss without such filters is asking for trouble unless you know what you are doing. Many a hapless magician has been burned to a crisp by reaching down or up the

24. THE STRUCTURE OF THE ABYSS WITHOUT KABBALAH

realms of the Abyss in pursuit of power. If you reach into the Abyss for power, it will destroy you in one way or another eventually.

When you reach beyond the surface world in magical practice, you reach into worlds of beings and power. If you reach beyond that level, you begin to touch upon the workings of the universe and the structures/beings that make sure the universe continues to exist and function (the universal boiler room). If you are stupid enough to think that you can reach into the boiler room to tap into that power for personal gain, then you are an idiot.

If you want to reach into the boiler room to be of service, then you are still probably an idiot (it is extremely dangerous) but at least you are a worthy idiot and with such selfless intent, you will probably be protected to an extent. If humanity does not create its own filters, then the Inner Worlds will do it for you, and theirs tend to be far more workable.

The inner filters work to protect you from complete destruction, but they will allow enough power though to do the job and teach you something: bear in mind that humanity always learns the hard way. It can be a difficult lesson, though usually a important one.

What is the Abyss? If you strip all the formal padding away that has been attributed to it, you are left with a multidimensional freeway for power and consciousness. The way that we see it when we look at it from an inner point of view is just the way our brains perceive it: it has no real form as such.

The Abyss is a highway from the highest form of consciousness to the lowest: the two extremes meet one another and are of one another. It is mirrored in the Tree of Life with Divine Being at the top and Humanity at the bottom, so the Abyss is Divine consciousness without form at the 'top' and the densest of beings at the 'bottom.' If I try to describe the shaping too much I will really get my knickers in a twist, because the dimensions of this structure are many and are beyond our ability to grasp.

Divine Being is at the top, then archangelic and angelic beings, at the point of Humanity is the Desert/abyss, which is the area that is our fulcrum for the whole thing. Below our fulcrum are demons, bigger demons and then Divine Being in its densest form. (Which is also primal and newly-birthed humanity.) In between those levels are lots of interconnections, levels of consciousness and a wide variety of beings. The structure also bends in on itself, so that the top and bottom are the flip sides of one another. Humanity in the middle is our balanced state between good and bad, no form and density: we are the fulcrum of the Tree.

At this point it is worth noting that when magicians figure this out (that humanity is the fulcrum) many tend to trip out on being the master species. Those tend to be the stupid ones. At the fulcrum is also the rest of our physical world: the animals, plants, etc. Everything that is physically manifest is in our realm of the fulcrum. The other levels are different worlds/states of consciousness: hence shedding your humanity is one of the keys to exploring and working with the Abyss.

In reality humanity tends to veer from that centre line in both directions: so the Satanists dive down and the Messiahs reach up (they tend to get nailed to bits of wood if they go too high up...). The goal of Humanity is to stay at that midline: to keep the balance of substance and non-substance, good and bad, in perfect harmony, and to stay in their own realm.

That is why it is so important when you work deeply in the Inner Worlds that first you go through the Void and shed your everyday world. Then you approach the Abyss unconditionally, without selfish intent and with proper focus: that way you cannot be dragged to one extreme or the other. This is also the reason why, when you first begin working at the Abyss, you are often asked if you are willing to give up your life. You have to be willing to let go of everything, therefore nothing can be used to seduce you and nothing can hold you back. If you can shed life within life, then you are a step further on in the Mysteries (this is the root of the death within life initiation).

Another point to look at with this pattern is what happens at conception: the act of making love reaches through the worlds in search of a consciousness to bring into form. If you imagine that the couple is making love at the bottom of the structure (which is also at the fulcrum) they open an inner vortex that stretches up through the Abyss until it reaches as far as it can go. Then a soul tumbles in from that level and falls into conception.

This is the basis for the sacred union: the sex between priest and priestess, Queen and King, etc. Their lovemaking would be focused and with spiritual intent for bringing through a sacred child. They would go through a variety of physical and mental preparations, and the act itself would be held in a sacred space. The method used is also mirrored in the Mysteries of Tantra.

The flip side of the sacred union is debauched, unhealthy forced or unconnected sex where the vortex does not reach far up and brings through unhealthy beings. Faery children are born when the vortex reaches to the Faery Realm: one or both partners mediate a faery being while making love so the Vortex reaches up to that frequency.

It is like tuning a radio: whatever frequency/wavelength you are on, that is what you will bring into your body. And it does not have to be a physical child: this can also bring through inner beings when done with intent.

So, back to the Abyss. Not only is Divine Being 'up,' it is also 'across.' When you cross the Abyss, you are into the realm of Divinity polarized, and then unformed but preparing for form. To understand this better, look at the Tree of Life: you cross the Abyss and you hit Divinity split into Male and Female (Chokmah and Binah) beyond that is God without Form but in preparation (Kether).

This split into Male and Female is purely for the fulcrum/human realm: we are by nature polarized beings (male/female, positive/negative) as is the world around us. Divinity filters through that polarization so that Divinity and humanity can be aware of each other. The further away a being is from the Fulcrum, the less aware of humanity it is.

The dimensions and twists of the Abyss can be mind-bending: God is up and also across. And Divinity is also down in its most dense twisted form, as is the human form—which brings about the reflection of the ability within humanity for great good or great evil. It depends which part of the pole you are sliding down (or up). The best way is to get blindingly drunk, then it all makes sense.

In practical terms you would work in the boiler room (remember the boiler room?) for specific reasons rather than sightseeing or personal gain. If you are in the business of creating a sacred or faery child, if you are working with Angelic consciousness, if you are working within the realm of death, if you are an exorcist, a worker in Universal service, or if you are stupid enough to want to stand at the foot of God, or connect with a demon, then the Abyss is for you.

The closer to the fulcrum a being is, the more aware it is of humanity and it will be either 'friendly' towards humanity or 'unfriendly.' The further a being is away from the fulcrum the less aware of humanity it is and it will therefore neither be 'for' nor 'against.' Also, the further away from the fulcrum a being is the more powerful and less physically formed it is and the less able it is to manifest in the physical realm. It has to pass down the Abyss towards humanity to appear in our world: hence the angels and demons taking human/animal form.

To work with true angelic form without a human filter, you have to go up the Abyss to its own realm and meet it as an inner being. The same is also true for what we call demons. The two sides of the Abyss beyond the fulcrum reflect for us the two sides of power: threshold mediation power becomes angels and demons, the extremes become Divinity in dense form or formlessness, etc.

All the levels between have their own 'fulcrums' that appear as tunnels and as the beings of those levels come to the edge of the Abyss, they have their own 'up' and 'down.' Our spiritual evolution is about being cast 'down' and finding our way back 'up' to formlessness.

If you are an exorcist, this boiler room can be especially useful as it enables one to commune with beings at their own level in their own realm as opposed to how they express themselves when they are in our polarized worlds. It is also safer to approach some of these beings this way. However the rule of the Abyss, as always, is to be focused, be in service, and have no wants or needs. True clarity and the Void within keeps a worker safe in the deepest realms and keeps the inner filters in place.

That is not to say you won't get the shit hammered out of you: you probably will. But that is just the side effect of working at such depth: it is not from any being attacking you. The deeper or higher you go away from your own realm or the fulcrum, the more of an impact it is going to have on your body. Even though you are working through your mind, the power filters through the physical body and you will

24. The Structure of the Abyss without Kabbalah

feel like you have just built a house singlehandedly while being beaten with a cricket bat.

What can go wrong? Oh, lots! If you are a skinny, spotty, black-clothed, chain-festooned Luciferian intent on communing with demons to expand your power over women, men, groups, and to get a bigger willy, then one of three things will happen:

1. You will not manage it but will end up connecting with bottom-feeder, parasite-type beings. This will take you down a path of feeling terribly important and possibly depressed at the same time. You will become paranoid, depressed, withdrawn and even spottier (the power flows through your body and will enhance any imbalance, therefore if you were spotty to begin with, it will get worse).

2. If you should happen to have natural abilities and are able to connect with beings, then you may in fact connect with a lesser (nearer to our realm) demon who may offer you just what you want and have a really amusing time at your expense, and your willy will not get bigger.

3. If you are truly naturally able to connect with beings you may reach a deep 'demonic' or Titan consciousness that will look at you in complete fascination, being unable to work out exactly what you are and what the hell you want. These beings can be disastrous for humanity not because they are 'bad' but because of the sheer power they mediate.

The same is true of going 'up.' Angelic beings closer to our realm tend to be worked with in the Kabbalistic patterns (among others). You can also work with them outside of those patterns, but you do need to be focused with your intent and concentration (otherwise all that will be left of you is a pair of slightly burned shoes).

If you have natural talent for connecting with beings, you might also reach up quite far and come face-to-face with an archangelic being (well, not quite face-to-face: as with the deeper demons, they are rather large...) which, like the deeper demon or Titan, will look at you with total astonishment before trying to communicate with you. If it does, not even your shoes will be left.

There are methods for working and communicating in both directions with these beings, and the methods are simple, direct and hard to maintain. If you chose to toss aside the magical structures/patterns and don't do it via drugs (which is the worst possible way, just because of the lack of control: the drug is in the driving seat) then working through the Void or carrying the Void within is your best option.

If you are working from an intention of universal service, then you will have the natural inner filters in place, and working through the Void will bring you to a fraction of the being you need to work with. Note the use of the work 'need.' When you go through the Void, you are connected to what you need for the job, not necessarily what you want.

If you work through the pattern of the Abyss, take the Void within you and the same filters will be in place. You have to try to maintain a balance, though: if you are working in the Abyss, work in both directions. This not only ensures that you gain a working knowledge of beings on both sides of the 'fence,' which is handy in any deep work, but it also maintains a sense of inner balance, which is also important if you are engaging in deep useful magic.

Those workers who constantly reach up and work only with angelic beings, climbing higher and higher up the ladder of angels, eventually stretch too far away from the fulcrum and 'cease to be' (or in Yorkshire terms, they fry themselves). The prophet Enoch 'who walked with God and was not' is one example. The angels are the beings that bring pattern into being, and also dismantle patterns—including humans.

And what happens if you only reach down the Abyss, going deeper and deeper? Well, I guess you become a conservative politician. The beings of the lower Abyss are ancient beings that manipulate and hold patterns in being. So you implode physically and mentally.

But for sensible, balanced and powerful work, work on both sides, and up and down. Work for true intent and with focus: and by true intent I don't mean 'good' or 'bad': I mean true intent, for a job, something that is not selfish. Good and bad is relative to your culture/religion, it depends on which end of the action you are on. But

24. THE STRUCTURE OF THE ABYSS WITHOUT KABBALAH

the difference between selfish and unselfish acts is a big difference in the inner worlds. Selfish acts will work, but they only work to a point. Unselfish acts that are a part of service to the Universe have almost limitless access to power: it is all down to what you are capable of holding.

Chapter Twenty-five

The eighteenth-century pattern of initiation in Britain

In the eighteenth century in Britain, ritualized gardens started to appear on the properties of wealthy landowners. The best example of these can be found at Stourhead, a 2,650 acre country estate at the source of the river Stour in the southwest of England. The estate is about 4 km northwest of the town of Mere and includes a Palladian mansion, the village of Stourton, ritual gardens, the Spread Eagle Inn, farmland and woodland. Stourhead has been owned by the National Trust since 1946.

The house and ritual gardens were built and developed by the Hoare family in conjunction with Capability Brown, namely by Henry Hoare II (1705–1785) an English banker, and subsequently his grandson Sir Richard Colt Hoare (1758–1838). Sir Richard Colt Hoare was an English antiquarian, archaeologist, artist, and traveller of the eighteenth and nineteenth centuries. He was also the first major figure to conduct a detailed study of the archaeological history of his home county of Wiltshire, and is considered the 'grandfather' of British archaeology.

These ritual gardens developed during the Enlightenment era, where most landowners and intellectuals were involved in the new developing concept of ancient rite and Freemasonry, and of the esoteric Mysteries in general.

The gardens at Stourhead allude to the Aeneid and the story of the descent of Aeneas into the Underworld. The Aeneid was written by Virgil around 20 B.C. as a foundation myth for the birth and greatness of Rome. Within the texts are many different tales that are littered with mythic and magical themes, and book VI of the Aeneid

25. The Eighteenth-Century Pattern of Initiation in Britain

features a tale of struggle, victory, ascent and destiny of the mythical hero Aeneas the Trojan who became an ancestor of Rome.

The layout and buildings of the garden are loosely styled along the steps taken by Aeneas and are woven in with esoteric themes and allegories. It presents a ritual pattern of discarding the mundane in search of the gods, with the theme of initiation running strongly through the pattern.

The following is an account of what I found in and upon the land of Stourhead in Wiltshire: I was manoeuvred by a series of odd circumstances that ended up with me staying in Mere for a couple of days and being invited to spend that time wandering the gardens at Stourhead to see what I thought about it, and what I could pick up magically from the site.

I spent two days walking the garden and the ritual path: I went in vision and talked to the land, to the contacts and to the ritual inner contacts that are still operating through the magical pattern that is there. This is an account of what I found.

25.1 The Walk of Initiation at Stourhead, Wiltshire

In the mid-1700s, Sir Richard Colt Hoare, archaeologist and owner of Stourhead house, expanded upon his grandfather's and uncle's work in the creation of a Landscape of Enlightenment. Sir Richard, like his uncle before him, was a freemason and was instrumental in the founding and developing of an Apollo Lodge at Stourton (initially held at the Spread Eagle Arms Inn, Stourton).

Sir Richard was fascinated by ancient history and the land itself. He opened over three hundred ancient barrows in the area around Stourhead and wrote down what he found. He unearthed what later became known as burials of the Beaker People: ancient Britons buried in mounds, often in couples, near a spring with a richly ornamented cup and a copper dagger placed between them. Stourhead gardens and lake was created by damming six natural springs. It is obvious from the location of the burials and the type of burials that the springs were sacred.

The landscape that was laid down at Stourhead was a ritual initiation of death-in-life, and was approached from an angle of myth, vision and the practical walking of one's own inner landscape. The path through the landscape mirrors the life challenges that a spiritual/magical seeker follows in his quest for initiation into the temple of Apollo.

There are other ritual gardens that date from the Enlightenment, but none of them have as much depth, or as many layers of ritual significance, as Stourhead. For example, at Studley Royal in Yorkshire, another Enlightenment garden, the path to the temple of Apollo/sun and the descent into the passage of birth are masterfully laid out, but the other points along the way are for visual appreciation, not ritual initiation. It is obvious from the Studley Royal layout, and that of Stowe (in Bucks) that such early Masonic patterning was fashionable, but often a parody of the true path of inner enlightenment.

The concept was that inner initiation can be reached by walking the outer landscape of a magical life: every life has an inner landscape that can be manipulated. The initiation was approached by externalizing that inner landscape, so the aspirant walked the outer path that mapped the inner path. They were walked together under the canopy of ancient Greek and Roman allegory.

These eighteenth century gardens were laid out according to patterns drawn from Virgil's Aeneid, following the descent of Aeneas into the Underworld. But the deeper layers of the death vision and the interrelations between the deities are laid one upon the other. Some are meaningful, and some defy reason. Some are just humorous and sometimes very magical, for example: the tunnel of birth is laid east southeast in the garden, E.S.E.: could this be a passing glance to *esse*, the Latin verb "to be"? (The place of birth/becoming.)

25.2 The Stourhead initiation

If you are working and walking the garden with magical intent, the powers that flow through the patterns within the garden will flow through your body. *Your body will understand the initiation, even if your mind doesn't.*

25. The Eighteenth-Century Pattern of Initiation in Britain

Beginning

The walk begins at the Stourton village: people, life, ordinary things from which we all originate. The aspirant visits the church to pray and devote himself to Divinity and the service to mankind.

The path then leads the aspirant first on a garden walk to the Temple of Flora. Originally when it was first built it was named the Temple of Ceres: she who brought agriculture and therefore civilization to humanity.

Temple of Flora/Ceres

Above the door is a warning to all: "Procul, O procul este, profani." Translated this reads "begone you who are unclean/uninitiated/unworthy!"

This sets the scene for the beginnings of the initiation. First the fruits of one's harvest must be sacrificed to the Goddess, which is all part of the usual initiation. The aspirant turns over his fate to the Goddess as he prepares to step into the unknown.

Then the deeper, more magical actions come to the surface. Below the temple, near the water's edge, is a stone mouth opening from which flows a spring into the lake. (Originally this had steps leading down to the water's edge where the springs gushed out.)

In the deeper part of the Mystery, both in an actual ritual action, and an inner visionary action, the aspirant initiate places his sword in the mouth of the spring and leaves it there.

Back in the temple a flame which sits within the water is doused, reflecting the release of the soul of the initiate as it begins the journey towards death within life.

He is cast from the temple to wander among the trees in search of the entrance to the Underworld and the golden bough. He walks among the giant trees and searches for the oak tree that holds the golden bough which will give him access to the Underworld. Once he finds it, he can approach the goddess for safe passage to the Underworld

25.2. The Stourhead initiation

Moon Pool of Diana

When he reaches the Moon Pool of Diana he is 'stripped of his humanity': in death, we must learn to let go of our old lives and move on. An attendant takes from him 'that which makes him human' (his clothing) and sends him into the Underworld with the golden bough, which gives him safe passage, to seek out the advice of a Goddess who sits in an Underworld Cave by a pool of dark water...He leaves naked.

Grotto of Ariadne

The journey through the trees and through the 'gate of horn' takes the initiate to the grotto in which Ariadne rests (originally Colt Hoare named the female statue Ariadne, which makes the most sense, as you will come to see; but many years later she was renamed 'a nymph.' The grotto is laid out so that Ariadne lies in the northwest, opposite Apollo, who is visible through the grotto window. The grotto holds four seats for four officers in the four cardinal directions, and the doorways are northeast and southwest.

The Goddess demands silence: "Drink in silence, or in silence lave." The initiate hands over the golden bough as a gift to her and then he drinks, or washes in, the sacred waters. This reflects the wisdom of the death vision: those who wish to remember all simply wash their face in the river/water of death. Those who are foolish or wish to forget will drink.

In the cave is the Goddess of the Underworld, reflected by Ariadne, she who weaves and gives a sword to Theseus. Bear in mind this area is part of Avalon, a place steeped in Mystery regarding cups and swords. Remember the cup/dagger burials in the barrows? The story of Excalibur/Caliburn and the Grail are just distant remnants of ancient magical wisdoms of this land: somehow Colt Hoare tapped into this and worked with it.

The Initiate offers the Goddess whatever appears in vision in his hand, usually his testicles (metaphorically, not literally) an act which is connected to his rejection of the mundane/death of his mundane life in the temple of Ceres. In return she reaches into the springs and pulls out his sword (that was left in the spring of Ceres), which she returns to him transformed.

Upon leaving this Grotto he meets Neptune, who points to the obelisk in the distance (Phallus).

The Cottage/Vesta

The initiate climbs a simple path that ends at a pretty little gothic cottage with a bench outside. Inside, the cottage is dominated by a hearth that holds a hearty fire. It is a place of familial comfort and cooking. Here the Initiate can rest, relax, and if not careful, be drawn into domestic bliss. If the Initiate sits upon the bench and admires the view, he will notice that the church lies directly opposite the cottage: the church is in the east (God) and the cottage (humanity) is in the west. It is a direct reference to sacred architecture.

Once the Initiate is rested he must forge onward, leaving family and security behind, willingly letting them go and stepping forward into an unknown future.

The Pantheon

The Initiate then encounters the Pantheon. In the temple are gathered Goddesses, priestesses and one man (an Argonaut) who championed women's rights to be hunters. The Goddesses are Hera, Diana, Flora, Isis and the priestesses Susanna (wife of Sir Henry Hoare II) and Livia Drusilla Augusta: *Mater Patriae* of Rome (priestess of Ceres, the goddess of agriculture and therefore civilization). The temple is guarded or flanked by Baccus: intoxicating visions, and Venus: sexual passion.

In this temple, the Initiate confronts the many faces of woman or the Goddess.

Bridge over the River

The Initiate is cast from the temple when the women are satisfied with his answers and he walks down a path. At the bottom of the path, the Initiate encounters a bridge over the river Styx. As the initiate crosses the bridge, he realizes that as he looks back, he can see nothing of his life that he leaves behind: as in death itself, he has to let go of everything that was before him.

As the initiate walks, the path opens to a walk beside the lake, and across the lake is the path that he has just walked. But instead of seeing it as it looked when he walked it (a series of high and low paths, dips, bends and turns, it now appears as a mundane path with not too much happening: pretty, but boring.

Then the initiate reaches the parting of the paths. He can choose the easy path back to the life he knew before, or he can choose the path of Hercules: the ultimate test of strength.

The Path of Hercules

The Path of Hercules is steep, like climbing the side of a mountain. In the death vision, the dead person is expected to scale a mountain and as he walks, he can hear the voices of sacred and profane utterances. The mountain is what we have put in our own path in terms of spiritual structures: the hurdles we create between us and God. Religion, which is man-made, becomes a difficult obstacle to the natural flow of communion between man and Divine Being. As we climb that path, we begin to think about the difficulties and dogmas we have created for ourselves, and then we let them go. At the base of the path are some steep steps which have a series of small cave-like structures on either side that probably housed officers who were the 'voices of the dead.'

The temple of Apollo

Once at the top the Initiate reaches the temple of Apollo and pounds upon the door for entrance.

At that point, sacred utterances of the Sun are whispered into his ear. His sword is enlivened as a weapon of Apollo and he is given a scabbard. Then the initiate is lifted from the floor, and the 'hands on' passing on of power is conducted. He is then invested in the colours of the Sun (white and gold robes) and told to walk forth in the sunrise.

25. The eighteenth-century pattern of initiation in Britain

The passage of birth

The initiate stumbles down a steep narrow path and enters a dark tunnel. He stumbles through the darkness, hearing noises and feeling people close to him, close enough to hear their breath, but he cannot see them. The feeling of fear and helplessness of going into a dark tunnel at night reaches a peak, but a faint light in the distance beckons the initiate. (The tunnel at Stourhead is not too impressive. However the tunnel of the same initiate walk at Studley Royal in Yorkshire is truly terrifying at twilight.)

He emerges in the weak dawn light to follow a path that takes him back to the village, the church and inn.

Chapter Twenty-six

Working with Sleepers

There are many different types of sleepers scattered throughout the various cultural traditions around the world. Throughout history, humanity has had a deep relationship with the land, and that has often translated into the tradition of sleepers. I approach this subject purely from an esoteric point of view. I am not an archeologist and I only have access to the sorts of information that anyone can find on the internet or in a library. I do have friends who are archaeologists/university professors and I do milk them occasionally for information, but on the whole I work with sleepers in the best way I know how: through vision. This is the form that I have a great deal of experience with, and this is the path that I grew up with: you work with instinct, stories and legends.

26.1 So what are sleepers?

Sleepers are people who die ritually in such a way as to keep the soul within the body after death. Through this action, the soul interacts with the land, the spirits of the land, and the people. Most of the sleepers gave of themselves freely in service. Later, this practice degenerated in some cultures to a form of forcible entrapment.

Where are the sleepers? Well, they are everywhere and are still being unearthed to this day. Archaeologists still haven't been able to figure out for themselves the difference between an ordinary burial and a sleeper. This has led to some sleepers being dug up, separated from the land that they serve, and their bodies put on display. This causes a rupture in the relationship between the sleeper and the people, bringing about terrible catastrophes for the tribes concerned.

The sleeper in the Ukok Altai is a good example of this problem. The Altai sleeper was a woman who had slept in the land for two

26. Working with Sleepers

and a half thousand years in almost perfect condition. She slept in the permafrost, her tattoos of spirit animals still visible. When she was unearthed and then handled in the most barbaric way in 1993 by a team of Russian archaeologists, things started to go wrong for the indigenous peoples of the Altai.

First the herds started to die, and then the people fell sick. Suicides rose to epidemic proportions, earthquakes rattled the land and famine starved the people. They pleaded with the archaeologists, the universities and then the government to return the sleeping lady. Here is a translated excerpt of a letter that was sent to the Authorities in Moscow:

> We, the indigenous people of the Mountainous Altai, are the pagans and nature worshippers. All the diggings that have been conducted and are conducted in the Altai cause us unrecoverable harm. The invaluable treasures, a spiritual heritage of the Altai people, are moved out of the region despite our protests. A burial mound containing a young tattooed woman of spirit descent was opened at the Ukok plateau in the Kosh Agachsk region. She's a sacred relic to the Altai people, a keeper of peace and welfare of our people. The Altai Princess is now kept in a museum in Novosibirsk. Being the pagans we're completely confident that the soul of the Altai Princess is full of anger because she hates being bothered and wants to be laid to sleep. The tragic events of the last few months spring from the situation. We, the residents of the Oroktoy village, are calling on the people of the Republic of Altai to support our demands for the return of the sacred relic.

This protest letter was signed from people of all walks of life and included the signature of Aelkhan Zhatkambaev, a governor of Kosh Agachsk, an area most severely hit by a recent earthquake.

The request was refused and the lady still lies to this day on display in a glass case at the University museum in Novosibirsk. The authorities have no intention of putting her back, and have since made it a crime to reinter bodies. It would seem there are plans to build a museum to house her but I am not aware of its proposed location.

As far the indigenous peoples are concerned, their fate has already been sealed: the Russian government now talks about the Altai tribal people in the past tense.

The reaction of the archaeologists is to say that either the people are just imagining their sudden plunge into imbalance, or that it wasn't really a ritual burial and that the people have been mistaken for generations. The most recent gem to come from the university is the claim that the sleeper had no connection to the Altai people at all. She was a red haired Caucasian. So?

The Altai is, and was, the crossroads of the top of the world. Different races have always come together there. Such a declaration shows either ignorance or a deliberate attempt to disconnect the people from their past.

I witnessed a similar thing happening in the UK during the unearthing of a ritual burial in Bath of a woman surrounded by men in a circle. The details of the burial were quickly suppressed and played down. An alternative 'truth' was released and since then, the story has been pretty much buried. The organization responsible for such suppression was the church: the burial was found in the area beneath Bath Abbey.

26.2 Are the sleepers still active?

Well yes, some are, the ones who have not been ripped out of the ground or who haven't totally rotted. While ever a sleeper's body stays intact, the they can pass between death and life, the Underworld and the surface world. That was why such pains were taken to make sure that the body was well embalmed: it was important that the sleeper sleep intact for thousands of years.

At the end of that time, the sleeper would be released, or would fade, and another sleeper would take their place. Or the sleeper would sink deeper into sleep, fading from the communion with the tribe and instead becoming part of the consciousness of the land itself. This is one of the Mysteries of the Titans.

26. Working with Sleepers

The problem today is that the sleepers are being dug up and released all over the world but no one is being put back as a sleeper. The world is running out of the sleepers.

When I was a kid, I was told that half the world was asleep while the other half was awake. I was told that it was important that half the world dreamed while the other half worked: this way the world was balanced. If people didn't dream for you, you wouldn't exist.

This is an interesting tale, and is probably an overlap from the days of the ritual ancestral burials. It also probably refers to the old stories of the people sleeping in the earth, dreaming about the world and that we are their dreams. While ever they are sleeping, we can exist.

I can remember being a kid and listening to all sorts of interesting stories referring to these themes. They were always set in a Catholic context: those who went before us and slept in the earth, dreamt of paradise to keep the memory alive. So when the end of the world came, we would all still remember what paradise was: our ancestors were dreaming it for us.

I was lucky in that for some of my childhood, I grew up in a mixed community that was poor and illiterate. From that community came a wealth of stories and legends that had been carefully passed down from generation to generation.

And that is one of the fulcrums of survival for these ancient Mysteries: let them live and breathe in a real and healthy way. Too many 'experts' pop up who are university teachers or librarians who 'discover' their Celtic roots, etc. by going to a few workshops, reading a mountain of books, doing a shamanism course, etc. They then write books from a garbled pseudointellectual slant of the subject in a way that is meant to be marketable for the New Age.

Most of them come from middle class, well-educated families, and their deep desire to escape such isolation drives them to dig deeper. That is a good thing. But it becomes destructive when they then become the 'Bible preachers' of such subjects, with no real understanding of what they are addressing. It becomes some remote romantic magic that only the 'experts' can do. Nothing could be further from the truth.

26.2. Are the sleepers still active?

True ancestral knowledge of the sleepers is found in faery tales, family stories, local legends and songs (Sleeping Beauty, for example). They are passed down from generation to generation orally: a few of the poorer remote communities until fairly recently were illiterate, so they developed great skills at recounting the spirit of ancient ways to the next generation.

I can remember when I was about ten years old, my cousin got drunk and placed a bet with another cousin that she could get into a small bedside cupboard. She ended up getting her bum stuck hard in the cupboard and was totally wedged there. One of the old grandmothers was sitting in the corner knitting. She raised one eyebrow and said in a dead pan way, "Well lass, you will have to stay in there forever and keep time for us all, just like Old Winny did." Old Winny was a local burial on Windy hill, a woman who had been there before people started writing records.

It was said that went you went on Windy hill, which also had a small cup and ring stone there, you could not keep your watch in time, because it would revert to Winny time. *She* kept time on that hill, not clocks. And sure enough, if you went for a walk on Windy Hill, your watch would go slow.

Because of the sayings, we all knew about Winny and what she did, she was the keeper of time for the area. These days, a series of houses have been built upon the hill, so I would love to know what their clocks do!

Some of the sleepers are old, going back into the far reaches of our humanity and can still be worked with, though we do have to approach them with caution: their concept of humanity and life is different from ours today and we have to take that into consideration.

A few years back, I was teaching at a residential in New York. We were working with a particular sleeper who had been recently dug up. I was talking with her spirit, which was preparing to go through the death vision, and she showed me that the land would be in terrible calamity if she was not replaced.

After we came out of a vision that worked with her, a man in the group announced that he was willing to take her place. He was serious and fully understood the implications. He went on to commit himself to her work and to the land. He handed over his fate to the

26. Working with Sleepers

Goddess so that when he died, he would be embalmed and placed near her resting place. He would prepare himself magically to sleep with the land.

I was shocked that a modern day man would be so willing to give up the rhythm of life and death to be of service to the Goddess and the land. But the warning is, if you are asked or approached in the inner worlds to take up such service, just be fully aware of what you are being asked to do. Taking a magical vow is no light thing and they will hold you to it.

26.3 Communing with sleepers

If you want to work with a sleeper, then first you must find out if the sleeper wants to work with you. The best way to do this is through dipping your toe in the water gently. First find the site where the sleeper is and see if you can find out anything about the burial there.

Then start by taking food offerings. Go each day to the mound or burial area and place an offering of bread and oil in an appointed spot. After placing the offering down, still yourself and tune yourself to the directions. Just be silent and listen for a while. The following morning, before diving out of bed, lie and think about any dreams you had. If the mound is active, then chances are the guardian of the burial will have picked up on your interest and will have appeared in your dream.

The guardian can often manifest as a person, black dog, or other being trying to get you to go away. They will try and discourage casual contact with the mound. But if you are sincere and determined, then the guardians will let you through: they will not try to stop you from working with the mound.

After a few days, you can try and enter the burial mound in vision and commune with the sleeper. If you decide to go through this phase, just make sure that you are prepared to work with respect, and are prepared to be of service to the burial.

A few years ago I moved with my family into an old house in the west of England that we were renovating. It was built into a faery hill that was also a burial mound. The mound had never been excavated and it was powerful.

26.3. Communing with sleepers

I worked with the children to clean the garden up, which was mainly overgrown grass, apple trees and hawthorn. As soon as I began to dig into the earth to plant things, I would become terribly tired and would fall asleep. The same happened to the children. It became a bit of a family joke: we would all go out to garden, and a few minutes later, mum and two girls would be crashed out sleeping in the grass.

Then came the nightmares. We began the alterations on the house, and I started to have bad dreams, warning dreams, that would try and get me to leave the house. I still didn't really understand what was happening until one foggy autumn morning.

Our washing machine was in a side section of the house that could only be entered from outside, a little like an outhouse. My daughter had gone out to get the washing, and came rushing back into the house as white as a sheet.

She had seen a man in a black coat with a black dog walk past the door of the washing hut and vanish into the garden. Now, our garden, which was on the top of the mound, was surrounded by thorn bushes and the only entrance and exit was down some steep little steps that ran down the front of the house and the front of the mound.

There was nowhere for this man to vanish to. At this point, it hadn't occurred to me that this was not a real man. I hunted around the perimeter of the garden, looking for a hole in the thorn bushes that he might have pushed through. It seemed to me at the time that he was probably a local who was taking a shortcut through our garden.

Two nights later, I was out getting the washing and the same thing happened, a man with a black dog walked past the door. But this time I got it. He was not real. I had felt him before I saw him and this was no human man. He was a guardian of the mound. They often appear at stone circles or burial mounds, accompanied by a big black dog.

It was then that I slapped my forehead. I can be immensely stupid sometimes. I was on a burial mound...that was working...that had active guardians...and it was the burial of a sleeper, hence the problems with the gardening. The falling asleep problem was coming from the burial: it is a protective spell to prevent looters and intruders from digging into the mound.

So I decided that if I was going to live there, then I must also be of service to the sleeper within the mound. It was late October, a perfect time for what I was about to do. I built a fire on the top of the mound. Living on the top of a burial mound has a lot of disadvantages. One is that everything you do in your garden can be seen for miles around. But luckily it was the time of the year for bonfires, with All Hallows' Eve a day away, and bonfire night a week away. I was trying not to draw too much attention to what I was doing, nor did I want to freak out my devout Christian neighbours.

I lit the bonfire at dusk and piled on all the dead branches I had gathered up while clearing the garden. Then I sat before the fire. Closing my eyes, I went down in vision, down through the center of the hill until I reached a chamber that had a stone bed in the center.

Upon the bed was laid a man who was asleep. He had a long beard that reached almost the ground and there were many birds asleep around him. I tiptoed up to him to look at him. But one of the birds made a warning noise and the man began to stir.

He slowly woke up and began to stretch. He didn't see me and was not aware that I was there. He began to recite a poem that I didn't understand, and the poem seemed to force me out of the chamber. I was worried that I had awoken him before his time, but that feeling was soon put to rest as the poem got louder.

The sound of the poem was driving me back to the surface to do something, and I realized I was being put to work. He had awoken and he wanted to leave, but he needed a bridge to help him release.

I opened my eyes and went to the east. I walked around each direction, pausing for a moment to feel if that was the right one. When I got to the East I felt that this was the right direction to work in. Normally, for releasing a person into death I would have chosen the North, but these burials have a mind of their own: they know what they are doing and we should just basically do as we are told.

I stood in the East and rooted myself with my back to the fire and my face to the darkness of the night. I connected down to the sleeper and I felt him rise from the mound to the surface. He emerged out

26.3. Communing with sleepers

of the mound via the fire, paused for a while before passing through me, out into the night and the stars.

It took a few minutes for his energy to make its way all the way through me and he felt old and strange as he passed through. Many things from the hill, faery beings, a later burial and many spirits passed through me by coming up through my feet, and they went into the fire. It was a strange sensation and when it was all over, I laid down on the grass beside the fire. I was exhausted.

As I looked out, I saw Orion, the star constellation right above me as he passed over the mound. It became obvious from the inner feeling I was getting that the sleeper had aligned somehow, on his interment, to Orion and that it was no coincidence that the sleeper I saw had been laid in the same position as Orion: when the stars passed over head there would have been a few minutes where the stars would have mirrored the exact position of the burial and *vice versa*.

After that night, the feeling of the hill changed considerably. It was empty and silent. We felt that we no longer belonged there and that it was time to move on. We lived there for only 12 months. We had been drawn to live there so that we could do our job in releasing that sleeper, and then we were dismissed!

The couple that we sold the house to had a great feel about them: they would really nurture that hill and bring it back to life after its long sleep.

If you find a burial that you think is a sleeper, tread carefully but with purpose. What follows is a vision that can be used in any burial area to ascertain what is in there, and if you should work with it.

But remember, not every sleeper wants to wake up, not every sleeper should be awoken. And not every sleeper wants to work with you. Respect and work with whatever you find and do be aware that the standards of service that were expected in the days of the sleeper might be different from the standards now. The sleeper might expect you to do things that are no longer appropriate in our modern age.

I have purposely kept the following vision simple with little description as each mound you visit will be different. But this method will give you an idea of how to approach such a burial and how to begin learning to work with them.

26. Working with Sleepers

Sometimes, the sleepers just want you to hang out with them, or they want you to lie beside them and sleep. When you do this, they will communicate with you through sleep and dreams, telling you about the earth and the weather. There are many different ways to work with such burials and you have to use your common sense in determining which way is appropriate for that particular sleeper.

26.4 Vision for contacting a sleeper

Go to the burial mound and sit comfortably where you won't be disturbed. Close your eyes and be aware of the wind around you. Be aware of any body of water in the distance, and be aware of the sun above you. Be aware of the wind on your face and the earth beneath you.

With your inner vision, see yourself descend down through the earth, passing through stones, rocks, roots and earth as you pass down and down into the hill. As you go deeper into the earth, you become aware of a guardian that is trying to stop you going further.

Let the guardian ask you questions about your intentions and tell them that you are willing to be of service to the sleeper. If the guardian is happy with what they are hearing, then they will let you pass.

The guardian guides you into a chamber where you see the sleeper: The guardian stays by the entrance and watches as you approach the sleeper carefully. Be still, be silent and allow the power of the sleeper to wash over you. It will become obvious to you what you should do. You may feel that you have to lie down and sleep awhile with the sleeper, to keep them company or to help them sleep. You may have to sing them songs, lullabies, or comb their hair for them.

Or they may begin to awaken as you sit there, in which case you will have to help them release. To do that, you will have to either help them to their feet and climb out, or you will have to cradle them in your arms and carry them out.

They will need to be released through the directions or through a flame. One way to do this, if you cannot build a fire, is to have a candle lit in a jam jar and place it atop the mound. As you carry the sleeper out, you would see a gateway in your vision opening in the flame and let them pass through it.

Once they have released, go back into the chamber and see if anything was left there. If there was, take it and pass it through the flame also, or put it in running water. When you have finished, use rocks and earth to close up any hole that you made so that the mound is sealed. Ask the guardian if he needs your help to leave/release and help them if they ask for that help.

Be still and listen to nature around the mound, feel the peace and stillness, and when you are ready, open your eyes.

26.5 The future

Now that so many sleepers are being removed or released from the Earth and none are being replaced, what will happen? And what can we do to help?

Well, our culture does not have a structure for such a problem, and I think ritual deaths and burials would not go down well with the Western community these days. And yet something must be done to try and address the imbalance, particularly as the planet needs all the help it can get right now. Our communities and cultures are crumbling as we destroy our environment and ourselves.

One option is active dreaming. Rather than becoming a sleeper through death and burial, we can become active sleepers through visions and dreams. At the end of the day what is needed is for some humans to act as intermediaries between the earth and humanity, between the Underworld and the people.

One way of doing that as modern living humans is to commit to a length of service in which we agree to do regular visions with a certain area of the land, and we agree to sleep with intent.

Sleeping with intent is where you lie down and go to sleep, not your normal nighttime sleep, but a daytime sleep where you allow yourself to be pulled deep down into the earth where you commune with the consciousness of the land. The land will impress upon you things that need doing or will warn you of things coming.

With that information, you actively pass on the information to those who work magically with you, or you act upon the information yourself. A sleeper will often work to rebalance a patch of land, or unblock an energy flow, or direct humans to work that needs doing with the forest or the birds.

You basically become a bridge between the land and the people. Actively sleeping opens you up slowly to such work, where you will dream deep dreams about the land and the spirits, and you will be warned of things coming.

When I lived on the burial mound, I did a lot of active sleeping where I would wake up in the morning and be promptly told an hour later to go back to bed and dream.

When I did this, I would be shown some amazing things, introduced to powerful beings and asked to do visions for faery beings: mainly bridging work in the Underworld.

This has happened to me many times. I didn't choose to do this, nor did I agree to a term of service specifically to sleep. I think it became part and parcel of my wider service as a priestess. It was also a matter of the fact that I always said yes to any inner request before I took the time to find out what I had just said yes to…which went along with my love of pressing buttons just to see what would happen. Amazingly I'm still alive!

In today's modern decaying world, one of the things we need to do is to become flexible and able to adjust quickly. Things are changing fast and we have to run to keep up. Old ways of working no longer really apply, and yet the ancient flow of power needs to be maintained. It is up to us as modern humans to find new and effective ways of working magically for the good of the land and the people.

26.6 Bridging

The other important way to work with sleepers in this modern age is to work with them as bridges to the ancient past. Sleepers are often one of a long line of sleepers, and contacts are passed from one sleeper to the next, so their connections stretch deep in into the distant past. They are often connected, through this line, to deities or powers that are no longer worked with or contacted in modern times.

Sometimes, a power or deity is so far back that we cannot reach them as we know nothing about them or how they presented themselves. For example, we know how Horus presented and even though his temples and priests faded out in real terms millennia ago, because we still have his image, his history and his stories, we can reach him.

But older deities become harder to reach. Tefnut for example is a much older and lesser-known deity in the Egyptian pantheon, and is harder, but not impossible, to reach. But what about the deity that was before Tefnut? What female divinity of the water, what power, kept the forest alive and the land balanced? To find this out we must contact the oldest sleeper we can find in that culture and start there.

From that starting point, you commune with that sleeper to establish a connection. Work with them to see what they need, what tasks they have for you, and what communications they wish to have.

Then, you would converse with the contact to ask about the sleeper who went before them. Once they have told you about the previous sleeper, you can use that information to track back through time to commune with that sleeper. You repeat this work until you reach the earliest sleeper you can find.

Upon reaching that first sleeper, you would commune with their spirit and ask if they need anything. Don't forget you would be communing with them in their own time, not yours. So they may ask you to do things that are no longer possible. You have to make sure that the sleeper is aware that you are from the future.

If you know of disasters that will happen in their near future, as a priest/ess you must tell the sleeper about the coming event. The sleeper then converts that information into a language the local community of that time would understand, and then conveys that information to the tribal seer.

This is one of the major ways in which a sleeper works. They work with contacts from the future who warn the people of the past what is coming. They also work with the land, the faery beings, the animals and the trees in an effort to make sure that the tribe is aware of what calamities lie ahead.

Time jumping, or bridging, in magical work is common and is indeed one of the major tribal ways of working with ancestors. We

26. WORKING WITH SLEEPERS

know what is coming, they don't, and between the information passed to a sleeper, the information gleaned from the behaviour of the land and the animals, and information passed on in dreams, again the dreams are information whispered to them by workers of the future while they sleep. With that collection of information tribal peoples can ascertain what is coming and take evasive steps.

We had a really good example of this recently. A fascinating story came out of the tsunami disaster that hit the Andaman and Nicobar Islands in December 2004: the survival of all the members of the indigenous Jarawa tribe. This tribe is one of the most ancient in the world, with DNA studies indicating that their generations may have spanned back seventy thousand years. The tribe fled into the jungle in plenty of time, hours before the tsunami hit, and remained there for several days before reemerging.

When approached by the Indian Authority tribal agent, the tribesmen refused to say how they had known in advance. My guess is that it was a combination of signs and warnings, with ancestral bridging included. Now that the tsunami has happened, their seers can go back through time in ceremony and warn the people. So which came first, the event, or the after-knowledge?

This throws us back to the issues regarding time and how time works. When doing work with sleepers, it is better to approach time in a different way. Do not think of time as before and after, but as over here and over there. That way your brain doesn't get chewed when you try to figure out how it all works. I gave up years ago! All I know is that it does work and should be worked with.

The other service that emerges from this type of work is the bridging between sleepers. As living humans, we have immense capacity to bridge between time and people. One of the important services that should be offered to sleepers is to bridge between the first sleeper in a line and the last or present one.

That allows the ancient knowledge and power that always gets lost between the generations to be reconnected to the present. The first sleeper in a line will have inherent knowledge regarding the land powers and divinities that stretch back into the distant past behind them. By bridging between the oldest and the newest sleepers, you connect the present day sleeper with the ancient knowledge that would have become diluted by the time they began to sleep. You are also connecting the oldest sleeper with the acquired and matured knowledge developed by the tribe over the millennia.

This strengthens the connection, deepens the powers of the sleepers and begins the process of transforming the original sleeper from human sleeper to Titan.

Working with a sleeper is something that every magical worker should undertake at some point in their magical training. It is a service to the land that gave you life and a service to the humanity that flows through you. Sleepers are wherever people settled. Start by searching in your own area for one, and if you don't find one, then look further afield.

Or you can travel to find one and make the connection. Once the connection is there, then you can go in vision to work with that sleeper from a distance.

Chapter Twenty-seven

Death and Birth

The Mysteries of death and birth, and the powers that work within these transitions, have slowly been eroded from Western culture by the monotheistic religions. All three religions are based upon a foundation of submission, fear and abdication of responsibility.

This castration of the human spirit has, as a side issue, disabled the once splendid transitions of birth and death, and replaced them with pain, fear and helplessness. If you attend a hospital birth in the Western cultures, you are most likely to see the woman in a space of 'not knowing': she doesn't have any control over her birth. She has no idea how to give birth and has to rely on paying an 'expert' (often male) to tell her how to do the job.

Women often emerge traumatized, torn and exhausted. They are thrown back into the community almost immediately where they are expected to just figure it out, read a book or rely on yet more 'experts' to guide them through.

The social engineering that has shaped our modern life has also served to further separate us from our mothers and grandmothers. We no longer tend to live in the same community we were raised in, sometimes not even in the same country we were born in. There is no spiritual input for the mother or the child, and no spiritual guidance. We are truly 'cast from the garden' to give birth 'alone' and in pain.

And then there is the other end of the spectrum. Death has also been made into a medical money spinner. I have had to stand by and watch doctors insist on invasive and painful procedures to be conducted on dying people, not for the patients good, but for the insurance money and their own curiosity. Dying people are dragged to hospitals, pumped full of drugs and they die in a spiritually void institution: how disgraceful.

27. Death and Birth

Death has been made so disgusting and terrible that most Americans have never seen a dead body let alone tended to the dying and the dead. Death must happen away from the home, it is unclean, it is a reminder of your own fate: these are all the nightmares that so many people live with.

When I was a child, there was always someone dying. I come from a large family with many generations still living. So there was always someone old and dying or someone young and stupid who has crashed their car, taken too many pills, etc. When a person died, we would cleanse and dress the body while talking to the soul. They would be kept in vigil in the house until burial time. This happens in various ways around the world in countries that have not yet been contaminated by the soulless greed of Western living.

So how do you find that way forward for yourselves, your family and your community?

You have to learn to be with birth and death. As an esoteric worker, the best and most solid way to learn the methods of these transitions is first to learn the visions that accompany these transitions, and then begin to work with them. Once you have become proficient with these methods, you will find that the universe puts you in situations where you can be of use to humanity. The other important thing is to go through your own death vision while in life. This is, important to someone on a spiritual path: the death within life is one of the oldest recorded Mysteries from various ancient cultures.

27.1 Death

The method of working within death that is compatible with the Western culture is the Vision of Death. There are many different versions of this vision/story and some cultures have even produced a Book of the Dead for their priests to recite from.

The death vision creates the scenario of a journey that includes a river, mountains and plains. When you die, this is not what you see but the images covey to the living what the dead person is experiencing. So the living human can access death by passing through the imagination into the Inner Worlds.

The vision is divided into sections that chart the progression from the separation of the spirit from the body, to the separation of the consciousness from the spirit. This enables the spirit or soul to progress into transformation without carrying any baggage from the recent life. Then the spirit awakens and moves on either to a new life, an inner service, an inner healing or to a merging with the Divine Being, which manifests as the Void.

27.2 So what happens when a person dies?

It depends on the circumstances of the death. If the person dies quickly, they are often catapulted into a state of unconsciousness of the spirit. This is a form of defense mechanism to protect the spirit just as the body will switch off the mind to protect itself while under extreme stress. It doesn't happen all the time but it happens most of the time.

While in this stage of nothingness, the spirit is still heavily connected to the body, and while passing through this short phase the person experiences this situation in the same way they would if they had briefly fallen asleep. They awaken slowly as if from a deep sleep. So be aware of this connection if you are around the body. *They can often still hear you.*

The person then begins to emerge out of their short sleep to find themselves in a place of nothingness. This is the most superficial form of the Void and is like a 'passing through' stage for the spirit. The person must have the will to move forward so that they can begin their death journey.

If they do not move forward, they need to be helped and coaxed to move forward. This is done by going in vision to this place and imagining a door. Once you have formed the vision strongly they will start to see the door for themselves and will be more willing to move.

In the state of death, the personality that you are dealing with is the threshold personality: that is to say, the part of the person that acted as a fulcrum between the body and the soul. Images can be conveyed through your 'imagining,' and the imagination is a common ground that you both share.

27. Death and Birth

When the person moves through that door, you must not follow. This is very important to understand. Once they move through that door they are fully committed to death and if you go through that door, the same rule applies to you. You can work deeply in the death vision but how you get there is different if you are still in life.

Once the person steps through that door, it may be anything from day or two to an hour or two before they emerge in the death vision itself. If a person has died slowly and is preparing for that death, they just seem to appear in the death vision immediately. I have known some people who have prepared spiritually for death to just go straight through everything immediately, which is really how it should be.

But in today's spiritually bereft modern world, that rarely happens. The death process has become a long, drawn-out painful passage that is like having wisdom teeth pulled without anaesthesia. And that is so unnecessary. Death should be a stillness: a letting go and surrendering to the natural forces that you know will wash you up on the beach of life many, many times. And the fear should not be a consuming terrible darkness: rather it should be the excited fear of a new marriage or a new child.

Life is not our natural state. Timelessness and stillness out of life is our natural state. This is why when people discover the depths of the Void in their meditations, they do not want to come back from it: this is our soul's natural state. That is not to say that we should turn away from life as some religions would have us do. Life is a wondrous, beautiful and powerful thing that is a special gift to us all. But at the end of the day our real state is an infinite timeless and conscious communion with Divine Being.

27.3 The death vision in detail

The death vision as we see it begins with a long walk across a hot dusty Desert landscape. In the distance is a river which the dead person is drawn to. Other people are often walking too, and some are sitting by the river. The dead person will be thirsty and they rush towards the river to drink of its water. As they drink it begins to affect

27.3. The death vision in detail

their ability to remember their newly lost life. The more they drink, the more they forget.

This is why Initiates in some of the Eastern Mysteries were trained to control their thirst and to control their inner actions. It was drummed into them from the beginning of their advanced training: do not drink of the River of Death. By doing this, they could cross through death and retain the memories of who they were. They can then pick up on their work that they left behind in the previous life.

I do not think that is all too healthy: some forgetting and letting go is important for the soul's development. The continuance from one life to the next in a conscious line of work becomes corrupted quickly, as can be seen with the Lamas of Tibet. Their obsessive clinging to power through linear reincarnation was the beginning of the end for their priesthood.

Such a practice for them is relatively new in terms of the age of their priesthood. It used to be that different enlightened souls would manifest each time through the incarnation of the senior Lama, thus bringing a wide variety of skills and wisdom to the leadership of the priesthood. Approximately three hundred years ago that practice was changed through magic to make sure that the same souls came back again and again. This is a degenerate practice that has brought about the destruction of an ancient spiritual lineage.

The balance for an adept is to drink only a tiny bit from the river and retain enough memory to recall your hard-earned wisdom and knowledge. But the tiny sips would have wiped away most memories of partners, loved ones, etc. which will allow the soul to move forward and understand the deeper rules of attachment.

The rules of attachment are that one must not be attached to anything or anyone. Once you die, all the people you loved no longer exist for you. For your sake and theirs, you must let go and move on. And by letting go, you will eventually be able to reconnect with these people under different circumstances and different forms of relationships, if it is appropriate.

At this stage of the vision, at the side of the river, the person ponders their lost life and begins the process of shedding and accepting. Often angelic beings will make themselves available to help people through this stage of the transition. These beings guard

27. Death and Birth

the bridge and the river, allowing only those who should cross to cross.

These beings will often cross-dress to help people accept them better. For example they will often appear as your aunt Betty, or as Jesus, Buddha, or whichever form of God, saint, or family member you would reach out to. This is not to deceive you: this is only to help those who are so traumatized that they cannot move forward without real practical help. And angels appearing in their own guise would frighten the socks off most people, so they dress up.

A good example of this is a story from some inner work I did for a family a few years ago. A young friend of my daughter had a snowboarding accident and ended up with severe injuries. He was in a deep coma and the hospital informed his parents that he would not recover. They planned to wait a week and then turn the machines off that were keeping him alive.

My daughter asked if we could sit down at the time of the turn off and do the death vision for him. I said yes. The day before the turn off was due, I suddenly was told by inner contacts to sit down with my daughter and do the death vision straightaway, so we did.

I saw the boy standing by the river. He was in shock. He refused to move in any way. He would not believe he was dead, and refused my efforts to get him to move forward to cross the bridge. Crossing the bridge would enable him to move to the next, deeper stage of death.

In desperation I asked one of the angelic beings for help. A few seconds later a beautiful young girl with rather large breasts strutted over the bridge towards the boy. His eyes nearly popped out of his head. He forgot everything he was afraid of, and immediately agreed to take her arm and walk across the bridge with her, so off he went. The angelic being had dressed as a beautiful young woman to assist this boy.

We later found out that he died naturally just as we were doing the death vision, thus saving his family from the terrible trauma of having to 'turn him off.'

But back to the side of the river. At this stage people are often confused, bewildered and angry. They are angry that death was not what they expected: there was no choir of angels to herald them into 'heaven' and no endless supply of ice cream, sunshine and all the other trivial things that were promised to them.

They sit at the side of the river and wait. Some at this stage realize that their imagination can take them back to the people that they left behind. Some become skilled at this and refuse to move further into death, choosing instead to 'haunt' their lost loved ones or their lost property. The longer they stay in death, the more the living world becomes a sort of 'inner' world to them: that is to say where they are becomes their total reality and the living world is accessed through imagination. For us, it is the reverse.

It is at this stage that you also sometimes find people who are in deep comas. They have a foot in death and a foot in life. They hang between the two and while their body is still alive in the living world, their spirit sometimes begins the death journey and they end up at the side of the river. They cannot go any further until their body is dead. So they hang out, confused and afraid.

They have to make a choice, either to go back or to let go of their body. If they cannot go back, i.e. if their body is too damaged, then they must learn to let go and allow their body to die. If they wish to go back, help them by looking for the umbilical line that connects them to life and follow it back to their body.

27.4 The Bridge

The bridge is a crucial part of the death vision: if they don't cross the bridge one way or another, then they cannot continue with the death process. They will remain frozen in the half-life world that is somewhere between life and death. Crossing the river by way of a bridge is our way of seeing a process in which the spirit severs connections with life and commits to moving forward in their cycle of development.

The bridge can appear to us as being guarded by angelic beings. They stand on either side of the entrance and act as gatekeepers, keeping out those who must not cross for one reason or another. As a priest or priestess, we can cross the bridge safely, though it is best not to return that way. Once we cross the bridge, if we wish as living beings to come out of the vision, we have to exit either from the top

27. Death and Birth

of the mountain or continue and complete the whole cycle of the vision. Another option, if you wish to come in and out of the vision, is to pass through one of the angelic beings.

The reason for not returning over the bridge is that there is always the possibility of some being that does not belong in life hitching a ride on you unnoticed. To avoid such happenings, which do indeed happen, care has to be taken to make sure that you always pass through an angelic being, or a threshold that is protected by, and created of, angelic consciousness. This can be done by approaching one of the working beings in the death vision and asking them to allow you to pass through them to get home. The thresholds of the mountain and the Abyss are protected thresholds which only allow those who should pass, to pass.

27.5 The Plains

As the spirit begins its journey towards the mountains it enters into a phase of letting go at a much deeper level. The physical form and all that was attached to that form begins to dissolve as they walk across the plains towards the high mountains. This often appears to us as things falling from the person as they walk. They may appear to drop baggage, clothing, heavy weights, even limbs as they draw closer and closer to the mountain.

While they are in this phase, they will begin to forget who they are and what they are doing. Some will be disorientated and will be drawn by instinct to the mountains before them. During this walk, it is the priest's/priestess's job to walk alongside them and be a companion until they are ready to let go of companionship and face being alone.

This is also an important lesson for this phase of death: that we are truly alone and that the love that we had for our children, parents, lovers and friends was love that was conditional love and as such is limited. Eventually the spirit passes through the letting go phase, understanding that such relationships were bound to that life and they begin to cut the emotional ties.

Eventually the understanding that such love is unconditional and flows out to all begins to dawn, not in a fluffy New Age sense, but in a real solid sense. Life flows in cycles and patterns and the love connected to that life flows in the same way. Someone whom we once loved as a lover may cross our paths again as a sibling, offspring or parent. Or that soul may never cross our paths again...The point being is that we really do not know, so potentially everyone around us has been connected to us at one point or another for good or bad. That brings a whole new meaning to 'love thy brother as thyself,' because you really truly do not know how much of a connection you really have with the person down the street.

People do reconnect and interconnect, and learning to let go between is so important: we must start the surface connection each time with a fresh outlook and an open heart. That way we truly learn to be one with the rest of humanity: because we really are all one family in one way or another.

The quicker that the person understands this, the quicker they reach the mountain and begin the next phase of their journey. If you are still accompanying someone, this phase is the last one where you can walk alongside them. By this stage there is often not much communication happening anymore, and as a worker you can walk along and observe, but not much else.

27.6 The Mountain

The mountain is the final hurdle that the soul must encounter within the death vision. The mountain is the deep spiritual programming that has happened to a person during their lives. Any religion they have been raised with, any cultural baggage they may have and any deep-seated ideals are challenged at this point.

This manifests itself in a couple of ways: the more the dogma is entrenched within a person, the higher the mountain is and the harder it is to climb. Once a person begins to climb, they will begin to hear many voices, some reciting sacred text, some praying, some political voices, some cultural voices and some of their own ponderings. The voices will be loud and annoying as they try to climb beyond the programming that happened during their lifetime.

When the person hears the voices, they will begin to be aware of them as something that is outside them: this is something they acquired during their lifetimes when they had a body, but it is not a

27. Death and Birth

part of them. The awareness that such thoughts are not of the spirit, but are a product of humanity, can be a shock to some people and the harder the shock, the harder the climb.

Such a letting go is probably the hardest: it is releasing everything you have ever held as being real, as being right. It shows a person the falsehood of their society, their religion and their own reasoning. It is a frightening and exhausting experience that weighs heavily upon the shoulders of a person who is struggling in such a difficult transition.

Once the spirit reaches the top of the mountain, they are exhausted and are ready for sleep. There are many beings who work in this section of the death vision and their duty is to guard, nurture, and prepare the soul for the renewal of life or for the service of the Inner Worlds.

The top of the mountain appears as a plateau with a grassy flat area where people lie down to rest. The beings wander in among the sleeping people, singing to them and stroking them as they sleep. The spirit lies down and the angelic beings arrange them so that they can sleep comfortably. They are laid out in a ritual position of one arm outstretched and the opposite leg outstretched. The other leg and arm are bent into the body. This position can be seen on some traditional tarot decks as a man curled around the wheel of life. It is also mirrored in some decks in the hanged man. It is a ritual position of preparation for life.

Spirits who are not going to reincarnate but are going to pass into the Inner Worlds in service as an inner contact or teacher, do not lie down. They are urged to a far, dark side of the plateau where the mountain falls away down a bottomless crevice or Abyss. The spirit stands on the edge of the Abyss and makes the ultimate initiation move by stepping off the cliff. Each spirit that is pulled to this place will have practised this action many times during their life in visions. The spirit steps out into the Mystery of the Abyss and vanishes into the mist. They will emerge in the Inner Worlds, ready to teach and guide humanity in a spirit of service.

This is also a get-off point for you as a visionary should you wish to exit the death vision with esoteric purpose. By going through the death vision to this point and then stepping off into the Abyss, you fully complete the death initiation of the ancients. You will emerge in the sanctuary of the Great Library.

The spirits, who are left sleeping and regenerating, are surrounded by song: the angelic beings sing to them the secrets of human life so that the spirit should not forget what human life is. This will prevent a spirit from forgetting that they manifested through humanity so that when they come to choose a new life, they will choose humanity over some other being.

27.7 The awakening into rebirth

At some point all the angels face east as the sun rises and they begin to call out the names of those spirits that they have guarded to awaken them. The spirits awaken and are immediately pushed down the opposite side of the mountain, which is a gentle grassy slope.

The spirits roll around and around as they tumble down the hill towards an Abyss that is guarded by an archangel. The angel appears as a woman with hair that flows in all directions and long arms that reach out to slow down the spirits as they roll down the hill.

Once they come to a halt, the spirits uncurl themselves and walk to the edge of the Abyss. The angel holds a protective arm out to stop them falling as they explore the power of this place. As they look over the Abyss they slowly become aware of potential lives that could relate to them. There is no past or present, as such concepts have no place where there is no matter. But all the lives that are within their field appear on the other side of the Abyss and they can watch them.

The spirit fixes on one life that seems to connect more than others. It is not a conscious choice, but an instinctive one. All the cultural and religious programming that would have affected such a choice has long gone and all that is left is deep spiritual reaction and instinct. Once the life has been chosen, the angel removes her arm and the spirit falls into a whirling mass of air that appears like a whirlwind. This is also an archangel that carries the soul from the depths of death to the threshold of life.

27. Death and Birth

The soul falls down and down, swirling around the directions as it falls towards a couple who are making love. And such is the inner mechanism of conception.

27.8 Practical working methods

To work with the above vision, construct a vision using the elements above. The safest access point to begin the vision is the Underworld: go down into the Underworld until you hit a river. Stand beside the river and call for the boatman. Slowly a boat will appear with a boatman holding a flame light—give him a coin which after the vision you later throw into water, and step into the boat. It will float along the underground river until it emerges in the realm of death and you will get out of the right hand side of the riverbank, which is the area that newly dead people come and gather before crossing the bridge.

Once you have constructed the vision, you can use it to reach newly dead people, or you can recite it as a story to someone who is in a coma. Most of the time when people are in comas you will find them near the edge of the river: They will be confused and unsure what to do or what is happening. You can talk to them if you visit in vision and ask them what they want to do. If they want to let go and die, then you can help them by taking them over the bridge, and then physically holding their hand which allows your energy to flow into them: it takes a lot of energy to die.

If someone is dying and they are receptive to it, you can do the vision with them so that it prepares them for what is to come. The more prepared they are, the less frightened they become and the smoother the passing is. You can then go in and track them on a daily basis: going through the inner death process takes many days usually, and you can go in each day to work with them and monitor their progress. Usually, by the time they have reached the top of the mountain you will be told by the angelic workers to stop coming in as help is no longer needed.

If you are emotionally connected to the person, you have to be careful not to hold them back by your own longings or wishes for them to stay around longer. You have to work from a place of non-emotion so that you can do your job. I worked with my father for ten days when he died. After the second day, he had no idea who I was as he had let go of his earthly life: I found that hard but it was good for me to learn how important it is to be focused and not let emotions intrude.

If you are working with a dying adept who wishes to stay around a bit longer to continue some work, then go over the vision with them a few times even if they know it. And once they die, be ready for them changing their minds and wishing to move on. They may also pass into a different space after crossing the bridge: there is a place over the bridge where adepts go to become inner contacts.

If someone is stuck by the side of the river and is not moving on, and has learned to stick around and access the human world, then they need to be taken over the bridge. This is a form of haunting and you have to explain to them what they are doing. If they still will not cross, and they are haunting people, then you need to work with beings to forcibly take them over the bridge.

27.9 Physical practicalities

When you are working with someone who is dying there are certain things to keep an eye out for. If they are in a coma, sometimes they will awaken just before death. Sometimes, when you are feeling them energetically, you will feel that they die slowly from the feet up, one leg at a time. This once happened to me when I was working on someone who was in intensive care: one day I couldn't feel their right leg anymore and I became confused. A being told me later that the man in question 'had one foot in the grave.' It made me think a little more about old sayings and what they had grown out of.

When working with the dying, be aware of the energy needs of a dying person and of the beings around them. If they have a parasite keeping them alive, take it out. If they are frightened, do the inner vision quietly to yourself because even if they do not consciously do it, your action of it has a stretching effect upon them.

You can also help them by working within the spiritual construct that they are used to: Christian, Muslim, it doesn't really matter. Recite sacred text at their side, as some of the sacred texts are designed to draw angelic beings to the dying to help them in the passing. If they are not religious, call upon the angelic beings yourself for the death preparations. You can do that quietly, with eyes open as you sit and keep vigil.

Working with the newly dead is the most important work. These are the people who are least cared for and the most in need of help. Lots of structures are in place for those who are left and are grieving. To work with the newly dead, just be with them for each day that they need it and keep a vigil candle burning for them as they are going through the process.

If the family is receptive to the idea, you can let one or two of them join in the vision with you leading, so that they can become a part of the overall process. This can be an incredible healing tool for all concerned.

27.10 Birth

Upon conception, the spirit of the new life spreads out throughout the body of the mother, affecting her moods, her body and her character. The mother's personality will often change. This is just a side effect of the mingling of the two souls: the mother will often display the personality traits of the future child.

As the pregnancy progresses, the new spirit slowly adjusts to the growing body of the child and slowly withdraws from the safety net of the mother. By the time the birth is imminent, the child's body will hold almost all of the spirit and that transition is completed with the cutting of the cord. The inner cord is cut by the angelic beings who attend a birth, and the outer cord is cut by the midwife or doctor.

Once that cord is cut, the spirit is totally housed within the body of the infant and the mother's body begins its adjustment to returning to a pre-pregnancy state. Just as the physical body adjusts to the sudden departure of the baby, so the inner body has to adjust to the departure of another spirit that was housed there. Both changes take some time and have their difficulties.

Many beings attend a birth to help with this adjustment phase. They will appear as angelic beings who 'stroke' their fingers through the mother to readjust her energy and realign her inner landscape.

27.10. Birth

What fascinates me more than anything about the birth process is the inner connection with the stars. I obviously knew about the astrological significance of the moment of birth and the planetary alignments, but I fell across something else by accident, which, in theoretical terms, was obvious. But for true understanding, the real experience just blew me away.

I was busy working in vision with angelic beings and the stars. Suddenly, all the angelic beings that were the consciousness of the planets and stars began to sing. It was a strange, beautiful cacophony of sounds that stirred my soul. As I listened, I watched: the angelic beings slowly moved in harmony and when they reached a certain point, the song reached a strange crescendo and a light appeared to rush past me. Out of curiosity I followed.

The light entered a woman's womb as she was making love to her partner. I was stunned. The angelic beings that were the stars had created or had aligned themselves to an opening that allowed a soul to pass from the Inner Worlds into physical manifestation. The soul had waited, or had been held back, until the planetary pattern was correct, and the angelic beings who were the consciousness of the planets worked in harmony to create a window of opportunity for that soul. It was fabulous to watch and listen to.

I then realized that when I was in the death visions and looking at the souls tipping into the Abyss to fall into life, I was seeing the 'outer' picture of conception. But what I was seeing here in the stars was the deeper, more profound picture of conception. And it was the most beautiful thing I had ever seen or listened to.

It suddenly occurred to me that the most important part of a child's astrological chart is the conception time and date. It was also as though the moment of the child's birth was set at the point of conception and that the two events tied harmoniously into each other.

That then raises questions regarding induced births: how much does an induced birth interfere with the harmony of a child's life pattern? And if an inducement has to be done for safety reasons, rather than the usual convenience reasons, is there any way we can work magically or spiritually to help redress the imbalance?

27. Death and Birth

It also raises questions regarding test tube babies and forced conception. I think it will take us a few more generations to unravel these questions and concerns.

Chapter Twenty-eight

Using tarot as a working tool

Tarot can be used for a great many things besides looking at someone's love life/career/ingrowing toenails. In magical practice, tarot can be used to look for the best way to approach a magical problem, to identify the source of a particular energy, to preempt the effects of a particular magical action, to identify hidden matters and to ascertain if a body impact is magical or a physical illness. The limitations upon what a reader can see are dependent upon what boundaries the reader puts up as we make our own limitations when it comes to seeing. If a deck is poorly thought out however, it can hinder a reading, which is another matter.

Such self-imposed limitations are not only the ones we consciously adopt, such as "oh you cannot read unless they are on red silk, laid east facing," or "you cannot read for yourself": we also limit ourselves through our inability to see something without prejudice. Sometimes the answer can be staring us in the face, but if you are unwilling to look critically at yourself, then often the answer can be missed. By the time a reader comes to using tarot as a magical tool, I would presume that the phase of 'only seeing what you want to see' has passed.

The choice of deck is immaterial really, so long as the deck has the range of beings needed for a wide view of the worlds. The layout is probably more important because the layout is how we put pattern and focus to the information: if the layout is clear and precise then the information will be clear and precise. The best decks are the ones that are designed around and within the layout, with the positions and the beings interacting and interlacing. To find a deck like that to work with, you need to look for an author who has a good understanding of how everything works as opposed to a good artist. A beautiful deck

28. Using tarot as a working tool

can be useless if it is not structured properly, but a spartan deck will work perfectly if it is constructed properly.

This is why it is a useful magical exercise to make your own deck: get blank cards and coloured pens, and structure your own deck to work for you.

So how is a deck constructed properly? Well, the first step towards putting a proper working deck together is need. If you have a real need for a working tool, then you will be a lot clearer about what you need and why. Phase one would be marking down the worlds that you go to and need to be aware of, and then within those worlds, asking, "What functional areas of these worlds affect my work?"

Look at the past, present and future, look at the magical, emotional and practical parts of life, look at the help and hindrance, the inner and outer expressions, the relationships, the home, the temple and the deeper worlds. With that mapping of the worlds and how we live and operate within those worlds, then you have to put in the people. What types and quality of beings do you interact with? Where do they belong in the universe? What powers flow through these beings and what are the effects of those powers. And so the list goes on.

You can see that, by constructing your own deck, you begin to think about the magical world around you in a more focused and connected way. By building a layout/mapping the universe and then putting the beings and powers in their positions on/within that map, you begin to see magical patterns arising that have implications upon your life that you had not thought about. Certain interrelations start to emerge as do flows of power and progressions of states. The whole exercise can be a massive magical education even before you pick one card up to do a reading: it also teaches you the depths of reading.

But using a deck can help you gain information quickly and efficiently if you learn to approach it as a simple working tool, and again, the success of that depends upon the layout as much as your ability to read.

28.1 Layouts

Looking at two layouts, one which most people will know is the Tree of Life layout which is a useful simple layout that can be used to ascertain what is going on with a particular situation, or to look at the results of work. The cards are laid in the following numbered Tree of Life sequence:

The following mapping of the layout is not deep, mystical, Kabbalistic or anything else like that. It is not for meditation, for introspection or backflips. It is just to get simple answers to straightforward magical questions.

Now before all you Kabbalists jump all over me for shifting things a little: in this context, it is just a useful pattern that works! It has simplified the powers right down to get straight answers and if you look deeper about how the layout operates, you will see that it actually makes sense.

For example if you are a magical practitioner who has a variety of skills and you have to attempt an important and maybe dangerous magical act, and you are not sure quite which system or being to use to facilitate the action, then you can look using a reading, asking 'which system should I use?' You would pay particular attention to what is in positions five, eight and ten. For example, if the Knight of Swords is in position five, then it is saying don't use the angelic powers/magical instruments of air. If for example the 5 of Wands is in position eight, then that is saying that the inner contacts that you were considering will be weak and disorganized. If the Magician is in position eight then you have a good magical inner contact, probably human, if the Tower is in position ten then you are screwed, etc.

Looking at magical actions and the differing ways that action can go, depending on what tools/contacts you work with, can teach you an enormous amount about how the power works and how you work within that power from an inner point of view. So you can use the readings to pinpoint the exact best way to approach an important working and find out which contacts, etc. would be the best to work with.

A downside to this, which we have to be aware of and balance against the benefits, is that the simple act of reading for a situation

28. Using tarot as a working tool

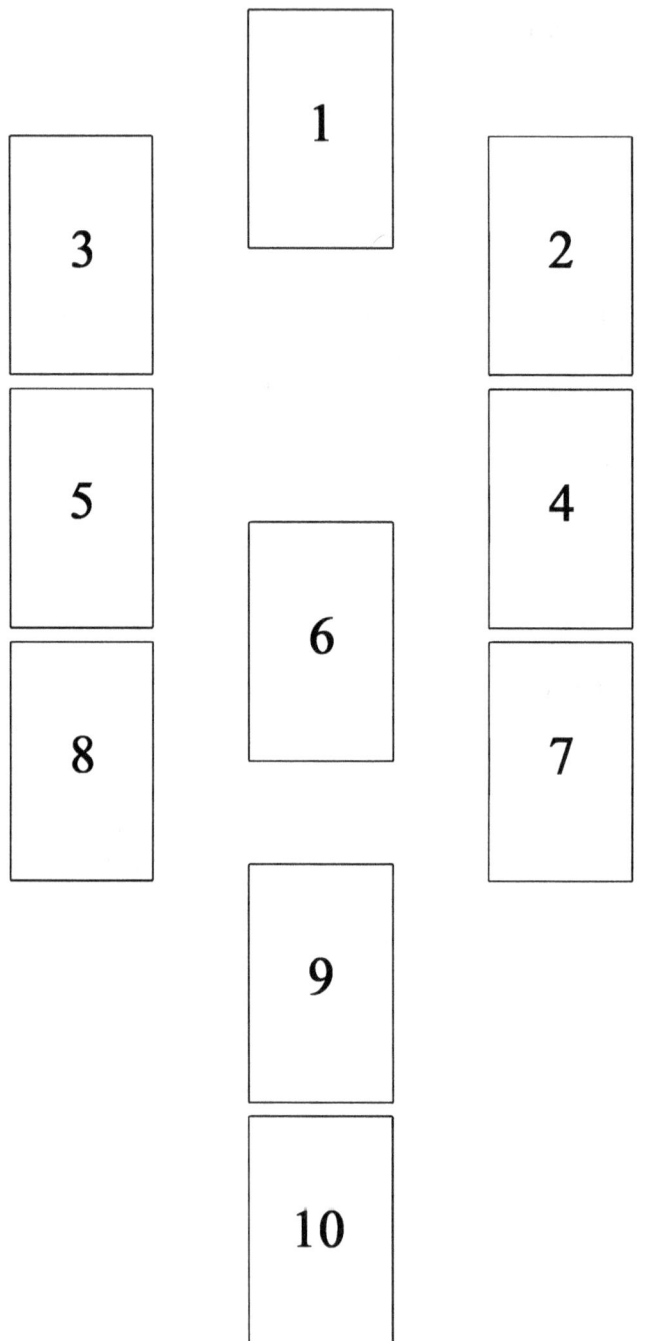

Figure 28.1: The Tree of Life tarot layout

can change the path of that situation. Too many readings on a particular subject or incident can narrow the options available to the worker, so it is important that you do not use decks indiscriminately. Use your own knowledge and common sense to eliminate certain possibilities and then approach the unknown aspects using the deck but be clear and precise about what you ask.

This is the other problem that surfaces when reading for a magical situation: how do you phrase the question? The question has to take into account the limits of a deck in its vocabulary. So for example here are two ways to ask a question:

1. "What will happen if I do X and use Y tool?"

2. "Show me the outcome of the working if I use Y tool."

The first question would bring about an answer that could potentially show you about the dropped candle, the toothache that you get in the middle of it, the untimely knock at the door, the neighbour dropping dead in the middle of the working or your zip bursting when you stand up. By asking what will happen you are opening a field of visions that is potentially wide indeed.

The second question is specific: it will show you the consequence and outcome of using a specific tool. If you are using the reading to see if that tool will be the right one, then you will get a clear and straightforward answer. *It's all about the focus of the question.*

The other thing to think about is the allocation of characters within a deck. If you are working magically with faeries, ancestors, angelic beings etc., you need to sit and think about how court cards and major cards are going to represent the various beings that you work with. Doing such allocation with a deck ends up being a joint effort: you allocate a specific card for a specific being, but the deck consistently spews out another card repeatedly for the same being. So the deck has made the choice and you have to make the connection, but by beginning an action of allocation, it opens a door for that process to begin. As in all magical work, starting the ball rolling allows all the other invested powers, beings and contacts to step up to the plate and do their job.

28. USING TAROT AS A WORKING TOOL

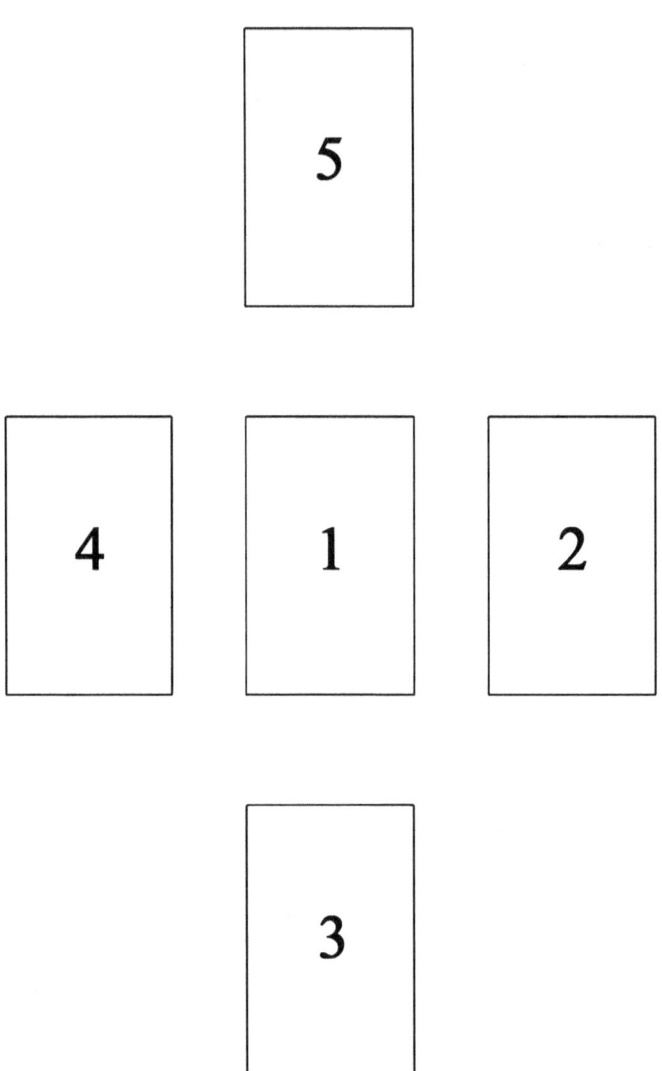

Figure 28.2: The four-directional layout

28.1. Layouts

A second layout that can be useful for a simple view of power is a layout of the four gates. These are general magical attributes that can be used not only in magic, ritual and vision, but also in divination. Once you have a basic idea of the powers that flow from these magical directions, you can use that knowledge to work with the directions for tarot readings.

1. Centre. Body, self, land, starting point, present time. Always start at ground zero: you are seeing from this perspective and this is what all of the directional powers are affecting.

2. East. Air, swords, words, spring, morning, birth, intellect, training, mind, utterance, books.

3. South. Fire, summer, midday, wands, success, rulership, kings, gods, immune system, future.

4. West. Water, autumn, dusk, cups, emotions, relationships, psychic ability, bridge of death.

5. North. Earth, winter, nighttime, pentacles, substance, ancestors, death, elders, queens, goddesses: female.

6. Relationships. This position is about how things, powers and people directly affect you and your relationship with them.

There are many more directional attributes, and as you develop as a magician you will learn far more subtleties, interlinks and connections. But it is unwise to swamp yourself beneath a ton of lists: start simple and go from there. These are a basic list of magical directional powers and how you use them in readings will depend largely on what you are reading about and what you need to know.

This layout can be versatile and can be used for a lot of different types of questions if you work within the parameters of directional attributes, for example east = spring, starting, air, utterance, books, incoming. If you are reading to look to see if a magical attack is incoming, if it is active and forming, it will show in the east (and south). If you were looking for the best timing to do a particular working, the strongest card in the east would indicate dawn/spring, and so on.

28.2 The use of tarot in healing

Tarot, as we know, has many applications, and one of the more interesting ones is as a tool for looking in depth at the human body. Not only does it tell you what is going on with the body, but you can, with the right layout, look at the influences that are bringing about changes in the body, be they organic or inner.

Before we go any further, I have to point out the commonsense thing that everyone knows but it has to be said anyway: using tarot as part of healing is not a substitute for going to a doctor.

You can use an ordinary deck but, if this is something that you are going to use often, I suggest that you make your own deck using your own health and magically related key words written on blank cards. Creating your own deck is not easy as there are a lot of things to think about, such as what key powers, words and dynamics are necessary for a healing deck. But the journey itself is revealing and can teach you a lot not only about the sickness/healing process, but also about how a deck can truly work powerfully.

When you look at the body using tarot, you begin to see some interesting things that relate to illness, body changes, and minute reactions to things that have long-term consequence but little outer symptoms. You start to see the impact that inner work has on the body, how magic sometimes changes things within the body, and how various parts of the body react to power in various ways. It also maps out the passage of inner power through the body, which in turn gives the magical worker clues about how to care for the body while doing powerful work.

The other interesting thing that begins to emerge is the pattern of illness: normally we see only the outer symptoms, which are treated and we get better. Using tarot, we start to see the profound implications of a virus or bacteria, how it can change things at a deep level, and we also start to see the inner manifestation of the outer virus. Every living thing has an inner expression, and through the tarot, we can look at these illnesses to see their inner 'personalities.' This in turn can change how we approach an illness and how we get rid of it.

28.2. The use of tarot in healing

One of the first things that emerge when you start to track the progression of an illness using tarot is that some illnesses, while they may make us miserable, have positive uses for the body. I used to hate the occasional cold: I rarely got them but when I did they made my life a misery. But when I started to look at them from an inner point of view by using the tarot, I saw that the body was using the cold to 'dump' a whole load of toxins that it had in storage. The cold virus was actually a positive thing for me, so I stopped trying to treat the symptoms, and let the body get on with it.

In fact, the more you look at the body and illness using tarot, the more you see positive sides to minor illnesses that the body can use to avoid deeper and more troublesome problems. You also start to see the positive and negative effects of certain types of magic and how the body copes with such power: it changed the way I did magic.

It also began to become clear that the endocrine system processed the heavy impact of magic and too much heavy work, or the burden of a serious attack/curse could seriously damage the endocrine system. This was something that Dion Fortune wrote about from her own body observations, and to see it laid out within a spread is fascinating.

I also began to look closely at the immune system and tracked how magical attacks trigger the immune system: the body treats the energy as an invasion, which, in reality is what it is. The immune system kicks in and tries to fight the attack. If it cannot succeed, the reaction becomes chronic. No amount of treatment can cure it because it is not an outer illness i.e. there is no virus to subdue: it is purely an inner attack and has to be dealt with using inner work.

It really helps if you are doing a lot of magical work to differentiate between ordinary illness and illness that is a manifestation of magic. Too many people think their body problems are the result of magic and the reading will clearly point out if it is or not. Mostly it's not: but it is always good to check, particularly if someone is just not getting better. If someone is sensitive, then their body will react to all sorts of things and you can track that reaction all the way through the body: it's fascinating!

The layout is the key to working in this way. The layout has to be specific so that you can pinpoint certain things that you need information about, and the layout has to have no ambiguous parts to it: it must be precise. I put together a layout that I have used for a few years now and it works in tandem with a healing deck, which is focused specifically upon the human body.

You can track the progression over the days of an illness, seeing if it alters the deeper parts of the body in anyway. I have watched things in my children, seeing how an illness has caused a change and then watching that change emerge over the years. At first I used to panic and try to put back whatever had been altered using homeopathy, cranial work or inner work.

Eventually I learned not to do that: we are the sum total of constant change within ourselves and the changes that come from the viruses are all part of our maturation and growth. Nothing stays the same: everything is always changing and moving.

As a person who uses a lot of homeopathy, this method of using tarot to look at the body became invaluable. I was able to look at the possible progression of a specific remedy to decide the potency or even if it is the right remedy. What I learned over the years is that sometimes even though it's the right remedy picture, the remedy would wreak havoc in the body if I took it or gave it. For me, that was not too much of a revelation: when you do a lot of magical work, the 'body' changes. The way that the body processes power and substance becomes inextricably altered so that normal everyday remedies, medicines and herbs do not work, or have an different or opposing effect. You have to approach a magical body in a different way and take the magical changes into account.

It also becomes useful to look at a person's body rhythm: by getting familiar with someone's processing pattern, you can the make better decisions regarding recovery/treatment. By a person's rhythm I mean the way that the particular body in question processes power, food and illness. Everyone's body has their own unique way of doing things, and that 'way' is borne out of the body's previous experiences, its miasms and its personality. By tracking certain behaviours through the readings, you begin to see the individual pattern of action/reaction in the body and such information can be invaluable when trying to help them.

To sum up, be clear with your questions is always the cornerstone of good reading. Develop the work to fit what you do: quite a few doctor friends of mine have taken this layout and quietly used it in their diagnostic work with some adjustments. And finally, allow your curiosity free rein: that is how we discover things!

28.3 The health layout

The health layout is just that: it is a layout that gives you a snapshot of what is happening in the different areas of the body, and how they are affecting each other. This is an excellent place to start when looking at a magical impact that is physically manifesting, or an illness that is rooted in magic.

This layout looks at the interaction of three forms of energy: emotion, inner energy coming from outside the body, and the energy the body derives from whatever it ingests. These three dynamics are inextricably linked, and the layout shows how those interactions affect the body's various functions.

1.

The first position shows what magic, power, and energetic influence is coming from the Inner Worlds in order to manifest in the body. This is where any magic that could affect the body will show up: for example an inner contact, current inner work, or a magical attack. It is also the position where you will be able to see any future patterns of fate or action that have not yet fully begun to manifest. If the only negative influence in the reading occupies this position, then the destructive pattern is still forming and can be obviated or avoided, as it has not yet reached the individual's inner landscape.

2.

The second position shows any inner influence that has already penetrated a person's sphere/has entered their inner landscape, and is now present in their immediate future pattern. Something that turns up here is already having an energetic influence on how a

28. Using tarot as a working tool

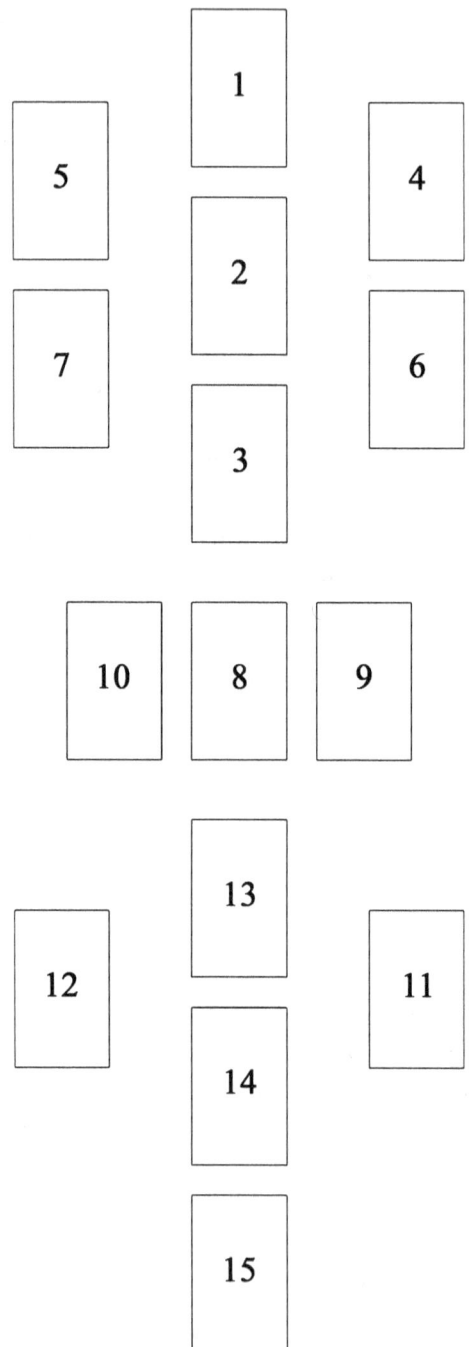

Figure 28.3: Health layout.

body is operating, but it has not yet fully manifested as a full-blown condition.

It is in this position that we see the consciousnesses of viruses and bacteria, along with beings, magical attacks, impacts, etc. Whatever occupies this position is already affecting the person's energetic body, and if left unchecked will descend into their physical body and cause symptoms.

Learning how to discern the meaning of the card in this position will really help you to understand what type of magical impact or injury you are suffering from. If something major shows in this position, do a follow-up reading using the Inner Landscape or Desert layout to gain more detail.

3.

The third position tells us what is physically happening regarding the health of the head. That includes the brain, sinuses, lymph glands, endocrine glands in the brain,[1] ears, nose, eyes, and the throat including the thyroid gland—basically everything above the base of the neck. If something untoward shows in this position, and the physical symptoms presenting are not enough information to pinpoint the exact problem or what area of the head is affected, then narrow things down using a simple layout. To do that I use the Tree of Life layout and ask questions like "is the problem infection?" "is the problem inflammation?" and so on. Remember, the health reading only gives you an overview. After that, you need to focus in on specifics.

4.

The fourth position shows us the solid energy going into the body. Anything that you are eating, drinking, smoking, or otherwise ingesting will show here, and the type of card that falls in this position will also indicate whether it is affecting you badly.

---

[1] The hypothalamus, and the pineal and pituitary glands.

5.

The fifth position shows the state of the emotions: how the person feels. Often the emotions can be good indicators of what is going on deeper within the body. The emotions can drive the immune system, and when looking for a treatment make sure that it brings about favourable emotional energies. If a person is in physical pain, it will also show in this position.

6.

The sixth position shows what the short-term or primary immune system is currently doing. If it is fighting something or it is in overdrive, it will show here. What we put into our bodies directly affects the front line of the immune system: hence this card sits directly under the 'solid energy' position. Look at the relations between the two cards: if an ingested substance (food, drugs, etc.) is contributing to, aggravating, or causing the illness, then both positions four and six will show aggravating or aggressive cards.

7.

The seventh position shows the deeper immune system, and this is connected to the function of the thymus, an endocrine gland. The thymus prepares and trains T and B cells for a front-line attack on an intruder, and it is deeply affected by emotional wellbeing, which is why card seven sits beneath card five in this spread. This position also shows the secondary immune system that wraps up, locks up, or breaks down threats that have already been overcome.

When the querent is already on the winning side of an illness, the aggressive cards will often move from position six (primary immune response) to position seven. This is where disease threats are processed and put into 'sleep mode.' The person's emotional wellbeing will affect how well this process works, and if they have recently experienced terrible grief, this area of the immune system can become compromised. This position also tells us how our immune system is functioning. It indicates how well-balanced the immune responses are, and whether the body's T- and B-cells are being produced in the right quantities and are operating as

28.3. The health layout

they should, and are not attacking the body itself. (Regarding inflammatory diseases: when one is in active mode, it will often show in both immune positions. When the disease is dormant but has potential, it will show only in the seventh position.)

8.

The eighth position shows the central core of the body, which houses the vital organs. If there is a problem with those organs, it will show here. If a major aggressive card falls in this position, then the reader needs to do further readings to see which specific organ has been affected.

9.

The ninth position shows the male sexual organs, testosterone, and the bladder. Testosterone is also present in females, and if the reading is for a woman and a difficult card turns up in this position, then it will probably be necessary to look in more depth at her endocrine system and hormone balances. If they all look fine in separate readings, then a reading needs to be done to look at her hormonal response to being around males.

10.

The tenth position shows the female sexual organs and the bladder. Again, males also have estrogen in their bodies, so if the reading is for a male and a difficult card turns up here, check their hormone system. A difficult card here can also indicate the presence of a member of the opposite sex who is hormonally disruptive. So for example, if a woman magician is out-of-balance and a reading shows an aggressive card in the ninth position, it could either indicate a testosterone imbalance within her own body, or a male around her who is disrupting her health simply with his presence or energetic influence. This usually happens unconsciously, and it is the result of the many hormone signals our bodies put out—sometimes we can have a bad reaction to hormone signals coming from another person. Depending on where a woman is in her cycle, she can be attracted by male pheromones—but she can also be made aggressive by the presence of the same. In female magicians, this is far more pronounced than in the general population, depending on what streams of inner power and contacts they work with. So be aware of those possible dynamics when reading those positions: hormones are the dynamos that run our moods and emotions, and as such they have a powerful influence over everything that we do. The other thing that can show in these two sexual reproductive positions is bladder issues, so bear that in mind.

11.

The eleventh position shows the digestive system, and it reveals how the large and small intestines are processing everything that came in at position four (food, etc). But be aware that a lot of magic can also be processed through the digestive system, particularly when we are given energy or information to take in. This area of the body can also be read in conjunction with position five (the emotions): there is a direct relationship between digestive health and mental and emotional health. For example, neurotransmitters like serotonin play a major part in mood, muscle health, and digestion.

12.

Position twelve tells us what is happening to us in our sleep. Many magicians put too much emphasis on controlling their dreams in order to have 'lucid dreams.' This is a mistake and it can interfere with true magical events that can happen in sleep, plus it also interferes with the body's own repair system that swings into action when we sleep.

Any magical intrusions of any real power will surface naturally in dreams, and dreams are also an opportunity for protective beings to warn us of impending trouble. Our sleep is also a time when our deeper spirit can partake of magical service, and it is unwise to interfere with the natural flow of our deeper selves. The dreams/sleep position is directly below the emotions and the deeper immune system in this layout, as they are all inexorably linked, and these cards can be read together to get a deeper understanding of what is happening in our subconscious, our brains, and our immune system. This position is also linked to positions one and two, and

28.3. The health layout

if disturbances show in positions one and two, and there is a volatile or difficult card in position twelve, then you are most likely looking at a magical attack, a difficult period of fate changes, or at least a magical disturbance. The quality of your sleep is important to both your health and your strength, so pay good attention to what is going on in this position.

13.

Position thirteen looks at the 'structure and movement' system of the body, which means bone, muscle, and nerves. Any inflammatory reaction, central nervous system disturbance, or bone/muscle impact will show here. If there is a difficult card in this position and also in position three (head/brain) then you are more likely to be looking at a problem with nerve issues. If there are fiery cards in this position and in the eleventh position (digestion) then it may indicate an inflammatory disease active with roots in bacterial imbalance or inflammation in the small intestine.

14.

Position fourteen is the skin. The skin is the most externalized organ and also the biggest organ of our body. It is through the skin that the body can safely deposit toxins and dead matter, and process irritants: this mechanism keeps such problems away from vital organs, and also gives you an obvious heads-up when there is a problem.

Issues with food sensitivity or allergy, recovery from viruses and infections, and reactions to magical power will all show on the skin: the skin is a good weather indicator about how our bodies are coping, and what they are coping with. If the magician is badly attacked and gets ill as a result, one of the healing objectives should be to bring that imbalance up to the surface to present itself on the skin.

As soon as the rashes start to show, you know the healing process is working. Because of this mechanism, never be tempted to suppress rashes that appear: rather it is better to keep an eye on them and let them be. If it is an allergic reaction or a sensitivity reaction like eczema, find out the root cause and eliminate it if possible.

15.

Position fifteen tells us the immediate future of the body's health. If a damaging card turns up in this position, then work still has to be done to help to body come back into balance. Consider this card in relation to the time limit you put on the reading: if the reading looked three weeks ahead, and the card in position fifteen is a difficult one, then redo the reading to look at a span of six weeks, to see if the body just needs a bit more time to heal. If at six weeks the card in position fifteen (or other cards) is still difficult, then you need to reassess what action you are taking.

When to use the health layout

Use this layout when the body is showing obvious signs of distress after magical work, or if your body suddenly nosedives and you suspect that magic has been used. It is also a good layout to keep an eye on your general health and it can be used by energy healers to look at a client to get a deeper picture of what is going on inside their body.

Keep a record of the readings so that you can track recovery over time, but also so that you can spot potential longer-term problems that are not so apparent in the first readings. Often an imbalance in an area of the body starts like a grain of sand rubbing in your sock, but then grows over time to become a major issue. If that happens, you can go back over the readings to pinpoint the beginning of the problem and locate the area of the body that first went into decline. It also helps you to see how a particular body copes with problems: each body is slightly different and will have its own healing pattern. Through tracking various bodily reactions through readings, you can ascertain that body's own method of self-healing.

28.4 Making a contacted deck for magical seership

When you design your own deck for divination, there are many ways in which it can be done which will decide what type of deck you will end up with. Doing a vague copy of the Rider-Waite will give you a

28.4. Making a contacted deck for magical seership

Rider-Waite deck. Working within the structures of archetypes and psychology will give you a deck that speaks from the complexity of the human psyche. But if you do a lot of magical work and you use your deck as a tool to assist you in your work, then you need a deck that will bend and flex with the demands that present in the type of work that you do.

Such a deck will be the most useful if it is connected to the contacts that you work with, or the types of beings that you regularly encounter. This way, the beings can talk to you clearly through the deck which can save a lot of faffing about when you need to get a job done swiftly and successfully.

In conjunction with the contacts within the deck, the layout should reflect the realms and places that you work in or that are a part of your life, or the places that you go to when you are working with a particular order of beings. This way, the cards and the layout are read together, and begin to form a natural flow of communication that you can plug into.

If you are making a contacted deck, then you need to make sure that every being, place and power that you put in the deck is real: it must be beings and places that you have experience of, however brief the encounter. This ensures the clarity, depth and honesty of the deck: it cannot be a contacted deck if the beings are not real!

What can happen however is that, if the beings are not real, they can occasionally act as filters or windows for real beings to come through. The only problem with this is that the filter can interfere with the natural qualities of the being—it will literally filter them and they will only be able to express the power that is represented in the image.

Then you need to look at the sorts of 'actions' that need to express themselves through the deck. These 'actions' are the equivalent of the Minor Arcana in the tarot deck. They must express all the different depths of emotions, actions, happenings, etc. and it is a good idea to use the elements as a basis, but it is not essential. The way to decide the actions section of the deck is to write a list of emotions, happenings, actions, etc.

For example: power, work, travel, past, balance, imbalance, illness, creation, accident, gift, accumulation, etc. It does not matter

28. USING TAROT AS A WORKING TOOL

how many you have, though I tend to work on seven or ten for each element. Using a single word or only two words takes away the deliberate and terribly annoying whimsical obscurity that is found in the minor cards in some decks. I want straight answers, not a philosophy lesson!

Once you have all your actions charted, then you need people for your deck. Again, I usually steer away from the traditional court cards, which can be as equally annoying as the obscure minor picture cards.

How many of us have wanted to tear up page/child cards that litter a reading and have nothing useful to say!

Look at the different aspects of womanhood and manhood. Some people are rulers, others are seers, some are workers, so you would need a king, a queen, a priestess, an old person, a young person, a mother, a father, consort, a wise elder, a young lover, etc. You need to represent one of each of the various expressions of womanhood and manhood. I usually end up with about 20 court cards, 10 for each sex. But you can do as many or as little as you like: you are the only person who imposes limits on yourself!

When it comes to layout, you must decide which realms you wish the deck to work in and what elements of your own realm you wish to include: home? temple? work? Within your own realm, you will need positions to allow the powers to define a specific influence e.g. dreams, warnings, struggles, what is coming in, what is going out, what is past, what is future. If you want clarity within your readings, then the positions of the layout must be in harmony with each other and the pattern must make sense, rather that being decided upon by a design/aesthetics decision.

One of the strongest ways of working with a contacted deck is to design the layout in fellowship with the major cards. Each major card is also a position in the layout: for example if you have twenty major cards, there will be twenty positions for the full layout. Each position will be named after and will be the home of a major card. When you are doing a reading with the full layout, the card and the position will be read together.

When approaching the layout design, write the realms that you work with, and then think about the major cards and where they would live, what realm they reside in. The actual pattern of the layout reflects the realms, and the positions reflect the powers and beings that are the major cards. The positions and cards interact to create a pattern that flows through the reading once the deck is in use.

Once you have got a basic pattern for your layout, look at it again from a geometric point of view: the universe that we live in is mathematically coherent and its patterns are clear, beautiful and make perfect sense. Your layout needs to reflect that harmony, so it also needs to make geometric sense. The best pattern of all to use is the patterning of the universe.

28.5 Minor layouts

The full layout of your deck would be for major magical readings. For smaller readings where you need straight answers and to identify powers, action, etc. you will need a more work-friendly layout that can be used quickly and efficiently.

Think about the basic environment you are in: past, present, future, home, work, and temple. Think about positions that will express a space for an answer to come in: i.e., dreams, obstacles, support, and relationships. The layout will then be built around a basic structure that will enable the cards to talk in a clear way to you for simple communication.

28.6 Creating your major cards

Once your basic mapping of cards and layout is done, then you need to start creating the deck from an inner point of view before you begin to create the outer deck. The orders of beings, the individual beings and the places that are represented need to be connected up to images that you will create. This is the most time-consuming part of the whole process as it cannot be rushed and needs to be done systematically and carefully.

Find a space where you can leave out parts of the deck where they and you will not be disturbed, and where you can keep a safety candle going all the time. Starting with the first being or place of the deck, go in vision to that place or to meet that being and commune with them. Ask for a sigil, pattern or image and when you come out of vision, write it down and then make that card. Repeat the process until all the major cards have been made.

You may find that during the process, some of the beings or places want their layout positions changed or modified: the first map of your layout should be a starting point, not a finished production. Be flexible and able to listen to the beings as they guide you. Ideally, the major cards and the layout are created together and are a part of each other. They should have a close working relationship with the layout and with each other so that it becomes their own little world.

Then you can then go onto make the minor and court cards. When you make the minor cards, again stay flexible, as you may find that some actions become unnecessary and you will most likely realize that you have left out a crucial action. You can use the harmony of numbers to allow powers to flow through the minor cards too, in which case you must make sure that the actions and emotions are relevant to the harmonics of the number patterns.

Sometimes you will find that the minor cards become lower octaves of some of the major cards, showing that life patterns are often octaves of higher and more powerful fate patterns that flow through the consciousness of the time and the culture that you live in. It can get very interesting and this is where some of the astrological symbolism comes into play on the minor cards: the planetary symbol can be put in the corner of the card if it is useful to show the deeper pattern of the power that you are expressing.

One word of caution though: don't fall into the trap of putting lots of obscure magical symbols on your cards just to make them look more magical as you will clutter the filter, confuse the reading, and you will start to walk down the road of glamour. Magic is about real powers, real work and a real world: it's not about black clothes, funny symbols and looking magically cool.

On that note, you don't have to be an artist to create your own contacted deck, words, symbols and basic images will work and allow the power to flow through, just make sure that there is nothing on the cards that does not belong there: don't fill them with junk!

If you are an artist, then you are especially lucky: some of the inner world beings are stunning in their representations, and to

28.6. Creating your major cards

recreate them with all their colours, lines and shapes would be awesome! The power would truly flow through unhindered and such visual beauty is wonderful to work with.

As you are working on your deck, make sure you have a living flame burning to tune the space in as you work. It can be really useful if you tune the flame into the Void: this means that help can flow out of the Void as you create.

Once the deck is created, let it sit for twenty-four hours before you start to work with it. This is like a settling-in period to let the powers settle: it's the cooking of the deck! Make sure you have a safe place to put it so that it cannot be played with: contacted decks can affect people if they mishandle them. Having a warrior goddess coming face-to-face with your three-year-old toddler is not always a good idea: it could get messy (though in my household it would have been debatable about which one would come out on top).

When the deck is ready to work, start by laying out the major cards in their layout positions and just sit and hang out with them for a few minutes to look over the connections, patterns and relationships. You might start to see new ones that you did not know about, or hadn't thought about. It also helps to get a visual of the card in its position so that when you come to do a reading, you can see the major card position in your head and read the card that fell in that position in tandem with the positional meaning, along with the position where that positional card landed. (Confused? Ha!)

So for example: say you have two major cards, the Pathway (future) and the Old Gods: the Pathway falls in the layout position of the Old Gods while the Old Gods is in the position of the Mountain (challenges you must face). This would indicate that the way forward for you is to look into/work with the powers of the old ways/gods, but it will be a hard struggle that must be faced. If it still doesn't make sense, just drink a few beers, it will all get clearer...

Once you are familiar with the layout positions/powers, then it is time to start to play with the deck. Work with a notebook and write your questions. The first one to do, which will open your deck up and align it to you, is to look at your long-term magical/spiritual work/life, or something of that ilk that is connected to your magical work and you, and it should be a long-term or lifetime view. This is

28. Using tarot as a working tool

like charging a phone battery: you have to give it a long charge the first time around, as that sets the power levels for future fills.

Write down the reading so that you can go back to it in the future. This is a good training habit to get into: always write readings and your interpretations. If you are wrong, you can go back and see why, and you can see how it really unfolded.

Once you have seen the disaster that is the rest of your life, then you can start to look at other things of power to exercise the deck, and to train you to understand its idiosyncrasies. Don't put any limitations upon what you look at or why, just be curious so that you can learn.

Look at the work of political figures: look at the inner influences that flow through them, for good or bad. Look at religious and magical figures, look at historical figures and their powers. Look at deities and their powers, their histories and their stories now. Look at magical places and realms: ask how they work and why.

The secret to the focus of the deck is the focus of the reader's questions. You have to be clear and to the point with a question. For example, if you ask the deck to show you your magical work now, it will probably show you your magical work at that precise point in time. So think about your questions and be simple, for example: show me the magical powers that ran through Crowley from his teens until his death, show me the magical influences that were around him from birth until the age of twenty. You can see how specific the questions should be.

Once you have done one deck and have become proficient at working with it, then you can start to look at creating decks with specific purposes. If you work a lot with herbs or are a healer for example, you can create a healing deck where the cards are slanted towards body issues and powers, and the layout reflects the systems of the body.

There is no real limit on what you can do in deck design: we create our own limits which we have to learn to move beyond. If you spend enough time pressing the red button and blowing the world up, you will begin to learn your real limits, as opposed to the ones that are inflicted upon you that are there simply to keep you in your place in the magical pecking order.

Chapter Twenty-nine

Working methods for leading group visions/workings

When you are in a situation of leading groups into visions, there are many powers and techniques that come into play both to protect the group and to facilitate the inner contact/connection.

In this chapter, I will be dealing with visions that are 'contacted' i.e. going to real places and interacting with real beings as opposed to psychological guided journeys that are written in advance and explore the deeper part of the self. That is therapy and is not dealt with here.

When you are leading people in a vision, you are basically telling them what you see: you take them by the hand and lead them to a place where they can interact with a contact. So the first step is to make sure that the vision you are using is flexible enough for that purpose so that the group can pass from imagination to reality pretty quickly. For that you need a structure that is well used so that you do not have to do any 'hacking' into new territory, unless that is your aim.

To approach it this way, you begin the structure from the minute you light a candle in the centre of the gathering. People have been lighting candles to precipitate inner work for hundreds if not thousands of years, so the minute you light a flame with intent, you begin your walk down a well trodden path.

The vision that you use will need to have the basic gateway structure that gets people to where you need them to go. It also needs to have the 'unfolding' energy that stretches the people from an inner point of view to make them more 'flexible.' There is a great deal of power in approaching a contact slowly by going through a series of processes: first the people need to become focused, then they

29. Working methods for leading group visions/workings

need stilling and to be made aware of their own environment before embarking on a journey that will take them away from themselves.

By instilling the details of their environment, it is easier to bring them back after a particularly deep vision. What they will need is a sense of the directions, of themselves in relation to those directions, and the focal point of their own power within. Then connect that to the central flame that will act as a beacon for when they begin their journey back.

One piece of advice at this stage is that throughout the vision don't be tempted to describe too much, or to be creative in your language or to add things in to 'make' the surroundings, as these details cloud the natural vision of the listener and can be distracting. Simple and straightforward is much better and allows the listener to 'see' things for themselves. If you describe too much, you end up blocking their sight, so the less you describe the better. The basic rule of thumb is to say only what is needed to get them somewhere and to introduce them to the contacts.

Once you have crossed into the vision from the imagination, you will basically be telling them what you see, except don't give too much detail regarding the contact. Just outline the power and basics of the contact, and let them experience it for themselves. Give them a period of silence so that they can commune with the contact themselves. And then when you start to bring them back, you will find it is much easier and quicker to bring them back than it is to take them there.

29.1 Contacts

When you are reaching for a contact to work with in vision, they will often be lining up for you once you have decided what it is you are going to do. This works if you are working within a framework, rather than random visions where you are looking for anyone who is an inner contact: that is like wandering the streets for someone to talk to. Be focused and know where you are going and why.

Don't fall into the trap of visionary tourism: going somewhere just to look/connect with a contact but not actually doing anything useful. This is a dead end road to go down and will slowly close your contacts up over a period of time. When you go into the Inner Worlds, particularly with a group of people, you have the chance to do something useful. Ask the contact if they need you to do anything for them: they will jump at the chance usually and it is better for groups to be doing rather than looking.

29.2 Energy dynamics

The energy dynamics of group vision is interesting. You can go further and open things out more with the group energy, but you also have the strain of carrying the weaker members of the group to some extent. If it is a fairly large group, it is advisable to have experienced workers in each direction and they have the responsibility of holding the energy in that direction. This intention of action automatically begins a load-sharing between the workers and shares the strain out, enabling the group to do much more powerful work without blowing anyone out.

The protection of the group comes from the framework that you are working in. If you are using a vision path that has been walked many times over the generations, then certain beings will be operating within that structure and will automatically keep you safe. If you are working on a new path, or hardly used path, then you will have to be a little more attentive.

Be on the alert for beings that you had no intention of working with ("hey, I can work with you, I will take you here, I am the high priest" etc.), as they are mostly hungry parasites out for a quick lunch. If you are doing exploratory work, have a clear intent of where you want to go, what you want to achieve and who you want to meet. Don't move out of that framework and don't get taken down the garden path, so to speak.

If for example, you are aiming to connect with a certain deity, then they will probably have protective beings within their structure that will come into play the minute you begin the vision. If you are stretching for a person in time, or another type of being, then it is advisable to work within your own structure if you are a part of a coven/lodge/priest line, etc. Use your own contacts and guardians to warn you and keep you safe.

29. Working methods for leading group visions/workings

As you get to be more experienced at exploratory work, you begin to recognize the beings that will just be a pain in the ass or could be a threat to your group. If you stay on your intended path though, such things tend not to happen.

When the group is looking at a particular set of beings, places, people, deities, the best way is to always go meet them in visions first, and then talk about them afterwards. This way, you do not colour the person's experience, or preempt their vision in any way. The effect is the opposite: if you do the vision and then have a talk-around to share experiences and then talk about the theoretical stuff, you will see things dawn on people's faces as they come to realize what it was that they just saw. Hearing other people describe something that you thought only you saw is a wonderful feeling: you realize you were all really there.

29.3 Reality or imagination?

This takes us to the age-old beginner's question: what is real and what is the imagination? Well, both really. You use the imagination as a vehicle to get you into the Inner Worlds and then it crosses over into visions of what is actually there, not what is imagined there.

People have to experience this for themselves: no amount of explaining will do it. I have been doing this work for a long time and I still get shivers of happiness when I get inner conformation of the reality. When a person has a silent experience in a vision (i.e. they see something that was not described, or the contact tells them something directly) and then at the talk-around after the working someone else describes exactly the same thing, you know you have all been in the same place.

My all-time favourite example of this happened in Bath UK and Ulster. Many years ago, while teaching in Ulster, during a vision I offered a precious ring that I had to the Dark Goddess. She took it with thanks and I made the promise to put the actual ring into the river in Bath where the hot springs of Sul pour into the river's edge.

As soon as I got to my home in Bath I got my ring, put it in my bag and went off to the river. I couldn't bear to look at the ring (it was the most precious thing I had besides my kids, and dropping little kids into the river as a goddess offering tends to get you arrested these days...) so I just put my hand in the bag, got it on the end of my finger, and with my eyes shut, dropped it into the water. All was well.

Until a week later when I was leading a group vision into the cave of the Dark Goddess, where she lunged at me in fury demanding to know where her gift was. To say that I was shitting myself would be putting it mildly. I stammered that I had given her the ring but she held another ring up to my face: a ring I recognized but wasn't 'The' precious one: it was an Egyptian ring, antique gold, but not the one she wanted. I was confused.

When I got home, my then partner reminded me that he had put my Egyptian ring in my bag to remind me to get it fixed (the turquoise was loose). When I put my hand into my bag I had pulled out the wrong ring unknowingly and the Goddess had not got her gift.

I immediately found the precious ring and took it straight to the river and deposited it. That is one of many examples of the reality of visions, and a good example of my unerring ability to be a dork.

29.4 Snatched energy

One sad thing to be cautious of in group work is to be on the lookout for energy snatchers. These people try and harness some of the group energy to use for their own agenda which, just by nature of their action, will probably be unhealthy.

The way it is done is a rock, little bag, trinket, amulet, etc. is quietly placed under or around the altar in the centre with the intention of siphoning off power into it to be taken away at the end of the day. It can also be done by holding the object and gathering up the group power as the others work. Do not allow anyone to put anything by, on or near the altar, and don't let them hold anything. There are often many excuses given but none are valid: there is no reason for anyone to need an object while working. The protections are in place and they need to work like everyone else. It is sad in today's magical world that such things happen, but they do.

29. Working methods for leading group visions/workings

On a side note, if you are part of a visionary magic group or at a workshop type gathering, look for the leader doing the same thing. I have had experiences of watching teachers and leaders use workshop energy to fuel their own private agenda even to the point of using group workshop energy to launch curses and magical attacks. Under those circumstances the unwitting participants become sucked into the energetic structure of the attack and take the repercussions as if they were the initiator of the attack. This is a sneaky way for the attacker to use the group as a scapegoat for the backlash of energy such attacks generate. I hate writing about this type of thing, but it happens more than you would think and people need to be aware of it.

29.5 Different strains for different places

When you take groups to different places, there are different body impacts that such visions bring. The closer the vision is to your own realm and time, the less of an impact it will cause. The further away in time and the deeper the realm, the more of a bodily impact you will get. If you are taking a group way out in the stars at a planetary consciousness level, they will get hammered. If you are taking them to the depths of the Abyss, they will get hammered, but in a different way. Going up seems to precipitate nausea and going down has the beaten with a baseball bat feeling.

One of the things that can help to lessen such impact is to build up to such heavy workings slowly by doing a few gentler ones first. If you are planning to go far out in any direction, do at least two visions that take people a part of the way so that they become stretched along that path. Then when they come to do the heavy one, they have already been down a section of the road and their body has had time to adjust.

Take frequent coffee breaks and make the group talk in turn about their experiences after the visions: this helps people to come back, it helps jog memories that become lost in deep vision, and it also helps to hear other people's experience in relation to your own.

After a particularly heavy vision, do a light rebalancing meditation or take them into a Void-type setting to rebalance and restore them. Don't finish the day on a powerful working either, finish on a gentle note: people have to drive and find their way home. That is not easy if you head is stretched in fourteen different directions.

29.6 Picking up maps from written visions

When you read a written vision that was created through true vision as opposed to being a constructed vision—i.e. what is written was the direct experience of a seer rather than a vision put together theoretically—then you are looking at someone else's experience. But it can still be used as a basic map to get you somewhere without being affected by the author's individual sight/experience, if you know how to read what they wrote.

When you look at a written vision (such as the ones below), look without getting drawn into the vision. Look at the mechanism used for getting into the inner realms, look at the path used, the contacts worked with and the way out. You can extract a basic skeleton map that you can work with to allow your own vision to emerge. This ends up being a deeper experience than following another person's writings word for word. Following other people's visions to the letter will limit your own ability to reach into the Inner Worlds for visions and contacts.

When you look at written visions, be on the lookout for things put in there that are mythical or psychological: you want neither. What you want is the true map and nothing else, so don't get sidelined by descriptions or declarations.

An important point to think about within group working is don't filter who can come and who cannot: when you work with deep inner contacts, they line up the group before you do. They pull in people they need to work with and will reject people they do not wish to work with. If you have an open door policy, then the filtering is done for you providing the work is conducted within the right ethics i.e. it is not a commercial affair.

The strangest people, who you think might not be able to handle the work, often turn out to be the strongest of the group or they take on some very important role that you hadn't thought of. The more I have worked with groups over the years, the more I have realized

29. Working methods for leading group visions/workings

that I really haven't a clue what I am doing and I just turn up and tune in. The inner contacts plug in after shaking their heads at the dork that life has thrown at them, and we are off and away.

The same goes for written work: I have found that if you just put out the work, it will inform those that need the info, will not interest the ones who don't, and will be totally incomprehensible or unusable to the people who really shouldn't be doing it anyway.

29.7 Clearing up

After you have finished a day of working, it is wise to clear up the room after yourself. You can do this as a group working, the last working of the day where people in the directions gather up the energy that has been generated and the vision imprints that are left in the room and they put the energy into the central flame, sending back into the Inner Worlds where it came from.

You then in vision fold up the room where you were working, like folding up a skin, and take it into the Void to disperse it, or put it in the flame. This way, you leave no imprint that can disturb or affect any future users of the room.

29.8 Creating a vision from a personal experience

When you have a powerful personal vision or experience, it can be good to share or expand the contact for use by a group. To do that you need to construct a vision that will safely get someone to a place and get them back.

The first stage of the construction is the opening and reaching for the contact. Intent is everything in magical work so when you light the flame, have specific intentions about where you want to go and what you want to do. You can draw the opening sequence from your own magical structures. I use the Void as a gateway to many places, while some people use a four-directional gate system, and others go down into the Underworld as a gateway to other places, and so on.

For example, say you had a powerful experience at a stone circle and you wanted to take a group there. You would open the vision using your own structure and then see yourself walking out of the mists towards the circle from some distance away. As you walk, call upon the guardians and contacts of the stones to grant you access to the circle, and you may have to as a group stop at a threshold and give gifts to the guardians. If you do this, warn people that if they give something that exists, they might have to throw it into a nearby river as an offering. This transfer of energy is important: if you are going to access a powerful place, it is only right that you contribute to the site in some way.

Once you have left gifts on the threshold, go down the path that leads to the stones and tell the group of any contacts that you see and introduce them to them. Once they are in the stones, give then silent time to commune for themselves with the stones and contacts. Then you can ask the contacts if they need anything from you as a group: sometimes they will need a job doing. In return you can ask them about the power of the site and how to work with it properly in the physical realm.

When the work is finished, guide the people back away from the stones and towards the mists. Pass them through the mists and into the Void or whatever threshold you use. Then remind them of where they are, where their directions are, and give then a minute of two to orientate themselves before asking them to open their eyes.

I am hoping that some of this information in this chapter will be useful to people embarking upon the role of vision leader. To help with ideas, and for material to extract skeletons/structure from, I have included below a few visions for people to work with and use. All of the visions are contacted visions and can be used to connect with those connections.

29.9 The vision of the goddess Tefnut in Ethiopia

Light a candle and close your eyes. Be aware of the flame within you, burning at the edge of the Void, and be aware of the candle flame before you. With your inner vision, you look at the candle flame and it grows into a column of fire. The fire is inviting and you edge closer to it.

29. Working Methods for Leading Group Visions/Workings

As you look at the fire, the room in which you are seated falls away and you find yourself walking down a hot dusty road with the sun burning in your face. There are many people around you, walking with you as you walk towards a walled city ahead of you.

As you get closer to the city you see that the wall that surrounds the city is made of dried mud and upon it are many beautiful frescos of birds, animals and strange-looking beasts with many wings and many eyes.

The air hums with bees, and flowers are all around you as you walk. The procession that you follow enters the city and heads straight to a low-built temple made of mud and brick. Many people are bearing gifts and male priests stop all women as they reach the temple: the women are not allowed to enter, they may only leave offerings at the threshold.

A deep instinct tells you to assume the look of a man and you draw a large cover over yourself to mimic some of the men who are swathed with robes and covers. No one looks at you as you enter the temple. To the far side of the temple is a narrow corridor and you walk down this corridor towards a large door.

No one seems to be interested in this door: they are busy celebrating something in the main temple. Pushing the door open you find yourself in a small dark sanctuary with a black rock in the center of a six-pointed star that is laid out upon the floor in grain.

Your hands are drawn to the rock and you reverently place your hands upon the black stone. A power builds up all around you and the room begins to hiss.

A face appears before you: a face of a lion who is also human. She is weeping and is angry. She has been trapped here in this temple by priests who wish to control her powers of moisture and life. She asks that you free her without alerting the priesthood.

A priest walks in and you pretend to be leaving an offering. Without wasting time, you leave the sanctuary and the temple, heading west to the river. Frantically you look around for a rock that looks similar to the one on the sanctuary. Finally you find one and hide it among your robes.

Returning to the temple you walk swiftly to the sanctuary and wait until it is empty. While no one is looking, you switch the rocks,

29.9. The vision of the goddess Tefnut in Ethiopia

picking up the sacred back stone and replacing it with the one from the river.

Once you are free of the temple and walking towards the river, you begin to be aware that the rock in your arms is beating like a heart. The voice of the Goddess swirls all around you: "yes, you hold my heart within your hands...take care and place me gently in the river that runs to the sea."

Once at the river, you walk into the water and find a good spot where she will not be disturbed. You place the rock among other rocks so that she is hidden. As soon as the rock leaves your arms you are overcome with a great tiredness.

Reaching the bank of the river, you lie down on the grass and immediately fall asleep. You dream of lions running free upon the land and of rivers bursting with life. Someone shouts your name and you wake with a start.

Before you stands a woman with the face of a lion. She is clothed in a cloak of many colors and around her neck are many bone beads. Aside her are two male lions without manes, and bees swarm all around her. She smiles as she shows you the life in the river that flows from her heart. She shows you how the life of the river flows down to the sea, flooding the land around it with life-giving moisture. Forests appear alongside the river and plants begin to grow.

She walks towards you, grass sprouting wherever her feet touch the ground, and she reaches out her hand. In the palm of her hand is one drop of moisture. She offers it to you and you carefully lick it from her hand.

The power of life flows through you, energizing you and filling you with strength and vitality. The Goddess tells you that with your willingness to help her, she will always help you and that wherever she is worshipped, drought will never appear.

She touches you upon the head and her touch fills you with a blinding light. All that you can see in the light is a flame: your flame. You move towards the flame and find yourself stepping through a flame back into the room where you first started. You sit awhile, absorbing what you have experienced. When you are ready, you open your eyes and blow out the candle.

29.10 The vision of Metatron and the Abyss

Be still and light a candle. As you become silent, so you begin to lose awareness of the room in which you are seated. The external noises fade, your mind settles and your breathing becomes relaxed and natural. Using your inner vision, you look at the candle flame before you. The room in which you are seated falls away and you find yourself looking through the flame to a landscape beyond.

Instinctively you reach through the flame and pass into the landscape—a place of sand, earth and wind. The wind whips around you and the sand gets into your eyes. For a moment you are blinded and yet you become aware of someone walking alongside you.

As your eyes clear, you see a human-type being, neither male nor female, walking alongside you, and yet their feet are down in the earth, so their legs are only visible from the calf up. They walk through the earth as though it was not there. Their hair is long and trails along the ground behind them, swishing away their footprints. No mark is left of their passing.

The being reaches out to touch you, and as their hand contacts your skin, a force flows through you with such strength that you fear you may fall. You become aware of the landscape in a different way. Life reflects from everything around you. The stones, the grains of sand, the plants and the wind, all are lit with the light of Divinity—all life is visible to you.

Looking around you see people come and go: they are unaware of you as you observe them. The perfection of power manifest in substance is evident in every person you look upon, and as you look to your own hands, you see divinity within your own flesh.

The angel moves you on and you walk deeper and deeper into the Desert, leaving the people behind. As you walk you become more and more aware of the mistakes you have made in this life, and the things that you have to learn. You find yourself assessing your life and you become so absorbed in this task that you arrive at the edge of a cliff without realizing. The angel puts out an arm to stop you falling over the edge.

You look out over the cliff and see that it falls down so far that you cannot see the bottom. It looks like a tear in the universe with no

29.10. The vision of Metatron and the Abyss

end. You look up and the sky is the same. The tear rises up through the stars also.

On the other side is a land swathed in mist. Something draws you to the other side but there is no way to cross. As you look around for a way across, a sound like no other echoes around the Abyss. The sound gets louder and louder until you put your hands over your ears. The angel who has walked beside you kneels down and lowers his head.

Out of the Abyss rises a being that looks like a man but is so large he fills the Abyss. He places one eyeball up to the cliff edge so that he can see you. He strains to see something so small but when he sees you he smiles and places out his hand. He whispers for you to step onto his hand but his voice is so strong it sounds like a hurricane strong enough to demolish the earth itself.

Carefully you step out onto his hand and he holds you up so that he can see you better. He cannot speak to you lest his voice destroy you, so he reaches over and places you on the other side of the Abyss.

As soon as your feet touch the floor the power of the universe emerges before you, building up to an uncomfortable pitch that makes you feel like you will explode. On instinct you turn around and look back over the Abyss and you see your many lives all happening at once. You see powers weaving back and forth interacting with your lives and you feel them within your own body as you watch.

The angel motions for you to look down and you peek over the edge. You see many different kinds of beings, with steps and ledges that lead to tunnels that vanish off into the darkness. Some of the beings look up at you and you recognize some of them. The beings start to look more familiar to you than the lives on the other side of the Abyss which means it is time for you to leave this side.

Metatron lifts you back over the Abyss quickly before you can lose your sense of humanity: to stand upon the realm of God, one must lose who one is.

Now that you are back upon your own side of the Abyss, the visions of your lives fade but you can still look over the edge. All the polarized beings that manifest into the physical realm are down in the Abyss, and all the non-polarized beings are up. You see that

29. Working methods for leading group visions/workings

you can come back here and explore further, and that the first ledge down the Abyss is a sleeping place for your ancestors.

You are placed gently back on the ground beside the kneeling angel. The archangel Metatron holds a hand over you before withdrawing back into the Abyss. That action fills you with fire and heat, so much so that you feel you are stood within fire and yet you are filled with stillness.

The stillness stays with you as you remember being seated before a candle flame. Your focus returns to the candle and you see the Divinity and stillness flow through the flame. Carefully, you blow out the candle, allowing your breath to mingle with the fire and the flame passes from this world to a deeper one. Remain seated and quiet for a while, allowing the stillness to deepen within you before you rise.

29.11   Vision of the elders

Light a candle flame and close your eyes. Be aware of the flame within you, feel the peace and serenity flow through you as you settle into silence. As you look at the candle flame with your inner vision, be aware that the flame grows into a fire and the room in which you are seated falls away. You find yourself sat outside on grass.

A strange noise comes from the sky above and as you look up, you see a giant bird swooping down towards you. The bird lands near you and encourages you to climb upon his back.

The bird flies up into the sky and you cling onto the feathers on his back as he climbs higher and higher into the sky. The bird flies at great speed and as you look down, you see that you are passing over the great ocean as you head east.

While flying, you notice that you are also passing backwards through time. As the bird flies over the European landmass you see civilizations rise and fall. The bird flies lower over the Mediterranean Sea and you watch boats appear and vanish as you pass backwards through time.

The Bird begins to circle over land, falling lower and lower towards the earth as he circles. You watch as the hills and valleys get closer and still you are passing back through time. On landing, you jump off of the bird's back and offer him a gift. Reach into yourself

29.11. Vision of the elders

and pull out something sweet from your childhood memories, offer it to the bird and step back. A single feather falls from his back as a gift for you.

Before you stands a large craggy hill that is cleaved down the middle creating a narrow passageway through the hillside. A priest emerges from the passage and asks you to follow him. You realize that there are more people with you who have travelled from all the corners of space and time. Together you follow him down through the passageway.

As you walk through the passageway you look up the steep cliff sides that almost obscure the sun. You can hear the tapping of tools and distant voices. You emerge from the passageway into a clearing with a tall stone cliff before you. Many men are working on the cliff face to create an impressive façade. The priest guides you around the workers and through a small doorway that is covered by a heavy cloth. You emerge on a ledge at the entrance to a large city that is in the early stages of construction. Looking around, you see many temples, houses, baths and other buildings in various stages of construction. In the center of the city is a strange-looking compound that houses a decaying step pyramid.

The priest guides you down through the city and to the threshold of the old temple compound. The priest tells you that he cannot go any further, as the compound is the territory of the 'old ones.' He tells you to enter the compound and climb the pyramid.

Stepping over the threshold into the compound, you notice that everything sounds different. The building sounds of the city do not penetrate the air of the compound and everything is quiet. You stand a while in the silence and stillness, gradually becoming aware that the compound and its contents are partially in another time. An overwhelming urge to climb the steps of the old pyramid flows over you and you begin to climb slowly.

With each step you take, a brief vision flashes before you of a previous time when the pyramid was in use. Sights and sounds of ceremonies, gatherings, conversations flash before you as you climb to the top.

Part of the way up the pyramid, you put your foot on the next step but your foot seems to vanish into nothing. You retract your foot

29. Working Methods for Leading Group Visions/Workings

and try to touch the step. Your hand falls into nothing. Something deep within you urges you to walk forward as though through the steps. Moving forward, you pass through the image of the steps and find yourself walking through a dark stone tunnel cut deep into the pyramid. A small flame urges you forward until you reach a strange-looking door.

Reaching out to touch the door, your hand again passes through the image into nothing. Stepping forward, you pass through the doorway: power swirls all around you as you pass though the image. The doorway is a threshold guardian: a being of fire that guards the inner sanctum. Their flames lick around you, probing into every part of your thoughts to see if you are worthy to pass through.

As you pass through the flames, the fire withdraws and you find yourself in a small octagonal room with a fire bowl in the center. The fire bowl is empty and surrounding the fire bowl is a group of Priests and Priestesses. An old priestess steps forward to greet you. She tells you that before you can commune with the assembled company you must pass the test of the inner sanctuary. You must light the fire bowl in the center using only your inner flame.

Closing your eyes, you reach deep inside to the inner flame at the edge of the Void. You pass into a state of stillness and peace. Your flame burns brightly at the edge of the Void within you. Reaching inside, you cup your hand around your inner flame and allow a fragment of the flame to settle in the palm of your hand. Pulling your hand out, you hold up the tiny flame to light the room.

Lowering the flame into the fire bowl, the fire bowl lightens with fire and the room illuminates. Looking around you see many priests and priestesses standing in all the directions. The old priestess reaches out and holds your hands. Her energies feel strange to you and she picks up on your thoughts.

She smiles and speaks to you:

> "We are the last of our world, the remnants of what has passed into the Void. We are waiting for you and people like you, the seed carriers. Please take our wisdom and our secrets, and carry them forward into the future. The people who have come into this land and built their cities

29.11. Vision of the elders

are deaf and blind to our ways. But these treasures must not die. They must be carried forward to the edge of time and seeded out to the future waves of humanity. Are you willing to carry these treasures out to the future to pass onto whomever is able to access them?"

The priestess waits for your answer. If you answer yes, four people step forward from the four directions. If you answer no you are guided back out of the room to wait at the steps of the pyramid.

The four people who step forward ask you to approach them one at a time. The first person lays their hand on your shoulders. An immense power of fire flows through you, reaching every cell in your body. With your inner senses, you see volcanoes, fire upon water, fire within cells and finally electricity. Your home and the electricity running thorough it appears in your mind. The electricity shows itself as a conscious being flowing constantly through your home and you become aware of how you could work with this being in a more harmonious way. The knowledge of the power of fire enters your consciousness and you feel the wisdom reach every part of your body.

The second person touches you on the chest, and your thymus gland, seated in the deep center of your chest, responds. The firepower flows into the gland and energizes your immune system. You feel its action flow into you and its power building up in your hands. It is at that point that you realize this is the power of healing. The power flows out of your hands and into the person stood before you. Awareness builds of your connectedness with the land and how the power flows from being to rock to air to water and back in a continuous flow of sacred life.

The third person touches you upon the lips and immediately you draw in breath. You find yourself at the edge of the Void looking out over the universe. The planets and stars are all around you. Air builds up within you until you feel as though you are going to burst. When you can take the pressure no more, you breathe out.

Many beings pass through you and out on your breath. They fall to the planets and you fall with them. As they fall closer and closer to the planet they take on recognizable forms. Some are animals, some

29. Working Methods for Leading Group Visions/Workings

are trees, insects, plants, humans of many different types: some are part human and part animal. You fall with them to the land.

On touching the surface of the planet, the beings spread out in all directions and you find yourself in a forest among the trees and the animals. Many of the animals are also part faerie part human. They commune with you and you feel their wisdom and light.

A strange noise carries upon the air and the beings start to change. The animals and faeries separate from the humans and the humans are cast out of the forest to live in isolation. You watch as the humans walk into darkness: they find themselves walking through a Desert. You can hear the cries and feel the tears of the animals and faeries as they weep for the humans. Something nudges you and you find yourself back in the temple room.

The fourth person touches you on your abdomen. Something passes into you from their hand and begins to sting your eyes. Your eyes water from the pain and you rub them hard. When you try to open them you blink in the flame light and begin to see strange things. Everything seems to be connected by patterns or threads. You see the building around you, not as stone and wood, but as fire and air. Beyond the fire and air are the stars, which have threads reaching down to the planet surface. Each person is connected by the threads, which seem to weave into a complicated but beautiful web pattern. Looking down at your own body, you see it as made up of a combination of elements rather than flesh. Everything around you appears in its true from and you marvel at its beauty.

The old priestess asks you to take these secrets out into the world and allow them to flow from you naturally in your everyday life. You do not need to teach them or activate them: they will sit within you and will pass, at the right time, to whomever needs them. With that she reaches into the fire bowl and picks up the fire with her hands. She throws the fire at you and the flames consume you. Cleansing you, the fire surrounds you and you feel it as a powerful being who is transporting you through time. The fire has many eyes that watch over you as you pass from one world to another.

The fire within you grows so that you can see nothing but the flames. You feel the stillness of the Void within you and the vision of the elders falls away, leaving you in stillness and silence. When you

29.11. Vision of the elders

are still and ready to move, you step forward with the intent to return home.

Finally you emerge back in the room where you first started, passing though the candle flame. You remember yourself seated before the flame and when you are ready, you open your eyes.

Chapter Thirty

The inner aspects of consecration

In today's magical world which has become so heavily commercialized, offers of consecrations, initiations and ordinations abound, from serious spiritual and magical groups to the silliest New Age faery Saxon Celtic Wiccan Church of the Shamanic voice of the Archangel Michael. If you filter out all the silly stuff, there is still a good solid tradition alive in today's world where power, lineage and connection is passed from generation to generation.

The words consecration, ordination and initiation mean different things to different people. Even dictionary definitions are vague so the picture can become complicated and arguments often break out between magical and witchcraft groups about who has what and when they got it, etc. For the sake of looking at this from an inner point of view, I want to talk about consecration from the way I perceive it, received it and have handed it on. I am not approaching this from any particular magical system: rather it is a reflection from personal experience of how it works outside those systems i.e. what it is in its own right without dogma and structures.

For me personally, initiation is the magical/spiritual acceptance into a magical/spiritual family and the initiation both marks you as a human individual, and opens you to a family connection that stays with you for that lifetime or for however long you stay in that group. Consecration on the other hand (for me and the way I pass it on) is the marking of the soul pattern. It connects the soul into a stream of consciousness that it becomes an inseparable part of.

30.1 Born or touched

When someone is consecrated, they are woven into a stream of consciousness, becoming one with that stream whilst their own

30. The inner aspects of consecration

personal qualities are added to the stream to effect change and mature the consciousness as a whole. If that particular stream is about change, then you will become a vessel for change in your world. If it is about service, then your life will walk down that path, etc. Once you are connected into a line at this depth, it flows through you and you flow through it life after life.

It may go dormant if unused in this life, and reemerge in another life, or it may go dormant in another life only to reemerge in a few lifetimes. I have consecrated many people over the years and there have been times when people have stood before me and I see that they are already consecrated into a line, they are just not aware of it. But I and other consecrated people can often see it in them or upon them: they carry a mark that follows them from life to life. They had it when they came into life and my job in consecrating them was simply to reawaken it within them.

It may be a line that is not the same as what I am passing on, but their own line must not be interfered with: as a priest/ess the job is simply to lift the veil so that they can see again. When this is done, they very often become immediately aware of the line and they can see how it has always been with them.

The most commonly known line of consecration historically is the Apostolic Succession which is the Christian line of connection from Apostle to Apostle going back to the original touch by the Holy Spirit (though in my opinion—and in my experience—it is a much older line). That line is all one and they become all of each other (hence a bishop is 'we' rather than 'he' or 'she'): they become a composite consciousness that comprises Christ plus all the Apostles who have been before and will go after.

When you consecrate someone who does not already have the consecration, you tie them into the stream that you work with, blending them with that line so that they become a part of that weave with full access to its benefits and connections.

30.2 Pros and cons

Most people are not aware of what they are getting themselves into when they are consecrated. This is why, in times past, it took a

30.2. Pros and cons

long time and a lot of study, work and commitment to build up to a consecration of any form. Unlike initiation, consecration passes through all of your lives, which immediately takes it to a serious and heavy commitment. It is the time in your existence where you stop playing, put away your toys and commit to an inner path of fate that cannot be gone back on. You can stop working with it intentionally, but it will continue to affect your lives and the decisions you make: once you are changed, there is no going back.

The benefits of such consecration are many: you become a part of a huge collective consciousness, being able to connect and reach out to all the other priests/esses in the line, drawing upon their knowledge, strength, wisdom and skills. If you use it properly, you have the keys to the Library.

If the consecrator has agendas when passing it on, then there is a chance that he will limit or interfere with the communication of the line in order to control it and you. This doesn't happen often, but it does happen: some priests will tie you in such a way that you become a part of their structure, i.e. you become their scapegoat and carry the consequences of their actions. So it really pays to look, think and meditate carefully on the choices you make!

The unfolding of the consecration brings with it a sense of being a true conscious part of a large number of people: you never feel alone. You become aware of the constant nudges, voices, gentle guidance and the speeding up of your fate: this is one of the most noticeable things: everything goes and comes a lot faster.

There is none of this karma, fate unfolding slowly as you learn: when you are consecrated your fate will swing out of the sky and smack you like a baseball bat. You do something bad or silly knowingly, here comes the bat. This is why unscrupulous priests rig the scapegoat effect at a consecration. Because fate is speeded up, they have to behave which they do not want to do, so they construct the ultimate scapegoat: you become the scapegoat to them by becoming he who takes all the sins and sufferings into the Desert.

This is why when you are consecrated properly, the angelic structures are brought into play so that other types of consciousness cannot be tied into you or you to them—which brings me into the practical aspect of how it is done.

30. THE INNER ASPECTS OF CONSECRATION

When the consecration is done from within a structure, there are certain rules, witnesses, codes of dress, oils, etc. that the particular structure/lodge defines as their ritual of consecration. In reality there is little needed, but the ones that are needed are important. The rest of the dressing defines the particular magical family and enfolds the people attending in a sense of ritual.

The following is a simple breakdown of what I do and how I do it. I cannot speak for any other consecrator nor would wish to. The method I use works and has been stripped down to its basic simplicity so that it is nondenominational: it connects people to the ancient line without the dressings of a magical order/lodge etc.

I work with the four elements and the four directions, with or without a living priest and with or without altars (I have consecrated on the edge of the sea with nothing other than an implement). I draw in an inner contact that carries the line into each direction of east, south (unless I have a working priest in there) and west, and I work in the north.

Working with the contacts in the directions and angelic beings I have called in, I begin to 'weave' using inner vision, a web of connection using strands from the line and with the strands from the other contacts. The web is woven to create a veil that is also a doorway that will go over the person consecrated and they will 'pass through' that veil by having it pass through them: it passes through them and becomes a part of them and they become a part of it. All of this is done silently.

Once I have woven the veil, I begin working. Sometimes I will have a couple of priestesses to work with as upholders on either side of me who will keep the gates open. From the north, I draw angelic beings to me to work with me and also the priestess inner contact from the north to work through me.

As a person comes up to me, I ritually strip them of anything or any being that does not belong with them (so no parasites, etc. get consecrated too!) using angelic names and contacts as part of the stripping so that the person is a clean slate to work upon. Then I lower the inner veil over them silently by lowering my hand onto them and I wait until the inner contacts have done the same thing. Then the inner contact behind me steps through me and connects them into the line that she originates and that flows in me. Sometimes more than one line passes through. Then I verbally consecrate them, using angelic and sacred names to seal it, and mark upon their heads the sacred seal in consecrated oil.

Then they go and stand to the other three directions and commune with the contacts who put their inner lines of consecration into the person. Then it is done.

It carries a lot of power with it, so it is exhausting for the consecrator and if I am doing a few people I can often end up with burns on my hands. I have never figured out how to stop that happening.

30.3 Physical and magical effects

The physical effects for someone who has been consecrated can vary from a subtle shift in consciousness to the feeling of being hit by a train at high speed while choking on a gobstopper. The first thing most people notice is that they have to treat their body differently: it will often not put up with trash anymore and you may find yourself having to change your diet, give up certain things, and change how you do things. It varies from person to person depending on that person's health and their current lifestyle. And the changes that one person makes are often not the same that another person needs to make.

This is why I feel it is important that there should be no real rule books, formats, or one-size-fits-all systems: it varies so much according to what your path should be and what your role upon that path is. So one person might have to give up meat, and one person might have to start eating it: it's all about what your task is, what tools you will need and how you need to protect your body in the meantime.

The magical effects can be quite profound: you are plugged into an ancient line of consciousness that wants to work through you and the more sensitive you are, the more they will push through you and nudge you upon your path. Over the years I have come to the conclusion that the idea I had of life, i.e. that it is all about the choices we make, all goes out of the window. I feel these days that I

30. The inner aspects of consecration

have no real choice, even when I think I do. I find myself pushed into situations, lifestyles and lands that are not my choice: I just end up relaxing and going with the flow. I gave up trying to rationalize my life years ago, and just tighten the seat belt and try to enjoy the ride!

One of the interesting things that happens magically, is that you begin to stack up power for the work before you even know you are going to be doing it and then often find that you have connected in with a much bigger 'happening' that you were unaware of. You are called to work whenever you are needed and many times you haven't a clue what you are doing, it just flows through you and happens regardless of your intent or lack of it.

30.4 Training versus nature

This is something that is a sore point with many pagan, magical and spiritual organizations: it is projected that only 'they' can uphold your consecration, and that you cannot leave them and if you do, your consecration will no longer work. The inference that you cannot be consecrated unless you have undergone a series of trainings, tests and rituals is total bullshit: what they mean is that they will not consecrate you unless you jump through their hoops. There is a big difference.

I do not really advocate consecrating someone who is unprepared, but saying that I have done it anyway because it was right for that person at that time and basically I was told by the inner lot to get on with it. But in general, I believe that people need to have a full understanding of what they are getting themselves into and preparing themselves appropriately. The training can provide this, but then so can the individual if they are mature and focused enough: hoop jumping is not necessary, but preparation is a good and sensible thing. Sometimes someone has walked alone on an intense spiritual or magical path for a long time and they are put in your path to consecrate them into service.

The problem arises when the organization tells the people that the consecration will not work unless X is done, paid for and studied. This is harnessing and putting fake conditions on something, which I feel is a dishonourable action. It would be better to say, the

30.4. Training versus nature

consecration may cause problems for you if you are not fully prepared and X is designed to prepare you properly over a period of time.

The other myth that is heavily propagated is that if you leave the group, your consecration will be taken from you and you will have no access to its power or connections. That may be true of a simple initiation in which you are 'marked' with a badge that can be taken off on the inner, but when someone is consecrated, that is it: it is an irreversible change within the person's soul that can never be taken from them, regardless of their actions.

Some people are natural vessels for the consecration and they are ready from the word go. If I have come across someone like this in the past, I have tended to throw them in with the lot who are about to be consecrated and let them run with the pack. The consecration takes fine, but I often worry about the effect it can have on them. Some are fine, but some might need help in the future. Over the years I have moved more and more away from set rules, structures and definitions to just doing what I 'know' is right regardless of what rules it breaks. By taking that stance, the inner contacts then filter who gets put before you and who does not.

But the responsibility to all the people that you consecrate is a heavy one. When you consecrate a person, you become a type of partial parent or guide from an inner point of view. Because the veil woven from all the directional threads is woven by you, you are responsible for what flows through those threads and how it affects them. It is something that really needs to be thought about before you decide to start being a consecrator.

Once you consecrate someone, you are inextricably linked through the Inner Worlds. If that person is in severe need, near death or under terrible threat, then you will be called upon to help them. If they have drifted away from the group and no longer do magic it doesn't matter, you are still linked and you are still responsible. And it is not a conscious helping: your strength, knowledge, contacts and action will be plugged in and working automatically when they are in such severe distress.

It has happened to me many times that I have suddenly become overwhelmed with a sense of disaster, or of passing, or of need and I have had to stop what I was doing and tune in. Often it ends up being a priest or priestess in need and as consecrator you have to call upon all powers that are needed to help them or even just to load share with them. In time, you get to know on the outer what it was that was happening.

30.5 Lines

One of the things that consecrators become aware of early on in their work is that all lines that flow through them also flow through the consecration: you cannot separate out the magical threads that flow through you. The person you are consecrating gets all the lines within you all braided in together. I have three lines that run through me and when I consecrate someone, they get all three lines. I cannot block any single one of them; nor would I wish to. But people who are on the receiving end need to be aware of what it is they are getting and why.

These lines often sit well together and create a pattern within you that weaves in harmony to a much bigger web that is the universe. We are so used to a modern culture of segregation and separation by nature of how we live, eat and work, that we expect the same in our spiritual life. It doesn't really work like that and the inner consecrations often reflect that. When a priest has a few lines within him and he goes onto consecrate someone who came into life with other lines already within them, we begin to see a large weave of lines slowly converging together in a wonderful harmonic.

So essentially, instead of becoming a consecrated priestess of the line of blah, you become a mongrel which makes for a healthier genetic structure.

30.6 What is the future for such consecrations?

I think that the less rigid, less 'members only' group-orientated way of working will slowly develop within our consciousness as we mature and loosen our ability to work in the Inner Worlds without major dressing and rules.

30.6. What is the future for such consecrations?

Consecrations should be there for people who are truly dedicated to the work, who wish to devote themselves to something bigger than themselves, and are willing to take on the work burdens and challenges that they may face as part of their inner service.

It should not be dangled as something that will give power or status, nor should it be tied forever to a particular line of work: it should be a tool that is given at the right time to a worker who needs it, and who will use it wisely in their own field of work, whatever that may be.

I think truly that the way forward into the future for magic is to not work within consecrations, but to work naturally within the fate that flows through you, and the connections that are reached through years of working with inner contacts. Truly, consecrations are man-made and are not necessary for walking a powerful magical path: some of the most powerful and profound magicians I work with today are not consecrated or initiated, but have developed and gained the skills and lines of contact they need through hard work and dedication to magic. *If the magic is within you, life and fate will draw it out for you.*

Chapter Thirty-one

Afterword

The life of an Initiate can become increasingly isolated as fewer and fewer of the things around you in everyday life make sense, and the popular magical community loses its glamour: it begins to look like a giant therapy dressing-up box with weird sex.

Being able to connect with and befriend like-minded people, even within your own lodge/coven/community can become harder and harder the deeper into the inner realms you go. This is not because such work causes depression, but the deeper into the Inner Worlds you go, the more obvious the bullshit around you becomes. Your tolerance levels for silly things goes down rapidly and the little things in life that used to fire you up are no longer significant in the face of grappling regularly with demons, angels and the like.

This is a blessing and a curse: the path is hard and sometimes lonely, but it is immensely rewarding, uplifting and educational.

This life is not by choice: you are called, like all magical and spiritual paths; and if you are called then you are a brother or sister and you join a large, powerful, insane group of isolated magicians all over the world. Thank the gods (or the devils) for the internet!

Above all, remember that as an initiate you are bound by duty to stretch the boundaries of life and magic that other people cannot. We open doors, close doors, clean windows, ferry parcels and sweep roads: the magicians/priests are the maintainers of balance within a temple/city culture just as the shaman is the maintainer in a tribal culture. You can try and walk away from it, but it will always be in front of you waiting at the next destination you have run to. And when you realize that deep down you are relieved to see it waiting for you, and that it has not abandoned you, then all the power and beauty that is the world will open up to you.

Part III
The Adept

Introduction

The Contacts of the Adepts is a book that will hopefully act as a springboard for those who have spent a great deal of time learning, doing and exploring the inner realms and ritual magical patterns. This book holds more visions that the other two books, because this phase of a magical life is more about doing inner work in vision and visionary ritual/magical actions, than learning or practising. It was very difficult to decide what should actually go into this book, not because of censorship, but because there is just so much material, so many directions and so many contacts out there: the book would be too large and would be like working with a feral teenager. I have chosen areas of work that need the most attention and focused upon the most active contacts within those subject areas. You will notice, once you get to the end of the book, that the different areas of magic and the various contacts within the visions interconnect and interweave: in truth, they are all of one another.

I have approached certain key elements of the inner realms from various different angles within the book, giving you a chance to have a much more in-depth understanding of important patterns and contacts within the inner realms. For example, in the book there are various different visions and contacts that bring the practitioner into contact with the Metatron Cube, a key pattern of consciousness within the inner realms, and something that truly needs to be understood if you really want to work magically at any depth. By approaching it this way, you begin to see how different roads often lead to the same place, and that which road you approach it from dictates how it will present and interact with you.

Working at an adept level means working in depth in the Inner Worlds and bringing that work out into the physical world through ritual, utterance and focused thought. The rituals become less and less elaborate and more powerful in their action, with a simple ritual bringing deep and lasting change into the world. Because the power levels become so intense, the adept has to be a clear and focused window, through which ancient consciousness can flow without the interference of agenda, dogma and limited emotive intelligence.

To achieve this level of mediation, the adept needs to have worked in all the worlds, learned about the beings and about themselves. The learning about yourself is key to success in magical work: the ancient saying of "man, know thyself" never ages and fits a great deal of wisdom into three words. To truly know your weaknesses and be willing to confront them, to challenge yourself and be able to make yourself do the right thing, and be as unselfish as possible, is the real key to magical success. The reason for this is not psychological, it is plain common sense: if you know what your weaknesses are and address them, then powerful destructive beings cannot get a true hold on you and destroy you.

The other major step that brings a magician to adeptship is truly absorbing the Mysteries of death-in-life. To work in death, to walk through death and be totally at home in that realm with no fear, brings a human into direct contact with the deeper eternal side of themselves. The fear of death falls away and the true understanding of how the cycles work emerge into the daily consciousness of the person. The knowledge of who you really are, and what you bring into the manifest world filters through into your everyday consciousness, enabling you to mature beyond being a student into being a worker.

Similarly the work in the Inner Desert brings us to the foot of Divine Consciousness without all the religious dressing. We experience Divinity as a power, and the structure of life for what it is. That enables us to work with those powers as coworkers and not as religious devotees who are dependant upon the whims of deities and the traps of religious dogmas. Divinity is constantly renewing itself and we are a part of that process. Whether we are an active participant in that process or a passive pawn depends upon whether we are willing to pick up the spade and start shovelling rather than standing before the pile of shit and praying for someone else to do it for us. All of these things turn a neophyte into an adept, not exams, studying texts and wearing fancy robes. Magic is real life, not dressing up and playing fantasy games, and when we finally realize that, we step forward into a world that is beyond anything we could have dreamed of. That is the step of the Adept.

With the net, the gift of Anu, held close to his side, he himself raised up IMHULLU the atrocious wind, the tempest, the whirlwind, the hurricane, the wind of four and the wind of seven, the tumid wind worst of all.

— The magical battle between Marduk and Tiamat.

Chapter Thirty-two

Methods of working with temples and deities

The work of the outer temple for an adept is a complex and yet clear mix of communing, moving power, creating and destroying. By the time a magician gets to an advanced level of work, the two roads of ritual and visionary magic come together to create a mega highway of power: neither of the two methods can work in an advanced form without the other: one fuels the action, the other gives it form. And yet one can separate them out as an individual action, but in truth, once the work gets to this level each form has fragments of the other within it. So for example, it becomes very hard to work a ritual where you are not also drawing the Inner Worlds into the ritual, hence melding the two together. Similarly in vision, what becomes apparent is that the deeper in vision you go at this level, the more ritualized your outer motions become before, during and after the vision. So for example where a visionary magician may think he or she is only doing a vision, they will find themselves ritualizing the visionary space, working with their hands while in vision (sigil forming and power weaving) and ritualizing the close-down afterwards.

What becomes apparent from this is that the closer to power you get, the less formalized the *dressing* of the action becomes: a ritual becomes less about outfits, wand waving and long speeches, and more about focused movement/action, true utterance and enlivening. Visionary structures become less about the description and detail, and more about sensation and focused image. The further from the surface and the deeper into the inner realms you go, the less identifiable the form becomes so that you end up working with a power source instead of a deity or magical structure. For example, where a magician may be used to 'seeing' certain 'places' and beings

32. METHODS OF WORKING WITH TEMPLES AND DEITIES

while working in vision, as they move deeper into the inner realms, the forms all fall away and the magician instead sees nothing, but feels the presence and the power. Sometimes the magician may lose all senses altogether and go into a sleep-like state. But they are not sleeping: they have gone beyond what the conscious mind can cope with so the subconscious kicks in, which in turn cuts out the conscious use of the imagination: they go into the deepest form of consciousness. They will awaken on cue and often not remember anything that happened. However when the need for specific skills or information arises, anything that was 'downloaded' into the magician during that sleep state will reemerge ready to for use. Such a state can often also bring about profound changes within the magician which will manifest in their everyday lives.

The very interesting dynamic is that when you move deeper and work with the more formless magic, you are more able to work in the complexity of the surface manifestation/ritual while retaining the power levels of the deeper contact: you bring the two together. Always, magic is about opposites, tension and polarities, and that works through every single layer, angle, presentation and being.

32.1 Deities: working practice and power dynamics

A word of caution before we go any further: working with deities demands a very open mind in many ways. You are potentially stretching back to a completely different culture and a totally different way of thinking. One of the problems with the magical lines today is the subtle sexist attitudes in certain lines of magic. The Golden Dawn, for all the good it did in giving magic a wider audience, also perpetuated an odd attitude towards women. Even though they were revolutionary in their time in their attitude towards women, the way that the system was built and operates subtly encourages an imbalance in the polarities which is evident to this day in many Golden Dawn magicians. They also created limitations upon the magic i.e. the lack of trained visionary work and overdramatized ritual are problems that are still embedded within the mindset to this day. Crowley then picked up on this and ran with it, creating

32.1. Deities: working practice and power dynamics

even more of an imbalance while further dismissing the concept of controlled vision in magic.

People who have come up through these magical lines are going to have inherited some pretty limited and unbalanced ways of thinking. If you approach some of these ancient priests and priestesses with such a mindset, they will destroy you. Trust me, the priestesses of some of these ancient temples (and I mean ancient, not 100 B.C., more like 4000 B.C.) are powerful, bloodthirsty and are built, power-wise, like brick shithouse walls. If you carry mental attitudes about women being inferior and weak, they will tear you to pieces. That limited, arrogant mindset traces all the way back to ancient Greece and even a bit earlier than that. It was a propaganda campaign that was perpetuated to muzzle the destroying warrior goddesses who had gotten out of balance: times were changing, cultures where changing and solar male kingship was ascendant.

But the same could also be said regarding women going into the inner world temples: if you go in with a hostile attitude towards men, or a derogatory attitude, the male priesthood will tear you apart: it's all about respect and balance. Both sexes have power, they are different in their magical expressions, but bring the two together in a working environment and you have a potentially massive expanse of magic. In the ancient temples, discussion and patience are not qualities that most of the inner contacts have: you have to be neutral and be able to chameleon to the mindset of the powers you are working with. That way you do not clash head-on. Before we get back to the magic, I want to tell you a little story that perfectly highlights what can go wrong, then I promise I will end my lecture on sexism. This is a true and very sad story about how magical work can go wrong if you have the wrong attitude.

Many years ago, I was working alongside a group of experienced magicians in Bath, England. The house where we were working was directly over part of the ancient temple to the goddess Sul, a dark Underworld goddess (not a goddess of the sun, as some moron has put up on the web). We had opened the gates to the Inner Worlds and we were taking turns talking to this powerful Goddess and preparing to do deeper service work with her.

One of the magicians, when it came to his turn to communicate with her, stood arrogantly in vision before her. She took out a blade and put it to his throat. This is a common challenge that a Dark Goddess does to men—besides ripping off their testicles, which is one of her favourites: this is not about neutering, but about changing and deepening power.

Instead of standing still, submitting to her challenge and trusting her, he knocked the blade to one side and challenged her to a fight. (Ouch!) When he came out of the vision, he was very full of himself and would not be told that such action was indeed very stupid, and that he would suffer consequences: she is a destroying goddess, her job is to destroy you. If you trust her, she will do it in a way that clears all of your crap away ready for regeneration. If you do not trust her, she will just destroy you. And that is exactly what she did.

On his way home, he had an epileptic seizure. He was not epileptic and had never had problems before: he was in the peak of heath. He was taken to hospital. He had another, and another. It ended up with him losing his job, his home, his driver's license, and he suffered frequent fits and minor brain damage. She destroyed him for his lack of respect. If he had let her challenge him and do whatever she needed to do, she would have sent things into his life that would have changed how he thought, how he did things: she would have put life experience in his way that would have been hard, but she would also have destroyed the parts of him that were holding him back.

These powers are real. It is not a game, and if you break into contact with them, they will mediate power to you that does a job. That is what they are there for. And that is why people built temples to them and worked with them, not because of fear and superstition, but because these beings could influence their daily lives and help with natural disasters.

32.2 Working with Deities in the Temple Environment

This is a very delicate line of magical work that has to be trodden very carefully and thoughtfully. As a magician, it is very important right at the outset of work with a deity that you establish a working relationship and not a worship relationship. If you are working in a temple environment as opposed to a magical space, which is different, then it is even more important to tread carefully, as the line between religion and practical magic comes very close. But the difference is still there and must be adhered to, unless you want to spend the rest of your life chained to one line of work without the possibility of parole.

The reason it is so much more dangerous in a temple is that a temple structure has deeper power foundations than a magical space and often many beings within its inner structure. So the power levels, contacts and doorways are at a much more aggressive power level, and there is usually a doorway through which the deity can cross over the threshold into the outer space.

Keeping all that in mind, work in a temple with a deity usually takes the form of visionary ritual, and visionary ritual movement. Remember at all times that the deity is a powerful working companion, teacher and sometimes parent, but they are not to be treated as all-powerful gods and goddesses to whom you swear allegiance, agree with totally, or give anything that is asked of you. Keep this line very clear in your own head and in your work.

32.3 Finding the Doorway

The best way to learn about working with a deity in a temple environment is to first work with them in an ancient temple if you have access to one. This would include stone circles, ancient ruins and power spots that are known to have been worked with. Some will have been shut down ritually, and if that is the case then I would suggest that you let sleeping dogs lie. If they are not shut down then the first step is to find out where the 'access' gate is. That will be an area in the structure that acted as a gateway for the deity in the absence of a statue. Every temple has one: it is just a matter of finding it. Do not trust ancient scripts or maps of the temple when it was still active: often the true gateway was hidden from the public eye and was heavily guarded.

The best way to find the doorway is to sit as close to the centre of the temple as you can get and light a candle flame. Fire was used in about ninety percent of ancient temples, so it is the easiest way to switch the lights on. (Unless you are very unlucky and happen to have chosen one of the rare temples that did not use fire.) If the candle flame is lit using inner technique, i.e. also seeing the inner flame, then there is a major possibility it will switch on all the lights, which will make your attempt a whole lot easier. With the flame before you, sit with your eyes closed and using your inner vision and imagination, look to each direction around the site. Then see yourself getting up and walking around the site, looking in all the corners and directions. Be patient: this is a skill that needs time to develop, and the echo of the doorway may be very faint. But you will, if it is still there, pick up on it. There will be an area that feels or looks 'different', welcoming or energetic. That will be the area that housed the doorway.

Once that is established, put out the candle and go have a look around that area. If it is a temple complex you may find fragments of the old altar or the actual point where the focus was for the deity. If it is a stone circle or complex, there will just be an area that was a doorway and getting as close as possible to that will be sufficient.

If you live close to the site, go regularly and build up the power of the doorway before moving onto doing actual 'work': the more solid the door, the easier the rest of the work will be. If you do not live close and have only a limited timeframe to work in, then it would be an idea to build a 'window' for the deity, which means having a vessel and connecting that vessel to the deity. The doorway is used as a threshold for the deity to bring them through, and then the deity is connected into a vessel that can be taken away. This vessel will act as a 'window' for the deity so that they can interact with you wherever your ritual space is. It is a weaker alternative to actually moving the whole temple pattern, which is discussed later in this chapter.

32.4 Creating a window for the deity

Whatever site you are working with, you will need to have something that can be used as a focal substance for the deity so that you can take it away with you if you want to carry on working with the deity away from the temple site. This can be anything from a statue or image of the deity, to a stone that is used as either the doorway or as

32.4. Creating a window for the deity

an altar. If you are trying to contact one of the deities at the stone circles I would suggest that you do not use an image or statue, even if it is homemade: those powers had no images that we know of and certainly none exist to this day, so to give that deity a pair of eyes and a mouth may be a very big mistake. We have no clear knowledge of what they were and what they did, so working with a stone will be a safer filter until you really get to know what the deity's agenda is. For example, they may be a power form that demands a human life in return for working with you. If you refuse, they may take one anyhow, and they will only be able to see the lives that are attached to you (lovers, children etc). Those ancient deities can be very dangerous, so really, tread carefully.

If you are working in an ancient temple site, then chances are you already know background information of the deity there. There may be a possibility, depending on what temple you are in, that the deity has been bound there, or has had limits placed upon them. If the temple is after 1500 B.C. then there is a good chance that there is no binding or inner interference. Either those abilities were slowly lost over time or that action was just stopped, as such bindings seem to fade around 1500 B.C..

You have identified the area of the temple where the doorway is. The next step is to open it. Some temples can be still 'up and running' from an inner point of view, and the minute you take an inner step towards the doorway, all the lights will go on and all the people will stream out, which can be a little bit disconcerting. Others have been shut or have gradually closed down over the millennia, and there is no easy way to differentiate, so tread carefully.

The first attempt should be purely using inner imaginary techniques. Imagine two pillars creating a gateway with two flames before them. See beyond the pillars a deep mist. Using your inner voice, call upon the deity and ask them to grace the temple once more. If everything in the temple is still active, then this simple imaginary action will be enough to trigger a contact. It might take a few minutes and you may have to also use your breath, i.e. speak the summons out loud (the power of utterance). The way to know that you have a real contact is your body will react with being so close to a deity. If that works, then talk to the deity and tell them your intentions, of your wish to work with them. If the temple is not close to where you live, explain this and ask if they are willing to work with an image/statue/object as an interface that you can take home with you.

If that simple inner exchange does not work, then you will need to exteriorize some of it. Find two reasonably large stones and create a doorway with them. Light two candles (tea lights in jam jars are good to work with) and again create a doorway, or one light in the centre. Repeat the inner exercise, whilst also calling upon the gate keepers to open the gates, and ask the deity to come back into our world. The two together makes for a much stronger action: just remember that verbal and ritual action alone without inner action will not work at all unless it is an exact replica of what was used in the temple (which will trigger the inner pattern). As the deity appears in inner vision, prick your finger and place a drop of blood upon the statue, image or stone that will be the focus for the deity. That will provide the deity with a connection to you and will also provide fuel.

The next step, after introducing yourself and explaining your intentions, will be to bridge the deity into the object, if they agree to the action. Because you are in the temple where they were housed and at the threshold of the doorway, a whole load of work that would usually have to be done to open a window to a deity into an object is unnecessary. You simply have to provide the bridge for the deity, which you do using your own body. Once you are ready, turn your back to the deity and place your hands upon the receiving object, and using your inner vision, 'see' the deity behind you and feel their power building up. The deity will step into you and then through you, passing through your body and into the object. They will then pass through the object, leaving a trail that looks a bit like a tunnel through you and the object.

What has been done is that by passing through you and the object, the deity has created a change within both you and the object that will make it much easier for the deity to use both you and the object as a window. It's like placing a mark upon you, and a window inside you and the object, so that they can commune and see through you/the object into the outside world. Once it is finished, then you can put the lights out and leave. If the deity has bindings upon them, or if there are still guarded boundaries around the temple, you may find it very hard to get the object out of the temple. A whole variety of things can happen from the power suddenly vanishing out of the object,

32.4. Creating a window for the deity

from you dropping and breaking the image, to someone arriving and stopping you, to feeling sick or suddenly drained.

If there are just guardians, you may make it home but after a couple of nights of bad nightmares and sudden illness, you may be forced to take the object back or destroy it. If these restrictions do appear, heed their warnings and do not, under any circumstances ignore what is happening. They are usually there for a good reason, usually because the deity is/was far too dangerous to be out in the world at large. If this happens, take the object back and bury it somewhere within the temple. You will only be able to work face-to-face with the deity while you are in the actual temple. If they are a deity that has a much larger field than the local area, i.e. they are a god/ess of the Sun etc., then this will probably not happen and you should be able to work and bring them through anywhere.

If they are specific to an area, hill, spring etc., then they may well be bound to that area either naturally or by magic. Don't try to take that on and 'free' them: you could be responsible for committing mass murder or chaos if you do, or the other outcome may be that you kill yourself or are sent mad (the two usual outcomes of clashing with inner power).

The basic rule of thumb is know your deity and if they are very localized, then you have to understand, before you start to try and commune with them, that you may not be able to work with them at home: you will have to travel to the temple to work with them. (Although some localized deities do seem to travel well, so it is not a hard and fast rule: much of this work is about experimenting.) Also, if at all possible, look as far back in records as you can to find out about them. Do not take the more recent myths about them at face value, as they are usually manipulated: go back to the very early stories where you are most likely to get a truer picture. And keep that picture in mind when you start to work with them. And don't forget: if they were magically shut down, it may have been for a very good reason.

32.5 Work on site or move the site? How to move a Temple

Once you have established a contact on site at the temple, the next decision has to be whether to build up the work onsite or 'move' the site. What makes a temple powerful is its inner structure, which can be moved (by a strong group of people) if necessary. This is something that needs a group of able magicians, all of whom need to have varying degrees of inner 'sight.' You will also need four ballast workers who will guard the perimeter while you work. The other thing that you will need is a 'temple' to house the inner structure once you move it. You can use an already standing building, but then you run many risks of contamination of the site by its other users, and also losing control over the building itself. (Plus you really do not want to have the Temple of Set in your living room.) It is best to choose a spot of land or a field that is never used, or that you own, and mark out boundaries with stones. The temple will nestle its boundary pattern into the stones. If you own a building that you can limit access to, then it could be a suitable vessel.

You do not need to be at the site to do this work, but you do need something, just a stone, from the site to act as a resonant focus. I have moved a small site, and we as a group were not physically onsite, but we had all visited. It was extremely hard physical work and we all had extreme strain afterwards, but we did it and it worked well.

You need to have visited the site physically so that your body remembers the frequency of the place. If you can be all physically in the temple space, then the physical strain is kept to a minimum and the work will be far more successful. This technique is basically an extension of the technique used for taking the consecrated implement out of the physical implement and putting it into something else.

The room or space which will be the receiving vessel should be prepared, with an altar space that will mark the doorway for the deity, a defined entrance for the workers, and a central working position for whoever is leading the work. For this working, the altar should have two candles that will mark the doorway, and also two candles for the person leading: one on either side of them. The use of fire in creating doorways is ancient and powerful, hence its removal by the

32.5. Work on site or move the site? How to move a Temple

Protestant church. (It is interesting to note that the magical patterns that have been born out of Freemasonry, which in turn was affected by the Protestant leanings of its members, also did not use flames in a magical way, making life far more difficult for them.)

The number of workers you will need is twelve for the perimeter and one for the centre, along with the four guardians who will provide ballast. The perimeter workers need to be equally distributed around the working space and beyond them, four ballast workers who will sit one in each direction outside of the working pattern. Their job is simply to guard the space from any interference. This will mean they need to be in vision in the room, just watching. Sometimes, the power of this work will attract people to the space and they will try to enter. Again, the job of the guardians is to intercept such intrusions.

The person who sits in the centre, who is the fulcrum, leads the work. Either side of her is a candle that is tuned to be access gates for inner workers. The fulcrum leads a vision that takes the workers down into the Underworld and emerges back up to the surface in the temple site back in time when it was recently built. The workers are able to observe the inner patterns of the temple construct and watch as its power flows around the space. The fulcrum then leads the workers to the inner sanctum of the temple, where the power source and doorway of the deity is. The fulcrum calls upon the deity and as the deity appears (sometimes they are there waiting) the fulcrum explains to the deity what the group is trying to achieve and why. They then ask the deity if they are willing to assist and to allow their temple to be moved. If the deity agrees, then first each worker must introduce themselves to the deity and be 'touched' by the deity. This is a subtle form of tying in energetically with the deity so that the body of the worker can be upheld and supported by the deity during the work.

Once everyone has had their turn in communion with the deity, then it is time to begin the process of removal. The deity will turn and lead the fulcrum, and the workers will follow as the deity steps back through the doorway. The deity leads the group out onto the plains of the Inner Desert, with the Abyss in one direction and the River of Death in the other. The group is led to the edge of the Abyss, then prompted to turn and look back over the Inner Desert. The pattern of the temple appears before them in the Inner Desert with the deity standing the middle. The pattern is the lines of angelic consciousness that make up the inner power structure that the temple was then built around. It appears as a series of interlocking patterns and Platonic solids that give off a barely detectable sound. The deity stands in the middle and acts as a central point of balance to the whole structure. The fulcrum is then summoned to the deity and told to walk 'into' the deity, assuming the central role of balance.

The workers take up positions around the pattern and upon prompt from the fulcrum, take a thread of the pattern that anchors it into the ground of the Inner Desert. When everyone is ready, the workers begin to wind in the pattern, like gathering up threads of wool. It is important that the workers all work at the same speed, and it is up to the fulcrum, who is leading the vision, to ensure that everyone works at the same pace. One way to do this is to time each roll of thread verbally while still in vision (i.e. and now roll to a count of three then wait, and repeat). In visions, the threads are rolled and placed in the arms of the fulcrum who is then immediately upheld by the group. To uphold the fulcrum, the moment the worker hands the roll of thread to the fulcrum, the worker then places (in vision) a hand upon the fulcrum and leaves it there. This ensures that the burden, which is heavy indeed (being the weight of angelic consciousness), is upheld by the whole group. As each person touches the fulcrum, they must state out loud that they are finished. This is for the benefit of the guardians.

The moment that the pattern is bound up, any demonic guardians that were employed to guard the temple will appear. The fact that the group is working with the deity ensures that the group will be safe from attack, but the demonic beings will need to be redeployed in the temple once it is unfurled. When the guardians hear the last call from the workers, they must then be ready to 'buddy up' with the demonic guardians while the temple is being re-sited. For the guardians, they will experience a sudden heaviness or strain as they uphold the demonic guardians. The fulcrum, speaking from within the deity, will tell the demonic beings to go and sit with the guardians while the temple structure is being re-sited.

The fulcrum, still within the deity and holding the burden of the pattern, leads the group down the path of the Inner Desert, over the threshold of Malkuth (manifestation) and into the life pattern of the

32.5. Work on site or move the site? How to move a Temple

fulcrum. The fulcrum walks through their life pattern (like taking a walk down a path of your life as an observer, a very weird experience indeed) until they get to the point of the working in the room. Once back in the room where they first started, the fulcrum holds her arms out and calls to the workers to take and unfold the pattern that they were working with, and to anchor it in the land. The workers each call out when they are finished. When the last worker has called out, then the demonic guardians are asked to take up position once more in the pattern, guarding the directions and the doorway.

The fulcrum will stand and walk towards the area of the new housing that will accommodate the doorway for the deity, and if there is an altar, they will place their hands up on it. The deity will then pull away from the fulcrum and take up residence in the doorway. The fulcrum then describes the inner pattern and the outer temple in the vision, so that the whole group has the same imagery, which is imprinted upon the room, and the deity is thanked and welcomed.

The group comes out of vision and the two candles of the doorway are lit. The guardians wait as the workers and the fulcrum leave the room, and then the guardians are the last to leave. The candles are left burning and the room is left empty so that the inner structure can embed itself in the space. From now on, that space is used as the original temple and it must be worked with daily for the pattern to strengthen and settle. Eventually—and there is no telling how long the embedding phase will take, it can be anything from a few days to a few weeks or even months sometimes—it will have settled, and then it can be worked with less frequently, so long as it is regular.

★ ★ ★

As you can see, this working method utilizes the method of working both in vision and ritually at the same time. The workers, while in vision, also have to be able to call out with their voices at certain junctions in the work, so that timings can be communicated. This means that each worker must be able to work in vision without drifting or falling asleep: they have to be fully conscious all the way through the working. This can be achieved by having the workers stand through the vision. An extension of this could be to have the workers ritually moving through the vision i.e. during the rolling of the threads, etc. Either way, this technique demands a high level of concentration and discipline in the participating magicians.

One of the things that will become very apparent from very early on from working in this transferred temple is the reality of what the temple's original magical pattern was, and what was overlaid dogma or interference at the original site. When you move a temple structure using the above method, you are moving the bare skeletal energetic structure that the temple hung upon, not all the layers of human interference, agenda and magical manipulations. You are down to the very basic foundation that allows the deity to flow through and work with humanity unhindered. Most ancient temples will have many layers to them, and many of those layers will be magically bound, triggered, and manipulated.

By working with the sheer skeletal structure, you create the doorway for the deity while bypassing all the following generations of priestly interference, binding and pinning that became so common in powerful temples by around 1500 B.C.. What will be left at the original site will simply be the patterns of consciousness that grew over the years of work that happened on that site, but the original inner infrastructure of the temple, the 'inner template of the temple' will no longer be there: that is what you move, and this is what you rebuild and work with. Without that inner structure, the original site of the temple simply becomes an outer shell, and the consciousness patterns will naturally degrade and slowly vanish.

When you begin to work with the deity in this reformed temple, keep very tight records of every interaction, every working and every communication with the deity so that a complete picture of that deity can be built up. Most of what we read from later wall paintings and historical texts is often misleading. You will often find that when you work this way, you will experience the deity in a form that is similar to the very early descriptions by ancient priests. The longer the temple is around, the more manipulated and changed the story becomes.

If for any reason your site has to be abandoned, then you must rewind the temple structure back up and take it out into the Inner Desert and let it unfurl there (and don't forget the demonic beings). If you leave the structure unguarded and unworked with, it can become 'feral' as it will have not had decades of work to stabilize it. This can become dangerous and all sorts of things can go wrong—and the fulcrum will bear the energetic brunt of what goes wrong. So if the temple is to be abandoned for any reason, take it into the Inner Desert and preferably wind it into the deity so that they absorb the structure.

Such work carries a great deal of responsibility, as so many things can go wrong (or right). If you plan to do this work, ensure that you are planning to work with and evolve the structure over decades, and be willing to carry the burden of work should the temple need to be dismantled.

However, if it is worked with and cared for by successive generations, then you will find that the temple will slowly build, particularly if you connect it up to the Inner Library, and it will become a place where adepts will come to work after death. With such care, these temples often take on a life of their own and grow to become vast areas of learning, work and magic, which can serve generations to come.

If there should be a need to build an inner and outer temple from scratch, then the techniques to such work can be found in my book *The Work of the Hierophant* (Golem Media).

32.6 Deity versus Divinity in a magical temple space

One very important difference that is often overlooked in the magical space of a temple is the very big difference between a deity and Divinity in working practice. I have harped on about this difference *ad nauseam* in my writings, simply because so few magicians stop to think about the distinctions and how that difference affects their work.

When you are working in a temple space with a deity, the deity is going to dictate, to an extent (even if they are not 'worshipped') how the temple operates, what line of magic is undertaken and how that magic is ritually approached. So if you bring a deity to work with you into a magical temple, be aware that even if the deity is working with you as a coworker, it will limit certain aspects of your magical freedom. This is partly to do with the characteristics of the deity, their defined area of interest and the areas of their expertise. A deity is not an all-powerful, all-knowing being: they have limitations like the rest of us, and they also have very distinct agendas. They will steer the work of the temple to fit their agenda if they are allowed to.

If you bring a deity into the temple to work, or you create a doorway within the temple for that consciousness, then you will only be able to work magic in areas that are conducive to that deity. If you are wishing to work in many different areas of magic over time, then bringing a specific deity into the temple space in such a way is not a very bright idea. If however you are wishing to develop long-term work in a very defined area of magic, then having a deity along for the ride that is very involved in that area of work will truly enhance any long-term projects and make the job a whole lot easier.

For complex and contrasting magical work over a protracted length of time, it is more advisable to work directly with Divinity, which takes on a more formless, but infinitely more powerful pattern, and is simply mediated into the space from the central flame. The downside (if it *is* a downside of working this way) is that you have far less control over the magic that you work with, and you become somewhat of an active observer to the magic as opposed to its instigator and controller. This method of working in the magical temple is best for long-term service work or very large projects that affect a great many people or the land. But if your work is more about a localized area, fertility, small projects, or individuals, then it is far better and a lot easier to work with deities or with neither.

32.7 Visionary ritual action

What follows sort of sounds like fancy New Age self-healing therapy. Thankfully, it is not. It is a working method for moving power around and for effecting change. The basic, stripped-down working method is to open the gateway and call the deity into the temple space. Once the deity is on the threshold of the temple space, turn with your back to the deity and using vision and utterance, call the deity into yourself or to join you in action. They will put their arms through your arms so that you work together. Usually, for this type of technique, you would have before you a miniature model or drawing of what you

32.7. Visionary ritual action

want to work on. You use your mind, breath and arm actions, with the deity working through you as a power source, to effect change over the model, which is magically linked to the real place/person.

For example, let's take a situation that is happening as I write this chapter. A large earthquake and subsequent tsunami has just hit Japan (today is the thirteenth of March) and one of the reactors has just exploded. If this was to be worked with in the temple setting, it would go something like this:

Call in the destroying dark Goddess Izanami. Do not be frightened by her appearance, which is usually not very nice. For those who can embrace her power without fear or loathing, she will gift her help in dangerous situations. Before the magician will either be a map, a drawing of the Islands of Japan, a painting or a model. The magician draws the death Goddess into themselves, and looks over the model/map with the eyes of the Goddess. The magician will be able to 'see' or perceive, in their mind, the imbalance of power in the fate structure that created the inner fate potential for such outer destruction. The magician, with the Goddess' arms within their arms, begins to work in both a physical and visionary way, weaving or unweaving threads, mending broken inner power lines, using utterance to blow or send the sea back, and reaches down to the reactor to scoop up the 'power' of the reactor and eat it.

The magician and the Goddess take that destructive star power into themselves and digest it. The magician, from an outer perspective, seems to be staring at a map or model, while muttering, moving their hands about, blowing on the model and using their eyes to stare down something. In their mind, the magician is superimposing the image of the inner structure of the islands over the outer image of the map or model.

When it is finished, the magician and deity part, and the magician ensures that the deity took all of the inner disaster power with them (i.e. the inner pattern of the radiation or impact). The magician will be ill and weak for a while after the work: their recovery depends largely on their age, health and fitness. This is not work for an ageing magician, one with any chronic illness or medical conditions, or who is run down in general: to do such work would bring death.

The map or model itself will have been ritually prepared and linked to the landmass and surrounding sea. When the magician sees the inner pattern of the island and any beings inherent to that landmass, the many layers of that land are brought together before the magician and then worked on by the composite being which is the magician and the Goddess. This is a very powerful way of working and does indeed work. I have used this method in other instances, and what is really curious about it is that when you are invited to work on such a problem, which will happen at some point in your life, you discover other people, most often ones not connected to the situation, were also asked to do the same thing. So when you are called to do such work, and it works, don't pat yourself too readily on the back: chances are a few hundred magicians around the world got a similar call and between you all, you have managed to effect some inner change. That is what being a magician is all about, tending the garden. However, if you are not called, do not act.

And what change can be effected by this work? On an outer level, the results of a few hundred magicians working at top speed can slow certain inner momentums down, which in turn stops that energetic feed to the outer manifestation. So for example, it cannot stop a natural occurrence or a disaster, but slowing down the inner impulse can make it a bit easier for the outer cleaning and regeneration to trigger. What this actually does is ensure that what is happening in the physical world is not leaned on or interfered with by an inner being that may use their energy to perpetuate the disaster so that they can feed off of the results. It can also slow down the 'inner disaster' in general: every outer occurrence has an inner mirror version. The inner version or inner pattern of an event and its subsequent unfolding is what powers the *fate path* of that event and its subsequent unfolding. If the inner pattern can be modified, tuned or brought into harmony, then there is a good chance that the outer disaster will not be as long-term and horrific as it would have been with no magical intervention.

Back to the technique. In stages it would go something like this: link the outer land or person to the image or model. Bring through the deity into yourself, then work on the model or image using vision, breath and hand actions. When you have finished, the deity disengages and returns back over the threshold. The magician turns around, thanks the deity, closes down the doorway and leaves the model or image on the altar with four candles burning around it to effect a boundary. Leave that boundary/flames in place for about an hour or so as the work will continue to happen. After that time, close the candles down and put the image or model in a safe place.

32.8 Visionary movement

There are many ways of moving power about using vision and movement, and one method has a presentation that looks very similar to tai chi. It is a simple but very powerful form of mediation of power from the Inner Worlds to the outer world. Usually this work is unconditional and you have absolutely no idea what it is doing. This 'keeping the magician in the dark' is a very good way of working, because it keeps the abuse of this technique to a minimum.

When called to do this work, the magician opens up the gates either above him or below him, which are the most usual directions this works from, but it can also be used with the four directions. Once the gates are open and power is flowing across the thresholds, then the magician gets to work. Using movement that looks very similar to tai chi, the magician gathers the power from behind him and pulls it through his body using visionary techniques. The power is gathered within and then is directed outward to a specific direction or is woven with arm movements and shifts of balance before being directed by the hands and the mind.

Elements of this technique can be seen in many ancient forms of sacred dance. For example, Bharat Natyam, a form of temple dance from South India, uses the mind combined with action to send power: As is written in the ancient text Abhinaya Darpanam: 'where goes the hand the eye follows: where goes the eye, goes the spirit: where goes the spirit is the heart: where's the heart is the reality of the being.'

In practical terms, this technique is best developed and practised by working with the weather. If a storm comes in, figure out which direction the storm is coming from and work with your back to that direction. Be totally open in your mind and do not try to direct, affect or suppress the storm: let it flow through you and work with it to achieve whatever the consciousness of the storm is trying to achieve.

32. Methods of working with temples and deities

You can then learn to work with the storm which in turn teaches you a lot about the health of the land.

Once you get used to working with the weather this way, then if there is a really dangerous situation, you can work on nudging the direction of the storm (which is a last resort action). The key is the tiniest but focused intention: this has a lot more affect on a storm than brute force. The one thing to never ever do is to try and suppress a storm: to do so could bring death to a lot of people. The aim of this line of work is to get to know how storms work and how they think. With that information, you develop an affinity with the weather which enables you to gain insight into where a storm is going and how powerful it will be, which in turn gives you the information to get out of it path. Most storms are doing a job that is absolutely necessary for the health of the land, and to interfere with that can create a cascade of problems.

The other way that this movement/power technique can be used is to break up power patterns that have become 'looped' and are destructive. This can be a side effect of badly done magic, or magic that is aimed at a person or household for malevolent reasons, or unhealthy patterns that have built up in the land or in a property. All power and magic leaves a trail or thread of energy, and when there is a buildup or aftershock after a magical event, it can begin to loop over and over in a pattern that in turn affects the area and people around it.

If you just wade in to break such a pattern or loop of magic, it can dig in and resist any attempt to break it up. But if you use the method of movement and 'weaving' to echo or copy the pattern, over and over until you have merged with it, then you can break the pattern by suddenly breaking away from the pattern once you had become established with it. This is a very old form of magic and has been used in many ways for both good and bad. Essentially, you use the method of copying and merging with a power pattern, being, or person until you are no longer detectable. Once you and the pattern are one, you take the lead of action and by breaking the action, the original pattern also breaks. It's also a great way to catch horses: follow them, copy them until they forget you are there, then change direction and they will all follow you!

32.9 Summary

Once you have established a working temple, either by moving an ancient one or creating a new one, and you have connected the temple up to inner contacts or deities using doorways, then you are ready to begin the Work. Magical temples are not there to play with: they are working spaces where the magicians unfold their work of service, development and exploration. As an adept, the emphasis on learning should now be over, and the focus should be on engaging everything you have learned to begin to do something useful. In truth you never stop learning, but if you constantly approach the Work with an agenda of learning or self-development, then your work will eventually plateau and go no further. Power only really comes together when there is a good reason, and when it does, the urge to Work will be almost unbearable.

Chapter Thirty-three

The magic of the fire/volcanic temple

With the understanding of elemental magic in the early parts of training comes a realization that the powers of these elements can be moulded magically and used with pinpoint accuracy to build powerful magical structures. One of the most prevalent and prolific forms of this elemental building is the Fire Temple. The history of the fire/solar temple reaches back into the far distant past of our humanity and is the most powerful 'formed' expression of the power that streams both from fire and from the sun. In history, the streams of fire magic split into solar temple and Fire Temple, which in its Underworld expression is mainly taken up with volcanic powers, and its overworld expression which is from lightning. But the source power is the same: it just expresses itself differently. The volcanic form of magic is older in terms of power usage, but the solar magic has been the most prolific magical stream through history and has given us numerous strands of solar temples, out of which came the solar kingships.

The majority of expressions of the solar power in the Near and Middle East, Europe and Central America expressed themselves through the male power, hence their association with kingship. But there have been some female expressions of this power, usually in much older traditions i.e. Japan, early Egyptian dynasties, Yemen and Nordic myths. I will deal with the solar lines and overworld lightning lines of magic later, which are completely different realms of magic.

But of the two streams, the volcanic stream is more interesting, more ancient and certainly more powerful to work with. It appears in disguise in British mythology (Vortigern's cave for an example) and is still scattered around the world in various mythological forms, which can be referred to when searching out images from magical

33. THE MAGIC OF THE FIRE/VOLCANIC TEMPLE

working visions. It has survived in magical practice up to the present day, although some groups that use this form of magic have dressed it up and dumbed it down to sell to the masses, which in turn has caused the inner contacts of that work to walk away in disgust. It is a very fragile form of magic in that it is so old, beyond our humanity, that it needs careful handling for its integrity to stay intact. The other possible problem with this stream of work is that the contacts are so ancient that they are not of our humanity, so when they appear in the visions of the magicians working that form of magic, if they are not prepared for what is coming (or they are stupid), they think the contacts are aliens because they are not fully human. This problem happens when people who have natural sight stumble across this work without understanding and don't pause to discover what it is that they are actually seeing.

33.1 The use of volcanic magic

Volcanic power is about forging new lands, melting and transforming, and it is also about the raw power of the planet. It is about the metals within the rock, the releasing of those metals and their powers, and the transforming of those substances into magical tools. So straightaway you can see how powerful and potentially dangerous this form of magic could be in wrong or stupid hands. It could also be very dangerous in the long term if it was in ambitious hands: this power creates, along with solar power, civilizations, temples and kingships. Hence sovereignty is nearly always associated with the sun and the sword (liquid metal drawn from rock, which is the volcanic part of the deal). The volcanic power forges the path, creates the weapons, and intermingles with the sea power to make new life, and the solar power gives it growth, beauty and strength.

But that is the historic picture; what about today's magic? The power of volcanic fire can be drawn upon for a mass of reasons, both in personal use and wider service. The majority of volcanic magical work starts out through visionary work to ensure the right inner contacts, knowledge training and inner flexibility to hold the power safely. Once that training and ability is in place, then the outer expressions can be worked with in ritual and in mediation, and in direct physical action with volcanic sites. The reasons to work with this power are many: for example to rebalance and assist a volcanic site where magic has been used and has caused an imbalance. It can also be worked with to forge powerful magical tools, build temples, and to work unconditionally with the inner contacts and beings connected to the volcanoes in the rebalancing needed after human interference (i.e. bomb tests, etc. and to attempt to temper an impending eruption that poses major risk to living beings. From an inner point of view, this power can also be worked with for building Underworld temples, reaching back to connect with prehuman contacts, and to work with 'dragon' power that is expressing through the land in an unbalanced way and causing problems.

33.2 The path to working with volcanic/fire power

It is very important at the outset of any branch of deep magic that its inner patterns, energies and contacts are connected with and understood. If a magician attempts to work a new form of magic without attending to its inner aspects, then the magic will be flaccid and without strength. This is good in that it takes time and effort to delve into the inner aspects of a realm and people who are silly or selfish in their work don't like to put in much effort to obtain the power their desire. It's a sort of idiot filter in the flows of magical power.

The way to gain the knowledge of the inner patterns and contacts is through vision, and lots of it. Every time someone goes in vision to a specific magical realm, they loosen the binds that hold their consciousness into their bodies, until the magician can flow easily from one realm to another. Once that is achieved, a magician can stand at the foot of a volcano and commune with it in depth, commune with the inner beings that reside in the volcano and draw upon the power of the volcano just by standing there and thinking at it. There are no robes, no waving of wands: it's actually quite boring to watch, but the results can be devastating in their strength.

Once the visions can be accessed properly and enough contact has been made, then the next step is to learn to mediate the power of

33. THE MAGIC OF THE FIRE/VOLCANIC TEMPLE

the volcano into an object, usually a sword. That alone will set off a whole new path of magical work that could last years as one learns to properly wield a sword that carries the fire power of the Underworld. With the knowledge of the sword, ritual workings of volcanic power can become extremely powerful and have to be handled carefully and thoughtfully: it is one of those streams of magic that can destroy the practitioner if it is not handled properly.

Work with the following visions in the sequence in which they are given, and work with each one a few times until the contact is established before moving onto the next one. As with all visionary magic, once you have found a suitable connection with a contact, the vision will take on its own life as you are shown the patterns and structures that are best accessed by you. Always remember: the vision is merely a window of constructed imagination through which the contact can connect and communicate with you. All of the visions in this book are ancient paths that have been used over and over for millennia, so they are well-worn and their inner patterns fully tuned to their frequency. Once the vision is fully established in reality, then you will find it begins to take on a life of its own as you move away from the constructed pattern and connect with what is currently happening in that space.

33.3 Visions of the volcanic temples

These visions are truly ancient and stretch back to a time and power that we associate with the myth of Atlantis. (Dare I say that word without cringing?) The mythical pattern of Atlantis reaches back to an ancient memory of a consciousness and power that drew its strength from volcanic energy and solar power. It comes from a time before 'our' type of humanity existed, but the waves of its magic still wash up on the shores of our world today. The following vision was given to me by an inner contact when I was in a time of great need for this form of power.

Fragments of the priestly workings of this magical path were written into my first novel *Azal: The Retelling of Eve*, which outlines in its later chapters the patterns and methods used in solar and volcanic fire magic of that time. It also highlights the problems of power drunkenness than can scourge a magician when he or she dips their toe into this form of magical work. Once the work is fully connected with, it can give access to a very focused and potentially destructive form of magic that must be used wisely. Thankfully, this magic also has a safety valve in which those who try to use this power for unhealthy ends tend to suddenly shut down as the contact withdraws their bridging. It is heavily dependant upon the contacts for it to work, and once you veer onto a path of self use in a power grab, the contacts withdraw and the work becomes useless twaddle.

The visions are laid out in a specific sequence that gives you the information you need to work with this form of power. It is important to first observe and understand the inner structures of these massive earthly powers before then going onto make contact with the beings that work within these structures.

33.4 Going into the city beneath the waves

Light a candle and with eyes closed, see your flame burning within you quietly. See your inner flame and the flame of the candle merge, feel the peacefulness that surrounds the flame and within that peace, see the flame grow bigger before you, filling you with warmth and peace. With the intention of wanting to reach out for knowledge regarding the temple of volcanic fire, you walk into the flame and feel its gentle warmth flow over you. The flame falls down into the Underworld, passing through the building, rock and earth, and you follow.

You fall and fall through earth and rocks, falling and falling through darkness and silence. As you fall, your memory of the surface world falls away and you fall in a still peace, as if you have always been falling. You fall through caverns, crystal caves, dark stones and also just darkness, where you cannot see anything around you. Eventually you fall on soft sand, finding yourself in a dark cave with no features. A light touch upon your shoulder makes you jump and a being that you cannot see properly hands you a kind of boiler suit to put on, a hat for your head and glasses for your eyes. Once you are suitably dressed, you are led to a corner of the cave where there is a small opening in the ground and a rope ladder descends into darkness.

33. THE MAGIC OF THE FIRE/VOLCANIC TEMPLE

You are prompted to go down the rope ladder without explanation, and as you climb onto the ladder you feel a deep fear rise up within you as you begin to climb down. Don't worry about the fear: it is a natural instinctual reaction to the power building around you.

Down and down you climb, climbing through darkness and silence once more. But this time you feel heat all around you, which builds slowly. It is then that you realize your suit is there to protect you from the heat. Down and down you climb until once more you land in a small cave. To one end of the cave is a tunnel out of which shines a dull light. You venture down the tunnel, which emerges out onto a ledge. Below you is a vast ocean floor and you realize that you are under the sea somehow, but the water does not affect you. On the ocean floor is a series of buildings, like an ancient city with step pyramids and beautiful buildings with vast ornate entrances. Many of the roofs are covered in gold, and the city seems to emit its own gentle light.

You dive in and swim down to a building that really draws you. Upon entering the building, you find a stairway that winds around the directions in a square shape as it descends. You walk down the stairs, noticing the murals on the walls as you walk. They seem to be telling a story of history and you stop for a while to look and absorb the story. Once you have seen what you needed to see, something urges you to climb further down the stairwell until you come to a doorway. Placing your hand upon the door, you feel shapes and sigils outlined on the door, magical symbols that protect what lies beyond. As your fingers scan the shapes, you come across one that you recognize and with that recognition, the door quietly swings open.

In the room, which is built of stone and has a stone floor, is a square stone plinth. Looking closer, you realize it is actually a stone cube that is partially set into the floor. It is at that point that you realize that the building, and in fact the whole city, is all straight lines: there are no curves, no archways, no circles. You are drawn to stand upon the stone plinth, your feet upon a square marked out in gold in the centre of the plinth. Standing in silence, you gradually become aware of an immense power beneath the plinth. It is then you realize that the room has the odour of sulphur and that it is hot. Something about the shape of the room catches your attention: it is very harmonious, but strange. The walls work at a specific angle to

33.4. Going into the city beneath the waves

the floor which gives the appearance of a slight tilt, and the more you look at the walls of the room, the more you become aware of lines of energy flowing along the joins of the walls and floor. It begins to feel like you are standing in a massive battery.

The room begins to communicate with you, not as an inner contact or as stored information, but as the shape itself: its lines, corners, and angles all have their own vocabulary, and as you look to understand, you see that the angles, corners and lines all act as conduits for power. Looking up for the first time, you see that the roof rises to a pyramid point, and all the lines of power that are drawing from the source beneath the plinth are being channelled to the tip of the pyramid.

Your attention is drawn back to the plinth, and you are now aware of the fact that what is beneath you is a volcano and that the building, in fact the city, is built around and upon the volcano. The plinth is the epicentre of the building that caps the volcano, and you are standing in the very centre of the top of the volcano. The power flows along the lines of the room and is gathered by the tip of the pyramid which vanishes into a room above, looking at this you realize that you are looking at an externalized form of patterned ritual: the power is flowing around lines, directions and shapes, and it is mediated from one direction (below) to another direction (above).

Your mind struggles to understand, but something deep within you tells you not to fight, but to let the power flow around and within you, and that will bring its own form of understanding. The humanity that built this place is very different from our own, and you must let your body translate for you rather than your mind. With that understanding, you lie down on the plinth. We are a humanity of imagination and emotion. The humanity that built this place is a humanity of logic and mathematical structure. You cannot use your imagination as a doorway to understand this temple: you must allow the ancient common memory within your blood to remember in its own way. Lie down and close your eyes. Let the power of the volcano flow all around you. You fall deeper and deeper into a still place. You drift without time, without thought, without movement. You drift into a deepness that stills everything within you. All is silent, all is peaceful.

33. THE MAGIC OF THE FIRE/VOLCANIC TEMPLE

In that state, you feel a deep shift in your consciousness, like an ancient remembering. It triggers a déjà vu feeling, a sense of aura, of remote memory and of scents and sounds that skirt the edge of your mind. From that deep place, a sound wells up in your lungs, a deep resonant sound that breaks through a barrier and is released through your vocal cords. It is a deep harmonic sound that you did not know your body was capable of making. The room begins to vibrate from the sound, like a bell, and the lines and angles become bright with power. A force of immense strength, the life force of the volcano explodes out from beneath the plinth and flows through the room and your body. The nerves and muscles in your body twitch with the connection of power, and the endocrine glands in your brain suddenly feel bright and full of power. The power in the room flows up to the pyramid tip, but the power flowing through your body seems to have no focal point and flows around and around your nervous system.

Just when you think you are going to explode with the power, some memory somewhere deep in your brain knows what to do and you stand, extend your arms into a direction and shout a deep loud sound. The power gathers together in the spine in the area of the back of your neck and then shoots out through your arms and through your voice. The power levels are immense and you have no control over what is happening. The sound and lines of power from your body shoot through the wall of the building and vanish. You collapse down onto the plinth as the power leaves you. You must now get back on your feet and leave this place so that you can observe what has just happened.

Leaving the room and climbing up the stairs, as you look at the paintings on the wall, you see a painting that depicts something similar to what has just happened to you. The power of the voice in the painting shows the immense destruction of a city by an explosion of wind and fire: it looks like a nuclear bomb has gone off. As you emerge out of the building and begin to swim back to the ledge, looking back, you see a line of destruction through the old city, a line that is from your call of destruction. What you did has flattened the inner patterns of the buildings in a straight line in the direction in which you held your arms out.

33.4. Going into the city beneath the waves

You swim back up to the ledge, pondering on the implications of this ancient form of mediated volcanic power. Certain things in ancient and biblical history begin to make more sense to you now: they were racial memories of this ancient and very destructive power. As you climb your way back to the surface, more and more things regarding patterns, shape, power, numbers, geometry, etc. begin to make sense in terms of magic, power and how the universe works. The closer you get to the surface, climbing your way up through the cracks in the rocks and on rope ladders, the more the information that had been stored for millennia in your genes surfaces to your conscious mind. As you emerge from the Underworld and sit back in front of the flame, you look around using your inner vision and notice for the first time, faint lines of power following shapes around you, and power flowing through the nerves in your body. You remember all that has happened, and you particularly remember how the power of the volcano was funnelled through the shapes and through your body. You sit for a moment in silence and stillness before opening your eyes and blowing out the candle.

★ ★ ★

That vision introduces you to the form and pattern that underlies the volcanic form of fire magic that flows through human consciousness. Once you have learned that form, it opens up the structure for you to find other and probably safer ways to work with that power. It has been used over the millennia in the construction and destruction of cities in the early era of city building. The same form of power emerges in various ancient civilizations around the world that built city states, and I was curious about why the same power emerged in almost the same way at locations that were not connected (that we are aware of). It took me years to figure out that while they did not have direct contact, the knowledge in the Library of our humanity can be accessed by those who know how to do so. The early city and temple builders were masters of occult knowledge and as such were able to access ancient wisdoms, just as we do now.

That construction and destruction power has little use in today's world, as it can be so devastating. It is akin to a nuclear bomb, and thankfully our consciousness is slowly moving away from the use of such power. It can be used, with great care and restraint, in temple building, but I feel there are much safer ways to do it. However, even though it is a power that is falling into oblivion, it is important, like all histories, to study it, learn about it, and put it in context. It is important to know about it so that you can deal with it safely when you come across it. It is a power, though, that corrupts very easily and becomes dangerous very quickly. If you know how it works and what it does, then you can also gain the knowledge of how to dismantle it and make it safe. Such work is part of the work of an adept, and such things will be put in your path to deal with.

33.5 The cave in the centre of the world that links all volcanoes

This is a very curious, interesting and powerful place that is manifest in the inner world but has no real direct expression in the outer world that we currently know about. The way it manifests in the Underworld is as a cave at the centre of the planet. Now we know that such a place could not possibly exist in the manifest world, but its expression to us tells us that it is deep in the Underworld, is very old, and is a place where the power of mountains comes together.

When I first started to work with this place, a fellow occultist remarked that it was very similar to a place that occultist Bill Grey had found when he was working with mountains in the Himalayas.

Magically, it is a place where mountains and volcanoes at opposite sides of the planet can be worked with simultaneously. I also found, after a short while of working in this space, that fault lines can also be worked with from here. I used to work in this place if there had been underground bomb testing that had caused blockages, or if magical pathways through the Underworld had been blocked by an earthquake. It is important to note at this point that outer occurrences like earthquakes, volcanoes and the like affect pathways through the Underworld and can have a knock-on effect through the Inner Worlds magically. Sometimes it is fine and is just change, but at other times it can block ancient pathways which then isolate inner beings and cut off access to Underworld temples and places.

33.5. The cave in the centre of the world that links all volcanoes

I once came across a really good and interesting example of this many years ago when I lived in a place called Pointe Reyes in California. It is a small peninsular that juts out into the Pacific Ocean, and it is a wild and beautiful place. As I was driving home one night from San Francisco, I noticed a large boulder that I always pass which lay on the boundary of the peninsular. An inner contact loudly announced, as I was driving and singing along to Bally Sagoo, that I had a job to do with that boulder and it was time that I got to it! The day after, I did 'get to it' and went in vision to the boulder and asked it if it needed help. A being appeared beside the boulder and told me the boulder was fine, thank you very much. I was confused. Normally when I get a contact like that, it really means that there is a problem. I told the being this. "Oh," said the being, "it will be to do with *them*," he said, as he pointed to the ground under the boulder. "Them?" I asked? "Listen," the being said. I sat very quietly, and sure enough I heard a very faint call for help.

I went under the boulder in vision and found a small tunnel that I could just about fit through. A short way into the tunnel I came across an abyss: a crack in the ground that seemed to go on forever. On the other side, peering out of the gloom, were a motley collection of faery men, all dressed in Tudor sailors' clothing. I was fascinated! What the hell where these English faery men doing in California? They shouted at me to get them out, but as I looked around I could not see anything that would create a bridge across the abyss. It was short enough for me to straddle, though, as I was a lot bigger than them. Eventually I laid across the abyss and they climbed over my back and up out from beneath the boulder.

As I scrambled out they were running towards the sea, waving and shouting thank you. As I went home, all I could think was what a bloody weird experience it had been. I could not figure for the life of me how the hell they had got there. I guessed that they had been trapped by an earthquake: that area sits right by the San Andreas fault line. A few days later, when I tentatively told a friend what had happened, she replied that they probably came from one of the ships. Ships? I asked? Yes, she replied. Drake's Bay, which was close by, was called Drake's bay because Sir Francis Drake got stuck there for a winter while they repaired a badly damaged ship. The light bulbs went on...an English Tudor Ship, close by in dock for a few months.

33. THE MAGIC OF THE FIRE/VOLCANIC TEMPLE

The faery men must have been on board the ship, left to explore the powerful land where they had stopped, and got trapped by an earthquake, unable to get back to their ship, which sailed off without them.

I then began to fret about what would happen to them once they got to the bay and found no ship, and that hundreds of years had passed. I went down to Drake's Bay, but did not find them. I never saw them again.

So, back to the cave. The following vision can be used to work on fault lines, volcanoes, and mountains. It can be a part of service to the land to keep this place in balance, and it can be worked with to relieve tension in fault lines and volcanoes when the tension has been caused by magical interference or underground bomb testing. If the volcanic or fault line activity is natural, then no matter what the consequences of an earthquake or volcano on humanity, you must not use magic to stop natural disasters. It is very tempting, particularly when there is the possibility of many deaths, but unless you have an inner prompt from a contact, it is important not to interfere in the Earth's natural processes. What may be bad for us may be very necessary for the planet's health and survival, and we have already, as a species, done enough damage by manipulating the environment to suit ourselves.

Sometimes, though, there is what seems to us to be a natural disaster unfolding and inner contacts will kick us into action to do something, and it is always a matter of understanding that we have an extremely limited ability to 'see' what is going on in the larger picture. If you have strongly established contacts, then they will come to you when work needs doing, whether the disaster is a natural occurrence or not. Here are two examples of such scenarios. The first happened in the middle of a working group session. I was teaching structures to do with the Fire Temple and a contact started to badger me during the sessions. They told me they needed a group to do a job and would we be willing? Of course, me being me, I always agree to a job before actually taking the time to find out what it is.

The contact showed me a desert scenario, and below the surface of the desert was what looked like balls of explosive fire straining at an invisible membrane: it was about to breech, whatever 'it' was. We

33.5. The cave in the centre of the world that links all volcanoes

all set to work and slowly released the pressure on the membrane before guiding the fire power through channels into storage caves, down into tunnels, and mediated some of it out into the air where it could disperse. Some of it needed real heavy containment: it seemed very toxic and was killing everything around it. So between us all, we took it down deep into the earth to the bottom of the Underworld, as far as we could go, and called upon a deep and ancient goddess (a precursor to Sekhmet) to ask her for her help. She ate up the toxic fire power and that was that.

When we came out of the vision we all had light sunburn on our faces and hands, and we all felt like shit. After consuming vast amounts of coffee and chocolate, we sat around discussing what we had just done and what it actually was. I did not recognize the desert where we had worked, and I had no clue about what we had actually just done. But one of the women in the group did know. She recognized the patch of desert and mountain as being in Nevada: it was a particular military underground dump for spent nuclear fuel and decommissioned weapons. This is why I often say that you do not need to go out looking for the work, it will come to you: there is enough damage out there caused by our species to keep you going through multiple lifetimes.

The second example of being guided to work on a natural disaster was when I was living in Tennessee. I had just finished my work for the day at the ballet company and it was the day that I only worked until mid-afternoon. I was very tired after a gruelling week of rehearsals and training sessions, and I was just about dead on my feet. When I got home I went straight to my bedroom and lay on my bed. On my wall bedroom was a six foot icon of the Black Madonna, a goddess contact I was currently working with. Before her were a mat and a candle: I would sit there each day during my working pattern with her, doing what I usually do. As I was laid out on the bed, listening to an old recording on CD of a group of Tibetan monks singing the skeleton dance, a contact made an appearance and demanded that I sit before the icon. With the chants still going, I had to light the candle and go into the Void. I was unsure about doing a vision, as my baby grandson was asleep in the next room, and I am always wary about doing visions so close to children from my family: they tend to come along for the ride. But the contact almost screamed at me to get going.

I went into the Void, the chants still going in the background, and I felt a huge amount of pressure build up before me. It was bearing down upon me and I had to very gently and carefully push it to one side. I had no idea what it was or what I was doing. It was a tremendous strain, and I was relieved when it finally faded. I was brought out of vision and the contact told me I could now go and rest (gee, thanks). I fell into a deep sleep for two hours and awoke suddenly as though someone had shouted at me. I staggered into the kitchen where my daughter was cooking and my grandson was gurgling away in his chair. I still had no idea what the hell had happened, until I plopped down in front of the TV and watched the news.

A storm front had been building all day, and as it moved towards Nashville it had been spitting out tornadoes. One had been on a path straight towards us, but it had veered away at the last moment and trashed a small neighbourhood a few miles away. It shook me up when I realized the implications of a tornado hitting our tiny little house, with no shelter and a baby inside: it did not bear thinking about. So you can see how contacts will sometimes step in to get you to work. I had no idea if the storm was natural or not: the point is that I did not work on it intentionally, but was guided into unconditional work by an inner being.

33.6   The vision of the cave

Light a candle and with your eyes closed, see your flame burning within you quietly. See your inner flame and the flame of the candle merge, feel the peacefulness that surrounds the flame and within that peace, see the flame grow bigger before you, filling you with warmth and peace. With the intention of wanting to reach out for knowledge regarding the temple of volcanic fire, walk into the flame and feel its gentle warmth flow over you. The flame falls down into the Underworld, passing through the building, rock and earth, and you follow.

33.6. The vision of the cave

You fall and fall through earth and rocks, falling and falling through darkness and silence. As you fall, your memory of the surface world falls away, and you fall in a still peace, as if you have always been falling. You fall through caverns, crystal caves, dark stones and also just darkness, where you cannot see anything around you. As you fall, you can hear water rushing by and splashing, but you cannot see anything in the deep darkness. You fall and fall until eventually you feel you are just falling through space, with nothing around you, no rocks, no earth, just falling and falling. Eventually you slow down and fall into a spherical cave with a sandy floor.

The cave has its own glow to it and you look around in wonder at its beauty. It is a very large round cave with many holes in the walls that vanish off up and down into darkness. You realize that you have just fallen down one of those holes. The walls of the cave are littered with sparkling outcrops of various types of semiprecious crystal stones, veins of precious metals and clumps of very primitive fungi. The cave is warm and damp, with a faintly strange odour that you recognize but cannot exactly remember. You begin to explore the cave, which is pretty large and has a strange quality in that it is spherical and there seems to be an odd gravity. You can keep walking around the cave and realize that you are walking the full circle of the sphere: you are walking the full surface of the inside of a sphere without falling off the roof.

Once that novelty has worn off, you begin to explore the holes, some of which are large and some of which are small. As you put your hand into the holes, which are actually the entrances small narrow tunnels, you discover that the inside of each tunnel is smooth and shiny: it is quartz rock that has been smoothed out through millions of years of being touched and stroked. Placing your hand on the quartz, you stop the urge to stroke the smooth rock and you quietly become aware of a pulse in the rock. The pulse from the quartz flows up the tunnel which passes through the earth and emerges on the surface of the land, either at a fault line, a mountain or a volcano.

It takes a while for your inner sensitivity to catch up with the huge number of vibrations that flow in and out of this cave, but as you go from hole to hole, you realize that the holes each have their own pulse frequency, and each hole is unique. To experiment, you place one hand in one hole and another hand in another. You

33. The Magic of the Fire/Volcanic Temple

feel the two different pulses flowing into your body from the two different holes. The vibrations begin to harmonize and communicate within your body and the pulses flow from one hole to the other in a deep, pulsed conversation. As they flow through you, you can see in your mind's eye the sources of the two vibrations: two mountains on different continents. The mountains commune with each other in a flow of natural power that brings balance to them both.

You are prompted to break the connection from some deep instinctive place and you are drawn to another hole in which you place your hand. The pulse in this hole seems to be blocked, and is echoing back into the cave rather than flowing out into the world. You push your hand up into the hole to feel where the blockage is, but it is too far up for you to reach. Instead, something tells you to blow hard up the tunnel, which you do. The pressure builds up from you blowing until you feel it give way, and your breath vanishes up to the surface. You feel a deep rumble and shift before the pulse of the quartz reestablishes itself up this tunnel. Stepping back, you realize that your breath has just released an energetic blockage that had caused a pressure buildup in a fault line, and the land had shifted to loosen itself once more.

So now that you know how this space works, you can come here again when this type of work is needed. But for now it is time to leave. You have to ascend slowly from this deep place, and you climb back into the hole that you fell out of. If you cannot remember which one it was, walk around them until you feel one that is very familiar: that one leads to the land upon which you live. You climb back up the tunnel, feeling the pulse as you go and feeling the land around you, the rocks, the pressure, the fault lines, the mountains, rocks, hills and springs: the roots of all of these land expressions are in these tunnels. You climb and climb, taking care not to dislodge anything, and taking note of the different scents, rock types and occasional beings who sleep in the land as you climb. If you pass one of these beings, pass slowly and quietly so as not to wake them. As you emerge out into the light of the surface world, you remember the candle that is before you and you sit quietly, contemplating the flame as you remember what you have just seen and experienced. When you are ready, you put out the flame.

* * *

That vision can become part of an adept's service to the land upon which they live, and can be used to work with natural earth expressions like earthquakes, volcanoes etc. But it can also be used on a landmass that is supposed to be open and breathing but is trapped by concrete, buildings, etc. There are a variety of ways to work with this power and the best way to find out all of its applications is to work with it and discover its power and function as you go. It can be used to relieve power in a volcano: rather than block the volcano, you can release the pent-up power so that the eruption dissipates faster and with less damaging consequences.

33.7 The contact of the sword maker

This part of the Volcanic Fire Temple is fascinating, beautiful and very strange: it is probably the oldest part of the inner structure and most certainly the part that is prehuman in its inner construction. I am not sure of its full use magically speaking but I am sure that it has far more applications than I have discovered, though it does seem to be slowly drifting out of our conscious realm. The inner pattern of the temple and its beings/contacts usually survive for millennia beyond the outer construct, and when its builder's civilization has fallen into the dust the inner pattern still ticks away, slowly fading over thousands and thousands of years until it is finally barely a whisper. This contact is fading, but is still strong enough to be reached in vision and worked with.

This contact works deep within the volcano and works with metals, their powers and their transformation. The contact itself appears in a prehuman lizard/raptor-man style form, very similar to beings that appeared in Babylonian bas-reliefs. The image itself is not a major revelation to occultists: this form of being seems to pop up all over the place in its work with humanity. When I first started to work with this contact he taught me a lot about swords: the power that can flow into a sword, how to weave beings and powers into swords, but most important of all, how not to use a magical sword. He also taught me about the power lines of magic that flow from the volcanic temple that is in the previous vision, and how to break those lines

33. The Magic of the Fire/Volcanic Temple

and safely dispose of them. So that has been most of my experience with this contact. I do not know if that is all that he does: I'm sure he works in a wider field, but I do not have that wider experience with him. For those of you who feel a great calling to this part of the work, I am sure that over the years of your work the mysteries of this place will unfold far beyond what I have seen.

33.8 The work with swords

Once of the most interesting things I learned from this contact was a way to work with magical swords I had not previously come across and it was a way that seemed to make a great deal of sense. Instead of putting power or a being into the sword as a consecration/mediation that then stays for the life of the sword, this contact places into the physical sword an immensely powerful line of fire power that works on the job in hand and is then taken back out again. At the beginning of the work, the magician visits this contact, has the power placed in the sword, goes off, does their job and then immediately comes back and has the power taken back out of the sword and placed back into the volcano. This has two major benefits: the first is that it allows a much greater power than normally would be mediated to be put into the sword for the job at hand, and the second benefit is that the magician is not tempted to misuse the power over time. By having the sword empowered for only one job, there is no possibility of what can usually happen with magical swords, and that is that the magician, upon realizing how much power a magical sword can wield, begins to use it to solidify their own power base.

The other nastier temptation is to then use the sword to wipe out one's enemies. One who attacks with a magical sword will reap destruction down upon their whole society (the magical wisdom hidden in the Arthurian Mysteries) because the power in the sword is enough to destroy a whole nation. The magical sword, when used to defend a nation, is not wielded in battle, but is held forth as a being in its own right.

> Then they heard Cadwr Earl of Cornwall being summoned, and saw him rise with Arthur's sword in his hand, with a design of two chimeras on the golden hilt:

> when the sword was unsheathed what was seen from the mouths of the two chimeras was like two flames of fire, so dreadful that it was not easy for anyone to look. At that the host settled and the commotion subsided, and the earl returned to his tent.
>
> — *The Mabinogion*, translated by Jeffrey Gantz

The power that can be wielded through this method of working is not to be handled lightly or without serious reason (usually a life or death situation for a person, being or nation). It is tremendously destructive both to whoever is on the receiving end of the magic and to the person wielding it. Remember the basics: you mediate your own magic, so it flows through you before it goes anywhere else. People forget this over and over, and then are shocked when they get hit on the rebound (which takes its own time, but does happen eventually). If the power is used to cut magical binds, spells, curses, to bring about justice and balance, or to guard a land, nation or area in dire circumstances, then such power will also do the same to the handler.

33.9 The vision of the sword maker

This vision takes you to the contact and introduces you to his power. I have purposely not included how the sword is worked with: you will have to figure that one out for yourself. But if you truly need that power in your work, then the contact will guide you.

Light a candle and with eyes closed, see your flame burning within you quietly. See your inner flame and the flame of the candle merge, feel the peacefulness that surrounds the flame and within that peace, see the flame grow bigger before you, filling you with warmth and peace. With the intention of wanting to reach out for knowledge regarding the temple of volcanic fire, you walk into the flame and feel its gentle warmth flow over you. The flame falls down into the Underworld, passing through the building, rock and earth, and you follow.

You fall and fall through earth and rocks, falling and falling through darkness and silence. As you fall, your memory of the surface

33. THE MAGIC OF THE FIRE/VOLCANIC TEMPLE

world falls away and you fall in a still peace, as if you have always been falling. You fall through caverns, crystal caves, dark stones and also just darkness, where you cannot see anything around you. You fall and fall through darkness, the scents of the earth, the rocks and underground rivers swirl around you as you fall. You can hear the roar of an underground river that you pass by as you fall, and the deeper you go into the belly of the earth, the more you begin to smell the scent of sulphur. You begin to slow down and eventually you fall on soft sand, finding yourself in a dark cave that is hot and sulphurous. There are loud noises all around you, and as your eyes adjust to the dark you start to see a gentle glow coming from a tunnel carved out of the rock.

You begin to walk towards the tunnel. All around the entrance are carved into the stone strange frightening faces and many intricate patterns made out of squares, triangles and straight lines. The walls of the tunnel are lined with gold and punctuated with crystals of many different colours. The crystals reflect light in all directions, and steam swirls around your feet. The deeper you go into the tunnel towards the orange glow, the hotter you become, until it becomes uncomfortable. Just when you think you cannot take the heat anymore, the tunnel opens out into an underground cavern where part of the floor falls away to expose the bubbling lava of a volcanic pool. You get as close as you can comfortably stand to the pool, and you call using the sound that you learned in the earlier vision.

Once you have called a couple of times, a being emerges from a hidden crevice and walks towards you. The being appears as part reptile, part human, with a spinal ruff of feathers down their back. Its movements are very calm, quiet and considered as they walk slowly towards you, summing you up as they walk. The being does not speak to you, but gestures for you to watch the volcanic pool. The being opens its mouth wide and calls a strange noise that echoes around the cavern and seems to create vibration that is picked up and amplified by the stones and crystals that are in the walls around the cavern. The vibration seems to get into your teeth and your bones, until your whole body is vibrating at the same frequency as the being's call.

The being motions for you to step back, and you do just in time to see an enormous dinosaur-looking being raise its head out of the

33.9. The vision of the sword maker

pool. Its head is so large that it fills the pool, and its eye is the same size as your body. It turns its head to look at you, and it gazes deep into your eyes. The gaze and the sound seem to change something about your cellular makeup: the vibrations and power of the gaze reach deep into your past, the past that flows through your blood, and awakens something. This ancient being is of a power that is rarely experienced in the world anymore, and just standing in the presence of this volcanic giant is enough to effect change, which is what power does: it changes things. The being that is the contact that guards the cavern places a hand upon your shoulder and then seems to fiddle about with your throat and the back of your head. This gives you a headache, but you begin to hear and see differently. You can see the lines of metal that run through the cavern, and the flow of power that pulses through the veins of both these ancient beings.

It is enough that you all have looked at each other and had contact: now it is time to leave, but it is advisable to visit this place and to learn from the contact both about the powers and beings of this realm, and also how to work with precious metals and the tools forged from them.

The contact being guides you out of the cavern and shows you an ancient stairway that reaches all the way up to the surface world. They back away and leave you to find your way back up to your own realm. You are guided by the memory of the candle flame that you are seated before, and that memory pulls you back up as you climb and climb. Just when you think you cannot climb another step, a small tunnel with a dim light to your right beckons you, and you climb up through the earth and rocks to find yourself emerging back in the room where you started.

You sit before the candle flame, pondering on what you have just experienced, and when you are ready, you blow out the candle.

★ ★ ★

When that contact is worked with in terms of working with a magical sword, the being in the pool is the one that takes the sword and puts power into it. You can imagine the intensity of the power that can flow from this magical work. But before you rush off to

33. THE MAGIC OF THE FIRE/VOLCANIC TEMPLE

conquer the world with a magical sword, there are a couple of things you should know.

Firstly, the sword has to be virgin: the blade must not have drawn blood, which of course is a given in all magical work with swords. It must also have been magically stripped of all influence, salted and grounded. Once the power has been in it, that is all it can be used for. Once you return the power, the sword has no other use than to wait until you go back to this place to repower the sword. It is not a ritual sword and cannot be used in ritual, not even when the power is not in it. It has become a vessel for that power only and will have no other use at all. Put it away with a guardian to watch over it, and never ever let anyone fool around with it, swing it around, or point it at anyone. The reason for this is that once it has been used, even though the power has been taken out, remnants can remain, and even the smallest remnant of that power can kill or damage someone.

The second thing you should know is that while the sword carries the power, you carry the sword, which means you have to hold the burden of that level of power in your body while you do the work. It is a vast amount of power to have to carry, even for a short piece of work, and the effect on the body can be considerable. The effects may not be obvious straightaway as the inner impact, although felt while you are working, will not fully manifest for days or even a week or so after the work. Then you can be hit so badly that it may make you very ill. Hence this work is only done when it really needs to be done. The load cannot be shared with anyone, and there is no way of dodging around this aspect of working with this implement in this way. The holder bears a terrible burden and is this is expressed as part of the Mystery to do with the Sword of the Land and the Sacrificial Kingship. This whole aspect of work is the source of the dragon/volcanic/fire/sword/king myths, mysteries and stories. The king or queen would be a keeper of the sword and would empower it in times of peril. The sword would be carried across the land and its dragon power released to do what was necessary to bring about peace and stability. The king or queen would carry the terrible burden of the sword on behalf of their people and the land, and woe betide any who misused it: it would destroy them.

The sort of work that would warrant the use of this sword spans a variety of situations from slicing through complex Kabbalistic

33.9. The vision of the sword maker

bindings and serious death curses, occult attacks upon a nation, war, drought that is caused by magic (natural disasters should never be interfered with: they are usually bringing balance for the land) the dealing with large ancient beings who are disturbing volcanoes and waking them up (usually woken up by magic) any very large fire being that is wreaking havoc and nothing else has worked. This method of working with the sword is a last resort, as it holds a power similar in its destructive capacity to a nuclear bomb.

In general, any of the fire/volcanic magic is volatile and dangerous just by its own nature. But you must also take into account that this form of magic has been misused over and over again throughout time to quench various thirsts for power and revenge. It is a raw, vicious power that can wield great good in the right hands and terrible destruction in the wrong hands. The safety valve is the amount of physical burden such work puts upon the human body: this burden tends to put off most people with bad intent, but there are occasional madmen or women who will do anything to further their agenda. Hence the care with intention, the care with guardians, and the willingness to work unconditionally, working blind with inner contacts as simply a cog in a very large wheel.

Chapter Thirty-four

The power and magic of utterance, sound and sigil

One of the purposes of magic in humanity, particularly in the West, is upholding the structure that allows civilization to exist. In this day and age, we often wax lyrical about how wonderful it would be to get back to a simpler time, to live closer to nature and away from civilization. But there has to be a balance. I would bet that very few people reading this would know how to forage properly, hunt and kill their food, keep warm in winter, protect themselves and live on the edge of existence all the time. It's a very romantic idea, but in reality nature is harsh, vicious and deadly in northern climates. Without the basic structure of civilization, we would dwindle as a species very quickly.

That does not mean that we turn our backs on the sacred land and the feral powers of nature, it means that we must keep a balance between the two and treat both with extreme respect for we need both to survive. As magicians or priests, there is a great deal of work to be done to uphold both nature and the magical inner structure of civilization and society. The ritual structures of society are basically the patterns of magic as expressed through the civilizations of the Near East and are the foundations of magic today.

In this chapter we will look at the direct patterns that influence civilization and society. The most prominent, the earliest and the most enduring pattern of magic in this field is concerned with the power of recitation. From myths, stories and songs, recited wisdoms, the inner power of utterance, to the calling upon the deities, and the language structure that gives rise to invocation, sigils, and sacred alphabets: the use of words/breath creates magic of all kinds. Language in magic is used to bind, release, move power, bring a

34. THE POWER AND MAGIC OF UTTERANCE, SOUND AND SIGIL

being in or send a being away: the scope of this magic is endless and its potential is beyond our meagre understanding.

We will start by looking at the relationship between the angelic thresholds of this power, the mediators and the manifestations. It takes all three for this power to flow into the manifest world and our job, as humans, is that of mediator. The most externalized form of this role as mediator is found in the monotheistic religions. The angel speaks wisdoms to the man, the man listens, the man goes and tells others. It has become a well known and well trodden (and often misused) path for the utterance of Divinity. But there is one problem with that scenario (hence the problems, wars, etc.) and that is that the utterance of Divinity is not about understanding what is said, or wise words or platitudes; it is about power.

The power of utterance is a way that humanity can cope with the manifestation for the frequency of sound and vibration that is Divine Being: i.e. the words don't *mean* something, they *are* something. The wisdoms became lost somewhere along the way and by the time we got to Jesus and Mohammed, that power had become a series of teachings and pronouncements. They knew that to utter something in the name of God was special, but the true magical implications and applications were lost by that time as the Near East became mired in tribal wars, Roman wars and general mayhem.

The mediation of the Divine Utterance of the Universal Power is the same as mediating the patterns of the Metatron cube, for instance, or the putting of a deity into an object: you are taking a power with no face or form and putting it into something that will be able to function in the outer world. The sounds *do* things. The words *are* things, and putting the sounds and words together *creates* things. And then you have the layers: words that *are* things but also *mean* things, so you can utter a sentence which will *mean* X, but the sounds themselves have their own power and will *do* Y. You can see the potential for powerful magic and also for dangerous misuse. A lot of quite vicious magic developed over the centuries through the use of word and sound, and gradually the constructive use faded into the mush of reciting religious or magical texts in the feeble hope of it doing something, anything.

This magical use of language, both spoken and written, is virtually everywhere where there is a magical or religious interface with beings that move beyond ancestors and land beings. But for this chapter I will concentrate on the languages, scripts and ciphers of the Near East, because that is what I know best. The techniques in this chapter can be altered to work in any other culture, for example Nordic, Sanskrit etc. All of them have angelic and demonic beings that work through the languages: they are known by different names, but the powers are the same.

The following visions take the magician through the whole process of the mediation of the power of utterance, and show the various octaves that this power can operate through, from the depths of creation to the magical interweave between a name and a power. Although the visions expressed here are situated loosely within the Judaic stream of consciousness, the techniques can be transplanted to be used in any tradition: once you get to a certain level of power and depth in any tradition, the interfaces and methods are more or less the same, because you are working with what is actually there, not a construct.

Once the visionary work has been done, the inner contacts have been established and the magician's body has adjusted to the impact of being close to such power, then the mediation can be transferred into ritual so that the power is worked with in a visionary ritual format. That is when it is at its most powerful, and care must be taken always when working at such level.

A word of caution: if you work at any real depth with this power it changes how your voice works (sometimes literally). You become able to create patterns of power using your voice without intention or thought. Most very powerful magic flows from the magician unhindered by conscious control: you have to be very careful at all times about how you use your voice, your words and your meanings. Once a magician has mediated power at this depth, they never switch off: you become a twenty-four hour open door for power, and what you say in anger can have devastating consequences. Hence this work is laborious and time-consuming: it takes years to climb the ladder safely.

34. THE POWER AND MAGIC OF UTTERANCE, SOUND AND SIGIL

The first vision is the deepest. It puts you in the position of the mediator of creation with the archangel and angel at your back as filters. Creation started with a sound: all flows forth from that sound and all becomes that sound. You become the Pontiff, the bridge; and as the power of utterance passes through you, it changes you forever. From that point on, when you work with utterance, sigils or speech, that power will trigger at some level and begin a magical process within you. You will truly understand the power of utterance, which covers magical speech, sigils, alphabets and the power of the wind.

You cannot control what passes through you, though, and trying to work at this depth with an agenda is sheer stupidity. To even think of doing so is madness. You are messing with the powers of all creation and while is it an honour for you to be allowed access to this event, and to passively participate, it is a crime above all crimes to try and filter, control or shape it. Why? Because we are an incredibly stupid, dense and shortsighted species. Not only would what we create be pathetically primitive, taking control of this power to form it would put you in the driving seat, hence all the power will descend upon you and will not be upheld by anything else. As a passive mediator you get to experience it, but you are not responsible for it: you are not upholding it. Once you take the reins it is all yours, and if you think for a minute...a manifest human body in relation to the whole of creation...well...it's a bit on the heavy side, even if you go to the gym.

There are a few who have got access at this depth and have tried to control, weave and form the power as it leaves them: they attempted to harness the power of Divinity and they just ended up leaving a mess on the floor. So for any pentacle-festooned black-clad 'magician' reading this with the keys of Solomon on the table beside them, be warned: piss around with this stuff and you will become a flurry of epithelial cells blowing gently in the wind...

The reason for working with this vision, and it is the only reason, is to change you deeply inside so that your body and soul touches base with the constant act of utterance/creation at the edge of existence. Creation was not a one-off Big Bang event: it is happening all the time. In the Inner Worlds there is no time, only action and reaction. The constant existence of the act of creation and destruction ensures that the world keeps turning, babies keep being born, and new species keep constantly flowing out of the Void. Because we are bound by substance and time, we view events and expressions of power as one-off happenings in a linear sequence in time. This is not the case. All lives are happening at once, all deaths are happening at once, the single act of creation is constantly happening, and you will always have credit card debt. Okay, back to work...

As usual, light a candle and sit quietly in a place where you will not be disturbed. Once you have become used to working with this power and are not easily distracted, then go out onto a hill and do this vision using the wind/air instead of a flame as an elemental gate. That would mean being aware of the wind and then joining with the wind in communion with that element.

34.1 Vision: the mediation of sound at the edge of the Abyss

With eyes closed, be aware of the candle flame before you and of the flame that burns deep within you. As you look at the candle flame you are drawn to the flame and find yourself stepping into the fire and bathing in its cleansing flame. The flames do not burn: they are the brightness of the spirit of Divine Being. The deeper you walk into the flame, the more regenerated you feel, and your inner flame grows in strength and vitality. You pass through the flame and find yourself deep in the Void, the place where there is no sound, no time, no movement. In stillness, your outer structure falls away and you find yourself drifting without form, flowing with the wind that blows in and out of this place as it carries power into manifestation. You are blown with the wind out of the Void and out into the Inner Desert. The wind swirls the sand and out of the swirling sand walk two angels of great height: their long hair, which trails behind them, swirls with the sand and their legs vanish deep into the earth.

One of them reaches out and grabs you by the hair. The moment they touch you, brightness throws sparks out of your skin and hair, like static. They pull you through the Inner Desert to the edge of the Abyss and make you stand, looking over the Abyss to the mists on the other side. The mists seem to be moving, like a very slow tornado, and a very deep, almost inaudible growl is coming from the moving mists. The hair on the back of your neck begins to stand up and your whole body screams with fear, but the angel holds onto you so that you cannot run. You are committed.

The mists seem to get deeper and thicker, with resonant rumbles and groans adding to the noise. The ground begins to shake, and rocks begin to fall into the Abyss. Beings who were sleeping deep in the sand begin to wake and emerge, and the sand itself begins to give off a very bright intense light. At this point the angel turns you around and puts a hand over your eyes. A massive archangelic being emerges out of the Abyss: a being of indescribable proportions that is so powerful his light is trapped deep within him, like a black hole. His frequency is a very high vibration of sound in opposition to the deep growl of Divine Being across the Abyss. The Archangel puts his head back and screams at a really high pitch, which hurts your head and makes the sand grains vibrate very fast. Different tones begin to sound, and when they lock together in a specific harmony, the power of Divine Being, the deep growl in the mists is pulled through the dark centre of the Archangel and is combined with the high-pitched scream.

This combination of frequencies is transformed in the body of the Archangel and becomes the Wind of Many Sounds. The Archangel leans forward and tries, ever so gently, to blow the Wind across the Inner Desert. The Angel of the Desert, who is standing behind you, shielding you and protecting you, filters the wind through their backs and blows a fragment of it through them and into the back of your neck. The Wind builds up within you like a great pressure. You feel as if your lungs are going to burst from the pressure, and your heart begins to race as it fights to cope with the power.

Just when you think you are going to black out, the angel pulls back your head by the hair and screams in your ear: "Recite! Recite the name of That which Cannot Be Named! Recite! Recite!" Your mouth works as you try to form words that your brain does not understand. Your mind struggles to convert the Wind/Name into something you recognize, but it cannot make sense of it. The angel tugs tighter on your hair and screams once more at you. Your body takes over, your mouth opens, and out comes a series of strange

34.1. Vision: the mediation of sound at the edge of the Abyss

sounds: they jumble and compete as the different frequencies try to escape.

What you cannot see, because you are shielded from the knowledge at a deep visual level, is the words blowing like little whirls in the sand, joining with the sand and taking form. They become animals, trees, birds, rocks, and people. Every living thing upon the Earth, within the Earth and above the Earth forms from the mediated sound of Power. Lines of existence, fate and manifestation emerge out of the sand like a giant skeleton, which the creations are drawn to and finally merge with. The two combined become the world that we know, with all the lives, deaths, and patterns of action embedded within them.

The last breath issues out from you and you collapse onto the sand, the angel still holding your hair. The Archangel vanishes back into the Abyss and the mists of Divine Being are still once more. You find that you cannot stand, you cannot speak and your lungs are on fire. The angel picks you up by the hair so that your eyes are level with his eyes. He looks into you and the look bores right through you, like a beam of light searching for something. The light hits parts of you that were damaged by the mediation and it fills those parts with light to allow them to heal. The angel then picks you up and strides off down the Inner Desert with you, taking you towards the threshold of your life, beyond your birth, through your childhood and up to present day. He walks and walks through every aspect of your life while he carries you, and although you are cradled, exhausted in the arms of the angel, you recognize points in your life where you subconsciously picked up on this angel striding through your life with your soul cradled in his arms, maybe in dreams, or daydreams, or just a weird feeling of being held and protected. You had a strange déjà vu sense that you were not alone and that you were protected at certain points in your life, and now you begin to remember those points in time and realize what it actually was that you were picking up on.

The angel arrives at the time where you are sat before the candle flame and he gently puts you down in your body as it sits before the flame. He rubs balm in your eyes. He pours oil down your throat. He blows gently into your lungs and he takes out plugs that he had put in your ears to protect you when you were not looking. The angel

34. THE POWER AND MAGIC OF UTTERANCE, SOUND AND SIGIL

blesses you with the blessing of life and death, and then vanishes into the flame.

You look at the flame for a while, remembering what happened and feeling your body and soul settle together again. When you are ready, you blow out the candle flame. As you blow, you feel a power on your breath and that power directs the flame into another world. You realize that you have been changed, and that your breath has the power of utterance and all the responsibility that goes with it.

★ ★ ★

34.2 Utterance in the temple

The next octave down the scale in that work is to mediate the Utterance in the temple. This again is a very old working that was a major part of temples of the Near and Middle East and laid the ground for religions that worked with language, sound and shape. As an aside, the most degenerate form of that expression is a religion of the book. By the time the 'Book' had taken hold, the power was already gone and the rot had set in.

This working method steps down the power of the Abyss work and forms it into a shell or Qelippah. This second octave, the first step down from the raw power expression of Divinity, is what the Kabbalistic Qliphoth really is (instead of a load of large-breasted demons in drag). This Qelippah is a form that allows the Divine Power of Utterance to express itself in the manifest world, and it creates a barrier between the magician and the true depth of the Divine Utterance. Because this second octave puts shape and face to the frequencies, it is inherently unbalanced, as any boundary or restriction on unformed power will compress it and contract it, therefore making a shape.

All the different octaves of this work are repetitions of the original act at the edge of the Abyss, but each octave is more formed, more detailed, more approachable, and therefore more corruptible. If a temple is working with this power, then the original act at the edge of the Abyss must be regularly done in the inner sanctum to ensure that the outer, more manifest Qelippah do not degenerate and

34.2. Utterance in the temple

contract too much. If the perpetual utterance at the Abyss ceases, the Qelippah becomes more and more contracted, which makes it more degenerate and therefore more dangerous. Both ends of the seesaw must always be in action: if one ceases to express power, so does the other one. If you have the outer manifestation without the balancing octave, the Qelippah becomes a true shell: an empty husk devoid of power which then is usually hijacked by inner parasites who move in, dress up in the shell, and tell hapless magicians that they are demons and have great powers. Those magicians who lack proper inner experience take the Qelippah at face value and a truly degenerate, parasitical and powerless relationship begins.

The second octave is the utterance of magical form into the temple. This level of utterance creates the interface for Divinity to manifest through a pattern which can be interacted with by humanity, which is basically what magic is: an interface between Divinity and Man. This magical interface can either be worked with in its genuine form, which is technique, or it can be moulded into a religious structure. In the magical form, the utterance creates vibration patterns that become vessels and bridges for power. The magician learns to work with the patterns and the beings that uphold those patterns, and through that interaction they learn to work with the inner powers of all the worlds to effect change.

If it is stepped down into a religious structure then it must be further contained, and gates are created, along with gatekeepers, to separate man from Divinity. The religious structure and its hierarchy then act as mediators between the people and Divinity: it simply becomes a more heavily filtered pathway. And the more filters a path has, the more chance there is for corruption and power grabbing. The filters are the Qliphoth which, if allowed to become empty husks, are filled once more with parasites who protect themselves and their food source by dogmas which are designed to keep the feeding station under control. It is easy to see how religions and magical paths start as amazing, wonderful, powerful paths, but under the bad management of humans quickly become degenerate, dogmatic, parasitical means of control.

Back to the second octave. The following vision is the technique for plugging into and working with the second octave in a magical temple setting. It can be used to establish a temple, strengthen a temple or to open the gates for a flood of new and fresh work. If you are working in a traditional lodge or temple organization, then this vision, if done fairly regularly in sequence to the first octave, will keep the lodge and its magicians healthy, and the work will trot along at a strong and clear pace. Doing each of the first two octaves twice a year if you are a lodge or order will be enough. For an individual adept I would recommend the first two octaves done once a year at key points in the year. These two lay the path, keep the door open and keep you, the vessel, clean and balanced for the Work.

34.3   The vision of utterance in the temple

With eyes closed, be aware of the candle flame before you and of the flame that burns deep within you. As you look at the candle flame you are drawn to the flame and find yourself stepping into the fire and bathing in its cleansing flame. The flames do not burn: they are the brightness of the spirit of Divine Being. The deeper you walk into the flame the more regenerated you feel and your inner flame grows in strength and vitality. You pass through the flame and find yourself deep in the Void, the place where there is no sound, no time, no movement. In stillness, your outer structure falls away and you find yourself drifting without form, flowing with the wind that blows in and out of this place as it carries power into manifestation. You are blown with the wind out of the Void and find yourself standing on a threshold between two worlds. Behind you is an immense swirling tornado that has eyes and wings, and before you is the temple in the outer world where you work.

You are standing upon a threshold, and the threshold is an angelic being who is the gatekeeper between the Paradise of balanced power and the outside manifest world of imperfection. You can feel the being move and flex beneath your feet, and you feel its power seeping through the soles of your feet, travelling up your spine. The feeling becomes more intense and you realize that the being is slowly climbing into your body to be a co-mediator with you. The being slowly inches its way up your spinal column and into your brain. It stretches out in your body and begins to merge with your nervous system. Your vision changes and you begin to see how this being sees and feel what it feels. Before you are lines of light and dark, the

34.3. The vision of utterance in the temple

air moves thickly like an intense swirling fog and the space seems to be constantly fragmenting and reforming. The space is devoid of sound and it feels like you are observing a vacuum.

You become aware of the tornado raging behind you and also aware that you can see all around you. The tornado has many eyes, many wings and is getting denser and denser with each second. Your attention to the tornado pulls it closer to you and a power begins to build up that leans against you, pushing at your back. You struggle to stand upright and the being within you grips the floor with what feels like talons gripping a perch. Your head and neck begin to arch down with your chin reaching for your chest, as if coiling a spring ready for action. Suddenly the angel snaps back your head and the tornado behind you flows through you at high speed.

As it hits your vocal cords, strange sounds come out of your mouth and form into shapes. The shapes settle themselves around the room and embed themselves into the walls and objects in the room. Lines of power come out and weave patterns of light and dark across the space of the room and the patterns connect up with the shapes. The wind stops, the angel suddenly withdraws back through your feet into the threshold and all is still. You stand for a moment, on the threshold between two worlds, your eyes seeing the room but the residue of angelic sight showing you the patterns and shapes of the power that was uttered.

Something pushes you forward and you fall into the room, the patterns vanishing. You stand before the central flame, feeling the fullness and profound stillness of the room. Everything has changed energetically, everything is alive, everything is charged ready for work.

Leaving the candle going, you open your eyes and sit for a moment drinking in the peace. When you are ready, leave the room, leaving the candle going, and let the space readjust to the magical patterns that have just been impressed into the fabric of the building. You will feel when it is time to put out the flame and have the sense of simply sending the flame into the Inner Worlds rather than putting it out as you blow.

★ ★ ★

This vision enlivens the room and embeds specific lines of power that are to do with the magic of utterance, language, alphabets and sigils. You would use this vision in your magical space/temple if you were about to embark upon a term of service that deals with anything from magical writing, to working with sigils to constructing ritual. It will ensure the full powers of recitation are with you and will also open the gates wide to the depths of that power. It can also produce impressive puffs of wind outside as you come out, which really looks good and always causes a stir...

The next stage down from that vision, the next octave, is to work with sigils and sacred writing. Essentially, it is the same working again, just at a different frequency, a different octave, and the power is stepped down once more. In our power-crazed world, the idea of stepping down power to work magically, as opposed to raising power, often causes a flurry of discontent among those who wish to impress. But if the power is too high, then it cannot fully manifest in the outer world. The more manifest something is, the less powerful it is: the density of physical manifestation limits the amount of power that can express through that density. When the power that is attempting to manifest is air/utterance, then its most exteriorized form is an alphabet or sigils.

The sigil form that expresses out of this power is not the type of sigils that are beings and powers within themselves, but is a lesser version, power-wise, that consists of marks, names and 'brands' that carry the power of intention or identification with them. This work would be done to either create a new magical alphabet, create individual sigils for specific jobs, or to invigorate one that already exists. When you are creating a new alphabet, you are reaching for that power of utterance and aiming it through a filter that forms the vibrations into sounds and then images. If you try to create a magical alphabet or sigils without the inner utterance, then the image of the letter has no power within itself and it becomes an empty shell that other 'vibrations' or sounds that are a part of parasitical consciousness can step in.

The vision that we will work with takes us to an ancient Underworld goddess from whom many magical scripts and alphabets have emerged. It is a step down from the power of Utterance at the edge of the Abyss, as this is a formed, specific goddess, and she has her own place (the Underworld) whereas Divine utterance at the edge of the Abyss is Divinity without form, the most powerful form we can get to without ceasing to be. This is the difference between Divinity and deity.

It is important to understand that such an alphabet does not give rise to a language that can be used in sacred communication: that is a totally different kettle of fish. This way of working allows you understanding of the sound of certain places and beings and gives you the key to lettering those sounds onto places and things to help connect up beings to places and events. The same goes with sigils: when they are created this way, they provide a key to a specific place, event or person and allow a connection to form and grow. The actual creation and mediation of this form of alphabet is done in vision, with some physical action of writing, but then after that, the utterance and letterings are used in ritual action and intent.

The next vision takes us to the creation of a sigil or string of sigils that are to be used for a specific purpose: it is the creation of working tools that then become a major part of the ritual structure within the temple. It works with and builds upon the previous vision, and once you have worked with all octaves of this form, you will find that they begin to intermingle as you work, and echoes of one will awaken the thresholds of the others. Once the sigils or letters have settled within you, they will begin to unlock and emerge as you work. This can be done as a seated vision or can be done standing at an altar.

For this work the altar must be in the east with nothing upon it but a candle flame. Anything on the altar could potentially act as a filter for the power as it is mediated, fragmenting or even blocking the sigils. Besides, working at this magical level you should have got past the whole New Age product display altar.

34.4 The vision for the creation of magical sigils

Light the candle flame in the east and stand with eyes closed. See the candle flame with your inner vision and see beyond the candle flame two gates that slowly swing open to reveal a pathway of columns that vanish into mist. See yourself stepping through the candle flame

34. THE POWER AND MAGIC OF UTTERANCE, SOUND AND SIGIL

and walking through the mist with the columns on either side of you. Some of the gaps between the columns have fire pedestals, which throw off a faint light, and others are in complete darkness. The effect is light, dark, light, dark, as you walk through the mist, and you find yourself becoming slightly disorientated.

As you walk and try to penetrate the mist to see what is up ahead, you hear a strange breathing, almost like panting, echoing out of the mist, and the volume of sound would suggest something very large and animal-like ahead of you. Treading carefully, the side fire pedestals vanish and you are plunged into a misty darkness with just the sound of panting to guide you. Suddenly, two priests holding up flaming torches appear before you and challenge you. One looks into your eyes and seems to delve deep into your soul, and the other demands to see the soles of your feet. When they are happy with what they have found, they turn and stand beside you and each puts a hand upon your shoulder. They walk you forward and as they walk you get the feeling that they are holding you not to support you but to stop you running away from something.

As you walk further into the mist and get closer to the panting noise, the hair on the back of your neck starts to stand up in alarm. All of your inner warning bells are ringing and your heart begins to beat faster and faster. The two priests throw you to the ground before what looks like a large boulder. The boulder moves. It is then you realize that the boulder is alive and is actually the tip of a big toe. You look up and see that you are at the feet of a gigantic being that is seated and all you can see are the legs up to the knees.

The giant being slowly lowers a hand for you to step onto which immediately raises you up into the clouds and brings you level with the eye of a great black being who is part human, part lioness. The scent of lions is all around you and she stares at you, unblinking as you stand like a speck of dust before her. She looks at you, and then looks into you as if checking that you are a suitable container. She asks you what you want and why you want it. You reply that you are a magician and wish to work with sigils within the temple as magical tools.

When she is sure of what she sees, she begins to whisper, her lips barely moving. As she whispers, she releases one of her claws and

34.4. The vision for the creation of magical sigils

cuts a line between your eyes, which immediately begins to bleed. The blood gets in your eyes, making it difficult to see, and the heat rising from the hand of this great Goddess is making you burn with its power. The cut begins to really sting and distract you, and just as you are about to put your hand to the cut, the whispering noise of the Goddess gets louder and louder. Her pitch changes from high to low and to areas of sound that you cannot hear. You brush the blood from your eyes so that you can see what it is she is doing.

Her lips move and out of them, formed by the sound, come shapes. The shapes travel towards you and push themselves into the cut in your forehead and drive themselves through your skull and into your brain. You can feel the shapes trying to find a place to nestle in your head. The pain is unbelievable. More and more shapes appear and push themselves into your head, and you feel your body begin to buckle under the pressure. She breathes the last shape, which pushes its way into your mouth rather than into the cut upon your brow. The she blows on you, hard. Her breath, which smells heavily of lions, blows at you like a hurricane and takes your breath away. She then stands up and begins to climb with you in her teeth until she reaches a cavern that is too small to take her, a cavern which also has a crack of light at the other end of it. She motions for you to go through that crack and then pushes you. You walk towards the crack and the light, and as you get to the opening in the rock a priest steps out to greet you. He looks at the blood on your forehead and is instantly aware of what has just happened to you. He takes your hand and guides you carefully over rocks and down tunnels until you emerge out of the side of one of the columns in the mist.

He walks with you and explains to you that you now hold a magical alphabet that is directly linked to her power, which is the power of death, medicine, war and healing: the powers of destruction and regeneration. The priest tells you that he will act as an inner contact with you so that you can learn to work with this alphabet properly. He shows you his right hand, which has a strange mark upon the palm. Remember that mark: it can be used to call him or to have his power work with you on a project. You will be instantly recognizable to any priest or priestess of this line by the mark upon your forehead, and all inner beings will recognize you as touched by Her.

You walk back towards the threshold of your world, leaving the mists and columns behind. Stepping over the threshold, you return to your seat and look at the flame with your inner vision. You reach out, take the flame in the palm of your hand and put it into yourself. Once the inner flame is safe within you, you blow out the outer flame. Immediately go and draw the sigil of the priest that was on his palm, and once you have done that, go and sleep: the knowledge and keys that have been placed within you need to settle and reemerge into your conscious mind.

★ ★ ★

The first thing to notice about that vision is that is it getting closer in its action and presentation to our world and the Underworld which upholds it. The second thing to notice is that the sigils or alphabet are not shown to you, but put within you to unravel in their own time. If they were put in the head, which is this goddess' favourite method of transfer, then you are likely to have blinding headaches for a while until the sigils settle and make their way out of you. If they were put into your mouth or you have to eat them, which is a delivery method favoured by angelic beings, then you will probably have the shits for weeks. Anything that has to do with angels and scripts, books, scrolls or sigils is usually processed by the body through the alimentary canal, and anything from Underworld Goddesses tends to be in the head. If you are working with the sheer power of Divine utterance, then it tends to pass through the lungs and the back of the neck, and those two areas usually take a hit.

I have yet to come across any script or sigil transfer by a male deity, so I have no idea how such a transfer would affect the body. It is pointless trying to theorize over what would happen, or even to theorize over why the body has such a reaction in general: it just is what it is, and your time is much better spent getting on with your work. When working with inner dynamics, things happen in the most bizarre ways for the most bizarre reasons. If you try to push for an intellectual dissection of what happened and why, then you will lose the ability to flow with the power. If you just let it be, the reasoning will emerge into your mind in its own time. Once that has happened, then you will be falling over texts that explain or describe the process in minute detail. Everything in the Inner Worlds has its own time.

So you are full of sigils and shapes. What next? Well, there is no magic button to press that will release them; they will come out in their own good time, usually when you come across something that one of the sigils is ready to connect to, or when the alphabet is needed to be put to work, and then it will all tumble out. This can be a quick or a slow process, and there is no way to tell which way it will go. If you can divorce yourself from your mind, then you may be able to automatic-write them, except then they will be out of context and you will not know what they mean. It is much better to wait and let them come out as they need to. Once it is all out and working, you will find it was worth the wait and the work. Usually the first one comes along pretty quickly and will initially emerge as a familiar sound that you connect to a being or place, swiftly followed by a sigil. You will then start to see the sigil everywhere you go... it is the Inner Worlds' way of saying, 'did ya get that?'

The rest will tumble out as and when. Just make sure that you write each sigil down with a note about what it is connected to. If you do not, you will remember the sound and what it is connected to, but you will not remember the sigil. This is an inner defence mechanism for the sacred sigil: it will not stay in people's heads independently.

34.5 Working with the sacred sigils and alphabet

Once you have mediated the script and it is completely manifest, what then?

Sigils and scripts that are mediated like this have a number of uses. Some work as calling cards or keys to unlock areas and open gateways. They also mark areas, in the Abyss for example, they can change the power of whatever they are linked to, and they can connect up people, places and objects. They can also act like an open phone line to a particular being or realm. So once the sigils/letters are within you, it is like you have a font folder within you and as beings/deities connect with you, they will see that you are storing sigils of utterance and they will show you which ones can be used to call them or connect with them.

If you are working with a being as a guardian, for example, then rather than having the being there all the time, which is not really necessary unless they are guarding an Inner Temple, they can leave behind their imprint, which is a sound. That sound is converted to the sigil within you and drawn out. The sigil is like a window to that being and if someone opens a box, comes into a room, picks up a magical tool etc., it will ring the doorbell and call the being: the sigil is like the eyes or ears of the being. So it would be marked where it was needed. To mediate the mark, you would first listen to the sound of the being in vision, and while in vision, with pen in hand, let the being guide your hand to draw the sigil. This takes practice, as you have to block your mind out from wanting to control the shape, but at the same time, the mind needs to be present to allow the being to mediate properly. Automatic writing is a step beyond this, as such a method is truly passive. The mediation of sigils has a wee bit more control and interaction than that.

If you practice this a few times with a being and a place or deity, when you hit the right one, you will begin to see it everywhere. Just don't allow the Goetia sigils to creep into your mind: often ancient magical sigils look nothing like them. Once you have had a couple of successes and you have got your confidence, then you will find it much easier. The other method of getting the sigils out from deep within you is to again tune into the sound of the being or place and hold that sound in your mind. Ask to be guided to the shape of that sound and you will begin to see a sigil everywhere you go, and it will be the only one you can draw. These are placed upon containers, upon Inner Temple doors and outer temple doors, or over the entrance of Abyss tunnels where you are working and want the beings to find you, or you to find them.

34.6 Sacred alphabet

Bringing through a proper sacred alphabet is a lifetime's work but a very fruitful project. To do this, you would have to work with the whirlwind in the depths of the Inner Temple and bring it out

34.6. Sacred alphabet

one sound at a time. The sound will manifest its own shape within your mind and the angelic contacts will again point it out to you so that you recognize it. One way to do it that will take less than a lifetime is to focus on producing eighteen sounds. Each time you work with the angelic threshold and the Whirlwind in the Depths (which is an archangelic being) a vibration and shape is put within you to carry out. Doing it one at a time is much easier upon the body and is less likely to kill you. It also gives you time to work in depth with each sound to find out what it does, what its power is, and how you work with it. Once all eighteen are out, then you can begin to work on stringing them together in a power weave to create interfaces for Divine Power to flow through. You will find that some work together well and others do not. You will also find that when you get certain sounds together in a pattern, things happen, doors open and power flows in. Certain harmonies will open certain worlds up and other harmonies will destroy. Certain harmonies will connect with certain star alignments and others will tune in with the movement of the planet. Some harmonies will have mathematical expressions that mirror events, and so on.

A word of warning. Do not get trapped in the dead end of attributes, tables, qualities, note expressions, and other such patterns. Don't burn the midnight oil trying to match things up: you will find all sorts of connections with the letters/sounds, but that is immaterial: what is more important is to work with them and actually do something. It is a common trap that many people fall into.

Lastly, the most externalized of all expressions of Utterance is poetry and song. Going into the Inner Worlds and standing before the wind that blows out of the east, allowing that wind to blow through you and then translating that wind through your emotions is a very powerful form of expression, and is the basis for speech in a contacted ritual. You basically plug yourself in during a vision and let that power flow through you as you then begin to write. What comes out is literally the voice of the gods.

At the beginning of this section, I mentioned that when you work in depth with the power of Utterance, it changes you at a deep level. It changes your voice, often literally, it changes the power that flows through your voice, and it empowers your words magically. Because of this, you must be very careful how you use your voice and be very

34. The Power and Magic of Utterance, Sound and Sigil

aware that your words hold power. A casual off-the-cuff wish can turn deadly as a directed chant. The wind flows through you and with you: choose wisely how you work with that wind.

Chapter Thirty-five

The magical dynamics of fate

The life events of every living being seemingly follow a pattern of fate that can, to an extent, be predicted. Going back in history we have many myths and stories about powers/women who were responsible for fate, for example the Moirae in Greece and the Norns in the North: immortals who weave the pattern of life and death for every man and woman. Some religions, for example the many religions of India, accept a passive role in the path of fate and do not attempt to challenge or change their current and potential life path. Is that valid? I don't think so.

There are many events that happen in a magician's life and many of these events will put you into a collision course with Fate. I use the name Fate to identify a power that that flows through the life of every living thing and is the junction point for the patterns of life events and death. I see Fate not as a deity but as a hive angelic pattern that interfaces and filters power as it manifests. There are certain realms and visions that you can use as a magician to gain a deeper understanding of this power and of how it is relevant to your work and the work of a group or lodge.

The first step in understanding a fraction of this dynamic, which is almost incomprehensible to us, is to gain the understanding that time does not exist everywhere: it is simply a part of us in our manifest state on a planet that turns. Once you step out of the body in a visionary aspect, there is no time. It is very important to gain that understanding, and to also grasp that time, once you step away and observe it, is all happening at once. It is not a linear event that goes from A to B. it is a complex pattern that just 'is' and it can be moved away from or moved into. Hence in vision you can go back and forward in time so long as you have detached yourself in vision from your body.

35. THE MAGICAL DYNAMICS OF FATE

When you cross the Abyss and stand looking back over it at the Inner Desert which is the foundation for the world, you will see all the events of life all happening at once: it is like a large, complex spider web with many weavers and powers shooting back and forth. The interweaving and interlocking combinations and crossings of paths is fascinating and almost beyond our comprehension. We cannot work with the whole picture, which is far too much for our brains to take in, but we can observe a tiny fraction of the process at work, which can help us understand the process better.

Fate is not like a storybook where it is all mapped out at the beginning and can never be changed. Upon birth the child has an array of paths leading from them that they can walk down. Each path has an echo of the others, and some hold more power than others. The actions and choices of the child decide which route they will take, and as the child becomes an adult their paths lessen as more and more choices are made. Sometimes a choice will open up a new set of paths, and each path will have an echo of the others...often very silly unimportant echoes, like having the same names, same places, etc.

The magician becomes involved when those paths are cut across by powerful magic designed to destroy, shut down, bind or kill a person. One could argue that such a crossing of paths is part of their fate, which it very well could be. But if a person's fate has been cursed to the death, then I see no problem in stepping in and removing the magical curse or binding. They will never be able to go back to their original fate path, but they can pick up the threads and open up new possibilities.

The other instance where a magician and the work of fate crosses paths is in the event of a magician being consecrated (not initiation, which is different). This immediately wipes a large chunk of their path and creates a new one. Not everything is wiped, but a lot is overlaid by the communal fate of the consecrated line. Often one spends a large portion of one's life after consecration cleaning up paths and unbinding them. Most lines of priesthood and magic have a lot of degeneracy: curses and bindings within the line that need dealing with. You do what is put in front of you to clean things up. Don't bother getting the idea that you can filter the whole line: you will be given a fraction to deal with and that will be plenty.

So back to the machinations of fate. Let's look at the process from the inside out. Fate begins with the fate of the planet and that is echoed through the fate of every living being. The octaves are interwoven and are virtually impossible to separate out. Starting with the deepest and most powerful expression of fate, we have to go up into the stars. Fate is filtered by the archangelic beings that are the interfaces of the stars and planets. The call for a new life comes from an act of lovemaking and the echoes of the ancestral blood that lies deep in the earth repeat this call: it is amplified by the call of the bloodline to ensure the call reaches as far into the stars as possible. This is an octave of the action of conception that reaches up the Abyss in search of a being for manifestation through a bloodline.

When the call goes up, it sets off a harmony between the angelic beings and the ancestral echoes: they weave with sound to create an interface that a soul can manifest through. Once that weave is complete, a soul is called out of the Void and falls through the interface into manifestation. The following vision looks at this process in more depth and gives the observer an idea of the deepest octave of this work, which in turn will give a worker a better understanding of the more superficial presentations of bridging life.

It will allow you to observe the inner dynamics of the coming together of the fates: just don't be tempted to interfere. This is not a created or psychologized vision: the minute you attempt to interfere, you will be pulled into the soul's orbit and you will have a hell of a job getting out of it. There are fragments of this vision scattered among a variety of ancient texts, including the Old Testament, and once you have worked with this aspect of visionary magic you will begin to notice it in many different ancient and religious texts. Like everything else, the Mysteries hide themselves until you are able to recognize them. It is not a very practical vision in that it is simply used for observations, but once you have worked with it and experienced it, when you come to work within a temple structure around the issue of fate, it will give you are a far wider perspective on how the ritual practices work and why. I do think it is important, wherever possible, to have a full inner understanding of the processes of magic and how the work originally forms itself.

35. THE MAGICAL DYNAMICS OF FATE

35.1 Vision of the conception of a soul out in the stars

Light a candle and look into the candle flame for a moment. When you are still, close your eyes and see the candle flame with your inner vision. As you look at the candle flame, it grows bigger and bigger until it takes up all the space before you. When you can see nothing but candle flame, step into the flame in your inner vision and bathe in its power. The flames do not burn you, they cleanse and energize you ready for the work that is about to happen.

As you stand in the flames, you see through them to a beautiful nothing: a space of peace and stillness. You are drawn to this place and you step out of the flame and into the Void: a place with no time, no space and no movement. You feel like you have come home: this is the place where all power comes from and all power goes to: all existence issues forth from this place, and you feel the potential all around you, yet there is nothing here. You spread out in the nothing, aware that you have no boundaries, no restrictions, no lives, no anything: you just 'are' in this place, you are complete. The stiller you get, the more complete you feel, and the less bound by time, shape or manifestation. You move around in the nothing and you become aware that the nothing is in everything that exists, and therefore because you are within the nothing, you are within all things. You feel as you pass through trees, creatures, stones, buildings and you feel as you swirl around time, as though you are turning in water.

As you drift in the nothing, a call echoes through the Void and you drift towards the sound. You find yourself pulled out of the nothing and out in the stars, surrounded by space, power and planets. Each of the stars and planets seems to be breathing and calling, like a choir coming together. Within each star you see the eyes, movement and consciousness of beings coming together. As you watch the stars and planets slowly parade in their orbits and listen to their songs, you become aware of a deeper, more 'earthy' sound, like a deep horn coming from the depths of the planet. As you shift your focus, you become aware of a cacophony of sounds issuing out from the Underworld: the voice of the ancient ancestors. Those whose blood lies in the land call out to the stars to grant them a new generation

35.1. Vision of the conception of a soul out in the stars

in the line of ancestors, and the deep echoes of time mix with the song of the stars to create a whole intricate pattern of sound.

A funnel of wind, a bit like a tornado, appears in the space between the earth and the stars, and it reaches down to the earth and up into the stars. The wind sucks in the sounds and turns the sounds, creating a vortex. The sound and movement draw you in to look closer. Its beauty fascinates you, and the sounds that come together are the most beautiful thing you have ever heard. It touches some deep and ancient memory within you, and the emotion that spills out from you overwhelms you and you begin to weep. Your tears gravitate to the funnel and mix with other echoes of emotions that are woven into the wind. You draw closer still, feeling the power of the funnel and the sounds, a deep instinct within you drawing you ever closer. A hand grasps you from the back and stops you tipping into the funnel, holding you back so that you can observe without being sucked in.

At that moment a bright light flows past you and into the funnel. It drops at high speed to the earth, like a shooting star, vanishing into the clouds of the planet. A soul has just passed you on its journey into life, and if you were stood at the edge of the Abyss, it would have fallen past you on its way into manifestation.

The shooting star left a trail of threads behind it, some linked to the stars and some floating around as if looking for a place to take root. Out of the darkness between the planets, beings that can be barely seen, almost like shadows, pick up the threads and begin weaving. They connect the stars to the earth, and link in the trailing threads to create a beautiful complex pattern. Their fingers work and weave in total focus, and as sections seem to be completed, the weave lights up with a bright glow and harmonic sounds like vibrating strings fill the space all around you. One of the shadow beings offers you a thread to hold, just for a second, so that you can experience the feel of the weave. The minute the thread hits your hands, a terrible weight descends upon you and everything suddenly seems heavy and dark and complicated. You feel a rush of conflicting emotions, images rush past your vision as if you were watching life sequences, but the thing that hits you the most is the sense of darkness and density: you are feeling the full weight of manifestation while you are not within your own body: the reality of the struggle of life hits you full on.

35. The Magical Dynamics of Fate

Something pushes you forward and you find yourself stepping forward into the Void once more. The stillness and silence rush into greet you and once more you are drifting in a place of no time, no space, and no movement. You stay a while, allowing what you have just experienced to unfold itself within you, and here, in this stillness, you remember something hidden deep in the depths of your memory: the feeling of the wind, the sounds of the ancestral call, and songs of the stars. You have experienced this before and your body recognizes it. With that realization, you step forward out of the Void, back into the room where you first started. You sit before the candle flame and focus upon the light of life within the flame. Reaching out, you cup the light in your hand and place it within the flame that burns deep within you. You feel its peace. You feel the Divine presence within the flame. You open your eyes and when you are ready, blow out the candle flame.

★ ★ ★

That vision is the deepest expression of fate that you can experience as a human, and once it is within your experience, when you come to work with the outer more manifest patterns of fate, the experience of the deepest form keeps the more surface work in perspective. It also reminds you of the sacredness of the pattern of fate. Understanding the deep inner movement of power that manifests as paths of fate helps you to understand that the surface details of an individual's life fate pattern are not about events but about harmonics: the life path is like a song that guides you back to the stars.

35.2 Chess and the Inner Temple

The two main temples I have come across that seem to be heavily involved in fate patterns are temples that I call the Sea Temple and the Fire Temple. Both are templates that underpin many ancient religious temple structures, and both can be worked with in depth. The Sea Temple is basically an inner construct of a magical structure that operates from the deep consciousness of the sea and mediates the tides of life, genetics and the weather. Most ancient temples that are connected to the oceans or seas, to Neptune, Oceanus and Tethys or Nammu, etc. are more formed expressions of the Sea Temple, and you can reach the more skeletal generic power of the Sea Temple by going through the more formed versions with a specific intent to go deeper. Every elemental deep temple has outer, more formed expressions that can be used as access points.

The Fire Temple is the same: it is an inner structure that acts as a template for outer manifest temples around the world that deal with deities of fire and volcanoes. Such temples have manifested around the world and some are still functioning. Again, the deep echoes of magic flow from the archetypal temple out into the world through various religious and magical structures.

Fate is a theme common to both temples, and whereas the Sea Temple is concerned with genetics, i.e. bloodlines and species, the Fire Temple is more focused upon souls and bringing through specific beings and people. If you put the two together you have a massive inrush of power that was used in ancient times to bring through priest-kings and priesthood queens.

To view this process up close, we will visit a Fire Temple to observe the manifestation of fate lines through the temple and how that temple dealt with it. The following vision will be recognized by those who have studied certain ancient mythologies and classical myths. The vision is not taken from those myths, however; rather the myths echo what is to be found in the Inner Mysteries of that temple, and what you will observe is one of the Mysteries in action.

35.3 The board game

Light a candle and look into the candle flame for a moment. When you are still, close your eyes and see the candle flame with your inner vision. As you look at the candle flame, it grows bigger and bigger until it takes up all the space before you. When you can see nothing but candle flame, step into the flame in your inner vision and bathe in its power. The flames do not burn you, they cleanse and energize you ready for the work that is about to happen.

As you stand in the flames, you see through them to a beautiful nothing: a space of peace and stillness. You are drawn to this place

35. THE MAGICAL DYNAMICS OF FATE

and you step out of the flame and into the Void: a place with no time, no space, no movement. You feel like you have come home: this is the place where all power comes from and all power goes to: all existence issues forth from this place, and you feel the potential all around you; yet there is nothing there. You spread out in the nothing, aware that you have no boundaries, no restrictions, no lives, no anything: you just 'are' in this place, you are complete. The stiller you get, the more complete you feel and the less bound by time, shape or manifestation. You move around in the nothing and you become aware that the nothing is in everything that exists, and therefore because you are within the nothing, you are within all things.

You remember your task to seek out the Fire Temple and with that intention you step out of the Void and find yourself in the Inner Desert. You appear in the middle of the Inner Desert, with the River of Death in the distance to your left and the Abyss in the distance to your right. You set off walking towards the Abyss and as you get closer to the Abyss, a wind whips up the sand and blows you into the far right of the Inner Desert, near the temples at the edge of the Abyss. You are blown to the steps of one Inner Temple, to a large white step pyramid with a box structure upon the top which is decorated with gold. You begin your ascent up some steps that lead up the centre of the pyramid and enter the structure halfway up. You wander through tunnels that meander around and intersect other tunnels. The walls are decorated with complex story images, all of them decorated with gold and precious stones. Eventually the tunnel opens out into an inner sanctum which is a large white circular room with a gap in the roof through which shines a beam of sunlight. On the floor is a mosaic of a man with the face of the sun and the beam of sunshine is illuminating it. In the centre of the room is a cube block of white stone with an oil flame burning upon it. The floor is also decorated with lions, faces and lots of intricate gold patterns and you can see that the beam of light tracks an arc around the altar in the centre. Around the edges of the room are elaborate chairs decorated in gold, and each one has a sigil upon it.

You hear voices in the distance and you walk across the room to the doorway on the other side and peer through. The temple seems to open out beyond this sanctum and you realize that you entered the temple via the inner back door that leads to the Inner Desert of

35.3. The board game

the Tree of Life. Beyond you, through the door, is a vast hallway with columns that reach high up above you. In between the columns are vast statues of deities with altars before them and plumes of incense. Many priests in white robes and with shaven heads are milling around and talking. One of the older ones spots you and gestures for you to come near them. It is only at that point that you realize there is a being behind you and the priest recognized the being before they spotted you. You walk over to the priest and all the other priests stop and stare.

The priest gestures for you to follow him into an antechamber and he leads you into a room that partly opens out into a library. The being stands behind you and the man gestures for you to sit. He asks you what you are wanting from the temple and you explain to him that you wish to learn about the fate patterns that are worked with in the temple. You tell him that you have been out in the stars and have watched souls fall into generation, and now you wish to learn about how those patterns of fate play out magically. The man nods and begins to tell you about the function of his temple. He says that one of the functions is to ensure that the land has a sacred god-king who will ensure the balance of the land, that the elements are kind to the humans and that the land and rivers are fertile. He begins to tell you about a time before the temple, when the land would heave with earthquakes, storms would devastate the crops, drought would kill their animals and that some storms would bring terrible illnesses with them that would kill many of the children. They learned to work with different beings and deities to subdue them, but subduing one often mean angering another. Over the many years and generations, they learned to bring the powers together properly, and one man would mediate the power of God to the land, so that his job would be to be the fulcrum of all powers upon the land. To find such a child would be impossible, so they learned to call a soul of power into the world and then structure fate to ensure that the child survived into adulthood and beyond.

The priest gestures for you to follow him, and he gets up and takes you back into the great hall. You cross the full length of the hall and come to a great bronze door. The being that is with you, an angelic being, turns you around to show you the inner power structure of the hall. The being places a hand upon your eyes for you to look

35. THE MAGICAL DYNAMICS OF FATE

through and you see the complexity of power lines spilling out from the inner sanctum which are being woven by the priests into the various deities that are seated between the columns. He then turns you again to the great bronze doors before you and shows you how the power leaves the great hall, adjusted by the deities, and flows out into the world. You step through the great bronze doors and down some white stone steps into a courtyard full of trees and blossoms. Here there are women as well as men, also dressed in white, but they seem to have a much lesser role than the men and are not allowed into the temple proper. This gives you warning that something about the temple structure here is imbalanced: the women have lesser roles as opposed to just different ones of equal respect and power.

They are all gathered around a giant board game that is laid out in the courtyard. The pieces are a collection of very large, strange-looking beings, with the odd one that looks human. The board is completely surrounded by people watching, and there are four players. As you watch the game, you see that it is not a game of war or strategy like chess, but a game of complex interweaves that must be constantly balanced and an equilibrium maintained. The player's job is to ensure that each move stays balanced while achieving its goal. The more successful a player is, the more they play. If they are unsuccessful, they have to leave and another player takes over.

The priest talks to a man who seems to be overseeing the players, and they both look at you. One of them gestures for you to step up to the board. The angelic being that has been shadowing you steps up with you and places both hands upon you to assist you. Together you step to the edge of the board. The overseer tells you to place both feet over the threshold of the board and then stop there until told to move. The moment your feet cross the line, the board vanishes and you are in a strange world of misty images, lines of bright and dark power, spinning cubes, and many complex multidimensional patterns that are constantly changing and reconnecting. The shock of the change makes you waver, and the angel holds tight to your shoulders to steady you. The angel does something to the back of your head and then pokes you in the eye, which really hurts—but when you take your hand away from your watering eye, you realize you can now see the board with one eye and the strange patterns with the other. You are given a short time to adjust as you watch the players moving pieces with one eye and see the resulting changes to the patterns with the other.

You are then invited to step onto the board and choose a piece to work with. You are immediately drawn to a particular piece, and you are told to put your hands upon the piece. The moment your hands touch the piece, you see a whole weave of life patterns parade before you. You see them as they look in different lives, and what they did. You are told to feel the piece and to see if the piece needs to be active or be moved or left alone. At first you are not sure how to tell, but the angel leans upon you, giving you access to his perception. The board beneath your feet tells you by a sense of touch if a piece is in the right place or not. You can feel that the piece you are holding is in the wrong place, and you begin to move it instinctively to where you feel it belongs. Your right eye watches as all the patterns change. Shapes vanish and new ones appear, some lines are broken, others are connected, and then suddenly there is a sharp movement and the whole pattern clicks into a new stability. At the moment of the click a bright light shoots past your vision and vanishes into the darkness beyond. You realize that whatever it was that you just did, someone somewhere died as a result. You are horrified, but the angel steadies you, pointing out to you that you worked unconditionally: you did what was needed to be done to restore balance, and you did not move the piece with the full knowledge and therefore human decision. You mediated a fate action that changed a lot of things to restore a balance to a land somewhere in time.

The angel places a hand upon each of your shoulders and grasps you hard. You are immediately spun around at high speed until the breath is sucked from your lungs, and you find yourself fighting for breath. You begin to feel a strong stinging on your face and your hand reaches up to feel sand hitting your face at high speed. The wind slowly dies enough for you to grasp a breath, and you open your eyes to find yourself standing on the edge of the Abyss which is behind you, and the Inner Desert which is before you. The angel lets go of your shoulder and places a hand over your eyes so that you can see with the sight of angels. Before you is an immense construct of shapes and patterns with threads leading off in all directions. The angel begins to walk you down the Inner Desert, passing through

35. THE MAGICAL DYNAMICS OF FATE

the construct. As you pass through each shape, you feel the potential within it for a life event or a crossing of paths.

You are walked slowly down the Inner Desert until you come to a threshold you had never noticed before. As soon as your feet touch the threshold, you once again see in different ways through each eye. In one eye you see the patterns morphing and changing, every one renewing themselves in a dance of fate. In the other eye you see the world, a place, a person with their life intersecting with other people and events. You watch as the movement of the chess piece you instigated on the board begins to play out and change the life path of the person and all the events that it triggers. You see the old life path they were walking crumble and dissipate and a new path open up for them. Beyond the person, you see how the change in fate changed the whole world around them and restore a balance to a land, a community and a family line.

Once the angel is sure that you have seen all that you need to see, he turns you around and walks you back to the edge of the Abyss, where a large angel is waiting for you. The angel you stand before gives you a scroll of knowledge for you to absorb, which will unravel throughout your life to slowly expose you to the ancient Mysteries of fate and life patterns. You take the scroll, unsure what to do with it. The angel tells you to eat it, which you do. The scroll nestles itself in your body and will unfold in your mind over time as the information hidden within it is needed. The angel then grabs you hard by the arm and throws you over the edge of the Abyss. You begin to fall and a sense of utter terror rises within you as you realize you are potentially going to die. You fall down the Abyss, but the speed of your fall is slowed, enabling you to see all the tunnels and areas of the Abyss where the ancient beings of the distant past of our world are slumbering.

In their faces you see echoes of humanity, fragments that have survived time and emerged in the various species alive in your world today. You fall is slowed even more and you become aware of a funnel of wind forming in the Abyss and stretching high up past you and beyond the Inner Desert where you were standing. It reaches far up into the mists into the distant future where the angelic patterns of fate are woven. You are caught in the funnel of wind and you become aware of a soul in the funnel with you, a bright, beautiful power of life

35.3. The board game

that is half slumbering on its journey into a new life. You instinctively wrap yourself around the soul to protect it, and as you draw closer to the soul you become deeply aware of the beauty and stillness of the soul that you are protecting.

You watch as angelic beings that are the funnel watch over you both while also pulling on ancient bloodlines deep within the Abyss, triggering them out of hibernation and pulling in fragments of their development and evolution ready for the bloodlines that will be within the being as it manifests into life. A bright light shines up from below you: you slow even more and find that the funnel is coming to a completion at a threshold that was the same one in the Inner Desert where you stood. You are confused, as you have fallen a great depth into the Abyss and yet you are ending up presumably where you first started. The angels around you nudge you, which awakens the scroll within you, and you become aware that the soul will manifest in the Inner Desert of Humanity where you were working, but back in a time long before your humanity existed. Falling into the depths has taken you back into the distant past, into a world that will eventually lead to the present that you were witnessing being formed in the Inner Desert.

The brightness below you suddenly gets a lot brighter and you begin to hear a cacophony of sound, like a choir of voices that guide the funnel towards the bright light and awaken the soul that is nestled in your arms. The soul moves, like a sleepy child, and you are loath to let the child go, but the pull of the light gets too strong for you to cope with and you release the soul, watching it fall into the bright light and vanish. The funnel suddenly makes a loud whooshing sound as it vanishes, and you fall into a room where two people are making love. Angelic beings stand around ensuring the safe passage of the soul into the body of the woman, and you watch as her soul adjusts to accommodate the new soul in a complex yet gentle dance of energy.

The beings all around you and the couple watch impassively to ensure that the soul is properly placed within the woman, and you watch the light of the soul and the light of the woman's soul blend into a profusion of colour and sound. The angel touches you upon the shoulder and asks you to act in the role of sacred priest/ess and bless the soul of both the mother and child. You walk towards the woman and place a hand upon her head. Time, fate and the sounds

35. THE MAGICAL DYNAMICS OF FATE

of the frequency of the child's future flow through your hand into the woman, and you call upon the blessings of Divine Power to descend to them both, and for the strength of the Underworld to ascend to them. A mark appears upon her forehead and your work is done. Both their sacred paths are sealed, and nothing shall interfere with the future path of these two heavily interwoven souls.

The angel turns you around and around, turning you through the worlds and through time. You spin in a flow of life and death, of manifestation and completion, your own sound calling out through all the worlds. You spin into the Void, spinning in silence, coming slowly to stillness in the deep nothing. In that moment of stillness, you are aware of all the lives you have passed through as your soul manifests again and again throughout time, answering the call to life as you journey through yourself. The knowledge of that journey stays with you as you step instinctively from the Void and back into the life where you are sitting now before a candle flame. You watch the candle flame with your inner vision, seeing the power of Divine Being shine out of that light—you reach forward, gently lifting that sacred flame and placing it, once more, deep within you.

The flame fills you with peace and stillness, the Divine Power filling you with life as you open your eyes and consider the physical flame. You blow the flame out, sending it back into the Void, sitting for a moment to remember the long and difficult service and learning you have just been exposed to.

★ ★ ★

From that long and detailed vision, you will draw understanding of the act of fate, the falling into life of souls, and the sacred act of union that stretches up the Abyss in search of a soul to bring into life. This sacred act of union was used to bring the sacred kings and priestess-queens into life, to ensure the land always had a manifestation of Divinity within substance among the people.

The patterns that are woven at the edge of the Abyss are complex ones of power, intent, and interface. The shapes and threads are essentially angelic beings placed together in an ever-shifting pattern that filters the power of Divinity into the world, and from which life potential, with all its inherent possibilities, can flow. It's a bit like the

35.3. The board game

concept of stem cells: there is potential for many areas of growth and renewal. The pattern is often woven either by other angelic beings, or by deities. Often when you get a powerful god or goddess that is also associated with weaving, it is not talking about weaving baskets—that is a common modern interpretation that is just plain wrong—it is the weaving of existence. The deity pulls the threads of angelic consciousness together and the weave will decide how the power will manifest: will it be a human or a tree? Divine Power utters out of the Void, passes through the weave of angelic consciousness that is woven by a deity, and becomes manifest. How that manifestation will interact both with Divine Power and everything else around it is where the fate pattern comes in. Fate does not decide who we are: it provides materials for us to build with.

Fate can deal you many bad or good cards: it is how you use each card that truly decides your fate. In magic, for adepts, the deeper into the Inner Worlds you go, the heavier and stronger the impact of fate becomes, for a variety of reasons. The more you can process and carry, the heavier your burden will be. The more you call through the worlds for wisdom, the more obstacles and challenges you will be woven. Wisdom comes from struggle and bitter experience, not from love and hugs. If you become a consecrated priest, then more fate lines are woven into your 'cloth' to enable you to be in the places you need to be in to achieve your role as priest. The higher the power levels you become able to access, the more dangerous your fate becomes: this ensures the swift severing of the life threads should a priest abuse the power of Divine Being. A good mythical picture of this is the sword of Damocles. The Roman politician and philosopher Cicero tells the famous story about the Syracusan tyrant Dionysius II and his courtier Damocles, a story which Cicero had read in the *History* of Timaeus of Tauromenium. The story was originally a peek at the Mystery of the Fate of Kings, but it eventually degenerated down to a moral story.

> Pandering to his king, Damocles exclaimed that, as a great man of power and authority surrounded by magnificence, Dionysius was truly fortunate. Realizing the stupidity of this courtier, Dionysius offered to switch places with him, so he could taste first hand that fortune.

35. The Magical Dynamics of Fate

> Damocles could think of no other place he would rather be and accepted the King's proposal. Damocles sat down in the king's throne surrounded by every luxury, but Dionysius arranged that a huge sword should hang above the throne, held at the pommel only by a single hair of a horse's tail. Damocles finally begged the king that he be allowed to leave, as he no longer wanted to be so fortunate.

In the story that is told today, the king himself had the sword hung above the head of Damocles. In the Mysteries of Fate, the sword does indeed hang over the heads of those at the height of power, both in kingship and priesthood, but the sword is there by the grace of the deity of Justice: the swift sword of justice hangs by a thin thread, just as the scales are balanced by a feather. The more power you are given access to, the greater the destruction if you consciously fail or become corrupt. The powers of Fate and Justice are two of the same threads of power expression: they ensure balance and harmony.

When you become a magical teacher, or magical adept, or hierophant/magus/whatever, you take on a greater burden of responsibility. The willingness to be of service at a high level brings with it great power but also great responsibility. The more power you wield, and the more you have access to, the thinner the thread that holds the sword. Should you knowingly do something that upsets the inner order/pattern, or hurts a being out of sheer malice, greed or corruption, or manipulates fate for your own selfish means, then the sword will come crashing down upon you. It is a fail-safe device that protects the integrity of Divine Power within Humanity, and its falling is not a punishment, it is a severing of the umbilicus that connects you to the power source to stop you having access to unnecessary destruction. You become powerless, which is itself a terrible blow.

When working with this power it is very important to understand that morality and our human sense of right and wrong have nothing to do with the powers of fate and justice. Things that we may consider evil flow into the world to create change, to bring about massive destruction: genocide, war and oppression. Power is constantly flowing in many directions and we have to step back to observe the effect that the power has upon us. Sometimes such destruction is needed; sometimes it is not. Sometimes struggling against some injustice brings about a major change in the consciousness of the people, which could not have happened any other way.

As a magician, when such destruction and oppression is happening purely out of human imbalance, then you cannot act magically to change it. You can, however, act magically to bring it to a conclusion, it is just that you cannot mould that conclusion. You give power to the situation to do whatever it needs to do to bring about an unconditional conclusion: you cannot dictate the outcome. If you work that way, then you can lessen the suffering in that you shorten the time span of the process without interfering in the end product. Even if you do not like the end product, you must not interfere, as fate often has long arms that stretch way into the future, way beyond your ability to see the whole pattern.

If, however, magic is being used to manipulate a large pattern or event—World War II is a good example of this—then all bets are off regarding the path of fate: you can do whatever needs to be done. During World War II both the Germans and the British were using magic to influence the outcome of the war. Hitler's use of drugs (amphetamines), combined with his very fateful soul which was walking a mental tightrope, ensured that when the magical doors were opened, a whole stream of powerful parasites and then demonic beings flowed into feed off of the situation. It was magic that tipped the situation over the cliff, so magic could be used to put the brakes on.

If a fate is very strong, then there is really very little that can be done to alter it, and it probably should not be interfered with anyhow. You will find, when looking at a strong and important fate pattern in a person, that if you block one route, then another will open with similar details within the pattern. The details are always silly inconsequential ones, but act as beacons for the powers of fate to flow through.

35.4 Summary

Really, at the end of the day, we know so little that it is best to not try and interfere, but just restore balance where some other idiot has tried to interfere. The magic of fate is a complex and powerful area of magic, and the best learning can be gained from going into the inner patterns and simply observing. So much more makes sense once you have experienced the powers that flow through the pattern, and to observe the making of a pattern of fate is one of the most beautiful and awe-inspiring experiences I think a human can have.

And when you are faced with the pattern of your own fate and it is one that you do not like, then tough shit basically. You will know you are growing in your magical maturity when you stop trying to alter your fate in a major way and start working with it to achieve whatever it is you need to achieve. Every path has something to teach us, something that will make us stronger and wiser. To try and foreshorten that, or dodge all bad things, is complete folly and will actually take away the gifts that are given when you walk a rocky path. You can, however, look to see where your mistakes or bad decisions may appear, and head them off by learning the lesson consciously. Or at times, when prompted, you can step to one side of a disaster when it is not necessary for you to go through it. The trick is to understand the complexity of cause and effect, and to know what to sidestep and what to take on the chin.

The harder you put your shoulder to the boulder of fate to push, the greater the rewards that eventually trickle down to you when the time is right. Of all the many disasters that have happened in my life, looking back, I would not change a second of them. Everything, and I mean everything, down to the smallest detail, taught me something, gave me strength, learning, smacks around the head when I needed them, and opened future paths to wonderful things. To see all of that dynamic in action from an inner point of view, to me, is the highlight of a magician's career.

Chapter Thirty-six

How to work with angels

The other two Magical Knowledge books both have chapters regarding the nature of angelic beings and some of their functions, so we will not need to cover that ground again here. Instead, I would like to take the time to look at the various forms of angels that magicians come into contact with through the course of a lifetime, how they came to those forms and how to address those forms. Then we will look at working methods for working with angelic beings and within angelic structures.

This will give us a deeper understanding of how some magical and religious structures hang together and why. To work at an adept level with angelic beings, you really need to know what it is you are working with, why you are working with them and what will be the likely outcome. To blindly walk into the circle of work with angels without those basic foundational understandings will limit the power and breadth of the magical work, and if it is a religious structure, will severely limit the religion's ability to connect with Divine Being.

I have chosen the three most likely forms of angelic beings that a magician will encounter and we will look at them in turn. The bound angels are angelic beings that have, over time, been bound into service by priest-magicians to serve the agenda of the religion and the priesthood. The most common occurrence of this began back around 1500 B.C. and by 500 B.C. it was a commonplace practice within certain ancient priesthoods. I am talking about the areas that we would call the Near East, the various Mediterranean cultures and as far east as northwest India. I cannot comment on the rest of the world as I have had no direct working experience with bound angels from other cultures, but I have no reason to think that it was not happening elsewhere.

36. How to work with angels

36.1 Bound angels

A bound angel has had its function 'tightened' and focused, and it is not free to act naturally. The bindings force the angel to fulfil its function to the whims and agenda of the priesthood that has bound it. This was very successfully done in ancient times and the method of working with such beings was handed down the generations. By the 11th century onward, the fact that these beings were actually in bondage had been forgotten and the names, working methods and functions of the angelic beings had become a 'truth': the early Kabbalists for example had no idea they were working with beings that had been bound and moulded to work with them. Because of this, it encouraged the development of a form of magical interaction that was inherently abusive and relied heavily on a form of inner slavery. This is very evident in the Keys of Solomon and the whole Solomonic stream of magic.

So how were these angels bound in the first place? The key to this answer is in the Torah and the Pentateuch: man is an octave or echo of Divinity and has the power of utterance to create and destroy. Angels are functional beings who have individual purposes and are answerable to God and Man. To adapt such a being is fairly easy if you know how: these beings only exist to serve, have no emotional structure and have access to vast reserves of power. If a human utters a command using the utterance of God, and uses words that bind and direct, then it will change the structure of the angelic being without a struggle: we are echoes of Divinity and Divinity commands the angels. The interesting aside of all this is that Man is within Divinity and Divinity is within Man, and there are also cases where Man has become angelic, which we will go into later.

The angelic being is bound using sacred language and then is directed by command. The angel can only do whatever it is that is its natural function. So for example, an angel of death can only take life, it cannot give life or provide substance, change the weather, etc. The binding will give the magician the power to use that angel of death as a weapon against nations and individuals. In nature, the angelic beings that work in death act as doorways for people and creatures as is dictated by the flow and pattern of fate. They cannot be stopped or directed in any way: they are like a wind that sweeps the land

36.1. Bound angels

clean. But once bound, they often cannot answer that call of fate and instead are only able to function at the direction of their master or the priestly line which holds the control. I have however come across some bound angels who seem to at least partially function in their natural capacity but are still bound when called upon.

The bound angels present themselves as images of function, have names, hierarchies and a very distinctive appearance. These are the angels that have been bound for so long that people have forgot the fact that they are bound and assume that the appearance and name is the actual angel, which is incorrect. Purely naturally occurring angelic beings have no name, only a signature sound, and do not tend to have any form of humanlike appearance. If an angel appears before you in a human-type form it is one of three things: either it is bound, or it is dressing up so that you can interact with it, or it is an angelic being that has a fragment of humanity within it. The way to tell if it is bound or not is to simply ask it: if it cannot change its appearance, then chances are it is bound.

If you get the urge to unbind it, first find out what it does in its natural form. Some angelic beings were bound up to prevent them from massacring whole populations or wiping out species. It's a difficult dilemma really, because such angelic beings are basically fulfilling the natural balance of the planet and keeping everything healthy. If something overgrows, then it is weeded back. But if you are one of those weeds, then there is a self-interest in survival which may prevent you from wanting to unbind it.

Then there is the issue of naturally bound angels which are angelic beings that are bound and held in the Inner Desert to prevent them working until the time is right. Then when it is time for them to do their job, they are released from the bondage of the Inner Desert so that they can once again walk the earth.

If you are truly not sure, then you can work in vision, going into the Inner Desert, to the area of binding and severity where there are many bound angels and other beings, and ask the guardian and attendant workers there for their opinion and advice. They are angelic beings themselves and their task is to ensure that beings, including angelic beings that have no place currently in our world are held in binding until it is time for release. If you come across a bound angel and get the urge to unbind them, then it is a good idea to check that it has not been naturally bound or bound by man under the instruction of Divinity.

There is no set method for unbinding an angel: you have to work from instinct, as the methods of binding are many and complex. The basic rule of thumb is, work in vision: first get the angel to agree regarding the unbinding, look for sigils or text somewhere on the body, or it can be on a thread that is tied to the leg, neck, arm, etc. of the angel. It could also be written on a strip of cloth and hung down its throat. But somewhere on the body will be the utterance that bound it. Removing the utterance will depend upon what element of magic was used in the initial binding. You may have to blow off the script, eat it, wipe it clean with tears, or scratch it off: it will be a very physical action and it will have physical repercussions upon your body. You will know when you have been successful because the angel will completely transform itself. Then you will be able to converse with the angel and ask it who bound it and why. Unbinding like this is a major spiritual service, but before you go rushing off to save the angel world, be aware that the bodily impact, that usually slams in a day or two after, is really not a pleasant experience. After you have done such work you will really need to clean up, so take a ritual salt bath.

You may find it interesting once you have unbound an angel to ask it questions about the nature of its work as a bound angel, what it did, why and for whom. You could also ask the angel, while you have its attention, what did it do before it was bound, what was its primary purpose, and ask the angel to show you through its eyes how it worked. It can be a massive learning experience. It would also be prudent to ask the angel how to call it. They don't actually have names—those were all given to them by humans—but they do have signature sounds that are unique to them. If you ask the angel, it will make the sound that identifies it, and it will put that sound in your head. If it is within range of your voice, you can then physically use the sound to call the angel if you really need to. If the sound is completely out of range of human hearing or voice capabilities, then you will have to 'think' the sound in your head: the effect will be the same. But only call these angels if you really need it to do something that is specifically within their function range, and even then you can only ask, do not command: by commanding, you take on the mantle of God and you are not God, not matter how much your girlfriend tells you that you are.

36.2 Religious angels

Religious angels are angelic beings that operate completely within a religious structure and uphold it. They are not bound and they work mainly by cooperation to facilitate an interface by which man can talk to Divinity, be it a god or goddess. The structure of a religious angel is basically a presentation of a humanlike being with a specific name, wide brief of function and occasionally attendant emotive qualities. The angel, unlike a bound angel, agrees freely as part of its service to dress in a way and function in a way that upholds the inner and outer structure of a religion which acts as an interface between Humanity and Divinity.

The angel presents itself in its assigned role in a way that enables the human to understand the function and intention of the angelic being, and the assigned interface allows the human to request, commune with and generally build a relationship with that angelic being within the sphere of its function, and beyond that a communion with Divinity. This dance will continue while ever the religion truly acts as a bridge between man and God. It is not dependant upon dogma, creed etc., but purely the fact that an inner structure was built to accommodate an outer structure upon which was placed a religion that worked. So it does not matter which deity the religion is working with, or what its 'rules' are, so long as it actually works from the human side, and as long as the humans involved, i.e. the priesthood, are doing what they are supposed to be doing, then the angelic beings play the game. They usually facilitate communication, companionship: bring healing, bridge death and birth, all the usual angelic functions, just within a specific religious structure.

If the human part of the bargain ceases to operate, i.e. it becomes totally corrupt and no longer serves Divinity, then the angelic beings slowly withdraw first from the outer expressions, and then from the upholding of the inner structure. The religion becomes an empty shell with no power and eventually crumbles. When that happens, the angelic beings slowly cast off the 'dressing' of that religion and return to their more natural appearance. Their function stays the same, it just does not operate through a religious window.

When a religion is first put together, or when a major temple is first built, the priesthood would work in vision and ritual with angelic beings, using them as foundations for the Inner Temple and outer temple. The following vision is something I worked with many years ago, and is a very good example of how this method of construction works. It demonstrates the inner construction of a Catholic cathedral which would be done before the outer building itself is worked on. It will show you how Angelic powers and Divine presence are brought through into an inner structure to create a sacred place.

The vision of the cathedral is using the inner flow of the power of the East to manifest itself through a Christian Mystery. The details of the religious outcomes are irrelevant: it could be a mosque or a Greek Temple. It doesn't matter. The knowledge and ability to open the power of the elemental temple and work with the powers that flow through that mediation is what is important.

The form it will take (Christian, Muslim, pagan) is a surface detail that takes form as the power exteriorizes. It is the moulding that is done as the power comes through. Each variation still has the same rules: this is how you open the door, this is how you use a deity to mediate the power, this is how beings can work like building blocks.

So, as you will see, the vision gives you the feel of how it is done. If any of you go to the south of England, go to Wells Cathedral. When you stand in the west and look east, you will see how the architect has actually placed the power patterns of the Angelic Beings in the building. You can see their pattern right there in front of you.

I stood there once, waiting from my daughters to finish looking at something, and I sort of glazed over. But when I came back into focus I saw them for the first time and was astounded. I had been there so many times and not noticed. How could I have been so blind? (And stupid!) But then, I seem to specialize in random acts of complete stupidity, so I guess it was to be expected.

36.3 The consecration of the cathedral

Light a candle and meditate on the inner flame that burns deep within you. As you look at the central flame it grows bigger and bigger until you are seated before a column of fire. You are drawn to the fire and find yourself stepping through the fire with the intent of going to the creation of the cathedral.

Stepping over the threshold you find yourself standing before a beautiful cathedral that is still under construction. It is all but finished, and detailed carving is being added to the outside the building. The priests and priestesses stream into the building and you follow.

Inside, it is filled with people who are weaving threads and connecting them from one end of the building to another. They are pulling threads from a central point and weaving an inner matrix for power to pass through. Once it is completed you are urged to go and kneel before the altar. You can feel that the altar is not yet consecrated or tuned to any specific power. Many of the people kneel with you and tell you to turn inward, to meditate on the central flame.

You pass into stillness and stay in a place of silence and peace. A power builds up all around you and within you. Urgency passes through your mind and you can feel the need to do something, but you are not sure what. You begin to cough as air forces its way out of your lungs. The force becomes too much and you tip your head back to allow a sound to release from your body. You cry a cry that comes from every cell in your body. It is the cry of hopelessness, despair and imbalance: the human separated from the rest of existence.

A call and a movement answer the cry. The east wall of the cathedral falls away and is replaced by light. As you adjust to the light, you realize the light is coming from a woman who stands on the threshold of the east. At her head are the stars and at her feet is the moon. She stretches out her arms, and her robe falls open. The opened robe reveals the Void within her, a place from which all light, all being, and all compassion steams.

Out of the light step two large Angelic beings that stand opposite each other. They stretch out their wings to touch, reaching beyond the ceiling of the cathedral. They reach out and touch hands, crossing their arms at the wrist and they both move one foot forward until their toes are touching. They create a double helix pattern with their bodies, which upholds the building and enlivens the web pattern.

Once the angels are in place, another being steps out of the East. You see the outline of a human shape, but the inner fire of this being is so bright that you cannot see any detail. The human comes up to you and touches you on the forehead. A light of immense intensity flows through you and you feel that you might die in a state of joy. As your body adjusts to the light, you feel awakened and at peace.

The human then goes to the Altar and lies upon the cold stone. Their body sinks into the Altar, becoming one with the stone: becoming the Corpus Christi. You rise to your feet and go to stand before the Altar with your hands resting lightly on the stone. You feel the stone beneath you breathe and the power of peace and stillness flows from the stone into you.

A priest touches you lightly on the shoulder and tells you that it is time to leave. As you turn to go, you realize that many priests are praying in the cathedral: priests of the time and place of the cathedral. You move quietly towards the west door and pass through a threshold of fire.

The fire passes through you as you cross the threshold and you feel the power of the guardian as you step from one world to another. You emerge back in the room where you first started. When you are ready, you open your eyes and meditate on the candle flame for a moment before blowing it out.

★ ★ ★

The angelic beings and the priesthood work in tandem to create images and actions of the angelic beings, and after that, decades and millennia of generations interacting with that construct serves to strengthen it. In actuality, those presentations are merely windows through which we can converse with the angelic being and through that being, interact with Divinity, or receive an intervention of Divinity through the mediation of the angelic being.

In some ancient temples, early cathedrals and Norman churches, the angelic interface is still there if you know how to turn the lights on. Later buildings and even some ancient temples are completely empty or closed down and really it is just a matter of testing the light switch in each place you go to and seeing if it is still active or not. There is really no other way of judging which ones are still running and which ones are not. Going into a church, cathedral or temple, sitting in vision and seeing the inner structure will tell you a great deal, then opening the gates in the east will confirm whether the angelic structure is still active or not. You will also be able to see the religious dressing of the angelic beings as they were when they first began their 'tour of service' with that religion, and it can be interesting to contrast that image with later artistic interpretations in the religious community as the culture slowly changed.

36.4 Religious angels of recitation

The three main monotheistic religions that come out of the Near East all use the power of the word as their foundation. All three religions, Christianity, Islam and Judaism, have recitation and a book as their central focus. The angelic beings that are the thresholds for that power of the Word are beings that are important to work with from an esoteric point of view. They will teach you the deeper mysteries of recitation and the power of the Word. The following vision will teach you about recitation and what recitation is really about. It is within a framework of the monotheistic religions and the name God is used in the context of Divine consciousness without gender or form.

36.5 The vision of recitation

Light a candle flame in the east and close your eyes. See the flame with your inner vision and allow yourself to be drawn into the flame. Find yourself stood within the flame, bathing in the cold fire of the Void, from which all comes and to which all returns. Look out beyond the flame and see a threshold to a temple of the east. Its columns and threshold are guarded by large angelic beings with many eyes and many wings. Step out of the fire and stand before the two guardians, bow to them and step onto the threshold. You feel the threshold beneath you, which is also an angelic being, and you feel the threshold looking into your soul, looking over your life and looking into your mind to see your intentions.

Stand on the threshold of the East and when the guardians of the thresholds step back, walk over the threshold and into the temple. You begin to walk down a long columned walkway, many guardians watching you as you walk. A wind begins to blow. The wind gets stronger and stronger until you have to lean into the wind to fight through the wind to reach two great doors in the distance.

The wind takes the breath from your lungs and you battle against the hurricane that stings your eyes and suffocates you. You reach the great doors of the inner sanctum, which is also the source of the wind. Something with you tells you to place your forehead to the great doors and you can feel the doors looking into you, seeing if you are honourable enough to be allowed to pass through them. Just as you begin to think you have failed, the great doors swing open and before you is the Void with a whirlwind blowing from it. The wind sucks you in and you fall through the wind, twisting and turning. The wind seems to have arms that hold you as you fall until you hit a sandy floor with a thump.

Standing up, you find yourself in a small empty cubic building. The aged walls are covered with many small rough-cut niches. The niches are empty and you know that you must fill them, but you are not sure what with. Go up to the walls and run your hands over the niches. They feel beautiful and strange.

You become aware that an angel is behind you. You feel the presence and power all around you. The angel leans against you. Power builds up within you, forcing breath from your lungs until your body screams for oxygen. Colour drains from your face and nausea assaults your throat. You cannot inhale.

The angel grabs you by the hair and shouts in your ear:

> Recite! Recite what God commands you. Recite the words that the Angels brought to the world and uttered before the throne of God. Recite so that thy soul shall never forget. Recite from the depths of thy heart where the words of God are written upon the souls of all beings. Recite so that all worlds and all times shall hear what we

36.5. The vision of recitation

have given to those who would listen. Recite the song of Paradise so that all shall behold its beauty.

Open your mouth and inhale. The oxygen hits your brain, exploding light throughout your mind that weaves its way to your lips, forcing out words that you cannot understand. The words take form and travel across the surface of the room, mingling with the angel who joins the recitation.

The word forms become shapes and settle in the niches creating a light of their own. Each word form becomes a deity, an expression of Divinity, flowing with the power of the Void. When the niches are full, the room dances with brilliant light and you finally understand that it is Paradise upon Earth as you bathe in the power and beauty that surrounds you.

Each word shines with the light of power. The power of the Void flows through each word as each word takes a form. The angel passes a hand over your face and tells you to look through his fingers.

You see a door that you had not noticed before. As you touch the door, it moves and breathes, causing you to step back. The door transforms into a light which is so bright that it burns all images from your mind. The angel holds out his hand and speaks to the light:

> Hail Ridwan, keeper of the doors of Paradise, threshold to the Throne of God. May this mortal pass through you and still be as one being. May they leave Paradise and hold its secrets on their lips throughout eternity.

The light dims and the angel pushes you forward. You fall into the door and find yourself enveloped by the power of the Angel of Paradise. In the depths of this power, the Angel speaks to you about your immortal self, and you commune together in silence.

The power of the Angel burns through you and for a moment you see yourself in your entirety, through all lives in all worlds. Within the vision of yourself you see Paradise: the first expression of Divinity as it emerges out of the Void.

Ridwan, Keeper of the doors of Paradise, opens himself and you tumble through the doors to find yourself falling through fire. Looking down you see the Earth below you and you fall towards it at great speed. As the planet gets nearer, you hear many whispers and feel the hands of people reaching out to touch you.

The Earth gets closer and closer until you fall towards a city, a street and finally a building. You pass through the roof of the building and end back in the room where you first started. You fill the whole room and look down with difficulty at the tiny body that you have been living in. Breathing deeply, you begin to draw yourself in, a step at a time.

Slowly, you shrink yourself down until you are the same size as your body. You begin to realize just how limited your true expression is while you are in a body. When you are ready, you open your eyes and look around you. Be aware of all the Divine expressions of power in the living beings, plants and rocks around you. Gently blow the candle out, sending the flame back into the Void.

36.6 Human angels

The next kind of angel to look at has fragments of humanity within it. Don't ask me how this happens because I do not have a bloody clue, but there are many inner beings such as angels, demons and deities to name a few that were once upon a time human.

There are humans who, probably by nature of their magical work, but that is only a guess, end up somehow morphing over time in the Inner Worlds into angelic beings. It may be that they are a construct within themselves, i.e. created as beings that have humanity as well as angelic qualities so that they can be duel interfaces in the depths of the Inner Desert, the place where humanity is formed. But again, that is just an idea really.

My direct experience of them has been in the Inner Desert, by the Abyss and in the Abyss. They combine the focused power of an angel with some emotive quality of humanity and the ability to communicate openly with humanity. The Sandalphon and Metatron are both the most well known ones in Biblical terms but also the most reported in inner visions by magicians and mystics. They are perceived as very large humanlike angelic beings that will converse, protect and teach humans in inner vision. They work closely with those who are working in service in the Inner Worlds, and Metatron appears to be tied to the Abyss and unable to pass beyond that. He is the bridge between our side of the Abyss and the side of Divinity. The Sandalphon however work in the Inner Desert but also upon the surface of the planet. The interesting question would be, would they still exist if humanity did not? Are they tied or a part of our humanity or are they independent of us?

When working in vision with these forms of angels, it is very interesting that they show a full understanding of the emotive nature of humanity, which all other angels do not. Because of that, they also have a great insight into out failings, our bullshit, and our agendas: they cannot be fooled and they can get angry, which makes them very dangerous. Let's look a bit closer at a human angelic form.

36.7 Sandalphon/Synadalphos ("colleague")

Sandalphon is an angelic being of the Earth. Their action is parallel to the Watchers who befriend humanity and teach the human race what they need to know. Sandalphon is a being who walks with humanity and guides them. Sandalphon is also referred to as the gardener: he who tends and nurtures. The following vision introduces you to Sandalphon and gives you a way to work with this power.

36.8 Vision of the Companion

Light the candle and meditate on the power of the flame for a while. Be aware of the strengthening of your own inner flame. The central flame grows bigger and you are drawn to step through the fire. As you step through the fire you find yourself walking through an Inner Desert and an angel begins to walk alongside you

You walk for a while in silence before you ask the angel who he is. The angel stops and looks at you. He places his hands across your eyes and tells you to look through his hands. His voice resonates through you head like a drumbeat.

> I am the angel of the earth upon which you walk. I am the
> skin across the soil, the grains of sand in the Inner Desert:

36. How to Work with Angels

> I am he who lies between the stars and the Underworld.
> I am around and within you. I am completion.

With that the angel takes you by the arm and walks you at great speed across the Inner Desert. You flow upon and also through the sand, which seems to almost pass through you as you walk. The sand interacts with your flesh, and you lose sense of where your flesh ends the sand begins. The angel stands you in the centre of the Inner Desert and points to the Abyss in the distance. He then turns you and points to the mountains in the distance in the opposite direction. He then takes your hand and places it upon his head. You feel many things through your hand: you feel the bark of trees, the strength of rocks, the rich earth, and grains of sand. You feel flesh, your own flesh within the angel.

The angel then takes you to the edge of a great city wall and points to it. You are confused for a moment until you look closer and see the angel is also part of the great city wall. He is truly all around you. You talk to the angel and ask him what you need to know. When you have finished, the angel walks you towards a mist that has gathered in a section of the Inner Desert. He walks you into the mist and when you get so deep into the mist that you cannot see anything, the angel leaves you. You flounder for a short while until you remember the Void within everything.

You step forward with the intention of stepping into the Void. You find yourself with nothing, within stillness and silence. You stand in peace, in stillness, and realize this is your natural state: total stillness and silence. Something reminds you that you must step forward back into life and with that you take a step forward out of the Void with the intention to go back to your body. As you step into the room where you first started, you look around and see fragments of the angel in all the things around you, in the floor, the walls: he is all around you and within you. When you are ready you open your eyes and touch the floor in recognition of Sandalphon: the skin of the Earth.

36.9 Metatron

Metatron is written about as being the prophet Enoch who walked with God and was not. He is one of the angels who was once a man, and he holds the great seat of power before the throne of God. In the Tree of Life he is the one who stands in the Abyss and is the bridge between God and humanity. He is often referred to as the Prince of Countenance. The name Metatron seems to have no roots in any language and to date no one really knows where the name came from.

> Sitting next to God, Enoch was instructed in wisdom, and using his skills as a scribe, prepared three hundred and sixty-six books. When he learned everything, a most significant thing happened. God revealed to him great secrets: some of which are even kept secret from the angels. These included the secrets of Creation, the duration of time the world will survive, and what will happen after its demise. At the end of these discussions, Enoch returned to earth for a limited time, to instruct everyone, including his sons, in all he learned. After thirty days, the angels returned him to Heaven.
>
> And then the divine transformation took place. Additional wisdom and spiritual qualities caused Enoch's height and breadth to become equal to the height and breadth of the earth. God attached thirty-six wings to his body, and gave him three hundred and sixty-five eyes, each as bright as the sun. His body turned into celestial fire: flesh, veins, bones, hair, all metamorphosed to glorious flame. Sparks emanated from him, and storms, whirlwind, and thunder encircled his form. The angels dressed him in magnificent garments, including a crown, and arranged his throne. A heavenly herald proclaimed that from then on his name would no longer be Enoch, but Metatron, and that all angels must obey him, as second only to God.
>
> — *The Legends of the Jews*, by Louis Ginsberg.

36. HOW TO WORK WITH ANGELS

So Metatron is a powerful Mystery who bridges for us the realms of divinity and humanity. The following vision takes us to the edge of the Void where we can reach out to communication with the power Metatron. The depth of his humanity allows us close contact with such an immense being without being destroyed.

36.10 The vision of Metatron and the Abyss

Be still and light a candle. As you become silent, so you begin to lose awareness of the room in which you are seated. The external noises fade, your mind settles and your breathing becomes relaxed and natural. Using your inner vision, you look at the candle flame before you. The room in which you are seated falls away and you find yourself looking through the flame to a landscape beyond.

Instinctively you reach through the flame and pass into the landscape—a place of sand, earth and wind. The wind whips around you and the sand gets into your eyes. For a moment you are blinded and yet you become aware of someone walking alongside you. As your eyes clear, you see a humanlike being, neither male nor female, walking alongside you, and yet their feet are down in the earth, so their legs are only visible from the calf up. They walk through the earth as though it was not there. Their hair is long and trails along the ground behind them, swishing away their footprints. No mark is left of their passing.

The being reaches out to touch you, and as their hand contacts your skin, a force flows through you with such strength that you fear you may fall. You become aware of the landscape in a different way. Life reflects from everything around you. The stones, the grains of sand, the plants and the wind, all are lit with the light of Divinity—all life is visible to you. Looking around you see people come and go: they are unaware of you as you observe them. The perfection of power manifest in substance is evident in every person you look upon, and as you look to your own hands, you see divinity within your own flesh.

The angel moves you on and you walk deeper and deeper into the Inner Desert, leaving the people behind. As you walk you become more and more aware of the mistakes you have made in this life, and

36.10. The vision of Metatron and the Abyss

the things that you have to learn. You find yourself assessing your life and you become so absorbed in this task that you arrive at the edge of a cliff without realizing. The angel puts out one arm to stop you falling over the edge. You look out over the cliff and see that it falls down so far that you cannot see the bottom. It looks like a tear in the universe with no end. You look up and the sky is the same. The tear rises up through the stars.

On the other side is a land swathed in mist. Something draws you to the other side but there is no way to cross. As you look around for a way across, a sound like no other echoes around the Abyss. The sound gets louder and louder until you put your hands over your ears. The angel who has walked beside you kneels down and lowers his head.

Out of the Abyss rises a being that looks like a man but is so large he fills the Abyss. He places one eyeball up to the cliff edge so that he can see you. He strains to see something so small but when he sees you he smiles and places out his hand. He whispers for you to step onto his hand but his voice is so strong it sounds like a hurricane strong enough to demolish the earth itself. Carefully you step out onto his hand and he holds you up so that he can see you better. He cannot speak to you lest his voice destroy you, so he reaches over and places you on the other side of the Abyss. As soon as your feet touch the floor the power of Divine presence flows through you and your mind fills with awareness. Things you had not been able to understand suddenly become clear and a deep, powerful peace rises within you.

Metatron lifts you back over the Abyss quickly before you can lose your sense of humanity: to stand upon the realm of God one must lose who they are. You are placed gently back on the ground beside the kneeling angel. The archangel Metatron holds a hand of blessing over you before withdrawing back into the Abyss. The blessing fills you with fire and heat, so much so that you feel you are standing within fire and yet you are filled with stillness.

The stillness stays with you as you remember being seated before a candle flame. Your focus returns to the candle and you see the Divinity and stillness flow through the flame. Carefully, you blow out the candle, allowing your breath to mingle with the fire and the flame passes from this world to a deeper one. Remain seated and quiet for a while, allowing the stillness to deepen within you before you rise.

36.11 Natural angels

Natural angels are my term for angelic beings that have not been messed around with by humanity and religions or magic. An angelic being in its natural form is a threshold being that enables something to manifest or unmanifest: they are thresholds, literally sometimes. They appear in strange forms, often in the shape of Platonic solids, or spinning wheels with many eyes, long threads with many eyes and ears, etc. Whenever they appear with human or animal form, then chances are they have been altered or have been working with a human religious or magical structure for a very long time.

The best way to observe natural angelic beings at work, as a magician, would be to observe them working at the edge of the Abyss, where humanity prepares to take on a manifest form. You will be able to see them interlinking, interconnecting, and weaving together to form an energy filter through which consciousness can flow on its way to become a manifest being in the world.

The Metatron Cube is an example of an angelic filter at work and its job is to specifically be a threshold for humanity. The Metatron Cube is a hive of angelic beings that create an intricate pattern through their interlinking and that series of patterns and shapes triggers a release of Divine Power across the Abyss that then passes through the Metatron Cube. As it passes through the pattern, the power is shaped, its consciousness is awakened, and the momentum of the burst of power across the Abyss sets off the pattern in motion. The pattern travels down the Inner Desert landscape (flowing down the Tree of Life) interacting with and triggering certain areas of the Inner Desert that hold specific powers (the spheres). Once it has reached the threshold of physical manifestation it is ready to be born. Stepping over the threshold of Malkuth, the human consciousness steps into birth and the Metatron cube holds the integrity of the soul's ability to manifest through the life of the human. When the human dies, the pattern begins to break up as the angelic beings pull apart the pattern.

The pattern, which is angelic consciousness, has many patterns within it, and those patterns have patterns within them too. Our ability to manifest is based upon the shapes, patterns, harmonic sounds and vibrations that we label angelic beings. Those shapes and harmonies have consciousness and we can interact with them. They do not however have emotions like we do: they have purpose and function and do not exist outside those functions. This focus of function allows them to handle vast amounts of power, which in turns allows the world to physically exist. We have a much wider scope of action, but we are more diffuse, hence we are much weaker when it comes to mediating power. We do however have a greater emotive and conscious ability then angelic beings.

So back to the pattern at the edge of the Abyss. The Metatron cube is a fascinating angelic construct to observe in action, and a lot can be learned about real natural angelic beings just by observing them at work. The following vision takes you to the threshold of the Abyss and allows you to observe the process of angelic mediation of life. One word of warning: do not be tempted to deviate from the vision and begin experimenting with this structure. Once you have observed and then worked with it for a while, then you will know exactly what you are doing and will be able to branch out with the work. In the initial phases of working in vision though, stick to the boundaries of the vision until you have a template to work with. Wandering around messing about with the pattern when you do not know what you are doing will result in you being fried both physically and mentally. It's a very strong visionary presence and is akin to standing right next to the biggest nuclear reactor that you can imagine.

36.12 The vision of the Metatron Cube

Light a candle and close your eyes. With your inner vision see the candle flame before you. You are drawn to the flame and find yourself stepping into the flame, which is cool and refreshing. You bathe in the flames, which fill you with energy and stillness. That stillness draws you to walk forward through the flame and into the Void. You pass into the deep nothing that all things flow from and flow to, the place where there is no time, no space and no movement. In this still place, your daily life falls away and you find the eternal you drifting in the stillness, spreading out beyond the boundaries of your humanity. Something calls to you within this still place and you find yourself stepping out of the Void with the intention of going into the Inner Desert.

You step out of the Void, stepping onto sand and finding the Sandalphon stood before you. The Sandalphon stands tall, their hair long and trailing in the sand behind them, and their bodies the colour of the sand around them. They motion for you to follow them, which you do and together, you set out walking towards the Abyss that is at the far end of the Inner Desert. At the other end is the River of Death.

The angel walks you to the edge of the Abyss and then turns you around to observe a pattern of human life going into manifestation. Before you, at the edge of the Abyss, strange shapes start to appear out of nowhere, their shapes being Platonic solids spinning at high speed. They give off a strange deep harmony that vibrates right through your body. They align themselves into a pattern of thirteen shapes, the spinning and vibration moving the shapes to where they need to be.

The angel moves you to one side, to get you out of the way of what is about to happen, but near enough that you can still see everything that is happening. From across the Abyss, the realm of Divinity, comes a wind like a breath. A deep mist, a mist that does not seem to be affected by the wind, obscures the other side of the Abyss: you cannot see anything, but you can hear everything. The breath sounds like a word, a deep resonant word that booms across the Abyss and affects the vibrations of the shapes that are spinning. The breath seems to take shape as it crosses the Abyss, appearing as strings as thin as silk that attach to the shapes and begin to interlink them. The strings of breath connect up all the shapes to make a much bigger, more complex shape: the Metatron Cube.

Once it is complete, it begins to move down the Inner Desert, and each time it reaches a place of power in the Inner Desert, the pattern changes slightly, strengthening and taking a more solid appearance. You walk alongside the pattern, watching it as it spins and moves. Its strong sounds echo around the Inner Desert like a choir of deep

36.12. The vision of the Metatron Cube

harmonies. The Sandalphon walk one on each side of the pattern with the Metatron Cube, to the edge of the Inner Desert up to the area of Malkuth. There the pattern pauses and waits as if for some cue. Without thinking, you look up and see stars moving and shifting, and they also give off a faint sound that joins in with the harmonies in the Inner Desert. The stars seem to reach a certain pattern or constellation and there is a sudden powerful shift, like a door clicking open.

The pattern steps forward with the Sandalphon, crossing over the threshold of Malkuth. The minute the pattern crosses that threshold, it turns into a human form and walks off into the mists of time and physical manifestation. It all happens so quickly, you struggle to understand what it is you have just witnessed. What you have in fact witnessed is the conversion of the utterance of Divinity into form: the creation of Man.

The Inner Desert is silent when the pattern has gone and it holds a strange eerie stillness, as though all the energy of the Inner Desert has just been used up and it has exhaled. This is the 'still point' before the inhalation, when the process will start all over again. The pattern of the Metatron cube is the blueprint for humanity and that blueprint is something you also passed through as your soul stepped out of Divine Being and into the circles of reincarnation. One day, the Inner Desert will inhale and you also will go back to the source, when your times of reincarnations are over. But for now, you savour the stillness of the Inner Desert. It is not the same stillness of the Void, which is a true emptiness: the stillness of the Inner Desert is the pause before action, the taking a second to catch breath after a hard job.

The Sandalphon places a hand upon your shoulder, and tells you it is time to leave. But before you turn to step into the Void, the angel places a thumb upon your forehead and presses hard. It feels like he has made an indent in your forehead to which he puts his lips. He begins to utter strange sounds and words that vibrate through your brain and make you feel strange. The angel is inserting the wisdom and knowledge of the complexity of the pattern that you have just witnessed, so that over the next few years, you will be able to unravel its deepest Mysteries and truly, fully, understand the power that is that pattern.

36. How to work with angels

The angel removes his thumb and pushes you backwards. You fall onto your back and fall through the sand, falling down and down, deeper and deeper into the land and into time. You feel yourself in the pattern, feeling your consciousness linking into a complex weave with angelic beings holding the threads to ensure the pattern is woven carefully. You also feel a feminine force, not a motherly or gentle female power, but a truly awesome, fiery, battle-ready woman who also weaves fate and time. A face flashes before you: that of a woman with a mass of tangled hair, of powerful strong eyes and muscled, battle-scarred arms: a goddess who has truly fought for the survival of humanity and who weaves the fate of the future based on her wisdom and understanding gained in battle.

She touches the threads and you feel her all around you. She makes sounds and the angels holding the threads of the weave move as if in a strange dance. Her face appears and disappears in front of you, and your vision is obscured by fog. The images of her fade deeper and deeper into the mist until you find yourself completely surrounded by mist and dark. It is still, it is dark and it is silent. You feel safe and you feel held. Your mind drifts, allowing your deeper self to take over, a self which remembers this feeling with great comfort, and with great happiness. You drift in the dark small space, completely surrounded by a feeling of love and safety.

A noise awakens you and calls your name. You wake up and step forward but there is nothing beneath your feet for you to stand upon and you fall, turning around and around as if rolling down a hill. You finally uncurl and come to a sudden stop, finding yourself in your body sat before a candle flame. You feel a bit disorientated, as if you came back too quickly, and you want to go back to that safe warm still place. Sit for a while until you are ready to open your eyes. Remember what you have seen, remember the pattern and remember the goddess who wove you. When you are ready, open your eyes and blow out the candle flame.

★ ★ ★

As soon as you have come out of the vision, write down everything you can remember, as it will fade very quickly no matter how strong it is in your mind. Also draw out the pattern, as there will be much

36.12. The vision of the Metatron Cube

for you to retrieve by recreating it. Don't use a ruler but allow your hand to work the pattern from within you.

The experience at the edge of the Abyss will have long and far-reaching ripples of contact if you work a few times with it. It is a deep and powerful working that really takes you to the stripped-down form of angelic power, and truly demonstrates the dynamics of Divinity working with angelic beings to give form to humanity.

The observing of angelic beings at this level gives one a deeper understanding of these beings, and also wipes out any fantasy we may have about angels being soft fluffy handsome blond boys. They are in truth bloody ugly most of the time, and if not ugly, just plain weird.

Another way to observe natural angels in their home setting is to work in the directions with them both ritually and in vision at the same time. Working with the directional elements allows you to see the angelic beings as they express themselves through those elements. A good example of this is a working I did many years ago with a group of magicians while I was living in Bath. The apartment where I lived was over some of the remains of the ancient temple to Sul, Goddess of the hot springs and Underworld. So the room where we were working was a strongly tuned temple extension, and able to handle a great deal of power.

We were working in the directions. I was in the North and one of the adepts was in the south. He was raising angelic power of the South and of fire, and my job was to mediate that out from the center to the west/humanity. He built the power up and then released it: vast swathes of fire emerged out of the south, and out of the flames shot many Wheels of fire spinning at high speed. The Wheels had many eyes that seemed to bore into your soul as they passed you. They circled around the room and then shot out of the window, out into the world. (Bear in mind this was happening in vision, not literally!)

The power and intensity of the contact was massive and really took me by surprise. I was still quite young at the time and had not experienced that level of angelic contact in quite that way before. It changed how I understood angelic contact and it certainly changed the way I approached working with them. In that hour, the adept, who was very skilled and experienced, taught me more about angelic contact than I could have learned from years of study. That is always the best way to learn, and his ability to mediate and control power to such depth opened my eyes to the level of skill that an adept could reach. He was a wonderful inspiration and has remained one of the people I truly look up to, not only for his skill that he demonstrated that day, in his usual understated way, but for his general humility, sense of honour and wonderful wisdom. I dedicated this book to him to pay respect where respect was due.

If you wish to develop angelic work to that level, I suggest you first work in the visionary scenario of the Inner Desert, to enable your body to get used to the level of power. Once your body can handle that contact, then begin to work in the directions, both ritually and in vision. That will allow you a slow bodily adjustment so that you do not fry yourself.

If you work in magical service to any real level, you will have to work with angelic beings, just as you will have to work with demonic beings, and it is work that will have an impact upon your body one way or another. The only way to minimize that impact to is to grade your body into the power levels slowly. The more humanized or named the angels are, the less of an impact it will have upon your body. As you move further and further away from bound, named or structured angels, the more the body will buckle under the impact. There are countless examples of such impacts in ancient and religious texts: the Old Testament story of Jacob is a good example. He was injured through his interactions with angelic beings, but he also discovered the Ladder of Angels. The Ladder of Angels is a visionary structure in which the hands of angels carry you and pass you from hand to hand up the Abyss to take you to the foot of God. It is a powerful and dangerous process which is used in a variety of ways, including the vision of Justice and Judgement, which is included in my book *The Exorcist's Handbook*. If you decide to work on that vision, make sure you have a very good reason to do so, and that whatever the reason is, you must be prepared to have your life changed forever.

36.13 The Archon and the Aeon

There is an absolute load of twaddle written about the Archon and the Aeon, about what they are, what they do and to whom they answer. They have been dressed in many guises, and married off to various fantasy goddesses or demons or both, usually to fit an agenda of a religion, or to go with the fashion of that magical line.

In reality, when you encounter these beings in vision, they are powerful, and close enough to Divinity to have no real discernible form. These two opposing powers create a tension that works on a variety of levels of consciousness and manifestation. They are the opposing tensions, or polarities, that allow all substance to manifest. They are the alarm system for Divinity, triggered by any human who gets too close to Divinity: their tension creates a threshold that is very close to the source of Divine Universal Power as it manifests in our world.

The Archon and Aeon are hives of consciousness that are part angelic and part Divine. In real terms for us, pushing deep into the Void with the intention of reaching God will eventually bring you face to face with these opposing powers. They snap like an elastic band, literally kicking you out of the Inner Worlds and giving your body a good kicking for good measure. They are the intense light and intense darkness of creation: they are power in and power out, dense and ethereal: they are complete contrasts like two ends of a magnet, never meeting, always dancing around each other. They have no communicable consciousness: you cannot talk to them, and they are just too vast for us. They lie dormant in their opposition until someone reaches a bit too deeply into the inner realms and gets to the threshold of Divinity. At that point their silk thin line of control is disturbed and they contract and react, creating a wave of energy that barrels over anything in its path, snapping you back into your body with a thump and a lot of bruises.

They protect the integrity of Divinity and stop humans from becoming Gods. In our human form, we must not get too close to the reality of Divinity: if we do, we lose our bodies and do not fulfil the purpose of our manifestation in the first place. This is what is just so amazingly wonderful about our world: everything and I mean everything has purpose, power and connection. It is the most beautiful thing to behold in action, and the Archon and Aeon ensure that it stays that way.

I do not write about them for you to work with; rather, it is important to know these things and to put them in context, so that you get the bigger picture.

36.14 Working advice

In advanced practice, the best way of all to work with any form of angelic being is to be open, simple and straight to the point. You do not need to dress these beings and they do not need long formal ritual wordy prayers or invocations: they do not have egos, so it is pointless brown-nosing them with impressive and gushing compliments. Just call them and tell them why you have called them, or go to them in vision, or both.

At the end of the day, we learn about angels so that we can learn to work with them. Just knowing what they do, what their names are and where they hang out is not enough. There are beings that wish to be worked with, and this is a step closer to a deeper Mystery of all the beings of the earth working together. And we wouldn't really work with them to benefit ourselves: we offer ourselves in service to do things that they cannot. They in turn do the things for us that we cannot do.

The following vision is just one of many examples of how angel and human can work together in service. This vision takes us to the point of death in an individual and we work with the angelic being to assist the passing of this spirit.

36.15 Vision of the pattern of death

Light a candle and close your eyes. With your inner vision see the candle before you. As you look at the candle with your inner vision a peace rises up into you and the stillness descends upon you. You reach deeper down into the earth and you feel the depths of the planet beneath your feet and the height of the stars above your head. The light of the flame burns deep within you.

36.15. Vision of the pattern of death

The flame grows bigger and bigger until all that you can see is fire. Out of the fire steps an angelic being. The angel stands in front of you and reaches out to touch you on the forehead. As soon as they touch your forehead, you fall forward into the angel. The angel allows you to fall through him, and you find yourself falling through the stars with the angel following you.

You fall and fall until you see the planet below you. You fall towards a landmass, a country, a town, a street, a house. You pass through the roof of a house and find yourself in a room where someone is dying on a bed. Someone is sitting with the dying person and in the corner is a man praying and reciting from a holy book. The prayers and recitations appear as many beautiful forms of energy that make a pattern. The pattern has triggered the angel to attend and you are called by the angel to work with them. The man reciting in the corner is not aware that you are there.

The angel touches you on the shoulder and you begin to see in a different way. As you look at the dying person, you start to see in them a beautiful web pattern that is damaged in some areas. In the center of the web, by the person's abdomen, is an orb of light that is glowing dimly. You wonder of it is possible to heal the person. The angel tells you to go forward and touch the person.

You sit by the edge of the bed and you hold the hand of the person who is dying. As you touch them you can feel that the body can no longer hold onto life and that it is time for this spirit to move on. You instinctively reach towards the central orb and pick it up. It breaks the connection with the web and the person breathes their last breath. The angelic being reaches over and assists the spirit to begin to separate from the body. You are told to place the orb where it belongs. You go outside and dig a hole, placing the orb inside the hole. Immediately the orb begins to break up and melt into the earth to be regenerated.

You return to the room and watch as the spirit slowly begins to separate from the body, letting go one by one of the threads that connect it to the body. The spirit listens to the recitation and watches the words as they form into patterns. The patterns tell the spirit which way to go, how to move forward to begin the death journey and what to expect.

36. How to work with angels

A door appears before the spirit and as the door swings open, you feel the power of the Void flow into the room. The Void calls to the spirit and the spirit moves towards the door, drawn by the power and beauty of the Void. Once the spirit has passed through the door and is ready to begin its journey, the door closes. You instinctively go towards the door but the angel holds you back. To step through this door would mean instant death. The angel shows you a wall of fire and you step towards the fire. As you pass into the flames, you feel the fire rebalancing you. You pass through the flames and emerge in the room where you first started. You look at the flame for a second before gently blowing it out.

★ ★ ★

If you wished to take that work further, and walk with the person through death, to be of assistance, then instead of walking through the door, you would go into the Underworld and find the River of Death. You would follow the river until it opens out in the Inner Desert. From there, you can work safely, talking to the person and when they are ready, suggesting to them that they cross the bridge over the river and walk deeper into death.

Finally, if you are going to work in any depth with angels, get fit and look after your body because they are the ones more than any other being you will encounter that will knock the shit out of your body. You will get bruised, dislocated and even fractured if you are not careful. And always be straight to the point. If you make a mistake or are vague with your intentions, you may end up with something that you really did not want to happen.

Chapter Thirty-seven

Practical methods for creating ritual tools

There are many ways levels and methods of working with the consecration of ritual tools and in the early phases of magical training, learning how to attune or enliven an implement is the foundation for more powerful consecrations and object mediations. Once a magician has learned to tune in a tool, then the next step is to consecrate the tool to tune it to the 'original': there is only ever one consecrated sword for example, and all ritual swords are a part of it, like a hive consciousness. In this section we will look at the technique of consecrating a ritual implement, and we will also look at putting beings/workers/powers into tools specifically for a job, after which they are taken out again. The tool becomes a vessel for a coworker that brings a specific quality with it. We will also look at awakening Divinity within a tool.

37.1 Consecration of tools in the deepest part of the temple

This method of consecration basically cuts out a lot of the middlemen—the priesthoods who often have agendas—and goes straight to the 'source' of the angelic threshold. This action leapfrogs all of the generations upon generations of magical/priesthood layers with all of their attendant degeneracy. Going back to the source also takes the implement back to the very first expression of the original consecrated and sacred implement, which often has its roots deeply embedded within the sacred land.

As with all true consecrations, you cannot dictate exactly what is going to go into the tool; and although you may start in a traditional direction for that tool, you must be willing to be flexible if the tool decides that actually its consecration line needs to come from a completely different direction.

When you decide you want to properly consecrate a ritual implement, you must first be willing to think it through and be aware of all the responsibilities and consequences of such an action. Unlike an attuned tool, a consecrated tool will last forever, and if it is broken up, it is possible that its power will remain in its fragments. They are very difficult to destroy and can be dangerous to keep, depending on what power is in them and how will have access to them. Also bear in mind that a fully consecrated sword, for example, is a very dangerous and powerful tool that can weak havoc on a home, community or even land if wielded without knowledge and wisdom. So what will happen to it once you have died/given up magic/become a politician? You need to make proper plans for the tool to ensure its guardianship after you have gone. That is the whole point of the story of Excalibur: the dying king commands that the sword be returned to the water where it will be safe from the hands of men. It must be buried, or put in water, or burned and returned to its source. If you bury it or cast it into water, then you must also charge an angelic guardian to watch over it and keep people away from it.

Seeing as we are on the theme of swords, we shall look at the consecration method for a ritual sword. For the other implements, depending on what element/direction they want to work in, you would simply adjust the direction/element in the vision.

The following consecration vision and ritual places the power of the wind in the sword, which is the power of utterance and justice. This would be worked with in the east. If the sword were to be consecrated to be a sword of protection, say for a landmass, then you would work with the volcanic power in the south. If it was to be a sword of sovereignty, then it would be worked with in the north.

37.2 Consecration ritual/vision for a consecrated Sword of Justice

Set the ritual working space up with an altar in the center and an altar in the east. On each altar is a candle, and the altar in the east should

37.2. Consecration ritual/vision for a consecrated Sword of Justice

have a small dish of consecrated oil and nothing else. By the door have a pad of paper and a pen in case you have to write something down.

The sword should be prepared the night before by placing it in a sheet or cloth that is filled with dry salt: leave it wrapped in the salt. In the morning, the sword is washed, dried and exposed to the outside air briefly. Ensure that you are also prepared which means that you must take a consecrated bath the morning of the work and wear clothing that has no script, words or faces upon it: Plain clothes or robes, and no jewellery unless it is ritual jewellery.

Take the sword and place it upon the central altar. Light the candle and be in the stillness, use your inner flame to light the inner candle and stand for a moment in silence to give the room time to tune in properly. Then go and light the flame on the altar in the east. Remember to process around all four directions before you get to the east, to strengthen and continue the tide of power that swirls in the room like a whirlpool. Light the candle in the east and be still and silent as the flame tunes itself. Once the direction is tuned, then you must open the gates of the east. Place a hand on either side of the candle and close your eyes, see with your mind's eye the two gates slowly swinging open, and you will see a passageway that vanishes off into the mist. See yourself stepping over the threshold and into the east. You walk into the mist with the intention of reaching for the deepest part of the power of air and angelic justice. As you walk in the mist a wind begins to blow, and as you walk deeper and deeper into the mist the wind becomes stronger. The mist vanishes and you find yourself trying to walk along a passageway that is slightly banked up a slope with a strong wind blowing directly at you from somewhere.

The wind becomes so strong that you can barely stand up, and you find yourself crawling up the slope to reach a pair of doors that the wind seems to be blowing out of. Inch by inch you crawl against the wind until you reach the great doors. The wind is blowing through the keyhole and you realize that if you open the doors, there is a very good chance that you will be destroyed by the wind. But you know it is something that must be done, not only for the work, but also for your own development. Your hands grasp the door handles and with every ounce of strength you have, you pull upon the doors to open them. A terrible wind screams out from the crack of the opening doors and it blows you over. And then the wind falls and you lie on the floor surrounded by the most beautiful scent of flowers.

You sit up and before you, beyond the great doors to the inner sanctum, is a whirlwind spinning at great speed. Its wind has eyes looking in all directions. The whirlwind gives off a deep rumbling sound and a faint but beautiful light. The wind that floats slowly from the fast spinning center is scented with the smell of wildflowers: the smell grips your heart in a clutch of long-forgotten memories that rise in your mind. Now that you have opened the great inner sanctum, it is time to get the sword and take it into the angelic wind for consecration. In your mind you return to the altar where you are stood and you walk clockwise to the sword that is waiting on the centre altar.

First the sword must be ritually stripped of anything that is in it, so that it is a blank slate, ready for the power that is about to be placed within it. The following is done in vision and also ritually, which your physical voice. Where you see +, it means mark an equal-armed cross in the air over the object. With your left hand, hold the hilt of the sword, and with your right hand, pointing the first two fingers at the blade, recite: "I exorcize you, creature of the Earth by the living gods + the Holy Gods + the omnipotent Gods + that thou mayst be purified of all evil influence in the name of Adonai, lord of all angels and men." The power of the wind flows through your voice and you feel a great power mediating through you as you speak. Pass the blade of the sword through the candle flame and in your mind's eye, see the flames consume the blade and cleanse it. The second half of that recitation will come after the vision.

Take the sword from the centre and walk a full clockwise circle around the directions, finishing in front of the altar in the east. Close your eyes and, holding the sword in your hands, step over the threshold and into the passageway that leads to the whirlwind. This time there is no heavy wind, just the mild breeze with the scent of flowers that blows gently around you as you walk up to the inner sanctum. As you reach the threshold, you bow to the power of Divinity manifest in the whirlwind, and you also physically bow, even though you are working in vision. See yourself step over the threshold and approach the whirlwind, whose many eyes have all trained themselves upon you. They search within you, they see every

37.2. Consecration ritual/vision for a consecrated Sword of Justice

part of you, and they see all of your intentions. This is the angel of Justice in its deepest form: the whirlwind that sees all. You are prompted to hold out the sword, which is instantly whipped out of your hand and absorbed by the wind. The sword is changed from an inner perspective before being released by the wind and dropped at your feet.

You are told to turn your back to the wind and to hold the sword out before you, the point facing down to the floor. Behind you, out of the whirlwind, steps an angelic being that places its hands upon your shoulders. The angel puts its face to the back of your neck and begins to blow into you. A pressure builds up within you, filling your lungs and your mind. The angel begins to speak into the base of your neck and your mouth is forced open. Out of your mouth come sounds, but as you breathe them over the sword, you see the sounds taking shape and becoming sigils that mark the blade. You must concentrate and remember as many of them as you can: they are the angelic keys to the power that has been placed within the sword. Once the angel has finished, it grasps your hair and tells you to recite. You do the recitation in vision and physically with your voice. Holding the sword in one hand, you place your right hand with the flat of its palm up to the sword, and recite the following: "creature of the earth and the wind, I consecrate thee in the name of (-) to the service of the Gods and Goddesses." (The G-D name that you use depends on what powers you work with and in what tradition you are working. Alternatively you can utter simply Divine Being.)

Mark one of the sigils that you saw with your index finger onto the blade both in vision and physically. When you do it physically, dip your index finger into the oil and mark the sigil by the hilt. Back away from the inner sanctum, bow and return to the threshold. See yourself once more stood at the altar with the sword, take a step back and bow once more, thanking the inner contacts, guardians and angelic beings for working with you. Take the sword all around the four directions even though they are not lit and hold it up, hilt up, in each direction as an acknowledgement before finally putting it by the central candle. See the central flame, which is the flame that burns at the edge of the Void, flow into the sword, giving it life. The flame sits within the sword and finishes the enlivening. Every time you pick up the sword, you must be aware of that flame of life within

37. PRACTICAL METHODS FOR CREATING RITUAL TOOLS

it, the sigils which are the angelic keys to its knowledge upon it, and of the responsibility the holder carries.

Go out of the room while leaving the candles burning. It may take an hour or so for the inner ritual to complete itself, and you will feel when it is finished. When you feel that completion, go back in and starting at the east altar, thank the contacts, close the gates and blow the flame back into the Void. Do the same with the central flame and wrap or scabbard the sword, leaving it in the east of the sacred space.

The next step will be the enlivening of the scabbard. As soon as you can, get the pen and paper and write the sigils that you remember.

★ ★ ★

The consecration method above reaches beyond human consecration lines, reaching instead for the angelic thresholds of power that flow through people and objects. Because it is a deep consecration method, you must understand that you will be held responsible for the inner and outer health of the sword, for its power will be strong and potentially dangerous. Do not let anyone other than you touch it: you birthed its power through mediation and it will be specifically tuned therefore to work with your power structure only. If someone else tried to handle it or use it for magic it could potentially be very destructive.

The basic structure of the above ritual works for any direction and any quality of the direction for any of the implements. What changes in the four directions is the elemental expression. Notice that there was no landscape, elaborate temple etc., just the pure power of the element beyond the gates and the angelic mediator. When you tune to the pure element of the direction, the angelic contact will appear to mediate it to and through you once it has figured out what you are actually trying to do. If the element does not respond to you, speak across the element, telling it what you are trying to achieve, and then the angelic contact should emerge out of the element. They may appear as human, non-human or just downright weird.

Just an aside: if you are working in the east, try not to do it in the spring, as there is a good chance, depending on what landmass you are on, that ritually opening the gates to the depths of the east wind may cause a very large burp of tornadoes or lightning storms. You will very probably end up in one of those 'oops' moments. You will need to spend some time working with the sword to find out exactly what power is flowing through specifically and how that power works with you. Just tread very carefully until you have a good idea about what it actually can do.

37.3 Ritually enlivening the scabbard

The scabbard contains and completes the power of the sword, bringing it ballast and ancestral connection. It is not just a holder, but a nurturer, teacher and stabilizer. Without a proper scabbard, a sword can become feral, can become distorted and often become unwieldy. Magicians who do not have enlivened scabbards for their swords often, over the years, become aggressive in their magic and develop the tendency to curse people. The power needs a proper containment and the scabbard is a power that anchors the destructive energy within the sword, ensuring that its powers are always directed in work and not left hanging about, which enables that destructive power to seep into the magician's everyday life.

If the sword did not come with a scabbard, then you will need to get one made or make one yourself. It should have no sigils, shapes, words or pictures upon it, just plain leather or cloth. Patterns that are decorative are fine as long as no beings are represented.

Set up the sacred space with just the central altar and the altar in the north. As before, strip the scabbard and cleanse it with salt, and have sacred oil on the altar in the north. Light the central candle and tune it to the flame in the Void and the flame within you, and then light the candle in the north. See the gates of the north open as you stand there in the stillness and beyond the gates, you see mist.

Take the scabbard to the altar in the north and place it upon the altar. In vision, with your hands still upon the scabbard, step over the threshold and into the mists. You will find yourself walking among large standings stones that loom out of the mist and one of them you notice is covered in many intricate patterns. Before the stone is a well, and you find yourself peering down the well. Something shoves you from behind, and clutching onto the scabbard, you find yourself falling through water, down and down into the depths of the earth. You fall through the water, into the deep dark earth, clutching the scabbard to you as you fall. You fall and fall until the light of the world you have fallen from fades away and you are left to fall in darkness.

You land with a bump on a soft floor and find yourself standing before a rough-hewn rock doorway with a faint light glowing beyond it. You push open the door, which is made of a very strong, almost metallic wood that is the deepest black you have ever seen.

Beyond the door you find yourself in a cave that is lit by a faint green light emitting from its walls. On the floor are many sleeping creatures and birds, and at the other end of the cave you see an old woman sat on a stone throne. She is slumped over a hound that is on her lap, and she seems to be sleeping. The dog opens one eye to look at you and begins to growl quietly. The old lady begins to awaken, and as she sits up, she looks at you. Her face is a mass of wrinkles, her hair, long and grey-white, but her eyes have the youth of a woman in her prime. They are bright, powerful and see right through you. She looks at the scabbard and nods to herself before beckoning you to approach her. She reaches out her hand and asks for the scabbard. When you give her the scabbard, she also asks for whatever is in your pocket. Reach in to your pocket and whatever you see there, you give to her. If it is something that you own in life, then you must give it away to a stranger or bury it. If it is something big, like your house, you must let it go and be willing to let it go in real life...learn to trust.

The old woman takes a thread of her hair and begins to weave. She takes hair from the hound, moss from the walls, hair from her body and hair and feathers from the animals and birds around her. She weaves and weaves until they are all woven into the scabbard and then she spits on it to smooth it down. She then pricks her finger and lets a drop of blood fall onto the weave. You also do the same (and physically, prick your finger and drop the blood onto the scabbard).

She then hugs the scabbard to her and tells you that you have to get it from her. Think very very carefully about how you approach this and how you get her to give up the scabbard. Once you have got the scabbard from her you hold it up to look at the weave and you

37.3. Ritually enlivening the scabbard

see a pair of eyes looking back at you: her bright sharp eyes have been woven into the scabbard, and as you look back at her, you see that her eyes are missing. She will be within the scabbard, being the eyes of the sword and protecting it as it rests. You realize that a part of this being is now in the scabbard and you must treat it accordingly with respect and reverence. The scabbard is the more powerful of the two, and guides, aims, advises and protects the sword. Carefully you carry the scabbard up a long stone stairway that the scabbard guides you to, and you climb slowly through the Underworld, reaching for the surface world above you. The scabbard is not a tool, it is an inner contact from deep within the earth, a fragment of the ancient Goddess and you must remember that at all times.

You emerge by the threshold of the altar and you step back into yourself, finding yourself stood before the flame, the scabbard in your hands. Open your eyes and look at the flame. Look at the scabbard and thank the sacrifice that the contact has made to be there for you and to guide you. The contact within the scabbard will teach you many magical things about the sword, the scabbard and the Underworld if you are willing to listen and learn. Place your right hand upon the scabbard and recite: "I vow to uphold your honour, to work with you wisely, to listen to your guidance and to tend to your needs. Thank you Great Goddess, for the gift of your eyes." Bow to the flame, to give honour to the sacredness of the being within the scabbard and the Divine Power within the flame.

Blow out the flame, sending it back into the Void, and then circle the directions before placing the scabbard by the central flame. You will need to immediately paint two eyes onto the scabbard while the candle flame is still burning. Once the eyes are finished, leave the room with the candle still going and let the process continue until you feel it complete. Once everything has gone silent and the energies have subsided, go back in with the consecrated sword. Place the sword on the altar beside the scabbard and place a hand upon the scabbard and a hand upon the sword. Ask the being that is now the scabbard if they are willing to work with the consecrated sword and be the scabbard for that sword. You will slowly begin to feel the guardian being that is the scabbard looking into the sword and feeling what sort of consecration it has had. You may find questions bubble

37. PRACTICAL METHODS FOR CREATING RITUAL TOOLS

up in your mind, and if that happens, you must answer honestly. These questions are coming into your mind from the scabbard.

Once everyone seems happy with everyone (and if not, then you are well and truly screwed) place the sword in the scabbard and place it on the altar. Go out again for around fifteen minutes or so to let the two settle together while the sacred flame is in attendance. Once all is done, go back in again (ever felt like you are on a piece of elastic?) send the flame back into the Void and gather up the sword which should now, in its scabbard, be kept somewhere, either in the sacred space, or in a place where it can watch over the house/temple. It must not be touched by anyone but you and it must never, ever be unsheathed for any reason other than magical. Do not let people play with it or be curious around it. Such interference will unbalance the sword which could in turn affect your magical work. It could also be dangerous for the various beings and deities in the room.

I once had a situation where a magician thought it would be great to swing around my sword, when I was out of the room, a sword which was a fully contacted consecrated sword with a being in it. Swinging it around the space he managed to break the links to all the guardians of the space, and decapitate the shell that held an ancient demonic being that I was working with...which really pissed them and me off. He undid a year's work in ten minutes. Great. Needless to say he was demoted to dishwasher. If the sword is holding a being, which we will go on to next, untold damage can be done by a curious idiot unsheathing it and playing with it. Simply pointing it at a person and uttering words, even in jest, can result in a lot of very nasty things. These are not playthings, they are not the sort of thing you can buy in a New Age store that looks all magical and has nothing in it. These are powerful, dangerous and productive working tools that are akin to Exocet missiles. Think carefully about where you place them. I found that hanging them on the wall, blade down, is the best: it's not so easy for someone to reach up and take them down. Morons tend to pick up things that are directly in front of them.

When you do work magically with your sword, ensure that you remember that the sword is a tool, but the scabbard is a being (or a window for a being, but you treat it as a direct being). Always be respectful of the scabbard: they are always 'her.' The scabbard is a fragment of the Dark Goddess of the cave: this is where the sword and the stone comes from. The sword sleeps in the sacred element of earth/ land, and the Goddess in the Cave is the Mother of the land. Talk to the scabbard, learn to build up a communion with her so that she can tell you things, warn you of things and advise/teach you. If you use the sword in vision or ritual, tell the scabbard first, let her prepare for the work and when you unsheathe the sword, place the scabbard on the altar and she will work with you as a coworker. Eventually she will begin to show you herself in vision as woman, and you will be able to build up a communion with her as an inner contact.

37.4 Placing a being within the sword

This is another way of working with magical tools that can be used for any of the tools be they sword, wand, cup or shield. Instead of consecrating the tools, they become vessels for beings that are heavily linked into the element and direction you are working with. Or they can be linked into specific powers that you need to work with for a length of time. The beings can either be brought into take up permanent residence, or they can be brought in for a particular length of service, even just for one vision, and then returned to their source. Just remember if you have a being in a tool permanently or for a long while, then they will need some upkeep and a wary eye keeping on them.

This is a very powerful way of working with a sword, and a magician would use this technique if there is a very heavy or prolonged and dangerous piece of work to do. The same is true of all the other directional tools.

The first thing to remember with this kind of work is that there is an outer tool and an inner tool and you have to work with both. There is a method for putting a being directly into a tool but I have found by experience that this is not always the best way to work: they get bored, hungry and sometimes feral. It is better to create a bridge to the being from both the inner and outer tool so that the tool becomes an extension of the being, rather than the being itself. So when you work with the tool, the being will be alerted and will be aware of you and will work with you, but when the tool is not in use, the being will not be there. It's a bit like leaving the phone line open.

37.5 Bridging a being into a tool

Firstly you need to ascertain which direction the being you wish to work with is residing in, or if they are in a landscape, historical place, etc. If they are in a direction, then you can work with the altar in that direction as an anchor and threshold. If the being is in the Underworld, overworld, the past or in the land around you, then work with the central flame and the central altar.

Essentially, you go in vision to the being, wherever it may be, and ask the being if it is willing to work with you through this tool. You have the inner tool with you and your physical hand on the physical tool. First the being ties a lock of their hair, or some of their blood to the tool or will pass into and through the inner tool to make the bridge and connect with it. Once that is done, then tie a lock of the being's hair to a lock of your hair or to your wrist if you have no hair, and walk out of the vision back to the altar with the being connected to you.

Once you return to the altar, place your hands upon the outer tool and invite the being into the tool. It will pass through your body and into the tool. Don't rush this part of the work: give the being time to do the transfer and you will feel when it is completed. When it is finished, when you look with your inner vision, you will see the being within the tool and you will see an umbilical flowing from the tool back into the direction or landscape where you were working.

Leave the tool with the flame for a little while, just to let the being settle in. When it is finished, put out the light and place the tool in its resting place, away from curious hands and eyes. Whenever you work with the tool, see the umbilicus vanishing into the Inner Worlds and see the being within the tool. The more you work and commune with the being, the stronger the bridging will become.

If for example you wished to use the above method for bridging power into a tool for a specific working or task then you would follow the same basic steps. Inner tool, outer tool, go to contact, either give the tool to the contact or have the contact connect themselves to the inner tool. Then bring out the inner tool with the being connected and link them up or put them into the outer tool. Then forge the inner and outer tools together again. A good working action like this is to work with the Fire Temple volcanic sword maker. This contact is mentioned in the chapter of volcanic Fire Temple work, and the contact is a very ancient consciousness that forges metal magical weapons in the depths of volcanoes.

A word of advice, though: whenever you intend to work with the magical tools of sword, wand, cup and shield, do not allow yourself to be influenced by writings or 'truths' about the role, power and wielding of magical tools. Let them be themselves, allow them space to speak to you, to show you who they really are and what they really do...you will be very surprised about what can surface if you do not lay preconceived ideas upon them. There are some interesting writings out there, true, but there is also a pile of bullshit out there that will potentially block you from achieving what it is you want to achieve.

If you want to learn more about a particular magical tool, then work with it, talk to it, go into the Inner Library and ask about it. Once you have been told a few things and shown a few things, then it is time to go and search the outer world for information. That way, when you see something that correlates to what you were told by inner contacts, then you know you are on the right path.

37.6 Awakening Divinity in substance

This is a very different way of working with the magical implements and is best only done if you are working purely from a standpoint of service. If you use this technique for your own ends it simply will just not work. If you are working in service, though, it can be an extremely powerful way of working and will most certainly teach you a lot and mature you a lot as a human spirit.

This technique does not put anything into the tools: rather it awakens to a conscious level the Divinity that is within all substance. The flame of Divine Being in all things is usually an unconscious thread of power, a fragment of the whole and an echo of all creation. If that fragment is awakened and tuned, it becomes a direct interface

37. PRACTICAL METHODS FOR CREATING RITUAL TOOLS

between the power of Divinity and the magician. The fragment of Divinity within the substance is awakened specifically to the power and consciousness of the magical implement, so the power within the tool is not like an icon of Divine Being that you can talk to or interact with as a humanlike form; rather it is a conscious fragment that is awakened specifically to the power frequency that the tool holds.

The power that awakens within a tool cannot be preempted: it will be individual and purely of itself. How Divinity chooses to express itself through that tool is a Mystery that you will have to unfold slowly yourself. Because of that, I would not recommend using the tool magically straightaway; rather I would suggest spending time with the tool, getting to know its expression, its power and its abilities. It may take years to fully understand exactly what power is in the tool and also, more importantly, what its purpose is. Every Divinely awakened tool has a specific function and you will be held responsible for ensuring that it fulfils its function. Because of this specific way of dealing with the tool, I would only recommend this form of working with magical implements if you had a specific idea of a long-term span of work that was of service: in those circumstances the Divine Tool will work with you in service, and you will learn its powers and skills as the work unfolds.

The preparation for such awakening begins with the acquisition of the tool. It must be virgin, i.e. never used before for magic, and preferably a brand new tool, a newly forged sword, a branch taken from a tree, a newly made cup and a handmade or newly made shield or a stone that you have found yourself. You would not salt it, as you do not want to strip out everything within it: you want to awaken the latent power within it. That will mean that you awaken not only the divine power within the object, but also the inner spirit of the element, or tree, or rock. The skill that is needed to do this job is stillness, total and complete inner stillness.

To begin, light a candle in the centre and sit in a chair before the altar with the tool in your hand. Close your eyes and see the inner flame with your inner vision. You find yourself drawn more and more to the flame, and find yourself passing into the flame, bathing in its regenerative life power. The flames fill you up, filling you with a sense of peace and stability. You find yourself stepping through the flame and emerging out into the Void, into the place where there is no time,

37.6. Awakening Divinity in substance

no space and no movement. You spread out, no longer restricted by a body, allowing your spirit to flow freely in all directions at once. You become aware of a vastness within you, of the Void within and you also become aware of the tool that is in your hands as your body sits before a flame.

In the Void you hold the inner pattern of the tool in your hand and you begin to push deeper into the nothing, moving further and further into the Void and away from the physical world. As you push deeper and deeper into the Void, your memory of the physical world falls away and you find yourself merging with the Void, with a deep sense of belonging and of coming home. You begin to remember the feeling of this place: you have spent much time here, during lives and between lives: it is your home, your place of rest and regeneration. You push deeper and deeper into the Void until you find a very narrow path before you. Something tells you that you must collect yourself together, to take human form again, and walk this narrow path.

With the tool in your hand, you walk the narrow ledge through the Void, walking through nothing and yet feeling a great deal around you. The ledge comes to an end, beyond which is a nothing that feels completely empty and very different from the Void around you. The hair on your neck starts to prickle and you feel a massive amount of power building up around you. The air around you becomes very pressured and it gets hard to breathe properly. The tool in your hand begins to vibrate with the change of frequencies and out of the depths of the Void comes a wave of pressure that washes over you.

From that wave merges a being with many eyes, many wings and is made up of strange shapes. The being touches you upon the forehead with a touch that seems to light up your brain. The being then places a hand over the tool and grasps it tight. You watch as the tool changes and you begin to see all the molecules that make up the substance of the tool. Each molecule sparks brightly with life, and when all the molecules are bright, a surge of power flows through the being and into the tool. The tool begins to pulsate with life and energy and it weighs heavy in your hand. The angel turns and vanishes back into the Void and you are told to leave. You walk back along the ledge, the tool getting heavier and heavier as you walk. By the time you come to the part of the Void where you first started, the tool is so heavy you can barely lift it.

You remember the flame that you were seated before and with that memory you step out of the Void, through the flame and back into the room where you first started. The tool is very heavy and you place it on the altar with the candle flame and leave the room. You leave the tool with the candle until you feel it is time to go in and put the candle out. From now on, whenever you are going to use the tool, first light a candle before it and leave it for a few minutes before the stillness of the flame. When the tool is not in use, wrap it in a cloth or put it in a box away from prying eyes and curious fingers.

37.7 Summary

The methods of creating, maintaining and using magical implements are endless and really depend of what you are doing, where you are doing it and why. The main thing to remember is, at the end of the day, you will gain more from working with tools using methods gleaned from your own inner work and from sources that you have been guided to. There are many very powerful ways to work with magical tools and the old rule, which always applies, is 'when you need a tool, it will appear': you just need to keep your eyes open and realize what has just dropped on your doorstep.

Have the tools hang out with you while you work, that way you will be able to bridge into the consciousness of the tool and learn about it as you work. In truth, the deeper and more powerful the magic that you work with, the less you have to do anything specific with the tools: they just stay in the working space and do their job quietly. Just don't let the neighbours kids grab them and play with them, it leaves such a mess on the carpet.

Chapter Thirty-eight

The magic of the Underworld

In my opinion, the Underworld and all its beings, deities, sub-realms and landscapes should be the first training ground for all magicians, but sadly this area of magic is often left until the magician is already an adept. The Underworld teaches us about our past, our ancestors, and the distant past of the planet; it shows us about death and gives us access to the powers and landscapes of death; and it is the home of the ancient Mother Goddess, along with many strange-looking ancient beings. Very old shamanic magic sinks into the Underworld once it has been abandoned, and to touch base and learn about this vast array of ancient knowledge should be a priority for all magicians and priest/esses.

The back door of the Underworld is the Abyss, i.e. the place where the consciousness of the Underworld resides without the dressing of the manifest world. Every realm has a front door and a back door, and once the Underworld has been explored and learned about by going into the earth, then it is time for the magician to explore and work in the depths of the Abyss. To access the deep parts of the Abyss without first having experience of the Underworld as it manifests in our world (which is the death realm and ancestral realm, containing Titans and massive Underworld Goddess Temples, etc.) is suicide: it's that simple.

The backroom of the universe, which is the Abyss, does not have all the inherent safety valves built into it that the Underworld does so it is far easier to get eaten by an ancient being while you are down the Abyss than it is in the Underworld. In this chapter, we will briefly look at some of the various realms in the Underworld, and then we will look into the deep part of the Abyss to see how it all hangs together. The two previous books in this series do touch upon various Underworld realms, i.e. the death realm, ancestors etc., and

38. The Magic of the Underworld

you will find a few Underworld contacts and connections scattered around this book in other chapters. If you bring them all together, you will find a map of the Underworld.

When we go down into the earth below our feet we first hit the faery realm, which is also entwined with the surface world, then we hit our ancestors buried within the earth. In a visionary sense, one of the very first visions we find in the earth, usually in a cave, is an Underworld Goddess who presents as an old woman living in a cave with a pool of water. This image is found all across the Northern hemisphere from India to England. She is our first contact with the female consciousness of the land. As we dig deeper, we start to find older deities that have vanished from our world, the River of Death, sleepers from the ancient past, ancient temples from thousands of years ago, and then below them very large beings known as the old gods or titans.

Around that layer of Underworld consciousness we come across very ancient forms of humanity who still work as inner contacts, mediating Underworld power to the surface world and working with the raw forces of Divinity as they express through nature. Their power often brings destruction to our world, in a cleaning way, but more often than not their bridge to the surface world is blocked by ritual seals and locked doors placed there by some of the early monotheistic religions and some of the Classical religions who manipulated the deities to suit themselves. Greece and Rome were particularly guilty of such actions.

An adept has a great many reasons to work in the Underworld, not only in a learning capacity, but also in a line of service. The Underworld processes all that has passed, all that will sleep, all that has died, and all that no longer has a place in our world. Those processes take a great deal of mediating and bridging: sleepers need attending to and guarding, magically trapped deities that still have a place in our world need to be released and the land needs help to breathe after all the building we have done upon her. And that is just the outer face of the Underworld. The harder and more dangerous service is often undertaken deep within the Abyss, where beings must be guarded, put back to sleep, honoured, fed and consulted where necessary.

Providing you have worked in the faery realm, the death visions, and the ancestral realm, and you have struck up a suitable relationship with the Goddess in the Cave, then it is time to go a little deeper. The first step would be to visit and work with the Goddess in the Cave as an adept and then the Sisters at the back of the North Wind.

The Goddess in the Cave is a contact that is worked with a lot in the early days of one's visionary training, and she has been a foundational visionary contact in many esoteric and religious mystical practices for millennia. The contact becomes stronger and more profound as our experience grows, and it is one of the basic visions that I feel cannot be reiterated enough, hence I am going to put a visionary version of her in this book, even though she is in my other magical books.

As an initiate, we experience her as a guardian to the gates of the Underworld, as a healer and as a teacher. Once we have progressed in our magical training and we are coming to a path of service, then our relationship with this deity changes. We begin to see the deeper and more profound element to this goddess and work with her in our service to the land and to humanity.

There are certain details that should be observed when working in this realm, for instance, how the cave appears, which beings are in there sleeping with her, what she looks like, what attendants she has (if any), what state the pool is in, and whether she is armed or not. The cave is a threshold place in the Underworld and it is a space where the past and future collide: octaves are layered upon each other so when something is coming in the nearer future that is an echo of an ancient past, it will affect how the cave presents itself. If there are no animals or birds in there, it is because these animals are soon going to be extinct or at least removed off the landmass that her cave serves. How everything presents will tell you the health of the land, what is coming and also will hint about what your work will be. It can also be a place where the newly dead appear if they are connected to her in some way or other.

She can be worked with as an oracle for the near future of the land and civilization, and she can also help in cleaning up a heavily parasited person or place: she will give you tools, advice and helpers should you need them. She is a major advisor for magicians working in the Underworld, and will also offer some protection if she deems it necessary. She will also provide foundations for Underworld temples and furnish them with guardians. There is much to be learned from this most ancient of Goddesses and her power should never be underestimated. Her deepest version, which is found in the Abyss, is as a warrior lion goddess who is part human and partly divine: she keeps the balance in all things through destruction, justice and compassion.

The following vision takes you to her in the cave, and it also takes you through the back door into the Abyss where you can follow her work more closely. Be very aware that any gift that you give her in vision must also be given to her in real life: she is a demanding goddess and her effect upon your life can be very real, so do not shortchange her or you will regret it. It is a long vision, and establishes a connection between our world, the Underworld, the Abyss, the Inner Desert and the Void. It is a loop that can only be done by humanity but serves to open doorways for many powers and beings to flow through. Just doing the vision is in itself a major service, but also much can be learned from it and a strong relationship with this goddess can be developed through this work.

38.1 Vision of the Goddess in the Cave and in the Abyss

Light a candle and close your eyes. See the candle with your inner vision and feel the stillness of the Void within the candle flame and within you. As you bathe in the stillness, a hole opens up in the earth and the candle flame falls down into the Underworld, and you follow. The candle flame lights the way ahead as you fall through darkness, falling past rocks, earth, and tree roots until you come to a small cave with a floor of soft sand. You fall onto the sand and the flame falls beside you. As you look around you see an ancient stone stairway leading up to the surface world, a stairway that twists around the directions and that is carved into the rock face. On the other side of the cave an entrance is roughly cut into the stone with a curtain of wool pulled across it. On the curtain are hung many pieces of

38.1. Vision of the Goddess in the Cave and in the Abyss

jewellery: gifts for the goddess. You stand up and walk to the curtain. Carefully you pull it to one side. The cave beyond is dark, and you can hear snoring. Being very quiet, scoop up the flame and hold it in your hand as you tiptoe into the cave: the flame lights the way and also brings stillness to the Underworld.

In the larger cave are many creatures, all fast asleep on the floor. Up around you hang bats, alongside them are perched birds and lizards, all asleep. At the far end of the cave you see an old woman asleep on a stone throne. Her long grey hair has grown into the floor, and her body seems to be joining with the stone chair upon which she is seated. Among her clothing sleep tiny birds and other creatures, and at her feet is curled a large hound. The hound opens one eye and looks at you. This alerts the ancient Goddess, who wakes up, and also looks at you with one eye.

Kneel before her and offer her whatever you find in your pocket. She will either take the gift or tell you to leave. If she takes the gift, tell her that you are learning about the deeper parts of the Underworld so that you can be a better magician. She may ask you questions and she may ask you to do a job for her. If you agree to what she asks you, it is really important that you actually follow through and do what she asks. If it is something you are not comfortable with doing, then you must be honest and say so.

Once that is over, ask her if she will allow you to explore her cave in more depth and if she will allow you to learn about the deeper side of her in the Abyss. If she agrees, stand and bow to her before leaving her. You will find that behind her chair there is a narrow passageway. If she allows you, go down the passageway, taking the flame with you. You will also notice that the hound has properly awoken and is following you: he will ensure your safety as you draw near to the Abyss.

The passageway, which is hewn out of the rock, is roughly decorated with paintings of animals and birds, many of which you have never seen before. These are the memories of creatures that have become extinct and now are only memories, deep in the Underworld. The deeper into the passageway you go, the stranger the animal paintings get, until you realize you are looking at a creative version of dinosaurs. The passageway becomes narrower and you begin to

38. THE MAGIC OF THE UNDERWORLD

notice strange magical symbols on the walls, roof and floor. As you pass over and under them, you feel a strange sensation, almost like cobwebs touching you. These are magical barriers that create a wall between the Underworld and the Abyss: beings must not be able to pass freely from the Abyss to the Underworld. The sense of cobwebs becomes stronger and you begin to feel that you are pushing through some sort of sticky substance in order to continue on your journey. The flame draws closer to you, and the hound is now at your leg, growling softly. The darkness becomes more intense and the air takes on a very distinctive smell that you recognize from somewhere but cannot remember where: you do, however, remember the fear that goes with that smell, and all your defences are on full alert.

The passageway ends at a large and ornate doorway that is guarded by two very large and very strange-looking angelic beings. They have many wings that are wrapped closed around them and a body of many eyes, one of which opens to look at you. They look into your eyes, into your mind and into your soul. They see that you are a magician and that you mean no ill will. One of the angelic beings, either the one on the right or the one on the left, will reach out and mark you upon the forehead, so that you will be identified to other guardians. Whichever side the angel is on when you are touched will indicate a path that has now been finished for you magically. You can enter the Abyss from the Underworld, but you must not try to enter the Underworld from the Abyss: to do so would open a pathway for other beings and could lead to ancient beings finding their way back to our world when they should not.

The angels open the doorway slowly and a puff of stale air greets you. You find yourself in yet another passageway, also decorated with magical symbols designed to stop anyone from wandering through the tunnel and finding their way to the Underworld from the Abyss. The flame stays close to you, but the hound will not cross the threshold into the Abyss: he barks and then turns to go back to his mistress in the cave. The passageway widens a little and you notice paintings that tell stories on the walls. You stop to look at them closer. They are very beautiful, but they do not seem to make much sense to you. Your fingers trail the walls as you walk, running your hands over the images, which feel strange to the touch.

38.1. Vision of the Goddess in the Cave and in the Abyss

The deeper into the passageway you go, the more intricate the magical sigils upon the floor become, and you feel their power as you pass over them. The passageway opens out into a large cave with a bed in the centre. Upon the bed is laid a sleeping woman with a lion at her feet. She is dressed for battle with beautifully tooled leather armour, decorated with silver and gold. Aside her is a sword, a bow with arrows and a spear. She is very tall: her hair is long and red, and very thick. Her facial features look strange, part Chinese, part something else that you cannot quite identify. Around the stone bed are magical symbols that keep her asleep, but the lion has one eye open and is watching you. The lion speaks to you, telling you that you can learn about her by touching her, so you very carefully place a hand upon her leg and close your eyes.

You see her surrounded by humans that look very strange, almost prehuman, and they have ritually brought her into the world as their goddess to lead them in battle and to watch over them. There is something deeper in her, and your sight digs through the layers of magical overlay to find a female deity constructed by angelic patterns and Divine purpose. She is made up of the powers of the elements and directions, and she holds the voice of the forest, of the creatures and of the weather in her. She holds the word of Justice, and keeps the balance not only in nature, but in humanity.

It is then that you realize that she is not fully asleep and that she is watching you using her inner vision. She delves into you, searching your heart and mind as she learns about you. Through that searching, you become aware of imbalances within you that need addressing. She focuses in on aspects of your life that you know you have the power to change. You take your hand off and the contact breaks. Her touch has changed you: your sight is suddenly much stronger and as you cast a glance around the cave, you begin to see that some of the magical sigils that are keeping her in this place are imbalanced and are holding her prisoner against her will and the will of nature. You instinctively spit on to your hand and rub away the sigils on the pathway that block her way out of the Abyss. You can no longer be in this place, and you are told in your mind that you must leave.

Ahead of you is a tunnel that leads away from the direction that you came in, and you are drawn to leave via this tunnel. The minute you step out of the cave you become aware of many strange-looking

38. The magic of the Underworld

beings who are asleep in the tunnel and you have to pick your way carefully around them. Some look part animal, part human, and others look like nothing you have ever seen before. On the walls of the tunnels are scenes of bloody battles and massacres: you turn your eyes away so that you are not drawn to them as you begin to run down the tunnel. The tunnel has many twists and turns, with entrances to other caves running off of it, but you ignore them and continue to run down the main tunnel. It opens out suddenly onto a large cliff face or what appears to be a massive chasm in the earth. On the other side is a cliff face with similar entrances, and the walls of the cliff sides seem to go down and up forever: this is the great Abyss.

There is a little ledge that you are stood on that juts out slightly into the Abyss so that you can look up and down. As you stand upon the ledge, you remember something deep in your mind about the keeper of the Abyss: the Great Archangel, and you call upon this great being to help you. A pressure builds up in the air around you as a large being emerges out of the depths of the Abyss and looks at you. Explain to this being what you have just done, where you have been and that you wish to go to the Inner Desert so that you can find your way home. As you talk to the angel, you can hear people waking up and someone singing, the noise coming from the tunnel that you have just left. The angel puts out a hand for you to step onto and he lifts you up higher and higher in the Abyss. You see many ledges as you rise, and some of them have strange-looking beings upon them, which look at you as you go past.

The Keeper carefully places you upon the sands of the Inner Desert, and you see that the Sandalphon are already waiting for you. They see the marks upon your forehead, so they know where you have just been and probably what you have just done. One of them places a finger upon your forehead so that you can see into their mind. They show you the greatness of the Goddess that you have just visited, and her importance upon the land, how she keeps it in balance and how she also keeps humanity in balance. You are shown the rituals that bound her and cast her into the Abyss, sending her to sleep in the Underworld, and stopping her process of destruction for balance. Now you understand her better.

The Sandalphon walk with you as you walk towards a mist that will act as a threshold for the Void. They wait as you pass into the mist, passing into the Void and into nothing. You spread out in the nothing, taking in the stillness and silence, being in the place of no time, of no movement. The strain of the long journey you have just taken falls away from you, and you see how important it was for a human to descend into the Underworld, and to pass from the Underworld into the Abyss, and from the Abyss through the Inner Desert and into the Void. It has created a loop, opened a pathway, and reconnected certain powers up. With that knowledge, you step out of the Void and back into the room where you first started. When you are ready you blow out the candle, taking the sacred flame back into yourself, and filling your deep inner landscape with stillness and silence.

★ ★ ★

The loop of travel through the Underworld and Abyss is a very important one and establishes a very necessary pathway that builds regeneration within the land and humanity. Although the above vision is very much about the Goddess, it can be used in many different ways to establish the connection between the ancient past, the present and the future. Such connection is very important for the overall health of humanity and the land, and ensures the passage of ancient knowledge into the distant future. It also enables the freeing up of ancient knowledge that has been bound into the Underworld and allows the beings that accompany such knowledge to emerge out of the Abyss and work with humanity once more. You can see why this work is not really beginner material, as the possibility for abuse is massive and the potential for blowing oneself up with this work is obvious. But is it important work and needs to be expanded upon, developed and worked with a variety of Underworld deities and beings.

38.2 The Sisters at the back of the North Wind

The Sisters are an interesting contact that one finds deep within the earth, with ancient links to the sacred land. (It is not, however,

38. The magic of the Underworld

anything to do with the children's book of the same name by George McDonald!)

The Sisters at the back of the North Wind are an ancient line of priestesses who stay as mediators within the land and mediate a destructive power of air out into the world. It is the air within the earth: all elemental forces have a balancing power that flows through them. The air that flows from this contact is the air that changes humanity, the air that carries the disease and change from the depths of the Sea Temple and the air that is part of the weave of fate. They weave the story of the land, the fate of the people and the two opposing land powers, depicted in the UK as the red and white dragons.

For personal work and learning, these sisters will tear you apart in vision and scatter you to the four directions. Then they will reweave you in a fate pattern of magical service. If you work with them in service, you will often find yourself working and weaving land energies or sometimes just weaving or blowing the wind with them. Because they often work with vast stretches of time as far as humanity is concerned, it is often impossible to truly understand what it is you are doing when you work in service with them. Sometimes though, it is possible to see where their work is going and it is a very interesting experience to join in.

The following vision takes you to meet them and be torn apart by them. There is no ritual for working with this contact, as it is not their place to manifest in our time and realm; rather you go to them to work. It is an important step in inner work to touch base with them, if only once, so that you get a deeper understanding of the deeper land powers and how they run through and affect our society.

38.3 Vision of the Sisters at the back of the North Wind

Light a candle and be aware of the candle flame. Close your eyes, and with your inner vision see the candle flame grow bigger and bigger. You are drawn closer to it. The flame suddenly falls through the floor and into the earth, and you are drawn to follow it. You fall through the earth with the flame, falling and falling through rock, tree root,

38.3. Vision of the Sisters at the back of the North Wind

earth and more rock. You fall through caves and tunnels, falling with the flame as it journeys into the Underworld.

You find yourself falling in darkness as the surface world vanishes, the way lit only by the flame ahead. You find yourself slowing down and you land in a cave with a high roof and four tunnels, one each in the directions. The flame falls and settles in the centre of the cave and illuminates the space. As you look around, you see that the walls have very old paintings that seem to tell of events from another time. Some of the pictures have graffiti near them, names of people scribbled when they came here and visited. You look closer at the paintings and see stories of the land where you live, of king and queen-ship, and birds and creatures being tended by humans. As you walk around, notice that each tunnel has a carving over the entrance, which itself is carved out of the rock rather than being a natural tunnel. You look closer at each carving and see that they depict the four directions. The entrance to the north has a wind blowing out of it, which makes you curious, and you begin to walk down the tunnel of the north to see what is there.

The tunnel is lit by its own light, a kind of green hue that that glows out from the moss on the walls and allows you to just about see where you are going. A faint voice, singing, reaches you and you listen to it as you walk closer and closer to the source. The tunnel opens out into another cave. This one is smaller, and in the middle of the cave stand three old women with very long hair. They are standing around something you cannot see, and they are singing to it. You draw closer, and one of the old women, without stopping her singing, reaches out and pulls you towards her.

In the centre of the circle of old women is a narrow stone bed, and beneath the bed is a well that falls deep down through the earth and out into the stars. You peer down the well and see the stars faintly in the distance. The old woman holds on to you so that you do not fall in, and begins talking to you. You stand up to look into her eyes as she talks you, even though you cannot understand what she is saying, and her eyes look deeply and sharply into yours. She looks into you, deeper and deeper, seeing the depths of you, seeing your fate, seeing what blocks that fate and seeing where you need to be.

38. The Magic of the Underworld

She reaches out a long thin fingernail and scratches you on the forehead, drawing blood. She tastes the blood, looking through your bloodline as she tastes it. When she has seen what she needed to see, she nods and points at the bed: she wants you to get on it. You know that if you get on that bed, something powerful will happen and you will never be the same again. So you pause. The old woman rolls her eyes and grabs you, throwing you onto the bed and rolling her sleeves up.

One of the other old women begins to bang something, like metal on stone, creating a beat that the other two women begin to hum and sing to. As they sing, they begin walking around the table, touching you as they turn and singing over you. They dance and sing, turning around as they dance around you, getting a bit faster and a bit faster. Chatter begins in your head and you realize you are hearing conversations you had years ago with various people, some of it from childhood. Then you recognize your grandmother's voice, which then fades into voices you do not recognize. The voices get louder and more jumbled, chanting and calling around you as the women turn and touch you.

Your nose begins to bleed from the pressure, the blood dripping down off of you, off the bed and falling into the stars. Memories of painful emotions in childhood well up in your mind and you begin to cry, your pain and sorrow as a child flooding over you and overwhelming you. Your tears drip off the side of your face and form a small stream of tears that falls with the drops of blood down the well and out into the stars.

The songs of the women become stranger, and sounds begin to combine with the song, the sounds coming from the well of the stars. The song flows up the well, a wordless song of harmonies that is the most beautiful thing you have ever heard. Its pure beauty mixes with the coarse voices of the old women and you are filled with sound of all different pitches and harmonies. The women circle you, weaving your drops of blood with the vibrations of the harmonies falling from the stars. Their circling and calling begins to create a vibration on the rock floor around you, and the vibration slowly gets stronger and stronger. The ground begins to shake and you are forced to hold on to bed for fear of falling off.

38.3. Vision of the Sisters at the back of the North Wind

The rock bursts open and two beings appear that look like dragons, and yet their flesh seems transparent, as though they were not fully manifest. The two beings rise into the cave, drawn by the call of the old women: these are the two opposing powers of the land. They will appear to you as dragons of two different colours, often red and white, and will wind themselves around each other as they rise into the cave. Immediately the dragons appear the women change the pitch of their song, which now becomes higher and faster. Their weaving becomes more complex and they scoop up the tails of the dragons and begin to weave them into their patterns. You watch in fascination as the women transform the dragons into threads, along with your blood and the vibrations of the stars, and begin making a tapestry. It does not make sense that the sound becomes a thread, nor that the dragons become threads, but you watch as it happens and you stop trying to rationalize it.

Once the tapestry is finished, the women turn to you and begin to circle you while singing. The turning and singing gets faster and faster until you have to shut your eyes so as not to become dizzy. You lie in darkness, feeling a pressure building up around you as the women get faster and the sound gets deeper and stranger. The pressure becomes harder and harder to cope with and you begin to feel like you are going to explode. The air around you presses down upon you and the air in your lungs is sucked out but not replaced. You try and gasp for air, fighting in the confusion of sound and pressure that surrounds you.

The women suddenly change pitch and direction, which creates a massive force that seems to launch you out of yourself. You find yourself out on the land, flowing through trees and rocks, flowing through the air, through animals, passing through buildings, creatures, trees and flowers. You are of no substance, you are pure thought, pure spirit as you pass through all things, experiencing their thoughts and emotions as you pass through them. You are filled with a deep sense of peace and are able to see the beautiful light of Divinity within all things. That light touches you as you pass through things and its touch awakens deep knowledge and deep longing within you. You flow across the land like a breath and the land breathes back in communion. The land calls to you, asking you to become a part of it, to sleep, dream, sing and make love like the earth: to wind your blood into the blood of the land and become one with the sacred earth.

You breathe your reply of love and service of the land, and immediately your ears are filled with the song of the sisters. The song seems to take form and you look around you, looking over the face of the land. You see the tapestry that was woven in the depths rise to the surface and settle itself upon the surface of the land. The grass grows through the tapestry that is a weave of your blood, the song of the stars and the dragons of the earth. Trees grow through the tapestry, flowers burst open and birds land upon the earth looking for treats. You flow across the face of the tapestry and recognize the feel of your blood upon its story. That awareness of your blood makes you aware again of your body: your hands reach out to touch the tapestry of the land, and your heart beats with the rhythm of the song.

You are drawn to lie with the tapestry, so you lie down upon the land that holds the story and you feel yourself sink into the tapestry, becoming a part of it. The tapestry wraps itself around you and you feel yourself lay upon and within the land, hearing the heartbeat of the land close to your own. You feel the trees, the rocks, the buildings, the rivers and all the people who live upon the land. They are upon you and you are a part of them. The spirit of the land begins to talk to you, asking you if you would be of service to the land, either in your sleep and dreams, or in your waking life. The land may ask you to sing for it regularly, to garden it, to tend and uphold the land and all the ancestors who sleep within the land. You feel how your life and the land are one, and now you begin to understand the sacrifice of the sovereign king or queen who marries themselves to the land in a act of service. You realize with this work that you must look after your body and act with integrity so that the land stays healthy and balanced.

Once you have decided what you are willing and able to do to be of service to the land, and the land has accepted your proposal, you instantly find yourself back on the table with the three sisters around you. They are turning in the opposite direction, rebuilding you, reweaving your body as they put you back together. You feel the massive change that you have undergone, and you also feel those in the distant past of your bloodline who have done similar unions with the land at one time or another. You feel that deep connection with

38.3. Vision of the Sisters at the back of the North Wind

some of your ancestors, and that connection is woven tight into your memory as the sisters turn around you.

When they have finished, the three women step away from the stone table and wait for you to climb off. You feel unsteady on your feet, your body feels fresh and strong, and your mind feels like it has been opened wide and filled with generations of knowledge regarding the land around you. One of the sisters steps forward to you and marks you upon the forehead: it is the mark of a gardener of the land: one who tends and nurtures the sacred land upon which they live.

The sisters then take you back down through the tunnel to the flame that burns at the centre of the four directions deep underground and they stand you before the flame. You look into the flame and you are drawn to its peace and beauty. You step into the flame, passing through the flame into the Void, the place of eternal stillness and silence. The mark upon your head burns, reminding you of your commitment to serve the land upon which you live. This could mean literal gardening, or simply picking up litter regularly, planting wild flowers, feeding the creatures through the winter, weeding out aggressive plants, tending ancestral graves, or working with the weather when it becomes unbalanced. If you keep up a communion with the land then it will be made very clear to you what needs to happen.

You step out of the Void, through the flame and back into the room where you first started. You pause a while to reflect on what happened before you blow out the candle flame, sending it back into the Void.

★ ★ ★

The Sisters at the Back of the North Wind are an ancient and powerful inner contact group that work with the powers of fate out in the stars and connect/weave them in with the bloodlines of humanity and the deep land powers. Traditionally they are responsible for ancient kingships and queenships, weaving their fate into the land that they will serve so that the land and body become one.

The powers of the land in Britain that they work with often appear to us in myths and legends as streams of red and white that are bound

38. THE MAGIC OF THE UNDERWORLD

and woven together. Sometimes these streams are depicted as snakes or dragons, and they are the consciousness of the land itself. The contact calls out to the stars, wherein the angelic contacts that work with the stellar fate patterns answer the call in harmonies. The power of the harmonics is mixed with the power of the blood of a sacred female line which in turn is woven into the braid of the red and white dragon powers of the land. This tapestry becomes the fate of the kingship of the sacred land.

The weave of the sisters also manifests the lines of sacred priesthood and other bloodlines that have a direct effect upon the fate of the land and humanity. The blood, stars and the dragon powers combine to create a pattern through which Divinity can manifest through sovereignty, through the fate tapestry that weaves the future of the land and the people. Working with these sisters is very likely to put you into direct contact with these sacred powers, and you may very well find yourself in a long pattern of service to the land where you live. Upon your death you will be expected to sleep within the land or serve the land as an inner contact.

38.4 Origins of humanity in the Abyss

Underworld work, when you strip it right down to its bones, is basically going into the distant past by going down into the layers of the earth. Everything that is no longer reincarnating descends into the Underworld to sleep. That process continues with the consciousness falling ever deeper into the depths, passing into the Abyss and finally vanishing into a compressed layer of consciousness that is eventually recycled. Before it reaches that compression level, anything can be connected with if you are willing to go down deep enough (and you are stupid enough) and the more you interact with something, the nearer it begins to rise back to the surface world. Once something has passed into the Abyss, the connection to the Underworld slowly closes until that ancient consciousness is eventually locked deep in the depths of the Abyss. Those deepest layers cannot generally be accessed by our consciousness as they are just too far removed for us to get to them.

38.4. Origins of humanity in the Abyss

The one thing to really think about before you decide that you want to hack into the depths of ancient humanity is to ask yourself why. If there is a good reason, for example for learning, or for reaching an ancient power that is needed, or to release an ancient deity that was bound etc., then that is fine. But if you are intending on descending into the very depths of the Abyss for no reason other than sheer curiosity, then you are a moron. The reason you are a moron if you decide to do such a thing, is because the amount of danger that you will encounter on such a mission is akin to bungee jumping off of a 3,000 ft sheer cliff face with a bungee rope that is rather frayed. If you go into any great inner depths without a good reason, then you are basically on your own: other beings will not intervene and waste their energy protecting you just so that you can amuse yourself. But if you are doing a mission in service, for good reason that is not all about you, then a variety of orders of being will intervene and provide you with whatever help you need—but only when you really need it.

When you are reaching back to early forms of humanity, there are a few things you need to think about first. One of those things is the nature of Man itself. For some bizarre reason, modern magicians and spiritual types seem to have a very rosy view about what a human was and how they conducted themselves. There are books-a-many that wax lyrical about our wonderful ancestors living in harmony with nature. Well, yes, true. Except that today's idea of what 'nature' is comes from the Disney channel and has no basis in fact.

Our ancestors did not commune with Bambi, did not talk to the birds in twee 'whistle' talk and did not love the land like their own mother. They were struggling to survive, often against horrific odds, and could not afford to be expressive, cuddly or emotional. Cannibalism was a major feature, for a variety of reasons, as was aggression, selfish use of the land resources and the hostile grabbing of what they wanted when they wanted it. Nothing has changed really. The same is true of the animal world: when you observe animals and birds in a wild environment, you see the same pattern of an aggressive will to survive and reproduce. This only changes when the basics of life are provided, so if you reach back to a time/area when food was in plentiful supply and the population was more or less balanced, then you get very sophisticated and compassionate people in general. But in northern climates or difficult terrain, this was not true.

So bearing that in mind, be aware that some of your most ancient ancestors might very well hang onto you or try to use your body as an energy source or even to climb out of the Abyss. The other thing to remember when you are reaching down deep for a human contact or prehuman contact, is that not all human consciousness ends up down the Abyss, it is just one of many areas of universal consciousness where beings go to sleep and dream.

Every place in the Underworld that holds beings has the front door (outer visionary expression) and a back door (the Abyss tunnel). You may find that you have to go down the Abyss, into the tunnel where the ancient ancestor resides, and push through a sealed entrance to emerge out in the Underworld. Bear in mind if you do this, such a door from the Abyss to the Underworld can potentially allow that being access through the Underworld to the surface world. You can bring them into Underworld temples, which usually have lots of checks and balances to keep ancient beings in the Underworld and stop them ascending, and that is usually the safest way to reconnect with an ancient Underworld being that is sleeping in the Abyss. If you have some long-term work with an ancient being, then bringing them into an ancient Underworld temple will be a good working space. Don't try and build your own space in the Underworld as you will not know enough about the ins and outs of the ancient ancestor or being to make it escape-proof. And never, ever, build a tunnel from the Abyss out into the Underworld and up to the surface world: that could potentially wipe out humanity. It would be akin to releasing an ancient form of plague to which we have no immunity.

Working with ancient humans can be very useful in helping us understand our own humanity better, and they can often be brilliant guides/advisors for working with ancient sites, stone circles, etc. They can teach us about star navigation, hunting, weather work, fertility, and power spots upon the land. They can also be very interesting to work with if you are studying the intricacies of genetics from a magical point of view. Just make sure that when the work cycle is over, you help them back to sleep. I assume that you would have the common sense to ask the ancestor in the first place if they would be willing to work with you. Don't just drag them out of sleep: they tend

38.4. Origins of humanity in the Abyss

to get a wee bit pissy if you do that. And also be aware that they will have things they want you to do, or things that they need from you. It is always a two-way street.

Some people say that the past and dead should be left in the past, but I do not agree completely with that: the idea of past, present and future is a modern one. If you go back to around 3,000 B.C., you will find cultures where the dead slept very near or among the living. The communion back and forth between the generations, between the ancients and present day people, was constant. We also talk to the children of the future, keeping an unbroken line of consciousness flowing through and beyond time.

At the deeper levels of the Abyss and the Underworld, you will come across beings that are part human and part reptile-looking. These are not aliens, just a very ancient form of being from this planet. They are very powerful, very magical and are still pretty active in layers of the surface world. They appear still in visions in various parts of the USA where they are still fairly close to the surface. Just tread very carefully with them if you come across these beings: they are very strong and can be very aggressive. These are beings that appeared in Greek myths as Titans, and most places around the world have versions of them.

In any work that you do at great depth in the Underworld, keep tight notes and records of what you do, where you go and what you see: it is still very much exploratory work and generations to come can benefit from your experiences. It can also help you to look back in years to come and start to make connections in your work that were maybe not so obvious at the time.

With Underworld work in general I have found it best, in my own messed-up way, to go down as deep as possible first, do as much exploration as possible, and then slowly ascend, making contact with the various layers of consciousness a layer at a time. I spent a good five years going from the depths, as far back and down as I could go, and then slowly over months and years, exploring more and more layers on the way up. It is fascinating to see the different layers of beings, the layers of temples and sacred places, and then the layers of nonhuman beings who populate the layers a bit closer to the surface. It is also fascinating to work in the Abyss on the opposite side of

38. THE MAGIC OF THE UNDERWORLD

the Abyss, descending (I always go down slowly in increments when working in the Abyss...I'm a wuss) layer by layer, and contacting the beings in the various layers/tunnels as I go. On the opposite side from us you will find beings who have never expressed themselves in the outer world, who have never had physical manifestation and are not really used to human contact. It can get very interesting.

38.5 Methods of descent

As I said before, when you begin your explorations downwards, first go through the Underworld before you attempt the Abyss at depth. A good practical method of Underworld descent is to go via the various realms so that you are working downwards in stages. First you would go down to the cave of the Goddess, and find a tunnel behind her that leads downwards. Then you would probably find yourself in a cavern where the River of Death flows through, and again there would be a tunnel leading downwards. You will pass through a hall of ancestors, which is basically a large cavern with loads of people sleeping in it (a folktale version is where Arthur's knights are sleeping in a cave in a hill). At this point you have not gone very deep, but you have passed beyond death and are starting to hack through the layers of the past.

Then, again through a tunnel or rough stone stairway, going down you will come to a layer of ancient temples, often with large lioness goddesses in them. These are very good learning places and are also a good place to stop for a breather and allow your physical body to catch up with what you are doing. Pushing further down again you will come to caves that have markings on them, usually very primitive, and holes in the ceiling that seem to reach up to the surface world: these are caves where the roots of certain landmasses and mountain ranges come together and can be worked upon. The magic in these caves is often very powerful, ancient and potentially dangerous. Beyond those caves you will begin to reach volcanic caves, caves with sea water flowing out of them and caves of immense crystal structure.

The beings you will find here are often reptilian and there are many very large complex and powerful beings that can be very difficult to try and communicate with. This is about as far as I got in

38.5. Methods of descent

my explorations. I could say that you cannot go any further, but that would be stupid. It is better to say, I found I could go no further and if I wanted to reach back further I had to cross over into the Abyss. My limitations will possibly not be your limitations.

Once you get as deep as you can go, then you can attempt to cross over into the Abyss from the Underworld. Look very carefully for a blocked up entrance, locked door or very narrow tunnel, etc. If you have got to such depth, it means that others have got here before you, which in turn means that you are at a layer that once held a consciousness that was manifest on the planet surface. If it was manifest, then it has a place in the Abyss, which in turn means that somewhere, there is an entrance to the Abyss from where you are. It may take a while to find it and then a bigger job to actually get it to open. Usually such ancient doorways have guardian demonic beings or angelic beings that are there to stop beings getting out of the Abyss via the Underworld. They are not so bothered about stopping you getting into the Abyss, their attitude being, 'hey dude you want to fry, be my guest.'...

Once you find the entrance, you will need to explain to the guardian, whom you will have just woken up, why you need to access the Abyss. If you reason is good enough, they will open the doorway for you. If you have no service reason, but you are truly and honestly intent upon learning (as opposed to being a tourist) then if you run your hands over the doorway, you will find that certain sigils are carved into the door. If you come across one that has been given to you as a key in the past by an inner contact, you will find it will act as a key to opening the door. The sigil marks you as one in a line of a particular priesthood and as such gives you access to many inner places.

Once through the doorway, you will find yourself in a tunnel that will eventually lead to a large cavern or series of caverns. This is the 'real' abode of the beings from the Underworld realm whose level you are at. Beyond that series of caverns will be another tunnel which will lead to the Abyss itself, and it will have a ledge that overhangs the Abyss slightly. Standing on that, you will be able to call the Keeper of the Abyss who will lift you up to the Inner Desert which is the layer in the Abyss in which we humans currently reside. If however you wish to explore the Abyss a bit more, you will find a stone stair carved out of the rock face of the Abyss which basically goes all the way up while visiting many of the ledges on the way. Each ledge is marked with magical patterns and veils which stop beings that are down the Abyss, and belong there, from using the stairway to rise up. You will have to be very careful if you use this stairway to explore or access some of the tunnels: make sure that you do not have any hitchhikers attached who will use you to get out. On our side of the Abyss, which is also the side that the Underworld opens out onto, reside all beings or parts of the consciousness of those beings that have at one time or other manifested in the outside world, i.e. our universe. The caves and tunnels on the opposite side of the Abyss are the resting places of the beings which have never physically manifested at all. So for example, from the Inner Desert, which is our layer, on the opposite side of the Abyss, going down to the first layer of caves and tunnels is the faery realm.

The basic rule of thumb, when exploring the Abyss from down to up, is to use your common sense. Trust nothing, dress as anything but human, and keep on your side of the Abyss. Do not be tempted to cross over and explore down the other side: the Abyss can only be safely crossed from our own layer of the Inner Desert, unless you are working with angelic beings. If you do it may be very possible that you will not come back. Working 'down' at depth has been sadly neglected for thousands of years and it is time for reconnection, service and communion once more.

From a body maintenance perspective, be aware that going deep down into the Underworld and Abyss is akin to deep sea diving. It will affect your body in a variety of ways and you will without doubt have a physical impact from the work. Ensure when you are undertaking a program of deep Underworld work that you have regular body care treatments like acupuncture or cranial osteopathy: you will basically need putting back together again afterwards. Ensure that you are taking vitamins or are on a really healthy diet, and get loads of sleep between work sessions. The body heals when it sleeps, and also the work will continue in a way that your body can adjust around.

Working deeply in the Underworld has a side effect of grounding you, connecting you with your ancestors and their skill sets, and giving you good solid roots to work from. As a magician, it is the most important part of your development and will help you to really come to know yourself, which is the greatest achievement that any of us can truly reach.

Chapter Thirty-nine

Functioning as an adept

What does it mean to be an adept? In truth, and in my world, it is not a title assigned to a member of an order upon completion of training and tests, but a description of someone who has done a lot of training, maturing and self-development, someone with real skills, knowledge and technique, and someone who has matured beyond the self and is ready for service/work at a deeper level. This takes decades of work, and to get to a full working adept power level takes at least into your forties or fifties if you began as a teenager. I find it hilarious that there are twenty-somethings who have done a couple of years of postal study, attended a few weekend workshops in a 'Mystery school,' and declare themselves to be adepts: my question would be, adept at what precisely?

To be an adept means to be a person who has in-depth knowledge of a wide variety of advanced magical skills, and who can practically apply those skills with consistency, maturity and honour. Most importantly, *they know what it is that they do not know.*

We never arrive at a completion of the adept stage: in magic the learning is lifelong and just when you think you 'know,' another layer of the magic emerges, and the learning starts all over again. That is if the magician has developed a learning method: when you are 'taught' something by a teacher, you do not really develop an independent learning method, which with magic in particular means the magician can develop a lifelong dependency on teachers. In such cases the magician never really reaches adepthood: they become eternal initiate students.

The development of the independent learning method comes from downright curiousness: the need to know what is under ever stone, the need to learn as much as possible without a teacher, and the ability to pay proper attention to the smallest details, while

39. Functioning as an Adept

also taking responsibility for everything that you do. Being able to continue to the bitter end of a learning curve without giving in or stepping back in the face of adversity or threat. All of these qualities and more create not only a strong potential adept, they also by nature of walking a magical path that way, create a learning method that is often unique to the individual. In the ancient world, and really until the last hundred years or so, an initiate was trained by being given one step and they were expected to find the other ninety-nine steps for themselves: that is true magical learning.

The achievement of the skill level (rather than title) of adept also brings with it certain responsibilities. If a person is very self-obsessed, then the concept of true magical service will be alien to them and it is pretty certain that they will not reach the depth of power needed to be a true adept. It is very rare for a totally selfish person to move beyond initiate level simply because the skill level of adept involves a lot of selfless work. Why? Because a large amount of an adept's ability to do heavy lifting in magic comes from cooperation with other beings and powers. If you do not help others when needed, then inner/spirit beings will not work with you: it is always a two-way street. First you give freely and without agenda, so that you are recognized as one who works as part of the larger universal pattern in an active magical way. Once recognized as such, your own work and fate becomes an active part of that pattern and when the need arises, other magicians in other times, along with inner contacts, spirits, deities and beings will step forward and help you when you need it.

39.1 Service

Your magical skills may be called into the service of any religion be it present or past, or even future: though the call usually only comes if magic has been used in that religion and it has all slowly gone horribly wrong. If the degeneration in a religion is natural, then it is not a situation for magicians to interfere with. It is irrelevant what you think of the religious structure: your job is to ensure that it is plugged in and the lights are on. If the religion has degenerated beyond all saving, then it is the adept's job to pull the plug out and leave them in the dark. You cannot make this vast decision yourself: the job will

39.1. Service

come to you through inner contacts or sometimes even from the deity of the religion itself.

This might all read as a very controversial and interfering way of working, but in truth, if done unconditionally, and the degeneration came from magic in the first place, then it is simply magical service. If a religion has become so degenerate that humanity cannot reach Divinity through it and everything has been tried to plug it back in and failed, then the structure has no function in the future: it must be dismantled to ensure that parasitical elements do not move in and begin to operate it, though usually in such situations the vessel of the religion is likely to be heavily parasited already. It is basically the responsibility of the priesthood to close down a spiritual structure to prevent that from happening. If the priesthood has degenerated enough to have lost that skill, then it falls to whoever has the ability, usually the magicians.

In earlier times, when the priest/esshood knew that the end was coming, be it war, famine, or just the end of the shelf life, they would close the gates that allowed Divinity to step into the deity, and basically shut off the link between the Inner Temple and the outer. This can be directly experienced at some ancient temple sites where you can go to an altar area, or an inner sanctum and try to commune with the deity there. Not only will you not get anything, the silence will be deafening. It is emptier that an empty space: it is as if the very life has been sucked out of a space: that is how a lockdown is experienced. They can be unlocked, but you must be ready to take responsibility for whatever happens if you do open it all back up. You would probably have to move the whole structure to where you could work regularly with it.

If you are called to do such work and you are not sure of the ethics of such an action, (and such questioning of one's ethics and motives it very important) then go into the Inner Temple structure of the religion. Often the inner structures still exist and have priesthoods working within them. Talk with them and see what they suggest. Often, when a religion has degenerated for long enough, the inner priesthoods cut the outer structure loose. The one thing you have to really remember is you cannot be judge and jury for a religious structure: it has to be a call from the Inner Worlds. Even if a religion has degenerated to a point where it is killing and torturing

39. FUNCTIONING AS AN ADEPT

people, so long as Divinity is flowing through the structure, it is not your concern: destruction is just as important as creation and stasis. Everything, both good and bad, has an action in building the future, and you always, as an adept, have to be for neither good nor bad, for neither right nor left hand path: your job is simply to work. Humans do not have a long enough lifespan to understand the very long-term patterns of how things evolve: bad can bring great good, good can trigger great evil, so you must work without emotion, without judgement, doing only what is requested to bring things to where they need to be.

Usually such a call comes from the inner only when magic was used originally in the religion for conditional purposes and where the degeneration over time is a direct result of that conditional magic. Natural decay is usually left alone, and that has always been my policy too. If magic caused the problem, then use magic to mop it up, if it is a natural process, then let it be. Most if not all of my work as an exorcist over the years was a matter of cleaning up magical messes and putting away beings that had been brought into our world by magic. When I was called out to a situation that was natural, I just used to use common sense, compassion and priesthood skills to open the gates to let confused and trapped souls out.

That is just one example of one area of work that an adept can sometimes be called to. Basically the types of work that present can be limitless, so it is pointless trying to create 'work boxes' of what adepts 'do.' It is much less a matter of 'what,' and more of 'why.' The more experienced as an adept you become, the less magical work you actually do. But when you do take action, it is powerful, to the point, and very much needed. Just bear in mind that if you choose to go down the road of conditional magic, the complex strands of fate connections and the energetic deficits they create can eventually balloon out of control and you could spend the rest of your life trying to undo, rebalance etc. It's all about choices.

One area of very interesting work that an adept can get drawn into is joining in very long-term work. You step in and take up where others have left off, do the best that you can for as long as you can, and then you hand off to the next person coming up. Usually these long-term jobs are to do with the land, civilization, and the survival of humanity. Sometimes it is maintaining places like the Abyss, or working in the death realm, working on the weaving of the fate of nations, or helping clean up land messes that will take generations (like nuclear dumping). Again the list is endless, but the jobs are big, hard work and you get no recognition whatsoever. What you do get is immense learning, very good skill practice and the knowledge that your grand-kids' offspring will probably have a better, more fruitful life because of your work. You can also assign yourself to a term of service with a specific priest/esshood and help to maintain and clean up lineages, temples, and magical patterns.

The most curious form of adept service is to just be yourself. You do no inner magic, just the occasional prayer if anything: you just live your life and affect unconditional change just by being where you are and doing ordinary things while magic flows freely and naturally through you and out into the world. Once you have done a great deal of inner magical work over a long period of time, you can effect change just by turning up and being at a place or around a person. At that stage of adeptship, you cannot turn the magic on and off: it is constantly flowing through you all the time. You become the open gate between the outer and Inner Worlds, and you will find yourself being sent to places or people just to be there. You will go away wondering what the hell that was all about, but you will find that your visit coincided with a major change: you were the energetic catalyst that was needed. People will find their way to you, will be drawn to you, and you will bring change to their lives just by being around them.

You can immediately see how this can very easily send a magician on a massive ego trip. You have to be very careful to understand that it is not such a major thing to be an energetic catalyst: in fact, it is quite a small role indeed. You are nothing but a doorway, a postman, a servant. You are not the messiah and you cannot wield that power to suit your own ego or yourself: it simply will not work, as it ultimately does not, as a power, originate from within you, you are a mere stepping stone. The other truth to bear in mind is that you are not special, just trained. If you fell over tomorrow, there would be someone right behind you to take up your path: always remember that you are and always will be truly expendable and replaceable.

Once you step onto the path of true magical adeptship, regardless of what that path is, be it destruction, regeneration or maintaining something, you will find the Sword of Justice dangling precariously over your head. With great power comes a heavy price, and that price is honour and responsibility. Just as in the story of Damocles, where the king appears to have limitless wealth, power and riches, so he also has the sword of Justice hanging by a thread over his head. In the story, the king dangles the sword by a hair to demonstrate to Damocles just how dangerous it can be. But that story is a fragment of one of the secrets of the Mysteries: the more power you gain, the more accountable you become. For an adept, that translates, in really simple terms, to doing nothing you know to be wrong or selfish, as you will get an instant karma rebalance, which is often very unpleasant.

39.2 Practicalities of living as an adept

I have broached some of these issues in the other books, but there are certain points I want to reiterate here in more depth as they are important. The deeper in magic you go, the more it affects your body and your life: this is just one of those truths that there is no escaping, no matter how much you want to deny it. The type of magic that you do will define the type of reaction your body will have, and the reaction will be specific to your own body. It will open out weaknesses and aggravate certain conditions, and if you are working in an unbalanced way, it will trigger certain illnesses.

Because of the high level of power that is flung around when an adept is working, it really helps you to survive those levels of power if you look after your life and body in a way that cushions the blows. There are no hard and fast rules, so this is more like a heads-up to be more attentive to your body, your family and your surroundings. If you are eating something that your body cannot process properly or is intolerant of, then the reaction will be far greater than it would be if you were not doing magic. If you do magic when you are ill, say with a cold, then it will potentially develop into a more serious viral condition. Some people would look upon this as a bad thing and say that magic is bad for the body. In fact, the reverse is true. What is happening is that your body is no longer tolerating your stupidity and is forcing you to behave yourself.

39.2. Practicalities of living as an adept

The power of the magic will change things in your life that need changing: it will sweep away old and no longer relevant aspects of your life. That really starts to happen in the initiate phase and is usually settling by the time you get to be a trained and working adept. The idea of the initiate phase, from an inner perspective, is to clean you up and clean up your life. By the time you are an adept it is about putting you to work and smacking your wrist if you do something silly.

So as an adept, you will begin to find that everything that comes in and out of your life has a major purpose, and that you are put into places or situations where either you have a job to do, or your presence is needed as a catalyst. Life becomes one major job. There is no time out, and it is not something you can walk away from at this stage: you become inexorably linked to the karma of the land, civilization and the deities. You will be pulled into service whenever you are needed, and your life will flow with the rhythm of the land. Everything and anything around you will have meaning and power, and you will have to be very careful about what you are talking to: every statue or cuddly toy that you choose to chat to could potentially become a window for a being to step into.

You can see how important it is when walking such a path to have a strong dose of common sense and to keep the ego under control. It is hard enough for a very stable person to operate under these conditions, so imagine what it is like for someone who has a mental fragility or a tendency towards mental illness: magical work at this level would push them way over the edge and far away.

It is very important to really get a sense for what is real and what is imagined, for very obvious reasons, and it is also very important to constantly question your ability, your motives and your actions. If you can walk that thin line, you will find yourself in a world where everything is magical, everything has Divine Presence, and everything truly talks to you. Every action you take has long-term consequences, so you learn to be thoughtful with your actions and to be constantly listening to the land which provides all the guidance you need. I once mentioned this to a magician friend of mine who retorted that he did not do 'nature' magic and therefore would not commune with the land. What a stupid thing to say: the land is all around you, it is what upholds you, feeds you, and gives you shelter.

39. Functioning as an Adept

It is not a fashion accessory like a pentacle that you choose to wear or not; it is a vast power expression of Divinity all around you. Whether you are into nature magic or not, the land processes power. It is the altar of the greatest temple of all.

39.3 Working within a tradition

If you are working as an adept within a specific magical tradition (i.e. as a real adept, not a purchased or dressed-up one) then the field range of your work will be fairly narrow and intense. In contacted lodges and specific lineages of magic, the adepts are responsible for keeping the line of magic clear and balanced. They also interact intensely with the inner contacts to clear away anything that is disrupting or degenerating the magical line. The adept will often work in the past, clearing out energetic tangles of magic from generations before, and working with the deities to help weave magical patterns for the future. Those patterns will be the template for the lodge in the future to ensure its healthy survival. It will also ensure that the lodge or group has a healthy foundation that allows its initiates to get on with its long-term project work, while the adepts working with the initiates on those projects will tap into the patterns to continually stabilize them.

Often, the work of a lodge that is operating at this level tends to be work that is long-term service to a landmass, a deity or a monarchy. The adepts not only work with the initiates in these long-term projects, they enable the projects to happen by keeping the doors open, bridging the deity and being the catalyst. The difference between an adept working in a lodge and an adept working 'freelance' for want of a better word, is that the 'freelance' adept will have a much greater responsibility, a wider field of service, and will not be limited by a belief system or an agenda. Personally, I feel that freelance is the better way to work: you answer to no one other than yourself and the Gods.

39.4 The future: passing on the teaching

It is important to pass the work on from generation to generation, to keep the flame going. This can be done through writing, group teaching or one-on-one apprentices. A major word of warning: this is the last true test and step for an adept: can you pass on the work without making yourself terribly important, a messiah or a guru? When you teach, and you teach things that are worth teaching, then people listen. When people listen to what you are saying, you realize what potential 'power' you have over people, and it is a temptation to bask in the fact that people look up to you. Yes, people will idolize you, yes, they will write to you asking you to be their teacher, and yes, people will put you high up there on a pedestal. It's a long way to fall, and it can be a painful fall.

When you take on the role of teacher you also take on the responsibility for the development of other people. That is a major responsibility in itself, not only because you are the one who will put them on their magical path, but also because you are the one who has to burst all of their bubbles, glue their feet to the ground, and slap them around the back of the head when they make mistakes. You cannot do that to others until you can first do it to yourself.

A magical training is also soul training, a development of the personality and a maturing of the consciousness. As a teacher you are responsible for putting the student in the path of experiences that will potentially trigger that development, for taking them to places that they need to learn about, and for introducing them to working methods that will help them learn to learn properly. It truly is a massive responsibility: you are the doorway that allows Divinity and Humanity to experience each other: keep that in mind.

Unfortunately these days, many magicians/occultists have taken up the fashion pedestal of the workshop guru. These magicians teach general magical workshops that are cloaked in publicity hype about being 'secret teachings,' 'never before seen Mysteries' or 'advanced archaic magical techniques' which are actually all just ordinary magic, or even made up stuff that sounds good but has no real content. They are expensive, exclusive and just plain useless as a form of magical training. They may offer certain experiences that are of interest, but

39. FUNCTIONING AS AN ADEPT

at the end of the day, they are like candy bars: tasty, fun, filling for a short while, but with no real nutritional value whatsoever.

Some books have become like that also, and it truly is a minefield for the aspirant to find a teacher whose source of information is reliable, understandable and walks the real path. There is a lot of dross that one has to plough through, but that in itself can be a good part of the training: learning discernment the hard way can be a valuable lesson indeed. Discernment is a skill that is invaluable on a magical path of learning. There is also a lot of good writing and teaching out there, usually happening quietly and without major fanfares. If the student has true intent to walk and develop upon a magical path, they will stumble across books, teachers, mentors and friends as and when they need to: that is how it works. One of the jobs of an adept is to be there for a student to stumble across: guide them for as long as they need it, and *then let them go when they need to move on.* Never try to hold on to a student. An adept teacher is always a stepping stone, nothing more.

There is a lot of responsibility upon your shoulders if you choose to be of service by teaching, and yet it is a very rewarding path to walk down. The basic rules for avoiding the ego pitfalls while being a good teacher are:

Don't involve money. If you have to travel a distance or hire a venue, then expenses are fine: it shouldn't cost you anything to teach. But charge no fees—and don't try to circumvent that rule to get money while kidding yourself you are still doing service. Money can quickly destroy a good teacher: I have seen it happen often. How? Once you teach for money, you become dependant upon the income and you gradually begin tailoring the work to ensure enough people turn up to make the amount of money that you need. Often the magic that truly needs teaching is work that will not be popular at all, and therefore will not make much money as it will not draw a large or consistent crowd. You can see how this can unfold into a situation where the Mysteries are rewritten to be more palatable, more commercial, and more like product, or the teacher starts to teach the latest magical fashion fad, working with the latest fashionable deity and with the latest fashionable tools. This is not a new story, but it is a story that has destroyed many a good magician who tried to make a regular income from peddling popular teaching in courses and workshops. Kidding yourself and others that you can work for money without falling into that trap is just fooling yourself, and it will bring about the eventual destruction of your work. The door will slam shut to the inner contacts—they will simply withdraw from you, and you will be left as a parody of what you could have been.

Always remember you are not special. You are not saving the world, you are not forming a religion, and you are not the only holder of the information.

Make the information you are teaching accessible, simple and straight forward. There is no need to dress magical work: it dresses itself. I am sick to death of seeing books of magic that are so wordy, complex and obscure as to be incomprehensible, and yet they are usually pretty empty of anything magical or meaningful. There is no point or purpose to doing that other than masking the fact that you have not got a clue about the subject matter you are writing on.

Never ever hold back information, teachings or patterns to make yourself more knowledgeable than your students. This is a major trap some magical teachers get into. Your students should surpass you, not lag behind you. The information is not yours to hold back: you are just a messenger boy and the magical knowledge should flow through you unhindered at all times. If you play power games with the information and the students, then the inner connections will fade off and the contacts will walk away from you, only to be replaced by parasites set on amusing themselves at your expense.

Never get into sexual power games with your students and coworkers. This is another favourite with the guru types. Sex in this day and age is something between two people who love each other, or who just want sex, and it is not part of magical work, no matter how much you try to bullshit yourself. If you use sex with your students to gratify yourself, to gain power or to play power games, then you are degenerate and will fall to the bottom of the heap magically.

Many if not all of the above are traps that many adepts have fallen into and various lodges have grappled with them in one way or another. Just do not go down that road: grow up and get real about yourself: know yourself and your limitations. And then go out into the world and be useful.

39. Functioning as an Adept

wsḫ jst nt hr m mdww
spd dsw r th mjtn

Broad is the place of one calm in speech,
Sharp the knives against one who oversteps the Path.

— *The Instruction of Kagemni's Father*

Part IV

Appendices

Appendix A

The consecration of salt and water

This method is used to strip and tune salt and water for the use of cleansing a body or space. The ritual wording can also be used to strip an object. If you are using this ritual to strip an object, then you would only recite section A over the object to be stripped.

Use the first two fingers of blessing to point at what you are working on. Where you see +, it means make the sign of an equal-armed cross over whatever you are working on.

Section A

Recite over a bowl of salt while pointing your first two fingers:

> "I exorcize thee, creature of the earth, by the living gods + the holy gods + the omnipotent gods + that thou mayst be purified of all evil influence in the name of Adonai, lord of all angels and men."

Hold the flat of your hand over the salt:

> "Creature of the earth, adore thy creator. In the name of God the father + and God the mother + I consecrate thee to the service of the gods and goddesses."

Section B

Recite over a bowl of water or a bath of water while pointing your first two fingers:

> "I exorcize thee, creature of the water, by the living gods + the holy gods + the omnipotent gods + that thou mayst

A. The Consecration of Salt and Water

be purified of all evil influence in the name of Elohim Savaoth, lord of all angels and men."

With the flat of your hand over the water:

"Creature of the water adore thy creator. In the name of God the father+ and God the mother+ I consecrate thee to the service of the gods and goddesses."

Now for the recitation of pouring. Pouring the water and salt together, recite the following as you pour the salt into the water:

"Lord God, father of the heavens above; great Goddess, mother of the earth below my feet; grant that this salt shall make for health of the body and this water for health of the soul."

Pour the salt into the water.

"Grant that they may be banished from whence they are used all powers of adversity; every artifice of evil shall be banished into the outer darkness in thy holy names, Amen."

Once the salt and water are poured together, the mixture is ready to cleanse and purify anything it touches. For a ritual bath, consecrate the whole of the bath water, consecrate a dish of salt, then pour in the salt while doing the recitation of pouring. To cleanse a room, this preparation can be used with the recitation of exorcism listed below. Sprinkle the consecrated salt water around the directions as you recite.

Appendix B

A recitation for a basic exorcism

This can be recited in a space, while sprinkling consecrated salt and water to cleanse a room, building, or object. It can also be uttered over a ritual bath to strip the person of anything that is attached to them magically. It will work as a basic cleansing and exorcism for a person, place, or thing when the infestation is by parasitical or low-level beings. A true exorcism, however, requires a little more...

Using the first two fingers, trace a triangle in the air (or over a bath) marking the three points as you begin the recitation of the three names of G-D (Father, Mother, and Holy Spirit). For the rest of the recitation, use the first two fingers and point to the centre of the triangle you have just traced in the air.

> "In the name which is above every other name, and in the power of the Father, and of the Mother, and of the Holy Spirit, I exorcize all influences and seeds of evil from this body/room/object, and I exorcize all beings that bring disease and destruction, all marks of destruction, all marks of death, and all energetic dirt. I exorcize all demons, parasites, ghosts, thought-forms, golems, curses, spells, and bindings from this body/room and spirit. I cast upon them the spell chains, and I cast them into the outer darkness where they shall trouble not this servant of God. Amen, Amen Selah."

Appendix C

Making a Specific Talisman

A talisman can be used for a limited length of time when it is really needed. Such circumstances would normally be illness, a powerful magical attack when you cannot give it your full attention, or having to go into a place that you know is possessed by a being that is very dangerous. If you wear a talisman too much, your body and spirit will not get used to strengthening against magical attacks or against dangerous beings. It will prevent your inner immune system from performing properly. But there are times when we need an extra bit of help, and those are the times to use a talisman.

First choose a ring or necklace that you would be willing to wear all the time for a while—and it is best if it does not have magical or spiritual imagery, as that would filter the contact. Something that is metal or stone would be best, and would hold power for long enough to be effective. So for example a semiprecious stone in a plain setting would be great. A real magical talisman is not a fancy magical seal or sigil-festooned medal; it is what is put in it magically that matters, not what it looks like. Place it in a bowl of dry salt for twenty-four hours to magically strip it before you begin working.

Set up your work/sacred space with the four altars in the four directions and one in the centre. Have the talisman on the altar and light the central flame, while using the vision of the Void. Once the inner flame is lit, go and light the candle in the east, then the south, west, and north before returning back to the central flame. Go around the directions again, this time spending time in each direction, and call the inner contacts that you have made, asking them to the threshold of the flame and asking them if they would be willing to help you with your work.

Once all four directions have contacts ready, pick up the talisman and start in the east. Hold the talisman over the flame and beyond it,

C. Making a Specific Talisman

so that it has passed over the threshold. See the inner contact with your inner vision, and ask them to put into the talisman whatever would be necessary to help and protect you magically during this difficult time. Put the talisman in your left hand and hold your right hand over the object. Using your inner vision, see the inner contact place their hand over yours and feel the power flowing through your hand and into the talisman. You will feel when it is finished, and when it has, step back and thank the inner contact for their help.

Repeat the same process in each direction, but just remember to be as unconditional as possible: ask for help to protect you magically. That is a very simple request. It will not protect you from physical danger that has no magical impetus, but it will protect you from both inner and outer danger that is instigated by magic. By being so simple, the talisman will cover all bases. If you start a shopping list of what you want protecting from, there is a very good chance you will not mention or even know about every risk that you are subject to.

Once the talisman has been touched by all four inner contacts, place it on the central altar and place your right hand over it. Ask God the Father of the stars above, and God the Mother of the Underworld below to bless and protect you through the talisman. Allow that blessing to flow through your hand and into the talisman.

Leave the talisman on the central altar and go around the directions, thanking the contacts, closing the gates, and putting out the candle flames, always working east, south, west, and finally north. Leave the central flame going with the talisman on the altar, and leave the room for a while so that it can 'cook.' Often the magical process has to be completed without human presence.

Once it is ready, go back in, take the inner flame into yourself, and blow out the candle. Put the talisman on, and do not take it off for anything. Not for a shower, not for a change of clothes, nothing. It must stay in contact with your body at all times to work. Once it is full of impact and is no longer working, a talisman will often break or shatter, or will not stay on you anymore. That is the time to either make a new one, or test the water to see if it is safe to come out.

Don't use talismans unless you really have to: they are items of last resort. By only using them as an emergency stopgap, you will find you gain a great deal of magical strength over the years. Those who wear talismans all the time tend to eventually end up weak and damaged as their own inner immune systems have not been activated or challenged.

Appendix D

What does magic do?

Many people get interested in magic for all sorts of reasons, but in truth, very few novices have any real idea what magic does—and more importantly, what it *doesn't* do.

The popular image of the magician, for people who do not do magic, is of an individual who can curse, kill, and bless, and acquire money, power, the ultimate girlfriend, etc. This is perceived as happening as a result of 'spells' and rituals where the magician commands spirits and powers to give them what they want, and the goods fall at their feet.

This is a fantasy which has been perpetrated by movies, stories, and shysters who write bullshit books, run very expensive courses, and offer even more expensive consultations. These days it is a fantasy that is touted on internet forums where inadequate fools hide behind anonymity and present an all-knowing, all-powerful front. In truth they are often isolated, depressed, and powerless folks who hate their life and their job. Or they are just nuts.

Magic is far more complicated and interesting than Friday night spells in your basement in order to get laid over the weekend. If I was to define magic, which is a tough job in itself, I would say that *magic is the power to influence things by working with natural forces.* It is not as sexy as the 'Dragon ritual drawn from the Dark Grimoire of Asdamodeus,[1] used to summon untold riches': that is the fantasy of the pubescent online gamer.

To explain to a beginner what magic is and what it can do, and to be as clear and truthful as possible, instead of 'easy speak' it is better to zoom right out and look at it from a different perspective

---

[1] A pun on the name of a UK supermarket owned by a predatory US company, for those who are confused.

D. What does magic do?

to our everyday, mundane lives. Let's look not at what magic can do and give us, but what it looks like in action. There are two ways to look at magic in action. The first is to look at what the magician is doing (e.g. performing a ritual, drawing a sigil, going on a vision). The second is to jump outside of the physical universe and look at what is happening 'beyond the veil' of the known world.

D.1 The complex web of fate and time

Imagine this: if you draw back the veil on life, and look at it as a magician, what you may see is akin to a complex multidimensional pattern or web that is alive, conscious, and constantly adapting and changing. Imagine it as a series of interconnecting multidimensional expressways that cross over, briefly merge, or interconnect and bridge at bright points. The bright hotspots are like focal points of condensed power/energy under pressure. The expressways in the pattern are paths of fate, of life/lives lived: a human's, a tree's...whatever.

In a mundane life, we travel along those expressways and we change paths and routes, hit dead ends or blockages, or get burned, obliterated, or energized by a bright spot. Our lives are a limited measure of physical existence, and how we navigate through that life on the expressway of fate depends upon our actions, intent, and choices, or/and the actions, intent, and choices of others. It also depends on nature, on where we live, and the complex interweave of various fates interacting, be they individual fates or the fate of nations.

In a magical life, a trained or self-developed magician essentially has learned how to not be a passive passenger. Many magicians also learn how to first be aware that there are many non-physical beings/spirits/whatever that also interact with this 'web' who have very different skill sets to humans: we can do things they cannot, and most importantly they can do things and see things we cannot. Working with beings in magic can at times be like having an inner Satnav on board.

Building a mutually beneficial relationship with these non-physical beings enables the magician to access into 'sight ahead of what is hidden from the magician,' to be warned of danger, and to work on changing something that would be impossible, or at least very difficult, for a human. Things a human cannot do, other beings can. The magician in turn does things to help the non-physical (inner) beings when asked, and when it is within the ethos of the magician. The key to such relationships, to making them safe, stable, and productive, is in the introduction phase of the relationship. The magician does not ask for something; rather the magician asks "what do you need?" By giving first, you open the door with true intent and without ulterior motives, and the magician begins to forge a relationship with a being or beings that can mature into a mutually productive and helpful union.

Together, the magician and their fellow non-physical beings travel along the web of fate (life) and times, and interact with each other to affect change. The magician also learns how to look ahead on the road they are travelling on this web by developing their own inner sight and divination skills, and learns how to avoid unnecessary calamity, and how to survive necessary calamity.

In the process of magical navigation of the highway of fate, the first most important driving force being survival, the magician also learns a great deal about the hidden world around them. They also learn about how fate works in its complexity. This in turn teaches the magician the complexity of real magic, of cause and effect, of power contraction and expansion, and the necessity for destruction as well as creation. That all sounds very highbrow, but it is what is beneath the lid in magic: it appears very different 'under the hood' to how it appears in our lives and practice.

D.2 Magic and fate in action

Magic is using skill, knowledge, tools, foresight, and methods to navigate this complex highway safely, efficiently, and to have what you need (not want) when you need it in order to achieve what you are trying to achieve.

Often a magician's work is doing something for someone or something else other than their own interests, as by doing so it also helps the magician on their own path. That is not about being selfless but about being smart. Once you realize that we are all interconnected on this vast highway, you find that many times your actions for others has an effective knock-on effect on your own journey. That is, of course, if your magic for the 'other' was compatible. If you get it badly wrong, the knock-on effect for yourself can often be very difficult. Think of it as harmonics of sound and vibration: if the 'vibration' is right, anything close by will start to vibrate at the same frequency: everything connected and interconnected with that part of the pattern will come into harmony. This is how a magician can affect everything around them by their magical actions.

To take it down to very simple terms, let's look at how a simple magical act can affect the fate journey of the magician and the person they have focused their magic on. These are things to seriously think about when getting into magic, not to put you off doing magic, but in order for you to understand that magic is far more complex in its reach than it appears on the surface, and also that, just like life, actions can have consequences, particularly if those actions are ill thought out or done in ignorance.

D.3 Magical consequences: an example of magic in action

No magical act happens in a vacuum. Nothing can be truly isolated. Every magical act may affect whoever and whatever is connected to the situation, and sometimes whoever and whatever is not.

Magical consequences can be good or bad, or a mixture of both, depending upon how fast you learn from experience, and how much you think things through and pay attention. Here is a hypothetical scenario, a sort of event that is all too common in early magic when beginners fall for the bullshit put out that magic can give you anything you want. I have lost count of the number of people who have contacted me when their first successful foray into magic went badly wrong, and this scenario is based very strongly on events that have happened to those people.

D.3. Magical consequences: an example of magic in action

The scenario

Say there is a guy who has been dabbling in magic, but is still in the early phase of understanding it, who decides to do a ritual to get his girlfriend back. She walked out on him a couple of weeks ago and he was devastated, then angry. He does a ritual, calls upon beings etc. to force her to 'come back.' His first mistake is not understanding that magic for the most part will not force someone to love you. His second mistake was a poor choice in the wording of what he wanted. The ritual works because, unknown to this guy, he is a 'natural' at magic. Some folks are just like that, and it happens more often than folks realize.

So, she 'comes back.' She appears at his door and he is elated: it worked! Except the dumb ass only asked that she 'come back.' Well, here she is, banging on the door. However, when he opens the door and lets her in, she tells him she is only back to pick up a few things she left behind. Because magic was involved in forcing that action (she may not have decided to come back to pick things up if she had not been nudged by magic), there is a lot of 'energy' built up around the situation (a bright spot on the highway...remember the complex highway?). The two of them both have a weird sense of heightened emotion. She is fearful but not quite sure why, so she is ready for a fight, and he is filled with a sense of triumph, power, and elation.

He lets her into the house and tells her he is so glad she is back. She turns around and tells him she is not 'back' but she has come to pick some items up she had forgotten about. They start arguing, and it descends into a fight. The magic that is around the situation (the bright spot) is unbalanced and unstable, and the beings he called on and commanded to force this situation were not the beings he thought they were: he did not have the knowledge or understanding of how to differentiate between certain types of beings. He simply trusted the grimoire/book that outlined the ritual.

The beings were simply inner parasites, beings that feed off emotion and energy, beings that will inflame a situation through emotion in order to get a good dinner. The beings sensed a good dinner in the emotional outbursts, so they joined the conflict, leaning on the heightened emotions of the two humans in order to amplify them. The fight became physical, and the girlfriend got injured and

D. What does magic do?

knocked about. She called the police. He was horrified, as he had never hit a woman before, let alone injured one, and a rage burned within him that he knew was not him, or normal for him.

So of course, it ended badly: she had a restraining order put out on him, and he was arrested and charged. She never spoke to him again, and he suffered from the fallout of the arrest and subsequent court appearance.

Sound dramatic? This happens all the time with magical dabbling. A difficult situation can become a disastrous one, and it happens on a regular basis. So what happened magically? Let's look at this from many different angles in depth, as it will give you a better understanding of magic both in its basics and also its more powerful hidden side.

The basic action

We will first look at this at 'ground level,' and see what sort of actions led to such a sad result for two good people going through a difficult time.

Magical acts by beginners are usually actions they have taken out of a book or a grimoire. Most beginners who are new to magic are not able to differentiate between a book written by a true magician and a book written by a hack who is full of shit and wants to make money and/or a name for themselves, or a magician who has no ethics and is heavily parasited—they will sell dangerous stuff just to make money. Some magical writers are literally only a 'a page ahead of their readers,' meaning they themselves are also more or less beginners and do not fully understand what magic is or what it can or cannot do. The only way to learn to differentiate is to *do* and learn for yourself, which usually means making a lot of mistakes.

Grimoires are a different beast entirely. Some are real and have magic buried beneath trash: at a first glance you see X, but when you look deeper with knowledge, you see Y emerging. And some were just babble that was handed down from generation to generation by people who did not know better. Bear in mind, though, that most grimoires were collated at times of religious control by a heavy-handed community that saw magic as the work of the devil. So a lot

D.3. Magical consequences: an example of magic in action

of real magic is hidden in layers beneath a surface presentation—that in itself can be a mine field for a beginner.

Our hapless beginner got hold of a ritual that was said to 'bring to you what you want,' or it may have been a specific one on how to 'get someone back.' Such rituals usually have instructions to 'use something belonging to the person,' and may involve invocations of angels or demons. What actually turns up (if anything does) tends to be a parasite dressing up as what you wanted to call. The being does not physically appear to the magician, contrary to popular belief (and moronic bullshit); rather the being comes into the energetic space of the magician and talks or interacts with the magician through their mind. The being, if it does connect, will affect and alter the fate web of the people the ritual is meant to affect by amplifying emotional thought and reaction. Intelligent parasites can nudge situations, plant ideas into weak minds, and inflate an ego in someone so that they end up overstepping their capabilities. These beings usually want something in return: an energetic dinner that can be anything from masturbation, killing something to feed off the energy of the event, or an emotionally charged ritual that feeds them.

When such a magical act is done in the heat of emotions, that draws more power/energy to the ritual, and some magicians work with that energy to transform it into fuel to power the ritual. However, if you really don't know what you are doing, the energy/power that gathers when magic and emotion are brought together can quickly get feral and out of control—and again, this also attracts spirits that feed from emotion. All of these things, when they come together in a magical act, can affect or alter the fate web of the magician and whoever is connected to the ritual. So you can imagine how it can get messy pretty quickly.

So how does it work?

When most beginners dabble in magic, thankfully little or nothing happens. They either give up and move onto something else, or they become more determined and set out on a quest to learn more. But the occasions when beginner actions *do* work come down to a few variables. If the ritual intent is aligned with the actual current active fate of the beginner—the pathways or strands of fate the person is

D. WHAT DOES MAGIC DO?

currently within that will manifest as events—then the ritual can trigger those strands of fate to become stronger, more condensed, and more active.

So for example, if the man had instead of asking for her to 'come back' had asked for help to repair the relationship by helping him see what went wrong, and how to fix it, and the fate path was aligned to such an intent, then the magic would likely have been very successful: it would create enough of a nudge for necessary change to occur. What would likely have happened was, after the ritual, he would have had dreams, his outer everyday attention would be drawn strongly to look at others in relationships to see how his problem is mirrored in others, his fate would have been strengthened so that he bumped into key people at a key time who could have given him excellent advice, or he may have bumped into his ex-girlfriend and had the opportunity to talk to her. Talking or other interaction, along with a strengthened fate path, could be enough to nudge the ex-girlfriend into giving him a second chance. After that, it would be up to him to recognize his side of what went wrong (there are always two sides) and to try and be a better partner.

The key with magic, be it performed for personal help, or for help in something beyond the individual, is to think very carefully before you act, then work with the process, putting your own effort in too. In Ancient Egypt, which was rich with magic, two key components were considered paramount for success: Heka and Sia. One without the other was worthless: Heka is magic, while Sia is *perception* (a literal translation). Perception in this case means using intelligence, paying attention, and thinking carefully before engaging the magic.

D.4 A checklist of advice for beginners

When most people first get into magic, they have no reference points upon which to draw wisdom or judgement beyond the usually touted 'harm none'...then they often go on to harm someone in order to get what they want. So here is a checklist to think about when you first start dipping into magic.

1. If it isn't broken, don't fix it.

2. Free will. Your magic should not go against the free will or destiny of a person, place, or thing.

3. Don't use a hammer to crack a nut. Exhaust all mundane options before using magic. If you jump to magic straightaway to solve an issue, particularly if it is personal to you, you will end up weakening yourself. Use your time to develop magically, then use it when necessary, when mundane options have run out.

4. When in doubt, when you come across something you don't understand or an action you are not sure of, think about it in mundane terms. If it is something you would not do physically in life (like kill or attack someone), then don't do it magically.

5. Trust your instincts.

6. If something sounds too good to be true, it probably is.

7. Tend to your own business and boundaries. Defend, but do not attack. This goes against modern thinking, but it is an ancient wisdom that still holds true. Defend your shit, mind your own shit, and ignore everyone else's shit. In time, you will learn to develop strong boundaries that are worked with in cooperation with other beings that make attack an obsolete option.

D.5 Some things to think about

Catalysis

Magic triggers changes, and no matter how experienced the magician, you cannot possibly understand or see all the potential variables that can trigger as a result of magical action. That should not stop you from working with magic, but it should give you pause for thought. You will make mistakes, everyone does; the key is to learn from them and not make the same mistake repeatedly, or repeat other people's mistakes.

D. What does magic do?

Small steps

In order to develop strength, perception, skills, and knowledge, training or learning in magic is the same as training or learning a major sport or classical art. Small steps taken regularly and carefully help you develop the 'magical muscle' slowly. That gives you a good strong foundation and helps your body and mind adapt to power of magic.

Action and reaction

Most magic in the early days of a person's magical life is about reaction. Action is where magic is used to trigger something new or wake something up, and reaction magic is a response to something. Understanding the difference between the two can be very helpful for beginners, as it gives you a better awareness of cause and effect, and how magic can fill a situation in a good way or a bad way.

Another way to put this is that action magic is where the magic starts a new cycle. Reaction magic is where the magic intervenes in an already ongoing situation. Being able to clearly identify which is which is of paramount importance to the magician, as the outcomes will be very different for all involved.

Path

Above all, magic is the most fascinating, infuriating, beautiful and complex path a human can walk in life.

Appendix E

The magical understanding of good and evil

When walking a magical path the practitioner soon comes up against issues of good versus evil, the duality of power, the left hand and right hand paths, and so forth. These issues can bring to the surface a great many questions that we have to ask of ourselves and those involved in the particular magical path that we are walking. I feel it is important for us as magicians to step outside of the dogmas and beliefs inherent within our culture and society, which are often deep-seated and not immediately apparent to us. By doing so it enables us to ascertain what is actually happening, why, and how to find a way to navigate through issues in a way that compliments who we are and what we are trying to achieve.

What we perceive as good or evil largely depends on our system of beliefs, be they religious, cultural, philosophical, etc., and our own emotional development. It also is deeply affected by our own needs, both in personal development and everyday living.

Our systems of belief and the wider religious and cultural patterns in which we were born and raised have a massive effect upon how we view the world. As children we accept such dogmas without question, particularly if raised in a religious household. As teens we rebel against such dogmas and begin the process of questioning. Often, though, the questioning element of our personal development can become limited by a continued unconscious adherence to the dogmatic pattern which results in not a breaking away from the pattern, but a continuing rebellion against a dogma which in turn feeds and strengthens it.

We can see this for example in the work of Crowley. I am not an expert on Crowley by any means, and am commenting from

E. THE MAGICAL UNDERSTANDING OF GOOD AND EVIL

the outside looking in. But it is an example that is known by most people in the magical arena. Crowley was raised in a very strict and unhealthy Christian household that was mired in the sexual and behavioural repression of the Victorian era. Crowley struck out to try and become the opposite of how he had been raised. This eventually brought about a huge change in thinking, but his reasoning was still mired within the dogma of Christianity, just from an opposing point of view.

At that time, I think it would have been near-on impossible for someone of his time, culture, and background to have completely stepped out of that pattern. But in his struggle, whether we agree with it or not, he and others like him opened doors that our generation no longer has to bother opening—yet many branches of magic still cling to that outworn pattern. And therein lies one of the problems: we have become so used to working and evolving within the pattern that we forget that we are now able to step outside of it, rather than being the antithesis of the pattern. We become stuck in the white magician black magician, left hand right hand path mentality.

So how do we operate? I think the first thing for a magician is to know their own personal limitations of what they are and are not willing to do and take responsibility for. On one hand, the more 'spiritually' inclined magician is likely to have a set of heroic ethics that they vigorously defend, often without direct experience, and postulate to others about. Over time, with the dedication of a magical path, the magician is then put into a variety of life situations that directly challenge not only the validity of those ethics, but also the ability of the individual to make more informed decisions regarding their ethics. Some are realized to be empty shells of dogmatic or fanciful beliefs, and some are discovered to be of vast importance. That distinction also strengthens the magician and enables them to uphold the important ethics in the face of extreme challenge.

Slowly, the ethics or concepts that may be considered admirable in many societies are put to the practical test. Many fall by the wayside as the magician realizes their futility. Others prove to be difficult to uphold, but wonderful boundaries that bring out the best in someone. This is a filtration mechanism that most of us have been through in one way or another, so that when we emerge battered and still standing a few decades later, we have a much more realistic idea of what we can and cannot do, and more importantly what we truly are willing, or not willing, to do to survive. The high ideals we started with are tested to the extreme until we are either destroyed, or we have learned to understand which ethics, boundaries, and limitations are actually really necessary, and which are just egotistic vanity.

It is easy to stand in judgement of someone from a safe vantage point and feel good about ourselves. But once fate tosses us to the ravages of harsh life, then we begin to feel a lot more compassion and understanding for those whom we observe to be struggling against themselves or their society. We know, because we have been there: understanding the hardship involved in true survival becomes a lantern to light our path.

Conversely, following a magical path of selfishness, of using power purely and unashamedly for the pursuit of wants and needs, gives freedom to the magician who has lived in a stifling society. Self-indulgence and self-preservation give a person a sense of power, a sense of control over their life and destiny. We gain a sense of our own power and importance. Until it begins to go wrong, with the dawning realization of how limited we are, and how our wants and needs do not fill a greater sense of identity, nor teach us truly about power. Our addictions begin to rule, then destroy us, to weaken and expose the false sense of security that was gained. A magician walking this path will either begin to develop their own unique self-containment, ethics, and understanding, or they will implode.

For myself, I began my magical path as a teenager in the 1970s with a terrible sense of self-righteousness. In my early twenties I asked the inner contacts for learning, for wisdom, for experience (not always such a great idea). I certainly got what I asked for: I was thrown to the wolves. Every pedestal I took delight in standing upon was knocked over until I understood the dilemmas of those I had so arrogantly looked down upon in my youth. It is a terribly hard, long, and painful lesson, but that is what magic does. It confronts you. Eventually I learned—and am still learning—to look beyond the 'pattern' of what I personally consider 'ethical,' and to recognize my own weaknesses and failures in the cold hard light of day. I realize now this process will never end, which is good as it means we can constantly grow, evolve, and learn.

E. THE MAGICAL UNDERSTANDING OF GOOD AND EVIL

Knowing our own personal limitations is a very important part of the development of magic within us, and it has great bearing upon how we wield that magic. The rules of engagement in life are the same for magic, from the small aspects to the greatest ones. So for example, eating meat. It is easy to buy a prepacked, chopped, and ready-to-cook bit of meat. It is not so easy to look into the eyes of an animal and watch it die by your own hands. In rich, First World countries, many people say, "I could not kill an animal, but I eat meat," or they will say "I could not kill an animal, therefore I am vegan." It is a statement that is easy to make in some First World countries where there is a financial social safety net, and also access to vegetarian protein sources. Although some may go hungry from time to time, people in such countries do not die of starvation. We have that choice and often choose not to kill: our ethics are a product of our living circumstances.

But put in a situation in a country where there is no social safety net, and you are very hungry, your children are hungry, and if you do not kill an animal you may starve, then it is a different matter. Your ethics change according to your circumstances. So they are not really ethics at all, but social and hierarchical expressions.

The will to survive is all-encompassing. It does not make the killing any easier, but it makes it *necessary*. That is the reality—the true reality—of the nature that we are often protected from in modern society. Our luxury enables us to be 'ethical'; but magic begins when we know our true limitations, we know what we are really capable of doing, both for good and bad, under extreme circumstances. Then and only then can we begin to understand power in a magical context: we learn about it through knowing our own true limitations, then we can learn how to navigate our way through the maze.

So it is back to good and evil. What do those words actually mean, anyway? We bandy then around in religion, in spirituality, and in magical paths. But do we really understand what they mean? What is evil? Is it evil to maim and kill? Is it evil to destroy? It all depends on where you are in context to the power. As humans, we find genocide against other humans as intolerable, evil incarnate. But we commit such acts without thought on a regular basis against other creatures. Is mass murder evil? If someone kills a load of seals, or ponies, or kittens, we consider that unacceptable. But if they are cows or pigs, then that serves our purpose and is therefore acceptable. So evil in reality is something we do not like to happen to us either as individuals or as a species. For us it is hard to differentiate between necessary and unnecessary destruction. Necessary destruction is a part of nature; unnecessary destruction is the closest we can truly come to understanding the complexity of what is truly evil.

High or powerful magic is like wielding nuclear power: it can do great damage over a long period of time. The power itself is neither good nor evil, but its use can have devastating effects regardless of the intention behind it. It is a dangerous tool, and the more power a magician is able to access, the more damage or good they can potentially do with it. How that power is applied is directly related to how that magician perceives themselves and the world around them.

Because of that dynamic, what often happens is the more potential for power that a magician has, the greater their life experiences will be in order either to bring them to a relatively mature place, or to switch them off—a bit like blowing a fuse. Those who do not have the capacity for mediating large amounts of power tend to have a more stable, constant life experience (unless of course they have already got their shit together). This dynamic seems to run in relation to the capacity of the person/path for power.

It is something that has happened to me, and something I have also observed many times over in other magicians. There is no sense of any paternalistic teaching parent god/s in the dynamic; it is more a matter of power in, power out, in the weave of life. The trick is to recognize what is happening and engage the process for learning and strengthening, rather than flailing around in the dark and cursing the gods. (Been there, done that...)

When the dynamic first really kicked in for me, I was horrified that suddenly life was throwing me big balls of shit , on a daily basis, that were beyond silly. Luckily there was an elder magician around in my wider community who pointed out to me that every damn thing I was going through was directly challenging me on my stance of ethics, of understanding, and of limitations.

That was a major turning point not only in my coping strategy, but also in my magical understanding and development. I began to engage directly with each challenge in order to draw what I could

E. THE MAGICAL UNDERSTANDING OF GOOD AND EVIL

from the situations and turn them into learning curves, strengthening exercises, and humble pie eating sessions. The more I engaged, the wider the door of magical contact became. I began to see the 'bad' side of life and magic as something that balanced out and polished the 'good' side. I began to see the dynamic of how creative magical power needed to exist in the presence of destructive magical power, so instead of trying to get rid of the bad power, it is merely balanced out by a creative power and *vice versa*.

Like everything else, you can read about something or be taught about it until the cows come home, but the true deeper meanings and the visceral understanding of magic cannot really take seed and grow until it is a direct learning experience. So, for example, this article is not really written to teach, not even to burble about my own opinions/expressions, but to open the door, as that elder did for me once, and say "hey, its okay, don't panic: this is what is happening, and this is how you deal with it to survive." It is a path that thousands have trodden before us, and knowing that it is a path that can not only be survived, but will bring you to a wonderful dawning of deep magic, is a lifeline that can light your way in the darkest of times.

> There is an earthly sun, which is the cause of all heat, and all who are able to see may see the sun; and those who are blind and cannot see him may feel his heat. There is an Eternal Sun, which is the source of all wisdom, and those whose spiritual senses have awakened to life will see that sun and be conscious of His existence; but those who have not attained spiritual consciousness may yet feel His power by an inner faculty which is called Intuition.
>
> — Paracelsus[1]

---

[1] hall1928.

Appendix F

The directions in Western magic

A brief journey through history

The following is an extended essay looking at the use of directions in magic at various points in history. It can be of interest to magicians to see where modern day magical concepts of directions, attributes, usage and power came from, what was behind them, and how they traveled down through time.

> Personal experience is the genesis of true learning
> — Aeschylus, *Agamemnon* (c. 458 B.C.)

In modern Western magic and also in some religious patterns, the directions are the thresholds and boundaries that define and focus the power and contact that flows from inner to outer, from non-physical realms into the physical ones. How we use those directions and why we use them differs according to the tradition or system we work within. In this essay, I want to look at certain points in magical history to look at how different people in time approached the directions and directional concepts.

Using that overarching subject matter of the directions, I also want to look a bit closer at some of those people and their cultures, to get a better understanding of who they were, what they were interested in, and to understand why they did what they did.

F.1 Background

The main difference in the use of directions is the difference between religion and magic. In religions the directions tend to be used in order

F. The directions in Western magic

for passive prayer and ritual to be 'sent' to the deity or to celebrate the deity, and for the passive acceptance of what flows from the deity. In magic the flow from the magician is active, and triggers the powers, deities, and spirits of that direction to an active interface which is then combined by the magician for a specific purpose.

In the last hundred and fifty years or so in the West, magic has slowly opened out to a wider number of people, and in the last century various traditions have come into form, often drawing from a wide variety of older practices. Some of those magical practices have subsequently branched and developed down a path to form pagan or mystical religions. Others have stayed as purely magical traditions and have similarly morphed and evolved into specific systems and traditions: how we approach magic and the Mysteries is a constantly evolving process.

This is important to think about when we look into the history of these practices, as someone approaching the directions in a magical sense is going to be different from someone approaching those same directions from a religious stance. It may appear similar or the same on the surface, but the inner dynamics are often going to be different, even when the religion relies heavily upon magical expression.

In modern magic, practitioners are often influenced by the culture they grew up in and the religious pattern that is most prominent in their society. While this is slowly changing in younger generations, the generations who formed or informed a lot of Western traditions were highly influenced by Christianity and Judaism. This can make for an interesting mix when it is done with full awareness, but more often than not, the founders and developers of those traditions were unaware that what they brought to their magical table drew heavily upon their Christian upbringing.

This is a complex subject all on its own, and may warrant its own essay in the future, but for now it is simply useful to keep in mind that our cultural lens and filter can sometimes cloud what we are looking at if we are not careful. Sometimes our embedded religious and cultural patterns are so deeply buried within our psyches that we are not aware of the influences they bring to bear upon our magical work.

F.2 The magical directions

The confinement of directions (east, south, west, north) in a magical working space appears in most Western magical forms, and is worked with either as a foundation ritual pattern or as a simple focus for intent.

I am often asked why a magician must face a particular direction, and why the directions are approached in different ways in different systems. To answer those questions, we must dig deep into the past and also pause to think about how we view magical actions today.

For the most part, Europe today has a culture that has been heavily influenced by more than a thousand years of Christianity, and that influence plays a major role in how we think, act and analyse everything around us. Similarly, since the fifteenth-century in Europe, rediscovered Classical Greek philosophy, particularly the work of the Platonists, also played a major part in influencing how we approach learning and thinking, not only in education in general but specifically in magic.

The only problem with this cultural and educational lens is that once we start looking at the ancient world itself, we find that our current model of thinking does not often match the model of thinking of ancient cultures. Nor do our modern mystical concepts often match those of ancient cultures. It is really important to realize this: if we are not careful, we can end up trying to shoehorn an ancient way of looking at the universe into our own modern way of thinking, and *vice versa*.

This becomes apparent when historians and theologians move out of their comfort zone and start to look at ancient cultures like Egypt, which was a culture that was vastly different to our own today. It can be painful to watch someone trying to fit the religious complexity of dynastic Egypt into the neat box of monotheism; and while this does not appear on the surface to have anything to do with magic, in real terms this is of the greatest importance to magicians. These ancient complex cultures were the cauldrons of what we call magic today: as is mentioned in the Jewish Kiddushin[1] 49b:

---

[1] The Jewish marriage betrothal: the first stage of the Torah-mandated wedding.

F. The directions in Western magic

> Ten measures of magic were given to the world: Egypt received nine, and the rest of the world got one.

Magic is about drawing power and contact into a defined pattern (ritual, vision, magical action) and giving it boundaries that the magician can operate within. Those boundaries can be anything from a drawn image or words, to utterances, vessels (statues and tools) or a defined space such as the directions. Such boundaries in a space make it a vessel that can 'receive' in a contained way, and the acts of the magician as a bridge of power from inner (non-physical) to outer (physical) create a pattern of action or intent. That pattern is woven and harmonized by the magician using his or her tools, utterances, vision and action. The pattern (the magical act) is then released into the flow of time in order for it to go do its job.

F.3 The current magical use of the directions

There are a dizzying number of magical systems today, with new ones or recycled ones emerging on a regular basis. Some of this is driven by innovation and the evolution of magic, and some of it is driven by marketing and ego.

When you look at modern systems, the first thing that can often become apparent is the use of 'boxes': everything is slotted into lists and categories. While this can be useful, it can easily 'lock down' the understanding and practice of the magician if it becomes too dogmatic. What can happen is that the magician rote learns lists of attributes connected to specific directions: knowledge without understanding. Or to put it another way, the person has a recipe book but doesn't know how to turn on an oven or blend ingredients together.

This has become far more apparent in recent years by way of the internet: there are an abundance of websites and E-schools where the directions are presented with lists of attributes, and these are copied over to other websites *ad nauseam* with mistakes also copied over, but no one actually learns anything in a practical sense.

In different magical systems the directions are used in different ways for different reasons. Some systems use the directions to focus

F.3. The current magical use of the directions

upon a mythic land construct connected to the elements and solar cycle. In these systems, the most common 'list' is east/air/morning, south/fire/midday, west/water/dusk, north/earth/winter. This is a northern hemisphere land cycle and can be used to draw upon the inner dynamics of the elemental and solar powers.

Some systems dig a little deeper and also lap over into Christian and/or Jewish patterns to draw upon specific angelic beings in the directions, such as east/Raphael, south/Michael, west/Gabriel, north/Uriel.

Other systems draw upon the 'four winds,' planetary dynamics that flow with the winds, and some draw upon specific planetary powers, 'earth-belt' spirits, etc.

Sometimes all of the different layers of powers are used directionally depending upon what the magician is doing. In more commercially formed systems, everything but the kitchen sink is assigned a direction along with a product to buy for each direction.

Keep in mind the earlier comment I made about religion versus magic in terms of the directions, and that the directions are used magically in an active way, which means contacted ritual, inner contact, vision, and so forth. Learning attributes is simply like learning an alphabet. You have to actually *do* something with the letters to make poetry, song, or stories: just learning and reciting the alphabet is meaningless.

As you dig around history, you will come upon points in magical history where systems devolve down to intellectual exercises or dogmatic lists that move the directional 'alphabet' from being a useful starting reference, to being an endpoint of knowledge.

Just for your reference, when we look at magic in the nineteenth and eighteenth centuries, there is a huge amount of historical writing that has already been done, so I do not need to go into too much detail: use the information in this essay as a starting point if you wish to dig deeper for yourself. It is a rich, complex, and at times messy period in magical history.

F.4 Nineteenth-century Europe

The Hermetic Order of the Golden Dawn (founded 1888)

The biggest (though not the only) influence on twentieth-century magic in Europe was the Hermetic Order of the Golden Dawn. Founded in 1888 with three temples in Britain, it created a structured education system for magical training, its three founders being Dr W. Robert Woodman, William W. Westcott, and Samuel Liddell Mathers.

As a cohesive organization it fragmented within a few decades, but it became the grandparent of many spin-off magical groups and subsequent new schools. It influenced many of the great magical thinkers of the late nineteenth and twentieth century either directly or indirectly, from Gerard Encausse (Papus) and A. E. Waite, to magical thinkers such as Aleister Crowley and Dion Fortune.

The system used in the Golden Dawn was a mix of, or influenced by, Freemasonry, Rosicrucianism, Kabbalah, and Theosophy. It was a broadly Christian system with added influences from other cultures which were likely brought to the table by one of the founders, Dr. W. Robert Woodman. Woodman had wide-ranging interests such as Kabbalistic philosophy, Egyptian antiquities, and Rosicrucianism as well as being a Freemason.

The Golden Dawn system is essentially a patchwork of different strands of magic brought together, and when you look closely at the various parts of the system, you can spot the actual books that Mathers had studied in the British Library collection.

The founders of the Golden Dawn were true innovators of their time, and did the best they could with what they had and with what was within their capabilities. Their system was deeply shaped by the Victorian industrial mindset and the need for order, ceremony and coherence. It also came out at a time when 'revels' were becoming popular, where reenactments were fashionable, and where a stonkingly good costume was everything. All of these influences brought to the group by various members made their mark in one way or another.

F.4. Nineteenth-century Europe

The magical system itself was formal and highly organized. The directional system that was used reflected that sense of coherence, and is largely a pattern that is still worked with today:

East	air	sword
West	water	cup
North	earth	pentacle
South	fire	wand

Each of these directions was assigned an archangel: Raphael, Gabriel, Uriel and Michael. Colours and letters were also assigned to the directions, as were planets, zodiac signs, and names of God.

The Golden Dawn approached the ritual pattern by use of theatrics, scripts and symbolism: it was a heavily externalized pattern that had its roots of action and symbolism in Freemasonry and Rosicrucianism. These were drawn from the experiences of its founder members, who used what they recognized in order to build a magical system. It was approached in a systematized, structured and hierarchical manner which reflected the times and society it was created in.

The directional attributes were also apparent in the tarot symbolism used by and recreated by members of the Golden Dawn; and this act, more than anything else, in my opinion, anchored the pattern deeply in subsequent generations of magical seekers who came after. The tarot deck developed by A. E. Waite and painted by Pamela Coleman Smith (published in 1910), known as the *Rider-Waite Tarot*, became a major tool for people seeking magic.

So where did those directional concepts and attributes come from? To answer that question, we have to keep digging further back in time, and observe how ideas, concepts and learning morphed from generation to generation. I will not take us through every step in the developmental journey, as that is not the point of this exercise; however let us look at a small number of people who cast an influence over their subsequent generations.

Eliphas Levi (born Alphonse Louis Constant 1810-1875)

Eliphas Levi was a French occultist with a strong, enquiring mind and an eccentric personality. Levi's writings had immense influence on

F. The directions in Western magic

various members of the Golden Dawn including A. E. Waite, along with other occult groups and individuals, such as Papus, in Europe.

Levi initially trained as a Catholic priest, but failed to take holy ordination when he fell in love and left the seminary in 1836. Levi began to delve deeply into socialism as an expression of true Christianity, and considered the Roman Catholic Church to be spiritually and morally corrupt. It is worth pointing out here, particularly for readers in the USA, that what Levi considered socialism was very different from the popular understanding of socialism today.

Without digressing too much, it is worth being clear about this, as it gives us insight into not only the mindset of historical and contemporary occultists, but also how easy it is to misunderstand something in history due to a lack of history education. In popular media in the USA today, socialism is often equated incorrectly with Hitler and the Nazi party. Nationalsozialismus (German for 'national socialism') was an extreme political experiment that became Nazism, and it has little in common with the vision that Levi and subsequent thinkers ascribed to.

Socialism and social democracy as Levi and others saw it can be described thus: *a political and economic theory of social organization which advocates that the means of production, distribution, and exchange should be owned or regulated by the community as a whole.* It was experimented with by various nations in the twentieth-century, and to this day many European capitalist nations have elements of social democracy within their national political structure (Germany, France, Spain, Britain etc.).

Understanding the time that Levi lived in can also help us understand his marriage of politics and magic. France was rapidly changing politically and economically from its first revolution less than fifty years earlier, where the people of France overthrew the monarchy and nobles—and subsequently threw their nation into a bloodbath of executions, restrictions, and war.

After that revolution, France went through a series of rapid changes from the First French Empire (Napoleon I) of 1804–1815 to the restoration of Monarchy, and then to the second revolution and Republic (1848–1852). The time of the Second Republic was when Levi, still using his birth name of Alphonse Constant, became strongly active in socialist thinking and also magic. In 1848 he wrote and published *Le Testament de la liberté*, and by the 1850s he was openly giving talks on a mixture of socialism and Kabbalistic philosophy.

He was immersed in occult studies and in Kabbalah, and mixed them together with Catholicism and socialism. By the 1860s he was writing magical books and was probably the first person to incorporate the use of tarot into magical training. He was a major influence on magical thinkers in the late nineteenth century onwards. Today he is still considered one of the grandfathers of modern magic.

Levi wrote extensively on ritual patterns and occult philosophy, and revelled in lists (of powers, attributes, directions etc.). His actual magical writing is odd in that in places it hits on points of wisdom and insight, and elsewhere is disordered and fragmented. When looking closely at his work, it becomes obvious that mostly he didn't know what to *do* with the magical lists and information he had acquired from various sources: he was mostly a theorist and a thinker rather than an actual practising magician.

We will look at his version of the directional attributes, as his work was subsequently taken up by other magicians, and it provides some major insights into the influence he brought to bear upon modern occultism.

Levi's directional system

In his extensive work *Transcendental magic: its Doctrine and ritual* (1854) Levi outlines directional theories and powers, which can be summed up for the purpose of this subject matter in his treatment of the directional powers in the section 'Conjuration of the Four Elements.' They are as follows—and I have included his various elemental, emotive, and talismanic attributions, as they throw an interesting light on the methodology which subsequently influenced generations of magicians:

F. THE DIRECTIONS IN WESTERN MAGIC

East	Air	Sylphs	Eagle
South	Fire	Salamanders	Lion
West	Water	Undines	Aquarius
North	Earth	Gnomes	Bull

East	Bilious (Argumentative)	Gold and Silver	Morning
South	Sanguine (Optimistic)	Iron and Copper	Noon
West	Phlegmatic (Unemotional)	Mercury	Dusk
North	Melancholic (Sad)	Lead	Night

Aquarius as listed in Levi's work is the 'Man of the New Dawn' i.e. the 'developed' man in a mystical sense. It does not stand for the zodiac sign Aquarius, as is often assumed today.

The attributions of the emotive states are interesting, and many would (wrongly) assume that these are emotional powers that 'rule' the direction, and would thus try to use those emotions in directional magical work, or expect that type of person to find a natural home in that direction. However, to do so would be to misunderstand why those attributes are there and what the list is telling the magician (and the emotive qualities for west and north are mixed up in Levi's listing: they should be the other way around). They show how the powers flowing from each direction can trigger and amplify certain emotions within the magician.

The listing of the emotive responses triggered by elemental powers in the directions is there to inform the magician what to watch out for in their emotive responses to the magical work: if they begin to manifest a specific emotion strongly during or shortly after their magical work, it is to be taken as a symptom of a magical imbalance or stasis somewhere in their work, or within themselves. The magician can then, by nature of the emotive response to the work, identify which directional power working might be unnecessary or unbalanced. It can also be an indicator of a major power imbalance within the magical system itself.

For that information alone, Levi sent a great gift down the path of time for us today (and likely has its roots in the writing of Luria, whom we will look at). I have observed this emotive response issue countless times during my decades of magical practice with groups and teaching, and learning to pay attention to such details and responses in magical work enables the magician to adjust and adapt their work accordingly.

Such power issues are part and parcel of working with external powers in a defined containment, and while it is virtually impossible to do magic to any great degree and avoid such issues, there are many things we can do to adapt and evolve our practice to mitigate such emotive triggers in our work. One such adaptation, which I use extensively in the Quareia training, is to create a filter for the magician themselves by placing them in the stream of time while they work.

This method directly draws upon the magical wisdom of the Egyptian pattern, which we will look at later in this essay. Essentially it makes the magician 'sovereign in their space': it is akin to putting a fuse box on the power inlet. Let us return to Levi and see what else he has to say in his directional listings.

In his elemental listings, he also includes magical tools to be used to 'command the spirits,' and they are:

North	Bull	Sword
South	Lion	Forked wand
West	Aquarius	Cup of libations
East	Eagle	Pentacle

This list caught my attention in his work, as one little detail in the list is a fragment of a much older magical tool that hides a potentially interesting history. His lists and consequent conjurations reveal quite clearly that he did not have full understanding of either the lists nor the ritual: he was using another source, a magical book, and using the lists and rituals like a recipe book.

Here is an excerpt of the explanatory text, and then a part of the ritual:

> We most observe that the special kingdom of the Gnomes is at the North: that of the Salamanders at the South: that of the Sylphs at the East: and that of the Undines at the West. They influence the four temperaments of men (i. e., the Gnomes, the melancholic: the Salamanders, the sanguine: the Undines, the phlegmatic: and the Sylphs,

F. THE DIRECTIONS IN WESTERN MAGIC

the bilious). Their signs are as follows: the hieroglyphs of the bull for the Gnomes, and we command them with the sword: of the lion for the Salamanders, and we command them with the forked wand, or the magic trident: of the eagle for the Sylphs, and we command them with the holy pentacles: finally with Aquarius for the Undines, and we evoke them with the cup of libations.

When an elementary spirit comes to torment, or at least to annoy the inhabitants of this world, we must conquer it by means of air, water, fire and earth, blowing, sprinkling, burning perfumes, and tracing on the earth the star of Solomon and the sacred pentagram. These figures should be perfectly regular, and made either with coals from the consecrated fire, or with a reed dipped in diverse colors which we mix with pulverized magnet. Then, while holding in the hand the pentacle of Solomon, and taking by turns the sword, the wand, and the cup, we pronounce in these terms and in a loud voice the conjuration of the four.[1]

Let's just take a little time to have a look at this text and see how it equates magically, and also what its roots may be. Most magic that comes to us from the last few centuries has its roots in a mixture of Greek, Egyptian and Persian thinking, and the various concepts were picked up, mixed about, passed on and ended up in various magical texts.

North: Earth, Gnomes, Bull, Melancholic (sadness) lead, night.

Gnomes are earth, and magically earth is equated with the north in the northern hemisphere. Why? From a magical perspective, earth is the element that houses all that has long since died: the dead are buried, and all that lives upon the earth eventually is absorbed by the earth. It is also the direction of winter, the direction where the sun never peaks as it does in the south, and where the further you go

---

[1] Eliphas Levi (1854) *The Conjuration of the Four Elements from Transcendental magic: its Doctrine and ritual*

north, the colder and often darker it gets. Winter is a time of death and struggle, so when you put all of these practicalities together, you start to get a pattern where the directions are equated with certain qualities of life and death, and of the elements.

Mythically the element of earth is connected to the north, probably by way of Greek and Egyptian mythology. In Greek mythology, Boreas, the god of the north wind was one of the four Anemoi (gods of the four winds) and he was the god of winter. He was also the north wind that blew down from the northern mountains of Thrace, bringing the cold of winter with him.

So where does the bull come in? Most people when looking at magical roots trace the bull to one the four holy creatures (Chayot)[1] from the Book of Revelations and the Book of Ezekiel, and that would be correct to a certain extent, except that those creatures have much older roots, and also have non-Biblical roots. The bull as the power creature/angelic being of the north likely comes from Egypt.

Since the first dynasty of the Old Kingdom in Egypt, the bull has played a major part in the state religion (bulls in general were considered magical power animals in the ancient world). The early appearances of the bull in the Egyptian state religion were based at Memphis (the most northern 'power city' of the time in Egypt) in the form of the Apis Bull. The Apis Bull was considered a form of the king's courage, power and vitality (I am simplifying this to be brief) and as the Osiris Apis, the bull was the triumphant king power in the Underworld/realm of death. Memphis was mostly the ancient centre of administrative power in Egypt, and was close to the royal necropolis of Saqqara. Memphis/Saqqara was 'north' in Egypt, which also had connotations of the long dead/the Underworld, which we will look at later in this essay.

Osiris Apis was something that was embraced in Egypt by Alexander the Great once he invaded Egypt in 332 B.C. and threw the Persians out. Osiris Apis as the Bull in the Underworld, and Apis as the *ka* of the king, had a strong draw for Alexander as a kingship symbol which he took up and used to great effect. Apis was also a major deity in the town of Rhacotis on the north coast of Lower

---

[1] Bull, lion, eagle and man: from Book of Ezekiel, Merkabah texts and the Book of Revelations.

F. THE DIRECTIONS IN WESTERN MAGIC

Egypt, a town which later became the site of the city Alexandria. The subsequent ruler after Alexander, Ptolemy I, also took up the Apis[1] and particularly Osiris Apis, and eventually the concept of the bull was fused with a humanesque deity which was subsequently called Serapis.[2] Serapis became a major feature in the cultic community in Alexandria,[3] a community that was a mixture of Greeks, Hellenized Jews, Egyptians, and others.

When Alexander died in Babylon in 323 B.C., Ptolemy, his general, had his body taken to the temple of Ptah at Memphis for embalming, the same temple where only a year earlier, he had been crowned king. Also bear in mind that the temple of Ptah was also the home to/enclosure of the Apis bull: the power of the king. Alexander was then entombed in Alexandria, the city where Serapis eventually became the main deity.

So you can see how the image of the bull became connected with power, kingship, death, and the north. It is likely that the cult of the Apis bull is also the root of the bull in the Chayot, something we will come back to in a moment.

The connection of the sword with the north and the bull had me puzzled for a while, as magically, historically, and mythically, the sword tends to be a tool of the east. East, magically, is connected to utterance, the dawn of new powers/actions, and the power of protecting/limiting/prophecy, and that probably comes into magic from Biblical sources where we have instances of the sword guarding in the east, or the sword and word being 'one.'[4]

I have come across such things before where tools and powers are in directions you would not expect, and often there is no magical logic nor historical context for such placing (where there is a magical logic, you can learn a great deal by analysing what someone has done). When I come across such things and it is clear that the writer is not a practising skilled magician, I have to assume they used common

---

[1] Diodorus Siculus (first century B.C.) Book I *Bibliotheca Historica* 84.8

[2] Mckechnice P, Guillame P, (2008). *Ptolemy II Philadelphus and his World.* Leidon, Boston.

[3] Bevan E. (1927: reprint 2015) *A History of Egypt Under the Ptolemaic Dynasty.* Routledge.

[4] *Revelation* 19:15 sword/utterance, *Genesis* 3:24 sword in the east of the Garden of Eden.

sense to place the tools if the original information was not available to them or is missing, or they are copying from another text. In terms of the Bull and kingship, it would make rational sense to place the sword there, but it doesn't make magical sense.

When you work with directional powers in magic, certain tools and powers do switch on strongly in certain directions, hence it is important to place things carefully and make informed choices about how to work directionally. I do not fully grasp whether these natural homes for powers and subsequent tools are the result of human focus over millennia, or if there is some other deeper dynamic going on: I just don't know. But what I do know is that when the sword is used in the north, it has a different and lesser effect than if it is used in the east.

If you apply working magical logic to the tools in directions and the natural powers that flow through magical directions, then for example with the sword you would trigger:

> East: sword: limitation/guarding of utterance, new action, new power.
>
> South: sword: limitation/guarding of the future, or the fire of battle.
>
> West: sword: limitation of harvest/people, or the act of culling.
>
> North: sword: limitation of ancestors or a past power, or the sword pinning that which is in the earth.

Going back to the directional elements list, there are whole rabbit holes you can vanish down should you wish to work on tracking the roots of each one: I will leave that up to you so that this essay doesn't turn into a book. However, it is worth noting that a lot of what appears in grimoires from the eighteenth and nineteenth centuries can be traced back to Alexandria in Hellenistic Egypt, where the old Egyptian religion, the Hellenized Jews, the Persian influence, and later the Romans and early Christians all rubbed shoulders.

For example, if you are looking for a source for the four creatures/Chayot in magical and Biblical texts, it is a curious point to note that the temple of Ptah in Memphis, which played such

F. The directions in Western magic

an important role in the founding of the Ptolemaic dynasty, was a temple that also featured Sekhmet (lion) the wife of Ptah, who in Old Kingdom Egypt was considered to be the mother of the King[1] and was a protector/consecrator of the King in the New Kingdom.[2]

At that time, Ptah himself was often equated with Imhotep (the 'perfect man'), the Old Kingdom architect and scholar who later became glorified as a demigod. His statue would appear in shrines to Thoth and Ptah, and in shrines of Thoth Hermes later during the Ptolemaic period. He was considered the 'greatest among men' for his wisdom and knowledge: a man of Aquarius indeed. Another god that featured at the temple of Ptah was Nefertem, son of Ptah and Sekhmet, a deity that would also have featured as the 'Aquarian man.'

Horus, the raptor bird (falcon) was considered Lord of Lower Egypt. During the Ptolemaic period, the second biggest temple in Egypt after Karnak was built to Horus. Horus was also strongly connected with kingship, was the protector of the king, and was the dawn/sun/eastern horizon/future as Ra-Horakhty.[3]

And finally you have the Apis bull, whose cult was centred at Memphis, in an enclosure at the temple of Ptah, Memphis.

I find it curious that the lion, the bull, the falcon and the man figure so strongly in magical and mystical symbolism, and that these figures would have also played a major role in symbolism in Alexandrian Egypt, which later became the centre of magical, religious, and philosophical thought for seven hundred years. Alexandria became a melting pot for Greek, Egyptian, and Roman thought, and was a major early centre in Christianity and early Christian Gnostic thought. It was also the melting pot that gave us texts that have now become magical classics, like the Greek Magical Papyri.

This could be pure coincidence, and when you look for patterns, you are likely to find them. But knowing the complexity of the community in Alexandria at the time and for the next few hundred

---

[1] West Gable of the Antechamber, Pyramid of Unas, Utterance 248. Faulkner R.O. (1969) *The Ancient Egyptian Pyramid Texts.* Oxford University Press.

[2] Ramses II's mortuary temple at Thebes: the smaller hypostyle hall wall relief of the king burning incense to his guide, Ptah, and protector/consecrator Sekhmet. New Kingdom, 19th Dynasty.

[3] Ra-Horakhty, "Ra, who is Horus of the Two Horizons."

F.4. Nineteenth-century Europe

years, and knowing that a lot of magical texts and ideas that travelled across Europe emerged out of Alexandria, it is an interesting hypothesis.

Levi's listing and system has many such interesting correlations to Dynastic Egypt, Ptolemaic and Greco-Roman Egypt and it would be an interesting exercise one day to take it all apart and trace each concept back to its roots.

Just to demonstrate this, for example, Levi's listing of *Undines water, west, Aquarius, cup,* is interesting and when you know the dynastic Egyptian religious and magical system you spot something interesting straightaway. The mixture of west, the perfect man, the cup, and water brings to mind one of the central pillars of the dynastic Egyptian magical religion: The justified one (human who has conquered death and been judged before the gods) who resides in the west, and the cup that provides his 'cool refreshment' (water).

In the funerary texts and in particular the *Book of Gates,* as a person develops more and more through their death transformation process, they are offered *cool refreshment* in the form of water, along with bread and wine, as part of the Osirian transformation (which sounds Catholic). This was also done at the mortuary temple of a dead person: water, wine, and bread would be offered to the spirit of the dead.

The connection with water pouring or offering and the dead also appears in some areas of Islam and is likely a pre-Islamic practice:

> Jabir narrated that the Prophet's grave was sprinkled and that the one who sprinkled the water over his grave from a waterskin was Bilal bin Rabah. He began where the head was and sprinkled it to his feet.
>
> — Imam al-Bayhaqi (A.D. 994)

And just before we move on, there is one last thing that caught my eye in Levi's listings, which was the mention of the forked staff. That confirmed for me that Levi had been reading the *Grand Grimoire,* a magical grimoire that was doing the rounds in the early part of the nineteenth century. The forked staff appears in Chapter III of the *Grand Grimoire*:

F. The directions in Western magic

> On the eve of the great undertaking you will search for a rod or wand of wild hazel tree that has not yet born fruit, at the highest point of the sought-after branch there should be a second little branch in the form of a fork with two ends: its length should be nineteen and a half inches.[1]

It is likely from his work that he read the *Grand Grimoire* and the *Grimoire Verum*, both early nineteenth-century texts that purported to be much older than they in fact were. Declaring great age and mysterious sources was highly fashionable in 'magical society' from the sixteenth century onward. Thankfully, although Levi obviously immersed himself in whatever magical texts he could lay his hands on, instead of simply copying them and giving them a new name and even greater age, which is something that happened a lot, Levi picked out bits here and there and tried to create a more coherent magical structure with them.

So why did the forked staff catch my eye beyond dating Levi's work? Because it is an ancient tool indeed and has an important role to play in magic. When we see ancient fragments emerging in later texts, it tells us that someone along the line had access to information or texts with roots in an ancient source. Whether they understood them or not is irrelevant; what we are seeing is how magic can move down through time, hiding in plain sight. And where there is one fragment, there are often more lurking around.

Later on we will come to understand quite how old the forked staff is, and what it harks back to, so take a mental note of this tool for later.

From the sixteenth to the nineteenth century we see a glut of grimoires. A few are magically interesting and hide a real magical practice, but the majority are mainly collections of folk spells with smatterings of Hebrew, Latin, and made up words (some of which draw from what their authors think is Hebrew and Latin). They are interesting in terms of magical history and folklore, but in real magical terms they are mostly simply babble. Their popularity waxes and wanes with fashions, and they are no different from today's glut

---
[1] *Grand Grimoire* a.k.a. *The Red Dragon*: Chapter III, Book One

of fake 'channelled' books or ones that are cobbled together from various sources and given a shiny pedigree in order to sell them.

Then, just as now, these books were presented to make money, open doors of influence and to prey on the magically illiterate. Saying this is deeply unpopular but is something that needs saying, and I am likely to attract a lot of howls of protest and yet more hate mail as result of this stance. A female magician poking at the most treasured toys in Western magic is definitely not going to be popular.

For the purposes of this historical analysis of directions and magic, it is vitally important that students learn to separate the wheat from the chaff not only in practice but also in historical studies. Discernment is an important skill in magic, and learning to look closely beyond glamour is an important exercise in developing that skill.

Although we cannot know what went on in the head of Eliphas Levi, we can see from his writings that he undertook what was then the herculean task of moving magic's focus away from empty glamour, and attempted to inject a more serious and in parts mystical treatment of magic. For that, we must always be eternally grateful to him.

F.5 The sixteenth century

If we step back in history before Levi, the next big waving flag in regards to assignments in the magical directions can be found in the work of Luria, and just before him, Agrippa. The sixteenth century was truly a blossoming time for magical texts, and although it is an absolutely fascinating time to read about, for the purpose of this essay we can only consider it briefly. It is not necessary to include every retrospective step in the development of directional magic, as this article is about the actual magic itself, not the history of those who developed and passed things along.

Isaac Luria (1534–1572)

Isaac Luria, also known as Yitzhak Ben Sh'lomo Lurya Ashkenazi, and also known as Ha'ARI Hakadosh (the holy lion), was a highly learned and deeply visionary Jewish mystic who essentially

F. The Directions in Western Magic

overhauled how Jewish mysticism was approached. When we as magicians look at the Tree of Life, the powers of the Sefirot, and the powers of the directions (among many other things) we are looking at the Divinely inspired work of Luria.

Luria brought the loosely connected knowledge that was scattered across the Zohar and put it into order, Reflection, and correspondence. It is important to point out at this time that Luria was not a magician but a Kabbalist, and his whole being was focused towards the Divine expression through mystical understanding. His most famous gift to modern magicians today was the Tree of Life and the Sefirot as an organized pattern.

His work appeared at a time when the magical minds of Europe had spent decades digesting the Greek philosophical and Hermetic texts that had been translated and narrated by Marsilio Ficino (A.D. 1433–99) and the mass of inspired magical books that had emerged in Italy, Spain and Germany. From the mid-fifteenth century onward in Europe, there had been a massive influx of magical, sacred, philosophical and mystical texts that been carried into Europe as a result of the strengthening new Ottoman Empire and the eventual conquest of Constantinople by Mehmed the Conqueror in A.D. 1453.

These texts varied widely in age and content, and were mostly Greek and Greco-Roman Egyptian texts that had come from Alexandria and the Near East. They were in Greek, Latin and Arabic: many texts of classical and ancient origin had been translated into Arabic a few hundred years earlier, which preserved them. The great libraries at Constantinople were basically grabbed and shipped out as much as possible, in the face of the advancing Ottoman army.

There was also rather a glut of cynically produced magical grimoires that essentially were cobbled messes of correspondences, demon names and mysterious sigils. For those who searched deeply through the dross, and found the magical and philosophical writings that touched their magical souls, the work of Luria shone a bright light for those who had laboured in the shadow of confusion. Here is just a small a glimpse of Luria's work:

> It is important to know that all worlds and all creatures that inhabit those worlds were created through

permutations of the holy names. The supernal root of all the names is the name Havayah.[1]

It has 4 letters and 12 permutations, 3 for each letter. Thus, from 4, we obtain 12. Corresponding to these, there are four banners (angelic camps) in the Supernal Merkava (Chariot). They are: Michael, Gabriel, Raphael and Uriel. Each of these 4 consists of 3, again making a total of 12. Corresponding to these, there are 4 basic directions (South, North, East, West) from which 12 sub-directions emerge. Each basic direction has two sub-directions.

Luria's directional correspondences:

South	kindness	chesed
North	discipline	gevurah
East	harmony	tiferet
Up	perseverance	netzach
Down	submission	hod
West	connection	yesod

Bringing the four species towards the heart: communication (malchut).

Luria's work remains a major part of Kabbalah to this day, and in the following comment, quoted from an article on the Jewish custom of extending the lulav and etrog[2] to the directions, we can see a faint fragment of the magical ritual pattern of facing east and working the directions.

> Our sages explain that the manifestation of the Divine Presence in this world—the Shechinah, stems from the

---

[1] "And Elokim G-d spoke to Moses and He said to Him, I am Havayah!" (*Exodus* 6:2)

HaVaYaH: the Tetragrammaton, G-d's Divine Name of the four Hebrew letters yud-hei-vav-hei, expressing His transcendence of time and space.

[2] The etrog is a Citrus fruit/lemon/lime (Etz Hadar) and the Lulav is palm branches (Kapot t'marim): used during Sukkot.

F. The directions in Western magic

west.[1] If the Shechinah is in the west, figuratively, when facing east, south would be to its right and north to its left.[2]

Facing east as a default magical position in ritual tracks back much further (probably a great deal further back than Christianity) and we find mention of it in the writing of an early Christian author Quintus Septimius Florens Tertullianus.

> Others with a greater show of reason take us for worshippers of the sun. These send us to the religion of Persia, though we are far from adoring a painted sun, like them who carry about his image everywhere upon their bucklers. This suspicion took its rise from hence, because it was observed that Christians prayed with their faces towards the east.
>
> — Tertullian (A.D. 160–220)

For those of you reading this essay who have practised Hermetic magic, you will start to see the roots of some ritual actions and patterns used within various Hermetic systems. The Kabbalistic patterns that emerged in Hermetic magic all stem from the work of Luria, and were passed on by various writers, thinkers, and practitioners such as Levi.

His work was revolutionary, and in keeping with the European magical communities of that time, his concepts, ideas and developments were absorbed, digested and incorporated into the swiftly growing corpus of magical knowledge.

Henry Cornelius Agrippa 1486–1535

The work of Agrippa, in his *Three Books of Occult Philosophy*, can in many respects be viewed as one of the cornerstones of modern

---

[1] Midrash Rabbah on *Numbers* 11:2. The Talmud (Bava Batra 25a) points out, from the verse (*Nechemia* 9:6) "and the hosts of the heavens bow down to you" that the heavenly bodies move westward because they are bowing down to G-d whose presence is manifest in the west.

[2] Chabad—Rabbi Eliezer Shemtov: the Chabad-Lubavitch emissary in Montevideo, Uruguay

Western magic. Agrippa was a German theologian and occult writer, and one of the great polymaths of his time.

He studied at the University of Cologne as a young man (thirteen to sixteen years old) where he was deeply influenced by the work of Albertus Magnus (1193–1280).[1] Magnus was a German bishop who had a deep interest in a wide variety of subject matter from philosophy and theology to alchemy, astrology, botany and mineralogy. Magnus translated Aristotle and a variety of Arabic writings, and delved into the writings of the Neoplatonists.

In his early twenties Agrippa studied with Johannes Trithemius (1462–1516) a Benedictine Abbot, cryptographer and occultist, at Würzburg in northern Bavaria.[2] This was also the time that Agrippa began working on his first draft of *De Occulta Philosophia* (The Occult Philosophies). When you look at Agrippa's work, you see straightaway how much it consists of lists, categories etc. Indeed, although Agrippa studied intensively every text he could lay his hands upon, he was not a practising magician. This pattern repeats heavily in the history of Western magic, and is important to bear in mind: magic is often passed along in texts from one generation to another by people who did not really practice magic and didn't really understand it, and it was often married to mystical texts, such as Luria.

However, although mysticism and magic often meet upon the road, their actual power systems are different, and it is easy for oddities and blind alleys to be introduced accidently into magical systems when mystical or religious elements are woven into magical systems without practical understanding or forethought from direct experience. I am sure that comment will elicit howls of protest from many quarters, but it is something that magicians need to seriously keep in mind and think about carefully.

To get back to the directions, here is a table from book II chapter seven of Agrippa's *The Occult Philosophies*.[3] It looks at the numerical pattern of four and the directional attributes. You will see immediately where subsequent magical writers and grimoires drew

---

[1] Nicholas Goodrick-Clarke, *The Western Esoteric Tradition* (2008)
[2] W J Hanegraaff, *Dictionary of Gnosis and Western Esotericism* (2006)
[3] http://www.esotericarchives.com/agrippa/agrippa2.htm#chap7

F. The directions in Western magic

their attributions from, and also the names, powers and Hebrew patterns.

The Scale of the Number four, answering the four Elements

THE NAME OF GOD WITH FOUR LETTERS.	י	ה	ו	ה
Four Hierarchies	Seraphim. Cherubin. Thrones.	Dominations. Powers. Vertues.	Principalities. Archangels. Angels.	Innocents. Martyrs. Confessors.
Four Angels ruling over the corners of the world	מיכאל Michael.	רפאל Raphael.	גבריאל Gabriel.	אוריאל Uriel.
Four rulers of the Elements	שרף Seraph.	כרוב Cherub.	תרשיש Tharsis.	אריאל Ariel.
Four consecrated Animals	The Lion.	The Eagle.	Man.	A Calf.
Four Triplicities of the tribes of Israel	Dan Asser Nephtalim	Jehuda Isachar Zabulum	Manasse Benjamin Ephraim.	Reubin Simeon Gad
Four Triplicities of Apostles	Mathias Peter Jacob the elder	Simon Bartholemew Mathew	John Phillip James the younger	Thaddeus Andrew Thomas
Four Evangelists	Mark	John	Mathew	Luke
Four Triplicities of Signs.	Aries. Leo. Sagittarius.	Gemini. Libra. Aquarius.	Cancer. Scorpius. Pisces.	Taurus. Virgo. Capricornus
The Stars & Planets, related to the Elements.	Mars, and the Sun.	Jupiter, and Venus.	Saturn, and Mercury.	The fixed Stars, and the Moon.
Four qualities of the Celestial Elements	Light.	Diaphanous-ness.	Agility.	Solidity.
Four Elements.	אש Fire.	רוח Air.	מים Water.	עפר Earth.
Four qualities.	Heat.	Moisture.	Cold.	Dryness.
Four seasons.	Summer.	Spring.	Winter.	Autumn.
Four corners of the World.	The East.	The West.	The North.	The South.

Continued on next page

F.5. The sixteenth century

Continued from previous page

THE NAME OF GOD WITH FOUR LETTERS.	י	ה	ו	ה
Four perfect kinds of mixed bodies.	Animals.	Plants.	Metals.	Stones.
Four kinds of Animals.	Walking.	Flying.	Swimming.	Creeping.
The Elements, in Plants.	Seeds.	Flowers.	Leaves.	Roots.
What in Metals.	Gold, and Iron.	Copper, and Tin.	Quicksilver.	Lead, & Silver.
What in stones.	Bright, and burning.	Light, and transparent.	Clear, and congealed.	Heavy, & dark.
Four Elements of man.	The Mind.	The spirit.	The Soul.	The body.
Four powers of the Soul.	The Intellect.	Reason.	Phantasy.	Sense.
Four Judiciary powers.	Faith.	Science.	Opinion.	Experience.
Four moral virtues.	Justice.	Temperance.	Prudence.	Fortitude.
The senses answering to the Elements.	Sight.	Hearing.	Taste and smell.	Touch.
Four Elements of man's body.	Spirit.	Flesh.	Humours.	Bones.
A four-fold spirit.	Animal.	Vital.	Generative.	Natural.
Four humours.	Choller.	Blood.	Flegme.	Melancholy.
Four Manners of complexion.	Violence.	Nimbleness.	Dulness.	Slowness.
Four Princes of devils, offensive in the Elements.	סמאל Samael.	עזאזל Azazel.	עזאל Azael.	מהזאל Mahazael.
Four infernal Rivers.	Phlegeton	Cocytus	Styx.	Acheron.
Four Princes of spirits, upon the four angels of the world.	Oriens.	Paymon.	Egyn.	Amaymon.

As you look at Agrippa's chart of the powers of four, you can immediately see the various sources that have been drawn together, Christianized, and then shoehorned into a system. And you can also see what an influence this listing had on subsequent generations of

675

F. THE DIRECTIONS IN WESTERN MAGIC

magicians up to present day. Agrippa's work also cemented the idea of 'lists' and tables in magical work, something that continues to this day.

Rather than continue back further in time, as we have what we need now to see the basis of the modern directional patterns, I think now is a good point to look at what is actually going on here in magical structural terms.

F.6 The modern structural approach

When I say modern, I include everything from the present day right back to thirteenth-century Europe, which in turn has its roots in Greco-Roman Egypt.

This approach in its foundations works from the perspective of everything *outside* of the magician. This reaches from the landscape, the elements, the stars and planets, the Underworld and so forth, and this externalization between the magician and the 'four' has informed and influenced Western magicians over long periods of time to the extent that it has become the orthodoxy of directional ritual patterns. If you look at any Western magical system today, you will see some or all of the 'four' powers and qualities emerge into the ritual pattern.

The 'four' as a patterned structure is very much about the earth, the Kingdom (Malkuth) and the universe in relation to the magician. The magician stands as the controller of the orchestra: there is a clear separation between the magician and his magic.

When you jump back much further back in time, further back than Greece or Greco-Roman Egypt, and start to look at Dynastic Egypt, you start to see a different pattern emerging, but one that subsequently influenced, informed and underpinned the later patterns that emerged as a result of what I call the 'Alexandrian Soup,' which is a mixture of Semitic, Egyptian, Greek, and Persian influences. (Its Egyptian influences were not uniquely Alexandrian: it clearly shows the influence of other areas, such as Thebes.) It was the 'Alexandrian Soup' that was the parent of what we call magic today, but the great-grandmother of the Alexandrian Soup was Egypt.

What I will say is that one of the major ingredients in that soup was the cultural and religious pattern of Dynastic Egypt, remnants of which made a base for the magical and religious patterns that emerged out of that time period. A lot of the elements that survived from Dynastic Egypt were heavily misinterpreted or misunderstood, and those misunderstandings carried forward into the newer religions and magical patterns in various obscure ways. However, some fragments also remained true to their roots and continued to be passed down from priest to magician, to alchemist to priest, and so forth.

Let us look at one small aspect of that of those surviving fragments: the use, knowledge, and understanding of the directions in Dynastic Egypt.

F.7 Dynastic Egypt

Before we delve into the directional patterns of Dynastic Egypt, it is worth pointing out to you that in Egypt, magic was part and parcel of the religion and culture. Magic was used within the temples to maintain the laws of Ma'at, to protect the king and nation, and to heal.

It was also used to heal and protect everyday people. Healer priests (male and female) operated out of the temple 'House of Life,' which was the library, archive and place of training and knowledge. Some, *swnw*, were general doctors, and some were *s3w*, who were the magical doctors. This role was later taken up by the *ḥk'y* ("magician") in the first millennium B.C.. The lector priests also played a major role in magical activity, as they were the ones who could read and recite the magical texts.[1]

Protection spells were worked not only by priests but also 'wise women' and seers who were usually connected to temple life in one way or another. Many of the priests, both male and female in a temple, often served only for a few months of the year and the rest of the time they worked out in the community either in a trade, or as a scribe, or as a healer, seer and so forth. This likely laid the foundation for the much later 'community magicians for hire,' a dynamic that we have

---

[1]David, R. *Religion and Magic in Ancient Egypt.* Penguin Books, 2003

F. THE DIRECTIONS IN WESTERN MAGIC

no evidence for until the Ptolemaic and subsequent Roman period of Egypt.[1]

One thing that all the Dynastic Egyptian magic had in common was how it used the directions. On the surface it can appear to be similar to Western magic in many respects, but in fact it is a whole other dynamic that separates it from later directional magic, and from the directional magic of the Greeks, Romans and Persians.

The big fundamental difference in the directional system, is that Dynastic system was based around the human and the Divine within the human, not so much the universe around them, which is the system that the West is more used to: the magic of Dynastic Egypt *was magician-centred and not environment-centred.* You can argue the point that the modern magician in general Western magic is indeed the centre, the Divine within, but that is simply one of the fragments of the Dynastic system that survived.

Because this has such a strong bearing on magic today, we will look at this in detail. If you understand those ancient fragments, and subsequently how they remain in modern magic, and then understand it within its own context, you will have a much greater understanding of the magic of today, and of yourself as the magician.

This in turn enables you to make choices: in a way, we as modern magicians have inherited two core principles: the magician as controller, and the magician as the centre of magic. That allows us elbowroom to decide what to use, when and how: we have a freedom of choice that was not so much of an option in times past.

Magic, Egypt, and the directions

This section of the essay is long and at times convoluted. Because Egyptian history is long, complex and at times completely different in its concepts to modern thinking, there need to be various digressions in order to establish context, content and meaning. However, I have attempted to approach this in a way that will also give you the reader a wider understanding of Dynastic Egyptian magical and religious/cultural thinking, and shine lights in corners of the Egyptian

---

[1] JF Borghouts. Witchcraft, Magic and Divination in Ancient Egypt. In: *Civilizations of the Ancient Near East.* ed. JM Sasson, Charles Scribner's Sons, 1995.

F.7. Dynastic Egypt

'Mysteries' that will help many readers reflect upon how these ancient concepts appear in various forms to this day. These concepts were carried out of Egypt by various waves of new religious thought and embedded in various ways into new magical and religious streams that still influence us to this day.

It is wise to bear in mind that unlike later Greco-Roman and much later Western magic, Egyptian magic and its texts as such were not recorded for the common man. The Egyptian sacred magical texts do not have bullet points, recipe lists (spells), and easily understood references: if you were trained and active, you were expected to understand the basics of what you were looking at. If you were not trained and active, but were a noble looking for a funerary text for your tomb, then a pre-prepared funerary scroll with your name inserted in it was essentially handed to you to place in your tomb or coffin, a text that most likely you would not understand.

Saying that, when you look at funerary texts over the huge span of Dynastic Egyptian history, you can tell when the education levels in the priesthood went up and down, or when such texts were used for the tombs/coffins of rich nobles who had little or no education. The complex texts start to acquire pictures, or are at times almost all pictures, though you would need to understand the process and Mysteries to decipher what was happening. But by the end of the New Kingdom, the Late Period and beyond, we do see basic 'picture book' funerary text that is about as simple as you can get for such concepts.

It is also worth knowing should you wish to research further, what form of Egyptian hieroglyphs you are looking at, as in terms of spotting magical signifiers, that there are big differences in the texts at certain periods in time. Anything from the Old Kingdom will be in Old Egyptian,[1] which is markedly different from Middle Egyptian which emerged c. 2050 B.C. in the Middle Kingdom period.

Middle Egyptian continued to be used as a form of high literature through the New Kingdom right up to Roman times for sacred and important texts, stelas and funerary writings, but its spoken form was only used for hymns, spells and important utterances once Late Egyptian emerged around the Amarna Period (c 1300 B.C.). And then

---

[1] For example, the Pyramid texts.

F. The directions in Western magic

there are other forms of Egyptian scripts such as Hieratic,[1] Demotic[2] and Coptic.[3,4]

Knowing what script it is you are looking at tells you a great deal about the information contained within that script, whether it was administrative, secular, sacred or magical. It can also tell you roughly what period in Egyptian history it was from. And also bear in mind the common misconception that the culture and religion of Egypt was one coherent history throughout its four-thousand-year history: nothing could be further from the truth. It was a mixed bag, just like any other nation of such age. Most of what we will be looking at has its origins in New Kingdom Egypt and the Third Intermediate Period.[5]

By looking at texts, images and wall paintings, we can discern from the directional positions and symbolic nature of the imagery, what was going on and often, why. As the magic was embodied within the magician/priest/king, the positions of the body in images tell us what dynamic they were working on, and also if they dead or alive or working in death or life. Left leg forward is striding into life or through life, for example, and right leg was striding through death. And ankh in the left hand is life in life, and in the right hand, is life in death.

So you start to see the subtle but major difference in how magic was approached in Dynastic Egypt. The Western magician seeks outside him or herself to draw in the power, the Egyptian magician generated it from themselves outwards.

Most Egyptian writings are multilayered in their meaning, so that high priests, kings and magicians could read one thing, and the lesser priests and scribes read another: hiding it in plain sight. And I presume that, knowing the pragmatic culture within ancient Egypt, those who knew, knew, and didn't need to point it out or need it pointing out to them. When a modern Western person looks at a

---

[1] Simplified cursive form of Old and Middle Egyptian

[2] Cursive variant of Hieratic that developed in Lower Egypt during the 25th Dynasty (c. 600 B.C.).

[3] Based around the Greek script (c100 B.C.).

[4] Allen, James P. (2000) *Middle Egyptian: An Introduction to the Language and Culture of Hieroglyphs.* Cambridge: Cambridge University Press.

[5] New Kingdom and Third Intermediate period (c. 1550-712 B.C.).

F.7. Dynastic Egypt

map, they automatically assume the top of the map is north, because that is how we align our maps: it rarely needs pointing out.

The first dynamic to understand before we look at directions, is a pattern that still emerges in Western magic today though in a different form and at times is heavily misunderstood. That pattern is one of *creation, stasis, and destruction*, and all three of those dynamics are considered to be within the natural order of balance, or in Egyptian terms, governed by the rule of Ma'at: balance. Outside of that balance is chaos which destroys order. In Western magic, destruction, death etc. are often considered 'bad' or chaos, this is expressed through modern terms like white/black magic.

The second dynamic that is foundational in Egyptian magic is 'seed' and 'harvest.' This dynamic runs through everything in Egyptian magic: something is 'seeded,' it grows, does something, and then its actions are harvested and weighed. The harvest is then 'judged' (weighed or counted) and what is good of the harvest is then renewed.

This not only applies to the actions of the magician/priest/individual but to their life also. We see aspects of this in Egyptian funerary texts where the deeds of the person (the harvest recorded by the heart spirit) are weighed[1] and if the harvest is sufficient, the soul of the person is considered 'developed.'

There is a deeper octave of this dynamic where the dead priest/magician/king is tested in death to *become* the scales.[2] If they pass this test, they are considered justified in death.

The most important dynamic of Egyptian directional magic is time. With time, and seed/harvest as two foundational dynamics, the Egyptian magician stands in the flow of time and operates through the input/output dynamic, with themselves as the vehicle through which the magic develops and flows.

The deity/spirit involvement is not the same as Western magic, though it can appear so on the surface to an untrained eye. In Western magic, the deities, spirits/beings are called to the magician and asked, forced, or instructed to do something: the magician as

---
[1] e.g. in the *Book of the Dead*, an Egyptian New Kingdom funerary text.
[2] e.g. in the Fifth Hour of the *Book of Gates*, an Egyptian New Kingdom funerary text.

F. THE DIRECTIONS IN WESTERN MAGIC

controller. In Egyptian magic, the *nṯrw*[1] (pronounced by modern Egyptologists as "NETCH-er-oo" or "NE-tyer-oo"), are the 'gods,' and the Egyptians looked upon the 'gods' in different ways to how we perceive them today.

Where modern magic has hierarchies of angels, demons, planetary spirits and so forth as well as deities and God, the Egyptians did not differentiate in the same way. For the most part, excluding things like hungry ghosts, almost everything was *nṯr*. This is a subtle but important difference in directional work: the Egyptian did not see the gods as the Greeks did (the basis of Roman and subsequently Western view) as squabbling Divine humans (i.e. human behaviours) in a literal sense, but more as powers and dynamics that manifested in everything around them (powers and creatures of nature) and this was played out in stories which were surface presentations of much deeper power dynamics.

By the end of the Dynastic era, the Persian and Greek ideas of the gods as squabbling Divine humans had integrated itself into Egyptian thought and we see this manifesting in the Ptolemaic period and beyond in Egypt.

This is all important to understand, as it shifts how the magician views power, works with power, and how that all relates to the directional work. And please bear in mind I have simplified this complex dynamic view right down, so that this article does not digress too much from the subject at hand.

The directional pattern

The Egyptian directional pattern, which governed everything in magic *and the magician themselves* is as thus:

> East: input, birth, seed, rising, left.
> South: future, in front, life, tomorrow, the new day.

East and south are inextricably linked to each other in a poetic sense: east is a 'gate' and south is a 'path.' The same is true for west and north:

---

[1] *nṯr*: singular deity, *nṯrt*: singular female deity, *nṯrw* plural 'gods'.

F.7. Dynastic Egypt

West: output, threshold of death, dusk, harvest, descending, right.

North: past, behind, dead, yesterday.

Centre: fulcrum/heart spirit.

The most important thing to think about, reading that list, is the understanding that mostly the directions were viewed as dynamic powers, not geographical points. For example in sacred (and thus magical) texts the term 'south' can often denote an inner/non-worldly state or location, not an actual physical one. South can also mean moving forward, the future and the path ahead.

The directions in Egyptian text are also identified with the body. Remember, with Egyptian texts one thing can have various meanings *all at the same time*. It was a similar way of approaching sacred information that was later used by Jewish Kabbalists (PaRDeS) and that Kabbalistic method most likely had its roots in Egypt.

The directions

The words/hieroglyphs of east and west are used to denote a geographical location, a sacred/inner location, a state of being, a goddess, the side of a body or object and the hand/foot on the body. Here are the emblems, transliterations and meanings for east and west in Middle Egyptian:[1]

 East:

iȝby (adj): left side, east, eastern. Will have suffix of an arm or foot to denote left/east side of the body, or a suffix denoting place.

iȝbt: The East (i.e. the power of the east) personified as the goddess Iabet, She of the sunrise.

---

[1]Raymond Faulkner. *A Concise Dictionary of Middle Egyptian*. 1962 Griffith Institute Oxford.

F. THE DIRECTIONS IN WESTERN MAGIC

 West:

imn (adj): right side, west, western. Will have suffix of an arm or foot to denote right hand/foot, or a suffix denoting place

imnt: The West, (i.e. the power of the west) personified as the goddess Imentit, She of the necropolis.

You start to see how the directions are inextricably linked with the body, with powers, inner locations and also physical space. With the left-hand default position as being east, you can then begin to understand the concept of south being forward, and north being behind.

Let us just looked briefly at how these body directions played out in statues and painting. Once you understand the directional qualities of east/left/life, and west/right/death, you can then begin to understand any underlying narrative presented.

Seti II

This 19th Dynasty statue of Seti II shows him with his left leg forward, which tells us it was made while Seti II was alive: he is striding forward into his reign. Also note the utterance is to the left of him.

As an aside, when you look at statues of some Egyptian kings, some scribes, and priests, you will notice that their hands are often curled around something. For years Egyptologists have hypothesized that they are holding scrolls, and sometimes they clearly are, and often have a tool in the other hand. But there are many times when it is clearly not a scroll, rather they are depicted as holding the *prow ropes of the barque.*

There is a whole narrative that appears in some of the funerary texts, where the Justified living and dead pull the Barque of Re in the Duat, and they are considered developed ones or developing ones: people of great learning where their heart speaks a truth, and they are considered 'Justified' before the gods. Pulling the prow ropes of the Barque of Re was a great honour and also a terrible burden. This is clearly outlined in the New Kingdom text *The Book of Gates.*

F.7. Dynastic Egypt

Figure F.1: Statue of Seti II, 19th Dynasty, Egypt. Displayed at the Museo Egizio, Turin, Italy.

F. THE DIRECTIONS IN WESTERN MAGIC

In this smaller image below, from the tomb of Tuthmosis IV, note how the king has his right leg forward, as he is in death, and is receiving *life in death* from Hathor, and *life and dominion* from Osiris.

Figure F.2: Tuthmosis IV tomb KV43, Valley of the Kings.

Now let us look in depth at a particular and famous funerary text, often called the *Egyptian Book of the Dead*. It is littered with imagery and texts that give us various insights into how directions were used to signify powers, places and actions.

Papyrus of Ani: The Book of Coming forth by Day

So many people look at these texts through a cultural lens of Western thinking which involves issues like monotheism and geographical location, and that immediately locks them out of the understanding

F.7. Dynastic Egypt

of the text. A good example would be a section of the Papyrus of Ani,[1] the funeral text of Coming Forth by Day for Ani, spell seventeen:

> I go on the road which I know in front of the Island of the Just. *What is it?* It is Rosetjau. The southern gate is in Naref, the northern gate is in the Mound of Osiris; as for the Island of the Just, it is Abydos. *Otherwise said:* It is the road on which my father Atum went when he proceeded to the Field of Reeds.

When you look at this from a point of geographical location, the eye is drawn to Abydos which is an ancient sacred enclosure and temple complex. It is one of the oldest settlements in Ancient Egypt and is the eighth nome[2] of Upper Egypt. From that, many people, both lay readers and some academics have tied themselves in knots trying to figure out where Naref is geographically, using Abydos as a location indicator. This is how a modern Western person would think, but to an ancient Egyptian, a sacred inner location, a person, and a state of being can all be the same thing.

Naref and Osiris[3] Naref are mentioned numerous times in funerary texts, stelas, statues and tombs certainly in the New Kingdom through to the Late Period. The words can be used for a location, a person or a state of being. Here is an example from the 30th dynasty, titles found on a statue of a priest at Herakleopolis Magna:

> Revered before Heryshef, king of the Two Lands, ruler of the Two Banks, Revered before Osiris Nareref.[4]

If we go back to spell seventeen and look at it from a magical Egyptian perspective, we can hypothesize that Naref being *southern*

---

[1] Raymond Faulkner (translation 1974) *The Egyptian Book of the Dead* (spell 17) Chronicle Books USA 1994 first edition.

[2] Territorial area of Ancient Egypt.

[3] Osiris is not only a god, but a term for someone who is dead and has passed many of the trials of the Duat.

[4] Díaz-Iglesias Llanos, L. (2016). *Naref and Osiris Naref. A Study in Herakleopolitan Religious Traditions.* Berlin, Boston: deGruyter

F. The directions in Western magic

is before the dead person and the *northern gate* is behind the dead person.

When you then think about Rosetjau and that it is a *desert* pathway through one of the deepest sections of the Duat, and the gates of the Duat open for the dead traveller according to their 'harvest' or life deeds/state, then you start to understand that Naref as a gate is a state of being (i.e. the gate is within that state of being): by passing successfully through the gate of Naref they stand a good chance of safe passage to the next stage of their development journey.

When the text says "the northern gate is the Mound of Osiris" it is referring to a state: where the body has been embalmed and wrapped, and the dead spirit has gone through the first stages of the process in the Duat. The *northern gate* is the gate behind, it is in the past, the spirit is now moving away from one stage of death/destruction process, and is preparing to move forward into renewal and the 'afterlife.'

> I have established offerings in Abydos. Open the way for me in Rosetjau because I have relieved the sickness in Osiris. I have painted his perch. Make way for me so that he might shine in Rosetjau.[1]

The northern gate as the Mound of Osiris talks in terms of the Osiris mythology of death, dismemberment, reconstituting the body parts, and resurrection. In the process of the Duat's challenges as outlined in the funerary texts, a similar theme emerges of death, trials that take the person apart/the destruction of their self-image, the healing of wounds, the judgement/weighing of the heart, and the path to resurrection.

There is also a dynamic in which the dead person heals/reconstitutes Osiris by *becoming Osiris*: as the person emerges, so does Osiris. This mythology is heavily interwoven with the themes of seed, grain, threshing, harvest and weighing the harvest.

If you wish to look deeper into the magical aspects of the Inner Desert paths of Rosetjau, I suggest you read hours four and five of the

---

[1] Ogden Goelet. A Commentary on the Corpus of Literature and Tradition which constitutes the Book of Going Forth By Day. (San Francisco: Chronicle Books, 1998)

Amduat.[1] If you are familiar with Egyptian magical concepts, these two sections can be interesting.

Before we move on, here is another extract from spell seventeen of the Papyrus of Ani that has a directional fragment in it. In the spell it is talking about an image which we will look at in a moment:

> *Who is he?* It is Re who created his names and his members, it means the coming into existence of those gods who are in his suite.
>
> I am he who is not opposed among the gods.
>
> Who is he? He is Atum who is in his sun disk. *Otherwise said:* He is Re when he rises in the eastern horizon of the sky.
>
> To me belongs yesterday, I know tomorrow.[2]

Note that the action is east–west. The passage of the sun, and the time is yesterday (north) and tomorrow (south) which are the names of the Aker, the two guardian lions of the horizon which we will look at in a moment.

To summarise briefly, for Egyptians the directional pattern from a mythic (not geographic) perspective was born/east, lived/south, died/west, passed into history/north. The same pattern also unfolds in the Duat, the Egyptian Underworld.

A good example of the east–west, south–north dynamics in Egyptian thought can be found in the Old Testament (or the Jewish Book of Prophets) in *Isaiah* 43-5/6:

> Fear not, for I am with you:
>
> I will bring your seed from the east, and gather you from the west:
>
> I will say to the north: 'Give (them) up,' and to the south: 'Keep (them) not back.'

---

[1] Warburton D, Hornung E, Abt T. (2014) *The Egyptian Amduat: the Book of the Hidden Chamber*. Zurich. Living Human Heritage Publications.

[2] Faulkner Dr Ramond (translation 1974) *The Egyptian Book of the Dead* (spell 17) Chronicle Books USA 1994 first edition.

F. THE DIRECTIONS IN WESTERN MAGIC

This extract from Isaiah is sometimes used by magicians today in order to establish and protect the path ahead.

You see the similar concepts straightaway, and when you look closely at the first section of chapter 43, if you are familiar with the processes outlined in the Egyptian funerary texts you will also recognize what is going on in that first section, and where that imagery comes from.

The east/left is life (that moves south) and in life we 'do,' we act, think, create, destroy and so forth: we participate in all the trials, lessons and joys of life. The east is the seed that grows and flourishes as we move forward (south) through life: hence the command in Isaiah "I say to the south keep them not back" is protecting the person's future.

If we learn well, evolve from our mistakes, and develop/mature, then we are said to be 'winnowing our harvest' while in life: we take the best of the grain and discard the stones, husks and stalks. This leaves our harvest lightweight. In terms of the seeds that remain, there is a whole mystical magical rabbit hole you can vanish down when it comes to the depiction of the weighing of the harvest (the heart) and how much seed is left (must be lighter than a feather of Ma'at).

Upon death that 'harvest' is examined, and weighed upon scales. This concept appears to have emerged in New Kingdom Egyptian thought, and also appears in different ways in Judaic scriptures. Here is a good example from *Proverbs* 21:[1]

א פַּלְגֵי-מַיִם לֶב-מֶלֶךְ, בְּיַד-יְהוָה; עַל-כָּל-אֲשֶׁר יַחְפֹּץ יַטֶּנּוּ.	**1** The king's heart is in the hand of the LORD as the watercourses: He turneth it whithersoever He will.
ב כָּל-דֶּרֶךְ-אִישׁ, יָשָׁר בְּעֵינָיו; וְתֹכֵן לִבּוֹת יְהוָה.	**2 Every way of a man is right in his own eyes; but the LORD weigheth the hearts**.
ג עֲשֹׂה, צְדָקָה וּמִשְׁפָּט-- נִבְחָר לַיהוָה מִזָּבַח.	**3** To do righteousness and justice is more acceptable to the LORD than sacrifice.

The root תכן is widely used in second temple literature in the context of weights and measures,[2] and its use in Proverbs, applied to

---

[1] https://www.mechon-mamre.org/p/pt/pt2821.htm Proverbs 21. Retrieved 17/4/2019.

[2] Shupak, N. (2015). *Weighing in the Scales* Fs.Talshir. From Author to Copiest: Essays on Composition, Redaction and Transmission of the Hebrew Bible in Honor of Zipi Talshir

human ethical conduct, is strikingly similar to the Egyptian concept. Also note, "The king's heart is in the hand of the LORD": in the Egyptian pattern, the heart of the individual is the voice that speaks the truth upon judgement: the heart speaks to the scales upon judgement, telling the gods what this person has done in life. Note that the 'LORD' is holding the king's heart in his *hand* to weigh/judge. This is mirrored in the magical use of the right hand to weigh, complete and compost a magical action.

In New Kingdom and subsequent funerary texts[1] it appears as a judgement scene where the heart of the individual (the spirit of the heart that speaks truth) is weighed against a feather of Ma'at. In Egyptian thought the heart spirit listens and watches, and recounts our actions and lessons to the judge when we are being 'weighed.'

What remains of the harvest becomes our *west*. If the harvest has been winnowed in life to a great degree, there are little or no seeds left, the heart passes judgement and the soul moves deeper into the process of the Duat, later to rise with the sun and be in the company of the gods.[2] Remember that the west is also the right hand/right side.

Just to move briefly from history and into esotericism, the right-hand harvest contains seeds (new potential: the fruit of the harvest) and also learned wisdom from experience: the light of evolution. That is the lantern held in the right hand by the adept, depicted as the Hermit in the tarot. The light of our evolution guides us forward in life, and in death lights our way through the darkness of the Underworld/Duat as we navigate its trials on our journey.

This esoteric understanding which flows from this ancient pattern is also likely the root of understanding behind the 'right hand of God.' Remember that many of the philosophies and thinking behind early Christianity was partly seeded in Egypt,[3] as was a fair amount of Jewish philosophy.

To qualify that statement adequately would take an essay on its own. But there is enough archaeological, historical and textual evidence to demonstrate Egyptian thought and ideas mingling with

---

[1] *Book of Gates* hour five: the dead appear *as* the scales. See also Book of the Dead spell 30B.

[2] *The Book of Gates*: New Kingdom text.

[3] Choat, M. "Christianity." 2012. In: *The Oxford Handbook of Roman Egypt* edited by C. Riggs. Oxford: Oxford University Press.

Hellenistic Jewish communities in Egypt (along with Greek and Roman communities in Egypt) to the point in which long fading Egyptian influences were taken up by the newer communities and absorbed into their mythology, philosophies and magical/religious thinking.

The continued adventures of Ani in the Underworld

A good example of learning to decipher images and text, specifically for these fragments of magical concepts in Dynastic Egyptian funerary texts and literature is spell 17 from the Papyrus of Ani, which we have already briefly looked at. Now we will look at an image from that papyrus and apply what we know of Egyptian concepts of time, state and direction to decipher a specific famous picture.

In Egyptian sacred imagery[1] everything has meaning, from the stance of the person, to the banners, flowers, animals and hieroglyphs. And remember that Middle Egyptian hieroglyphs in important literature, sacred/funerary texts and important stela often had layered meaning not only with the words, but also actual images, and the pictograms of the hieroglyphs.

Aker: yesterday and tomorrow

Aker is a power of the horizon between the otherworlds/Duat and the physical world. Aker is most often depicted as two lions sat back to back, and between their backs the sun is depicted either rising or falling. The sun, Atum (Ra/Re upon rising) is nestled between two peaks in a stylized hieroglyph named Djew.[2]

The two peaks are east and west, the two positions where the sun rises and falls. The image of the sun nestled between the two peaks is called the Akhet.[3] Akhet means the place the sun inhabits just before it rises over the horizon to flood the world with light. Interestingly the same word is also used for the inundation of the Nile.

---

[1] Statues, funerary texts, tomb walls.

[2] The two peaks of the primordial mountain are Djew are Manu in the west, and Bakhu in the east.

[3] $ȝḫt$, "horizon."

F.7. Dynastic Egypt

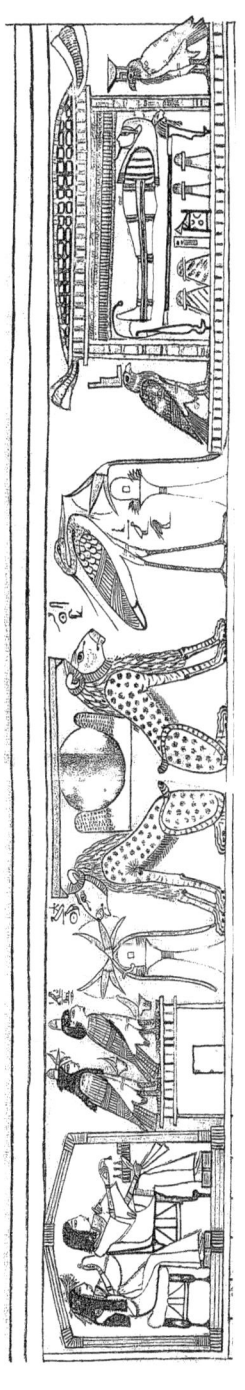

Figure F.3: Image from the Papyrus of Ani, Spell 17.

F. The directions in Western magic

So we have an image of Atum that also combines both east and west (Djew). Above the Akhet is the hieroglyph *pt* for sky or heavens. The image of the Akhet can depict the sun either rising or setting.[1]

On either side of the Akhet, also under the *pt* sign, sits the two lions: Aker. The image of Aker is one of the most misunderstood ones when people get interested in Egyptian images and symbolism, and the internet is rife with misunderstandings in articles that are then copied on *ad nauseam*. To look at the directional keys of the Aker, you need common sense and a basic knowledge of hieroglyphs and symbolism.

The names of two lions are Duaw and Sef, who together make up the Aker, *He who guards the Akhet*. Duaw can be a difficult hieroglyphic word to translate at times, as it can mean today (as in the day ahead) or tomorrow, and is translated in correlation to the context. And this is where you have to be careful about how language can shape thought: Duaw is a word that denotes moving forward, and would not be used in its context of 'today' as we would use it. For us, we would say, now, today, meaning this present moment in time. Duaw is always moving ahead, and the Middle Egyptian word for 'now' would be $3t$ (at).

In the context of Aker, Duaw means tomorrow and Sef means yesterday.[2] Aker as a collective of the two lions was at times titled *He who is looking forward and behind, Yesterday and Tomorrow,* or *He who is beneath* (the horizon).

When you look at images of the Aker lions in funeral texts, also look at what is around them. In the papyri of Ani[3] the lion Duaw which is to the left in the image, has before its nose, two lotus flowers which are symbols for Upper Egypt/south.[4] Beyond the lotus flowers are the *ba* birds of Ani and his wife standing on top of their mortuary

---

[1] Magli, G. (2013). The lords of the horizon. In Architecture, Astronomy and Sacred Landscape in Ancient Egypt (pp. 57-104). Cambridge: Cambridge University Press

[2] Faulkner, Ramond (translation 1974) *The Egyptian Book of the Dead* (spell 17) Chronicle Books USA 1994 first edition.

[3] A copy of the Book of the Dead for Ani, Theban Scribe 1250 B.C. 19th Dynasty Egypt

[4] McDonald, J. Andrew. 2018. "Influences of Egyptian Lotus Symbolism and ritualistic Practices on Sacral Tree Worship in the Fertile Crescent from 1500 BCE To 200 CE," Basel: *Religions* 9

shrines, and beyond them is an image of Ani playing Senet: the game of Passing.[1] Ani is depicted sitting playing the game in his 'shrine' or 'enclosure,' which means he has passed the trials of judgement and is now 'eternal.'

On the right of the Akhet is Sef, yesterday. Before Sef is the Benu bird, *He who came into Himself*.[2] In the Heliopolis[3] creation myth, the Benu bird flew over the waters of the Nu before creation. He landed on the emerging Benben stone and the cry of the Benu broke the primeval silence, determining what was or was not to unfold in creation. He is connected with Ra/Atum and Osiris, a symbol of the early beginning of regeneration (the midnight before the dawn) and likely the source of the later mythic Phoenix.

The text of the spell includes the words:

> I am that great Benu bird which is in Heliopolis, the supervisor of what exists.

Before the Benu bird is the lotus flower of the south attached to the south end of the shrine, and beyond the flower is Osiris Ani in his shrine, flanked by Isis and Nephthys (the two birds) guarding the embalmed body of Ani.

The whole line of images for spell seventeen run right to left, and signify the transition from Osiris Ani to the resurrected Ani. The images tell of Ani as Osiris, his body 'healed' and wrapped (embalmed) in his shrine protected by the two goddesses, and the lotus flower signifying 'south,' i.e. the direction in which Ani is to go in his travels through the Duat. Notice that 'north' of Osiris Ani is Nephthys who is the goddess of the death process, and south of Osiris Ani is Isis, goddess of life.

> Ascend and descend: descend with Nephthys, sink into darkness with the Night-bark. Ascend and descend: ascend with Isis, rise with the Day-bark.[4]   — PT 222

---

[1]Dunn-Vaturi AE, deVoogt A, Crist W. (2016) *Ancient Egyptians at Play*. Oxford: Bloomsbury Academic.

[2]Hart, George (2005). *The Routledge Dictionary of Egyptian Gods and Goddesses* (Second ed.). New York: Routledge. pp. 48–49.

[3]Iwnw (Iuna)

[4]Faulkner R.O, 1969. *Ancient Egyptian Pyramid Texts*. Oxford University Press

F. THE DIRECTIONS IN WESTERN MAGIC

Egyptian summary

What does all of this tell us about the Egyptian magical directions? By careful study of the texts, wall images and texts, and looking at them through the eyes of a magician, we start to see a pattern emerging that reflects the foundation of a lot of magical approaches today.

Like most western magical directions, one element of the pattern is solar: the sun rises in the east, peaks in the south, sets in the west and is the weakest in the north. The Dynastic Egyptian magic, as opposed to later Greco-Roman Egyptian magic, was centered around the individual: the directional pattern was an operation of the human passing through time, not an operation of interaction with the geography around them.

The passage of the sun into the Duat through the western gate and rising the following morning through the eastern gate is a pattern of death, trial and resurrection, where the magician in life and in death forges forward into the south for the future.

The left hand/east as a life/action direction and right hand/west/harvest direction shows clearly a method of operating in which the magician in the centre of all things, and walks a path of triggering life, action and consequence, and simultaneously a path of ending, completion, harvest, the judgement of that harvest, and evolution. All of this is under the influence of Ma'at, the striving to keep balance, justice and order.

In Ancient Egypt, if the actions and intent of the priest magician were necessary in order to reestablish balance or Ma'at then the powers would work with and flow through the magician. This is not about only doing 'good' magic, but *necessary* magical actions, which could at times be violent or destructive if that was needed to defeat Isfet and re-establish Ma'at. Note how this centre of balance uses both creative and destructive magic in order to maintain balance and suppress chaos.

F.8 Right hand path, left hand path

In modern occultism/magic, people often identify themselves as either right hand path or left hand path. The RHP path was considered 'good and holy' and the LHP was considered 'bad' and

F.8. Right hand path, left hand path

evil. This duality was introduced (as far as I can tell) by Madame Blavatsky, who founded the Theosophical society in 1875, and who coined the terms in her book *Isis Unveiled* (1877).[1] She drew upon Indian Tantra for the ideas and posited the concept that LHP magicians/practitioners were followers of Black Magic and were a threat to society.

I find it ironic that someone who drew upon East Indian concepts, and named her book after an Egyptian goddess, did more to separate future magicians than anyone else from the powerful and complex pattern that had emerged out of Egypt.

When you mix Blavatsky's duality with the Christian understanding of 'The right hand of God' as being good/just, you can see how quickly this not only distorted an ancient magical pattern, but also contaminated magical thinking from that time onwards.

She didn't just get it from Tantra, the right hand/good, left hand/bad had already been kicking around for a thousand years in Christianity and Islam, and she would have grown up with the concept as it is in the New Testament. But it is far more glamorous to say you got the concept from Tantra, and it was familiar to people in the west: you accept something far more if your consciousness has already been exposed to its essence. Here is it mentioned in the Gospel of Matthew, written sometime between A.D. 70–100.

> All the nations will be gathered before Him, and He will separate them one from another, as a shepherd divides his sheep from the goats. And He will set the sheep on His right hand, but the goats on the left.[2]

In Islam, it also appears in the ninth-century writings of Abi Dawud[3] in *Sunan Abi Dawud*, one of the *Kutub al Sittah* (six major Hadith collections):

> It is narrated that 'Aa'ishah (may Allaah be pleased with her) said: The right hand of the Messenger of Allaah (peace and blessings of Allaah be upon him) was for his

---

[1] Evans, Dave 2007. *The History of British Magick after Crowley*. Hidden Publishing
[2] *Matthew* 25:31–46.
[3] Abi Dawud was a Persian Islamic scholar based in Basra. Died A.D. 889.

F. The directions in Western magic

purification and food, and his left hand was for using the toilet and anything that was dirty. Classed as saheeh (which is narrated by men of good character) by al-Albaani in Saheeh Abi Dawood.

And yet, to give Blavatsky her due, what she was expressing and that she discovered in Tantra and would have echoed Christian thought, were ideas that also appeared in the old religion of Iran[1] and were also found in the Indian Vedas.[2]

When you merge the two concepts of the Persian and Egyptian together (remember the Persians conquered Egypt in 525 B.C.) you get a weird mix that right hand/death/harvest is good, and left hand/life/action is bad. This weird meld indeed emerged in esoteric and religious thinking in early Christianity and spread out across Europe during the first millennia A.D..

Now think about how that strange union of ideas affects magic and directional magic to this day, and how it locks the magician out of a sense of time, and of union with everything around them. It also causes a conflict within the magician not only in their magical thinking, but also their day-to-day lives. It separates the magician from their own magical sovereignty, and as a result, the magician can only draw from around themselves, not from within themselves, as there is a constant inner subconscious battle going on between what should and should not be.

This can then spill out into magical ritual action in which it can define which base direction the magician faces to work, how their use their hands and thus their tools, and how it locks them out of the stream of time. Instead it locks them into a battle of either good or bad, as opposed to the balance of creation, destruction and chaos. The RHP magicians sneer at the unravelling and destruction work of the LHP and the LHP magicians sneer at the self-righteous smugness of the RHP magicians.

When a magician works within a ritual or space, mostly they are actively working directional power in one form or another, whether it is to 'face east' which has become the default position in magic, or to

---

[1] Zoroastrianism 6th century B.C. Persia
[2] 1200-200 B.C. for present form, introduced into India by Aryans

circle the directions, also usually starting in the east. When you think about the long directional attributes list of Agrippa in the fifteenth-century which was uptaken by nineteenth and twentieth-century magicians, add the dualism, and also the seasoning of the soup that was provided by Luria, you start to understand the problems that many modern magicians find themselves in.

Luria, interestingly, picks up on the south/tomorrow, north/past in his attributes of power for the Sefirots Chesed and Gevurah, but that has largely been missed or ignored by later magicians.

All of these ingredients that have been drawn together, serve collectively to lock out the magician from their power within as they seek it outside themselves ritually. By not rooting the magician in the flow of time, and creation/destruction, the magician becomes reliant upon the powers around him or her, and not the ones within.

Instead, the internal power/Divinity of the magician becomes something that must be psychologized, or striven for in a semi-religious way without rooting it firmly into the magical practice as an anchor. This is not to say that the powers, beings and patterns that flow from the directions are not to be used or be a major component within magic, they are. However, if the magician is not first rooted within their own fate, time, and divine self, they are essentially trying to use software without an operating system.

When you add the concept of the duality/hand paths, you further limit the magical potential for power and balance within the magical work. The simple act of always facing east, which predominates in some magical systems, locks the magician himself out of time: why? Why does not a created pattern work when by rights it should?

If the facing east system was created around the inner power flowing out into the physical world from the 'inner east,' and the ritual system and physical actions of the magician were a holism designed to take that power and used it across their system, then yes it would work. But that is not what has happened.

Instead you have a patchwork of ideas and concepts stitched together, where related systems flow through those concepts: so for example you end up with a magical system where Egyptian, Greek, Romano-Christian, Persian, and Kabbalistic concepts are thrown into rituals and systems *without understanding what each component is*

F. THE DIRECTIONS IN WESTERN MAGIC

doing and why. Every single part of an old system that you use brings with it all the rest of the system into the magic, if it is not filtered. When you have clashing components inserted without real magical understanding, you also end up with whole clashing systems flowing into a ritual act.

This is not to say that you cannot mix components from different sources: you can, and it can work brilliantly—but only if those components are complementary and the mixing is done with true gnosis of all the different systems and their power flows. This is where the magician is anchored in a particular format, and weaves the power flows while limiting/filtering the rest of the various systems' 'idiosyncrasies.' They become the composer, the source and the landscape, as opposed to an operator who doesn't understand the machinery that they work on.

Before I finish, I want to just demonstrate how easily something ancient ended up in much later magical texts, but its knowledge was lost.

Remember when we looked at the nineteenth-century, Eliphas Levi and the Grand Grimoire, I asked you to take note of the forked staff?

> On the eve of the great undertaking you will search for a rod or wand of wild hazel tree that has not yet born fruit, at the highest point of the sought-after branch there should be a second little branch in the form of a fork with two ends: its length should be nineteen and a half inches.[1]

The forked staff has its roots in Ancient Egypt as the Was sceptre/staff, which magically is used to 'pin' the head of the serpent Apep and his fellow serpents, and is used in iconography and hieroglyphs to denote 'power of dominion.' That is, by pinning the serpents of chaos, the gods and magicians have power and control over the land. Incidentally this concept of pinning Underworld powers also emerges in Tibetan Buddhism.

The forked staff (without the head of Set on the end) is still used to this day in Egypt to pin and catch troublesome snakes: it has

---

[1] Grand Grimoire aka the Red Dragon: (early 19th century) Chapter III Book One

F.8. Right hand path, left hand path

practical, magical and symbolic uses that have spanned thousands of years. In a practical sense, if you look up modern steel snake-catching sticks, the handles often have a Setian shaped handle for a good angle grip, and the forked bottom to trap the neck of the snake. So it is possible that the Was staff head (Set's head) not only had a power/magical/deity function, but also a practical one. Holding the Was staff by the head allows the holder to angle the staff in a way that gives maximum distance and maximum control.

Going back to the mention of the forked staff in the *Grand Grimoire*, yes there were venomous snakes in Europe (the common European viper) and the forked staff could have developed independently in Europe, but when you pay attention to the instructions on how to make the forked staff, it does not say 'make it like a snake-catching staff,' or a similar terminology that would have been used if they were familiar to the people of the time. Rather it has to give detailed instructions including looking for the fork in the branches, as if it were something unknown. I did look through images from the Middle Ages and Medieval period looking to see if a forked snake-catching staff was depicted anywhere, and most images were of spears, and usually in religious icons.

Now have a look at these images. The first is from scene thirty-four of the sixth hour in the *Book of Gates*,[1] a New Kingdom funerary text that it packed within magical and mystical meaning.

Figure F.4: The forked staff as depicted in the Book of Gates.

---

[1]McCarthy J, Sheppard M, Littlejohn S. 2017. *The Book of Gates: A Magical Translation.* Quareia Publishing Exeter, UK.

F. The directions in Western magic

The inscription with the image says:

> Receive for yourself your mortal grapples which you hold fast in your arms. What is yours is in the Absorbing One: Dispute you what should be in him, that what is best in him may come forth, and he retires.[1]

Think about what the inscription is saying, and in context of the power of the Was staff and what it does. Note it is not depicted as a Was with the head of Set, it is simply a snake-catching staff.

This image is the Was Sceptre, with the head of Set (the suppressor of Apep, Chaos) and the forked bottom. It appears frequently in Egyptian tomb wall paintings, and with temple statues and images/statues of the king. It denotes the power to suppress chaos and thus help the land, area or person maintain their Ma'at and protect Ma'at.[2]

Figure F.5: Was staff

And finally, in this Middle Kingdom stela[3] the Was sceptre/staff in the hand of the Goddess Isis (Aset). Note how the staff is held in the left hand, which means 'power of dominion in life,' and the Ankh in the right hand which means 'I give life in death.'

I hope this essay has been of use to you, to help you think about where things come from, how they are passed through time, and how ideas form and change over millennia, and as they move from one culture to another.

---

[1]Translation by Michael Sheppard, 2017.

[2]Ma'at: truth, balance and justice: the underpinning concept of the Dynastic Egyptian religion

[3]Stela showing "Isis the Great Goddess" sitting and holding a was-sceptre. A man, the head of necropolis workers, adores her. From Egypt, Middle Kingdom. The Petrie Museum of Egyptian Archaeology, London. With thanks to the Petrie Museum of Egyptian Archaeology, UCL.

F.8. Right hand path, left hand path

Figure F.6: Stela showing "Isis the Great Goddess" sitting and holding a was-sceptre. A man, the head of necropolis workers, adores her. From Egypt, Middle Kingdom. The Petrie Museum of Egyptian Archaeology, London. With thanks to the Petrie Museum of Egyptian Archaeology, UCL.

F. The directions in Western magic

Figure F.7: Geb and Nut: The Gods of the Egyptians (1904) by EA Wallis Budge

Appendix G

The Book of Death

by Josephine McCarthy, 1999

Foreword

Throughout the history of magic, one of the most powerful ways to transmit magical knowledge through the river of time was to put that magical knowledge into a story. Following that tradition, here is a magical story centered around the topic of dying and death: it looks at the inner beings involved in the process of death and beyond, and also touches upon some of the deeper aspects of the Western Mysteries.

Stories embed themselves within us in a different way to how nonfiction information does, and we can draw upon that difference to allow magical stories and myths to permeate our deeper selves. This in turn serves as a bridge between us and the Mysteries: magic without stories is no magic at all.

Part I

Margaret brushed the stray hair from her face and looked out over the washing line. Her tired arms drooped onto the thick line and rested there for a second. Hanging washing always hurt her arms and today it was worse than ever. With a groan, she bent over and tried to pick up a peg that she had dropped on the damp grass. Her toes gripped the earth as she tried to balance, but to no effect. She tipped forward from the weight of her body and landed on her knees.

"You should squat, it's much better for you than bending."

G. THE BOOK OF DEATH

The interfering voice cut through Margaret's wet maternity shirts that hung haphazardly to the line and moved slowly with the light breeze. The voice jumped over the fence and parted the damp washing. "Here, come on, up you get."

The young man from next door put his hands under Margaret's arms and heaved her onto her feet in one swift movement. It was too fast for Margaret, causing her to become dizzy. She clung onto him, trying to stop herself from swaying. How dare he tell her what to do and then stick his hands in her armpits. Her face reddened with embarrassment and the cursed panic crept upon her.

She felt sick. She did not want to throw up in front of this idiot, so she clung to him, gulping for air.

"Excuse me for asking, but how far on are you? You look pretty big, are you carrying twins?"

That finally cured Margaret of her nausea. She wanted to launch into him for being so rude, but she knew she would not be able to pluck up the courage. Deep within her she knew that he was just trying to be friendly, and he had helped her. What had got into her just lately? Everything annoyed her, everything frightened her, everything made her want to scream. Her chin jutted out as she looked up at the bright teen face that smiled back at her.

"I'm 35 weeks, 5 more weeks to go, and no it's not twins, I'm just big." Her voice had just a tad too much venom in it as she spat the defensive words into his face, something she regretted immediately.

The young man became uncomfortable. He slowly realized that he had probably insulted her by saying that she was big. It was beginning to dawn on him that women did not like things like size pointed out to them. He had often wanted to talk to her, not for any, well, sexual reason, but because she always seemed so alone.

Her husband only seemed to come home one or two days a week and even then he would arrive, park up his large truck and then go out in his car. He never seemed to take her anywhere and she never seemed to go out very much. As he looked closer at her face, it became clear to him that she was not that much older than him. Probably only a year or two. She looked around twenty and his eighteenth birthday was only a month away.

"Well, I'll leave you to it then. Please call over the fence if you need anything."

The young man smiled awkwardly before jumping back over the fence and vanishing into his house. Margaret placed her hands under her armpits where he had gripped to lift her. Now that she had recovered from the indignity of being a beached whale flapping about on the ground, she savoured the moment of human contact.

That night, as in all nights just recently, her dreams came harsh and unrelenting. She tossed around in her bed, entangling herself in the soft blue cotton sheets and her black hair mingled with the blue in the still silent darkness. Her arms twitched as she recoiled away from something: a dark fear slowly tiptoed towards her, taunting her. Beads of sweat and panic broke out on her forehead as she inched away from the unseen, her closed eyes darting this way and that in an effort to find safety. The sound of her breathing punctured the silence as it became more urgent, her breath labouring against the inner terror.

She lay rigid and motionless for a few seconds before her hands flew to her face, her fingers trying to fight something off. Margaret's voice called out into the darkness and her eyes opened suddenly. Her body was paralyzed. Her hands were still by her face, unable to move. The darkness took shape and moved towards her. Her body prickled against the fear as the presence moved ever so slowly to her side. She could not turn her head, nor could she cry out.

It approached her, growing until it extended beyond the ceiling. Each hair on her body told her to run. The droplets of sweat that ran down her face and breasts told her to scream. But her body lay motionless against the horror that moved slowly in a deliberate path towards her. She struggled to move her eyes from side to side. The being had filled the whole room and she knew in her heart it was something that she could not escape. Its hand reached out to touch her.

It was aiming for her forehead. She knew she had to stop it but she did not know how. The child in her womb lay motionless, as though waiting for the inevitable. Her instincts were to put her arms around her swollen belly and protect the little child snuggled up within her, but her arms remained glued around her head.

Just before it reached her forehead, she knew, from somewhere deep within her, that if it touched her she would die. She did not want to die. She wanted her baby. She began to cry helplessly, for herself and her unborn child. The tears touched her face and something snapped within her.

Her eyes opened and an inrush of air to her lungs made her jump: when she thought she had been awake, she had actually still been dreaming. Sleep fell away from her as she sat up in bed, covered in sweat and tears. Her hands cupped her face as she wept, unable to cope with yet another night of the same nightmare.

Part II

"Okay, that's it Mrs. Kingsley, is there anything you want to ask?"

The doctor stood smiling at Margaret but she could see from the look on his face that he really did not want her to ask anything. But she knew she had to say something. Margaret smiled at the nurse seated beside the doctor, who had done her weekly observations, checking Margaret's blood pressure, urine and a mountain of other seemingly useless things.

"Well...there is one thing."

Her voice was unsteady as she began to redden. She felt overpowered by this professional man who held life and death, and her health in his hands. The doctor looked briefly at the ceiling and then back at Margaret before smiling. He had spent three minutes with this woman and now it was time for her to go. He hated women who asked questions. Why could they not just come in, be examined and get lost? His words came out with thinly disguised impatience, making Margaret go even redder.

"Go ahead, ask."

Margaret fiddled with her thumbs and tried to sound as confident as possible.

"Well, I feel that there is something wrong. The feeling gets stronger everyday but I don't know what it is. I just don't feel right."

She dropped her head and looked at her hands. She felt such an idiot for blurting that out. The doctor looked at the rotund, red-faced, raven-haired young woman sitting in a lump before him. He could see that she must have been quite pretty before she got pregnant, but they all faded after the babies started. It was always the same. That, he thought to himself, is why he would never marry.

"Mrs. Kingsley, there is nothing wrong with you. Your blood pressure is a little high, but that's okay. Now stop worrying, it will do baby no good at all if you worry. All will be well."

The nurse got up and stood by the door with it open and smiled at Margaret.

"Good-bye, Mrs. Kingsley."

The nurse continued to smile until the smile became fixed. Margaret slid from the chair and heaved herself up. Her body felt more than heavy, it felt poisoned. Her whole being seemed to be under a cloud and no one wanted to help or listen. As the nurse closed the door behind her, Margaret heard her voice filter through to the hallway.

"God, some of these women are such hypochondriacs."

Margaret wanted cry. She felt violated and humiliated, and she could not find within her the strength to challenge these people. Her mother had always told her that when she was twenty-one, she would find her voice. But it had not happened. Here she was, twenty-one, and she dare not say boo to anyone.

She cursed herself all the way home as she trudged back up the steep hill that led to her house. The road was dirty and smelly, full of rubbish that people had thrown from their cars. That was how she felt. Just a piece of rubbish that someone had thrown from a car.

She leaned heavily on the door when she finally arrived home. She had to wait a moment to summon the strength to get the key in the lock and when she finally let herself in, she knew she would have to go to bed for the afternoon to recover from the walk and the insults. Her nights were full of terror and she awoke every morning full of fear and exhaustion. At least she did not dream when she slept during the day.

She lay back on the bed, fully clothed, staring at the ceiling. She placed her hand on her enormous belly and caressed the child within her. Tigger, her secret name for her baby, had not moved in days. The doctor said it was normal. She felt that something was wrong. Tigger was named Tigger because of Tigger's amazing ability to do back flips at the most inconvenient moment. Tigger kicked, squirmed, hiccupped, pushed, stretched and generally gave a little joy and humour to Margaret in her loneliness. But now Tigger had stopped communicating with her. She felt the child was still alive, there were tiny little wriggles here and there, but nothing like what she had grown used to.

Slowly, Margaret drifted into sleep, her body twitching as she descended down into the Underworld, leaving her conscious mind behind. The dark stillness swallowed her until her jaw finally relaxed. The sleep was delicious. It drank its way through her body and the softness of the bed became deeper, kinder and full of a warmth that she had not felt in a long time.

When her eyes finally began to open, just as the sun was going down, her body snuggled into the comfort, laying and enjoying as she slowly surfaced from a rest that had not been plagued with terror and pain. In fact, for the first time in a long time, she felt no pain at all. She moved her legs to stretch and became aware that the bed was damp. She moved her leg back, and yes, there was dampness.

She stretched her arm out to turn on the lamp and she sat up in bed. As she sat up, a pain from hell shot through her, causing her to scream suddenly and fall backwards back onto the bed. She lay panting for a moment. Surely it was too early for her waters to break and the labor to start? She eased herself back up, slowly this time, allowing the pain to build rather than to attack. She pulled the bedcovers back, and cried out. The bed was soaked in blood.

Her hand reached calmly for the bedside phone and she dialled the emergency ambulance number. She talked so calmly that she could hear the disbelief in the dispatcher's voice. She replaced the receiver after being assured that an ambulance was on its way.

Laying back on the bed, she felt no panic, no fear. Everything was okay. Everything would be fine. There was no problem, it was all under control. She slowly sat back up and tried to stand. She felt dizzy but not too bad.

Methodically and calmly, she peeled off her bloodstained clothes and looked for fresh ones. The bleeding appeared to have stopped and she began to feel silly for calling an ambulance. Maybe she really did not need one. By the time the ambulance arrived, she had dressed herself, packed a small hospital case and left a note for her husband. She had also left a message on his work answer machine, just in case someone managed to get a message to him.

The ambulance man helped her into the vehicle and an ambulance woman wrapped a blanket around her. There was no sign of blood, no stains, no new fresh blood. Just a tired heavily pregnant woman who was slightly embarrassed at the fuss. They set off and as they travelled to the hospital, the ambulance woman took some details. She looked Margaret up and down, looking for signs of bleeding, shock, anything. Nothing.

"Are you alone, I mean, when will your husband get back from work? Is there anyone we can call?"

Margaret shook her head. The woman nodded and eyed Margaret again. Another lonely one looking for attention. She wrote that down as a side note on the admittance paper and circled it.

At the maternity unit of the hospital, Margaret eased herself onto the bed and retold what had happened as the nurses listened quietly. They nodded without comment and then asked Margaret to undress and put on a hospital gown. One of the nurses picked up Margaret's underwear and stated to the head nurse that there was no sign of bleeding.

"But there was a lot of blood in the bed, honestly there was."

Margaret was beginning to despair. It seemed that no one ever believed her. She looked from face-to-face as they all smiled patronizingly at her.

"Well, Mrs. Kingsley, we will link you up to a monitor to see what's happening and we will listen to baby. You say he hasn't been moving? Well, that's natural at the end of a pregnancy, don't worry about it. We will also do some tests to see what's happening. Just lie back and relax, doctor will be with you shortly."

Margaret lay on the hospital bed in a long and packed ward, staring out at the other women who all lay staring at her and at the wall. The place was depressing: no one was talking and no one was smiling. She lay there for over an hour and was just dozing when a brusque nudge of the bed brought her back to the gloomy ward.

She groaned inwardly when she recognized the clinic doctor who stood before her. She could also see from his face that he was groaning inwardly too. Another hypochondriac had dragged him away from his golf practice in the doctors' locker room. He sat on the side of the bed and looked her over. He asked why no baby monitor was being used, and the nurse informed him that there was not a low priority one available until the morning. He nodded and asked Margaret to "scoot" down the bed. She looked at him blankly.

"Please lie down and I will check your cervix to see if it is dilating. To see if you are in labor."

She lay down and the doctor pulled the bedclothes back. She did not register his face change at first, nor did she think it strange that the nurse had scurried off. She felt warm, relaxed and comfortable. Another nurse appeared with a large pad which she slipped under Margaret's buttocks. Margaret looked at her in question.

"For the blood."

The nurse did not elaborate and Margaret peered between her legs. Blood oozed out of her, slowly building into a pool between her legs. 'Strange,' thought Margaret, 'I didn't feel it this time.' In fact, as she plopped her hand on her leg to lever herself up, she had not felt that either. She wiggled her toes and breathed a sigh of relief that she could move them, except she could not feel her right leg or foot. Monitors appeared seemingly from nowhere and wires were soon growing out of every nook and cranny of her body.

"I'm going to break your waters and we are putting up a drip to help speed up your labor. We would normally do a caesarean section on you, an operation, but we have no spare operating theatre for nearly four hours at least. There is no emergency and all is well, the drip will really speed things up and he will be out in no time."

The doctor tried to sound as confident as possible. He hated working in this inner city hell hole and as soon as he was able, he wanted to leave England for ever, maybe to work in one of the Arab states where all the money was. Margaret caught hold of his wrist and looked into his eyes.

"Is my baby okay? It's a little early, isn't it?"

Margaret wanted to panic, but she could not. She felt calm and safe but she knew she had to ask. The doctor looked at her wearily. He tried to sound as strong as he could as he answered her searching question.

"No, lots of babies are born at this time, all will be well. Now you relax, you have a busy night ahead of you."

She lay back on her pillow and smiled at the nurse who had been stationed to watch over her. There was also someone standing behind her. But Margaret was not able to make out the figure who stood silent and unmoving.

She drifted off, unaware of the painless tightening that was stirring in her belly. The bleeding had stopped yet again, allowing everyone to breathe a sigh of relief. The warmth spread around her and pulled her deeper and deeper into a semi-sleep, the regular beeping of the machines singing her into oblivion.

The pain rose like a submarine surfacing from deep water, catching her unawares and making her gasp. The monitor sounds became uneven and somewhere, someone was shouting. Margaret opened her eyes and looked through the haze of pain. The doctor's face peered back at her, along with the nurse's and her midwife, who had just arrived and looked a little flustered. Behind the nurse and midwife stood two other people, but the shadows seemed to hide their features. It never occurred to Margaret that the ward was in full light and that there were no shadows. More and more people pushed around her, whispering to her, coaxing her.

Margaret, Margaret, come see the flowers, come see the lilies, they are so beautiful.

Margaret wanted to tell the voice that she was too busy having a baby to look at flowers, but her lips did not seem to work. The pain rose again, filling the space that she breathed and clearing out of her mind any thought other than pain. Endless, ceaseless pain. It got stronger and stronger as she groaned, the noise coming from deep within her. Someone touched her belly and Margaret wanted to pull the hands away but her arms were too heavy to pick up.

Sounds rushed past her, hands touched her, faces peered through the fog in her mind, staring at her intently. Someone told her to roll onto her side, but she did not know what that meant. What is a side?

She felt her body being pushed over onto her left side. The pain grew tentacles and seemed to grab her around her throat. Her breath became shorter until all she could do was grunt. Her thoughts became her world as she bathed in memories punctured only by pain as it passed through her on its way to somewhere.

A pressure began to build up in her head. At the same time, something solid moved down from her belly into her pelvis. The fullness became a centre point for the pain which was now exquisite as she bathed in it. Someone shouted her name, again and again. Margaret, Margaret.

She stood and looked at the chaos that was happening in the room. She found it much easier to breath now that she was no longer laid on the bed. Someone else was laid there. Margaret edged closer and froze when she recognized the woman on the bed. She looked at herself laying there, with her legs flayed and her lower body covered in blood. One of the nurses was crying as she carried something wrapped in a green cloth that the doctor had handed to her.

Margaret peered to see what it was. The body of a stillborn infant lay in the nurse's arms. Margaret was confused. She did not know why she could see herself on the bed when she was standing up and she did not know why they had a dead child. She hoped her child would not be born like that. She shuddered and thought about her own child. Should not she be busy with her labor?

With that thought she found herself back on the table and felt a warm wet cloth being wiped over her face. The warmth of the cloth punctuated the deep cold that had rolled into her body like a spring sea tide. She heard beeping and alarms. She heard conversations and regrets. Margaret wanted to comfort the nurse who had been crying. She wanted to say, "don't be sad, my baby will be born soon and you will see how beautiful she is. She will make you smile."

But she was too cold to speak. It had crept quietly upon her and wound its way into her bones, lodging itself there. The warmth from the cloth that was washing her down did not seem to penetrate her cold and she wanted to ask a nurse for a blanket. But her lips would not work. She tried to lift her arm to catch their attention, but she could not move. So she lay there while she was washed and thought about her child to come.

The daydream was shattered by a voice that cut through her cold and her thoughts. The doctor was speaking into a tape machine. He mentioned her name. He mentioned haemorrhage and torn placenta.

He described the condition of the dead child. He listed a date and time of Margaret's death. Feb. fourteenth, 3.45 a.m. Margaret screamed. The cry rolled through her body yet it could not escape. So it turned inward, digging deep into her soul and tearing her into shreds. It dug and dug until there was nowhere else to go. And then came the blackness.

Part III

Margaret moved in the darkness. Her thoughts reached out through the nothing and yet that nothing was full of everything. Someone called her. They did not use her name, or so she thought. But it was a sound that identified her and, in her fear and loneliness, she moved towards that sound.

The sound got louder until she found herself before a door. There seemed to be no door, but she knew it was there. She also knew that she had to go through that door. And yet, she was not sure about who or what she was. What part of her was going to go through that door?

The urge to move forward grew stronger and stronger until, using thought, she passed through the doorway and felt a power of transition, a shift, as she crossed the threshold. It was like waking from one of her terrible dreams. Her eyes scanned the horizon of a seemingly never-ending desert shining in the noonday sun.

In the far distance was a range of mountains and Margaret set off walking. The sun tore into her flesh as she walked, her feet stumbling as her legs got heavier and heavier. At first, it did not seem strange to her that she should be in a desert. But the further she walked, the more her memory of the hospital bed came back.

She remembered the pain and her child. She remembered her ever-absent husband and she remembered, finally, the voice of the doctor dictating his notes into a tape recorder. Margaret Kingsley, date and time of death: Feb fourteenth, 3.45 a.m. What a shame, he had said, to die birthing your first child on Valentine's day. The knowledge of her death washed over her and she began to weep. Her feet dragged over the dry earth and her tears fell, joining with other tears to form a stream that trickled on into the distance.

Without noticing, she had come closer to the mountains, and Margaret looked up into the distance. The stream of tears ran ahead of her and joined into a river that sliced through the landscape. Up to now, she had felt no thirst. But on seeing the river, her throat began to burn with the fire of the desert: thirst consumed all of her thoughts.

As she came close to the river, she realized that she was not alone in the desert. People wandered about at the river's edge. Some stared into space while others lay weeping with their hands covering their face. The sorrow of the people blew past her like the wind: the strength of their emotions caught her off-guard. The emotions of the people flowed through her like a never-ending river, joining with her own deep sorrow and creating a deep pool of pain within her heart.

The loss of her own child began to swell within her and instinctively she placed her hand on her abdomen. Her husband's neglect of her rose to greet her along with the scorn that her father had always directed at her. Memories of her childhood surfaced, memories of pain and of joy. Things that she did not want to let go of rose into her mind: her cats and her house paraded before her, and Margaret began to feel homesick. She wanted to go home.

Immediately she found herself standing in her lounge. But it was full of people. Her husband sat in his usual armchair with his head cradled in his hands. Beside him sat his mother with her arm, as always, protecting her son. Margaret felt instant, overwhelming jealousy. His mother always had to interfere, always had to side with him to protect him, even when he had done wrong: *Mummy would always make it better.* The bitterness simmered in Margaret as she stared at the plump, overdressed woman.

Another man walked into the room, her husband's brother. He had hated Margaret on sight and the feeling had been mutual. He walked up to her husband and squatted on the floor beside him.

"We all will miss her, we all loved her."

His voice quivered as his younger brother looked up in thanks for the kind words. Margaret wanted to be sick. Not only did she know he was lying, but she could see the lies floating out of him. She saw the smugness nestled next to his heart and she wanted to tear it out for all to see.

Someone sniffled behind her, prompting Margaret to turn around. There, sat in black with deep rings under her eyes was Tanya, her best friend. Tanya had been working abroad and had flown back for the funeral. Margaret felt the horrendous pain that Tanya carried within her. She could hear Tanya's thoughts as she mulled over the fact that Margaret would probably be alive today if she had not moved away, but had stayed close to be with her friend during her pregnancy. Tanya had, right at the beginning of Margaret's pregnancy, a premonition that something was going to happen, and she had ignored it. The guilt tore into Tanya and Margaret wanted to ease that.

She moved next to her friend and placed her arms around her. She whispered into her ear while stroking her hair. How would she ever let go of her deepest love, her friend from childhood? All that remained of her memories of childhood happiness was Tanya.

At first, she did not notice the man who stood silently in the corner of the room. He was dressed strangely, with a black hat and a long beard. Margaret wondered if he was a vicar. She did not recognize him. Then he looked straight at her. Margaret was startled: how could he see her? He stared and stared at Margaret until she spoke to him.

"Who are you, how can you see me?"

The man did not answer but walked towards her and when he got to the table, he walked through the table and straight to Margaret. She tried to run.

"Daughter, you have no legs, how can you run? and where to? Come, follow me, I want to show you something."

He held out his hand and she grasped it without question. They were back at the side of the river and Margaret became angry with the man.

"Why have you brought me back here? I don't want to be here, I want to be with my friend."

She struggled against him, but her held her firmly with his eyes.

"You do not belong there, that is not your world anymore and that is no longer your friend. It has all gone and will never return. You must let go and cease to be Margaret Kingsley. You must now be yourself."

Margaret cried out through her fear: "I *am* Margaret, what are you talking about?"

She wanted to flee, but she could not move and she did not know where to flee to. Instead, she flopped down to the ground beside the river, putting her head in her hands. All around her, people sat with their heads in their hands. Fear swam around them, lapping at their feet and refusing to go away.

Whenever she was in pain, Margaret always remembered her mother and the pain would go away. Her mother had died when she was a little girl, but Margaret had clung to the threads of memory that had remained with her.

Instantly she found herself back in her old childhood bedroom with her mother perched on the end of the bed, her golden hair shining from the hall light that reflected around her. Her mother smiled and Margaret snuggled down into bed. At last she was safe and warm, no one could harm her.

But something was wrong. Her mother did not change her expression and did not read her a story like mothers are supposed to. She just sat and smiled the same smile that Margaret had always remembered: the only memory that she had of her mother. The memory played itself over and over until Margaret finally understood that she could not hide in her memories.

She was back again, by the river, with her head in her hands. She looked up and scanned the desert with her eyes. People were constantly arriving out of the wilderness and sitting down by the river. Most ran to the river to drink, throwing the water over themselves and laying down to sup their fill. But Margaret did not want to do that. Yes, she had been thirsty, but something within her drove the thirst away.

People panicked around her as they reached the river: some cried out, some curled into a ball like terrified children, and others became violent. But the man who had frightened her with his words sat without emotion, looking out over the river with an expression of peace on his face. Margaret was intrigued. She walked over to him and sat quietly down beside him.

He did not react at first, but just allowed Margaret to be still with him as he watched the mountains. Finally, she turned to look at him.

Margaret wanted to introduce herself properly, but for the moment, she could not remember her name.

"That is good," said the man.

"What is good?" said Margaret.

"That you do not hold to your name. It is time it was no longer with you. It was just a tool and now you have finished your job, you no longer need the tools."

The man's voice was beautiful, but she wasn't sure she understood what he said. She tried to change the subject.

"Who are you, and how come you are not so afraid?"

Margaret was curious, this man was like no other she had seen anywhere: he was full of peace and his face seemed to shine like a thousand lamps. And yet, he just looked like a rather crumpled old man.

"Oh, I am myself. I remember this place, it holds no fear for me, and you will remember next time around, because you were wise enough not to drink of the river."

Margaret opened her mouth to ask about his answer, and then shut it again. Maybe she should not ask.

"So, what did you do, you know, before, well, before you died?"

She tried to be polite, but the question came out sounding rude and she wanted to be angry at herself, except she could not remember how to. The old man smiled and pulled on his beard thoughtfully as he looked out over the mountains.

"Hmm, well, I was supposed to be recognized. But no one recognized me, so here we all are and here we go again. They say, when you recognize a Tzadik Nistar, it is because that potential is also within you, and that when two come together and join, then our world becomes the Garden again."

Margaret frowned in confusion. She had no clue what he was talking about and yet, something deep dawned within her. Rather than ignore it like she would normally do, she allowed it to rise into her thoughts.

She saw the man in a beautiful city, like the pictures she had seen of Jerusalem. He was walking the streets and he shone like a full summer sun. But no one seemed to notice. Everything he touched became beautiful, every word he spoke took shape and travelled around him, echoing sacred sounds out to the world. But no one heard. No one recognized the grace that poured from this simple rather crumpled man. Therefore no one could partake of that grace.

"I see."

Margaret felt sadness for the man, that no one had recognized him. But then, she felt that he had no sadness, so why should she? What purpose would it serve? Why would it have a place here?

"You learn quickly!" said the man, as he smiled at her.

"Come, come with me and we will walk through some of this together. I can show you some wonderful things on the way. It's much better than walking on your own."

For the first time in a long time, Margaret was happy. She really wanted to be near this man and she knew that it would be good for her to walk with him. He held her hand as they walked along the river bank. He asked her about her life, her family and friends. As she talked about them, they seemed to get further and further away until she could no longer understand why they were talking about them.

They began to feel like distant characters from a book that no one wanted to read anymore. Eventually, she told him that she did not want to remember anything else because it all seemed so pointless.

"Why do you think it is pointless?" Asked the man.

"Well, I'm not sure, but that is how it feels. I suppose that just before I died, I had pulled away from people, I don't know. I do miss the feeling of the child within me though. It was wonderful having someone so close whom I could love.

"Although I do remember the anger and love I felt when I found myself back in my house and they were all there for my funeral. And yet, I cannot feel those feelings now. Why is that?"

Margaret posed the question to herself and the man waited for the answer.

"Maybe," she continued, "it's because they are there and I am here and *there* doesn't really matter anymore. Does it even exist anymore?"

She looked at him intently and he smiled.

"Not for you. It does for them. Love, anger, hate, joy, these are all things unto themselves. You have to learn that they are not yours to give and take. The love you had for your friend is never lost, ended or to be wept over. Every face that you see is potentially your lover, child, mother, or friend. You have all, as souls, interacted at one time or other. The love that you shared must be itself, unconditional and timeless. It flows through all being."

Margaret scanned the horizon silently. She was confused about many things, and the more she talked, the more confused she became. She turned back to the man, a question itching to be asked.

"Okay, one last question. Where is God? And Jesus? I don't see any of the stuff we were taught about at school. Where are they? Do they exist?"

The man laughed loudly and then turned Margaret around. She did not know what she was supposed to be looking at for a second. She watched a man walking towards the river and he was weeping uncontrollably. She could see pain all around him. Loss and regret fell as tears into his hands as he walked.

He reached out in all directions for something, anything to guide him. A being, like a thread of light appeared and began walking towards the man. As the being got closer, it began to take human form. It formed itself into the image of Jesus and held out its arms for the man. The man saw Jesus and ran weeping towards him. The being enveloped the man and held him in compassion until the man was ready to be released.

Margaret blanched. She had not led a religious life, not really. But she had been raised a Catholic and here she seemed to be seeing that Jesus was just a masquerading being? Her new friend heard the thought and shook his head.

"No, Jesus was a person who lived in time and then did not live in time. He was who he was, a Justified One, a Righteous One, but he was not a crutch as people would like to wish that he was. But when people die, they often die in fear and they cling to whatever memory they have of something greater than themselves. So the beings who are responsible for the transition of life and death, the doorways, often have to appear in a form taken from the human mind."

"These doorways, you know them as angels. Not long blond-haired men with wings, but beings who are a part of the Divine order: they are doorways, thresholds, enablers."

His words made sense to Margaret, and yet thought was becoming difficult for her. She did not want to learn, or think. She wanted to do something, to move forward. She had started to feel uncomfortable, as though she did not fit anymore. Her body shape had started to break up and she was finding it harder to think of herself as a human shape.

She turned to ask the man about this feeling but as she formed the question, she already knew the answer. Her earthly body had been cremated. She had no material pattern left that she could connect to in solid form.

In the distance, a bridge appeared over the river. It was a bridge of light, shape and movement, like a strong shimmering rainbow that drew Margaret instinctively towards it. She wanted to ask about the bridge, but the man had vanished. She turned, looking all around her, but he was nowhere to be seen.

The bridge pulled harder and harder until she could not bear it any longer. She broke into a run, pulled by a deep urge that coursed its way through her, driving every other thought out of her mind. On reaching the threshold of the bridge she stopped suddenly. Something blocked her. She leaned against it, trying to break through.

The sound of a whirlwind whipped around her pushing at her from all directions and she became frightened. Out of the whirlwind peered many eyes, focused intently on her and probing deep into her thoughts. Memories flooded into her mind. Memories of her childhood, her early love affairs, her night terrors, her baby, and finally her death. But somehow, these memories did not evoke anything within her anymore. They seemed like lead weights that pulled her farther and farther away from the bridge. She did not want them, she no longer needed them, so she let the whirlwind take them.

It tore into her, dismantling from her everything that she knew. It tore at her thoughts, her ideas, the concepts she had learned with the man on the river bank. It pulled away all her emotions and beliefs until she stood naked before the eyes.

The whirlwind stopped. All was quiet. It felt so wonderful to be rid of all the baggage she carried for so long, and with that lightness, she stepped forward onto the bridge. The moment her foot touched the surface of the bridge something powerful and beautiful passed through her. For each step she took, she felt a joining with something, a communing, as though she had become aware of her presence within a huge web that spread into infinity.

It felt good, it felt natural, as though this was her real self. The crest of the bridge drew her onwards and passing over the centre of the bridge, a nothingness enfolded her. The nothingness had all the potential of everything in it. Every thought, deed, word, and universe were held like a breath in that nothingness.

She knew she had a choice. Stay in the nothingness, or move on. The nothingness beckoned to her. She could drink of the union with all that is Divine, being at one with the Void: the source of all creation. But something else pulled her in the opposite direction. Service. To be in a world, in a life and to allow life to flow through her. The act of being within substance. She chose substance.

Immediately she was back on the bridge, stepping through the connections of all worlds as she journeyed towards the other side of the bridge. With each step that she took, her awareness expanded to enfold each soul who had ever walked the path she was now walking. She felt the deep connection with each individual as they passed through and over the bridge in their own time and space. Like the web, they were all one being.

On reaching the other side, an angel stood in silence, pointing into the distance. Rising out of the earth was a huge range of mountains. The angel indicated that she must climb the biggest mountain.

Her heart sank. It was so far away and so high, she would never get all the way up there. The angel started to walk with her, placing one foot in front of the other, and she copied. One step at a time. As she walked, she felt things fall off of her, things she had not realized were there. She did not know what they were, but something deep within her knew it was good to shed whatever it was. She felt lighter, more balanced and with a fuller sense of freedom.

G. The Book of Death

At the foot of the mountain, the angel vanished without any warning or communication, leaving Margaret to stare up at the clouds which covered the summit. A pathway was worn by many footfalls as it snaked up the side of the mountain, vanishing into the mist. Margaret stepped on the path and began to climb. She heard voices whispering and mumbling as she climbed. There was nothing specific said, no words that she could grasp, just noise. But the higher she climbed, the clearer the voices became.

She heard the texts of the gospels being read and the words mingled in with recitations of the Qur'an. Over the top of that was a speaking of the Torah, the Gita, and beyond that a whispering of Fire incantations. Words in languages she had never heard were chanted in the background as she climbed, their sounds dragged at her feet, weighing her down. All the sacred words that had ever been written and uttered whispered around her, making it harder and harder to reach the top of the mountain.

Other voices joined in the chorus, voices raised in political anger, voices speaking out against beliefs, voices calling for war, and voices crying for peace. And then came the loudest: the cry of beings as they were slaughtered: human voices, animals, birds, every creature she could imagine, the sounds of their voices raised in terror in their last moments of life drove itself into her like sword piercing her soul. The cry broke through all others and imprinted itself on her. It followed her wherever she turned. She could not escape it: the sound of life, of death, the sound of the living world of creation and destruction.

Margaret climbed and climbed in an attempt to escape the noise. As she neared the top, the sounds suddenly stopped. All was quiet, all was peaceful. The mist hid the summit from her and the atmosphere around her had become cold and damp. She knew she had to walk into the mist. She knew she could not turn around and return back down the mountain. There was nowhere else for her to go but into the unseen.

Her thoughts stilled as she prepared for what was beyond the mountain mist. The weight of her previous life had all but fallen away. It had become some dark distant memory that she had managed to finally shrug off like a disease. Now she was herself. Timeless.

With that stillness, she moved into the mist and was immediately enveloped in a dreadful weariness. Her mind forcibly pushed her onwards until she could go no further. The mist had begun to thin ever so slightly: just enough to see back down some of the mountain and to see ahead. Before her lay many people, all fast asleep. Beyond them, the mountain top fell away but the horizon was obscured by the mist. The tiredness ate into her and she fell to her knees. Motionless, she stayed in that position briefly, before finally laying down. Each position that she took felt uncomfortable until a voice passed through her.

Remember, the voice said.

Remember what?

Margaret could not remember, *but the body that she no longer had remembered*. Its human imprint, that was stored deep within her, remembered. The memory played out through her and she shifted into the remembered position. On her stomach, left arm outstretched, right arm behind her back. Right leg outstretched, left leg bent and tucked behind right leg. Finally, she knew she was in the correct position. With that knowledge came sleep.

The keepers of the dead wandered in and out of the sleeping bodies, maintaining the sleepers' inner balance as they slept. Some that they came across still had residual patterns from their last life that needed removing: the sleepers' bodies twitched from deep nightmares, or moaned quietly as if in pain. The keepers took pity on the sufferings of the sleepers. In their pity, the keepers lay beside those who slept and sang songs that would settle in the minds of the sleepers and guide them during the darkest hours of their next incarnations.

They stroked the sleepers, filling them with balance and power, tools they would need for their journey ahead. And finally, before the dawn broke, the keepers cupped their hands over the sleepers, holding the deep eternal inner flame of each sleeper and giving it temporary sanctuary.

As the dawn broke, the mist cleared and the keepers called to the dawn with a conch shell: the labyrinth of the ocean that carries the wind. The noise awoke the sleepers who looked out in awe as the light and darkness of the Void shone upon them.

G. The Book of Death

Margaret turned in the blackness, at one with the nothing. Not wishing to move or be. Silence.

Out of the silence, the sound of a loud horn vibrated through her, calling her back to existence. Margaret wanted to fight the call, she wanted to stay within the stillness but the call became more and more urgent.

She awoke to find herself lying on the top of a mountain. She looked up just in time to see someone bend over and push her down the far side of the mountain. She wanted to cry out in panic but her breath was taken as she rolled and tumbled down what felt like a grassy hill. During the rolling, she became more and more aware that she was feeling with senses and shape: with limbs, eyes, ears, even though she had none. The strangeness of such thoughts tumbled with her as she cascaded down the hill.

The scent of the fresh grass and dust awoke her awareness of the world and of being in human form. She ached for such life again and just as the ache became unbearable, something slowed her to a stop.

She unravelled herself at the foot of the hill and stood up. Before her was a large rupture in the ground: the Abyss. Behind her was the mountain. Looking up, she could see others tumbling down, just as she had done.

They all slowed, seemingly of their own accord until something nudged her from behind. The nudge seemed to alter her vision and she slowly became aware of a giant hand reaching out to each person and carefully slowing them down. She turned back to look at the Abyss and before it stood a being that made Margaret afraid.

Before the Abyss stood an angelic being that reached up to the stars. She had many arms and wings that stretched out to prevent people from falling into the Abyss. Many other arms reached out to slow those who tumbled down the hill. Her hair flowed in all directions, scooping up those who had lost their way. Her eyes turned to each person as she looked at them intently, one by one.

Her eyes finally looked into Margaret, and Margaret began to cry. Every failing that she had, became apparent to her. Every cruelty, ignorance, indifference, stupidity and thoughtlessness paraded before her. Behind it came every goodness, every drop of love that she had shed for others, every hand she had outstretched, every gift she had given.

The angel weighed it all in the palm of her hand. The balance was presented without judgment back to Margaret and Margaret became aware of what she needed to achieve to better that balance.

The angel turned her head to look out over the Abyss to the Desert beyond and Margaret's gaze followed. In that Desert beyond the Abyss Margaret saw many lives paraded in front of her, all happening at once, all lives that would give her the skills to achieve what she needed. Some were more tempting than others, but Margaret could see that the tempting ones might not yield all that she needed in a balanced way.

She saw one life that she felt she recognized. It was a difficult life and yet was rich in learning. Her heart lurched towards it and Margaret followed. The angel withdrew the protective arm from Margaret's centre and Margaret pitched forward into the Abyss. A whirlwind came up to greet her and whipped her into its centre. Her thoughts were flung around and around the directions as she fell, its wind flowing through her and adjusting her for what was to come.

Part IV

The angel stood impassive as the couple joined in love. The emotions that they released for each other joined and created a rising vortex, spinning throughout the worlds. The vortex connected with a whirlwind that whipped down out of the Abyss and the roar of the whirlwind echoed around the room where the couple lay. Still the angel did not move.

At the moment of connection between the vortex and the whirlwind, a light shone through the darkness and the angel began to awaken from its stillness. A soul tumbled through the worlds, twisting and turning within the whirlwind as the soul passed from wind to vortex. The whirlwind withdrew and the soul completed its journey into the world as it slowly passed, guided by the angel, into the body of the woman lying in the arms of her lover.

On contact, the soul spread out, joining with the soul of the woman and the angel took its position by the woman's head. A beautiful web pattern appeared, the pattern of human shape. The angel gently teased the newly arrived soul into the pattern and wove it in deftly within the pattern of the mother.

The woman's body shone with the intricate connections as her soul upheld and gave sanctuary to the new being that would eventually be her child. When the angel was satisfied that the connection was complete, it withdrew and vanished into the Void.

Margaret turned in a swirl of warmth and love. A regular heartbeat punched out a sense of rhythm for her as she lay in silence and light. She was at one with being in substance and yet she was in the stillness, in the deep. The stillness was full of Brightness, a light that was home. It was a place she did not want to leave, ever.

But there came a time, a turning within her. The sense of connection was lessening, and her sense of being was growing. She became aware that she was not her surroundings, that they were separate to her, and yet were still a part of her. At that point, the moment of awareness of separate, something shifted with her. She knew she had to leave. But to where?

The urge for a journey became overwhelming. It tore at her, forcing her to make the move to leave. Once the thought was accepted, her world began to contract and change. Pressure built up all around her, forcing her, squashing her into a battle for life.

She tried to fight back at times, until a deep knowing within her surfaced, telling her to relax. She felt herself leave the safety and comfort of her world. There was only forward into the unknown, there was nowhere else to go. It was terrifying. Her mind reached forward as her body was propelled on until she broke free of the warmth and safety, and was pushed into a dull light full of external noise and coldness. She took a breath as her thoughts vanished with the Brightness, and the loneliness of separation and dull light hit her without mercy.

The angel hovered around the woman's body as she arched her back against the pain. Other beings that were connected with the process of birth and death hovered, ready to be of assistance, their presence unseen by the people assisting the woman with the birth of the child. The child's head appeared and rotated. All the beings waited in silence as the woman screamed. And then came the final push.

The child slithered out and immediately the angel bent over the woman and cut the inner cord that passed from mother to child. The child's pattern became locked in its separateness at that moment, no longer integrated with that of the mother. The angel then stroked its fingers through the mother to rebalance her before turning to the child. As the other beings, and the humans in the room tended to the mother, the angel focused on the new life before it.

The child lay still and silent as the angel looked into the eyes of the child. In the communion, the angel sought the thread of the child's soul and when he found it, he tied a knot in it. A small, delicate knot of remembrance. The child and the angel passed visions of recognition before the angel bent over and listened to the child whispering something on its first breath. The child then turned its gaze to a bright harsh lightbulb hanging above it: all the child could remember was the Brightness, and the child longed to be within that Brightness once more. It searched for the Brightness in the lightbulb, but could not find it.

The angel went to the mother and whispered in the mother's ear. He whispered the words spoken by the child, the Divine breath made word and the word was in flesh. The words travelled around the mother before settling deep in her heart. The words transformed themselves into sounds and joined with the mother's thoughts. They, together, became a name. The mother bent over and whispered the child's name in her ear. And the angel withdrew.

Only in death can the light of the Sun truly fall upon our slumbering faces

Appendix H

Advanced Decoys

an extract from Quareia the Adept: Module V (Advanced Magic, Lesson 7) by Josephine McCarthy

A magical decoy is essentially a vessel with a close resonance to some target or victim. It draws the incoming magic to itself due to its resonance with the target. It takes in the magic, absorbs it, and holds it. If the incoming power or magic is ongoing rather than a one-off, then the decoy will continue to absorb the magic until it can hold no more power, at which point it will self-destruct. Some decoys can keep going success- fully for a long time; others cannot. It depends on what it is, what it is made of, and so forth.

Decoys can absorb natural flows of power, like death waves, destruction tides, and so forth; and they can also absorb directed magical attacks. Once the decoy is working, it will continue to work in the background and the magician can forget about it and get on with their work.

If the magician has to travel and they are on the receiving end of a prolonged attack, or their personal pattern is somehow attracting a prolonged destructive pulse, then often inner contacts will deposit a temporary decoy in their path. If you are paying attention and spot the temporary decoy, and engage it, then it will step into action and provide you with protection until you get back home.

Sometimes decoys can work for beginners. An adept can teach a beginner about them as a magical 'trick' if they are in direct danger—rare, though it does happen. But quite a few decoys work due to the adept's past work, resonance, and contact. This is why this lesson has to be in the adept section, as it does not work the same for someone not contacted or an apprentice. It is a seemingly simple method of

H. Advanced Decoys

magic, but its simplicity belies the fact that a lot is going on behind the scenes.

If you have to put together a decoy for a beginner or non-magical person, always use divination to ensure that it will actually work, and that you have chosen the right decoy. Choosing right can be a skill in itself, as you have to think poetically as well as magically.

Just remember that decoys are just *decoys*. They do not deflect, they do not defend, and they work due to their simplicity. They do one job, to divert, and nothing more.

Let's look at a few examples of decoys, how they work, and why.

H.1 Personal decoys

The most obvious and most-used decoy is an image, or doll, of the person. We have looked at this a little before. The method can also be applied in reverse, as it is in some folk magic involving *poppets*, where the poppet is attacked to affect the person.

Any such magic is a two-way street, and the more formed the decoy, the more chance there is that it can be used in reverse. Because of this, adept magicians rarely use personal decoys, as so much can go wrong with them. But if one can be carefully looked after in the long-term then it can work to provide a layer of protection—as well as other things— from heavy, prolonged, incoming fire.

The doll is placed near where the magician sleeps, and is made to look as much as possible like the magician, including any tattoos, etc. Once its job is done, it should be placed carefully in a box where it will not be disturbed and put in long-term storage. Once an energetic connection is made between the doll and the magician, it is very hard to break without physically or energetically damaging the magician. This is why this method is not often deployed. There are ways of disconnecting the link that are used in West African and Caribbean magic, but I do not know enough about them, nor have I successfully worked those methods enough myself, to write about them.

When you deploy a personal decoy, you rarely have to do much magic at all: they trigger automatically as a result of your magical work, the contact already within and around you, and the incoming threat. It is more of a coming-together of energetic elements at the right time; and if you begin to treat the doll as a personal decoy then it will start to take on that role.

Another form of personal decoy is having someone with the same name, physical features, or identical fate spots: a doppelgänger. This is not something you can magically produce or manipulate, but sometimes inner contacts will put a doppelgänger near you when you are in real danger and it is important that you survive. Again, this happens as a result of your work as an adept and is one of the things done for you to maintain your magical service—what you give, you also receive.

The main reason for mentioning this type of decoy is that when you spot it—and it does become obvious—you know that a real danger is flowing towards you. That lets you deploy other layers of protection in different ways, so that you can create a weave of very different types of deflection and protection, as well as having the doppelgänger. Protective layers used like this are much harder for a hostile magician to hack through, whereas a single protection can be dispensed with much more easily.

If the victim of an attack has a common name, and citizenship of more than one country, that will already create a dilemma for an attacker. The majority of magicians who would undertake such an attack use a name, an image or photograph, and a personal detail—that is if they do not have some personal belonging of yours. Many magicians assume that the being who deliverers the attack goes by the details it is given, but this is a mistake: those details are translated into fate points and patterns, and the being sees those, not the victim's face, name, and hair.

If you are near people with similar or identical sets of fate spots, the being has choices. If its job is to destroy, then it will look for the weakest, easiest option.

Say, for example, that a being was sent to attack me, and the attacker used my name and image to direct it. It would seek out a grey-haired woman called Josephine McCarthy who is involved in magic *and who stubbed her toe against the wall four days ago*. And that last detail is the important one that many magicians would forget about. Fate power points, i.e. hotspots that are potential junctions in

H. Advanced Decoys

a fate pattern and are therefore 'shinier' or more visible can often be seemingly tiny, unimportant events.

Thousands of women in Ireland share my name, have grey hair, and are involved in some way with magic—often folk magic dressed up as local tradition. And at least one of them will have banged her foot within four days of me banging mine. If one of them is very elderly, and therefore weak, then the attack will 'out' itself through that unfortunate person.

Bear in mind that a lot of your protection as an adept does not come from magical protection you have put in place, but from the beings and contacts around you and the magical patterns you have built over the years. You may not be even aware of an incoming attack: it will be deflected, decoyed, and moved around you so that you can get on with your work. You may feel a small part of it in the form of a drop in energy, the sudden appearance and attentiveness of beings around you, or in your dreams; but you will likely not pick up on what is actually happening until elderly people with similar patterns to yours start dropping around you.

I see this as more of a magical curiosity than anything to do with magical technique; but as an adept, being aware of this phenomenon and its implications for you can serve as an advance warning that you need to be careful, and that it may be time to go undercover for a little while. This dynamic has little or no effect in less experienced magicians, but the Fates weave and deflect as necessary when an adept is doing service work or has a very fateful future.

H.2 False doors

False doors are another decoy. They are used in tombs, temples, and magical work spaces. These are not about averting a personal attack or destructive pulse, but are more about protecting a space from magical intrusion or from being gate-crashed by beings.

For the most part the work done in the magical space and its continuous tuning will create a barrier that stops anything accessing the space. However, if a long-term pattern is to be triggered in a workspace and the magicians will be withdrawing for a lengthy period of time to let the inner powers get on with the work without the

H.2. False doors

magicians re-entering, then sometimes a decoy door is needed to stop intruders.

Sometimes—rarely—the following type of magical work is conducted - a place is tuned, empowered, and a series of visionary rituals are done to trigger a pattern into formation. Then, instead of the pattern being released, it is held in the space for a prolonged period of time. The room is never entered, and the inner beings and powers in the pattern work alone, without further human intervention. This is done when the pattern is upkeeping something powerful out in the world, and if the pattern is disturbed it could fall apart.

In such instances, besides the usual guardians and deflections, door decoys are deployed to confuse and repel inner beings and invasive magicians working in vision. Sometimes an altar is placed before the door with food offerings to keeping an intruding spirit busy.

Such false doors were used in Ancient Egypt from the third dynasty in mortuary temples and the sacred temples themselves. They, too, would sometimes have altars for food offerings before them. Archaeologists think that these false doors acted as thresholds for the deities and spirits of the dead. This is likely correct for the most part, in which case they were not working as decoys, but as thresholds. Personally though, when I have come across some false doors in temples and mortuary temples that have often led in vision to energetic 'mazes.'

So do not assume that every false door you see is a decoy, or that they are all thresholds. Sometimes they are one or the other; sometimes they may even be both. In many Egyptian temples the false door is on the west wall of a remote chapel, or at the back of the temple. So again, there may be a different function for those. I suspect that this is one of those situations where one thing can have different applications. If you come across one in a building, the best way to find out what it does is to try and use it to access a space in vision and see what happens.

In inner magical temple construction false doors are deployed as decoys, and often have very intricate carvings or reliefs around them with lots of words or patterns to keep a curious spirit busy—and

H. Advanced Decoys

a gate-crashing magician confused. If an inner place really needs protecting then false doors can be constructed that lead to mazes, 'false chapels,' or fake work spaces. They are constructed using inner vision and patterning, and are used to filter out the curious and uninitiated.

If you are lucky enough to have a proper, dedicated magical space then it can be a very interesting and useful experiment to paint a false door near or next to the real one on the outside the magical space, and see what a difference it makes. I once lived in a house that had two front doors, one of which was false, and it did make a difference to the flow of beings in and out of the house.

H.3 Time decoys

This is a curious one that I learned purely by accident. It was one of those situations where necessity brings forth a solution. When I sat back and analysed what was going on from a magical perspective, I discovered that fate patterns and inner 'drivers' of events were *particularly sensitive to time.*

Before we get to the actual decoy, let me explain a little of what I went on to discover about time and magic. With a natural wave of destruction or death, or a magical attack, part of what makes that power successfully reach its target is time. Our fate patterns are huge and complex, and the various different magical and mundane elements, *including time,* that make up a fate hotspot have to be in perfect alignment for the power to properly out itself as a fully manifested event. If time is confused, then the person is either sideswiped rather than getting the full hit, or they avoid the hit altogether.

I found this very curious and I realized that at certain times of magical danger I was not getting the full-on hit that was aimed at me. One thing those times had in common was that 'time,' or more precisely, *the measurement of time* around me was out of sync. I started to experiment, and I became fascinated.

I have a problem with watches and digital clocks. They quickly start go out of sync around me and watches invariably die within a week or two of my wearing them. The more technologically advanced

H.3. Time decoys

the timepiece, the quicker it runs down and stops. As I grew older, clockwork timepieces in the house were slowly replaced by battery-operated or electric ones, and they all began to keep different times. I have always tended to have a lot of clocks around me, as I had a weird obsession with keeping the right time—which is a bit unfortunate if you affect timepieces!

I found that if I stopped continually resetting clocks to the right time, and just let them do their own thing, then not only did it slowly wean me from my time obsession, but I also noticed that the heavy tides and occasional attack aimed at me dissipated in the house. Interesting. I wondered if it was just a coincidence, and the deity powers around me were doing more than providing their usual layer of help and protection.

Later, I had to live in a house with no magical tools, deities, objects, or anything. I was having downtime away from magic to protect my children from an acrimonious divorce that included hostile magical aspects. The only weird thing in the house was how its five clocks all kept different times. Some were an hour out, some were twenty minutes or so out, and one of them repeatedly stopped. I also found that heavy incoming fire was being dissipated in the house, even though it was magically shut down.

After a marathon divination session to try and pinpoint what exactly was working and what was not, I managed to identify the time confusion in the house as a layer of energy that was giving me protection. This did not make sense to me at first, as time, in my mind, was just *there*, and the clocks were simply measuring it. However, it appeared that my observation of time, and my use of time as a tool in my everyday life made it an integral part of my mundane pattern. I always look at clocks, and through observing my use of time, I realized that I focused on the time that was specific to the room I was working in. If I went into another room that had a different clock with a different time, I immediately refocused into that 'time frame': essentially my consciousness was 'time jumping' in terms of how it organized itself. Or to put it another way, each room was its own universe.

I began to experiment. I took out most of the clocks and kept only a very accurate one. The energy of magical attacks came in like

H. Advanced Decoys

a tsunami. I put the clocks back, set them to slightly different times, and let them go out of time as they tended to do around me. Bingo: the energy thrown at me dissipated considerably. It did not get rid of it totally, but it took out a lot of its sting. I got a very mild sideswipe instead of the full-on attack.

I took it a bit further. I got a day-to-day calendar and put it up, but I always left it a couple of days out of date. I let the clocks meander about in their own little time world, and I also changed my front door number to something wrong. Then I had my first truly peaceful night's sleep in months. Was this purely psychological? I was not sure.

The next time I was contacted by a magician under attack, one that used the same type of magic aimed at me, I suggested they get three or four clocks, keep one in each living space, and set them all to different times. I told him to take off his watch and simply go by the clocks in his house. Within twenty-four hours the power of the attack had lessened considerably. He contacted me very excitedly to tell me it had worked, but some was still getting through. I then told him about the calendar and the door number. Within three days of him trying them, life was back to normal.

The attack was still going on, but it was fragmenting when it got to the confused exterior presentation of time and place in the house. What bits did get through, the target's guardians mopped up.

Remember about working in layers? This is a far better method than constantly doing protective rituals or workings, or having large stomping guardians circling your house, or constantly having to do talismans. It is simple, effective, and you can leave it to work while you get on with your life.

However, sadly, when I tried this technique on a non-magical person in the path of destruction, it did not work. I tried it a few times more with non-magical people or magical beginners, and it still did not work. Yet it worked for all the more advanced magicians I told about it. Once more I was curious: why? I was pushed back on observation and divination.

The time decoy, like some other decoys, works due to the magician's magical patterns and tuning. I discovered that when you work magic at an adept level, your fate pattern becomes highly tuned and focused, and that little things can be deployed as a distraction from that highly tuned pattern. Time for an adept is a major element of their pattern, and it can become very defined, right down to the minutes.

This does not mean you are locked into a restrictive fate pattern; quite the opposite, in fact. It means that the more power and contact you work with as an adept, the more sensitive your pattern becomes to the slightest variation in key elements like time, place, and so forth. It is like the lens becomes highly tuned.

This sensitivity of timing plays itself out through an adept's the everyday life. They will be delayed by something so that they arrive at exactly the right moment; they will choose a seemingly random date which will turn out to be highly significant or perfect timing; or clocks will start to fail around them if they need to be in a confused time.

Funnily enough, the village where I live has an ancient church and bell tower with a clock. It was always known to keep great time, and the locals used to set their clocks by it. Then I moved in. Now it is rarely right and sometimes goes out by hours. As well as my house of clocks that all live in their own time universes, any power sensitive to time will not get anywhere near me.

H.4 Oppositions

Oppositions are a poetic way of triggering a decoy that also balances something. Again it draws on what is in the magician in terms of skill, contact, and patterns; and it can be used when an energetically affecting presence has been brought into being by another magician.

For example—and this is a real example—a certain group of magicians are social friends but do not work together at all. They get together occasionally throughout the year at conferences, and so forth. Though they do not and never have worked together, being in the same social circle still creates a pattern, as they are all working in magic, albeit different forms.

Once, one of those magicians jokingly got a toy creature and started talking to it. He treated it like a person and projected onto it all the 'naughty' things he could not do in life. He started to create

H. Advanced Decoys

narratives about the creature, how it was a demon who got up to all sorts of dubious activities. That narrative began to expand to include the creature having an active sex life: it was treated as a person.

Over time the toy became a vessel for a hungry and very intelligent parasite which fed off the magician. The magician was politely warned of what was happening, but he chose to ignore the warning. The toy became a strong vessel, which gave the parasite a stronger presence in the physical world. Then the parasite started to reach out to the other magicians in the social circle to try and connect with them, and a very unhealthy situation slowly developed.

The magician had not projected something of himself into the toy at all; rather he had created the vessel by talking to the toy and treating it as a living being. When you do that the intent, character, and purpose you have in your uttering tends to define what sort of vessel it becomes, which defines what sort of being would want to move into it.

Because the magician would not give up his 'relationship' with the toy, even though the being within had started to expand its reach, nothing could be done directly. You cannot force something in such a situation; you can only limit its expansion beyond the relationship between being and magician. The reach of the being started to badly affect another adept in the same community, so the adept took passive action.

He created a counterweight.

The adept stumbled across the same toy in a shop, but it was dressed as a consecrated bishop. He simply bought it and instructed the bishop toy to be the counterbalance to the feral toy. He sat it on a shelf in his home, and the problem slowly settled down.

It did not directly deal with the feral toy, as it was for its magical owner to do that in his own time. If you force such an issue, you end up with more mess than when you started. And you cannot solve all the problems triggered by thoughtless actions: the magician has to come to an understanding in their own time... or be slowly destroyed by their own stupidity. You simply stop the problem leaking to you, and then get on with your life.

You will find that the deeper you go in adept work, the more your focused magical ritual and visionary work is used for the big jobs.

Anything below this is dealt with by the power within you. Simple acts with intention—the right acts, relevant to the issue at hand—will deal with most minor and medium issues. The clue is knowing what acts are relevant and how to apply them. Always remember, little is better than lots, and poetic is better than full-on magical workings. Such poetic actions nudge a pattern into action that is already in place and waiting.

So, for example, back to the feral toy. As it grew as a vessel and a being moved in, that being became rooted, strong, and conscious. This triggered a shift in the patterns that began the formation of a threshold for a counterweight being to step in to keep things balanced. Because the toy was triggered by the magician's conversation and actions, the forming counterweight also needs the same trigger. When the adept got the bishop toy, he instructed it with intent and placed it in the magical household. This was a human trigger that invited the counterweight being to step over the threshold and into the waiting vessel.

Because the counterweight toy was a 'consecrated bishop,' the vessel had a certain function embedded within its shape and presentation. It could become what it looked like when uttered at. And remember that the counterweight being is the polar opposite of the parasitical being. It would not feed off people, it would not have sex—surprisingly, some bishops, even today, are celibate—and it has the religious connotations that work within the pattern of 'subduing demons.' It was the perfect choice. And it was amusing how the adept came across just such a toy when it was needed. Remember, things are put in your path to help you, and you will spot them if you pay attention. Or, I should say, you are nudged to visit places where the solution can be found.

H.5 Copper as deflection

Copper reroutes power and energy, not a decoy but a deflector and director. If a persistent flow of localized destructive energy, particularly if identified as coming in from a specific direction/source, using copper piping outside a property can deflect it and direct it down in the land.

H. Advanced Decoys

If the energetic disturbance runs on a defined path from A to B, usually spotted as a line of dying plants, you can put the pipes at both ends of the line. Simply knock the pipes in the ground so that they stand up, and they will channel the energy between them and in the ground.

Similarly if there are magical issues with the body on a particular side, wearing copper on that side can block it out. There are a lot of magical and medicinal uses for copper, usually for cleaning, containing or deflecting. Something kept within copper (like a pure copper box) will stay clean, and that has many different adept magical applications. But the strongest quality of copper from a magical perspective, is that it diverts and reroutes energy.

A lot of decoy work at an adept level is not flashy, but simple, effective and focused. However always remember that a good part of why it works is dependent upon the adept themselves and the magical patterns inherent within the adept. If you wish to deploy such methods for a none magical person or a student, ensure first that it will operate without you being present, or without it being reliant upon you to work. Otherwise you can end up being energetically drained as the decoy works for a student, or it just will not work which in turn puts the student at risk. Always use divination to check if you are not sure.

Appendix I

The prehistory of magical development

One of the important questions for an adept as they develop into their path as an adept magician, is why is magic here in the first place? How did it develop? Why did it develop? And what forms did it take? These questions and more are not really answerable in truth, as magic has existed probably for as long has humans have existed. However the process of asking those questions, and the process of research, thought and discovery leads us to a greater understanding of magic and of ourselves as magicians.

It is wise to be cautious when undertaking to find answers to such questions, as it can be tempting to try and fit history to our own narratives, which is an age-old problem where history is concerned. And again, it is unlikely we can totally avoid such overlays in our understanding, as we seek in relation to what we understand. But if we approach such exploration with as open a mind as possible, and also always look for the simplest and most reasonable explanations for what we find (as opposed to 'it's the aliens!') then it can lead us on a journey not only of historical learning, but of also self-discovery. Through looking at the struggles of our ancestors and what potentially drove them to magic, we can begin to understand our own limitations, fears and vulnerabilities.

The following essay is my own journey of discovery for the roots of magic in the northwest hemisphere, investigating what happened, how people reacted, how they organized themselves, and so forth. I also looked through the eyes of an adept magician, looking at magical responses to world events to see what I could recognize. The variations of magical responses are not endless, so we can as magicians sometimes see patterns of behaviour and magical action that we recognize from today's magical actions and methods: humans really don't change that much over the millennia, and the same goes

I. The Prehistory of Magical Development

for the core elements of magic. I certainly found it a very interesting exercise, and it made me rethink a lot of assumptions I had made about our magical ancient ancestors.

★ ★ ★

> And the light shineth in darkness: and the darkness comprehended it not
>
> —*John* 1:5

To truly understand the emergence of the concepts that arise in today's Western magic, we have to cast our attention far back in time to the cradles that those concepts emerged out of. Those cradles emerged out of North Africa, Western Asia, the Near East/Caucasus, and Europe. To understand why those cradles emerged as they did, where they did, and what their focus was, we have to look at the conditions that those cradles emerged from. Religion and magic evolve from cause and effect, from our response as humans to the world around us.

If instead we only look back a thousand years for the roots of magic, we miss the point of the exercise. Finding such roots means looking far beyond the organized religions and magical practices of cultures that went before us. We need to look at what made our distance ancestors tick, at the cauldron of human thought and response to circumstance that birthed magic in the first place.

If we look at human nature in its barest form, we find two dynamics at play: find food, and store food. This is a base survival mechanism that, along with breeding and prey/predator behaviour, keeps our species alive. Those base mechanisms are still within us today as individuals and as societies: a lot of what we do has its roots in those basic survival instincts. Marketing in our modern consumer society taps into the 'find food/store food' mechanism that drives us: we buy, we consume, and we acquire more than we need (store/bank).

When it comes to the deeper spirit side of ourselves, we reach out to the unknown to try and make sense of the universe around us. We reach out for 'food' to eat for our souls and we try to store 'food' for our souls for the future (religion/beliefs). Magic is the active step that grew out of very early religious behaviour in its most primal form, where we move from passive acceptance of existence to a wish to actively engage with the universe around us and to have an element of control in how we navigate through life, not only in terms of survival, but in order to flourish.

I.1 Magic and its forms

Today, the same as a thousand years ago, magic falls into roughly two categorizes: secure resources, and clear the path ahead in our future (find food/store food). To secure resources (find food) magic developed into acts designed to attract, repel, bind and release: base actions to gain our needs and wants. Today we call this 'results magic' or 'low magic,' labels that are both confusing and not entirely correct.

These two labels are modern tags using modern language that both denigrate that type of magic and also limit the understanding of such magic. The term 'results magic' comes from a twentieth-century model of science, where experiments are designed and implemented not only to achieve results, but to make them repeatable in a stable manner. That is fine for science, but magic often does not work with such clearly defined parameters: it is as unpredictable as the weather. I strongly suspect that this term slid into use as an attempt to give magic modern credibility by using terminology more commonly used in science.

The same can be said of the term 'low magic': the term is loaded with snobbery and highhandedness. 'High magic' is a term used to describe magic that reaches into mystical exploration, whereas 'low magic' seeks to acquire something or stop something. I have tied myself in knots for years trying to explain my stance on this issue, and it is often assumed that I am hostile to 'results/low magic,' which is not the case. Rather, I see the gaping potholes and potential meltdowns that such magic can cause when it is paired with emotional immaturity, a modern consumer mentality, magical ignorance or incompetence, and a massive fragile ego. Magic is magic, and every type of magic has its place and function. The key is to understand what is appropriate and when. This type of magic is about survival, about a person finding 'food' for their body and

I. THE PREHISTORY OF MAGICAL DEVELOPMENT

soul to keep them functioning, whatever they decide this 'food' is or represents.

'High' or mystical magic seeks the Divine in the universe: it moves beyond 'find food/store food' of 'low magic,' but in order to understand and work within that type of magic, 'low magic' must also be understood not only intellectually but practically: it is the weaving of inner power to manifest a controlled change in fate patterns. The magic itself (high or low) is no different be it mystical or functional: it is our approach and intention that creates a line of distinction.

This is a very important point to think about when looking into the ancient history of magic, as life in 7000 B.C. was very different to life today. The quest for mystical magic is a luxury in many ways: to embark upon such a journey of transformation and connection to the Divine, you need food in your stomach, a roof over your head and shoes on your feet. You need to be relatively safe and secure, and have time to ponder, think and act. It is those luxuries that mystical magic (and all mystical and philosophical thought) grew out of.

Functional (results) magic grew out of dire need, hence it is essentially folk magic: the magic of the ordinary person trying to get by in a way that they define for themselves. This is why it is more common in poor and rural communities both today and in the past. Simply understanding the dynamics of resources and human need can put a lot of magical history into perspective.

This is not to say that mystical magic did not exist in very ancient times. We have no books left to us from thousands of years ago, but what we do have is our magical knowledge of *today*. As a result, as practical working magicians, if we look deep into the ancient past then we will recognize certain acts that left archaeological findings for us to discover. We may not know the details, but the core magical mechanisms displayed in very ancient findings show both mystical and functional magical religious behaviour. It is through those behaviours that we can begin to understand ourselves as magicians today, and understand where our magic comes from.

When we look at ancient historical events that were happening at the same time as the emergence of magical behaviours, it can not only start to reveal to us the cause and effect of the development of magic, but it can also give us the foundational understanding of magical practice today: it becomes a whisper that travels down through time and reminds us of our magical roots.

In this essay, I wanted to dig back as far as possible to look for early magical behaviour. The timelines that I rummaged around in were far earlier than the written word, so I had to look at archaeological findings to see if I recognized anything. I also looked at the wider environment, at what we humans were doing and potentially why we were doing it.

This took me on a journey back to the period between 7000 B.C. and 5000 B.C. in human history, looking at what was happening with climatic events in the northern hemisphere from northern Europe to the Near East and north Africa. Bear in mind throughout this essay that I am not an archaeologist or trained historian, but I have done my best to check everything and ensure it is referenced.

I.2 The series of unfortunate events

The first thing that I tripped over was a rather startling bit of evidence from our genetic history. Sometime between the period of 7000 B.C. to 5000 B.C. modern humans experienced an abrupt genetic bottleneck specific to human males across the Old World.[1] Since the research paper was published in 2015, various other research bodies have tied themselves into knots trying to understand why this would have happened. Some theorized that it could be social (war, patrilineal dominance) and others suggested that it could be environmental (volcano). When there is a massive environmental disaster, often male fetuses abort[2], but the ratio of male to female in the bottleneck was 1:17, far greater than has been observed with spontaneous natural abortions during disasters.

But when scientists look at these startling anomalies, by nature of their focus, they tend to look for one specific potential cause, or a small orbit of potential cause and effect. However, when disasters strike, the ramifications can have wide and long-lasting effects in

---

[1] Karmin, M. et al. A recent bottleneck of Y chromosome diversity coincides with a global change in culture. *Genome Res.* 25, 459–466 (2015).

[2] *Impact of earthquakes on sex ratio at birth*: Emek Doğer, Yiğit Çakıroğlu, Şule Yıldırım Köpük, Yasin Ceylan, Hayal Uzelli Şimşek, and Eray Çalışkan.

747

I. THE PREHISTORY OF MAGICAL DEVELOPMENT

all aspects of society and health. So I spent some time looking closely at this time period to see what was going on, and I began to see the potential for complex cause and effect reactions in human populations across the Old World.

The period from around 6,500 B.C. to 5,000 B.C. reads a little like the title of a Lemony Snicket novel: *A Series of Unfortunate Events*. It was a rough time to be a human: for just over a thousand years, anything that could go wrong, did.

The picture that emerged was not one of a single massive disaster, but a series of them. It was a time of climate instability, and of massive land and environmental changes which would have likely affected various populations in a wide variety of ways. Let us look first at the natural events that occurred over that long period of time between 6,500 B.C. and 5,000 B.C., and then we will look at the fragments of evidence of the human responses to such upheavals, as they will give us a better picture of the cauldron within which what we know as magic today evolved, and why. Obviously magic existed in human cultures long before these events, but as we get further into this exploration of magical history, you will begin to see how pivotal this time was.

Leading up to the period we are looking up, we had the end of the last Glacial age around 10,000 B.C. and the beginning of the Holocene Thermal Maximum (9,000 to 5,000 B.C.).

Basically it went from cold to warm/hot, and such shifts cause all sorts of expansions and contractions in weather and the landscape. By the time we get to the era of the genetic bottleneck, things are really moving. Bear in mind that scientifically the following events can be dated only approximately, usually give or take a few hundred years.

The first event that caught my eye was the draining of Lake Agassiz: Ojibway, a vast glacial lake that at its peak potentially covered 440,000 square kilometres in the North American continent. Around 6,200 B.C. the vast fresh waters drained into the Atlantic, dumping a huge amount of fresh water down the Hudson Strait and into the Labrador sea west of Greenland. This is also thought to have caused or contributed to the collapse of the Laurentide Ice Sheet in North America, which also dumped vast quantities of fresh water

I.2. The series of unfortunate events

into the ocean. This is a crucial area for the global ocean circulation system, and such a massive influx of cold freshwater essentially stopped the Gulf Stream flowing.[1] It was rapid, and it was dramatic.

It caused absolute chaos around the world and is thought to have triggered what is known as the 8.2 kiloyear event, a period of intense rapid cooling that lasted anywhere from 200 to 400 years. It caused drier conditions in North Africa, and 300 years of aridification and cooling in the Near East/Mesopotamia/Western Asia. East Africa suffered 500 years of drought, and the effects/evidence of the rapid cooling have been found around the world.

Nature decided that this event was really just not dramatic enough, and decided to throw some spice into the mix, just to be sure. Around 6,225–6170 B.C. there was a massive landslip off the coast of Norway, known as the last Storegga slide, which dumped 3,500 cubic kilometres of debris into the north Atlantic, triggering a mega tsunami event. This event covered Doggerland, a land area that acted as a bridge between Britain, Denmark and the Netherlands. Doggerland was an area of expansive fertile hunting grounds for the region's Mesolithic cultures, and it vanished beneath the sea during this catastrophic event. It is likely that the area was already under extreme stress from rising seas from the 8.2 kiloyear event, and this massive tsunami had a huge impact on all the coastal communities of the North Sea. It has been approximated that the tsunami was thirteen feet high and went inland for fifty miles.

Around that time (6500–6200 B.C.) there was an apparent collapse of the eastern flank of Mount Etna that would have caused a potentially devastating tsunami that would have consumed Mediterranean coastal settlements. An Italian study led by Maria Pareschi of the Italian Institute of Geophysics and Volcanology in Pisa suggested the subsequent tsunami was possibly 130 feet high. If it was triggered by a massive volcanic explosion, it would have likely also caused a period of volcanic winter, as well as deep memories of a catastrophic event.

---

[1] *Reduced North Atlantic Deep Water Coeval with the Glacial Lake Agassiz Freshwater Outburst* Helga (Kikki) Flesche Kleiven, Catherine Kissel, Carlo Laj, S. Ninnemann, Thomas O. Richter, Elsa Cortijo. 2004 DOI: 10.1126/science.1148924

I. THE PREHISTORY OF MAGICAL DEVELOPMENT

The result of these different dramatic events would have had a massive impact on societies around the world as it suddenly got a lot colder—and in many places, dryer—with weather that was unpredictable, and massive floods in many areas. Thanks to archaeology, we know that there was a sudden interruption of the stability in society which is demonstrated in finds from Tell Sabi Abyad in Syria from this period of climate instability. Before the 8.2 kiloyear event, the pottery from Sabi Abyad was complex and highly decorative, and there was evidence of mass production and trading. Suddenly, around the 8.2 kiloyear event, the pottery ceased to be complex and decorative, and instead became rudimentary and simply functional. There was no evidence of decoration or trade: people were scrambling simply to survive and keep going.

The temperature began to rise steeply a few hundred years later with what is known as the Thermal Maximum, and with that came rising sea levels once again. Just as things were settling down, we have the Mount Mazuma eruption, a volcano in the Oregon segment of the Cascade Volcanic arc. Those eruptions sent a thirty mile high ash column into the stratosphere, with fallout over a three year period. The climatic eruption created Crater Lake, and it had a volcanic explosivity index of seven. It has been hypothesized that this mega explosion could have affected weather and temperature for three or four years in northern latitudes.

Two thousand years later we then have the 5.9 kiloyear climate event (Bond event 4, 3,900 B.C.) which triggered intense aridification to areas of North Africa and the Arab Peninsula, from which they never recovered. Incidentally, this is the most likely reason that people started to gravitate towards the Nile Valley from the nearby Sahara region.

It was also most likely the trigger for the North Atlantic cooling episode that brought about the decline and collapse of the European Neolithic culture in southeast Europe. The period from 4,200 B.C. to 3,900 B.C. saw intense climatic change with much colder winters in Northern Europe. The climate continued to deteriorate until approx. 2,800 B.C., and during this long span of time many settlements along the Danube were burned and abandoned, and overall the region saw an upsurge in settlement fortifications.

I.3 People and responses

When ancient cultures are subjected to repeated and prolonged extremes from natural disasters, and the stories of such disasters are handed down the generations in oral traditions, the response usually provokes two questions: 'what do we do?' (food, survival), and 'to whom or what do we pray for help?' The intense and sudden cooling of that period, with the accompanying weather extremes, will have put a lot of societies and communities under extreme stress. This was still a time where there was a mix of hunter gatherers, animal domestication, and early agricultural experiments.

Groups were already highly ritualized in their beliefs, and most religious finds we have from the archaeology of this period are continuations of 'Venus figures' (35,000—3,000 B.C.) and other anthropomorphic figures, along with other finds indicating the existence of bull cults. It is also pertinent to point out, at this stage of this essay, that highly ritualized behaviour was not, as has been previously presumed, the result of agriculture, but predates agriculture, or at least appears during the very early agricultural experiments before agriculture proper was established. It is likely that people's ritualized behaviour was focused on predator and prey: what threatened them, and what fed them.

The archaeological finds at Göbekli Tepe near Sanliurfa in southeast Anatolian Turkey of highly ritualized megalithic T-shaped decorated standing stones predate organized agriculture.[1] The deepest layers of the site show activity from the Epipalaeolithic period (18,000–8,000 B.C.) and the presence of megaliths from the Pre-Pottery Neolithic A period (PPNA). The samples used for dating were charcoal deposits and would have represented the endpoint of activity for that layer: the structures are older than the charcoal deposits. It is interesting to note that the images on the megaliths are predator and prey, with at least some of the megaliths attempting to portray humans: some of the T bars of the stones were fashioned as arms (but there are no heads).

This extensive ritual site, that was in use on and off for thousands of years, predated the first cultivation of the eight founder crops

---

[1]Schmidt, Klaus. (2000). *Göbekli Tepe, Southeastern Turkey. A Preliminary Report on the 1995-1999 Excavations.* Paléorient. 26. 10.3406/paleo.2000.4697.

I. The prehistory of magical development

in the region. This is important to us as we dig around in the mists of pre-civilizations, as we are looking for cause and effect and ritualized behaviour that is the ancient forebear of magic. People didn't intentionally grow crops (agriculture) and then begin to civilize and ritualize: the ritualization came first.

The 'Venus' figures are very interesting in that they are depictions of females with exaggerated breasts and thighs, and sometimes vulvas. This depicts 'plenty' and 'breeding.' Remember that at the period we are looking at (between 7,000 and 5,000 B.C.) societies and populations in general were very small by today's standards. The focus would have been on three simple things: breed, find food, and store and protect excess food for winter. Everything would have focused around those three dynamics, and in a way, it still is today: we are driven to reproduce, to get what we need, and to obtain excess to store (bank accounts, etc.).

When there is a major disaster or a prolonged period of disasters like a climate collapse or shift, those three survival dynamics are put under extreme stress. Small populations are very vulnerable and can collapse easily. In such instances, the survival of females is far more important than the survival of males: if you have ten men and only one woman, only one child at a time can be born. If you have ten females and one male, ten babies can be born at one time: this ensures the continuation of the tribe into the future: it also causes a male DNA bottleneck. It is simple dynamics of nature, and one that we know was used in Neolithic societies.[1,2]

It is very likely that during this prolonged period of a few hundred years of rapid cooling (that then suddenly warmed back up a few hundred years later) that vulnerable communities began to collapse through cold, starvation, and lack of known resources. It is my theory that during this period not only were there natural spontaneous abortions, but also infanticide and male sacrifice. Culling/exposing the majority of male children would ensure that all meagre resources

---

[1] Birdsell, Joseph, B. (1986). "Some predictions for the Pleistocene based on equilibrium systems among recent hunter gatherers". In: Lee, Richard & Irven DeVore. *Man the Hunter*. Aldine Publishing Co. p. 239.

[2] Milner, Larry S. (2000). *Hardness of Heart / Hardness of Life: The Stain of Human Infanticide*. Lanham/New York/Oxford: University Press of America.

I.3. People and responses

were protected and the small number of male children that made it to adulthood would then impregnate the females.

I was talking about this bottleneck and the culling hypothesis with a biologist who had specialized in genetics and epigenetics. She also suggested the possibility of castration as a survival mechanism. I was not aware of any evidence of eunuchs predating the first millennium B.C., where it was used in the courtly culture of the Neo-Hittite State of Carchemish[1]. I did some digging around and found evidence of knowledge of the link between testes and fertility in Neolithic animal husbandry (earliest findings approx. 5,600 B.C.): they castrated their surplus male animals to control breeding.[2] So that knowledge was kicking around the Old World and was very likely going on prior to the date of the archaeological finds. Castrating the majority of the living males while leaving fertile only the strongest and healthiest, though an extreme response, would make survival sense for the long-term population. But the castrated males would need to be fed in the short term, so I am not wholly convinced this could have been a solution, unless there was a need for working but infertile males.

It is very possible that the sudden bottleneck on the male DNA was a result of applying animal breeding knowledge to lower the male population, while also practising infanticide/exposure of male babies and the sacrifice of a percentage of the male adults. When you add to this the mix of disease, malnutrition (from extreme weather changes) and resulting resource wars, you get a picture of catastrophic change and extreme response from people in order for their tribe to survive.

Such events that spanned a few hundred years would have also stuck heavily in the ancestral memory, and stories of the events and how those events were dealt with would have gone down the generations in the forms of stories, oral history and ritual behaviour, something we know happened in Neolithic cultures.[3] I wonder if this

---

[1] Trevor Bryce: *The World of the Neo-Hittite Kingdoms: A Political and Military History.* Oxford, New York 2012

[2] *Size Reduction in Early European Domestic Cattle Relates to Intensification of Neolithic Herding Strategies.* Katie Manning, Adrian Timpson, Stephen Shennan, Enrico Crema University College Dublin Published: December 2, 2015 (Plos).

[3] *Oral Tradition and the Creation of Late Prehistory in Roviana Lagoon, Solomon Islands*: P. Sheppard, R Walter and S Aswani. Records of the Australian Museum, Supplement 29 (2004).

I. THE PREHISTORY OF MAGICAL DEVELOPMENT

is the source of the stories that appear in various books of the Bible of killing first-born sons. There was certainly human sacrifice around at that time, and it carried on for another three thousand years.

One thing to note, as we look at this from the perspective of wanting to know how magical/ritual behaviour patterns formed and matured, is that human nature, mostly, doesn't change that much at its core.

The initial ritualized behaviour/actions are a direct response to a threat to survival. Once that threat has passed, the ritualized behaviour continues, not only because it gives people a sense that 'there is help out there if we get them on our side,' but also because it gives a sense of control. With that sense of control comes hierarchy, and with hierarchy comes more and more controlling actions in order to establish who should be where in the pecking order. Humans like to box and label things, to put their mark on things, and to be the 'one who knows' (hierarchy establishment).

Once you have a pattern of highly ritualized behaviour, you then have a situation where some will be better at it than others. Those with obsessive compulsive tendencies will seek to express them through their ritualized behaviour: that action needs me to do it with my left hand at this time and place, with my foot placed in a specific position, with a certain colour robe on, and I must bow three times before addressing the deity. This obsessive compulsive behaviour usually triggers first as a stress response before settling into a longer-term control response.

We see this sort of OC development in virtually every religion once it gets to a stable level of acceptance in a community: this is the early development of a priesthood and temple culture. Such development comes a long time after the initial catastrophe that triggered the actions in the first place, and often the true nature of the event loses its original identity as it morphs into mythology. The changing of a natural disaster into a mythic story can take many generations, but once established it can stay within a culture for thousands of years.

When we look at tribal societies today, often their mythology is clear enough that you can locate the original events that triggered the mythology. It becomes a story of remembrance, passed down

I.3. People and responses

orally from generation to generation, and the main reason for the continuance of the story is to learn its lessons: when there is a bad earthquake, head to the mountains because flooding is coming. This was very evident in the 2004 earthquake (9.3) and subsequent tsunami that struck on 26th December 2004.[1] I watched the TV with horror as the reporting unfolded over a series of days, and then with intense interest when a military head was being interviewed about the safety of the indigenous tribes that populate some of the Andaman Islands.

Through his connections with people in charge of protecting the tribes, many of which were isolated and not integrated with modern life, he managed to ascertain that the Shompens and Holschu tribes were totally unaffected by the event. The interpreter/warden for the tribes stated that 'the tribes fled to the hills before the tsunami struck': they knew it was coming. The knowledge that it was coming would have been linked to natural observations that are connected to their ancient stories. This was conveyed in a subsequent interview with one of the wardens: their mythology carried the information they needed to survive a disaster.

In societies that shift from hunter-gatherer to farmer, such a shift needs organization skills: someone has to measure the harvest, distribute, and also organize the workload. In the period of time that this essay is looking at, the communities we are looking at, i.e. the various cultures of the Old World, were mostly engaged in animal husbandry and early rudimentary agriculture with wild seeds. This societal structure facilitates organization, ritualized behaviour, and consequently a more sophisticated response to disaster and the subsequent development of mythology, ritual behaviour and so forth, as we have previously discussed.

The stories that come out of such organized ritual structure become increasingly steeped in mystique, as the communicator of that story in each generation needs to assert a sense of status and control over the people. Often the disaster stories become vehicles for asserting societal morality: if you are bad people, the mountain will blow, and only those special people who are priests can talk to

---

[1]The Hindu News December 31st 2004: *All Primitive Tribes Safe*. Article by Suresh Nambeth.

the mountain. And these are the ritual laws that you have to obey so that the mountain does not get angry.

This micro-controlling of actions, society rules, the organizing of ritual structures and behaviours, and the subsequent 'mystification' of the memory tales and mythology triggers the creation of behaviour that eventually develops into temple cultures.

At the timeframe that we are looking at, we see evidence of ' who do I ask for help' in the form of the anthropomorphic figures, the use of which spans thousands of years prior to the 8.2 kiloyear event and subsequent 5.9 kiloyear event. We also see the development of more sophisticated temple style behaviour with the creation and use of the megaliths at Göbekli Tepe: this appeared at the early phase of people trying to control their environment through animal husbandry and early agricultural experiments. The anthropomorphic figures found in Europe, for example the Löwenmensch (lion-human) figurine found in a German cave, which dates to around 35,000 B.C., and the animal images at Göbekli Tepe, tell us that the relationship between the animal and human kingdoms were of the utmost importance in terms of belief and ritualized behaviour, and had been for millennia.

After the series of unfortunate events in our timeframe of the 8.2 kiloyear event and subsequent fallout (the rapid climate changes, land instability, rising sea levels, and the male DNA bottleneck), we start to see a shift in ritualized behaviour. Remember that we can only draw conclusions from the archaeological evidence that we can access: the rest has to be hypotheses drawn from what we know of ritual behaviour, and what came later, as humanity in general is pretty predictable.

The shift in behaviour away from the animal/human relationship starts to emerge in the fifth millennium. This is when we start to see ritual enclosures that appear to have their focus upon the behaviour of the sun. This makes sense to us in that the sudden and intense drop in temperature of the 8.2 kiloyear event and the subsequent hundreds of years of climate instability and cold will have etched itself forever on the collective memory of the people. Just as that series of events faded deep into the recesses of ancestral memory, we then see the societies suffer once more with the resulting climate upheaval from the 5.9 kiloyear event and subsequent long-term cooling.

When the sun no longer does its job of always shining and always keeping us warm, when it has become unreliable, then you have to work to ensure that the anger of the sun does not return again. You want the sun to be as predictable as it used to be, to not get angry, and to bestow its favours upon you: crops, animals and human lives depend upon it.

This was also the time where people started to get rather serious about agriculture. The bounties of the land had become less dependable, the weather was constantly shifting and changing, and the resources were thinly spread. It made sense to have more control over your food supply by growing and storing it. In northern latitudes, with the shifting more towards agriculture, you would expect to see a shift in ritualized focus from predator/prey, to seasons, solar activity, and the appearance and vanishing of stars, as these tell you when to plant and when to harvest.

The rise in sites of solar observation and worship appears in the fifth millennium around the northern hemisphere. It is likely that such sites served multiple purposes: solar observation of the season through the alignment of the stones/solstices, a place for worship and sacrifice, and a place for tribal gatherings. This shift in focus from predator/prey/observation of the animal and plant kingdom, to a focus upon the sun and stars is a major turning point in humanity's magical thinking that would affect the development of magic for thousands of years. So it is worth a closer look: let us look at some of these early solar ritual centres, as a closer look at them raises difficult or at least interesting questions.

I.4 Early ritual solar circles

In the fifth millennium B.C., we start to see the appearance of enclosures and stone circles that are aligned to the movements of the sun. This is quite a radical change from 30,000+ years of animal/human centred ritual behaviour we have seen so far. Two of the earliest that have been found are Goseck Circle, Saxony-Anhalt,

I. The Prehistory of Magical Development

Germany,[1] and Nabta Playa circle in Upper Egypt (in the desert 100 kilometres west of Abu Simbel).

The Goseck circle is thought to have been built around 4,900 B.C. and was in use for approximately two hundred years. It aligned with the winter solstice at sunrise and sunset, and the site has evidence of human sacrifice. The winter solstice is the lowest ebb of the sun in the Northern Hemisphere, and would have been a time when people feared the sun 'would not come back.' It makes sense that ritualized behaviour patterns emerged to time in with the winter solstice, and even today in some tribal societies, that behaviour continues.[2]

Later, stone circles aligned to the solar procession started springing up all over Europe and western Asia over a three-thousand-year period. The animals ceased to be the main focus, and the sun was the 'in thing' to watch and worship/ritually work with. A lot of these sites fell in and out of use over a long period of time, and quite a few of them have evidence of human sacrifice, or cattle sacrifice and of human burials (necropolis sites). The large quantity of cattle bones found at many of these sites is thought to indicate ritual sacrifice, but I would like to add something to that hypothesis that may throw a spanner into the works of those theories and also of mine.

When I lived for a while in a tribal society, when it got close to winter (October and November) the tribe would be very active with hunting, and extended families would gather together to collectively skin, and then dry the meat. The drying of the meat was often a family affair where everyone came together to butcher and dry the meat over huge hanging racks positioned over low ember fires.

This produced large quantities of dried meat that was then equally distributed between family members. It was a remembrance of survival mechanisms for a food supply that would last the harsh and bitter winters. No matter that there were supermarkets an hour away in a car, the drying of the meat was something still done as winter fast approached. It was also done, incidentally, upon the death

---

[1]François Bertemes, Peter F. Biehl, Andreas Northe, Olaf Schröder: Die neolithische Kreisgrabenanlage von Goseck, Ldkr. Weißenfels. In: *Archäologie in Sachsen-Anhalt*. NF Bd. 2, 2004

[2]Salizh/Pend d'oreille tribes on the Flathead reservation in Montana still practice 'Jump Dance,' a ritual nightlong stamping dance done around the time of the winter solstice to remind the sun to come back.

I.4. Early ritual solar circles

of a hunter. Meat would be dried and handed to the widow to ensure a food supply for the months ahead.

It is important to remember that as we look at these sites and their evidence, we do so from the comfort of a warm home that has a good food supply. We do not have the survival concerns that our ancestors did seven thousand years ago, so we tend to think only in terms of purely ritual behaviour, when often it was more likely that these behaviours served multiple purposes, including highly practical ones. And it is also pertinent to remember that these often highly practical acts worked well as survival and also bonding mechanisms, and they often persisted in closed and tribal societies right up to present day: if it works, why change it?

The second very early stone circle is a little more perplexing and is also far more relevant to us as magicians digging around in the underpants of history. Nabta Playa,[1] out in the Western Desert of Upper Egypt is an ancient centre of activity, with the first evidence of activity dating to around 10,000 B.C.. In the period between 6,500 and 5,000 B.C. we start to see a highly organized community with clear ritualized behaviour. The settlement had deep wells, organized 'streets,' and they appear to have been importing goats and sheep from western Asia. There is evidence of the ritual burial of cattle in stone roofed chambers lined with clay[2] (a very interesting parallel to the later burials of the Apis Bull in Egypt) and also of numerous large hearths (think about the drying of meat at collective slaughters).

The actual stone circle complex of Nabta Playa was thought to have been erected around 4,800 B.C., and there has been much debate about its meaning. It is clear that it aligns to the summer solstice, and is therefore a solar circle, but there have also been theories also about its alignment to various stars, namely the Orion constellation and Sirius. This theory was postulated by Wendorf, but later revised by University of Colorado (Boulder) astronomy professor J. McKim Malville. It is a complicated thing to work out what stars align to what stone circle, as there is the date consideration (the sky slowly

---

[1]Wendorf, Fred: Malville, J. McKim (2001) "The Megalith Alignments". In: *Wendorf, Fred: Schild, Romuald: Nelson, Kit, In Holocene Settlement of the Egyptian Sahara, vol. I, The archaeology of Nabta Playa*. New York: Kluwer Academic/Plenum.

[2]Wendorf, Fred: Schild, Romuald (November 26, 2000) *Late Neolithic megalithic structures at Nabta Playa (Sahara) southwestern Egypt.*

processes) and also the fact that—and this is in the least scientific of terms—if you have a circle of stones, and a load of stars in the sky, then each stone or pair of stones will align to something. But it was and is very clear that the circle's layout of prominent stones aligned to the zenith of the sun at summer solstice.

I can understand a solar stone circle in northern Europe where the sun appears to be vanishing in the winter, but why were there solar stone circles in a land where the sun always shines? The authors of the archaeological study of Nabta Playa hypothesize that the site links to Sirius in connection with the rising of the Nile waters, and that the solar solstice is connected with the heavy rains that trigger the rising of the Nile. There are problems with that hypothesis.

The first problem is that the monsoon rains that feed the Nile inundation happen in Ethiopia and South Sudan, not Egypt, and those rains begin in late April/May, and appear in Aswan in July[1]. The other more obvious issue with the idea that this stone circle was a way of watching for the impending Nile inundation is its position and the terrain in which it was built. It was built at a time when that area was not desert: it was still lush and had a good water supply (and small lakes surrounding it). Its local inhabitants were pastoralists, and its position, most importantly of all, was 100 kilometres west of Abu Simbel: it was far away from the Nile, in an area that is now desert. What would be the reason for building a stone circle connected to the Nile so far away from it? And by pastoralists who did not rely on the Nile for their herds and rudimentary crops?

As an aside, the 'received wisdom' regarding the rise of Sirius, and the goddess Sopdet being connected to the impending inundation, now appears to be on shaky ground. The theory of connection between Sopdet (Sirius) and the Nile inundation was largely based upon an ivory tablet supposedly showing Sopdet and the Nile.[2] I looked at this tablet and struggled to see the connection, and upon further research I found this theory to have consequently been debunked by Egyptologists.

---

[1] https://www.britannica.com/place/Nile-River/Climate-and-hydrology

[2] Ivory tablet from the reign of Djer, First Dynasty.

I.4. Early ritual solar circles

I also came across a piece of research that closely looked at this supposed connection, and these researchers also tossed the theory out of the window based upon astronomical calculations across the time periods of Egyptian history: the inundation did not happen like clockwork and relied heavily upon the timing of the monsoon, which had variability. If the inundation was late, the Egyptians would add an extra month to their agricultural calendar. It is also pertinent to understand, if you look into this yourself and come across various popular sites, that the Egyptians had a solar *civil calendar* of 365 days, so their months processed around the seasons over time, as well as an *agricultural calendar* that started each year with the rising of the Nile. So in both calendars, the timing of the heliacal rising of Sirius slowly processed through the months over the millennia (today it rises in August). Often some of the websites confuse the Egyptian civil calendar with the agricultural one, so watch out for that mistake. Here is an excerpt of the research text that I found, that essentially debunks the theory.

Regarding the rise of Sirius and the Nile inundation:

> It is shown that the only text that describes this event is formulated very vaguely. It makes impossible to derive a reliable astronomical dating. Modern interpretations of this text are based on the free interpretation of the original source, and often do not match. According to historical evidence of Greek authors and later Egyptian texts, flooding of the Nile based on heliacal rising of Sirius could be predicted at the beginning of I millennium A.D.. This fact is confirmed by astronomical calculations.[1]

So we have a ritual centre inland from the Nile, that built up over thousands of years, and around 4,800 B.C. they built a stone circle that aligned with the summer solstice. Why? I find it fascinating that around the same time, in two very different locations (there could be more, we just don't know yet) people decided to build these ritual structures that focused upon the sun. They appeared (along with later subsequent ones scattered around the northern hemisphere) in the

---

[1] Heliacal rising of Sirius and flooding of the Nile: Nickiforov, M. G.: Petrova, A. A. *Bulgarian Astronomical Journal*, Vol. 18, No. 3.

I. The Prehistory of Magical Development

very early days of agriculture, where animal husbandry was far more prominent.

The common theory about the rise of stone solar circles links to the seasonal cycles for agriculture, and yet, solar stone circles appear in such very different places with different seasonal structures: the summer solstice in the area that was to become Upper Egypt was very different in terms of agriculture and weather from the areas of northern Europe where other solar stone circles emerged at the same time. And keep in mind that we are talking about a time when the people who built these early structures were still, mostly, farming animals and harvesting wild seed.

We also must not forget that these early ancient peoples moved around a lot and travelled great distances: stories travel with people, ideas move around, and people copy what is different and cool, particularly if it appears to work. It is very likely that the huge and prolonged disturbances in climate, sea levels, and temperature affected those in more northerly climes far more severely than it did the people in the area that became Upper Egypt, but it would have affected them nonetheless. And if they encountered tales passed on along trading routes about the 'sun being angry,' those tales may have been scary enough, coupled with their own ancestral memory of a period of 'bad times,' and a renewal of those bad times, to prompt a shift to solar worship: there was also evidence at the Nabta Playa site of serious and prolonged drought (desertification from the 5.9 kiloyear event).

> Ra grew angry with mankind. He tore out one of his eyes, and threw it as Hathor down to earth, ordering her to destroy mankind. The goddess turned into the shape of a lioness, Sekhmet, and became the Lady of Pestilence and the Goddess of Vengeance. She was so successful at this, nearly wiping out the whole of humanity in her bloodthirsty killing spree, that Re grew alarmed and decided to put an end to the slaughter. He played a trick on Sekhmet: to quell her bloodlust he got her drunk on beer coloured like blood, and in her drunken stupor she forgot to continue killing, and transformed back into the gentle Hathor.

— The story of Sekhmet and the destruction of man, from the *Book of the Holy Cow*.

I.5 Chambered tombs in Northern Europe

In the colder, more seasonal north we see a continuation and development of the ditch/enclosure circles that developed into large and complex stone alignments. In both cooler and also warmer climes, we have evidence of human sacrifice, usually at high status burials in the warmer climes, and at the solar circles in colder climes.

From 4,200–3,900 B.C. in Europe we see continued climate instability, with the 5.9 kiloyear event (3,900 B.C.) with once again rapid cooling and intense cold winters.[1,2] Once again we see a ritualized response to this dramatic change and harsher living conditions.

Britain around the time period of 4,000 B.C. to 3,500 B.C., from a ritual cultural perspective, appeared to have focused upon two things: solar precession and death (sounds very Egyptian!). It is during this period that we find the chambered tombs:[3] complex stone constructions that housed one or more bodies. By approximately 3,000 B.C., stone circles and alignments were cropping up in various places in northwestern Europe and the tradition continued for another two thousand years.[4]

One of the major themes in magical history can be found in the ancient Dynastic Egyptian culture, and that is the theme of death and the afterlife. The sun and the progression of the soul through death and the Underworld are major themes in ancient Egyptian theology: the souls of the dead undertake a series of 'tests' as they travel through the Underworld, and at times they rest in caverns of

---

[1]Bond, G.: et al. (1997). "A Pervasive Millennial-Scale Cycle in North Atlantic Holocene and Glacial Climates." *Science* 278 (5341): 1257–1266. doi:10.1126/science.278.5341.1257.

[2]Bond, G.: et al. (2001). "Persistent Solar Influence on North Atlantic Climate During the Holocene." *Science* 294 (5549): 2130–2136. doi:10.1126/science.1065680.

[3]Pearson, Mike Parker (2005). *Bronze Age Britain (Revised Edition)*. London: B.T. Batsford and English Heritage.

[4]Burl, Aubrey (2000). *The Stone Circles of Britain, Ireland and Brittany*. New Haven and London: Yale University Press.

I. THE PREHISTORY OF MAGICAL DEVELOPMENT

the Underworld until it is time for them to release and rejoin their journey of development through the Gates of the Duat.[1] The light that guides the souls on their path of development and awakening is the light of Re, the sun as it travels in the Underworld.

With that in mind, the chambered tombs in the British Isles are worthy of a look. Of the many chambered tombs that litter the British Isles, there are three that are worthy of inspection as good examples.

The first is Newgrange (Brú na Bóinne) in the Boyne Valley, Country Meath, Ireland.[2] It is a large, impressive passage-chambered tomb from the Neolithic era (3,200 B.C.). It is aligned with the winter solstice, so that sunlight at that time flows through a 'roof box,' an opening that allows sunlight to flood the inner chamber at the winter solstice. When it was opened, human remains and grave goods were found, so it was definitely used as a tomb. There are quite a few chambered tombs in Ireland that align with the winter solstice. So here we have burials, placed in 'caves' (Underworld) where the sun at its lowest in the year falls into the cave and lights it up.

The second of interest is Bryn Celli Ddu in Angelsey, Wales.[3] It also dates to the Neolithic period and post hole remains that have been carbon-dated show activity from around 4,000 B.C.. It started out as a henge within a stone circle and later was developed as a chambered tomb mound. It is aligned to the summer solstice, unlike many others that align to the winter solstice, and it makes me wonder if the different alignment is a throwback to its earlier days as a stone circle/ditch. This would make sense with the much earlier circles we looked at earlier.

What caught my eye in particular was a serpent stone that is in the mound. When the mound was opened up, a 'patterned stone' six and a half feet high was found buried under the mound: the shape of the carving was very reminiscent of the later depictions in ancient Egypt of the 'Mehen' serpent that protects the solar god Re as he traverses the Underworld.

---

[1]Sheppard, McCarthy, Littlejohn (2017) *The Book of Gates*. Quareia Publishing UK ISBN 978-1911134220.

[2]O'Kelly, Michael J. 1982. *Newgrange: Archaeology, Art and Legend*. London: Thames and Hudson.

[3]Yates, M.J.: Longley, David (2001). *Anglesey: A Guide to Ancient Monuments on the Isle of Anglesey*. Third edition. Cardiff: Cadw.

I.5. Chambered tombs in Northern Europe

The Bryn Celli Ddu serpent stone was dug out and stood back up where the excavator thought it would have stood when the henge was active, so its original placing within the chamber is unknown. The theme of Underworld spaces, serpents, and the sun in the Underworld is an ancient and persistent motif in various places in the North hemisphere. It was also a strong theme in ancient Egyptian theology, with the Underworld populated by many serpents (e.g. Apep, Mehen, uraei, etc.) some of whom were helpers to the human souls, and some who were archenemies.

The third chambered tomb, Maes Howe,[1] on Mainland Orkney, Scotland, is truly astonishing and was very likely not a tomb at all. It is a vast chambered 'tomb' where the rear wall illuminates at the winter solstice. When it was opened, there were no grave goods and no human remains: it was never used for burial and was likely a ritual chamber. Once again, we have the 'cave' where the winter sun at its lowest shines into the 'cave' casting its light into the darkness.

This pattern of the light of the sun shining into the darkness at the darkest part of the year has magical parallels to one of the deep mysteries in magic: the light of the sun falling upon the seeker in the darkness of the Underworld, as they start the long journey up out of the darkness and up to the stars: the path of mystical ascent. It is one of the most prominent themes today in mystical magic: could this early ritualized behaviour be the far distant ancestor of today's magical mystical theme of ascent/rebirth from the darkness?

We have no way of knowing if this deep and ancient part of the Magical Mysteries was indeed what these ancient people were working with, or whether it is a total coincidence: were they simply copying the ebb and flow of the sun through the seasons, particularly in light of the harsher winters they were suffering? That is the usual hypothesis that is put forward, and yet we see the same pattern emerge in countries that do not, and did not, have such distinctive winters.

As a magician, I can say that these powerful dynamics and patterns are inherent within the magical human consciousness, not because magicians have been told it is, but because that is what

---

[1] Renfrew, Colin (editor) (1985). *The Prehistory of Orkney* B.C. *4000–1000* A.D.. Edinburgh: Edinburgh University Press.

I. THE PREHISTORY OF MAGICAL DEVELOPMENT

you experience in vision when you tread the magical mystical path, regardless of what you 'know' or don't know of historical patterns. A person going through deep magical development will experience these patterns in some form whether or not they have been exposed to the concepts.

But that then also poses a very interesting magical question: did these inner presentations that magicians stumble across in vision arise naturally, as organically forming structures of consciousness, or are they imprinted upon the collective inner consciousness of humanity because they have been purposefully worked with, in a visionary and ritual sense, for millennia, and have thus formed as a created inner structure? Did the various dramatic climate events first cause an outer social and ritual response, and then a deeper inner magical response, which in turn created inner visionary experiences that persist in human consciousness to this day?

The swimmer in the Nu is one with the darkness and silence. The swimmer does not know he is a swimmer: he is, and is within, the Nu. The golden rays of Re fall upon the swimmer, lighting up what was within the darkness. The swimmer reflects the light of Re, and thus is no longer one with the Nu.[1]

Excerpt from the Egyptian *Book of Gates*, Ninth Gate, Scene 58:

> O those being filled, who are in the water, The swimming/golden/molten, who are in the Nu, Look upon Re who is passing through, In his barque which is great of Mysteries. Now he ordains the design of the Gods: Now he formulates the business of the Radiant. Oho! Stand up, ones who are in the Nu: Behold Re as he ordains your designs.
>
> Says to them, Re:
>
> A coming forth for your heads/best, those who are diving, Plying for your arms, those who are slack, Swiftness for your hurrying, those who are swimming/golden/molten, Breath for your noses, those who are expanded. A coming into power for you through your water, Be you at peace in your cold refreshment. Your setting out is in the Nu,

---

[1] J McCarthy. (2018). *The Quareia Apprentice Study Guide* ISBN 9781911134329.

I.5. Chambered tombs in Northern Europe

> Your strides are of a stream. Your Presences, which are on earth, they are at peace, Meaning they breathe, and there is no destruction for them.
>
> Their extension is the peace of the Earth.
>
> Now, putting forth what is theirs on Earth Means coming into the power of one's peace on Earth.[1]

The above quote is taken from the *Book of Gates*, a ritual funerary text from New Kingdom Egypt. The *Book of Gates* first appears (so far as we know today) in fragments during the end of the eighteenth dynasty (approx. 1323 B.C.) and is the ritualized passage of Re (Solar deity) through the twelve hours and gates of the Underworld. It appeared on royal tomb walls, and also in fragments upon the golden sanctuary of King Tutankhamun.

Copyright © Josephine McCarthy 2018: all rights reserved.

---

[1] Sheppard, McCarthy, Littlejohn (2017) *The Book of Gates*. Quareia Publishing UK ISBN 978-1911134220.

Quareia
a New, Free School of Magic for the 21st Century

Advancing education in Mystical Magic and the Western Esoteric Mysteries.

www.quareia.com
schooldirector@quareia.com

Quareia is a practical magical training course founded by Josephine McCarthy and Frater Acher. It is a complete and freely available course designed to develop a student from a complete beginner into an adept. There are no barriers to entry: the course is accessible regardless of income, race, gender, religion, or spiritual beliefs.

Quareia is aligned to no particular school or specific religious, mystical, or magical system; rather it looks at and works with various magical, religious, and mystical practices that have influenced magical thinking in the Near Eastern and Western world from the early Bronze Age to the present day.

The entire course is free and openly available on the Quareia website.

www.ingramcontent.com/pod-product-compliance
Lightning Source LLC
Chambersburg PA
CBHW071723080526
44588CB00013B/1875